PEREGRINE BOOKS

ÉMILE DURKHEIM: HIS LIFE AND WORK

Generally regarded as one of the founders of sociology and social anthropology, Émile Durkheim dominated the sociological field in France before the First World War. He believed that society forms men's minds and controls their behaviour – which earned him the hostility of many who resented his apparent denigration of the individual. Durkheim, however, believed strongly in the sacredness of the individual, arguing that individualism was modern society's morality, or secular religion, with the schoolteacher taking the place of the priest.

Dr Lukes, in this major critical biography, analyses Durkheim's ideas and theories. Full consideration is given to his work on the division of labour, on suicide, on education, on the family and kinship, on crime and punishment, on law and politics, on socialism and on the sociology of knowledge and of religion. Dr Lukes pr[ ] l-heim's work within its historical, social and intellectual [ ] a fascinating account of a great sociologist [ ] ment of his work.

Steven [ ] or in Sociology and Politics at Balliol College, O[ ] ited, [ ] n Anthony Arblaster, *The Good Society: A book of readings* (1971) and has written an historical and analytical study of *Individualism* (1973), *Power; A Radical View* (1974) and *Essays in Social Theory* (1977). Steven Lukes has had articles published in *Political Studies*, *Philosophical Quarterly*, *European Journal of Sociology* (of which he is an editor), *British Journal of Sociology*, *Sociology* and the *Journal of the History of Ideas*.

STEVEN LUKES

Émile Durkheim
His Life and Work

A HISTORICAL
AND CRITICAL STUDY

PENGUIN BOOKS

Penguin Books Ltd, Harmondsworth, Middlesex, England
Penguin Books, 625 Madison Avenue, New York, New York 10022, U.S.A.
Penguin Books Australia Ltd, Ringwood, Victoria, Australia
Penguin Books Canada Ltd, 2801 John Street, Markham, Ontario, Canada L3R 1B4
Penguin Books (N.Z.) Ltd, 182–190 Wairau Road, Auckland 10, New Zealand

—

First published in Great Britain by Allen Lane 1973
First published in the United States of America by
Harper & Row, Publishers, Inc., 1973
Published in Peregrine Books in the United States of America by
arrangement with Harper & Row, Publishers, Inc.
Published in Peregrine Books 1975
Reprinted 1977

—

—

FOR J., WHOSE
CONTRIBUTION TO THIS WORK HAS
BEEN INCALCULABLE

—

Made and printed in Great Britain by
Hazell Watson & Viney Ltd
Aylesbury, Bucks
Set in Monotype Garamond

Contents

v

Contents

Preface

I WISH to express particular thanks to the following persons for their generous and valuable help in the course of my research: M. le Doyen Georges Davy, MM. les Professeurs Armand Cuvillier, Raymond Aron and Claude Lévi-Strauss, M. Raymond Lenoir, MM. Henri Durkheim, Étienne Halphen and Pierre Mauss, Mme J. S. Kennedy (*née* Raphaël), Mlle Jeanne Bouglé, Mlle Marcelle Fauconnet, Mme Y. Halbwachs, the late Mme H. Lévy-Bruhl, and Mlle Humbert, the extremely kind librarian of the Bibliothèque Victor Cousin. I am also very grateful for their comments, suggestions and criticisms to my wife and to Reinhard Bendix, Sir Isaiah Berlin, Tom Bottomore, Terry Clark, Jean Floud, Tony Giddens, Louis Greenberg, Jack Hayward, Robin Horton, Rodney Needham, John Peel, Melvin Richter, Alan Ryan, Raphael Samuel, Andrew Scull, Bryan Wilson and Theodore Zeldin. For secretarial help, I must thank Caroline Cumberbatch, Phyllis Jayakar and Pat Lloyd. I must also thank Deborah Thompson for doing the index. Above all, I am grateful for the scrupulous and inspiring advice of Sir Edward Evans-Pritchard, a not uncritical admirer of Durkheim.

Among the unpublished sources I have used are letters from Durkheim to Xavier Léon and Octave Hamelin (at the Bibliothèque Victor Cousin, MS nos. 361 and 357), to Louis Havet and François Simiand (at the Bibliothèque Nationale, côtes N.A.F. 24493(2) and N.A.F. 12855) and to Célestin Bouglé (made available by Mlle Bouglé); Durkheim's personal dossiers at the Archives Nationales (F17 25768), and at the University of Bordeaux (provided by M. le Professeur René Lacroze); the manuscripts made available to me by M. Raymond Lenoir (see Chapter 6); and the lecture-notes provided by M. Davy taken at Durkheim's lectures by himself and M. Cuvillier (see Chapter 21). Unfortunately, it is almost certain that all Durkheim's papers and remaining unpublished manuscripts were destroyed by the Germans during the Occupation.

I have throughout used the earliest editions of Durkheim's works that were not subsequently modified, except where otherwise indicated. I have consistently given references both to the original text and to the English translation, where available, but the generally, and alarmingly, poor quality of the latter (with some notable exceptions) has made re-translations necessary in very many cases, indicated by the addition of '(S.L.)'.

Most of the Introduction has appeared as an article entitled 'Prolegomena to the Interpretation of Durkheim' in the *Archives européennes de sociologie* (*European Journal of Sociology*), XII, 2, 1971; and a small part of Chapter 17 in a short article on Durkheim's 'Individualism and the Intellectuals' in *Political Studies*, XVII, 1, 1969.

List of Abbreviations

AFLB	*Annales de la Faculté des Lettres de Bordeaux*
AJS	*American Journal of Sociology*
AnS	*Annales sociologiques*
APDSJ	*Archives de philosophie du droit et de sociologie juridique*
AS	*Année sociologique*
ASR	*American Sociological Review*
BJS	*British Journal of Sociology*
BSFP	*Bulletin de la Société française de philosophie*
CIS	*Cahiers internationaux de sociologie*
EJS	*European Journal of Sociology (Archives européennes de sociologie)*
IESS	*International Encyclopedia of the Social Sciences* (New York, 1968)
JSSR	*Journal for the Scientific Study of Religions*
KZS	*Kölner Zeitschrift für Soziologie*
MF	*Mercure de France*
NC	*Notes critiques – sciences sociales*
PSQ	*Political Science Quarterly*
RB	*Revue bleue*
REP	*Revue d'économie politique*
RFS	*Revue française de sociologie*
RIE	*Revue internationale de l'enseignement*
Ri It S	*Rivista italiana di sociologia*
RIS	*Revue internationale de sociologie*
RMM	*Revue de métaphysique et de morale*
RNS	*Revue néo-scolastique*
RP	*Revue philosophique*
RS	*La riforma sociale*
RSH	*Revue de synthèse historique*
SP	*Sociological Papers*
SR	*Sociological Review*
*SR*ch	*Social Research*

Introduction

THIS study of Durkheim seeks to help the reader to achieve a historical understanding of his ideas and to form critical judgements about their value. To some extent these two aims are contradictory. On the one hand, one seeks to understand: what did Durkheim really mean, how did he see the world, how did his ideas relate to one another and how did they develop, how did they relate to their biographical and historical context, how were they received, what influence did they have and to what criticisms were they subjected, what was it like not to make certain distinctions, not to see certain errors, of fact or of logic, not to know what has subsequently become known? On the other hand, one seeks to assess: how valuable and how valid are the ideas, to what fruitful insights and explanations do they lead, how do they stand up to analysis and to the evidence, what is their present value? Yet it seems that it is only by inducing oneself not to see certain things that one can achieve a sympathetic understanding and only by seeing them that one can make a critical assessment. The only solution is to pursue both aims – seeing and not seeing – simultaneously. More particularly, this book has the primary object of achieving that sympathetic understanding without which no adequate critical assessment is possible. It is a study in intellectual history which is also intended as a contribution to sociological theory.

To this end, it is organized in a somewhat unorthodox manner. The overall framework is that of an intellectual biography, enabling one to consider Durkheim's thought as a developing whole, of which some aspects changed and others deepened. This framework allows one to give full weight to the historical context of Durkheim's ideas, the intellectual influences which helped to mould them and the criticisms to which they were subjected (and which were integral to their development, since Durkheim was a highly polemical, combative thinker), as well as the contemporary influence they had. On the other hand, critical analysis is introduced where appropriate, on the assumption that evaluation of the ideas considered cannot without artificiality be rigidly separated from their biographical and historical presentation. We are, after all, interested both in understanding and evaluating these ideas; it seemed best to integrate these processes rather than divorce them.

Durkheim's ideas have been paid the tribute of unrelenting criticism during his lifetime and ever since. Much of this criticism has been valid and some of it theoretically productive, but, equally, much of it has been based on misunderstandings and distortions. Moreover, despite the wide-ranging influence of Durkheim's thought on very many individual scholars,[1] its assimilation within France has been very partial and unsystematic[2]; while elsewhere it has been filtered through a number of sources which have themselves decisively influenced its interpretation and reception.[3] There is the sociologists' Durkheim (strongly coloured by the Parsonian interpretation), the social anthropologists' Durkheim (originally sketched in by Radcliffe-Brown, but progressively redrawn since), the Durkheim of anomie theory (deriving from Merton) and of suicide studies, the criminologists' Durkheim and the social psychologists' Durkheim, the educational sociologists' Durkheim and the human ecologists' Durkheim, Durkheim the sociologist of knowledge, and, most recently, the pre-structuralist Durkheim. Some see him as 'the spiritual heir of Comte',[4] while others stress the influence of Saint-Simon.[5] Some have seen in him a dangerous social realist, with a metaphysical belief in the group mind, one writer even putting him in the tradition of Fichte and the German Romantics,[6] another seeing him rather

---

1. See below, Chapter 20.
2. See Bouglé, 1935, and Bourdieu and Passeron, 1967.
3. See, for example, Hinkle, 1960, and Honigsheim, 1960a.
4. Parsons, 1937 (1949), p. 307.
5. For example, Gouldner, 1958.
6. Deploige, 1911. For Deploige, Catholicism was wholly opposed to Durkheim's ideas.

in the tradition of the French theocratic reactionaries and as 'the most important link between conservatism and the contemporary study of human behaviour'.[7] 'Durkheimism', according to another, 'is Kantism, revised and completed by Comtism',[8] and for yet another 'Durkheim has been the medium, so to speak, by which Rousseau has left his mark on modern social science'.[9] He has been variously called a materialist and an idealist, a positivist and a metaphysician, a rationalist and an irrationalist, a dogmatic atheist and a mystic, as well as a 'scholarly forerunner of Fascism',[10] an agent of 'bourgeois conservation',[11] a late-nineteenth-century liberal, a conservative and a socialist. It is clearly time to try to approach Durkheim's work as a whole, and for a full-scale consideration of its historical significance and its explanatory power.

There are, however, a number of preliminary difficulties that need to be faced at the outset. Durkheim's manner of thought and his style of expression have certain peculiar features the recognition of which can only clarify the interpretation of his ideas. First, there are certain concepts crucial to the understanding of his thought which need to be elucidated, either because they are ambiguous or because they are unfamiliar to a modern reader.[12] Second, underlying these concepts, there are a number of sharp dichotomies, or 'binary oppositions', on which his thought rests, which need to be made explicit and related to one another. Third, there are a number of characteristic, and often bad, arguments, which likewise need to be

7. Nisbet, 1952, p. 167. Cf. Nisbet, 1966. For Nisbet, Durkheim's ideas largely derived from Catholic counter-revolutionary thought.

8. Bouglé, 1930b, p. 283.

9. Wolin, 1960, p. 372.

10. Ranulf, 1939. See below, pp. 338–9, for a note on this extremely interesting question.

11. Nizan, P., *Les Chiens de garde* (Paris, 1932: 1971 edn), p. 98. See below, pp. 356–8.

12. And there is the further difficulty of translation from French to English. Sometimes what is perfectly intelligible in French cannot be directly translated into seemingly equivalent English words (such as '*conscience*' and 'conscience', or '*représentations*' and 'representations'). The French words map out a different conceptual structure from the English; they make different discriminations and carry different presuppositions and connotations.

brought to the surface and identified. And finally, Durkheim's style often tends to caricature his thought: he often expressed his ideas in an extreme or figurative manner, which distorted their meaning and concealed their significance. It is to these matters that the rest of this introduction is devoted.

CONCEPTS

Conscience collective

In *The Division of Labour*, Durkheim defines 'the *conscience collective* or *commune*' as 'the set of beliefs and sentiments common to the average members of a single society [which] forms a determinate system that has its own life'.[13] The French word '*conscience*' is ambiguous, embracing the meanings of the two English words 'conscience' and 'consciousness'. Thus the 'beliefs and sentiments' comprising the *conscience collective* are, on the one hand, moral and religious, and, on the other, cognitive.[14]

The *conscience collective* is, Durkheim writes, 'by definition, diffused throughout the whole society, but it none the less has specific features which make it a distinct reality'. It is 'independent of the particular conditions in which individuals are placed; they pass on and it remains'. It is common to North and South, to large and small towns, to different professions, and it links successive generations with one another. It is quite distinct from the individual *conscience*, though 'it can only be realized through individuals'.[15] Durkheim frequently denies hypostasizing the *conscience collective*: its distinctiveness is simply that

the states which constitute it differ specifically from those which constitute particular *consciences*. This specificity results from the fact that they are not formed from the same elements. The latter result

13. 1902b, p. 46: tr. 1933b, p. 79 (S.L.).

14. Larousse gives two main senses for '*conscience*': (1) '*Sentiment qu'on a de son existence et de celle du monde extérieur*; *représentation qu'on se fait de quelque chose*'; and (2) '*Sentiment qui fait qu'on porte un jugement moral sur ses actes, sens du bien et du mal*; *respect du devoir*'.

15. 1902b, p. 46: tr. pp. 79–80 (S.L.).

from the nature of the organico-psychic being taken in isolation, the former from the combination of a plurality of beings of this kind.[16]

We shall discuss below Durkheim's ways of drawing the distinction between social and individual phenomena. Here it is worth noting that he saw the *conscience collective* as 'the psychic type of society, with its own distinctive properties, conditions of existence and mode of development'. He also defined the term as meaning 'the totality of social resemblances'. Crime was an offence against 'strong and definite states of the *conscience collective*', which punishment restored and reinforced.[17]

Durkheim made great use of the concept of *conscience collective* in *The Division of Labour*. He used it very little thereafter, though he did come to see the state as 'the organ of social thought', concentrated, deliberate and reflective, distinct from the 'obscure *conscience collective*'[18] diffused throughout society; and he came to see democracy as consisting in a high degree of communication between the two, which rendered the latter more deliberate, reflective and critical.[19] His reasons for abandoning the concept were probably twofold. In the first place, the central thesis of *The Division of Labour* was that the division of labour is 'more and more filling the role that was once filled by the *conscience commune*; it is this that mainly holds together social aggregates of the more advanced type'.[20] In that book he claimed that the *conscience collective* is 'only a very restricted part' of the psychic life of advanced societies:[21] it becomes weaker and vaguer and ceases to attach men to transcendent ends, or indeed to society itself. Durkheim soon abandoned this thesis, in its simple form, and came to stress what he saw as the crucial role of collective beliefs and sentiments, and especially of morality and religion, in all societies. Hence he abandoned a concept which was tied to what he had seen as the distinctive mode of cohesion of less advanced societies (mechanical solidarity), characterized by 'social

16. 1901c, pp. 127–8: tr. 1938b, pp. 103–4 (S.L.).
17. 1902b, pp. 46–7: tr. p. 80 (S.L.).
18. 1950a, pp. 95, 97: tr. 1957a, pp. 79, 80 (S.L.).
19. See Chapter 13, below.
20. 1902b, p. 148: tr. p. 173 (S.L.).
21. ibid., p. 46: tr. p. 80.

resemblances' and repressive, punishment-centred law.

Secondly, and as a corollary of this, it was insufficiently analytical for his purposes subsequent to *The Division of Labour*. He wished to explore how individuals are attached to and controlled by societies, how collective beliefs and sentiments are inculcated, how they change, how they are affected by and how they affect other features of social life, how they are maintained and reinforced. The concept of *conscience collective* was too all-embracing and too static. It failed to discriminate between cognitive, moral and religious beliefs, between different beliefs and sentiments, and between the beliefs and sentiments associated with different stages of a society's development. To make such discriminations Durkheim used the concept of '*représentations collectives*'.

Représentations collectives[22]

Durkheim started using this concept in about 1897, when he wrote (in *Suicide*) that 'essentially social life is made up of *représentations*'.[23] Collective *représentations* are 'states of the *conscience collective*' which are 'different in nature from the states of the individual *conscience*'. They express 'the way in which the group conceives itself in its relations with the objects which affect it'.[24] Much of Durkheim's later work can be seen as the systematic study of collective *représentations*. Thus his sociology of knowledge examines the social origin and the social reference, and the social functions, of the forms of cognitive thought; his sociology of religion does the same for religious beliefs; and his projected sociology of morality would have done likewise for moral beliefs and ideals.[25] In this connection, it is worth noting two related ambiguities built into the concept of *représentation collective* which have significant consequences for Durkheim's theorizing. In the first

22. Durkheim wrote that it was Espinas who had shown that 'the essential object of sociology is to investigate how *représentations collectives* are formed and combine' (1900b, p. 648).
23. 1897a, p. 352: tr. 1951a, p. 312 (S.L.).
24. 1901c, p. xvi: tr. p. xlix (S.L.).
25. See Chapters 21, 22 and 23, below.

place, the concept *représentation* refers both to the mode of thinking, conceiving or perceiving[26] and to that which is thought, conceived or perceived.[27] (This ambiguity is significant in his sociology of knowledge.)[28] And second, the *représentation* is *collective* both in its origin, determining its mode or form, and in its reference or object (it is also, of course, collective in being common to the members of a society or group). Thus Durkheim wanted to say both that *représentations collectives* are socially generated and that they refer to, and are in some sense 'about', society. (This duality is clearest in his sociology of religion and in his sociology of morality.)

Durkheim made much of what he called the independent reality of *représentations collectives*.[29] He used the analogy of the individual's mental states, or individual *représentations*, which, though intimately related to their 'substratum', brain cells, from whose combined activity they result, cannot be reduced to and wholly explained by them, but have their own characteristics, are relatively autonomous, and can directly influence one another and combine according to their own laws. Similarly, he argued, *représentations collectives* result from the substratum of associated individuals (which 'varies according to their geographical disposition and the nature and number of their channels of communication'[30]) but they cannot be reduced to and wholly explained by features of individuals: they have *sui generis* characteristics. Durkheim's assumption here was that if a phenomenon has distinctive, or *sui generis*, characteristics, then it cannot be wholly explained in terms of its constituent elements, or 'substratum'. In other words, he equates the claims (a) that social facts are *sui generis* and (b) that

26. Thus, for example, 'concepts are collective *représentations* ... they correspond to the way in which that special being, society, conceives of the things that are part of its own experience' (1912a, p. 621: tr. 1915d, p. 435 – S.L.).

27. Thus 'myths, popular legends, religious conceptions of all sorts, moral beliefs, etc.' are all collective *représentations* (1901c, p. xvii: tr. p. 1).

28. Cf. Durkheim's confusion between the categories or fundamental forms of thought (for instance of space and time) and particular spatial and temporal divisions, that is, *beliefs about* how space and time are divided up (see Chapter 22, below).

29. See especially 1898b.   30. 1924a (1951 edn), p. 34: tr. 1953b, p. 24.

they cannot be wholly explained in terms of facts about individuals.

He claimed that their original and 'fundamental' forms 'bear the marks of their origin', so that 'the primary matter of all social consciousness is in close relation with the number of social elements, the way in which they are grouped and distributed, etc., that is with the nature of the substratum'. But, 'once a primary basis of *représentations* has thus been formed', they become 'partially autonomous realities which live their own life', with 'the power to attract and repel one another and form syntheses of all kinds' and engender new *représentations*.[31] Hence, for instance, 'the luxuriant growth of myths and legends, theogonic and cosmological systems, etc.',[32] and hence 'the way in which religious ideas . . . combine and separate and are transformed into one another, giving rise to contradictory complexes'.[33] There should, Durkheim argued, be a special branch of sociology (he called it 'social psychology') devoted to studying 'the laws of collective ideation' (which, there was every reason to believe, would be largely distinct from those of individual psychology), investigating 'by the comparison of mythical themes, popular legends and traditions, and languages, the ways in which social *représentations* attract and exclude one another, how they fuse together or become distinct, etc.'.[34]

How did Durkheim relate the *représentations collectives* to other features of social life? In order to answer this, it is necessary to turn to his conception of social phenomena in general, that is, to his concept of *faits sociaux*.

Faits sociaux[35]

Durkheim argued that the whole of sociology was based on

---

31. ibid., p. 43: tr. pp. 30–31 (S.L.).   32. ibid.: tr. p. 31.
33. 1901c, p. xix: tr. p. lii (S.L.).
34. ibid., p. xviii: tr. p. li (S.L.). But he also wrote that this social or collective psychology is 'the whole of sociology; why not use the latter term exclusively?' (1924a (1951 edn), p. 47fn.: tr. 1953b, p. 34 fn. – S.L.)
35. Cf. the excellent discussion in Lacombe, 1926, ch. 2; also the valuable comparison of Durkheim's and Weber's views of social facts in Bendix, 1971.

'our fundamental principle, the objective reality of social facts'.[36] For sociology to be possible, 'it must above all have an object all its own', a 'reality which is not in the domain of the other sciences'.[37] What did Durkheim count as social facts and how did he classify them? And what features did he believe mark them off from other phenomena or types of 'fact', the objects of other sciences? Before considering these questions, one should note the oddity to modern English-speaking readers of Durkheim's use of 'fact' here, which is only compounded by his rule that 'social facts must be studied as things'.[38] By 'social facts' he should be understood to mean social phenomena or factors or forces,[39] and by the rule that they should be studied as things he meant that they are to be seen as 'realities external to the individual' and independent of the observer's conceptual apparatus.[40]

Durkheim saw social facts as lying along a continuum. At one end are structural, 'anatomical or morphological' social phenomena, making up the 'substratum (*substrat*) of collective life': these consist in

the number and nature of the elementary parts of which society is composed, the way they are arranged, the degree of coalescence they have attained, the distribution of population over the surface of the territory, the number and nature of channels of communication, the form of dwellings, etc.[41]

Then there are what one might call institutionalized norms, which may be more, or less, formal – 'legal and moral rules,

36. 1901c, p. xxiii: tr. p. lvii.   37. 1897a, p. ix: tr. 1951a, p. 38.
38. ibid.: tr. pp. 37–8. Cf. 1901c, ch. II.
39. '*Fait*' has a somewhat different meaning from 'fact', signifying 'that which exists or occurs or is real' rather than 'that which is the case'. None the less, we will, for simplicity, use the term 'social fact'.
40. ibid. Durkheim uses 'things (*choses*)' here in at least four senses, viz.: (1) phenomena with characteristics independent of the observer; (2) phenomena whose characteristics can only be ascertained by empirical investigation (that is, as opposed to *a priori* reasoning or intuition); (3) phenomena whose existence is independent of individuals' wills; and (4) phenomena which can only be studied through 'external' observation – that is, by means of indicators, such as legal codes, statistics, etc. (Cf. Benoît-Smullyan, 1948, p. 501).
41. 1901c, p. 17: part of paragraph missing from English translation.

religious dogmas, financial systems, etc.' – 'established beliefs and practices' which have their origin or 'substratum' either in 'the political society as a whole, or in one of the partial groups which comprise it'.[42] Finally, occupying the rest of the continuum, are social facts which are not institutionalized, but 'without presenting these crystallized forms, have both the same objectivity and the same ascendancy over the individual'. These are 'social currents'; and these may be relatively stable 'currents of opinion' or, at the extreme, 'transitory outbreaks' such as occur when 'in an assembly of people, great movements of enthusiasm, of indignation or of pity are generated'.[43] Durkheim argued that 'a whole series of degrees without a break in continuity links facts of the most clearly structural character with those free currents of social life that are not yet caught within any definite mould. The differences between them are, therefore, only differences in the degree of consolidation they present.'[44] In this classificatory scheme, the *représentations collectives* were, then, social facts located in the superstructure.

As we shall see, the focus of Durkheim's attention shifted, during the course of his life, from the structural to superstructural phenomena, as the explanatory weight he accorded the latter increased. However, it is worth noting that, even at the time of *The Rules of Sociological Method*, he saw them both as intimately interrelated and of the same generic type. Political divisions, he there argued, are moral, not merely material and geographical, and social organization can only be studied via public law, which determines it; while population movements, for instance from the country into the towns, result from currents of opinion, and types of dwelling and communication channels are formed by custom and habit. These structural or morphological 'ways of being are only consolidated ways of acting'.[45]

What, then, distinguishes social facts from other sorts of fact? In *The Rules* Durkheim defined a social fact as '*every way of acting, fixed or not, capable of exercising over the individual an*

42. ibid., pp. 9, 8: tr. pp. 4, 3 (S.L.).
43. ibid., pp. 9–10: tr. pp. 4–5 (S.L.).
44. ibid., p. 19: tr. p. 12 (S.L.).   45. ibid., p. 18: tr. p. 12 (S.L.).

external constraint' and further as ' [*every way of acting*] *which is general throughout a given society, while existing in its own right, independent of its individual manifestations'*.[46] He intended this only as a 'preliminary definition': as he later protested, he did not mean it as an intuitive, essentialist definition, summing up all the features of the social fact, but simply as a sign by which to recognize sociological phenomena.[47] Other definitions were possible: he claimed his own was a useful guide to research.

Durkheim's definition embodies three distinguishing criteria: externality, constraint and generality-plus-independence. Let us look at these in turn.

Social facts, Durkheim wrote, exist 'outside individual *consciences'*. Thus, for example, domestic or civic or contractual obligations are defined, externally to the individual, in law and custom; religious beliefs and practices 'exist prior to the individual, because they exist outside him'; language and currency, as well as professional practices 'function independently of my use of them'.[48] Durkheim here perpetrated an important ambiguity, of which he was only half-aware, and which is responsible for much of the criticism that his 'social realism' implies the existence of a 'group mind', distinct from that of its members taken together. Social facts could be 'external' to any given individual, or else to all individuals in a given society or group: to speak of them as 'outside individual *consciences'* leaves both interpretations open. He obviously meant the former, but he frequently used forms of expression which implied the latter. He repeatedly denied reifying or hypostasizing society and wrote that 'there is nothing in social life that is not in individual *consciences'*[49]; on the other hand, he did use terms such as '*conscience collective'* and '*l'âme collective'* and wrote of 'that conscious being which is society . . . a *sui generis* being with its own special nature, distinct from that of its members, and a personality of its own different from individual personalities'.[50] As Georges Sorel put it, Durkheim

46. ibid., p. 19: tr. p. 13 (S.L.).
47. ibid., p. xx: tr. p. liii. Cf. 1924a (1951 edn), p. 35 fn.: tr. 1953b, p. 25 fn. 48. 1901c, p. 6: tr. pp. 1-2 (S.L.).
49. 1902b, p. 342: tr. 1933b, p. 350.
50. 1925a, p. 69: tr. 1961a, p. 60 (S.L.).

said that it was unnecessary to introduce the notion of a social mind but reasoned as if he were introducing it.[51] In claiming that social facts (and in particular *représentations collectives*) are external to individuals, Durkheim should have said that they are both external to and internal to (that is, internalized by) any given individual; and that they are only external to all existing individuals in so far as they have been culturally transmitted to them from the past.

The notion of 'constraint' is even more ambiguous. He uses it in the following senses, without seeming to realize that they are distinct: (1) the authority of legal rules, moral maxims and conventions or customs, as manifested by the sanctions brought to bear when the attempt is made to violate them; (2) the need to follow certain rules, procedures or methods in order to carry out certain activities successfully (for instance a Frenchman must speak French to be understood; and the industrialist must use current methods or else face ruin); (3) the causal influence of ecological, or 'morphological', factors (such as the influence of channels of communication on the direction and intensity of migration and commerce); (4) psychological compulsion in a crowd situation (as when collective movements of 'enthusiasm, indignation and pity . . . come to each of us from without and carry us away despite ourselves'[52]); and (5) cultural determination and the influence of socialization (as when certain socially given ideas and values are internalized by individuals who thereby acquire certain beliefs, wants and feelings and act in certain ways; thus education is 'a continuous effort to impose on the child ways of seeing, feeling and acting at which he would not have arrived spontaneously'[53]).

As Sorel, once more, observed, Durkheim extended the meaning of 'constraint' too far.[54] Certainly senses (1) – (5) are very different from one another. In particular, (1) refers to the enforcement of obligation through the fear of sanctions; (2) to a means-end relation (x is the only way to achieve y); and (3) – (5) point to different ways in which men's thoughts and

51. Sorel, 1895, p. 19.   52. 1901c, p. 9; tr. p. 4 (S.L.).
53. ibid., p. 11: tr. p. 6 (S.L.).
54. Sorel, 1895, p. 17. In Durkheim's mind (1) – (5) were forms of, rather than different *senses* of, 'constraint'.

actions are determined. To call them all 'constraint' is, at the very least, confusing. One naturally understands 'constraint' in sense (1), that is, to refer to cases where an individual who wishes to act in one way is made to act in another: hence Durkheim's stress on the link between social constraint and 'the prestige with which certain *représentations* are invested' and his talk of a 'power of coercion' by means of which 'ways of acting, thinking and feeling' are 'imposed' on the individual.⁵⁵ Even here there would seem to be a distinction to be drawn (which Durkheim half-sees) between cases of pure authority at one extreme (where compliance occurs because of the voluntary acceptance of legitimacy) and of coercive power at the other (where it occurs because negative sanctions are feared). However, it seems clear that Durkheim's paradigm sense of 'constraint' is the exercise of authority, backed by sanctions, to get individuals to conform to rules. It is obviously stretching the meaning of the word somewhat to apply it to sense (2), according to which I am under 'constraint' to speak French if I wish to be understood by Frenchmen (though one does naturally speak of, for instance, the 'constraints of the market'). But to apply it to senses (3) – (5) is even more misleading, since these refer to what influences men's desires not to what thwarts them, to the determination of how men think, feel and act, not to the modification of behaviour, getting men to conform to rules they would otherwise break. (And one might add that one type of 'social fact' Durkheim was soon to study, namely the so-called 'suicidogenic currents' leading men to commit suicide, were, in his view, causal factors inducing men – in the cases of anomie and egoism – to *break* the rules.)

In fact, Durkheim's central interest was in the ways in which social and cultural factors influence, indeed largely constitute, individuals. In the course of his career, he became more and more preoccupied with senses (4) and (5) above, which he saw as closely linked, (4) characterizing the periods of creation and renewal ('collective effervescences') of the ideas and values transmitted through (5). In fact, after *The Rules*, he eventually ceased to stress the criterion of 'constraint'. He had intended

55. 1901c, pp. xxi, 8: tr. pp. lv, 3 (S.L.).

it, he wrote, only as part of a preliminary, indicative definition of social facts: these latter, he admitted, can 'equally present the opposite characteristic' – that is, opposite to constraint in sense (1) – namely, the attractive power of (internalized) ideals to which men are attached and which thereby influence their behaviour, the opposite pole of the moral life to 'duty', namely, 'the good'.[56] 'Constraint' was, in general, too narrow a notion to identify all the ways in which Durkheim saw the individual as affected by social factors.

Finally, the criterion of 'generality-plus-independence' requires explication. A social fact could further be defined, Durkheim wrote, 'by the fact that it is general within the group' *and*, importantly, that 'it exists independently of the forms it assumes in being generalized'.[57] By generality Durkheim was here seeking to identify factors that are specific to particular societies; that is are neither strictly personal features of individuals nor universal attributes of human nature. Fauconnet and Mauss isolated this feature of social facts when they characterized them as 'certain ways of feeling, thinking and acting' which individuals would not have had 'if they had lived in other human groups'.[58]

Yet generality in this sense is not, Durkheim argued, enough to characterize social facts, since it does not distinguish them from their 'individual incarnations'. They are 'beliefs, tendencies, practices of the group taken collectively' as opposed to 'the forms collective states assume when refracted by individuals'. Examples are 'legal and moral rules, popular aphorisms and sayings, articles of faith in which religious or political sects condense their beliefs, standards of taste established by literary schools, etc.'[59] – as opposed to their individual applications. Durkheim was here pointing to *norms* as distinct from, and governing, individual behaviour. In the preface to the second edition of *The Rules* he extended this idea, and, following Fauconnet and Mauss, wrote of 'institutions' ('all the beliefs and modes of conduct instituted by

56. ibid., pp. xx–xxi fn.: tr. p. liv fn. (S.L.).
57. ibid., pp. 15–16: tr. p. 10 (S.L.).
58. Mauss and Fauconnet, 1901, p. 166.
59. 1901c, p. 12: tr. p. 7 (S.L.).

the collectivity') as the very subject-matter of sociology.[60]

But norms and institutions were not the only forms in which Durkheim saw social facts as identifiable independently of their individual incarnations. Statistics of marriage, suicide or birth rates register 'currents of opinion' (whose intensity varies according to time and country), since he believed that in the aggregate statistics individual circumstances cancel each other out. Durkheim was here pointing to social causes (inferred from the statistics) which, he claimed, influence individual behaviour.

The criterion of generality, then, is combined by Durkheim with the idea that the general form is independent of and governs individual behaviour: the social fact is not social because it is general but rather 'general because it is collective (that is, more or less obligatory) . . . it is a state of the group which is repeated among individuals because it is imposed on them'.[61] And Durkheim gives as further examples beliefs and practices transmitted by education from the past, and collective sentiments in crowd situations. But all this is merely to reproduce the ambiguity we have already detected in the notion of constraint: norms may be 'imposed' on individuals who wish to deviate from them by means of sanctions; currents of opinion, beliefs and practices, collective sentiments are 'imposed' on individuals when, once internalized, they influence them to think, feel and act in certain ways.[62]

The concepts we have been examining clearly presuppose a number of central dichotomies, chief among them those between sociology and psychology, and between the social and the individual. At this point it will be useful to examine the role of these, and other, dichotomies in Durkheim's thought and their relations to one another.

60. ibid., pp. xxii-xxiii: tr. p. lvi.
61. ibid., p. 14: tr. p. 9 (S.L.).
62. At one point Durkheim writes that the 'essential characteristic' of 'sociological phenomena' is their 'power of exerting external pressure on individual *consciences* . . .' (ibid., pp. 124–5: tr. p. 101 – S.L.). This repeats the same ambiguity.

DICHOTOMIES

Sociology-Psychology

In proclaiming sociology an independent science, Durkheim thought it necessary to declare it independent of psychology.[63] There was, he claimed, between them 'the same break in continuity as between biology and the physico-chemical sciences. Consequently, every time that a social phenomenon is directly explained by a psychological phenomenon, we may be sure that the explanation is false'.[64] How exactly did he draw this sharp line between sociology and psychology?

He in fact drew it in a number of ways and thus conflated a number of different distinctions. This can best be shown by bringing out the four different ways in which, at various points, Durkheim conceived of 'psychology', the first in terms of its *explananda*, the remaining three in terms of its distinctive type of *explanans*.

(1) In the first place he defined it by its object, or *explananda*. On this view psychology is 'the science of the mind of the individual (*de l'individu mental*)', concerned with 'states of the individual *conscience*' as opposed to those of the 'collective *conscience*', with individual as opposed to collective *représentations*.[65] In the course of his career he became increasingly insistent that the realities studied by sociology and psychology were equally mental, though of a different nature and governed by different laws. Though he raised the question whether a single 'formal' psychology might not ultimately encompass the behaviour of collective and individual *représentations*, he was doubtful this would occur.[66] This distinction rests entirely on Durkheim's thesis about different levels of reality, considered below, and his assumption that sociology must have its

63. In this he was a good disciple of Comte, who had banned psychology from the hierarchy of the sciences; but, unlike Comte, who had subjected the psychology (or '*idéologie*') of his time to detailed criticisms on the grounds that it 'mutilated' man, Durkheim never attempted a critique of contemporary psychology. For a good discussion, see Essertier, 1927b.

64. 1901c, p. 128: tr. p. 104.

65. ibid., p. xvi: tr. p. xlix (S.L.).

66. ibid., pp. xvii-xix: tr. pp. l-liii.

own such level (for sociology to exist it must 'take cognizance of a reality not in the domain of the other sciences').[67] Abandon that thesis and that assumption, and the plausibility, coherence and value of this sharp dichotomy disappear. Although one can distinguish different levels of what is to be explained, from the purely personal via inter-personal relations, small groups, organizations and institutions to the macro-level of society as a whole, one will no longer postulate merely two levels, attaching one to psychology and the other to sociology.

But Durkheim also saw psychology as consisting in a particular type of explanation, as advancing a distinctive type of *explanans*. In fact, he offered a number of alternative accounts of distinctively psychological explanation without realizing they were distinct, and therefore supposed he had shown them all to be equally inapplicable to social phenomena.

(2) On the one hand, he saw psychological explanation as explanation in terms of what he called 'organico-psychic' factors, that is (pre-social) features of the individual organism, given at birth and independent of social influences. Thus he wrote that if 'social phenomena . . . derived directly from the organic or physical constitution of man without any other factor intervening in their development, sociology would dissolve into psychology'.[68] Examples he gave of this type of *explanans* were psychopathic dispositions, race and heredity. His case for distinguishing this kind of explanation from sociology was both empirical and conceptual. Empirically, he claimed that organico-psychic factors could not, for instance, explain differential suicide rates, and that racial differences could not account for differences in social organization and culture.[69] Conceptually, he maintained that explanations of this type tend to use ambiguous and non-operational concepts (such as race) and fail to identify independent variables, and thus easily become circular (such as explaining the artistic character of Athenian civilization in terms of congenital aesthetic faculties). On the other hand, Durkheim was always equivocal about the role of 'organico-psychic' factors. He wrote of 'individual natures' as 'merely the indeterminate

67. 1897a, p. ix: tr. 1951a, p. 38. 68. 1900c: tr. 1960c, p. 363.
69. 1901c, pp. 132f: tr. p. 108f.

material which the social factor determines and transforms'[70];
yet pre-social, organically given factors play a crucial role at
various points in his theories – as, for example, in one major
strand in his account of anomie, namely the notion of unrestrained and limitless (organico-psychic) desires, and also in his
conception of a natural distribution of talents and his doctrine
about the biologically given characteristics of womanhood.

(3) Next, he sometimes saw psychological explanation as
explanation in terms of particular or 'individual' as opposed to
general or 'social' conditions: thus he argued that conditions
which cause 'this or that individual to kill himself . . . concern
the psychologist not the sociologist' as opposed to 'the
causes capable of affecting not the separate individuals but the
group'.[71] The justification for this distinction is either circular
or arbitrary. Circular if 'particular' is defined as what does not
enter into sociological explanations; arbitrary since it is hard
to see where the line is to be drawn between general and
particular, and, in any case, as Halbwachs argued concerning
Suicide, particular circumstances can certainly be related to the
organization of society.[72]

(4) Finally, and most often, he saw psychological explanation as explanation in terms of individual mental states or
dispositions – as when social contract theorists explain society
as 'a system of means instituted by men to attain certain
ends',[73] or when Comte appeals to man's innate tendency towards progress or Spencer to the fear of the living and
of the dead and the desire for happiness, or when sociologists
explain the organization of the family by parental and filial
sentiments, or the incest taboo by instinctive aversion, or
economic life by the desire for wealth, or religion by religious
sentiments. His case for ruling out individual mental states and
dispositions as explanatory of social phenomena was that they
are either too general to account for the differences between

70. ibid., p. 130: tr. p. 106 (S.L.).
71. 1897a, p. 15: tr. 1951a, pp. 50–51. Durkheim frequently argues or
implies that anything that is 'individual' in this sense must derive from
the 'organico-psychic' constitution of the organism.
72. See below, Chapter 9, and Halbwachs, 1930, p. 13.
73. 1901c, p. 120: tr. p. 97.

institutions and societies, or else that they are themselves the consequence of what they purport to explain: as he put it,

history shows that these inclinations, far from being inherent in human nature, are either entirely absent in certain social conditions, or else present such variations from one society to another that the residue which remains after eliminating all these differences – and which alone can be considered of psychological origin – is reduced to something vague and schematic which is infinitely far removed from the facts requiring explanation. Thus these sentiments result from collective organization, far from being its basis.[74]

And indeed some of the best critical passages in Durkheim are those in which he attacks explanations of this type, which he saw as lazy and facile, in the essay on *Incest*, for example, and in *The Elementary Forms of the Religious Life*.

These, then, were the ways in which Durkheim distinguished sociology from psychology. He did, of course, concede that collective and individual factors are 'closely inter-related' and even that the latter can 'facilitate the explanation' of the former. But he always insisted that the 'two sciences are . . . as clearly distinct as two sciences can be, whatever relations there may otherwise be between them'.[75]

Social-Individual

Durkheim held that this methodological distinction followed from an underlying ontological distinction between levels of reality: 'society is not a mere sum of individuals; rather the system formed by their association represents a specific reality which has its own characteristics' and it was 'in the nature of this individuality, not in that of its component units, that one must seek the immediate and determining causes of the facts appearing there'.[76] And he used a number of analogies of 'creative synthesis' to support this ontological thesis – the properties of the living cell are not in its component mineral

74. ibid., pp. 131–2: tr. p. 107 (S.L.).
75. ibid., p. 136, xvi: tr. pp. 111, xlix (S.L.).
76. ibid., pp. 127–8: tr. pp. 103–4 (S.L.). It is perhaps on this point that Weber and Durkheim diverged most sharply. For Durkheim, sociological explanation involved seeking 'immediate and determining [social] causes'; for Weber, 'subjective understanding is the specific characteristic

particles, the hardness of bronze is not found in copper and tin, nor the properties of water in hydrogen and oxygen.

Durkheim was mistaken in believing that his attack on methodological individualism and defence of sociological explanation required him to defend this strong form of social realism and to claim that social facts were *sui generis*, and could only be explained in terms of other social facts. This sharp bifurcation into kinds, or levels, of facts (social *versus* individual) was, as we shall see, conceptually confused, but, in any case, it led him to overstate his case. He need only have claimed that 'social' facts cannot be wholly explained in terms of 'individual' facts; instead he claimed that they can only be explained in terms of social facts. Denying methodological individualism does not entail acceptance of 'methodological socialism' or holism.[77] In other words, it would have been enough to have claimed that no social phenomenon, indeed few human activities, can be either identified or satisfactorily explained without reference, explicit or implicit, to social factors. Furthermore, it is very important to see that, in drawing this very sharp line between the social and the individual, Durkheim was, once more, conflating a number of (importantly) different distinctions. This seemingly innocent dichotomy encompasses at least the following distinctions:

(i) between the socially determined and the organically or biologically given;
(ii) between factors specific to particular societies, and abstracted or postulated features of 'human nature';
(iii) between factors that are general within a given society or group and those that are particular to one or several individuals;
(iv) between the experience and behaviour of associated indi-

---

of sociological knowledge' (M. Weber, *Economy and Society*, ed. and tr. G. Roth and C. Wittich, New York, 1968, vol. 1, p. 15). For Durkheim, social phenomena are *sui generis* realities that can only be explained by other social phenomena and not by features of individuals; for Weber, 'these collectives must be treated as *solely* the resultants and modes of organization of the particular acts of individual persons, since these alone can be treated as agents in a course of subjectively understandable action' (Weber, op. cit., vol. 1, p. 13). See Bendix, 1971.   77. Cf. Lukes, 1968c.

viduals as opposed to those of isolated individuals;
(v) between socially prescribed obligations and spontaneous
desires and behaviour;
(vi) between factors coming from 'outside' the individual and
those generated within his consciousness;
(vii) between thoughts and actions directed towards social or
public objects and those which are purely personal and private;
(viii) between altruistic and egocentric behaviour.

Durkheim conflated these distinctions; furthermore, he
reified them into the abstractions of 'society' and 'the individual'. Indeed, as Morris Ginsberg justly observed, 'in
general "la société" had an intoxicating effect on his mind',
hindering further analysis.[78] By 'society' he sometimes meant
the social or cultural transmission or inculcation of beliefs and
practices ('a reality from which everything that matters to us
flows'[79]), sometimes the existence of association (for instance,
'Society . . . is nothing other than individuals assembled and
organized'[80]), sometimes the imposition of socially prescribed obligations ('Society . . . is a great moral power'[81]),
sometimes the object of thought, sentiment and action
('society constitutes an end that surpasses us and at the same
time appears to us as good and desirable'[82]) and sometimes
just simply a real, concrete society – though even here he was
ambiguous, using the term sometimes to mean society (France,
for example) as a whole, and sometimes particular groups and
institutions within it (the State, the family, etc.).[83] By 'the

78. Ginsberg, 1951 (1956), p. 51.
79. 1924a (1951 edn), p. 78: tr. 1953b, p. 54.
80. 1913b, p. 74. 81. 1924a (1951 edn), p. 77: tr. p. 54 (S.L.).
82. ibid., p. 80: tr. p. 56.
83. In fact, Durkheim had a strong tendency always to conceive of
'society' as a whole, rather than in terms, say, of a plurality of or conflict
between different social groups and forces. This is strikingly brought out
in a review he wrote of Bauer's *Les Classes sociales*. Bauer argued that
classes are the only proper object of social science. Durkheim wrote:
'Outside the life of each organ, there is the general life of society. There
are phenomena that are not localized in any occupational group, which
are present in them all and which are precisely the most essential of all
social facts: such as morality, religion, all common ideas, etc.' (1902f,
pp. 257–8).

individual' Durkheim meant sometimes the (pre-social) individual seen as a biologically given, organic unit, sometimes the (abstract) individual seen as possessing certain invariant properties (for example, utilitarian or economic man), sometimes the (extra-social) individual isolated from human association, and sometimes the real, concrete individual person, living in society – not to mention a further sense in which 'the individual' refers to a socially determined conception of the human person in general (as in the 'religion of the individual', which is 'the product of society itself', in which 'the individual' becomes a sacred object[84]).

Now this central, but, as we have seen, multiple, dichotomy between the social and the individual is, in a sense, the keystone of Durkheim's entire system of thought. In particular, it can be seen as crucial to his sociology of morality, his sociology of knowledge and his sociology of religion, since it underlies the distinctions he drew between moral rules and sensual appetites, between concepts and sensations, and between the sacred and the profane.[85]

Moral Rules and Sensual Appetites

Durkheim saw 'society' as 'the end and the source of morality'.[86] He thought of morality as 'social' in a number of senses. Moral rules are social in origin ('the rules of morality are norms that have been elaborated by society'[87]), they are general within a given society ('there is a general morality common to all individuals belonging to a collectivity'[88]), they presuppose human association ('Let all social life disappear, and moral life will disappear with it'[89]), they impose socially given obligations on the individual ('the obligatory character with which they are marked is nothing but the

84. 1924a (1951 edn), p. 84: tr. p. 59.
85. As Durkheim himself wrote: 'The soul and the body, sensation and reason, egoistic appetites and moral will are opposed and, at the same time, mutually related, just as the profane and the sacred, which are forbidden one to the other, nonetheless are forever intermingled' (1913b, p. 73). 86. 1924a (1951 edn), p. 84: tr. 1953b, p. 59 (S.L.).
87. 1914a: tr. 1960c, p. 338. 88. 1924a (1951 edn), p. 56: tr. p. 40.
89. 1902b, pp. 394–5: tr. 1933b, p. 399.

authority of society'[90]), they provide an external framework for the individual ('. . . like so many moulds with limiting boundaries into which we must pour our behaviour'[91]), they attach him to social goals ('Man . . . acts morally only when he takes a collectivity as the goal of his conduct'[92]) and they necessarily involve altruism ('The basis of the moral life is the sentiment that man does not belong to himself alone . . .'[93]). In contrast, Durkheim presents the individual's 'sensual appetites', 'rooted in our organisms'[94] as personal, spontaneous, private and egoistic – and our 'sensibilities . . . incline us toward individual, egoistic, irrational and immoral ends'.[95]

Durkheim was, however, unable to stick consistently to this series of contrasts. In particular, he made much of the personal autonomy of modern man, which he saw as a central feature of contemporary morality.[96] He saw that autonomy as itself socially generated and correlative with the development of the individual personality, social differentiation, and the morality of individualism or the 'cult of the individual'. But this, given his extreme social determinism, led him towards the position that the individual's personal, spontaneous, private or egoistic desires and activities are, themselves, socially generated, rather than 'rooted in the organism'. This issue arises especially clearly in the discussion of anomie in *Suicide*, where Durkheim maintains that the individual's anarchic and unrestrained passions are rooted in his organism, but also half-sees that they are social or cultural products of a particular type of society. And, in the same work, does 'egoism' result from the absence, or the presence, of social causes?

Concepts and Sensations

In 'the order of knowledge' there was, Durkheim argued, a parallel dichotomy: 'there are the senses and sensory thought,

90. 1914a: tr. 1960c, p. 338.   91. 1925a, p. 30: tr. 1961a, p. 26 (S.L.).
92. ibid., p. 294: tr. p. 256 (S.L.).   93. 1938a, vol. 2, p. 54.
94. 1914a: tr. 1961a, p. 337.   95. 1925a, p. 128: tr. p. 112 (S.L.).
96. See ibid., *leçons* 7–8.

on the one hand, and, on the other, the understanding and conceptual thought'.[97] Like moral rules, 'conceptual thought' was, he claimed, 'social and nothing but an extension of society'. Thus concepts, including the fundamental categories, were 'originally collective *représentations*'[98] – being socially caused ('the result of a collective elaboration'), 'modelled on' society ('formed on the model of social phenomena'), 'impersonal' and 'common to a plurality of men'. Contrasted with them are 'sensations', which are organically based ('A sensation of colour or sound is closely dependent on my individual organism'), as well as being personal ('a person's perceptions are his own work and will be distinctive to him') and private. Thus intellectual, like moral, life contains 'two poles' that are 'not only distinct from one another but opposed to one another'; and Durkheim came to see this 'duality of our nature' as 'only a particular case of that division of things into the sacred and the profane that is the foundation of all religions, and it must be explained on the basis of the same principles'.[99]

Sacred-Profane

What, then, *is* this division, which has been so influential and so much discussed within social anthropology and the sociology of religion? It is, Durkheim wrote,

a bipartite division of the whole universe, known and knowable, into two classes which embrace all that exists, but which radically exclude each other. Sacred things are those which the interdictions protect and isolate; profane things, those to which these interdictions are applied and which must remain at a distance from the first. Religious beliefs are the *représentations* which express the nature of sacred things and the relations which they sustain, either with each other or with profane things. Finally, rites are the rules of conduct which prescribe how men should behave in relation to sacred things.[1]

He laid very great stress on the sharpness of this division, which he held to be mutually exclusive and jointly exhaustive.

97. 1913b, p. 64.   98. 1914a: tr. 1960c, pp. 337–8.
99. ibid.: tr. pp. 327, 335 (S.L.).
1. 1912a, p. 56: tr. 1915d, pp. 40–41 (S.L.).

It marks a 'logical chasm', an 'abyss' between 'two hetero-geneous and incomparable worlds', indeed,

> In all the history of human thought, there exists no other example of two categories of things so profoundly differentiated, so radically opposed to one another ... the sacred and the profane have always and everywhere been conceived by the human mind as separate classes, as two worlds between which there is nothing in common.[2]

Beings can pass from one to the other but only through rituals (such as initiation rites) which signify 'a veritable metamor-phosis'; the 'two worlds are not only conceived of as separate, but as hostile and jealous rivals of each other', and 'the two classes cannot approach each other and keep their own natures at the same time'. We will consider, first, Durkheim's at-tempted explanation of the dichotomy, and then various empirical and conceptual difficulties which it raises.

Examples of sacred things are not only 'those personal beings which are called gods and spirits' but also 'a rock, a tree, a spring, a piece of wood, a house, in a word, anything can be sacred' – including rites and 'words, expressions and for-mulae which can be uttered only by consecrated persons': the extent of 'the circle of sacred objects ... varies infinitely, according to the different religions'.[3] What is sacred is 'set apart' and 'cannot, without losing its nature, be mixed with the profane'; it inspires us 'with respect that keeps us at a distance; and at the same time it is an object of love and aspira-tion that we are drawn towards'.[4] Now, Durkheim's thesis in *The Elementary Forms* is that 'sacred things are simply collective ideals that have fixed themselves on material objects'[5] and he attempts to explain their sacredness thus:

> they are only collective forces hypostasized, that is to say, moral forces; they are made up of the ideas and sentiments awakened in us by the spectacle of society, and not of sensations coming from the physical world.[6]

Durkheim accounted for the profane in a number of signi-ficantly different ways. It is made up of 'sensations coming

2. ibid., pp. 55, 454, 58, 53, 54: tr. pp. 40, 318, 42, 39, 40 (S.L.).
3. ibid., p. 51: tr. p. 37.
4. 1924a (1951 edn), pp. 103, 68: tr. 1953b, pp. 70, 48.
5. 1914a: tr. 1960c, p. 335. 6. 1912a, p. 461: tr. p. 322.

from the physical world' and of 'vulgar things that interest only our physical individualities'[7]; and it is located at the level of ordinary life, and our relations with ordinary things, where we are concerned with 'ourselves and our sensory interests (*nos intérêts sensibles*)', our private existence and our 'egoism'.[8]

Thus, on the one hand, there is the sacred – 'elaborated by a collectivity', hypostasizing collective forces, fusing individual *consciences* 'into communion', imposing respect and love, transferring 'society into us' and connecting 'us with something surpassing us'. On the other hand is the profane – expressing 'our organisms and the objects to which they are most directly related', and relating to men's ordinary life, which is seen as involving 'daily personal preoccupations', 'private existence' and 'egoistic passions'.[9]

It should by now be very clear that Durkheim's dichotomy between the sacred and the profane is isomorphic with the other dichotomies considered above; and that it derives from and is explained by the basic, and multiple, dichotomy between the social and the individual. It has, of course, been subjected to wide-ranging empirical and conceptual criticism. Empirically, it has been said to be 'unusable except at the cost of undue interference with the facts of observation'[10] – it does not allow for the existence of ordinary mundane objects that are neither affected by nor affect the sacred; it misrepresents the dualism found in aboriginal thought (which is not exclusive but interdependent) and it is of doubtful general ethnographic application; it confuses the different reasons for which things or persons are kept away from sacred objects or occasions; and it does not allow for situational flexibility, so that what is sacred in some contexts may not be so in others. Conceptually, it is problematic in a number of ways. For example, 'the profane' is a residual category which in fact includes a number of quite disparate classifications: namely, 'commonness (work is "an eminent form of profane activity")';

---

7. 1914a; tr. p. 336. 8. 1912a, p. 453: tr. p. 317.
9. 1914a: tr. 1960c, pp. 335–7.
10. Stanner, 1967, p. 229. I am much indebted in what follows to Stanner's discussion. Cf. also Evans-Pritchard, 1965, pp. 64–5.

minor sacredness (the less sacred is "profane" in relation to the more sacred); non-sacredness (the two classes have "nothing in common"); and anti-sacredness (profane things can "destroy" sacredness)'.[11] As Stanner has justly remarked, 'Things so disparate cannot form a class unless a class can be marked by a property, its absence and its contrary.'[12] Again, it is difficult to see how the dichotomy between sacred and profane can be reconciled with Durkheim's thesis (following Robertson Smith) that sacredness itself is ambiguous between the pure and the impure, the propitiously sacred and the unpropitiously sacred, such that there is a 'close kinship' between them, but also a contrast that is 'as complete as possible and even goes into the most radical antagonism', so that 'contact between them is considered the worst of profanations'.[13] (How, for instance, is the impurely sacred to be distinguished from the profane, a sacred profanation from a profane profanation?) Part of the whole trouble is that the dichotomy between sacred and profane is, on the one hand, a radical distinction (assumed to be made by the religious believers) between classes of 'things' (including persons, situations, etc.) of which some are 'set apart' from the rest; and, on the other hand, a distinction between the way men feel and act towards, and evaluate those things (such as whether or not they feel intense respect, or religious horror, or veneration, or love towards them). Now, clearly, the second distinction admits of degrees and situational flexibility; and, furthermore, it neither presupposes nor entails the first.

The Elementary Forms is a study of aboriginal religious beliefs and practices which Durkheim classified and interpreted in terms of this rigid and static dichotomy which he attempted to explain by linking the sacred to 'society' and the profane to 'individual' life, in all the senses we have specified above. In fact, though Durkheim's sociology of religion begins from this dichotomy, it does not end with it; and many of the ideas it contains can be considered independently of it. There is, however, no doubt that it vitiates his analysis in important

11. Stanner, 1967, p. 232.
12. ibid.
13. 1912a, pp. 586, 585; tr. pp. 410, 409.

ways. It is difficult to dissent from Stanner's judgement that this dichotomy is 'empirically inadequate' and 'caught up in conceptual and logical difficulties', that it makes for 'too many difficulties of classification and analysis, and the heuristic value is illusory'; and that it was due to following false ethnographic leads[14] – but, above all perhaps, to 'Durkheim's love of dualism'.[15]

Normal-Pathological

The last example of this dualism we shall consider is Durkheim's distinction between normal and pathological social phenomena, which he held to constitute 'two different varieties which it is important to distinguish'. Underlying this distinction – and the correlative distinction between social physiology and social pathology – is Durkheim's desire to give a scientific basis to his value judgements – or, as he preferred to put it, to give science 'practical effectiveness' – by finding 'an objective criterion, inherent in the facts themselves, which allows us scientifically to distinguish between health and sickness in the various orders of social phenomena'.[16]

In reality, Durkheim advanced two such criteria – one of which he enunciated in theory, while applying the other in practice. According to the first, one seeks 'to decide the normal or abnormal character of social facts according to their degree of generality'.[17] Thus a '*social fact is normal in relation to a given social type, at a given phase of its development, when it is present in the average of the societies of that type at the corresponding phase of their evolution*'.[18] Durkheim assumed that one could distinguish a class of social phenomena that are 'general throughout the species', found, if not in all, certainly in most cases and varying within very narrow limits, from the class of

14. Of the *noa-tabu* kind.
15. Stanner, 1967, pp. 234, 231. Stanner writes: 'Historians of ideas will no doubt wish to say much about Durkheim's inclination to dichotomism and dualism. The sacred-profane division is one of the most pre-emptive' (ibid., p. 229).
16. 1901c, pp. 59, 60, 61; tr. 1938b, pp. 47, 48, 49 (S.L.).
17. ibid., p. 91: tr. pp. 73-4 (S.L.).
18. ibid., p. 80: tr. p. 64 (S.L.).

'exceptional' phenomena, found in few cases and transient in duration; and he held that the 'average type' was an abstract model constructed from the items in the former class, at any given stage of the species' evolution. Pathological phenomena were those which diverged from the average type: 'every divergence from this standard of health is a morbid phenomenon'.[19] One trouble with this criterion – quite apart from the theoretical problems of constructing a satisfactory typology and specifying stages within it, and the logical difficulty of inferring health from generality – was that it could not be applied to existing, ongoing societies, subject to unforeseen and unforeseeable changes. As Durkheim himself put it, it was inapplicable to societies undergoing 'periods of transition where the entire species is in process of evolution, without yet being stabilized in a new form', societies which have 'not yet accomplished their entire course'.[20] (This incidentally reveals a further sharp dichotomy operative in Durkheim's thought, deriving from Saint-Simon: between 'stabilized', or 'organic', and 'transitional', or 'critical', societies).

In practice, Durkheim applied a different criterion (which he regarded as explaining the first), both to present and to past societies. This was that a social phenomenon is normal when it is tied to '*the general conditions of collective life in the social type considered*'.[21] He used this vague principle in an attempt to show, for instance, that in the 'organized' or modern industrial type of society, 'organic solidarity', planning and organization, normative regulation and social justice are normal, while economic anarchy, anomie, exploitation, the 'rising tide of suicides', etc. are abnormal. But of course these latter were all general throughout all actual, observable societies of this type; their abnormality was postulated rather in relation to a future integrated society held to be latent in the present, and it was attributed to the disappearance of the old social structure, or 'conditions of existence', and society's failure yet to adjust to the new. ('All of its traits have not been formed . . . disordered at certain points by a transitional crisis, it is itself in process of

19. ibid., pp. 69-70: tr. pp. 55-6 (S.L.).
20. ibid., pp. 75, 76; tr. pp. 60, 61 (S.L.).
21. ibid., p. 80: tr. p. 64 (S.L.).

development.')[22] Durkheim also applied this criterion to past
societies – as when he wrote of 'errors committed by the past'
and argued that human development 'has not always been
normal', as, for instance, when the Renaissance destroyed what
was of continuing value in the Scholastic educational system.[23]

Now, the trouble with this appeal to whether a phenomenon
is tied to a society's 'conditions of existence' is not merely
that it is extremely vague. It assumes that for any given society,
or social type at a given stage of development, there is a
unique set of social phenomena 'tied to its conditions of
existence', 'grounded in its normal nature'.[24] The conditions
of social health for each social type were determinate; the
latter was 'something that is definite and given in reality'.
This assumption blinded Durkheim to the possibility of real
historical alternatives at any given stage of development and
led him to see politics as analogous to medicine – a matter of
'working with steady perseverance to maintain the normal
state, or re-establishing it if it is threatened, and of rediscover-
ing its conditions if they change'.[25] The assumption derived
in part from his fundamentally dichotomizing temperament.
Any real society was bifurcated into (1) its normal, or ideally
integrated state and (2) the pathological conditions deviating
from that state. As a result, he tended to idealize societies he
thought of as integrated, ignoring the tensions and conflicts
within them, while seeing the realities of his own society
only as pathological deviations from its future, normal, ideally
integrated state.[26]

ARGUMENTS

We shall now briefly consider three characteristic forms of
argument to be found throughout Durkheim's writings. We

22. 1893b, p. 36: tr. 1933b, p. 434.

23. 1938a, I, pp. 22–3.

24. 1901c, p. 72: tr. p. 58.

25. ibid., p. 93: tr. p. 75 (S.L.). Cf. the discussion of Durkheim's view
of the relation between explanation and evaluation in Chapter 21, below.

26. Another central dichotomy in Durkheim's thought is that between
traditional and modern societies. This is discussed at length in Chapter 7,
below. It is also stressed in Giddens, 1971b.

shall here content ourselves with identifying them, rather than analysing them in detail, or explaining why Durkheim found them so convincing.

Petitio Principii

It has been said that '*petitio principii* may be considered a besetting scholarly vice' in Durkheim[27] – though it is arguably a vice more damaging to the presentation of his ideas than to the value of his explanations. Thus, for example, in *Suicide* he begins by offering a classification of suicides according to 'the causes which produce them' – so that his 'aetiological classification' presupposes the truth of his causal explanations of suicide, which the rest of the book is devoted to establishing. Again, in the same work, he argues that the currently high suicide rates must be abnormal because the vast and rapid social changes underlying contemporary suicide statistics cannot be normal.[28] In the essay on *Primitive Classification* he repeatedly presents types of classification as based on, modelled on or 'moulded by' forms of social organization – which is precisely the thesis he is seeking to establish. Again, in *The Elementary Forms*, the very definition of religion as uniting its adherents into a single moral community presupposes one of the central theses of the work, while his hypothesis that collective effervescences generate religious beliefs and rites presupposes those very beliefs and rites, since the effervescences are expressions of them.

Argument by Elimination

A second, very typical mode of argument in Durkheim is what has been called argument by elimination,[29] in which alternative explanations of a given phenomenon are systematically rejected in a way which is clearly meant to lend authority to the sole remaining candidate – Durkheim's own theory. Thus, in

27. Needham, 1963, p. xv. Cf. Lévi-Strauss, 1962a, p. 102, Stanner, 1967, pp. 237–40, and Douglas, 1967, p. 30.
28. 1897a, p. 423: tr. 1951a, p. 369.
29. Cf. Alpert, 1939a, pp. 87–8.

The Division of Labour Durkheim eliminates alternative accounts of its development, in *Suicide* he systematically eliminates explanations in terms of 'extra-social factors', in the essay on *Incest* he rules out the existing conjectural and instinct-aversion explanations, in *The Elementary Forms* he begins by ruling out animist and naturist theories of religion. The first trouble with this mode of argument is that the explanations reviewed may not be jointly exhaustive – that the rejected explanations may not include all possible candidates except Durkheim's. The second, more serious, trouble is that they may not be mutually exclusive – that the causes they separately postulate may in fact be interdependent, that, say, the environmental or psychopathic causes of suicide interact with the social causes. Indeed, Durkheim himself half-recognized this last possibility, when he wrote that suicide-proneness could itself be seen as (at least in part) socially caused, so that social factors 'predispose [individuals] to submit to the collective influence', helping for instance to render 'men's nervous systems sensitive and excessively delicate'.[30] Perhaps the main reason for Durkheim's insensitivity to this second difficulty lies in his doctrine that '*a given effect always has a single corresponding cause*'.[31] This doctrine (together with his view that they must be of the same nature) certainly allowed him to feel an unjustifiable degree of self-assurance that, in any given case, he had found the unique (social) cause of what he sought to explain.

Another form that this mode of argument by elimination takes in Durkheim is to seek to support his *definitions* by presenting the unacceptable alternatives as the only ones available. A good example is the following argument concerning the definition of morality, but the same holds for his definitions of socialism and religion:

(i) The qualification 'moral' has never been given to an act which has individual interests, or the perfection of the individual from a purely egoistic point of view, as its object; (ii) if I as an individual do not as an individual constitute an end having *in itself* a moral

30. 1897a, pp. 365–6: tr. p. 323 (S.L.).
31. 1901c, p. 157: tr. 1938b, p. 128.

character, this is necessarily also true of other individuals, who are the same as myself, differing only in degree; (iii) from which we conclude that, *if a morality exists*, it can only have as an objective the group formed by a plurality of associated individuals – that is to say, society, *but on condition that society be considered as a personality qualitatively different from the individual personalities who compose it.*[32]

Treatment of Evidence

Finally, we may allude to Durkheim's rather high-handed way with evidence – which is related to the above types of argument in springing from a remarkable confidence in his own theories. At the École Normale Supérieure when told that the facts contradicted his theories, he used to reply: 'The facts are wrong.'[33]

This approach is manifested either in the ignoring of negative instances or in what Evans-Pritchard has called 'Durkheim's irritating manoeuvre, when a fact contradicts his thesis, of asserting that its character and meaning have altered, that it is a secondary development and atypical, although there is no evidence whatsoever that such changes have taken place'.[34] There are many examples of both these moves in *Primitive Classification* (which ignores cases where social organization and symbolic classification do not correspond, and explains Arunta and Zuñi classification in terms of conjectural later developments in social structure) and in *The Elementary Forms* (which ignores clan societies without totems and totemic societies without clans, and which accounts for other totemic forms than the Central Australian as more advanced). Again, Durkheim often relied on very inadequate evidence – for example, in the discussion in *Suicide* of altruistic suicides in pre-industrial societies, in the central thesis of *Primitive Classification* that social organization corresponds to forms of classification, in the conjectural developments of beliefs in the essays on *Incest* and *Two Laws of Penal Evolution*, and in the theory in *The Elementary Forms* of the origins of

32. 1924a (1951 edn), pp. 52–3: tr. 1953b, p. 37 (S.L.).
33. Chevalier, J., *Entretiens avec Bergson* (Paris, 1959), p. 34.
34. Evans-Pritchard, 1960, p. 12.

totemism and of the genesis of the gods as syntheses of totems.[35]
In brief, Durkheim was a bold and adventurous theory-builder,
who, if he no longer claimed that 'the facts are wrong', was,
despite his aspirations toward objective, empirical science,
often surprisingly insensitive to their role in falsifying, or
verifying, his theories (though it can, of course, be entirely
rational for a scientist to place more confidence in his theories
than in some of the evidence at his disposal).

These methodological failings are, of course, very serious
(they are least evident in *Suicide* and most, perhaps, in *The
Elementary Forms*[36]); and they raise the whole question of how
his work is to be approached – as a body of explanations, or as
a body of ideas with explanatory possibilities. Certainly, many
of his own explanations are inadequate and often simply
wrong. Equally certainly, his ideas have had, and continue to
have, considerable power to organize, illuminate and suggest
explanations of many features of social life, from suicide and
deviance to ritual and religious beliefs.

DURKHEIM'S STYLE

In conclusion, a few words must be said about Durkheim's
style. It is a style that is both highly polemical and highly
metaphorical; and both the polemic and the metaphor tended
to betray Durkheim into misrepresenting his own ideas, and
into misleading himself and his readers as to their significance.

The polemic derived from Durkheim's embattled desire to
advance the claims of sociology as a science with its own
distinctive reality to study. Caught within the confines of the
dichotomy between social and individual phenomena, he was
single-mindedly, almost fanatically preoccupied with demonstrating the reality of the former. Hence his maxim that they
should be treated as things – and, even more important, the
realist language he used to characterize them. Hence, above all,
his talk of '*la société*' as a 'reality' distinct from the 'individual',
which led him to reify, even deify 'society', to treat it as a *deus*

---

35. Not, of course, that this was always his fault. Often, as with altruistic
suicide, the evidence was not available to him.
36. See below, pp. 477–81.

ex machina, to attribute to it 'powers and qualities as mysterious and baffling as any assigned to the gods by the religions of this world'.[37] He was led along this path, all the while denying any desire to hypostasize society, and was thus inclined to ignore aspects of social life not easily assimilable into the society-individual schema, such as interaction and relations *between* individuals, and relations between sub-societal groups and institutions. Moreover, his exclusive concentration on the society end of the schema, on the impact of social conditions on individuals rather than the ways individuals perceive, interpret and respond to social conditions, led him to leave inexplicit and unexamined the social-psychological assumptions on which his theories rested.

This last tendency was only reinforced by the metaphorical, figurative language he used to characterize social phenomena. In *The Division of Labour* it was the organic analogy which predominated[38]; subsequently he was increasingly attracted – far more than any of his interpreters have realized – by the language of 'collective forces' and 'social currents' and, in general, the analogy of thermodynamics and electricity.[39] *Suicide* is full of such language: for each people there was 'a collective force of a determinate amount of energy, impelling men to self-destruction' and such forces 'determine our behaviour from without, just like physico-chemical forces' and their strength can be measured 'as one does the strength of electric currents'.[40] He used this language very widely to describe the genesis and operation of collective ideas and sentiments, and the phenomenon of sacredness. For example, in discussing the origins of property rights, he described the

37. Ginsberg, 1955 (1956), p. 242. Cf. Evans-Pritchard's remark that 'it was Durkheim and not the savage who made society into a god' (Evans-Pritchard, E. E., *Nuer Religion*, Oxford, 1956, p. 313).

38. For example, 'What gives unity to organized societies, however, as to all organisms, is the spontaneous consensus of the parts' (1902b, p. 351: tr. 1933b, p. 360).

39. But see Needham, 1963, p. xxv, n. 1: 'It is intriguing to conjecture the effect of nineteenth-century physics on the development of such notions as "cause" and "force" in Durkheim's thought, and which led Mauss to look for a 'force' in a gift which compelled its return.'

40. 1897a, pp. 336, 348–9: tr. 1951a, pp. 299, 309–10.

ritual ceremonies of maintaining boundaries as relieving the field of

the excess of religiosity in order to make it profane or at least profanable, without incurring peril. The religiosity, however, is indestructible: it can therefore only be shifted from one point to another. This dreaded force dispersed about the field will be drawn off, but it has to be transferred elsewhere, so it is accumulated on the periphery. This is the purpose of the sacrifices described.[41]

There are continual appeals to 'collective' and 'moral forces' in Durkheim's writings on morality and on religion: thus, for instance, the 'extreme facility with which religious forces spread out and are diffused' is compared with the way in which 'heat or electricity which a body has received from some external source may be transmitted to the surrounding medium',[42] and religion in general is seen as consisting in 'religious forces ... human forces, moral forces'.[43] Indeed, 'behind [religious] beliefs there are forces' and a 'theory of religion must first of all show what these forces are, of what they are made and what their origins are'.[44]

Now, all this language of social currents and forces was a weapon in Durkheim's campaign to win recognition for sociology's scientific status. It was, however, a distinctly inappropriate way of expressing what he had to say: for *Suicide* is not about the operation of social currents, but about the social preconditions for psychological health, and *The Elementary Forms* is not about the impact of collective forces, but about the social origins of religious beliefs and rituals, the interpretation of their meaning and symbolism, and their consequences for individuals and for society as a whole.

41. 1950a, pp. 184–5: tr. 1957a, p. 156 (S.L.).
42. 1912a, p. 461: tr. 1915d, p. 322 (S.L.).
43. ibid., p. 599: tr. p. 419.
44. 1913b, p. 66. Likewise, he saw morality as 'a system of forces ... which draw all their power of action from *représentations*' (1910b, p. 60).

Part One
Youth: 1858-87

Chapter 1

Childhood

DAVID Émile Durkheim was born on 15 April 1858 at Épinal, capital town of the department of Vosges, in Lorraine. His father, Moïse Durkheim, had been the rabbi of Épinal since the 1830s and was Chief Rabbi of the Vosges and Haute-Marne; his grandfather, Israël David Durkheim, had been a rabbi in Mutzig (Alsace), as also had his great-grandfather Simon Simon, appointed in 1784. His mother, Mélanie *née* Isidor, was the daughter of a trader in beer (or horses). He grew up within the confines of a close-knit, orthodox and traditional Jewish family, part of the long-established Jewish community of Alsace-Lorraine that was notable for providing France with many army officers and civil servants at the end of the nineteenth century.[1] Durkheim, however, was destined for the rabbinate and his early education was directed to that end: he studied for a time at a rabbinical school.[2] Yet he soon decided, while still a schoolboy, not to follow the family tradition.[3]

The Durkheim family's resources were very modest and its manner of life austere. The father earned the meagre sum of 2,500 francs a year, which the mother supplemented by opening an embroidery workshop, like many other such wives in the Vosges, from which she earned the same as her husband. At the time of Durkheim's birth the embroiderers worked in the family house.[4] He grew up, the youngest child, with his brother, Félix, and two sisters, Rosine and Céline, in

1. See Aubery, P., *Milieux juifs de la France contemporaine* (2nd edn, Paris, 1962), p. 61, and Anchel, R., *Les juifs en France* (Paris, 1946), p. 18. See Appendix G in Lukes, 1968b, for a reproduction of Durkheim's family tree, which gives a striking picture of a sample of this community's upward social mobility over six generations.

2. M. Étienne Halphen, personal communication.

3. M. Georges Davy, personal communication.

4. M. Henri Durkheim, personal communication.

an atmosphere where 'the observance of the law was precept and example, where nothing intruded that might divert one from one's duty'.[5] This background, according to Georges Davy, marked him with several ineradicable traits: 'scorn for the inclination to conceal effort, disdain for success unachieved by effort, horror for everything that is not positively grounded: the life of the individual within the framework of the group, truths through their rationally established implications, conduct by its moral regulation'.[6] From the time of his childhood, he retained an exacting sense of duty and a serious, indeed austere, view of life[7]; he could never experience pleasure without a sense of remorse.[8]

He undoubtedly experienced what he later described as 'that tempering of character, that heightening of life which a strongly cohesive group communicates to its members'. He held this to be peculiarly evident among religious minorities, obliged, 'in order to combat hostility or ill-will from outside, to turn inwards'; among them, he wrote, social bonds are much tighter than otherwise, and 'this increased concentration leads to a feeling of relief that is immeasurably bracing and sustains one against the difficulties of life'.[9] Especially was this so among the Jews, with their 'need of resisting a general hostility, the very impossibility of free communication with the rest of the population'.[10] He later wrote of the typical Jewish community as 'a small society, compact and cohesive, with a very keen self-consciousness and sense of unity' and of Judaism as consisting 'like all early religions . . . of a body of practices minutely governing all the details of life and leaving little free room for individual judgement'.[11]

5. Davy, 1960a, p. 15.
6. ibid.
7. Davy, 1960b, p. 6.
8. Bouglé, 1930, p. 283.
9. 1925a, p. 274; tr. 1961a, p. 240 (S.L.).
10. 1897a, p. 159; tr. 1951a, p. 160.
11. ibid., pp. 159–60; tr. p. 160 (S.L.). On the special relevance of Durkheim's theory of religion to Judaism, see Scharf, B. R., 'Durkheimian and Freudian Theories of Religion: The Case for Judaism', *British Journal of Sociology*, 21 (1970), pp. 151–63.

Durkheim went to the local school, the Collège d'Épinal, where he was an outstanding pupil, skipping two classes and gaining his *baccalauréats* with ease. While at school he experienced a brief crisis of mysticism, under the influence of an old Catholic school-mistress, which he rapidly surmounted.[12] At a very early age he decided that he wanted to pursue his studies beyond school. His father agreed but made it clear that this would be conditional on his being serious and working hard. These conditions were fulfilled; his youth at Épinal was 'studious and serious'.[13]

During the Franco-Prussian war, when Durkheim was twelve years old, the Germans occupied the town of Épinal (which, after the armistice, became a French frontier-town). There is evidence that he witnessed, and was possibly subjected to, anti-semitism at this time, for he was later to write:

[Anti-semitism] had already been seen in the regions of the East at the time of the war of 1870; being myself of Jewish origin, I was then able to observe it at close hand. The Jews were blamed for defeats.[14]

His experience of the French defeat may have contributed to a strong (though in no way militant) patriotism, a defensive sense of national decadence and a consequent desire to contribute to the regeneration of France – sentiments that were, in different forms, prevalent among intellectuals of his generation.[15] The biographer of his contemporary, the historian

12. Davy, 1919, p. 183, and Davy, 1960b, p. 6.
13. Davy, 1960b, p. 7.
14. 1899d, p. 60. Anti-semitism had had a long history on the eastern border and had found a ready target in the Yiddish-speaking Ashkenazim who had settled there. Cf. Byrnes, R. F., *Antisemitism in Modern France* (New Brunswick, N. J., 1952), vol. I, pp. 260–61. But by the end of the nineteenth century, the Jews were fairly closely integrated with the rest of the community. In Épinal, the Durkheim family lived in the centre of the town and (on all accounts) did not speak Yiddish.
15. See Digeon, C., *La Crise allemande de la pensée française (1870–1914)* (Paris, 1959), ch. VIII, Swart, K. W., *The Sense of Decadence in Nineteenth Century France* (The Hague, 1964), chs. V and VI, and Girardet, R., *Le Nationalisme français: 1871–1914* (Paris, 1966).

Camille Jullian, recalled the 'long-suffering and easily offended patriotism' characteristic of that whole generation:

> Defeat in disorder, the mutilation of the country, the eloquent heroism of Gambetta, the improvised armies of the East and of the Loire fighting, until utterly exhausted, for the sake of honour even more than victory – was this not enough to produce in a child with an ardent imagination an impression that would last?[16]

Durkheim, like Jullian, was 'one of those whose task would consist in the revival of France'.[17]

Having gained his *baccalauréats* in Letters (in 1874) and in Sciences (in 1875), and distinguished himself in the *Concours Général*, it was necessary to leave Épinal for Paris in order to prepare for the École Normale Supérieure, on which he had set his sights. At this period his father became ill and he had to take on the considerable responsibilities of acting, in effect, as the head of the family. Having little money, it was only after difficult financial negotiations that he was admitted to a *pension* for students non-resident in Paris, the Institution Jauffret. He wrote subsequently of 'that feeling of emptiness and isolation familiar to all those who come to complete their studies in Paris'.[18] And indeed his days were passed in daily anguish,[19] partly because of the family responsibilities he carried and the insecurity of his own future, partly because of the uncongenial nature of the courses he had to follow, in conditions of the strictest discipline. His predilections were already scientific rather than literary; he suffered under the weight of the Latin verse and the principles of rhetoric which he had to master. At the end of the year he failed to be admitted to the École and he entered the Lycée Louis-le-Grand to continue his preparatory studies. There was, says Davy, 'only a single light in his sombre sky; it came from the professor of philosophy, Charpentier ... Without influencing the formation of his mind, this perspicacious philosopher advised him to persist in his design, sustained his courage, enabled him to enjoy domestic

16. Grenier, A., *Camille Jullian* (Paris, 1944), p. 16.
17. ibid.
18. 1887d, p. 51.
19. Davy, 1960a, p. 16.

pleasures and helped him with many lessons.'[20] After the
second year he was again unsuccessful. It was only after a
third that he was finally admitted to the École, in 1879.

20. Davy, 1919, p. 183. Charles Andler describes Charpentier as a man
of learning and integrity who had 'reflected a great deal on Infinity and
Quantity and on the fundamentals of various sciences' (Andler, C.,
Vie de Lucien Herr, Paris, 1932, p. 25). Cf. 1895b, p. 129, where Durkheim
writes caustically about the philosophy he was taught at the Lycée, with
its emphasis on intellectual gymnastics and novelty.

Chapter 2

The École Normale Supérieure

HENRI Bergson had been admitted the year before, and so also had Jean Jaurès, with whom Durkheim had established a friendship while at the Institution Jauffret, which was to continue until Jaurès' death. In those early years he was often in the company of Jaurès.[1] There is some reason to believe that it was the combined influence of Jaurès and Bergson on Durkheim while at the École that led to Durkheim's final break with Judaism.[2] That break was painful but decisive; henceforth he was to regard religious beliefs, not as simply false, but rather as a confused and distorted form of morality, a set of moral beliefs expressed in a theological or mythological rather than in a positive, or scientific, idiom.[3]

Durkheim suffered greatly from the strains of academic competition and the fear of failure. Davy writes that he experienced agonies at the pension Jauffret and during his first year at the École, which were to begin again after his *agrégation*. During his visit to German universities in 1885–6, he almost returned home for fear of not meeting the expectations of those who had sent him there.[4] Even when he had been appointed to the Faculty of Letters at Bordeaux, 'he spent his

1. M. Henri Durkheim, personal communication. It was Durkheim who influenced Jaurès to take a greater interest in social problems. See Goldberg, H., *The Life of Jean Jaurès* (Madison, 1962), p. 16, and Mauss, 1928, p. viii.

2. M. Étienne Halphen, personal communication. M. Davy has told me that this was '*une rupture pénible*'. His first taste of pork made him feel great remorse – see his use of dietary laws to illustrate the moral, obligatory character of religious rules in 1887b, p. 308, and 1902b, p. 76: tr. 1933b, p. 107.

3. Pécaut, 1918, p. 15. Cf. 1925a, pp. 12–13: tr. 1961a, p. 11, where Durkheim speaks of science having the task of uncovering those moral forces which 'hitherto men have only learned to conceive of in the form of religious allegories'.

4. Davy, 1960a, p. 17.

first year of teaching in the Faculty in dread of failure'.[5] At the
École, however, his anxiety was somewhat appeased after his
first year by the gaining of his *licence* with maximum honours,
though he remained apprehensive and always anxious.[6] Yet he
already felt inspired by a mission. He had determined, says
Davy, to be 'a teacher and a scholar, but also an apostle, so
vital did it seem to him to raise up the public spirit cast down
by defeat'.[7]

Durkheim's generation at the rue d'Ulm was a brilliant one:
apart from Bergson and Jaurès, it included, during his three
years, a great number of future academics of distinction,
among them the philosophers Gustave Belot, Edmond
Goblot, Félix Rauh and Maurice Blondel, the psychologist
Pierre Janet, the linguist Ferdinand Brunot, the historian Henri
Berr, the Roman historian Camille Jullian and the geographer
Lucien Gallois. On graduation, the students served as *professeurs de lycée*, after which, apart from those who became
academics, some went into industry and journalism, while
others eventally became politicians.[8]

Here was the French equivalent of Jowett's Balliol. The
students were 'the choicest and keenest young men of the
entire land, already well equipped, academically, for honourable positions in life'. The École Normale Supérieure 'provided for these the most learned masters and best teachers to be
found', and kept 'away from them all distractions of the outside world'.[9] Indeed, for much of the time, the students were
literally locked in the École; except for attending outside
courses, they were allowed out only on Sundays and Thursday
afternoons (and only once a month until midnight). Working
conditions were bare and sombre, badly lit, badly ventilated,

5. ibid.; the quotation is from a letter to Davy from Marcel Mauss.

6. Davy, 1960b, p. 7.

7. Davy, 1960a, p. 16.

8. See Hyppolite, J., quoting speech of Lucien Febvre in *Revue de
synthèse*, 3 série, no. 35 (July–September 1964), p. 156.

9. Ladd, A. J., *École Normale Supérieure: An Historical Sketch* (Grand
Forks, N. D., 1907), p. 3. There were 135 students, divided into science and
arts sections. See Peyrefitte, A., *Rue d'Ulm: Chroniques de la vie normalienne*
(Paris, new edn, 1963).

and remarkably unhygienic.[10] The École was really a 'total institution',[11] bringing the 'young men of the elite, from all over France' into close proximity and under rigorous discipline.[12] It had a powerful effect upon them: here were 'formed lasting friendships that are fruitful for science', and ex-students retained (as Durkheim later did) 'fond memories' of their intense years there.[13]

It was an exhilarating and closed world: as Jaurès was later to write, it was really 'a prolongation of school – a sort of intellectual boarding-school, animated sometimes by a marvellous effervescence of ideas and giving the mind a passion for the movement of history, but in no way educating it by immediate contact with men and events'.[14] Durkheim was fired by the feverish activity of the *normaliens*, especially when it took the form of arguments and discussions, which were as often political as philosophical.

Indeed, Durkheim, in Davy's words, 'did not conceive of a philosophy which did not end in a political and social application – nor, inversely, of a form of politics which did not have a philosophical basis'. He was later to see sociology as the 'philosophy which would contribute to giving the Republic a basis and inspiring in it rational reforms while giving to the nation a principle of order and a moral doctrine'.[15] He even formed the ambition to devote the first half of his life to pure, scientific research and the second half to politics.[16] He passionately enjoyed these discussions, at which he excelled in argument. Davy quotes the reminiscences of Durkheim's

10. Andler, op. cit., p. 22, and Frédéricq, P., 'L'Enseignement supérieure de l'histoire à Paris', *RIE*, 6 (July 1883), pp. 753–4.

11. See Goffman, Erving, *Asylums* (Chicago, 1962).

12. Frédéricq, loc. cit., p. 754. Its director in 1898, Perrot, was to write: 'Democracy needs an elite to represent the only superiority it recognizes, that of the mind. It is up to us to recruit that elite. . .' quoted in Zeldin, T., 'Higher Education in France, 1870–1940', *Journal of Contemporary History*, 2 (1967), p. 74.

13. Frédéricq, loc. cit., p. 754.

14. Quoted in Jackson, J. Hampden, *Jean Jaurès* (London, 1943), p. 28.

15. Davy, 1919, p. 188.

16. Halbwachs, 1918, p. 353.

friend and contemporary, the Hellenist Maurice Holleaux:

> He was at the École at the time of the ascendancy of Gambetta and the great reforms of Jules Ferry. At the École these were the subject of incessant discussions. Durkheim sought out these discussions, often starting them and throwing himself into them with true passion . . . I heard him discuss for hours with a logical fervour which was the marvel of his hearers – he could not have been more strained, more nervous, more eloquent. Yet he always remained on the summits and only debated principles. The political arena ('*la cuisine politique*') was always odious to him: he was unaware of questions of personalities and coteries. Gambetta was something of an idol to him: I believe he liked him so much for what he believed to be large and generous in him. Talking with him in 1914, I remember him saying that politics had become in our days 'a thing so small and mediocre'. He always wanted it to be a big thing; he saw it as such in his youth.[17]

Twenty years later, Durkheim recalled this period of triumph over the monarchist and Catholic right in these words: 'The men of my generation remember how great was our enthusiasm when, twenty years ago, we at last witnessed the collapse of the last barriers that resisted our impatient demands. But alas! disenchantment came quickly . . .'[18]

The hot-house atmosphere of the École did everything to encourage a view of politics from a high plane of principle. As Jaurès wrote, 'In minds nurtured in that fashion, the most subtle and profound knowledge is found side by side with the most extraordinary ignorance. It is like a vast secluded room where the light penetrates dimly. . . In my case . . . I did not know that there were Socialist groups in France and a whole agitation of propaganda and fervour of sectarian rivalry, from Guesde to Malon.'[19] Durkheim, like Jaurès at that time, was entirely persuaded by the rhetoric of republicanism and convinced of the need to establish a national creed based on 'liberty, equality, fraternity'; they both admired Gambetta as the spiritual embodiment of the Republic and thus as 'the heroic defender of the good society, who worked for justice at

17. Davy, 1919, pp. 188–9.
18. 1898c, p. 12.
19. Jackson, op. cit., p. 28.

home and peace abroad'.[20] Durkheim is reported to have spent the entire day demonstrating in the Paris streets during the fourteenth of July celebrations of 1880.[21]

Evidence is lacking concerning Durkheim's precise views about Jules Ferry's anticlerical educational reforms, which sharply divided the students at the École. Among the most controversial was Ferry's measure forbidding the administration of schools by unauthorized religious orders. Durkheim was presumably sympathetic, as was Jaurès, to the republican, positivist Ferry and his aim of creating a national system of secular education. He must have argued fiercely against the minority of the *normaliens* known as the 'Talas' (*'ceux qui vonT À LA messe'*); but we do not know whether, with the majority, he supported Ferry's measure, or whether he supported Jaurès in the view that the beliefs of others should be respected. Nor do we know whether he agreed with Jaurès in deploring Ferry's dismissal of the Catholic philosophy professor at the École, Léon Ollé-Laprune, for protesting against the measure, on the grounds that 'professors . . . were entitled to their freedom'.[22]

Durkheim's main preoccupations, however, were academic. He was a serious student and had no time for the irony and literary banter common among the *normaliens*; he hated all superficiality and dilettantism. As Holleaux writes,

I have seen him ardently wishing for the end of the year, the vacation time, the moment when he would be allowed to live again among 'good simple people' (his own expression). Being absolutely simple, he detested all affectation. Being deeply serious, he hated a flippant tone. Few people truly knew him. Few realized what an almost feminine sensibility was concealed by his severity and what treasures of tender goodness were hidden by that heart, hostile to easy outpourings.[23]

20. Goldberg, op. cit., p. 19. For a discussion of Jaurès' republicanism, see Brogan, D. W., *French Personalities and Problems* (London, 1946), ch. xi.

21. Davy, 1919, p. 188.

22. Quoted in Goldberg, op. cit., p. 20, which gives an account of these debates at the École.

23. Davy, 1919, p. 187. Cf. Jaurès' letters to Charles Salomon in Lévy-Bruhl, L., *Jean Jaurès, esquisse biographique* (Paris, 1924), expressing very similar sentiments.

Durkheim's closest friends at the École, apart from Jaurès and Holleaux, were Lucien Picard, another classical scholar, and, above all, Victor Hommay, who committed suicide in 1886. In the light of Durkheim's future interest in the subject of suicide, the intimacy of his friendship with Hommay and the sensitive account he wrote of the latter's life and death[24] acquire a special significance.

'I no longer know', he wrote,

how we came to be linked. One can only suppose that it happened by itself, little by little, for I cannot recall any particular circumstance giving birth to a friendship which soon became for me the sweetest intimacy. Throughout our three years at the École, we truly lived the same life; we worked in the same room, we pursued the same studies; we even spent together almost all our days of freedom. In the course of those long conversations, what plans did we not make for each other! I can now no longer recall them without sadness and bitterness.[25]

Before entering the École, Hommay had found life during his preparatory studies in Paris empty and isolated. 'Accustomed to a warm family life' and 'unable to live without a sense of secure affection around him, he felt himself surrounded by indifferent people unable perhaps to understand him'.[26] However, his three years at the École were 'three blessed years'. His teachers valued his originality and his 'very lively imagination'; his friends were most impressed by his open and ardent conversation – 'His speech had a strange charm; somewhat rough and jarring, it was full of warmth and life; sometimes, it came forth in sudden spurts, as though inspired; one always sensed a deep sincerity.' Hommay knew 'no greater happiness that that of being liked and appreciated by his teachers and friends'; it was 'only among us that he felt completely at home'. In the vacations,

in the remotest part of his native Brittany . . . he soon came to miss our good talks and our warm discussions. He entirely preferred this active, even rather feverish life. What delighted him above all was

24. 1887d.
25. ibid., p. 52.
26. ibid., p. 51.

the continuous contact with distinguished minds and outstanding teachers.[27]

On his leaving the École to teach in provincial lycées, there began 'what he himself called a period of ordeals, which he found hard to endure'. He enjoyed teaching itself, but 'he had a need for variety which provincial life, with its poverty of events and relationships, could hardly satisfy':

he also had a proud spirit and an independence of character which made all the little difficulties of secondary teaching very painful to him. Eager for change, he could not live without a certain amount of dreaming. And in those small towns, where people live rather on top of one another, where they see and observe one another at such close quarters, reality was too close to him not to bruise and wound him ceaselessly. 'When I think of those good years at the École,' he wrote to me, 'especially of that second year, when we really lived the true life, the only life that is worth the suffering one endures for it, when I think of our dreams of that time, of our preoccupations, of the work we did, then my present life appears to me pale, colourless, monotonous, insipid, and I wonder whether really the good times are not over for us, at least for a long time ... When my thoughts become too gloomy, I bury myself in my books which are now my only friends. We are indeed very fortunate to have this resource.'

Hommay, wrote Durkheim, 'recognized the danger' and became absorbed in his thesis (on the history of moral ideas). Things seemed to improve, and the tedium of daily life became less acute: 'he had a goal and advanced towards it with resolution'.[28] One day, Durkheim wrote to him somewhat despondently about their work, and Hommay replied: 'Doubtless the results of one's efforts, when one analyses them, are worth very little; but that very little, magnified by imagination, adds an element of the ideal to life and inspires activity: if life were reduced to the monotony of daily habits, it would seem to be so very little that one would cling onto it only by routine.' Hommay's life continued to grow 'less sad and

27. ibid., p. 52.
28. ibid., p. 53.

solitary', until it was suddenly ended by what Durkheim (tactfully) called 'a miserable and tragic accident':

On Tuesday 6th of July at about eight in the morning, he was getting ready to leave for the lycée. He was ... going out when, suddenly changing his mind, he said: 'I must give a lecture I have not sufficiently prepared. I must go up again and look again through my notes.' He entered his room, on the second floor, took his notebook and sat on the edge of a very low window without a balcony, which easily induced vertigo. He made a sudden and foolhardy movement, characteristic of him, and lost his balance. A few moments later, he was picked up in the courtyard, his book of notes beside him.[29]

One can only guess at the impact Hommay's life and death had upon Durkheim. But the emotion expressed in the obituary is unmistakable, as are the foreshadowings of the account Durkheim was later to give of the condition leading to egoistic suicide – 'the individual isolates himself ... because the ties linking him with others are slackened or broken'[30]; he is no longer part of 'a cohesive and animated society', providing 'a constant interchange of ideas and feelings' and a 'mutual moral support'[31]; he becomes 'bereft of reasons for existence', his efforts 'lose themselves in emptiness' and his activity lacks 'an object transcending it'[32]; all 'that remains is an artificial combination of illusory images' and 'the only life to which [he] could cling no longer corresponds to anything actual'[33]; life is deprived 'of object and meaning'[34] and 'the least causes of discouragement may easily give birth to desperate resolutions'.[35]

His fellow *normaliens* tended to regard Durkheim with some awe. In Holleaux's words,

It was in November 1879 that I made the acquaintance of Émile Durkheim. Physically he has changed very little in the course of his

29. ibid., p. 54.
30. 1897a, p. 317: tr. 1951a, p. 281.
31. ibid., p. 224: tr. p. 210.
32. ibid., p. 228: tr. p. 213.
33. ibid.
34. ibid., p. 288: tr. p. 258.
35. ibid., p. 228: tr. p. 213.

life. In 1879 he was 21 years old, the average age of his contemporaries, but he still seemed markedly older than most of them. His maturity was precocious. He already had that serious air which we have always known. Hence the nickname of 'the Metaphysician' which he was given.[36]

Holleaux writes, about a paper he delivered in his first year, that

We had the distinct feeling that the author far surpassed his contemporaries in maturity of mind. The style had already acquired that concentrated force and sober brilliance which one was to rediscover in all his later writings. But it was above all in his lectures that Durkheim showed from those early days what he was and would be. He was at once the teacher and the orator which he remained throughout his career. He spoke volubly, virtually without notes, with a passionate ardour and an imperious decisiveness. Those who had once heard him could not doubt his superiority.[37]

Bergson was, however, less generous. He spoke of him as bearing the marks of the future metaphysician and stunning dialectician:

His conversation was already nothing but polysyllogisms and sorites. Having [subsequently] taken as premisses the Totem and the Taboo, I am not surprised that he has been able to deduce the whole world from them. On the steps of the staircase and even at lunchtime, he would immobilize us with four-forked dilemmas.[38]

'I have always thought', Bergson recalled,

that he would be an abstraction-monger. I was not so mistaken. With him, one never encountered a fact. When we told him that the facts were in contradiction with his theories, he would reply: 'The facts are wrong.'[39]

Although he was very devoted to the École and afterwards felt greatly attached to it,[40] he was also disappointed by it and severely critical of its style of education, which he found too

36. Davy, 1919, p. 184.
37. ibid., p. 185.
38. Maire, G., *Bergson, mon maître* (Paris, 1935), pp. 143–4.
39. Chevalier, J., *Entretiens avec Bergson* (Paris, 1959), p. 34.
40. In 1905 he was opposed to projected measures that aimed to reduce the autonomy of the École *vis-à-vis* the Sorbonne; and he wanted his son to go there: see Davy, 1960a, p. 16.

humanistic and literary, and too hostile to scientific attitudes. Holleaux writes that Durkheim's first year at the École, most of which had to be devoted to Latin verse and Greek prose, brought him great disillusionments[41]:

> It was not only the rhetoric, which was bad enough, for it was imposed on young men already saturated with rhetoric. They also had to apply themselves to the most mediocre exercises of an antiquated humanism: Latin verses and Latin or French dissertations on more or less far-fetched witty conceits. Exercises of this sort were odious to Durkheim; they cost him a great and painful effort, which did not always meet with success. I saw him groan and vent his indignation over Latin verses from which he could not extricate himself.[42]

He found Ernest Bersot, the Director of the École until 1880, too literary and unmethodical, and he was critical, on similar grounds, of Ollé-Laprune and the literary scholar Delacrulouche. None the less, Holleaux reports that Durkheim read to his class towards the end of the first year a dissertation he had composed on the phrase of Schiller's Don Carlos, 'May you never despise the dreams you had in your youth!', which won admiration, and he also wrote a distinguished study of the Jews in the Roman Empire for Ernest Desjardins. His first year was completed by his *licence*, when he is said to have astonished Mézières by an ingenious oral improvisation on the genius of Molière.[43]

His second year was more secure. It was spent largely in personal research, as was the practice at the École, under Gaston Boissier, who taught Latin literature and had a great ascendancy there, but in his case too Durkheim reacted against the brilliant literary manner. He wrote for him a paper on Stoic morality among the Romans, which was greatly praised. He also gave a paper on the self which Émile Boutroux found so striking that he reminded Durkheim of it during his doctoral defence. He was greatly attracted by philosophy and psychology, though he approached the latter subject from a purely

41. The first two years were common to all students, being devoted to philology, literature, philosophy and history.
42. Davy, 1919, p. 185.
43. ibid.

philosophical point of view, and was afterwards to complain of having learnt nothing of the experimental research that was gaining much currency in France at that time: it was only after his *agrégation* that he came to know of the work of Charcot and Ribot in France and Wundt in Germany.[44] Indeed, for some time he intended to pursue psychological researches on 'quantity and quality'[45] but soon abandoned the idea, probably during the second year, and turned to the study of morality and society, and eventually to sociology.

RENOUVIER AND BOUTROUX

The writings of the neo-Kantian, or 'neo-criticist', Renouvier[46] excited him greatly and 'marked him with an imprint that he never erased'.[47] It was the thought of Renouvier (whom Taine called a 'republican Kant') rather than that of Kant himself that exercised the strongest immediate influence on him at this important period of his intellectual development.[48] He was later to say to Maublanc, 'If you wish to mature your thought, devote yourself to the study of a great master; take a system apart, laying bare its innermost secrets. That is what I did and my educator was Renouvier.'[49] Maublanc thinks that Durkheim owed most to Renouvier, and Davy writes that his

44. ibid. See Reuchlin, M., 'The Historical Background for National Trends in Psychology: France', *Journal of the History of the Behavioral Sciences*, 1,2 (1965), pp. 115–22.

45. Léon, 1917, p. 750.

46. On Renouvier, see Picard, R., *La Philosophie sociale de Renouvier* (Paris, 1908); Parodi, D., *Du positivisme à l'idéalisme* (Paris, 1930); Soltau, R., *French Political Thought in the Nineteenth Century* (New York, 1959), pp. 306–21; and Scott, J., *Republican Ideas and the Liberal Tradition in France, 1870–1914* (New York, 1951), pt. 1, ch. 1.

47. Davy, 1919, p. 185.

48. According to Davy, he 'mistrusted' Kant (Davy, 1919, p. 186); but it is clear that he was always well disposed towards Kantianism. As he wrote, in 1887, 'of all the philosophies Germany has produced, Kantianism is the one which, if wisely interpreted, can best be reconciled with the needs of science' (1887a, p. 330). Bouglé wrote: '*Le Durkheimisme, c'est encore du Kantisme, revu et complété par du Comtisme*' (Bouglé, 1930b, p. 283).

49. Maublanc, 1930, p. 299. Cf. 1955a, p. 76, where Durkheim calls Renouvier 'the greatest contemporary rationalist'.

Renouvierism was even to be increased later at Bordeaux, where he was much influenced by the Renouvierist philosopher Octave Hamelin.[50]

It would be hard to exaggerate Renouvier's influence on French liberal republicans at the end of the nineteenth century; indeed, it is not too much to say that his philosophy was 'the system from which the political culture and the official metaphysics of the Third Republic derived',[51] especially between 1870 and the turn of the century. It was particularly influential among academics, and especially philosophers. One can discern what Durkheim valued in Renouvier: his uncompromising rationalism; his central concern with morality[52] and his determination to study it 'scientifically'; his neo-Kantianism emphasizing the compatibility of the determinism of nature with the freedom presupposed by morality; his Kantian concern with the dignity and autonomy of the individual together with his theory of social cohesion based on the individual's sense of unity with and dependence on others; his preference for justice over utility, and denial that the first can be derived from the second; his notion of existing society being in a state of war and his view of the State's role being to establish 'social justice' in the economic sphere; his advocacy of associations, such as producers' co-operatives, independent of the State; his case for secular, republican education in state schools; and his underlying purpose of reconciling the sacredness of the individual with social solidarity.[53] Renouvier's

50. Davy, 1919, p. 185. Cf. Hamelin, O., *Le Système de Renouvier* (Paris, 1927). See below, Chapter 22.

51. Mariça, 1932, pp. 3–4. Cf. Parodi, 1919, p. 33: '. . . this singular and powerful system . . . has had so much influence in our time . . .' Louis Prat wrote that 'the most distinguished thinkers at the end of the nineteenth century were influenced by [Renouvier's] thought' (quoted in Scott, op. cit., p. 76).

52. 'In effect, the thesis of criticism is precisely the primary of morality in the human mind with regard to the possibility of establishing transcendental truths. . . Criticism subordinates all that is unknown to phenomena, all phenomena to the *conscience*, and, within the *conscience* itself, theoretical to practical reason' (Renouvier, C., *Science de la morale*, Paris, 1869, vol. I, p. 14).

53. There is 'no longer any guarantee of justice' when 'the individual's conscience, his reason and his right are not posed as the most general laws

thought must have strongly influenced Durkheim's attitude to 'that cult of the person, of individual dignity ... which henceforth is the unique rallying centre of so many minds'[54] and which he later described as 'the only system of beliefs which can ensure the moral unity of the country'.[55] One must also suppose that Durkheim found Renouvier's celebration of the bourgeois virtues congenial: 'respect for rights and obligations, regard for national traditions and customs, sincere attachment to the rule of law, and the observation of moderation in all things'.[56] It could, indeed, be argued that the essential political role of Renouvier's philosophy was to consolidate the Republic and to contain what were seen as its enemies, on both the right and the left. Mauss wrote of his period at the École that 'by vocation and in an atmosphere animated by political and moral interests, and together with Jaurès and his other friend Hommay ... he dedicated himself to the study of the social question'.[57] The ideas that guided them were, in no small measure, Renouvier's.

There is an even more fundamental respect in which Renouvier may well have influenced Durkheim. Kant had maintained that Reason, and in particular the categories of thought, are given *a priori*. Renouvier interpreted this position in a particular direction: 'criticism', he maintained, 'subordinates ... theoretical to practical reason',[58] thus stressing the role of will and choice in the constitution of Reason, in establishing the nature of the fundamental principles which order our experience. Renouvier's epistemology could thus be seen to imply that Reason, and the categories of thought (space, time, substance, cause, etc.), could be otherwise. One

---

of the moral order'; 'liberty as the basis of justice and even of reason, authority arising from the person and applying to free persons, all truths and all moral goods presupposing the person, and the establishment of legitimate social relations required for the free decisions of the person – that is the end and the means of all reasonable agents, the origin and the essence of the duty of each' (ibid., vol. I, p. 298, vol. II, p. 565).

54. 1893b in 1902b, p. 396: tr. 1933b, p. 400 (S.L.).
55. 1898c, p. 10: tr. 1969c, p. 25.
56. Quoted in Scott, op. cit., p. 66.
57. Mauss, 1928, p.v.
58. *Science de la morale*, I, p. 14.

can see that it is a relatively easy step from this to the socio-logical epistemology which Durkheim began to elaborate, first in his essay with Mauss on *Primitive Classification* and later in *The Elementary Forms of the Religious Life*.[59] If Reason was contingent in the sense that the categories ordering experience could be otherwise, then it was reasonable to argue that they varied with societies and were socially determined.

Durkheim also, as he later wrote, derived from Renouvier the axiom that a whole is greater than the sum of its parts, an axiom which he held to be presupposed by his own 'social realism'[60] (though Renouvier himself did not use the axiom in this way; indeed he criticized the social realism of Saint-Simon and Comte). A second principle that was to be central to his methodology he derived from his teacher, the philo-sopher Émile Boutroux, also a neo-Kantian, who believed that philosophy should be 'in direct touch with the realities of nature and life' and 'more particularly . . . should be grounded in the sciences'.[61] Boutroux followed Comte in arguing that the field of each science was irreducible to that of the preceding one, and Durkheim assimilated this as entailing the principle that if social science was to exist, it must have its own dis-tinctive subject matter and its own principles of explanation. As he later wrote,

I owe [the distinction between sociology and psychology] in the first place to my teacher M. Boutroux, who, at the École Normale Supérieure, often repeated to us that each science must explain by 'its own principles', as Aristotle put it: psychology by psychological principles, biology by biological principles. Very much impressed by this idea, I applied it to sociology. I was confirmed in this method by reading Comte, since, for him, sociology is irreducible to biology (and hence to psychology), just as biology is irreducible to the physico-chemical sciences.[62]

59. See Guitton, 1968, p. 75, and Chapter 22, below.
60. 1913a(ii) (15), p. 326.
61. Boutroux, É., *La Contingence des lois de la nature* (Paris, 1874): tr. as *The Contingency of the Laws of Nature* (Chicago and London, 1916), pp. v–vi. On Boutroux, see Parodi, 1919, ch. VI.
62. 1907b, p. 613, repr. in Deploige, 1911, p. 402. Cf. especially 1895a, ch. 5, and 1898b.

Boutroux maintained that there were different orders of
reality, and that each was contingent with respect to the order
below it: thus, physico-chemical phenomena formed the
basis of life, but they did not of themselves produce biological
phenomena, which were, therefore, contingent with respect
to them. This kind of argument, aiming to show the relative
autonomy of 'higher' *vis-à-vis* 'lower' orders of reality, each
with its own explanatory principles, was very influential in the
formation of Durkheim's thought. On the other hand, he was
not impressed by Boutroux's parallel claim that the role of
necessity diminished, and the role of contingency increased,
as one moved from lower to higher orders: for Durkheim,
laws were no less to be expected in sociology than in mechanics. Boutroux also taught that science proceeds by means of
hypotheses[63] and that its laws hold true generally but not
necessarily of all particular instances – whence, possibly,
Durkheim derived his tendency to identify the social or
collective, the general, and the objective. But Boutroux's
influence on Durkheim went further than this: as Davy writes,
'Boutroux . . . revealed to him the great philosophers of the
past . . . and, in his penetrating and objective fashion of
reconstructing and rethinking systems, revived and presented
scientifically before his pupils the history of philosophy.'[64]

FUSTEL DE COULANGES

Durkheim was also influenced by two historians at the
École: Gabriel Monod and Fustel de Coulanges, who became
its director in 1880. He admired their rigorous historical
methods, although he was later to criticize the latter ('despite
his profound historical understanding') for inadequate use of
the comparative method.[65]

63. Boutroux actually used the phrase 'hypothetico-deductive method':
see 'Histoire et synthèse', *Revue de synthèse historique*, 1 (1900), p. 10.

64. Davy, 1919, p. 187. Andler records that Boutroux was an exacting
teacher who 'pushed his students to extremes of personal effort' (op. cit.,
p. 25).

65. 1898a(i), p. ii: tr. 1960c. p. 342. (S.L.). Durkheim's criticism referred
to Fustel's account of the Roman *gens* as a large agnatic family, and his
failure to consider ethnographic analogies.

Monod exercised 'a considerable influence upon the scientific development of students of history, as much through his theoretical lectures as through the practical exercises he directed'.[66] His courses in 1880–82 surveyed the institutions of ancient France, from the Carolingian period to the eighteenth century. Monod

referred constantly to specialist works and to archives. He provided many colourful and very precise details. Here was an immense scientific work, disguised by extreme simplicity.[67]

His courses were 'solid, conscientious and engaging',[68] notable for their 'clarity and order, combined with a vivid, but balanced and subtle manner of characterizing men and epochs'.[69]

For Fustel, the 'most liberal-minded' teacher at the École,[70] author of *La Cité antique* and the monumental *Histoire des institutions politiques de l'ancienne France*, rigorous method was, indeed, a moral duty. Over his pupils, 'he exercised, above all, a moral influence. From him there emanated a sort of austere radiance which imparted intellectual asceticism as much as historical skill.'[71] History, he taught, 'is not an art, it is a pure science ... It consists, like all science, in ascertaining facts, analysing them, comparing them, and showing the relations between them'[72]; the historian

has, as such, no other ambition than to see the facts clearly and to understand them with precision. He does not seek them in his imagination or in his logic; he seeks them and finds them by the meticulous observation of texts, as the chemist finds his facts through meticulously conducted experiments.[73]

66. Frédéricq, loc. cit., p. 758.
67. ibid.
68. ibid.
69. ibid., p. 769.
70. ibid., p. 753.
71. Grenier, *Camille Jullian*, p. 122. Jullian recalled the respect surrounding him as 'the homage paid to the moral virtues of a superior mind. . .' (quoted ibid.).
72. Fustel de Coulanges, *Histoire des institutions politiques de l'ancienne France: la monarchie franque* (Paris, 1888), p. 32.
73. ibid., p. 33.

To his students Fustel communicated high seriousness and severe intellectual discipline. He

abhorred dilettantism and indifference; he incited his students to engage in controversy, to avoid generalization, to make detailed studies of small subjects based on original sources. He never spoke to them about their examinations; his lectures did not contain long recitals of facts, but enthusiastic extempore arguments, propounding one or two ideas.[74]

Durkheim, as Camille Jullian recalled, was

a pupil of Fustel de Coulanges, and a pupil of whom his teacher was fond. He dedicated one of his first works to Fustel.[75] From his time at the École Normale, he was profoundly affected by the influence of *The Ancient City*, and by the lectures and the example of its author. He himself has recognized this and proclaims it openly.[76]

Apart from generally reinforcing his sense of intellectual dedication and his commitment to scientific method, Fustel's influence on Durkheim can be discerned in a number of more specific respects. At the methodological level, compare Fustel's statement that 'preconceived ideas' were 'the most common evil of our time', and his plea for 'a mind absolutely independent and free, above all with regard to itself',[77] with Durkheim's rule that the sociologist '*must systematically discard all preconceptions*' and 'resolutely abstain from the use of concepts formed outside science and for purposes that have nothing to do with science'.[78] For Fustel, 'patriotism is a virtue, history is a science; the two must not be confused'[79]; for Durkheim, sentiment – such as 'one's idea of patriotism, or of individual dignity' – was 'the object of science, not the criterion of scientific truth'.[80] Durkheim also assimilated Fustel's distinction between the history of events and the history of institutions,

74. Zeldin, art. cit., pp. 72–3.

75. This was his Latin thesis on Montesquieu: 1892a.

76. Jullian, C., 'Le Cinquantenaire de *la Cité antique*', *Revue de Paris*, 23ᵉ année, no. 4 (15 February 1916), p. 857.

77. *La Monarchie franque*, pp. 30–31.

78. 1901c, pp. 40, 40–41: tr. 1938b, pp. 31, 32 (S.L.).

79. op. cit., p. 31.

80. 1901c, pp. 41, 43: tr. 1938b, pp. 32, 34 (S.L.).

as well as his concentration on the latter (Durkheim wrote in
1901 that sociology was 'the science of institutions, their
genesis and functioning'[81]); his sense of their reality, and their
complex relations with the rest of a given society's life; and his
conception of historical survivals – 'the past never completely
dies for man . . . take him at any epoch, and he is the product,
the epitome of all the earlier epochs'.[82] In important ways,
and though he rejected the term, Fustel's work was distinctly
sociological, with a keen sense of social complexity and the aim
of treating each society as a (changing) whole. Indeed, Fustel
himself wrote that 'history' had the same meaning as 'sociology': 'history is the science of social facts, that is sociology
itself'.[83] Finally, Fustel encouraged Durkheim's scepticism
towards unrestrained philosophical speculation: 'to philosophize', Fustel used to say, 'is to think what one wants'.[84]

At the substantive level, Fustel's influence on Durkheim was
similarly profound. A striking similarity can be seen between
Fustel's discussion of ancient Roman family worship within
the independent patriarchal household and its severe, expiatory morality, on the one hand, and Durkheim's conception
of mechanical solidarity, on the other.[85] Fustel's main substantive influence on Durkheim, however, was on the latter's
sociology of religion, though this influence was delayed.
In *The Division of Labour* Durkheim criticized Fustel's *The
Ancient City* for explaining social organization by religion,
rather than *vice versa*,[86] but, as we shall see, he himself subsequently moved much closer to Fustel's position, according

81. ibid., p. xxiii: tr. p. lvi (S.L.).

82. *La Cité antique* (Paris, 1864): tr. as *The Ancient City* by W. Small
(Doubleday Anchor Books, Garden City, N.Y., n.d.), p. 14.

83. Quoted in Grenier, *Camille Jullian*, p. 130. To which Durkheim
responded: 'nothing is more incontestable provided that history is
carried out sociologically' (1898a (i), p. iii: tr. 1960c, p. 343 – S.L.).

84. As Durkheim remarked to a doctoral candidate: see *RMM*, 18
(1910), Supp. January, p. 30, reproduced in Appendix B(11), below.

85. For instance: 'These gods belonged in common to all the members
of the same family; thus the family was united by a powerful tie. . . Duties,
clear, precise and imperious, appeared, but they were restricted within a
narrow circle' (*The Ancient City*, p. 100).

86. 1902b, p. 154: tr. 1933b, p. 179. See below, p. 230.

religious beliefs and sentiments an ever-greater degree of
relative autonomy, and an ever-greater explanatory role.
The Ancient City is a study of the central role of religion, in
particular the ancestor cult, in Greece and Rome ('The religious idea was, among the ancients, the inspiring breath and
organizer of society'), stressing the importance of sacredness
in the explanation of their institutions and beliefs, and the
pervasive predominance of ritual (religion 'signified rites,
ceremonies, acts of exterior worship. The doctrine was of
small account: the practices were the important part; these
were obligatory and bound men . . .').[87] These were the very
features which Durkheim's sociology of religion was to
emphasize. Its germs can be seen throughout Fustel's great
work: for example in its account of ancestor worship (establishing 'a powerful bond . . . among all the generations of the
same family, which made of it a body forever inseparable'[88]);
in its view of primitive religion as the source of 'all the institutions, as well as all the private law, of the ancients', the earliest
forms being 'the most important for us to know'[89]; in its
hypothesis that there might be a connection between the ideas
of economic value and of religious value[90]; and in its general
focus on 'the intimate relation which always exists between
men's ideas and their social state'.[91] And, like Durkheim,
Fustel spoke of the 'truth' underlying the 'legendary forms' of
religious beliefs: 'Social laws were the work of the gods; but

87. *The Ancient City*, pp. 132, 167.
88. ibid., p. 36. The ancient family was 'united by something more
powerful than birth, affection, or physical strength; this was the religion
of the sacred fire and of dead ancestors' (ibid., p. 42).
89. ibid., p. 13.
90. Cf. 1912a, p. 598 fn.: tr. 1915d, p. 419 fn.
91. *The Ancient City*, p. 12. In the beginning, wrote Fustel, 'the family
lived isolated and man knew only the domestic gods. . . Above the family
was formed the phratry with its god. . . Then came the tribe, and
the god of the tribe. . . Finally came the city and men conceived a god
whose providence embraced the entire city. . .; a hierarchy of creeds, and
a hierarchy of association' (ibid., p. 132). Cf. Durkheim, 1912a, bk. II,
ch. IX, which argues that 'the great god is the synthesis of all the totems
and consequently the personification of tribal unity' (p. 421: tr. 1915d,
p. 294).

those gods, so powerful and beneficent, were nothing else than the beliefs of men.'[92]

Fustel's admirer and interpreter, Jullian, writing in 1916, stressed the close relation he saw between *The Ancient City* and Durkheim's *Elementary Forms of the Religious Life*. Jullian presented Durkheim's view as follows:

that which creates a social unity – religion, the sacred and moral existence, the intimate and perpetual value of a savage tribe, is itself considered as a divine and magical essence; it is, in a sense, non-material, foreign and superior to all physical forces, common to all the members of a human group, and arises from the mutual understanding and union between the members of that group. Every tribe is at once a fraternity and a church. And there is a sacred ideal rising above the rudimentary societies of Africa or Australia.

But is this, he continued, 'not exactly what Fustel de Coulanges said of ancient cities?'[93] However, though these seeds were sown, Durkheim did not turn his attention to religion until 1895.

92. *The Ancient City*, p. 133. It is worth noting that Durkheim also accepted, in general, Fustel's account of the religious origins of the right of property (*The Ancient City*, bk 2, ch. VI) referring to the sacred nature of landed property among the Greeks and the Romans; but he criticized Fustel's account as based on too narrow a conception of the family cult. Fustel, he maintained, reduced the latter to 'the cult of the dead, when in reality it is far more complex. Family religion was not ancestor worship alone; it was the cult of all things that played a part in the life of the family...' (1950a, p. 183: tr. 1957a, p. 154; q.v. ch. 13 passim). For Durkheim's account of property, see below, Chapter 13.

93. art. cit., p. 857. On Durkheim and Fustel, see also Nisbet, 1966, pp. 238–43, and Momigliano, A., 'La Città Antica di Fustel de Coulanges', *Rivista storica italiana*, LXXXII (1970), pp. 81–98, especially Appendix 1: 'Fustel e Durkheim', pp. 95–7. Evans-Pritchard also stresses Fustel's influence on Durkheim's theory of religion (Evans-Pritchard, 1965, pp. 50–51), claiming that 'Fustel de Coulanges, and also, of course, Montesquieu, had a greater formative influence on Durkheim's thought than Saint-Simon and Comte' (Evans-Pritchard, 1960, p. 12 fn.). This last claim probably goes too far, though Evans-Pritchard is certainly right in seeing Fustel's *The Ancient City* as marking 'the dividing-point between the speculative and dogmatic treatises of such writers as Turgot, Condorcet, Saint-Simon and Comte on the one side, and on the other, for example, Durkheim's detailed analysis of systems of classification, totemism and incest prohibitions, and Hubert and Mauss's scholarly treatment of sacrifice and magic' (ibid., pp. 11–12).

After successfully taking his *agrégation* in 1882 despite a
serious illness during his last year at the École (he came second
to last in his year),[94] he became a philosophy teacher, first, in
October, at the Lycée de Puy and then, in November, at the
Lycée de Sens.[95] The philosopher André Lalande was in his
class there and recorded that he was an excellent and unusually
conscientious teacher, who gave his pupils a remarkable
example of 'systematic order in investigations and ... well-
organized ideas: at the end of each lesson he turned to the
blackboard and reconstructed its plan, composed of titles and
short, ordered formulae, which made concrete for his hearers
the structure, always precise and well-constructed, of what he
had just expounded in a free and continuous fashion'.[96] His
pupils had a great admiration and respect for him and were,
indeed, 'deeply attached to his person and his teaching',[97] some
of them even following him to the Lycée de Saint-Quentin,
where he moved in February 1884 to be nearer his family.
Here his teaching struck the Recteur as 'very sincere and very
methodical, but somewhat abstract and perhaps too elevated
for his pupils'.[98] The Inspecteur Jules Lachelier wrote a
report on his teaching that is more revealing:

M. Durkheim has a very serious and somewhat cold appearance.
He is conscientious, hard-working, well-informed and very clever,
though his mind is perhaps more rigorous than penetrating and

94. Fustel wrote a very warm reference for Durkheim on the latter's
departure from the École. He wrote: 'Excellent student; very vigorous
mind, at once accurate and original and of a maturity that is very remarkable. He has a real aptitude for philosophical and above all psychological
studies. His teachers have a high opinion of him. The École Normale has
just awarded him the Adolphe Garnier prize as the most hard-working
student, and the most deserving of his promotion. Only received 7th in
the *agrégation de philosophie*; his work and his merit led one to expect
one of the first ranks for him' (in Durkheim's dossier, Archives
Nationales).

95. Durkheim's dossier, Bordeaux.

96. Lalande, 1960, p.22.

97. ibid., p. 23 (see Durkheim, 1967a).

98. Recteur's report of 11 June 1885 in Durkheim's dossier, Archives
Nationales.

more capable of assimilation than invention: none the less, his teaching is very exact, very precise, very concise and perfectly clear, though the clarity is, it is true, of a scientific rather than a popular nature. His way of speaking is firm and clear-cut, though somewhat brief . . . M. Durkheim is, in short, one of the most serious of our young professors of philosophy . . .[99]

99. Report of 21 April 1885 in ibid.

Chapter 3

The New Science of Sociology

DURKHEIM had already decided by the time of his *agrégation* that the general area of research for his principal doctoral thesis was to be that of the relations between individualism and socialism.[1] Yet, though he had by this time read Comte,[2] he had not yet identified this field of interest as peculiarly socio-logical; he still defined it quite abstractly and philosophically. Sociology was in some disrepute in France at this time. Professional philosophers 'knew in general and quite vaguely that Comte had proposed this word to designate social science: they were unanimous in finding it bizarre and unwarranted'.[3] Sociology was, not unjustifiably, generally associated with the latter-day disciples of Comte, both orthodox and dissident,[4] and, apart from Le Play's monographic studies of the socio-economic aspects of family life, it had not yet gone beyond philosophical generalities.[5] It was in 1883 that Durkheim turned from the analysis of theories to the study of reality, defining his subject as 'the relations between the individual and society' and then, finally, as 'the relations of the individual personality to social solidarity'.[6] It was between the first plan in 1884 of what was to become *The Division of Labour* and

1. Mauss, 1928, p.v. Cf. Neyer, 1960. At that time doctoral candidates had to submit two theses, the subsidiary one being in Latin.

2. Davy (Davy, 1919, p. 186) is unsure of the date, but thinks that it was during 1880–81 or soon after. This is corroborated by 1913a (ii) (15), p. 326.

3. Espinas, A., 'Être ou ne pas être, ou du postulat de sociologie', *RP*, 51 (1901), p. 449.

4. See ch. 2 of Simon, 1963, and Charlton, D. G., *Positivist Thought in France during the Second Empire, 1852–1870* (Oxford, 1959).

5. See 1915a: repr. and tr. 1960c. This was, as Mauss observes, true of Comte, Spencer and Espinas, as well as of the Germans Schaeffle and Wundt (Mauss, 1928, p.v.). See below.

6. 1902b, p. xliii: tr. 1933b, p. 37 (S.L.).

its first draft in 1886 that, 'by a progressive analysis of his thought and the facts . . . he came to see that the solution to the problem belonged to a new science: sociology'.[7] During this period he set himself the task of establishing that science, of 'giving it a method and a body'.[8]

It was an aim peculiarly appropriate to the period, which one writer has described as follows:

Let us recall the intellectual atmosphere round about 1884. . . . One attitude of mind, one doctrine dominated and excited French intellectual life: scientistic positivism, issuing from Auguste Comte, and brilliantly represented at that time by two 'leading lights': Taine, the well-known *'cacique'* [top scholar] of [the École] Normale, and Renan, the 'priest of science'. The original ideas of Comtism had taken on the hues of Darwino-Spencerian evolutionism, as they were subsequently to take on those of Durkheimian sociologism. What, essentially, did Comtism claim? That a new era is unfolding; that the positive method is henceforth to guide human thought, that, if science has issued from religion, scientific knowledge is now replacing primitive imaginary beliefs. Philosophy itself is rendered null and void by science, for the latter is the sole instrument capable of resolving philosophical problems.[9]

COMTE, TAINE AND RENAN

This attitude of mind was certainly shared by Durkheim, though he never maintained it as uncritically or in so extreme a form as did Comte, Taine and Renan.[10] Durkheim, as we shall see, owed a great debt to the influence of Comte (a debt which

7. Mauss, 1928, p. v.

8. ibid., p. vi.

9. Bouvier, R., 'Henri Berr et son œuvre', *Revue de synthèse*, 3e série, no. 35 (July-September 1964), p. 40. Cf. Marc Bloch's comment that the generations of the last decades of the nineteenth century were 'as if mesmerized by a very rigid conception, a truly Comtian conception of natural science . . . Such was the nearly unanimous opinion at the time' (*Apologie pour l'histoire ou métier de l'historien*, Paris, 1949, p. xv).

10. For an excellent discussion of the scientism of Comte, Taine and Renan, see Charlton, D. G., *Secular Religions in France, 1815–1870* (London, 1963), ch. III: 'The Cult of Science', and *Positivist Thought in France*, chs. VI and VII.

he always freely acknowledged).[11] As he wrote to Lucien
Lévy-Bruhl in 1900, declaring his 'complete sympathy' with
the latter's book on Comte, 'I certainly believe that, in affirming the specificity of social facts, I am in accordance with the
Comtist tradition – a fact which contributes much to confirming me in my attitude.'[12]

Comte's influence on Durkheim was very much a formative
rather than a continuing one. Its most important element was
precisely the extension of the scientific attitude to the study of
society: as he wrote in his subsidiary doctoral thesis, a study of
Montesquieu's contribution to the rise of sociology:

> No further progress could be made until it was established that the
> laws of societies are no different from those governing the rest of
> nature and that the method by which they are discovered is identical
> with that of the other sciences. This was Auguste Comte's con-
> tribution.[13]

Durkheim agreed, moreover, with Lévy-Bruhl in maintaining
that 'basically the Positive Philosophy is entirely sociology:
the latter is everywhere', adding that 'true methodology is a
branch of social science, since science is a social phenomenon,
and even for Comte *the* social phenomenon'. Though this view
was as yet confused in Comte's work, Durkheim saw it as one
which 'would, I think, be worth taking up again today'.[14]

Yet though Comte argued for the possibility of sociology,
the sixth and last to enter the Hierarchy of the Sciences, its

11. For example, in 1914, Durkheim said, 'I have always acknowledged
what I have derived from Comte' (1914b, p. 35). For discussions of
Comte's influence on Durkheim, see Simon, 1963, pp. 144-5; d'Aranjo,
1899; Fink, Y., *Étude critique de la notion de loi chez Comte et de son influence*
(Paris, 1907); Lacombe, 1926a; Duprat, 1932; Delvolvé, J., *Reflexions sur
la pensée comtienne* (Paris, 1932); Hubert, 1938; Parsons, 1937; Bouglé,
1924; Davy, 1949 and 1950; Nisbet, 1952 and 1965; Ranulf, 1955; Peyre,
1960; Marjolin, 1937 (all mainly affirmative); Bréhier, É., *Histoire de la
philosophie* (Paris, n.d.); Deploige, 1911; Pécaut, 1921; Brunschvicg,
1927; Benrubi, 1933; Alpert, 1939; Gouldner, 1958 (all mainly negative);
Richard, 1932. For further references and details on this point, see Simon,
loc. cit.

12. 1969b.

13. 1892a, p. 133: tr. 1960b, pp. 63-4.

14. 1969b.

'crown and *pièce maîtresse*',[15] his own practice and cast of mind denied that very possibility. As John Stuart Mill had put it, 'It is one of M. Comte's mistakes that he never allows of open questions.'[16] Once sociology had been founded, it was to become 'the universal science, and in consequence a philosophy', since 'the other sciences can be regarded as great sociological facts'[17]; it was the key to a complete systematization of experience and the basis for a doctrine, a morality – even, in the end, a religion. Comte's own sociology was essentially dogmatic, above all in claiming that the Law of Three Stages applied to all aspects of human life; the progression of stages, from theological to metaphysical to positive, was inevitable and the differences between societies ignored. As Durkheim later wrote:

Now, social dynamics, as he explained it, presents in no degree 'that continuity and fertility' which, according to the criteria of Comte himself, constitute 'the least equivocal marks of every truly scientific conception'. For Comte considered the science as virtually completed by himself. In fact it is wholly contained in the law of the three stages; and this law once discovered, it is not easy to see how it would be possible to complete it, extend it, and still less what laws other than this could be discovered. The science was brought to a conclusion with its foundations barely laid ... A science cannot live and move when it is reduced to a single and unique problem, on which a mighty intellect sets his seal for ever and ever.[18]

As for that remarkably versatile psychologist, historian and critic of literature, art, philosophy and politics, Hyppolite Taine, science, rather loosely conceived, was both a method and a metaphysics, from which he ultimately hoped to derive 'a new art, morality, politics, religion ...'[19] He sought to synthesize German idealism and British empiricism, in the

15. 1905d, p. 259.

16. Mill, J. S., *Auguste Comte and Positivism* (London, 1865), p. 15.

17. Lévy-Bruhl, L., *La Philosophie d'Auguste Comte* (4th edn, Paris, 1921), p. 403.

18. 1905d, p. 264.

19. Taine, H., *Histoire de la littérature anglaise* (Paris, n.d.), vol.iv. p. 390, quoted in Charlton, *Secular Religions in France*, op. cit., p. 63.

belief that one could arrive at knowledge that was 'absolute and without limits'.[20] Durkheim was sympathetic to Taine's popularization of scientific attitudes, though he criticized him for lacking sufficient vigour of mind, comprehensiveness of vision and scientific culture, as well as for being too literary and too sympathetic to 'English empiricism'.[21] In Durkheim's view, Taine had introduced into France a philosophical tradition originating with Aristotle and passing through Hobbes and Spinoza, which Durkheim called 'rationalist empiricism' and whose fundamental principles he accepted.[22] These, as Durkheim interpreted them, amounted to the claim that phenomena are intelligibly related and can be rationally explained, while at the same time asserting that the sensible world is the real one, that science must concern itself with particular, concrete phenomena in all their complexity and must resort to observation and experiment. Taine, Durkheim thought, had provided a brilliant popular exposition of these ideas; as a result, they had become prevalent and in consequence 'one of the factors of our philosophical life'.[23] He also admired Taine's application of them in the context of experimental psychology, thereby showing how mistaken the introspectionist school were to suppose that the mind was simple and easy to understand, that 'it could be reduced to a small group of clear ideas and distinct states'; on the contrary, it had 'profound and hidden depths, into which, however, the light of reason can gradually penetrate'.[24] Yet there is no evidence of any direct influence of Taine on Durkheim, nor of any relationship between them. Indeed, Durkheim regarded Taine's attempted synthesis of rationalism and empiricism as ultimately a failure: he had juxtaposed rather than logically united these two tendencies and the task of reconciling them had to be taken up again. Taine's philosophy was, in the end, a dogmatic metaphysical system; as we shall see, Durkheim

20. Taine, H., *De l'Intelligence* (16th edn, Paris, n.d.), vol. ii, pp. 383–4, quoted in Charlton, ibid., p. 61.

21. 1897f, passim.

22. ibid., p. 290.

23. ibid.

24. ibid.

was to offer a sociological solution to the problem of recon- ciling rationalism and empiricism.

Durkheim had considerably less sympathy for Ernest Renan, who had made science into a sort of religion, specifying man's final end and the true meaning of life, with its own creed, morality and priesthood,[25] and had subsequently become the conservative, sceptical and dilettante 'lay saint of French literary life'.[26] As Maurice Barrès wrote, 'Renan's task was to find some provisional solution conciliating religious feeling and scientific analysis; he discovered the way of enabling the modern mind to keep the benefit of that wonderful Catholic sensitiveness most of us cannot do without.'[27] Renan's Romantic and confused celebration of 'science' and progress, a sort of surrogate theology, seeking to embrace 'the infinite' and give humanity 'a symbol and a law', had little to do with genuinely scientific or even empirical inquiry – though the very great popularity of Renan's writings doubtless contri- buted to the popularity of the idea of science and the spread of positivism.[28] Durkheim had first read Renan at the École Normale and had found the experience distasteful: Holleaux reports that he spoke of him with 'decided antipathy'.[29] He always thought of Renan as 'the author in whom one is sure of finding a number of assertions which clearly contradict one another'.[30] He particularly disliked Renan's cult of great men, his belief in an elite of superior minds holding itself aloof from the ignorant mass of men whose minds were 'invincibly

25. For example: 'Science is thus a religion; science alone will hence- forth provide symbols; science alone can resolve for man the eternal problems to which his nature imperiously demands the solution': *L'Avenir de la science – pensées de 1848* (Paris, 1890), p. 108.

26. Peyre, 1960, p. 30.

27. *Le Figaro*, 3 October 1892, quoted in Soltau, op. cit., p. 227.

28. Cf. Lévy-Bruhl, *La Philosophie d'Auguste Comte*, op. cit., p. 21: 'Renan and Taine, without being positivists, have perhaps done more to spread the ideas and method of Comte than Littré and all the other posi- tivists together.' In fact, Renan's view of science had more to do with philology than with any of the natural sciences.

29. Davy, 1919, p. 185.

30. ibid., p. 186. I can see no basis for Peyre's statement that 'In spite of his frank distaste for Renan's writings, Durkheim was influenced by them more than any historian of ideas has yet shown' (Peyre, 1960, p. 28).

refractory to science'.[31] He rejected Renan's view that the latter's ideal – 'the coming of reason and the reign of truth' – must be confined to 'a small number of privileged minds', that 'reason will only be incarnated in a few superior men who will realize the ideal and will thereby constitute the final end of human evolution'.[32] To these views Durkheim opposed an optimistic and universalized rationalism, reminiscent of John Stuart Mill. In a prize-giving speech to the *lycéens* of Sens[33] he countered Renan's view that 'the understanding of most men is not and will never be capable of receiving the truth', observing that 'one sees in history the innumerable sequence of ideas that [the human mind] has already traversed, rejecting successively all those whose falsity has been demonstrated to it and thus advancing, laboriously but continuously and persistently, towards the truth . . .'[34] Despite setbacks and resistance to such progress, there was no justification for Renan's aristocratic pessimism: 'all individuals, however humble, have a right to aspire to the higher life of the mind'.[35]

DURKHEIM'S SCIENTIFIC RATIONALISM

Bouglé has aptly characterized Durkheim's perspective as 'rationalism impregnated with positivism'.[36] Durkheim, however, always spoke of himself as a rationalist, never as a positivist. He also always objected to being labelled as either a 'materialist' or a 'spiritualist':

the sole [label] that we accept is that of *rationalist*. Indeed, our chief aim is to extend scientific rationalism to human behaviour by showing that, considered in the past, it is reducible to relations of

31. 1967a, p. 26.
32. ibid.
33. 1967a.
34. ibid., p. 28.
35. ibid. Durkheim continued, in a manner still reminiscent of Mill: 'Everyone has the right to aspire to this noble sorrow, which has, in any case, its own compensations; for once one has tasted it, one no longer even desires other pleasures that one henceforth finds to be lacking in savour and charm' (ibid.).
36. Bouglé, 1938, p. 31.

cause and effect – relations that a no less rational operation can then transform into rules of action for the future. Our so-called positivism is nothing but a consequence of this rationalism.[37]

This position, he stressed, 'must not be confused with the positivist metaphysics of Comte and M. Spencer'.[38] Indeed, he explicitly denied any kind of dogmatic scientism:

We do not make science into a sort of fetish or idol, whose in-fallible oracles may only be received on bended knee. We see it merely as a grade of knowledge, but it is the highest grade and there is nothing else beyond it. It is distinguished from the humbler forms of knowledge only by greater clarity and distinctness; but that is sufficient for it to be the ideal to which all self-critical thought aspires.[39]

Moreover, unlike so many nineteenth-century (and twentieth-century) social scientists, he made no overweening claims concerning the foreseeable possibilities of social science: 'we do not delude ourselves', he wrote, 'by the hope that, in the near future, the various sciences of man can arrive at propositions that are as certain and indisputable as those of mathematics and the physico-chemical sciences'.[40]

The relatively undogmatic character of Durkheim's 'scientific rationalism' is doubtless partly to be explained by his early exposure to the similarly undogmatic ideas of such writers on scientific method as Claude Bernard,[41] Boutroux and Renouvier. It is, in particular, most probable that he absorbed from Bernard and Boutroux a sense of the crucial role of hypothesis

37. 1901c, pp. vii–viii: tr. 1938b, pp. xxxix–xl (S.L.).
38. ibid.
39. 1895b, p. 146.
40. ibid., pp. 146–7.
41. See 1885a, p. 98: 'the great service Claude Bernard rendered to physiology was precisely to free it from all forms of domination, from that of physics and chemistry as much as from that of metaphysics, putting off the time for generalizations to the distant future. One should proceed with similar prudence in the study of societies.' For Bernard, scientific theories yielded 'partial and provisional truths', representing only 'the present state of our knowledge'; 'the unique and fundamental rule of scientific investigation comes down to doubt' (*Introduction à l'étude de la médecine expérimentale*, Paris, 1865, pp. 63, 86). For a brief discussion of Bernard and Durkheim, see Aimard, 1962, pp. 115–17.

in science, and from all three thinkers his frequently reiterated claim that determinism, seen as an indispensable assumption of scientific method, did not preclude the possibility of free-will.[42]

However, though his attitude towards science was un-dogmatic, his rationalism was quite uncompromising – if rationalism means that 'there is nothing in reality that one is justified in considering as fundamentally beyond the scope of human reason' and entails that 'there is no reason to set a limit to the progress of science'.[43] It was at once the most basic and the most unchanging element in his thought – a cartesian passion for clear and distinct ideas combined with a firm belief in scientific method.[44] Its systematic application to social life (as opposed to the idea of doing so) was at that time still both novel and controversial, and Durkheim was to apply it to the most controversial areas of social life – to the study of suicide, crime, the family and, above all, religion. He relished the challenge of putting 'received opinions'[45] to scientific test: as he wrote, 'one must have faith in the power of reason if one dares to undertake the task of submitting to its laws this sphere of social phenomena, in which events, because of their complexity, seem to shun the formulae of science'.[46]

The corollary of this attitude was a marked hostility to all forms of thought that appeared to fall short of, or conflict with, the rigorous standards of scientific inquiry. Durkheim's two most bitter terms of abuse were 'dilettante' and 'mystical'. As we have seen, he had from his earliest years as a student reacted against the lack of rigour, the aestheticism, what he later called the 'anarchic dilettantism'[47] of traditional French

42. See, for example, 1888a, pp. 27–8; 1953a, pp. 38–9: tr. 1960b, pp. 10–11; 1902b, p. xxxvii: tr. 1933b, p. 32; 1901c, p. 173: tr. 1938b, p. 141; 1897a, p. 368n.: tr. 1951a, p. 325n.

43. 1925a, pp. 4 and 304: tr. 1961a, pp. 4 and 265.

44. Cf. 1900b, p. 651.

45. 1901c, p. v.

46. 1900b, p. 651.

47. 1895b, p. 133. This article is a forceful critique of the current state of French philosophy and a statement of Durkheim's proposed remedies: a concentration on scientific method and the study of psychology and sociology to elucidate the nature of morality. On dilettantism generally, see the conclusion to *The Division of Labour*.

philosophy, which derived ultimately from the eclectic Victor Cousin. This philosophy, he thought, was too literary[48]: it could not put the mind into sufficient contact with reality for it to form an adequate conception of it.[49] As to the charge of mysticism, he was to advance it against all those thinkers whom he saw as a threat to clear scientific thinking – and there were many such in the late nineteenth and early twentieth centuries. This was the period of the Symbolist poets, with their cult of the mysterious; of the anti-positivist, and often pro-Catholic, reaction of many writers such as Bourget, Brunetière and Huysmans, Barrès and Péguy; and of Bergson and *bergsonisme*. Always Durkheim's view was that such thinkers were not only mistaken but dangerous. In subordinating science 'to some other source of knowledge', they were mixing 'shadows with the light on the pretext that the light is not bright enough'.[50] Instead of speculating on the lack of a science that might guide human conduct 'to the advantage of mystery and obscurantism', one should seek to construct such a science.[51] Durkheim often wrote of living in times of 'renascent mysticism'[52]; he was continually conscious of a threat from the forces of irrationalism.

We have seen that Durkheim held scientific rationalism to entail not only that human behaviour was reducible to relations of cause and effect, but also that, by 'a no less rational operation', these relations could be transformed into 'rules of action for the future'. He regarded the denial that science could provide such rules as a prejudice[53]: science was in principle of immense practical significance. Though the social sciences were as yet 'much too young to form the basis for practical doctrines',[54] this was a role they would ultimately fill. Indeed, as he wrote in the preface to *The Division of Labour*:

48. 1887a, pp. 438–9.
49. 1890a, pp. 455–6.
50. 1895b, p. 146.
51. 1897f, p. 291. The hero of Bourget's *Le Disciple*, both aware of the sciences and amoral, was 'a sad character . . . a mediocre mind, a bad student . . .' (ibid.).
52. 1901c, p. viii: tr. 1938b, p. xl.
53. 1902b, p. xxxix: tr. 1933b, p. 33.
54. 1928a, p. 7: tr. 1958a, p. 7 (S.L.).

We would not judge our researches to be worth an hour's trouble if they were bound to have no more than a speculative interest. If we take care to separate theoretical from practical problems, this is not in order to neglect the latter; it is, on the contrary, to enable us the better to resolve them.[55]

Anxiety about the uses to which science might be put was common among Durkheim's contemporaries. Andler has written of 'the young men of that generation' of Octave Hamelin, Lucien Lévy-Bruhl, Jean Jaurès, Félix Rauh, Lucien Herr, Durkheim and himself:

We believed in the future of science ... [but] there remained one final anxious preoccupation: that the resources of science should not be used to assist oppression and war. We needed, therefore, in addition to science, a doctrine which would justify science through reason and prescribe for it human ends ... everyone awaited a doctrine of action.[56]

Durkheim, in the mid-1880s, came to regard science itself – that is social science, or sociology, and in particular the scientific study of morality – as promising to provide the basis for such a doctrine. The day would certainly come, he believed, 'when the science of morality will be sufficiently far advanced for theory to govern practice'.[57]

THEORY AND PRACTICE

How did Durkheim conceive the role of science as a guide to action? How could social science itself provide 'rules of action for the future'? What relation did Durkheim see between theory and practice? The answer to these questions is not simple, and in any case it was not fully worked out at this early stage of his intellectual development. Moreover, as his ideas on this point became more complex, he also became more critical of his society. Between the mid-eighties and the mid-nineties he developed his conception of social pathology, of the sociologist as diagnostician, testing the social order

55. 1902b, p. xxxix: tr. 1933b, p. 33 (S.L.).
56. Andler, op. cit., p. 35.
57. 1887c, p. 284.

against a conception of 'normality', or health; during the same period he moved from a rather conservative liberal republicanism to a position close to the reformist socialism of Jean Jaurès.

However, the influence of Comte (and, behind this, that of Saint-Simon) was evident from the beginning. Like Comte, Durkheim believed that sociology could in principle identify the processes of social change and the conditions of social order, and further that it should be used to alleviate the former so as to achieve the latter. Yet he was always very far from Comte's conception of social order, with its positive valuation of hierarchy and ideological conformity, and its negative valuation of individual freedom and autonomy; and, as we have seen, he was never tempted, like Comte, to make a secular religion out of science. His view of social order, with respect to his own society, was governed by the ideals which he took to be operative, or at least immanent, in that society.

At this period he conceived of those ideals somewhat negatively. This was, after all, a time of republican consolidation, after the Republic's precarious and inauspicious beginnings. That consolidation was already threatened by increasingly evident corruption in high places under the regime of the 'Opportunists', by lack of loyalty to the Republic of nearly half the electorate (as shown in the elections of 1885) and by mounting attacks on it from the Right that were to culminate in *Boulangisme* and ultimately in the Dreyfus Affair. Like very many others, Durkheim was preoccupied with the need to save the Republic and what it seemed to stand for: that meant, above all, establishing a liberal secular, republican ideology, a new civic morality to be taught in all the nation's schools.[58] This preoccupation and this concern with civic morality never ceased actively to engage him; throughout his career, it took up much of his time and energy.

Durkheim's conservatism in this early period is well illustrated by the following strikingly Burkean passage, written in 1887:

58. See Weill, G., *L'Histoire de l'idée laïque en France au XIXe siècle* (Paris, 1925).

... one has the right to say to young people and even to their elders: our moral beliefs are the product of a long evolution; they result from an unending sequence of trials, struggles, rebuffs, experiments of all sorts. Because their origins are distant and very complex, we too often fail to see the causes which explain them. We ought, none the less, to submit to them with respect, since we know that humanity, after so much suffering and travail, has discovered nothing better. We may be certain that there is more wisdom accumulated here than in the mind of the greatest genius. It would be quite puerile to wish to rectify, through our small and particular judgement, the results of human experience.[59]

Furthermore, in the 1880s Durkheim was emphasizing a view of morality as essentially a form of discipline. As he wrote in 1886, morality must be a form of social discipline[60]: individuals in society must be bound together by solid and durable bonds. This conservatism and this view of morality remained as a central and essential element of his thought. Yet, by the mid-nineties they were tempered by a critical concern for social justice and the advocacy of extensive social change, as well as by a wider definition of morality, involving explicit reference to social ideals as well as social discipline, to values as well as norms.

As to the manner in which theory should relate to practice, Comte's view had been refreshingly simple: science would be the handmaiden of an enlightened elite that would impose order on society. On this issue Durkheim was as yet undecided. He experienced doubts about the possibility of achieving a

59. 1887c, p. 284. Cf.: 'We are afraid to put men to live and trade each on his own private stock of reason; because we suspect that this stock in each man is small, and that the individuals would do better to avail themselves of the general bank and capital of nations and of ages' (Burke, E., *Reflections on the Revolution in France* in *Works*, vol. 11, p. 359, London, 1790, edn of 1882).

60. 1886a, p. 75. Cf. Durkheim's advice to the schoolboys of Sens: 'Whenever you feel that a man is superior to you, do not be ashamed to accord him a suitable measure of deference. Without false modesty, make him your guide. There is a manner of letting oneself be guided which in no way detracts from one's independence. In a word, know how to respect all natural superiority, without ever losing respect for yourselves. That is how the future citizens of our democracy must be' (1967a, p. 32).

rational, enlightened citizenry; perhaps progress merely increased the number of men's prejudices.[61] In any case, how could a population of thirty to forty million persons have an adequate understanding of the conditions of social life and a rational concern for the public interest? If one eliminated people's instincts and habits by education, making them purely rational, how would they then be able to understand patriotism and the beauty of sacrifice and disinterestedness? 'A voluntary and reasoned faith', he wrote in 1885, could not be socially cohesive.[62] These doubts were to reappear, especially after Durkheim had turned his attention to religion. On the whole, however, it was an attitude of democratic optimism that chiefly characterized his thought: sociology would pervade the social consciousness and ideally the diagnosis and cure would be self-administered.

DURKHEIM'S 'SOCIAL REALISM'

The immediate task, however, was to establish its credentials – to give sociology 'a method and a body'. The first requirement appeared to be a distinctive and independently identifiable subject-matter. This is what was postulated by Durkheim's doctrine of 'social realism' (as it came to be called by its opponents). We have Durkheim's own explicit authority that he was directly influenced in adopting this doctrine, well before 1885, by three thinkers: Comte, Herbert Spencer (then at the height of his influence in France) and Alfred Espinas.[63]

To see the point of this doctrine for Durkheim, one must ask what he took it to be denying. If the first step towards the foundation of a positive science of sociology was to see society as similar to the rest of nature in being subject to laws, the second step was to see it as distinct: to regard social phenomena as real, causally operative forces. The classical economists had taken the first step; indeed they had been 'the first to proclaim that social laws are as necessary as physical laws, and

61. ibid., p. 69.
62. 1885a, pp. 99–100.
63. 1907b: repr. in Deploige, 1911, p. 401.

to make this axiom the basis of a science'.[64] But they had stopped short of the second step; for, according to them,

there is nothing real in society except the individual; it is from him that everything emanates and it is to him that everything returns ... The individual ... is the sole tangible reality that the observer can attain, and the only problem that science can pose is that of discovering how the individual must behave in the principal circumstances of economic life, given his nature. Economic laws and more generally social laws would not then be very general facts which the scientist induces from the observation of societies, but rather logical consequences which he deduces from the definition of the individual.[65]

Moreover, not only did the economists' method exclude the observation of reality: it seriously distorted it by abstracting 'from all circumstances of time, place and country in order to conceive of the abstract type of man in general; but, in that ideal type itself, they neglected all that did not relate to strictly individual life'. All that remained was 'the sad portrait of the pure egoist'.[66] For Durkheim, classical economics represented a stage in the study of society that urgently needed to be transcended. As he was to write to Bouglé in 1896,

... when I began fifteen years ago, I thought that I would find [among the economists] the answer to the questions that preoccupied me. I spent several years and derived nothing from them, except what one can learn from a negative experience.[67]

The step that needed to be taken was to abandon this 'abstract and deductive' approach[68] – typical, in Durkheim's view, of French economists and moralists[69] – with its unacceptable postulate of 'man in general'. Real man, on the contrary, was far more complex:

he is of a time and a place, he has a family, a city, a nation, a religious and political faith, and all these factors, and many others besides, mingle and combine in a thousand ways, interacting with one

64. 1888a, p. 25.
65. ibid., p. 28.
66. ibid., p. 29.
67. Letter dated 16 May 1896.
68. 1888a, p. 29.
69. See 1890a.

another in such a way that it is impossible to say at first glance where one begins and the other ends. Only after long and laborious analyses, as yet scarcely begun, will it one day be possible to estimate the part played by each.[70]

Social science needed 'a nature to observe'.[71] It was, in Durkheim's view, Comte who gave social science 'a concrete reality to know'.[72] There is some truth in this view, though it is also true that the according of priority in explanation to collective phenomena was common to a number of counter-revolutionary thinkers who were reacting against what they saw as the 'abstract', *simpliste*, radical theories of the Enlightenment.[73] Certainly it was Comte who had erected this into a principle of scientific explanation: a society, in his view, was 'no more decomposable into *individuals* than a geometric surface into lines or a line into points'.[74] For Comte, Durkheim observed, society was 'as real as a living organism',[75] though he recognized that it could not exist apart from individuals: Comte saw that the whole was greater than the sum of its parts, but also that without them it would be nothing. Likewise,

in coming together under a defined framework and with durable links men form a new being which has its own nature and laws. This is the social being. The phenomena which occur here certainly have their ultimate roots in the mind of the individual. None the less, collective life is not simply an enlarged image of individual life. It presents *sui generis* features which the inductions of psychology alone would not enable one to predict. Thus customs, and the prescriptions of law and morality would be impossible if man were

70. 1888a, p. 29. Cf. the critical starting-point of the early Marx, for whom '*man* is not an abstract being, squatting outside the world. Man is *the human world*, the state, society' (*Contribution to the Critique of Hegel's Philosophy of Right: Introduction* (1844) in *Karl Marx: Early Writings*, tr. and ed. Bottomore, T. B., London, 1963, p. 43).

71. ibid.

72. ibid., p. 30. He later (rightly) came to regard this as Saint-Simon's achievement, developed and systematized by Comte: see 1915a; tr. 1960c.

73. Cf. de Bonald and de Maistre. On this subject, see Wolin, 1960, and Nisbet, 1943, 1952, 1965 and 1966.

74. Comte, A., *Système de politique positive* (Paris, 1851–4), vol. II, p. 181.

75. 1888a, p. 30.

incapable of acquiring habits; but they are still something other than individual habits.[76]

Thus Comte gave 'the social' a determinate rank in the chain of being – indeed, the top rank, in virtue of its greater complexity, and because it implied and included all other ranks. As Durkheim noted, it was not reducible to, and thus could not be deduced from, any other: 'to know it, one must observe it'.[77] Thus with Comte sociology had found 'an object which belonged to it alone and a positive method for studying it'.[78] Moreover, Comte had a keen sense of the interconnectedness of social phenomena – 'that universal consensus which characterizes the various phenomena of living bodies and which social life necessarily manifests to the highest degree'.[79] Yet Durkheim was also critical of Comte's version of social realism: sociology had an object, but 'how indeterminate it remains!'[80] Comte made the mistake of fixing on Society, not societies classified into types and species; he thought only of one social type – Humanity – indeed he used the words 'society' and 'humanity' interchangeably. In the end, Durkheim concluded, Comte's sociology was 'less a special study of social beings than a philosophical meditation on human sociability in general'.[81]

Spencer's contribution to Durkheim's social realism chiefly lay in the greater specificity of his explanations, resulting from his application of the organic analogy to societies. Comte had merely postulated the social as being distinct from other levels of being; Spencer, though he proclaimed methodological individualism, maintaining that 'the properties of the aggregate are determined by the properties of its units',[82] none the less regarded society as a sort of organism, as 'itself an organism transformed and perfected',[83] continuous with, but also dis-

76. ibid.
77. ibid.
78. ibid.
79. ibid.: quotation from Comte.
80. ibid., p. 32.
81. ibid.
82. Spencer, H., *The Study of Sociology* (paperback, Ann Arbor, 1961), p. 111.
83. 1888a, p. 34.

tinct from, the biological organism.[84] Thus Spencer was able both to get the most out of the analogy and to qualify it where necessary.[85] As opposed to such extreme, literal organicists as Lilienfeld, Spencer was able to use the analogy as an explanatory instrument, as a 'treasure of insights and hypotheses'.[86] Thus in this early period, Durkheim tended to regard Spencer's theory as fruitful, chiefly because Spencer applied it to 'different social types which he classifies into groups and subgroups'[87] and because he investigated 'special questions'[88] and particular institutions. On the other hand, Durkheim felt that, like Comte, Spencer was essentially a philosopher, whose sole concern was to verify 'the grand hypothesis he has conceived and which must explain everything',[89] namely the law of universal evolution; indeed, this vitiated his sociology, which was never specific enough, but always too hasty with facts, offering 'a bird's-eye view of societies'.[90] He also felt that Spencer offered an extreme *laissez-faire* view of individual

---

84. For a discussion of the respects in which Spencer's Social Darwinism led him to violate the requirements of the analogy, see Simon, W. M., 'Herbert Spencer and the "Social Organism"', *Journal of the History of Ideas*, 21 (1960), pp. 294–9. On Spencer generally, see Rumney, 1934, Burrow, J. W., *Evolution and Society* (Cambridge, 1966), ch. 6, and Peel, J. D. Y., *Herbert Spencer: The Evolution of a Sociologist* (London, 1971).

85. For example: 'The structures and functions of the social organism are obviously far less specific, far more modifiable, far more dependent on conditions that are variable [than those of the individual organism]' (*The Study of Sociology*, New York, 1906, p. 52) and, most relevantly to Durkheim's differences with Spencer in *The Division of Labour*, 'One cardinal difference is that while, in the individual organism there is but one centre of consciousness . . . there are, in the social organism, as many such centres as there are individuals, and the aggregate of them has no consciousness . . .' (*Essays: Scientific, Political and Speculative*, London and Edinburgh, 1891, vol. III, p. 411).

86. 1888a, p. 35. Cf. Evans-Pritchard's claim that Spencer's biological analogy 'did much to further the use of the concepts of structure and function in social anthropology' (*Social Anthropology*, Oxford, 1954, p. 51).

87. ibid. But see below.

88. ibid.

89. ibid., p. 36. T. H. Huxley put it simply: 'Spencer's definition of a tragedy was the spectacle of a deduction killed by a fact.'

90. ibid.

liberty in industrial societies because he failed to appreciate
that as societies grew larger, the scale of social influence grew
alongside that of individual action: Spencer had missed the
properly social aspect of modern societies.[91] What Durkheim
assimilated from Spencer was basically his organic perspective
involving the examination of institutions in the light of their
functions and the classification of societies into genera and
species; he remained unimpressed both by Spencer's overall
hypothesis and by his particular social theories, especially his
view of industrial society.

Yet Spencer was still too general and philosophical. It was
in the work of Alfred Espinas that Durkheim found the first
example of the 'studies of detail and precision'[92] that were
necessary. Espinas' *Les Sociétés animales*[93] (written under the
influence of Spencer) treated animal societies as consisting of
living elements bound together in simpler types by material
ties and in more complex types by psychological ones. Durkheim regarded Espinas as 'the first to have studied social facts
in order to construct a science of them rather than to preserve
the symmetry of a great philosophical system'.[94] He had confined himself to

the study of one social type in particular; then within this type itself
he distinguished between different classes and species, describing
them with care, and from this painstaking observation of the facts
he derived a number of laws, whose scope he was careful to restrict
to the special order of phenomena just studied.[95]

For these reasons, Durkheim thought, Espinas' book constituted 'chapter one of sociology'.[96]

91. See ibid., p. 37.
92. ibid., p. 38. For Espinas, society was a 'natural organized body, to
which a special science must be attached' (quoted in Bouglé, 1938, p. 25).
93. Paris, 1877.
94. 1888a, p. 38.
95. ibid.
96. ibid. In 1901 Espinas observed that Durkheim 'said about states of
human consciousness what I had said about states of animal consciousness: [that they are] "products of group life, only the nature of the group
can explain them" and again "although society would be nothing without
individuals, each of them is much more a product of society than its
creator" [1893a, p. 391]' ('Être ou ne pas être', *RP*, 51 (1901), p. 450).

Sociology had a subject matter. Social phenomena were real; they could be studied as analogous, though not identical, to organs performing functions within societies that were to be fitted into a general scheme of classification; and this study was to be detailed and precise. By 1885 Durkheim was a proselytizing sociologist. As he wrote in his first publication, a review of a book by the German sociologist Albert Schaeffle, 'Sociology has now emerged from the heroic age ... Let it establish itself, become organized, draw up its programme and specify its method.'[97] To these tasks he henceforth applied himself.

He greatly admired Schaeffle's 'laborious and patient' work, which was a massively documented examination of modern European societies, making (restrained) use of the organic analogy, identifying 'social tissues' and 'social organs'. Durkheim commended Schaeffle for being aware of the metaphorical status of organicism (unlike Espinas and Spencer) and for perceiving (like Comte) the crucial differences between biological organisms and societies. He admired Schaeffle's book because it was full of 'erudition, details and observations' – features absent from French sociology, which was 'too thin, too meagre, too fond of simplicity'.[98] Schaeffle's dominating concern was to 'place himself as near as possible to the social facts, to observe them in themselves, to see them as they are and to reproduce them as he sees them'.[99] His book was 'guided throughout by a properly scientific method' and constituted 'a genuine treatise of positive sociology'.[1]

Durkheim was looking for examples of sociology at work, face to face with the 'infinite complexity of facts'.[2] It was entirely natural that he should turn to Germany, and that during the academic year 1885–6 he should spend a term visiting several German universities, among them Berlin, Marburg and Leipzig.

97. 1885a, p. 98.
98. ibid., p. 97.
99. 1888a, p. 38.
 1. ibid., p. 39.
 2. 1885a, p. 97.

Chapter 4

Visit to Germany

THE Ministry of Public Instruction had for some time – since the *année terrible* of 1870 – made a point of awarding scholarships to the brightest of the young *agrégés* to visit Germany and become acquainted with the latest scholarly and scientific work there.[1] On the whole, these young scholars were highly critical of what they saw: they were far from ready to grant German superiority either in content of research or method of instruction.[2] But Durkheim was impressed and wrote two articles[3] on his return that were full of admiring, though not uncritical, observations on the teaching of philosophy and the state of the social sciences in Germany, together with corresponding lessons that the French might profitably draw.

He admired the German universities for being 'alive': there was a sense of community and corporate life, which contrasted favourably with the French 'striving for individual distinction and originality'.[4] French philosophers worked apart

---

1. Andler, op. cit., p. 30.
2. On a similar journey in 1882–3, Jullian wrote: 'Every day I am convinced that our French institutions are excellent and that we have nothing to learn from, and nothing to envy in our enemies, except the patience and seriousness they bring to all they do. . .' (Grenier, *Camille Jullian*, p. 49). According to Digeon (op. cit., p. 383), 'the era of exuberant admiration was over. The German universities no longer played a dominating role for the young minds of continental Europe . . . [they] had lost their halo. . .' However, many still agreed with the sentiments of Renan, who had written that 'Germany's victory was the victory of science . . . If we wish to recover from our disasters, let us imitate the conduct of Prussia. The intelligence of France has declined: we must strengthen it. Our system of teaching, above all in higher education, is in need of radical reforms' (*La Réforme intellectuelle et morale*, Paris, 1872, pp. 55ff.). It was for long widely held that the 'Prussian Schoolmaster' had triumphed at Sedan.
3. 1887a and 1887c.
4. 1887a, p. 437.

as though they were alone in the world and as though philosophy were an art: in this respect they had much to learn from Germany. It was, he wrote, 'scarcely contestable that what we most need at the moment is to reawaken in ourselves the taste for collective life'⁵ and this applied equally to intellectual and academic activities. (He also admired the 'hard-working habits' held in honour in German universities by students, and above all by their teachers.) He criticized the Germans for their lack of centralization and general organization of courses and their excessive vocational specialization (leading, he said, to an absence of interest in politics, and trust in their rulers), but these were the consequences of their virtues: the living, complex, evolving character of their universities.

In general, he was struck by the generality, eclecticism and low level of German philosophical teaching and its hostility to the experimental spirit. He approved of the pervasive influence of Kantianism, though it tended to separate unduly 'the psychic from the logical life' and to militate against the empirical observation of the 'higher forms of the understanding'.⁶ It was, however, the philosophy of law and, above all, ethics that constituted the really fruitful and living sector of German philosophy, though here it drew its sustenance more and more from neighbouring sciences – from political economy, law and history. Moreover, it benefited, as did those sciences, from the absence of the typically French confusion between such inquiry and immediately applicable practical doctrines.

The article ends with a striking rationale for the teaching of philosophy, as he conceived it, in France: it should serve 'national education'. 'We wish', he wrote,

above all to know the *raisons d'être* of national sentiments and patriotic faith; whether they are founded in the nature of things or whether, as is maintained, openly or not, by so many doctrinaire persons, they are only prejudices and survivals of barbarism. Now these problems concern psychology. To answer them one must teach students to appreciate the nature of sympathy and sociability, and get them to see their reality and usefulness. It is necessary to

5. ibid. Cf. Grenier, *Camille Jullian*, p. 56.
6. ibid., p. 329.

explain to them that our personalities are for the most part composed of borrowings, and that when taken out of the physical and social environment which surrounds him, man is only an abstraction. It is necessary, finally, to show them that sympathy is only exercised within groups that are unequally extensive but always confined and closed, and to indicate the place of the nation among these groups. To the teacher of philosophy also belongs the task of awakening in the minds that are entrusted to his care the concept of a law; of making them understand that mental and social phenomena are like any other phenomena, subject to laws that the human will cannot upset simply by willing, and therefore that revolutions, taking the word literally, are as impossible as miracles.[7]

It was, he thought, right to teach such things, as part of moral education, to schoolchildren in lycées; but that required that the science of morality should first be well advanced in the universities. It was 'astonishing that we make so little effort to produce an enlightened public opinion, when the latter is the sovereign power amongst us'.[8] Politicians mostly came from Faculties of Law, but they learned nothing there about 'the nature of law, moral codes, customs, religions, the role and relations between the various functions of the social organism, etc.'.[9] It was odd, he thought, that the Germans attributed importance to the moral sciences, when it was the French who had undertaken to govern themselves democratically.

It was, however, what he saw as the German contribution to the nascent science of sociology that mainly excited him. In general, he viewed with favour what he called the new organic conception of society which he found there, interpreting it as entailing that the 'individual is an integral part of the society into which he is born; the latter pervades him from all sides; for him to isolate and abstract himself from it is to diminish himself'.[10] This, he observed, is how one should understand it, if one is to understand 'certain German political conceptions'. Moreover, one must not judge these

7. ibid., pp. 439–40. Cf. 1895b.
8. ibid., p. 440.
9. ibid.
10. ibid., p. 337.

with our French ideas. If the German conceives the State as a power superior to individuals, it is not because of mysticism or servility. It is merely that the State is not for him as it is for us a vast machine destined to repress that multitude of unsociable beings pictured by Rousseau and in which, to our misfortune, we continue to believe . . .; it is a spontaneous product of social life; though distinct from it, it results from it.[11]

An 'acute sense of collective life, of its reality and its advantages' seemed to have become the essential feature of German social thought. Perhaps this was because of the 'grave events' besetting Germany, in comparison with which incidents in French political life seemed superficial: the Germans had 'a rich store of facts to observe'.[12]

More particularly, he was impressed by various examples of 'the positive science of morality' that he discovered in Germany. First, there were the social economists, the Socialists of the Chair, in particular Wagner and Schmoller. He valued their critique of the economists of the Manchester School for taking no account of social context and only treating of 'individuals . . . who exchange their products . . . like Rousseau, they see in the social bond only a superficial form of association determined by meetings of interests'.[13] He valued their insistence on the reality of society, with its '*conscience sociale*', in which the whole is greater than the parts, but which is in part explained by how the parts are assembled; their denial of the possibility of radically separating moral from economic phenomena (for example, economic activities could become obligatory) and their assertion of the mutual influence of moral and economic causes[14]; and their moral relativism, postulating different moral codes for different societies. On the other hand, he criticized them for having too much faith in the possibilities of legislation and a predilection for

11. ibid., pp. 337–8.
12. ibid., p. 338.
13. 1887c, p. 37.
14. For example: the need for increased production requires greater personal incentives and thus the legal and moral recognition of personal liberty; but then a growing sense of the importance of individual dignity opposes the exploitation of women and children, thereby changing economic relations, and ultimately replacing men by machines.

'authoritarian' means. They underrated the complexity of social phenomena and failed to take account of 'the obscure causes, unconscious sentiments and motives unrelated to the effects they produce' that underlie social processes.[15] (Schaeffle, he felt, in recognizing the organic character of law and morality, avoided this error, but was still too intellectualistic.) He thought highly, too, of the jurists, in particular Jhering, who advanced the hypothesis that all phenomena which persist and become widespread are useful, and who treated law as a necessary condition of social life, integrating the study of it with that of morality and custom.

It was, however, in the work of Wilhelm Wundt that he found the greatest evidence of advance in the sociological treatment of morality. He also greatly admired Wundt's experimental work in psychology, with its concentration on 'precise and restricted' problems and its avoidance of 'vague generalizations and metaphysical possibilities'.[16] But it was

15. 1887c, p. 45. He subsequently denied having been influenced by these ideas: 'Basically, I have, on the contrary, an aversion for socialism of the chair, which itself has no sympathy for sociology, whose principle it denies' (1907b: repr. in Deploige, 1911, p. 403); and in 1913 he wrote that 'Comte's work had an altogether more profound influence on us than the somewhat indecisive and loose thought of Schmoller and, above all, of Wagner' (1913a (ii) (15), p. 326). Their effect was almost certainly entirely negative, reinforcing Durkheim's animus against the methodology of the liberal economists.

16. 1887a, p. 433. Cf. 1898b: repr. in 1924a (1951 edn), pp. 45–6. Wundt's teaching was at this time very fashionable in France, and generally among foreigners completing their philosophical education (cf. 1887a, pp. 314 and 331, and Andler, op. cit., pp. 32–7). For an interesting discussion of Wundt's influence on Durkheim, see Gisbert, 1959, where it is argued that 'Wundt's psychological system is the key that will lay open the philosophy of Durkheim'. Gisbert argues that Durkheim took over Wundt's 'principle of actuality' (that mind is process, not substance), his 'principle of creative synthesis' (that new syntheses can emerge from component elements), his tendency to hypostasize a group-mind and personality (though both thinkers denied doing this), and his 'principle of relating analysis' (that analysing a whole into its parts brings out the parts' relation to the whole and the special collective properties of the whole). All these ideas can be found in Durkheim's thought, but there is no particular evidence that they came directly from Wundt. (On Wundt's psychological work, see Boring, E. G., *History of Experimental Psychology*, 2nd edn, New York, 1950, pp. 334–7.)

Wundt's sociological work that excited, and influenced, him
the most.[17] Wundt had a sense of the independent reality of
social causes and the unimportance in explanations of individual calculation and will, while at the same time holding that
collective phenomena do not exist *outside* individual minds:
'Everything occurs mechanically, and customs produce moral
consequences, without the latter having been either wished or
foreseen.'[18] Durkheim was also impressed by Wundt's view of
an original fusion of morality, custom and religious practices
and their subsequent separation; his view of the progressive
development of individuality; his notion of the first form of
community resulting from the affinity of like for like, powerfully reinforced by religious sentiments, and the subsequent
development of a more impersonal morality, based on a
transcendent ideal of humanity. But he disagreed with Wundt's
explanation of the obligatory force of morality in terms of
men's need for a durable social ideal, an unattainable ideal
that is ever-receding, arguing that morality should rather be
seen as a social function, offering an attainable ideal that is a
function of a particular society and enables men's inclinations
to be satisfied. Against Wundt's postulate of a single ideal to
which all religions and moralities tend, and approximate more
or less, he argued that 'there are as many moralities as there are
social types, and the morality of inferior societies is as much a
morality as is that of cultivated societies'.[19]

Finally, he praised the attempts of all these German writers

17. Wundt was at this time engaged on his *Ethik* (Stuttgart, 1886).
Durkheim later criticized this work for offering too rapid and summary a
survey of the historical development of morality (1893b, p. 21: tr. 1933b,
p. 423).

18. 1887c, p. 120. Cf. Durkheim's observation, concerning the growth
of the division of labour: 'Everything occurs mechanically. A disequilibrium in the social mass produces conflicts that can only be resolved by a
more developed division of labour' (1902b, p. 253: tr. 1933b, p. 270 –
S.L.).

19. ibid., p. 142. Lucien Herr also objected to Wundt's evaluation of
societies against a single moral ideal. This led, he wrote, to 'the idea that
peoples, like men, are only worth what they represent. Whence the ideas
of superiority and inferiority, of wars justified by their results, of force
representing law, ends justifying means, etc. Very Prussian and pretty
old hat!' (Andler, op. cit., p. 37).

to give inductive accounts of complex, *sui generis* moral phenomena by means of observation, analysis and comparison, and thus to produce a social science of morality (only Leslie Stephen, he wrote, had attempted this outside Germany), but he still criticized them all for being, none the less, too general: they were still too concerned with arriving at the fundamental principle of morality. They did not go into the necessary detail of considering, for instance, the right of property, contract, crime, punishment, and so on. Only Albert Hermann Post had studied these detailed questions. Everything, in fact, remained to be done; and the method must be strictly scientific, using methodical comparisons and establishing classifications of human societies. The science of morality, he concluded, was in the process of being born.

Durkheim was inspired by what he found in Germany, but it would be a mistake to argue, as the Catholic apologist Simon Deploige did in a polemical attack on Durkheim, that his main ideas were basically all of German origin.[20] It is true that he was influenced by these German writers, but, essentially, they clarified and reinforced existing tendencies in his thought. As he himself was to write,

Personally, I owe much to the Germans. It is in part from their school that I acquired the sense of social reality, of its organic complexity and development. After contact with them, I understood better the exiguity of the conceptions of the French school, whose importance, however, I do not mean to belittle in saying that I recognize, in comparison with others, its excessive *simplisme*.[21]

This seems to be an accurate assessment, although he was afterwards to write of sociology as an exclusively French

20. Deploige, 1911 (first published in the *Revue néo-scolastique*, 1906–7). (This view is taken over by F. A. Hayek in *The Counter-Revolution of Science*, Glencoe, Ill., 1952, pp. 187 and 205.) Durkheim described Deploige's book as 'an apologetic pamphlet', whose purpose was 'to discredit our ideas, by all possible means, for the greater glory of the doctrine of St Thomas' (1913a (i) (15), p. 326).

21. 1902d, p. 647. Cf. Bouglé's similar estimate (Bouglé, 1938, pp. 26–8); and also Durkheim, 1907b: 'I am certainly in debt to Germany, but I owe much more to its historians than to its economists . . .' (repr. in Deploige, 1911, p. 403).

science.[22] The main lines of his sociological and methodological views were drawn before his German visit, but they were somewhat indefinite and wavering; he was clear about the independent reality of social phenomena, but not entirely sure of the relation between the whole and the parts and the extent to which sociological explanation was independent of reference to individuals[23]; he was inclined to see the '*conscience collective*' as a mere 'reflection' and was not yet prepared to grant it any autonomy[24]; he was clear that societies were held together by rules, custom, habit, prejudices and sympathy as opposed to reason and interests,[25] but he was unclear about the extent to which these socially cohesive forces must remain irrational[26]; he was clear that morality, law and religion

22. 1900b, p. 609; and 1915a: tr. 1960c. See below, Chapter 20.

23. See 1885c, pp. 632, 633: 'Since there are in society only individuals, it is they and they alone that are the factors of social life'; 'But, it is said, the individual is an effect, not a cause; he is a drop in the ocean, he does not act but is acted upon and it is the social environment which controls him. But of what is this environment composed if not of individuals? Thus we are at once active and passive, and each of us contributes in the formation of this irresistible current on which he is borne'; 'The whole can only change if the parts change, and to the same extent.'

24. See 1886a, p. 67: 'We believe that the role of the *conscience collective*, like that of the *conscience individuelle*, is reduced to recording phenomena without producing them. It produces more or less faithfully what occurs in the depths of the organism. But it does nothing more than that.' The Greeks, for example, abandoned their religion, he says, because it could no longer ensure the equilibrium of the large communities that resulted from the Roman conquest.

25. See 1885b, p. 453: '[For Fouillée] social harmony would result from the spontaneous accord of wills. There would be a sort of mild and enlightened democracy . . . unfortunately one fears that such an organization would be very precarious. Sentiments, however splendid, are fragile bonds. A society which is not more solidly cemented would risk being carried away by the first tempest'; 1886a, p. 69: 'A society without prejudices would resemble an organism without reflexes . . . there is a need for custom and habit'; p. 75: 'There must be social discipline . . . Individuals in a society must be bound by solid and durable links'; p. 77 : 'Men are drawn together by sympathy.'

26. See 1885a, pp. 100–101: 'We begin to feel that all is not clear and that reason does not cure all ills. We have reasoned so much!'; 1886a, p. 69: 'Progress can only augment the number of prejudices' and religion would survive the attacks on it.

had the function of ensuring social equilibrium[27] and that morality was a form of discipline and not a means to individual happiness or perfection,[28] but had not yet explored these hypotheses in any detail; he was clear that the organic analogy had *some* value,[29] but was not sure quite what – whether, in fact, it 'masks reality',[30] or provided a mass of fertile hypotheses.[31]

Some of these matters were clearer to him after his return in 1886. He had a firmer grasp of observable and comparable elements of social life – customs, moral and legal codes, religious beliefs and practices; he had become more keenly aware of the interdependence of economic and moral phenomena; he was clearer about the importance of looking for unintended consequences and at causes of which men are unconscious; he was even more firmly convinced of the usefulness of the organic analogy.[32] More generally, he was convinced of the basic importance of the scientific study of morality (by which he at this time chiefly meant obligatory social rules). As he was to say soon afterwards, morality was 'of all the parts of sociology, the one to which we are attracted by preference'.[33] This preoccupation was to remain

27. See 1886a, pp. 67, 69: 'Now law and morality have the aim of ensuring the equilibrium of society, of adapting it to the surrounding conditions. This must also be the social role of religion'; 'Law, morality and religion are the three great regulating functions of society.'

28. See 1885c, p. 632: 'Social morality has the essential function of allowing the greatest possible number of men to live in common intercourse, without using external constraint'; p. 75: 'Morality cannot have objective authority if it only aims at happiness and individual perfection. It is nothing if it is not a social discipline.'

29. 1885a, p. 98: 'We freely admit that society is a sort of organism . . .'

30. ibid., p. 99: 'These metaphors and analogies had their usefulness in the early stages of the science [of sociology]; following an expression of Spencer, they are useful scaffolds, but they mask reality from us. Is it not time to cast them aside and confront things directly?'

31. See 1886a, p. 78: 'Economic phenomena, the State, morality, law and religion are functions of the social organism . . .'

32. See 1888a, p. 35: 'Spencer's theory, if one knows how to use it, is very fertile in application.'

33. 1888a, p. 45.

central with him; as Davy has written, 'morality was the centre and the end of his work'.[34]

After his return, in October 1886, he was appointed philosophy teacher at the Lycée de Troyes. His articles on philosophy and social science in Germany attracted attention and in 1887 he was appointed *chargé de cours* of social science and pedagogy, a post specially created for him, at the Faculty of Letters at Bordeaux. He was appointed partly as a result of pressure by Louis Liard, the director of Higher Education in France (himself influenced by Renouvier), whom he had impressed with his republican idealism and his desire to establish a secular morality based on science,[35] and who strongly felt that the national interest demanded that German universities should not be allowed to retain their monopoly of the social sciences. There is, however, reason to think that the original initiative for the appointment came from Espinas at Bordeaux.[36]

34. Davy, 1920, p. 71.

35. Lenoir, 1930, p. 294. He had, in fact, gone to Germany as a result of a conversation with Liard on the need to introduce the social sciences into higher education and to bring about considerable changes in the philosophy course for the *agrégation* at the École Normale (ibid.). Cf. 1895b. On Liard, see Lavisse, E., 'Louis Liard', *RIE*, 72 (1918), pp. 81–99.

36. See Lacroze, 1960a, p. 1, and Alpert, 1937.

Part Two
Bordeaux: 1887-1902

Chapter 5

Durkheim at Bordeaux

IN 1887 Durkheim married Louise Dreyfus, whose family came from Wissembourg in Alsace and whose father ran a foundry in Paris.[1] His marriage, according to Davy, could not have been happier, both personally and in creating an atmosphere conducive to his work. His first year at Bordeaux, however, was one of considerable strain, for he worked ten hours a day.[2] He had two children, Marie and André, and of his domestic circumstances Davy has written that the domestic ideal that is evident in his writings (the family being his favourite subject of study and lecturing) was most clearly represented by his own home life.[3] Mauss writes, similarly, that his wife 'created for him the respectable and quiet familial existence which he considered the best guarantee of morality and of life. She removed from him every material care and all frivolity, and for his sake took charge of the education of Marie and André Durkheim.'[4] Confidential reports sent by the Recteur of Bordeaux to the Ministry of Public Instruction confirm this

1. See Appendix G in Lukes, 1968b (Durkheim's family tree).
2. Davy, personal communication.
3. Davy, 1919, p. 198.
4. Mauss, 1927a, p. 8. Mauss adds that she never left his side, and that, being well educated, she even collaborated with him in his work; she copied manuscripts, corrected proofs and shared in the administrative editorial work of the *Année sociologique*. M. Davy has permitted me to quote from a letter to him from Mauss, which describes Durkheim's working and domestic life. Mauss, who was Durkheim's nephew, wrote: '[My aunt] was a saint – and she was cheerful as well. My uncle made her lead a life that was more than austere, but she led it with gaiety. It was only when Marie and André were growing up that they drew my uncle out of his domestic and academic circle. A little gaiety and fresh air then came to refresh him. He only returned to the theatre, which he loved, in order to take André there.' M. Henri Durkheim, who lived with his uncle at Bordeaux, has told me that he worked according to a rigid timetable: he would talk at mealtimes, but not afterwards.

picture of immensely hard work allied with respectability. 'No teacher', according to the Recteur in 1893, 'works harder or gives more of himself. M. Durkheim's health has even been endangered'; while in 1889, he described him as 'recently married; conduct *très "comme il faut"* . . . excellent relations – character likeable and reserved'.[5]

Durkheim's fifteen years at Bordeaux were immensely productive. Some idea of the scale of his activity can be obtained by looking at the bibliography of his writings during this period. Apart from all his reviews and incidental articles, he published the following major studies: his two theses, *The Division of Labour* and the study of Montesquieu; *The Rules of Sociological Method*; *Suicide*; and the articles on incest, on individual and collective *représentations*, on the definition of religious phenomena, on the 'Two Laws of Penal Evolution' and on totemism. By 1902 he had founded, edited and abundantly contributed to the first five volumes of the *Année sociologique*. He lectured during these years on a vast range of subjects, including 'social solidarity', moral and intellectual education, the history of pedagogy, the family, suicide, legal and political sociology, psychology, criminology, religion, the history of socialism and the history of sociological theories.[6] Finally, he took an active part in university administration and educational reform, in the movement for secular education and, in a restrained but positive way, in the campaign of the Dreyfusards.[7]

The appointment of the young social scientist to the predominantly humanist Faculty of Letters caused a considerable stir. Espinas, the new Dean of the Faculty, officially welcomed him in the following words:

This is a great event, if one is to judge by the emotion it has caused . . . May social science be far from a supererogatory study here . . . it is – and one must say so boldly – the common basis of all the

5. *Renseignements confidentiels*, dated 1 July 1893 and 22 May 1889, in Durkheim's dossier, Archives Nationales.

6. See Appendix A, below, for a complete list of Durkheim's courses.

7. His work schedule was, indeed, truly amazing, both at Bordeaux and subsequently at Paris. His health undoubtedly suffered, and his letters reveal a number of mental breakdowns brought on by overwork.

studies to which you devote yourselves ... it is probable that sociology – since one must call it by its name – will assume a more and more important place in all our studies.[8]

Durkheim's opening public lecture staked out large claims for his subject; his arguments were both intellectual and moral. He began by saying, disarmingly, that sociology was a science that had just been born and that he proposed to develop it in the process of teaching it. He would regard his audience as collaborators. It was best to begin modestly, rather than indulging in abstract discussions about whether sociology is possible or not. After a comprehensive review of its history and subdivisions, he ended the lecture by urging that sociology was useful to philosophers, historians and lawyers. Philosophy, after all, was 'in the process of splitting into two groups of positive sciences: psychology on the one hand, and sociology on the other'.[9] Moreover, social science was particularly relevant to problems that had hitherto belonged exclusively to philosophical ethics. These should be treated scientifically: that is, 'observed as a system of natural phenomena which we will subject to analysis and whose causes we will seek'.[10] It was clear that 'before discovering what the family, property and society should be, one must discover what they are, to what needs they correspond, and to what conditions they must conform in order to exist'.[11] As to history, it was not merely descriptive: it required 'inductions and hypotheses'.[12] In selecting his evidence, the historian needed 'a guiding idea, a criterion which can only be found in sociology. It alone will

8. Lacroze, 1960a, p. 1. Espinas had had a famous battle with his examiners when he defended the first sociological doctoral thesis in France (*Les Sociétés animales*) in 1877. He was forced by Paul Janet to suppress his introduction to the first edition, because it discussed the ideas of Comte, and a reaction from the ecclesiastical authorities was feared; also the publisher added, without the author's knowledge, the sub-title *Essay in Comparative Psychology*, so that his future career would not be adversely affected (See Espinas, A., 'Être ou ne pas être: ou du postulat de la sociologie', *RP*, 51 (1901), p. 449, and Essertier, 1930, p. 6.).

9. 1888a, p. 45.
10. ibid.
11. ibid.
12. ibid., p. 46.

teach him what are the vital functions, the essential organs of society'[13]: sociology would pose the questions that would limit and guide his researches. The student of law also needed to learn 'how law is formed under the pressure of social needs, how it gradually becomes established, through what degrees of crystallization it successively passes and how it is transformed'.[14] The lawyer should be aware of how such great juridical institutions as the family, property and contract had been born, what were their causes, how they varied and how they were likely to vary in the future.

In a final peroration, he observed that sociology was further needed in order to enlighten opinion, for 'we live in a country recognizing no other master than opinion'. That master threatened to become an unintelligent despot for 'the spirit of the collectivity is weakened among us':

> Our society must regain the consciousness of its organic unity; the individual must feel the presence and influence of that social mass which envelops and penetrates him, and this feeling must continually govern his behaviour ... [sociology] will enable the individual to understand what society is, how it completes him and what a small thing he is when reduced to his own powers. It will teach him that he is not an empire enclosed within another empire, but the organ of an organism, and it will show him what is valuable in conscientiously performing one's role as an organ.[15]

These ideas, he concluded, would only be truly efficacious when 'they are spread throughout the deepest levels of the population', but before that they must first be 'elaborated scientifically within the university'.[16]

What his audience made of this manifesto it is impossible to know. Certainly the opposition within the university did not abate, for in the following year, in the opening lecture of his course on the sociology of the family, he was still defensively arguing the case for sociology's usefulness to philosophers, historians and lawyers and appealing for an end to the battle raging between the Faculties of Letters and of Law over which

13. ibid., p. 47.
14. ibid.
15. ibid., p. 48.
16. ibid.

should accommodate sociology: 'Let us', he said, 'not divide our forces and wrangle over details of organization. Let us work together.'[17]

Durkheim was, understandably, from this early stage open to the charge of sociological imperialism, as well as to the graver charge of 'collectivism', for reasons that will be evident from the foregoing quotations. As we shall see, he was to be attacked on these grounds, as well as on many others, throughout his career. The latter charge, to which *The Division of Labour* was held to be especially open by both moral philosophers and liberal economists, led to his being excluded for a long time from professorships in Paris, to which he aspired.[18] The former charge was often made by aggrieved specialists, but, none the less, he soon gained the sympathy and even to some extent the allegiance of colleagues at Bordeaux.

In particular, the distinguished legal theorist Léon Duguit came under his influence, even proclaiming himself a disciple,[19] and in 1891 began a seminar on sociology for advanced students.[20] Duguit later wrote that the constituent elements of social cohesion 'appear to me to have been definitely discovered by several sociologists and particularly by my eminent colleague and friend M. Durkheim . . . These elements consist in what is called social solidarity.'[21] Similarly, Camille Jullian (at Bordeaux since 1883) was 'very deeply impressed by the renewal brought by comparative sociology to the Roman history which he taught at Bordeaux'.[22] Also sympathetic to Durkheim's ideas were the rationalist philosopher Octave

17. 1888c, pp. 280–81.

18. Mauss, 1928, pp. vii-viii; though none existed in sociology, and there were only one or two openings in philosophy.

19. Davy, 1960b, p. 9. See Hayward, 1960, especially pp. 189–91; cf. also Lévy-Bruhl, H., 1960, p. 40, for a discussion of Duguit's attitude to Durkheim. Duguit never accepted any form of 'social realism' and insisted that only the *content* of the *conscience collective* was social. Duguit and Davy strongly disagreed over this issue, each defending his own interpretation of 'our common master', as Duguit put it (Hayward, 1960, p. 191).

20. See Duguit, 1893.

21. Duguit, L., *Les Transformations générales du droit privé depuis le Code Napoléon* (Paris, 1912), p. 26, quoted in Hayward, 1960, p. 190.

22. Grenier, *Camille Jullian*, p. 129.

Hamelin and (from 1894) Georges Rodier, the specialist on Greek philosophy and Aristotle. These last two, together with Durkheim, formed a brilliant and celebrated trio, linked by close ties of friendship and by a common devotion to rationalism and 'a common hostility to those philosophies of life and action which they accused of putting the intellect in shadows'.[23] Espinas, on the other hand, became increasingly less sympathetic.[24]

Durkheim's influence at Bordeaux was considerable. Mauss writes:

The few philosophy students of the Faculty of Letters at Bordeaux were not the whole of Durkheim's audience. His lectures were public and well attended. There were jurists, students of law, several colleagues – a public that was, fortunately, sufficiently demanding, on the one hand. But, on the other hand, there were also teachers, students of diverse subjects and, finally, that vague body of persons that peoples the benches of the amphitheatres of our large provincial Faculties. Durkheim, who was not only a marvellous lecturer, but even loved lecturing, sought at the same time – and it cost him much effort – both scientific truth and didactic effectiveness.[25]

His lectures were, indeed, reported as being of 'an unsurpassable clarity'.[26] One of those who heard them describes them as follows:

M. Durkheim speaks a language that is clear, precise and, as far as possible, technical. He uses concrete symbols and numerical specifications. If he is discussing the family, he has a chart showing successive phases which this social group has traversed, indicating them with a finger; if he is studying suicide, he has reproduced the figures furnished by the official statistics, and he writes them on the board. In short, whatever the subject, his effort to achieve definite expression and measurement is apparent. In listening to him, you would wait in vain for literary displays and rhetorical periods, appeals to sentiment and metaphysical flights, to which sociological subjects seem at first sight so well suited. It is obvious that M.

23. Lacroze, 1960a, p. 2.
24. Bourgin, 1938, pp. 90–91.
25. Mauss, 1925a, p. 16.
26. Lacroze, 1960a, p. 3.

Durkheim denies himself 'phrases', generalities, and vast syntheses' and that he wishes neither to generate 'problems' nor construct systems. He observes facts, he analyses them and explains them by laws. In brief, it is not so much conclusions he draws as results he records and expresses in propositions that qualify as 'formulae' by virtue of their precision and rigour. Certainly, M. Durkheim is always eloquent, and often to a rare degree. Whoever has heard him will not forget for a long time the irresistible enthusiasm which he can, when he wishes, arouse in his audience. But even at those moments, what moves that audience is the extreme interest of the ideas expressed; what excites them is the intensity of the discussion, concise, urgent and constantly straining towards a proof; what overcomes and overwhelms them is the speed of the lecture which, concentrated and concise, though abundant, is as though impatient to reach its end . . . Listening to M. Durkheim, one has the very clear sensation that he does not seek to persuade, but to convince, and that he addresses himself much less to men's feelings than to their reason.[27]

In his confidential reports to the Ministry, the Recteur of Bordeaux built up a revealing picture of Durkheim and the nature of his influence. He was 'an original thinker, a learned and vigorous writer', a 'rigid and powerful logician, who is absolute and systematic' with 'great self-possession', 'much vigour and authority' and a 'strong individuality to which the label "master" is suited'. He was a 'zealous teacher who has a very great influence over his disciples. And he is armed with an ardent and militant proselytism'; he conceived of his teaching as 'a kind of apostolate, which must extend its influence over his students outside the Faculté . . .', indeed he

plays at Bordeaux among his disciples the role of an oracle that has written with a sort of fervour, whether it is a question of sociology, or of militant politics or philosophy.[28]

Since his appointment was a joint one in social science and pedagogy, he decided from the beginning to give public

27. Delprat, G., 'L'Enseignement sociologique à l'Université de Bordeaux', *Revue philomatique de Bordeaux et du Sud-Ouest*, 3ᵉ année, August 1900, p. 357.

28. *Renseignements confidentiels*, dated 5 May 1900, 20 April 1901 and 25 April 1902, in Durkheim's dossier, Archives Nationales.

lectures on sociology and separate pedagogy lectures (the content of which will be indicated in the next chapter).[29] In addition to this, however, he took seriously the business of preparing his students for the *agrégation* in philosophy. He felt very strongly that the literary and unscientific character of philosophy as it was normally taught for this examination was pernicious: it made students prize dialectical skill above the patient and systematic understanding of facts, so that knowledge became a useless impediment and originality was at a premium. This was pernicious partly because it led to irrationalism; the dangers of dilettantism and mysticism were once more in evidence. Philosophy became 'a form of symbolism or impressionism' and '*le règne de bon plaisir*' prevailed in the world of the mind, while anti-scientific doctrines found ready recruits among the students, being, indeed, 'most evident in those who are the elite of our school teachers'.[30] To counter these tendencies, from 1888 onwards Durkheim gave special tuition on prepared texts by selected authors (which he helped to choose, as an examiner for the *agrégation*), along with his philosopher colleagues. Mauss wrote that the textual commentaries which he drew up for this tuition were

a model of direct exegesis, of the author interpreted by the author himself – of that exegesis which has, at last, under the impetus of a healthy philology and a healthy philosophy, under the impetus of Hamelin, Durkheim, Rodier and others, replaced the brilliant but irrelevant interpretations in which young philosophers used to allow themselves to indulge.[31]

Durkheim gave such courses on two books of Aristotle's *Politics*, on one book of the *Nicomachean Ethics*, two courses each on two books of Comte and on one book of Hobbes'

29. See Durkheim's dossier, Bordeaux, letter written in September or October 1887; 'My intention is to give a public course in *Social Science* and a series of lectures on pedagogy. It would be good, I think, to separate the two titles on the notice, since the public course will for a long time be devoted only to Social Science.'

30. 1895b, pp. 129–33.

31. Mauss, 1925a, p. 15.

De Cive,[32] but none of these has survived the Second World War.

Furthermore, as can be seen from his article on the teaching of philosophy for the *agrégation*, he believed that philosophy students should be taught about human and social phenomena as objects of science (for 'it is not by discussing whether the moral law is *a priori* or not that we will make citizens informed of their duties and ready to perform them with discernment'[33]) and that they should become aware of science, its procedures and its methods by direct experience of scientific study. Instead of problems of transcendental metaphysics, they should be taught to reflect on the nature of 'a type, a species, a law, an organ and a function, classification, mathematical reasoning, etc.'.[34] While 'not intending to disparage the study of the humanities', Durkheim believed that in his time there was

much less need for refined minds, capable of appreciating beautiful things and of expressing themselves well, than for men of sound judgement, who, not letting themselves be perturbed by the storms which menace us, are able to look fixedly ahead and mark out the direction that must be taken. Now one may be forgiven for supposing that the study of languages and literary masterpieces is not the best means of arriving at such a result. Doubtless, philosophy alone would not be enough for such a task; all the same, the role it has to play is of the first importance.[35]

He saw philosophy as essentially dependent upon science, and he held, further, that all meaningful philosophical questions (in particular those of epistemology and ethics) were answerable and that the conclusions of sciences were relevant to the answers; whereas those which could not be answered ('*tous ceux qui visent au delà de l'expérience*'[36]) were not meaningful, or at least not important, and *a fortiori* not worth teaching for the *agrégation*. Moreover, the most important part of philosophy was ethics and hence 'morality should constitute the object *par excellence* of the scientific teaching we would like to

32. ibid.
33. 1895b, p. 138.
34. ibid., p. 141.
35. ibid., p. 147.
36. ibid., p. 141.

see given in classes of philosophy' and, since 'social questions are in large part moral questions', social science, by 'showing how humanity has formed its basic beliefs and practices', must form an essential, indeed, the fundamental part of a training in philosophy.[37] Durkheim put these ideas into practical effect by proposing a resolution to the Faculty of Letters, which was passed in 1891, the effect of which was to include social science in the programme for the *agrégation* in philosophy. At the same time, he proposed a similar addition to the programme for the *agrégation* in law.[38]

37. ibid., pp. 138–9.
38. Durkheim's dossier, Bordeaux. As he explained in a letter to a local paper, he was against introducing an examination in sociology, either for students in philosophy or for those in law: it was a science still in the making. It should merely be included as part of the programme for each *agrégation* (ibid.).

Chapter 6

The Theory and Practice of Education[1]

THE title of Durkheim's Bordeaux appointment was 'Chargé d'un Cours de Science Sociale et de Pédagogie' (becoming a chair in Social Science in 1895). The course in pedagogy had begun in the Faculty of Letters in 1882, the first such course to be offered in France; and the State began to support it in 1884, as part of the national drive for a new system of republican, secular education. Espinas, who was in charge of it, started to give lectures which involved discussions of the practical questions of teaching with schoolmasters and schoolmistresses. It was, in the first place, specially to provide this teaching in succession to Espinas that Durkheim was appointed; this was the cover under which sociology was first officially introduced into a French university. Indeed it was only as a special favour that he was allowed to add the word 'Sociology' to 'Pedagogy' in the Faculty List.[2]

He gave lectures on education, in some years two a week, and these ranged from the more theoretical through the historical to the strictly practical. His audience regularly consisted of more than fifty young primary schoolteachers. Durkheim found the sympathy, enthusiasm, and intellectual liveliness of these young men and women highly congenial. He had, according to Mauss, a keen sense of the extent of his influence on them.[3] None the less, this teaching was a burden; he always felt, both at Bordeaux and Paris, that it meant a

1. Much of the historical information in this section comes from the *Revue internationale de l'enseignement* – especially for 1888. On Durkheim's pedagogical work as a whole see Fauconnet, 1922, Mauss, 1925a, pp. 17–19, and Halbwachs, 1938a; also Hueso, 1911, Case, 1924, Jacovella, 1925, Mackensie, 1925, Jyan, 1926, Ouy, 1926, Piaget, 1932, Ottaway, 1955, Lear, 1961, Wilson, 1961, Morrish, 1967, and Lourau, 1969. See also Chapters 17 and 19, below.

2. Mauss, 1925a, p. 17.

3. ibid.

fragmentation of his intellectual efforts. Indeed Mauss writes of '. . . this obligation he was under, for the whole of his life, to interrupt his preferred studies, those in which he felt himself alone to be responsible and in advance of everyone, in the interests of work that was less urgent, less important'.[4] Week after week, he had to devote at least a third, sometimes two-thirds, of his lecturing-time to this teaching,[5] and he did it with great conscientiousness. Mauss writes that he brought to it 'the same spirit, the same originality, the same personal, yet at the same time exclusively positive, thought that he brought to everything'.[6]

MORAL EDUCATION

The most important of the education courses was that on moral education. Its importance lies partly in its close relation to Durkheim's central sociological concerns, and partly in its central place within his educational thinking; it was delivered fairly regularly between 1889 and 1912, both at Bordeaux and Paris.[7] As Mauss observed, it was in this course that Durkheim 'connects his discoveries concerning the general nature of moral phenomena with his doctrine of education, itself a social phenomenon, and derives therefrom the consequent precepts of pedagogy'.[8] He viewed pedagogy as a 'practical theory' – 'neither the educational activity itself, nor the

4. ibid.

5. Fauconnet, 1922, p. 1: tr. 1956a, p. 27. See Appendix A, below.

6. Mauss, 1925a, pp. 17–18.

7. 1889–90, 1898–9, 1899–1900 (Bordeaux) and 1902–3, 1906–7, 1911–12 (Paris): see Appendix A, below. Cf. Fauconnet's discussion (Fauconnet, 1922, pp. 15–21: tr. 1956a, pp. 39–46). As of 1902–3, it consisted of twenty lectures, the first on the relations between pedagogy and sociology (1903b: repr. 1922a: tr. 1956a), the second on pedagogical methodology (not extant) and the remaining eighteen published as *L'Éducation morale* (1925a: tr. 1961a). However, M. Davy has told me that the text of this latter is a combination of the texts of various courses of different dates (I believe that M. Henri Durkheim possesses lecture-notes taken at an early delivery of this course, but I have not been able to make use of these). The following discussion is based on the published texts listed above (unchanged after 1902–3).

8. Mauss, 1925a, p. 18.

speculative science of education', but rather 'the systematic reaction of the second on the first, the product of thought which seeks in the findings of psychology and sociology principles for the practice or for the reform of education'.[9] It was here that he sought to put the scientific study of morality to applied use.

During the years at Bordeaux, this course developed into a clearly structured whole in which the bearing of sociological theory on educational practice was fully brought out. Both education and morality, Durkheim maintained, are social phenomena: both are relative to the needs and social structures of particular societies and both are open to systematic observation. He saw education as 'the means by which society perpetually re-creates the conditions of its very existence'[10]: it consists of 'a systematic socialization of the young generation'.[11] He thought it possible to distinguish analytically (though not in reality) between all those mental states which are private to the individual and 'a system of ideas, sentiments and practices which express in us ... the group or different groups of which we are part; these are religious beliefs, moral beliefs and practices, national or occupational traditions, collective opinions of every kind'.[12] The aim of education was to constitute that system within individuals.

What, then, was morality? This question was especially acute in the context of advancing secularization, and in particular its attempted enforcement by the State in the nation's public schools. It was no good merely stripping away the religious elements in traditional beliefs and practices:

9. Fauconnet, 1922, p. 11: tr. 1956a, p. 36 (S.L.). Cf. 1911c (3), repr. 1922a: tr. 1956a; and 1925a, p. 2: tr. 1961a, p. 2. Durkheim thus proposed a (very valuable) threefold distinction between: (1) the scientific study of education; (2) the art of education, consisting of 'ways of acting, practices, systematized skill' – the '*savoir faire* of the educator, the practical experience of the teacher'; and (3) pedagogy, seeking 'to combine, as conscientiously as possible, all the data science puts at its disposal, at a given time, as a guide to action'. Pedagogy is thus a 'practical theory' – 'an intermediary between art and science' (1925a, pp. 1–2: tr. 1961a, pp. 1–2 – S.L.).

10. 1922a, p. 119: tr. 1956a, p. 123.

11. ibid.: tr. p. 124

12. ibid., pp. 119–20: tr. p. 124.

morality and religion had been 'too inextricably bound together in history . . . for the separation to be so easily consum-
mated'.[13] The need was to 'discover the rational substitutes
for those religious notions that for a long time have served as
the vehicle for the most essential moral ideas'.[14] It was 'not
enough to cut out; we must replace'.[15] In order to do this, it
was crucial to provide a rational, not a symbolic or allegorical,
explanation of the nature of morality; one could then discern
what moral rules and ideals were latent in and appropriate to
the contemporary social situation. What was required was a
reform of educational methods in the light of sociological
inquiry that would discover within the old moral and religious
system 'moral forces hidden beneath forms which concealed
their true nature'.[16] Such inquiry would 'reveal their real
character and establish what they must become under present
conditions'.[17]

Durkheim's account of morality underwent a number of
changes, as we shall see, but by the end of the Bordeaux
period he had reached a clear-cut position, well expressed in
the published version of these lectures. He distinguished three
elements in morality. The first element, the spirit of discipline,
identified the imperative quality of moral rules: morality, he
argued, is 'a system of rules of action that predetermine
conduct'.[18] Far from being deduced from a general principle
within a philosophical system, such rules were to be seen as
'so many moulds, with given structures, which serve to shape
our behaviour'.[19] Arguing against Bentham, the utilitarians,
the classical economists and the 'major socialist theorists',
Durkheim postulated social and individual functions for
discipline, which he saw as presupposing regularity and
authority. As to its social function, regularity was essential to
social life: it was necessary that 'at each moment the functioning

---

13. 1925a, p. 9: tr. 1961a, p. 8.
14. ibid., p. 10: tr. p. 9.
15. ibid., p. 12: tr. p. 11.
16. ibid., p. 16: tr. p. 14 (S.L.).
17. ibid. (S.L.).
18. ibid., p. 27: tr. p. 24.
19. ibid., p. 30: tr. p. 26 (S.L.).

of domestic, professional and civic life be assured', that 'norms be established determining what these relations ought to be and that individuals submit to them'.[20] Its individual functions were no less important: it contained the latent anarchy of insatiable desires, affording mental equilibrium by preventing anomie – the Faustian 'malady of infinite aspiration'[21]; it provided behaviour with a 'clear-cut objective, which can be attained and which limits it by determining it'[22]; it constituted a precondition not only for happiness and moral health, but for 'all liberty worthy of the name',[23] since liberty was 'the fruit of regulation'.[24] ('To be free', he wrote elsewhere, echoing Montesquieu, 'is not to do as one pleases; it is to be master of oneself, it is the ability to act rationally and do one's duty.'[25]) Indeed, discipline performed 'an important function in forming character and personality in general',[26] since 'the most essential element of character is the disposition to self-mastery, that capacity of restraint or, as they say, inhibition, which allows us to contain our passions, desires, habits, and subject them to law'.[27]

The second element of morality concerned not the form but the content of morality: Durkheim called it 'attachment to social groups'. He answered the question 'what kind of acts are moral?' by specifying certain sorts of goal as peculiarly moral. This, he claimed, was a sociological kind of answer, rather than an *a priori* or stipulative one, since he sought it by asking 'What ways of behaving are approved as moral and what are the characteristics of these modes of behaviour?'[28] The answer he came up with was that 'moral goals are those

20. ibid., p. 42: tr. p. 37.
21. ibid., p. 45: tr. p. 40.
22. ibid., p. 46: tr. p. 40 (S.L.).
23. ibid., p. 51: tr. p. 45.
24. ibid., p. 62: tr. p. 54.
25. 1922a, p. 73: tr. 1956a, pp. 89–90 (S.L.). Cf. Montesquieu's *The Spirit of the Laws*, XI, 3:'. . . liberty can consist only in the power of doing what we ought to will, and in not being constrained to do what we ought not to will'.
26. 1925a, p. 52: tr. p. 46.
27. ibid. (S.L.).
28. ibid., p. 63: tr. p. 55.

the object of which is *a society*. To act morally is to act in the light of a collective interest'[29]: indeed, 'the domain of the moral begins where the domain of the social begins',[30] and 'we are moral beings only to the extent that we are social beings'.[31] Of course, the relevant groups to which individuals could be morally attached must vary with different types of society; one could, however, discern a progressive universalization of morality, from tribal morality to a sort of higher patriotism (since, in the absence of a world society, the state was the most inclusive and highly organized form of human organization in existence), the latter being committed to such universal ideals as justice, peace and the sacredness of the individual. Durkheim believed that 'New ideas of justice and solidarity are now developing and, sooner or later, will prompt the establishment of appropriate institutions' and that currently 'the most pressing goal of moral education is to work to unravel such notions, still confused and sometimes unconscious, to induce children to cherish them without provoking in them sentiments of anger against ideas and practices deriving from the past which were the precondition for those now forming before our eyes'.[32]

These first two elements of morality, discipline and the collective ideal, Duty and the Good, were reconciled in Durkheim's conception of authority. What, he asked, gives moral rules their peculiar authority? He regarded his answer to this question – 'society' – as reaching behind traditional mythical and symbolic forms to 'grasp the reality behind the symbolism'.[33] Many critics, as we shall see, regarded this answer as merely a new form of sociological myth-making, a hypostasization of society in place of the supernatural beings who had traditionally formed the source of authority.[34] It is, however (again, as we shall see), more accurate to see it as a breakthrough

29. ibid., p. 68: tr. p. 59 (S.L.).
30. ibid.: tr. p. 60.
31. ibid., p. 73: tr. p. 64. For a discussion of this argument, see Chapter 21, below.
32. ibid., pp. 117–18: tr. pp. 102–3 (S.L.).
33. ibid., p. 102: tr. p. 90.
34. See Chapters 16 and 25, below.

in social theory; for by 'society' Durkheim identified that supra-individual element in social life, which he elsewhere called *représentations collectives*, consisting of collective sentiments and beliefs, which was necessary to explain the authority of imperative rules and desired ideals.

The third element of morality, autonomy, concerned the state of mind of the moral agent; it had become a crucial element in morality only as a result of secularization and the advance of rationalism. To act morally,

it is not enough – above all it is no longer enough – to respect discipline and to be attached to a group; beyond this, we must, when deferring to a rule or devoting ourselves to a collective ideal, have as clear and complete an awareness as possible of the reasons for our conduct. For it is this awareness that confers on our action that autonomy which the public conscience henceforth requires of every truly and fully moral being. Hence we can say that the third element of morality is understanding morality. Morality no longer consists simply in performing, even intentionally, certain given actions; beyond this, the rule prescribing such behaviour must be freely willed, that is freely accepted, and this free acceptance is nothing else than an enlightened acceptance.[35]

Durkheim saw this striking conception of autonomy (reminiscent of Spinoza) as constituting 'the principal differentiating characteristic of a secular morality',[36] for religions put morality within the 'realm of mystery, where the ordinary procedures of scientific inquiry are no longer appropriate'.[37] Henceforth teaching morality would be 'neither to preach nor to indoctrinate, but to explain'.[38]

The second half of the course consisted of pedagogy proper, eliciting 'principles for the practice or for the reform of education' from the foregoing analysis. The school should serve as 'intermediary between the affective morality of the family and the more severe morality of civil life'.[39] The

35. 1925a, pp. 136–7: tr. 1961a, p. 120.
36. ibid., p. 138: tr. p. 121.
37. ibid., pp. 138–9: tr. p. 121.
38. ibid., p. 137: tr. p. 120. For a full discussion of Durkheim's sociology of morality, see Chapter 21, below.
39. ibid., p. 171: tr. 149.

schoolmaster was the secular successor to the priest, deriving his authority from that wider morality which he represented in the school: like the priest,

he is the instrument of a great moral reality which extends beyond himself and with which he communicates more directly than does the child, since it is through his intermediation that the child communicates with it. Just as the priest is the interpreter of God, so he is the interpreter of the great moral ideas of his time and country.[40]

What, Durkheim asked, was the best way to impart the elements of morality to the child in the France of his time? He went on to examine discipline in the school, the use of punishments and rewards, constantly emphasizing the need for the exercise of authority to be seen as legitimate and suggesting that it be used in a way that would elicit group sentiments and loyalties (for instance by collective punishments and rewards); he even applied in this context his sociological theory of punishment as the symbolic affirmation of social values, arguing that the best punishment was the most expressive and the least expensive. To punish, Durkheim argued, 'is to disapprove, to condemn'. When faced with a transgression, the teacher must unequivocally show that he 'disapproves of it with a disapproval proportionate to the importance of the offence' and thereby prevent any 'weakening of the moral convictions of the class'. Punishment is an 'affirmation of the rule the offence has denied': it is

a material sign which expresses an inner state; it is notation, a language by means of which either the public social *conscience* or the schoolmaster's *conscience* expresses the sentiment aroused in them by the censured act.[41]

Turning to the second element of morality, he examined ways of teaching the child 'the love of collective life' by getting him to 'live it, not only in his thoughts and imagination,

---

40. ibid., p. 177: tr. p. 155 (S.L.). It is certainly relevant to observe that Durkheim nowhere satisfactorily explains how the teacher is to acquire this moral authority, when it is lacking. See Floud, J. E., 'Teaching in the Affluent Society', *British Journal of Sociology*, 13 (1962), p. 300.

41. ibid., p. 200–201: tr. pp. 175–6 (S.L.).

but in reality'.[42] This was a particularly acute need at that time, Durkheim believed, because of the excessive individualism of French morality, the weakness of the 'spirit of association' and the absence of a network of secondary groups (other than the school) mediating between the family and the State. Although extensive social changes were needed, involving legislation, it was vital that 'the spirit of association come alive . . . in the deep mass of the population'.[43] Durkheim even treated the teaching of science, art and history in this connection: science (especially biology) should provide a sense of the real complexity of things and even had a role in the formation of moral character; art could eliminate self-centredness, opening the mind to disinterestedness and self-sacrifice; while history could give a sense of continuity with the past and of the principal traits of the national character.

As for autonomy, its particular implications for education were clear: the task was to make the child 'understand his country and times, to make him aware of its needs, to initiate him into its life, and in this way to prepare him for the collective tasks which await him'.[44] He needed, in short, to be taught about *morality*: about 'the nature of the social contexts in which he will be called to live: family, corporation, nation, the community of civilization that reaches towards including the whole of humanity; how they were formed and transformed, what effect they have on the individual and what role he plays in them'.[45] These ideas resulted in a separate course on 'The Teaching of Morality in the Primary School', which he developed at Bordeaux and was later to give at Paris.[46] In this

42. ibid., p. 262: tr. 229 (S.L.).
43. ibid., p. 273: tr. 238.
44. ibid., p. 141: tr. p. 124 (S.L.).
45. 1922a, p. 21: tr. 1956a, p. 45 (S.L.).
46. The manuscripts of this course of lectures (in the possession of M. Raymond Lenoir) are reproduced in Lukes, 1968b, vol. II, which contains further information relating to it. Parts of it have been published (by M. Lenoir), viz. 1958a, 1959a, 1960a. (It is worth noting here that the English translation of Fauconnet, 1922 (1956a, p. 45) misleadingly renders the title of this course as 'Moral Education in the Primary School', thereby confusing it with 1925a (tr. 1961a). I am grateful to Mrs J. E. Floud for having drawn my attention to this.)

course he aimed to show teachers how to communicate to children the results of his sociological study of modern societies, which he called the physics (and sometimes the physiology) of law and customs. As Fauçonnet wrote, this course was 'the popularization of the *science des mœurs* to which he devoted, elsewhere, the major part of his writings and his lectures'.[47]

This course is of considerable interest, because it shows in detail how Durkheim conceived of the various contexts of morality and how he proposed to make children aware of them and of their relations to one another. His picture of the modern family is particularly interesting. It was still, he thought, 'an essential organ of moral life', affected by all aspects of its members' lives and itself constituting a source of attachment, while imposing a whole range of rights and obligations on its members: it even imposed a kind of egalitarian justice in opposition to the inequalities of the wider society. He stressed the need for the various levels of social organization to balance one another so as to afford the individual a greater measure of freedom and justice; the State, for example, should prevent primary and secondary groups from being too oppressive to individuals. There is a characteristic lecture on 'The Country', which argues for the possibility of a non-exclusive patriotism committed to internationalist ideals; one on the State, stressing its role as the conscious centre of an organized society's life; and another on democracy, arguing against Rousseauist conceptions and in favour of a view of democracy as a well-functioning system of communication between society and State.

Perhaps the most striking of the lectures, and the most revealing about Durkheim's own moral views, is that on 'Duties of Man towards Himself'. Here he argues (in terms strongly reminiscent of Renouvier) that each man embodied a (socially given) ideal, 'something which goes beyond him and imposes respect', rendering him sacred. This was Durkheim's secular account of the soul: it explained the prohibition both of murder and of suicide. And Durkheim specified other

47. Fauçonnet, 1922, p. 21: tr. 1956a, pp. 45–6 (S.L.).

duties – 'not to abandon oneself to the propensities of the senses, to resist them, to make efforts, to be master of oneself': there was, he thought, 'no civilization without effort . . . to be excessively sparing towards oneself is to be lacking in dignity'. The tone throughout this course is that of a severe secular moralism, tempered by a concern for social justice and a respect for individual dignity and rights.

INTELLECTUAL EDUCATION

Durkheim also gave a course of lectures on intellectual education.[48] Mauss describes this course as 'powerfully original in parts' but 'less worked out and complete than other courses', for 'Durkheim, at the time he drew it up, was not yet the master of his thought concerning the social origins of reason, and he never had the time to develop [this material] in depth to the point where science can meet practice'.[49]

As in the moral education course, the first part concerned the general question of objectives. What was the aim of intellectual education? This required a sociological account of 'the intellectual type which our society is attempting to realize'.[50] Durkheim approached the problem by studying the origins of primary education and the way in which it had become conscious of its nature and role; in particular, he sought to trace the formation of this ideal in the writings of Comenius and Pestalozzi. But the trouble with Pestalozzi had been that he saw fundamental cognitive ideas as 'science's point of departure', whereas

48. 1888–9, 1890–1, 1900–1 (Bordeaux) and 1905–6, 1910–11 (Paris): see Appendix A, below. Cf. Fauconnet's discussion in Fauconnet, 1922, pp. 21–6: tr. 1956a, pp. 46–51 (on which I rely in the following discussion), and Mauss, 1925a, p. 18, and Halbwachs, 1938a. None of this was ever published. Fauconnet wrote of 'a complete manuscript' parallel to that on moral education and constructed according to an almost identical plan. But he adds that 'Durkheim was not satisfied with it; he found it difficult to reach an acceptable level of formulation in this work' (Fauconnet, 1922, p. 21: tr. 1956a, p. 46 – S.L.).

49. Mauss, 1925a, p. 18. Mauss is referring to Durkheim's sociology of knowledge: see below, Chapter 22.

50. Fauconnet, 1922, p. 21: tr. 1956a, p. 46 (S.L.).

It is science that elaborates the cardinal notions that govern our thought: notions of cause, of laws, of space, of number, notions of bodies, of life, of consciousness, of society, etc. All these fundamental ideas are constantly evolving, for they are the abridgement, the outcome of all scientific work ... We do not conceive of man, nature, cause, even space, as they were conceived in the Middle Ages ... Before the sciences were constituted, religion filled the same office; for every mythology consists of a conception, already well elaborated, of man and of the universe.[51]

Durkheim concluded that the intellectual ideal required of Frenchmen necessitated the acquisition of a given number of basic mental dispositions, or '*categories*, master-conceptions, foci of understanding, which are the frameworks and tools of logical thought' and which are not 'innate in the human mind' but 'have a history': such concepts as cause and substance, but also more particular ones such as '*our* idea of the physical world, *our* idea of life, *our* idea of man, for example'. These 'govern our interpretation of reality' and 'are in harmony with the fundamental sciences as they are presently constituted'.[52] These were 'collective ideas' that were to be transmitted to the child, and they were to be based on science. In arguing thus, Durkheim was opposing that tradition of educational thought reaching back to Montaigne and the Humanists which emphasized the (purely formal) virtues of literary study. The mind was rather to be trained through the acquisition of knowledge in a scientific form; indeed, he saw the assimilation of scientific knowledge as the precondition for a genuine intellectual training. Like Comte, he believed that the constitutive forms of the understanding can only be developed through a positive knowledge of the world. This theme was pursued through lectures on the development of memory and of perceptions, the various species of concepts (*représentations*), the development of the principal faculties, attention, judgement and reasoning, and the growth of intelligence in the child.[53]

51. 1922a, pp. 56–7: tr. 1956a, pp. 76–7 (S.L.).
52. Fauconnet, 1922, pp. 22–3. Cf. Thomas Kuhn's notion of 'paradigms' (Kuhn, T. S., *The Structure of Scientific Revolutions*, Chicago, 1962).
53. See Halbwachs, 1938a.

The second part of the course was again devoted to pedagogy proper: the derivation of practical principles of use to the educator. Here Durkheim dealt with the various disciplines in turn: among them, mathematics and the categories of number and form; physics and the notion of reality; geography and the notion of the natural environment; history and the notions of historical time and development, giving dates a meaning, and which are themselves historically relative.[54]

EDUCATIONAL PSYCHOLOGY: THE HISTORY OF EDUCATIONAL THEORIES

In addition to this, Durkheim lectured frequently at Bordeaux on the application of psychology to education.[55] He saw psychology, and in particular child psychology, as potentially furnishing

more complete and precise ideas about the class of phenomena that are called propensities, habits, desires, emotions, etc., about the various conditions on which they depend, and about the form they take in the child.

Although psychology was

incompetent to establish the end [of education] – since the end varies according to social conditions – there is no doubt that it has a useful role to play in establishing methods. And since no method can be applied in the same way to different children, it is psychology, too, that should help us to cope with the diversity of intelligence and character. Alas, we are still far from being in a position really to meet this requirement.[56]

54. Fauconnet, 1922, p. 24–6: tr. pp. 48–9 (S.L.).
55. 1892–8 and 1901–2: see Appendix A, below. None of these lectures has survived. Fauconnet singles out his work on attention as being particularly noteworthy (Fauconnet, 1922, p. 22: tr. 1956a, p. 46). He was to some extent influenced by the American psychologist James Sully, and by Guyau and Binet (see 1925a); and also by Herbart and Ribot (see Appendix B (5), below).
56. 1922a, pp. 101–2: tr. 1956a, pp. 111–12.

The few pages of Durkheim's which survive on this subject[57] reveal, not surprisingly, a preponderant stress on nurture as against nature, and a rudimentary developmental approach. He expressed himself on the former issue with differing degrees of extremism, writing in one place of society 'with each generation faced with a *tabula rasa*, very nearly, on which it must build anew',[58] but in another of education as 'not applied to a *tabula rasa*. The child has his own nature . . .'[59] His basic view was that it was only 'vague and uncertain propensities that can be attributed to heredity',[60] that pre-social 'individual nature' merely consisted in certain 'very general aptitudes' and that 'between these vague and confused dispositions (mixed, besides, with all kinds of contrary dispositions) and the very definite and very particular form they take under the influence of society, there is an abyss'. Indeed, he came near to saying that the former could not even be identified independently of their social realization, for

It is impossible for even the most penetrating analysis to perceive in advance, in these indistinct potentialities, what they will become once the collectivity has acted upon them.[61]

On the other hand,

The child's nature is not so malleable that one can make it take on forms for which it is in no way fitted. So there must be in the child . . .

57. ibid., 1925a, ch. IX; 1911c (2); and Appendix B (1), (2) and (12), below.

58. 1922a, p. 120: tr. 1956a, p. 125.

59. 1925a, p. 147: tr. 1961a, p. 129. Cf.: '. . . one can concede, in a general way, that these congenital tendencies are very strong, very difficult to destroy or to transform radically; for they depend upon organic conditions on which the educator has little influence' (1922a, p. 63: tr. p. 82).

60. 1922a, p. 120: tr. p. 125 (S.L.).

61. ibid., pp. 125–6; tr. pp. 128–9. Cf. ibid., pp. 64–7: tr. pp. 82–5, especially pp. 66–7: tr. pp. 84–5: 'To say that innate characteristics are for the most part very general, is to say that they are very malleable, very flexible, since they can assume very different forms. Between the vague potentialities which constitute man at the moment of his birth and the well-defined character that he must become in order to play a useful role in society, the distance is, then, considerable. It is this distance that education has to make the child travel.'

certain general predispositions that help us in achieving the goal [of moral education] and that act as levers through which educational influence is transmitted to the roots of the child's consciousness.[62]

Moreover, Durkheim saw the individual's development from birth to maturity as following a discernible pattern, which could be represented in stages; indeed, during the 'childhood' stage (roughly from four to thirteen), the educator should 'know, at each moment of this period, what precisely are the needs which correspond to it, what are the child's powers, and the exact degree and true extent of his faculties'. The 'first law of pedagogy is to adapt with maximum precision the education one gives to the child as he develops'.[63]

It should, Durkheim argued, initially give a place to 'the first of all the child's pleasures, the pleasure of varied activity, of free movement, of unrestrained impulse'. On the other hand, 'this lack of coherence and equilibrium constitute a state that cannot last and must be overcome. The child must learn to co-ordinate his acts and regulate them ... he must acquire self-mastery, self-restraint, self-domination, self-determination, the taste for discipline and order in behaviour.'[64] Fortunately nature provided the means, the 'levers', to achieve this transformation. The child's unstable mental life made him both suggestible and given to routine:

Thanks to the fact that habit so easily dominates the mind of the child, we can accustom him to regularity and develop his taste for it; thanks to his suggestibility, we can at the same time give him the first feeling for the moral forces which surround him and on which he depends.

In this way, the child's life would gradually acquire regularity and order, to be developed by moral education in the school into 'definite and complex sentiments'.[65]

A separate branch of psychology was, Durkheim thought,

62. 1925a, p. 153: tr. p. 134.
63. 1911c (2), p. 552.
64. ibid., p. 553.
65. 1925a, pp. 162–3: tr. p. 143.

also relevant here: namely, 'collective psychology'. Children in a class 'think, feel and behave otherwise than when they are alone. There are produced in a class phenomena of contagion, collective demoralization, mutual over-excitement, beneficial effervescence, that one must be able to identify, so as to prevent or oppose some, and make use of others.' Though very young, this science provided 'a number of propositions it is important not to ignore'.[66]

Finally, there were Durkheim's lecture-courses on the history of educational theories,[67] ranging from Antiquity to the nineteenth century. According to Mauss, the history was discontinuous, discussing in succession all the great writers in the field, concentrating on the French,[68] and Fauconnet wrote that he did not consider the theories he discussed purely analytically, but treated them rather as facts, using them to 'reveal the social forces that animate a system of education or work to modify it'.[69] Thus he sought to bring out the relation between the success of *Émile* and the prevailing tendencies of eighteenth-century European society,[70] the way in which the theories of Jouvency and Rollin 'reflect the pedagogical ideal of the Jesuits or the University of the seventeenth century',[71] and the significance of the two currents of Renaissance educational thought represented by Rabelais and Erasmus.[72]

66. 1922a, pp. 102–3: tr. p. 112 (S.L.).

67. 1888–93 (Bordeaux) and 1902–4, 1908–10, 1915–16 (Paris): see Appendix A, below. It was composed as follows: Greek and Roman education; Rabelais; Montaigne; Comenius; Port-Royal and the Jansenists; Locke; Fénelon; Mme de Maintenon; Rousseau; Pestalozzi and his school; German education in the eighteenth century; Kant; Herbart; and Spencer (Halbwachs, 1938a); also, according to Mauss, Condorcet and (possibly) Froebel (Mauss, 1925a, p. 18). (He gave a special course at the Sorbonne in 1903–4 on Pestalozzi and Herbart.) These lectures were never published (except for those on Rousseau: 1919a) and have not survived. Cf. Appendix B (5), below.

68. Mauss, 1925a, p. 18.

69. Fauconnet, 1922, p. 31: tr. 1956a, p. 55 (S.L.).

70. See 1919a.

71. Fauconnet, 1922, p. 31: tr. 1956a, p. 55 (S.L.).

72. At Paris he was to develop this work further in his course on the evolution and role of secondary education in France, discussed below in Chapter 19.

ROUSSEAU'S 'ÉMILE' AND DURKHEIM'S VIEW OF HUMAN NATURE

All that survives of these courses are Durkheim's notes for four lectures on Rousseau's *Émile*.[73] Xavier Léon, who published them, rightly stressed the interest of these notes. Apart from offering a valuable interpretation of Rousseau's educational thought (complementary to Durkheim's analysis of the *Social Contract*[74]), they reveal very clearly how much Durkheim's conception of human nature owes to Rousseau.

Durkheim, Léon noted, 'attached much importance to this side that he discerned in Rousseau's pedagogical work. Nothing was more false, in Durkheim's view, than the prevalent interpretation of Rousseau's doctrines which makes him into the precursor of individualism and anarchy'. For Durkheim, Rousseau's educational doctrines 'prove to what extent Rousseau had a sense of the social nature of man and of the reality of society, thereby confirming his view of the whole of Rousseau's work'.[75]

Durkheim penetrated behind Rousseau's 'ideal and abstract method' (dealing with 'man' in the abstract and seeking 'the essential, the rock on which human reality rests'[76]) and behind the current interpretations of his pedagogy as postulating the natural goodness of the child, entailing educational *laissez-faire*. Rousseau's thought was, he argued, much more complex: 'no one has a more lively sense of the power and necessity of education than Rousseau. Education transforms nature, it denatures it'.[77] For Rousseau, natural man was a 'self- sufficient whole', while civil man was a 'fractional unit':

Good social institutions are those which are best able to denature man, remove from him his absolute existence in order to give him a relative one, and transport the self into the common unity, so that

73. 1919a.
74. See 1918b: repr. 1953a: tr. 1960b, discussed below in Chapter 14.
75. 1919a, p. 153, fn.
76. ibid., p. 155.
77. ibid., p. 156.

every individual does not see himself as an isolated unit, but as part of the unity, and is no longer conscious except within the whole.[78]

Rousseau, Durkheim rightly observed, aimed 'to form the social man', and saw the educator as having 'a positive end to pursue', namely, 'to put the child in harmony with his environment'. This educational ideal, as Rousseau conceived it, comes very close to specifying Durkheim's own; and the conception of human fulfilment and satisfaction it implies lies at the heart of Durkheim's own conception of human nature, and thus of his whole system of thought.[79] Rousseau (as quoted by Durkheim) had written:

What then constitutes human wisdom or the path of true happiness? It is precisely not to diminish our desires, for if they were less than our powers, a part of our faculties would remain idle, and we would not be in enjoyment of all our being. Nor is it to extend our faculties; *for if our desires were at the same time increased* to a greater extent, we would only become more miserable. It is rather to diminish the excess of desires over faculties, and to put power and will into a relation of perfect equality. Only thus, with all his forces in play, will man's mind still be at peace and will he be well-regulated.[80]

(Compare with this Durkheim's argument in Chapter 5, Section 2, of *Suicide*.[81])

Durkheim then discussed Rousseau's reasons for 'taking nature as a guide', as a 'model' for the educator ('Let us postulate as an indisputable maxim that the first movements of nature are always right; there is no original perversity in the human heart'[82]). This was a question of reconciling 'natural' and 'human' education. Physical nature was 'stable, given', while social, human nature was 'variable, changing . . . changeable, dependent on us'; and the 'first must furnish the norm' for the second.[83] Rousseau, according to Durkheim, was here

78. *Émile* (Geneva, 1780), vol. 1, p. 9, quoted ibid., p. 156 (this and subsequent quotations from Rousseau checked with the original text: S.L.).

79. On Durkheim's conception of human nature, see Lukes, 1967a.

80. *Émile*, 1, pp. 126–7, quoted ibid., p. 157.

81. 1897a, pp. 272 ff.: tr. 1951a, pp. 246 ff.

82. *Émile*, 1, p. 164, quoted 1919a, p. 157.

83. 1919a, p. 158.

foreshadowing a scientific approach to pedagogy, seeking to base it on 'the objective study of a given reality': he had propounded 'the idea that *education, in order to be normal, must reproduce a model given in reality*'. It was true, Durkheim conceded, that Rousseau's idea of nature was 'very *a priori*', but it was 'nonetheless, in principle, an objective standard'.[84]

In examining Rousseau's conception of 'education by nature' as a 'prototype' for 'education by man', Durkheim showed how the educator would both follow nature (for example by allowing free expansion of the infant's activity) and provide the basis for its replication at the social level: 'In order that the civil being should be natural, he must feel moral force, comparable to physical forces, above him.' He needed to be 'limited' and 'checked', to achieve 'the ideal for every being – adaptation to his environment. Equilibrium between needs and means, faculties and desires . . . true power, true force, the condition of true happiness.'[85] As Rousseau had written: 'A conscious being whose faculties equal his desires would be an absolutely happy being.'[86] (Compare *Suicide*: 'No living being can be happy or even exist unless his needs are sufficiently proportioned to his means'; 'A regulative force must play the same role for moral needs which the organism plays for physical needs.'[87]) Rousseau's central aim was to prevent the limitless growth of unsatisfied desire, spurred on by imagination,

which extends for us the range of the possible whether for good or evil, and which in consequence excites and nourishes desires by the hope of satisfying them. But the object which at first appeared within reach escapes us more quickly than we can pursue it: when we think we have attained it, it changes and appears yet further ahead of us. No longer seeing the ground already traversed, we count it as nothing: that which remains to be covered grows and extends ceaselessly. We thus become exhausted without arriving at

84. ibid., p. 159.
85. ibid., p. 160.
86. *Émile*, 1, p. 126, quoted ibid., p. 161.
87. 1897a, p. 272, 275: tr. 1951a, p. 246, 248. Rousseau had written: 'All animals have exactly the faculties necessary to preserve themselves' (op. cit., p. 130); this is almost exactly echoed by Durkheim (ibid.).

a destination, and the more we gain in enjoyment, the more happiness eludes us.[88]

(Compare *Suicide*: 'Unlimited desires are insatiable by definition ... Being unlimited, they constantly and infinitely surpass the means at their command ...'; 'Even our glances behind and our feeling of pride at the distance covered can cause only deceptive satisfaction, since the remaining distance is not proportionately reduced. To pursue a goal which is by definition unattainable is to condemn oneself to a state of perpetual unhappiness.'[89])

Hence the need to instil in the child a sense of the 'resistance' of nature. Durkheim stressed what he called this 'little-known side of Rousseau', and reconciled it with the latter's view of liberty by showing this to be essentially 'contained; limited'.[90] Hence Rousseau's stress on the importance of education, not by (contingent) will, command, the issuing of orders, verbal lessons, emulation or the expression of opinion, but by means of 'things' – 'subject to necessary laws', thereby 'contributing to the preparation of the moral man'. Things 'act necessarily, impersonally' and 'give a sense of necessity',[91] thus preparing the child for a future appreciation of authority. Durkheim thought it debatable whether morality could be inculcated in this way, but he emphasized Rousseau's sense of 'indispensable discipline', of morality and authority, and his awareness, close to that of Kant, of 'the truly *general* and impersonal character of moral authority'.[92] Essentially, Durkheim argued, Rousseau was seeking to create 'civil man in the image of natural man' by instilling 'sentiments of discipline, equilibrium and moral order'.[93]

DURKHEIM'S SOCIOLOGY OF EDUCATION

Seen as a whole, Durkheim's educational sociology is highly general in character: essentially, it offers a conceptual

---

88. *Émile*, 1, pp. 127–8, quoted 1919a, p. 161.
89. 1897a, pp. 273–4, 274: tr. 1951a, pp. 247, 248.
90. 1919a, p. 162.
91. ibid., p. 164.
92. ibid., p. 166.
93. ibid., pp. 169, 171.

framework within which to think about education. Although its main emphases are the product of its time and place (secularization, the need to revive the 'spirit of association'), its value lies in the fruitfulness and subtlety of the questions and hypotheses it generates. Against this, however, one must set a number of important blind-spots and distortions. It will be useful to examine the central respects in which Durkheim's perspective is heuristically valuable, and then turn to its characteristic defects.

On the one hand, and most basic, is Durkheim's clear perception of education as a social reality ('a collection of practices and institutions that have been organized slowly in the course of time, which are integrated with all the other social institutions, and express them . . .'[94]). Durkheim conceived education as intimately related to each society's structure, which it reflects and maintains, and can only partially change ('It is only the image and reflection of society. It imitates and reproduces it in miniature; it does not create it'[95]). As a limited, though crucial, agency of social change, it can, at best, instil 'the inclination for collective life'[96] and transmit emergent cultural values and social ideals.[97]

Second, and as a corollary, Durkheim's view emphasizes the cultural relativity of educational ideals ('education has varied infinitely in different periods and countries'). Thus,

In the cities of Greece and Rome, education trained the individual to subordinate himself blindly to the collectivity, to become the creature of society. Today, it seeks to make of the individual an autonomous personality. The Athenians sought to form minds that were refined, clever, subtle, fond of moderation and harmony, capable of enjoying beauty and the joys of pure speculation; the Romans wanted children, above all, to become men of action, passionate for military glory, indifferent to letters and the arts. In the Middle Ages, education was primarily Christian; in the Renaissance, it became more secular and literary; today science tends to assume the place that the arts once occupied.[98]

94. 1922a, p. 40: tr. 1956a, p. 65 (S.L.).
95. 1897a, p. 427: tr. 1951a, p. 372 (S.L.).
96. 1925a, p. 273: tr. 1961a, p. 239.
97. See below, Chapter 17.
98. 1922a, p. 39: tr. 1956a, p. 64 (S.L.). For Durkheim's application of this perspective to the entire history of French education, see Chapter 19, below.

Moreover, this relativism is universal: 'our pedagogic ideal is explained by our social structure, just as those of the Greeks and Romans could only be understood through the organization of the city'.⁹⁹

Third, he stressed the complexity of the social determination of education. He saw it as 'both unity and multiplicity', for it is both 'society as a whole and each particular social milieu that determine the ideal that education realizes'. Each society 'sets up a certain ideal of man, or what he should be, as much from the intellectual point of view as from the physical and moral', an ideal which is 'to a certain extent the same for all citizens', but which 'beyond a certain point becomes differentiated according to the particular milieux that every society contains in its structure'. The function of education is thus to inculcate in the child

(1) a certain number of physical and mental states that the society to which he belongs considers should not be lacking in any of its members; (2) certain physical and mental states which the particular social group (caste, class, family, profession) considers, equally, ought to be found in all its members.¹

For Durkheim, the social divisions between city and country, bourgeois and worker were 'not morally justifiable' and 'a survival destined to disappear', but he maintained that even then, in a classless, differentiated society, 'the moral diversity of occupations would still result in considerable educational diversity'. That diversity would no longer rest on 'unjust inequalities; but it would be undiminished'.² Society would be both more unified and more specialized – a hypothesis directly contrary to that of Marx concerning the classless society.

Fourth, Durkheim's pedagogy should be seen in its complexity, as aiming to resolve a number of closely related contradictions: between an authoritarian and a child-centred approach to education; between education as social constraint, as 'a continuous effort to impose on the child ways of seeing, feeling

99. ibid., pp. 116–17: tr. p. 122.
 1. ibid., pp. 44–8: tr. pp. 67–70 (S.L.).
 2. ibid.

and behaving . . .',[3] and education as the development of 'personal autonomy' and self-determination; between socialization and individualization. Crucial to this attempt is Durkheim's use (worked out during the 1890s) of the notion of 'internalization', according to which socially given norms and values become an integral and constitutive part of the individual personality: in this way, while 'society is beyond us [and] commands us', it also 'penetrates us' and 'forms part of us'.[4] Thus, in societies which seek 'to make of the individual an autonomous personality', autonomy itself is imposed by society and internalized by the individual. It is worth adding that this view of education is intimately related to his similarly dual conception of morality, which was as central to his educational thinking as it was to his thought as a whole. Just as Pascal had stressed the contradictions within man, Durkheim stressed the contradictions within morality:

The ideal that it marks out for us is a peculiar combination of dependence and dignity, of submission and autonomy. When we try to rebel against it, we are harshly reminded of the necessity of the rule; when we conform to it, it liberates us from this dependence, by enabling reason to govern the very rule which constrains us.[5]

The main limitation of Durkheim's educational sociology results from the inadequacy of his conception of 'society', of which education is 'the image and reflection'. During the 1890s he increasingly stressed operative values and ideals as constitutive of society. 'Society' comprised not only a material side but (recalling Montesquieu) a 'spirit', an *âme*, which was 'nothing other than a complex of ideas' which transcend the individual and 'come into being and sustain themselves only through the interaction of a plurality of associated individuals'.[6] This introduced a certain degree of dynamism into the 'social' determinants and consequences of education. But at no point did Durkheim pursue the implications of seeing society as composed of conflicting groups with differential degrees of

3. 1901c, p. 11: tr. 1938b, p. 6 (S.L.).
4. 1925a, p. 113: tr. 1961a, p. 98 (S.L.).
5. ibid., p. 142: tr. pp. 124–5 (S.L.).
6. ibid., p. 140: tr. p. 123 (S.L.).

power; nor, therefore, did he allow that features of education might be seen as one form of the exercise of such power. He defined education as

the influence exercised by adult generations on those that are not yet ready for social life. Its object is to arouse and develop in the child a certain number of physical, intellectual and moral states which are required of him both by the political society as a whole and by the special milieu for which he is specifically destined.[7]

Yet he did not ask to what extent the states 'required . . . by the political society as a whole' are in fact determined by, or serve the interests of, particular dominant or hegemonic groups within that society. In fact, he did not carry his cultural relativism far enough: he did not examine the extent to which educational ideals vary, not only with 'different periods and countries', but with different social groups within society.

Durkheim assumed that educational practice is jointly determined by the demands of 'society as a whole' and of 'each particular social milieu', or social group, the former providing the necessary homogeneity for social survival, the latter the necessary diversity for social co-operation.[8] Leaving aside the unwarranted functionalist assumptions here (about what is 'necessary' for survival, and co-operation), this was to fail to explore the extent to which talk of 'society as a whole' is merely a legitimating expression of the dominance of particular forces within it. It is certainly plausible to see 'society' as playing this role in Durkheim's thought, even though he postulated an emergent social order based on equality of opportunity, the perfect adjustment of social functions to 'natural talents', the principle of 'each according to his works' and a spontaneous consensus about the justice of such a system. Such an interpretation is borne out by such passages as the following:

[Men] cannot assign themselves this law of justice. So they must receive it from an authority which they respect, to which they yield spontaneously. Society alone, whether directly and as a whole, or through the agency of one of its organs, can play this moderating

7. 1922a, p. 49: tr. p. 71 (S.L.).
8. ibid., p. 48: tr. pp. 70–71.

role; for it is the sole moral power superior to the individual, whose superiority he accepts. It alone has the necessary authority to stipulate the law and to set the point beyond which the passions must not go. It alone can gauge the reward to be offered prospectively to each order of functionaries, in the name of the common interest.[9]

Nowhere did Durkheim consider the role of ideology in maintaining consensus: he never saw the 'moral consciousness of societies'[10] as biased, systematically working in favour of the interests of some and against those of others.

As for the idea that education is in part determined by the requirements of the 'special milieu for which [the individual] is specifically destined', this too is to preclude further inquiry: namely, into the extent to which the education an individual receives helps to *determine* his social destination. Durkheim saw education purely as *adaptation* (in modern societies to national and occupational demands); he was blind to its role in predetermining and restricting life-chances. He saw it as adapting to an independently generated occupational diversity, not as helping to constitute and perpetuate social divisions.[11] Moreover, he never examined the relationship between the demands of the occupational structure for skills (to be inculcated by education) and the perpetuation of social hierarchies – that is, the relation between the technical and the social division of labour; nor did he consider the extent to which such skills are culturally defined in such a way as to create or maintain such hierarchies.

Durkheim evidently supposed there to be no basic contradiction between the demands of 'the political society as a whole' and those of 'the special milieu for which [a man] is specifically destined'. He did not consider the possibility that

9. 1897a, p. 275: tr. 1951a, p. 249 (S.L.).

10. ibid., p. 276: tr. p. 249.

11. Cf.: 'Man is destined to fulfil a special function in the social organism, and, consequently, he must learn, in advance, how to play his organic role. An education is as necessary for this as it is to teach him what one might call his role as a man. We do not, however, wish to imply that the child must be prematurely educated for a specific occupation, but that he must be made to like circumscribed tasks and limited horizons' (1902b, p. 398 fn.: tr. 1933b, p. 402 fn. – S.L.).

the content and form of education, ideologically sanctioned
within the society as a whole in terms of universalist values,
might create aptitudes and expectations which are irreconcilable with the requirements of specialization and the job
market. He thought that 'the part that is to be played by these
two opposing necessities . . . is determined by experience'[12]
and that an education could be inculcated which would both
instil universalist values and get people to 'like the idea of
circumscribed tasks and limited horizons'.[13] Moreover, in so
far as instilling 'general culture' made the acceptance of
specialization more problematic, it was harmful. ' No doubt',
he wrote, 'it is good if the worker can be interested in art,
literature, etc.' but, on the other hand,

If one becomes accustomed to vast horizons, broad views and fine
generalities, one will no longer allow oneself to be confined without
impatience within the narrow limits of a special task.[14]

He always assumed that these opposing tendencies could be
reconciled but never examined how.

Not only did Durkheim fail to explore contradictions
between the demands made upon education; he also failed to
consider the whole question of competing socializing influences upon the child, and the extent to which social contexts and institutions outside the school may affect its significance, militating against, and diminishing the potential
coherence of, what is taught there. He never saw the school
teacher as operating within an essentially conflictual situation,
having to combat other equally or more powerful agencies of
socialization. Indeed, there is something in the view that he
was inviting the teacher to embrace an exposed position in a
highly conflictual system, on the basis of an ideology which
concealed the conflicts of the real situation in which teacher
and pupil were placed.[15] In this sense, one can see Durkheim's
pedagogical doctrine as essentially conservative. The teacher

12. 1902b, p. 397: tr. 1933b, p. 401.
13. ibid., p. 398: tr. p. 402.
14. ibid., p. 364: tr. p. 372 (S.L.).
15. See Lourau, 1969. Cf. Nizan, P., *Les Chiens de garde* (Paris, 1932), and
Chapter 17, below.

was the agent, the 'intermediary' of 'society as a whole', even though the latter might be conceived in terms of emergent values and institutions.

Furthermore, despite its compexity, Durkheim's pedagogy relies upon an unduly narrow conception of education as socialization through the *authority* of the teacher, seen as the agent of 'society', the 'interpreter of the great moral ideas of his time and country'.[16] 'Moral authority', for Durkheim, 'is the main quality of the educator'; hence 'the imperàtive tone with which he addresses consciences, the respect he inspires in wills, which makes them yield once he has spoken'. Given 'the passivity' of the child, 'comparable [*sic*]' to that of the hypnotic subject, and given 'the ascendancy the teacher naturally has over his pupil', his influence will have 'the requisite efficacy'.[17] (Note that Durkheim saw this ascendancy as 'natural'.)

Durkheim nowhere examined other sorts of influence on the child than that of adults, nor any other adult influence than that of the teacher. Although he wrote that moral education could not be 'rigidly confined to the hour in the classroom' but should be 'mingled with the whole of school life' and be 'as manifold and varied as life itself', and although he saw his analysis as 'very probably incomplete',[18] nonetheless Piaget's criticism is fully justified:

Durkheim thinks of children as knowing no other society than adult society or the societies created by adults (schools), so that he entirely ignores the existence of spontaneously formed children's societies, and of the facts relating to mutual respect. Consequently, elastic though Durkheim's pedagogy may be in principle, it simply leads, for lack of being sufficiently informed on the subject of child sociology, to a defence of the methods of authority.[19]

Durkheim allowed no place for the co-operative activities, identified by Piaget, in which 'the child ties himself down to all sorts of rules in every sphere of his activity, and especially in that of play. These rules are no less social, but they rest on

16. 1925a, p. 177: tr. 1961a, p. 155.
17. 1922a, pp. 71, 68: tr. pp. 88, 85–6 (S.L.).
18. 1925a, p. 143: tr. p. 125 (S.L.).
19. Piaget, 1932 (English edn, 3rd imp., 1960), pp. 358–9.

different types of authority.'[20] Durkheim assumed that there is only one type of authority and one type of rule: he

settles the question almost without discussing it, and without seeming to suspect that alongside of the social relations between children and adults there exist social relations that apply distinctly to the groups which children form among themselves. The passages in which Durkheim commits this most disastrous *petitio principii* are probably among the most dogmatic in the whole of his works. All authority comes from Society with a big S ('la' société[21]); the schoolmaster is the priest who acts as an intermediary between society and the child[22]; everything therefore rests with the master,[23] and rules are a sort of revelation[24] which the adult dispenses to the child.[25]

In sum, Durkheim's commitment to the view that 'education must be essentially a matter of authority'[26] precluded him from even considering what other means there might be to achieve its object – 'to superimpose, on the individual and asocial being that man is at birth, an entirely new being'.[27]

20. ibid., p. 364. Cf. Durkheim: 'Life is not all play; the child must be prepared for effort and pain, and it would therefore be disastrous if he were allowed to believe that everything can be done as in a game' (1925a, p. 183: tr. p. 160 – S.L.).

21. 1925a, p. 103: tr. pp. 90–91.

22. ibid., p. 177: tr. pp. 154–5.

23. ibid., p. 176: tr. pp. 153–4.

24. ibid.

25. Piaget, 1932, p. 364.

26. 1922a, p. 69: tr. p. 87.

27. ibid., p. 70: tr. p. 87 (S.L.).

Chapter 7

Social Solidarity and the
Division of Labour

It was, however, not education but the public courses in 'social science' that were the focus of Durkheim's teaching during the years at Bordeaux. It was here, every Saturday morning, that his major ideas were expounded and developed. It was, together with his other duties, a tremendous burden. Mauss has written:

To entirely new subjects where no one had ever worked in this fashion; to problems which even today [1924] have been touched on by no one but him, and by an entirely new method; to facts which he was often the first to study: to all this it was necessary to bring, week after week, with a crushing and astonishing regularity, an intellectual content that was not only elaborated with a concern for the truth, but was also digested for the purposes of teaching – teaching that was itself very extensive in scope. Durkheim never weakened. For instance, his lectures on 'rule-governed authority' and on the 'rules concerning contravention' (1891–2) – what suffering they cost him! He had to be ready every Saturday. Once there was a serious objection – which he had raised himself – to which it was necessary to reply immediately if his whole 'theory of sanctions' was not to be called in question. The agony of [the prospect of] the lecture-hour compounded that of uncertainty. It was by the violence of continuous meditation maintained day and night for several weeks, that the solution was found in time, so that the plan of the lectures could be followed. It forms a simple passage in *The Division of Labour*.[1]

From the beginning, Durkheim kept to the promise made in his opening lecture: to engage in specialized studies of particular social phenomena, from the point of view of their functions, asking how, and how far, they perform them.

The age of the synthetic genius, he suggested to his first audience, was over; it was only by becoming more specialized

1. Mauss 1925a, pp. 16–17. M. Davy has told me that Durkheim was weighed down by his lecture-preparation.

that science became 'more objective, more impersonal and in consequence accessible to the variety of talents, to all workers of good will'.[2] He even offered his audience a tentative classification of fruitful areas for specialization, listing, first, 'social psychology' (the study of 'common ideas and sentiments passed from one generation to another which ensure both the unity and continuity of collective life')[3]; second, the science of morality (which sought 'the causes and laws' of 'maxims and moral beliefs'[4]); third, the closely related science of law, both penal and non-penal; and fourth, the study of economic phenomena, transformed into a branch of sociology.

There were, he thought, two alternative approaches open to the social scientist, as to the biologist: he could study functions (as in physiology) or structures (as in morphology). Durkheim firmly declared that 'it is to the study of functions that we must above all apply ourselves',[5] his reason being that in societies, unlike organisms, structures were flexible. Institutions and practices performed different functions in different societies; indeed, the forms of social life were secondary and derivative, and structure could be seen as 'function consolidated, that is action which has become habitual and crystallized'.[6]

SOCIAL SOLIDARITY

His first lecture-course, entitled 'Social Solidarity', sought to apply these principles.[7] In it he set out the argument of what was to become *The Division of Labour*. Though that argument was conducted at a fairly high level of generality, it advanced hypotheses within the four areas of specialization he had identified, and, further, it sought to establish the

2. 1888a, p. 41. He was later to write gratefully that his situation at Bordeaux had enabled him to abandon the over-general questions that had preoccupied Spencer, Mill and Comte, in order to 'embark on a number of particular problems' (1901c, p. 2: tr. 1938b, p. lx – S.L.).

3. ibid., p. 42.

4. ibid.

5. ibid., p. 45. See Pierce, 1960.

6. ibid.

7. For a summary of the 1887–8 course, see 1888c, pp. 257–9.

interrelations between them. Moreover, it was predominantly concerned with functional questions. Briefly, it advanced the claim that the functions once performed by 'common ideas and sentiments' were now, in industrial societies, largely performed by new social institutions and relations, among them economic ones; that this change involved a major change in the nature of morality; and that all these changes were best observed through studying changes in law.

The general problem on which he embarked in this first course was nothing less than the nature of social solidarity itself: 'what are the bonds which unite men one with another?'[8] This, indeed, was the problem that remained central to the whole of Durkheim's life work: as he was to write in a letter to Bouglé, 'the object of sociology as a whole is to determine the conditions for the conservation of societies'.[9] At this early period the problem posed itself as a question of determining the nature of social solidarity in industrial societies, as opposed to that in traditional or pre-industrial societies, and of accounting for the historical transition from the latter to the former. Later he was to turn to the study of 'elementary' or tribal societies, and in particular primitive religion, in order to determine the nature of social solidarity in general.

The form the problem took at this stage is made clear in a passage from *The Division of Labour*:

As to the question which gave rise to this work, it is that of the relations between the individual personality and social solidarity. What explains the fact that, while becoming more autonomous, the individual becomes more closely dependent on society? How can he simultaneously be more personally developed and more socially dependent? For it is undeniable that these two developments, however contradictory they may seem, are equally in evidence. That is the problem which we have set ourselves. What has seemed

8. 1888c, p. 257. Cf. Alpert, 1941 for a discussion of Durkheim's use of '*solidarité*' in an objective, relational, non-ethical sense, distinct from that of the Solidarists (on whom see Chapter 17, below). Cf. also Hayward, J. E. S., 'Solidarity: The Social History of an Idea in Nineteenth Century France', *International Review of Social History*, IV (1959), pp. 261–84.
9. Letter to Bouglé (undated; headed 'Épinal, Mercredi').

to us to resolve this apparent antinomy is a transformation of social solidarity due to the steadily growing development of the division of labour.[10]

Durkheim's account of this transformation, from mechanical to organic solidarity, was influenced by many thinkers and intellectual traditions. Quite apart from the general assumption, characteristic of Enlightenment philosophies of history, of a broad movement from religious traditionalism to secular rationalism, one can also detect the influence of Saint-Simon's view of the growth of organization in industrial societies and his view of the post-medieval period as 'critical' and transitional, that of the classical economists' account of the economic significance of the division of labour and the German jurists' of the cultural significance of law, that of Maine's theory of 'the movement of the progressive societies . . . from Status to Contract',[11] and that of a view, found in Wundt and ultimately derived from German Romanticism, of the historical process as the progressive unfolding of individuality from an initial primitive stage when the individual was indistinguishable from the group. Moreover, in assimilating all this, Durkheim was not free of an evolutionary perspective, though he constantly denied any simple unilinear evolutionism and was increasingly to shake it off. In all these ways Durkheim's thought was rooted in the nineteenth, and indeed the eighteenth centuries.

COMTE, SPENCER AND TÖNNIES

There were, however, three particular theories of which Durkheim was most clearly aware in developing the thesis of *The Division of Labour*: those of Comte, Spencer and Ferdinand Tönnies. By reacting against them (as he interpreted them), he was able partially to work out his relationship to the various intellectual traditions which they respectively embodied: French positivism and authoritarianism; English utilitarianism and *laissez-faire* liberalism; and German state socialism.

10. 1902b, xliii–xliv: tr. 1933b, p. 37 (S.L.).
11. Maine, H. S., *Ancient Law* (7th edn, London, 1878), p. 170.

Comte, Spencer and Tönnies all faced the basic question confronted, but only partially resolved, in *The Division of Labour*: if pre-industrial societies were held together by common ideas and sentiments, by shared norms and values, what holds an industrial society together? Or is it perhaps not being held together at all, but rather in the process of disintegration?

Comte's position was equivocal. On the one hand, he held that it was 'the continuous distribution of different human occupations that principally constitutes social solidarity and which becomes the primary cause of the extent and growing complexity of the social organism'.[12] As Durkheim pointed out, Comte's view was that modern large-scale societies 'can only maintain themselves in equilibrium through occupational specialization': in their case, 'the division of labour is the source, if not unique at least principal, of social solidarity'.[13]

On the other hand, Comte laid great stress on the dispersive effects of the division of labour. It had, he thought, 'a natural tendency to extinguish the sense of community, or at least seriously to impair it'.[14] Moreover

from the moral point of view, while each individual is thus made closely dependent on the mass, he is naturally drawn away from it by the nature of his special activity, constantly reminding him of his private interest, which he only very dimly perceives to be related to the public.[15]

There was thus a paradox: 'the same principle that alone has enabled society in general to advance and grow, threatens, from another point of view, to decompose it into a multitude of unconnected corporations which scarcely seem to belong to the same species.'[16]

Comte's solution was to point to the role of the State as a unifying force. The 'social destiny' of government was

12. Comte, A., *Cours de philosophie positive* (2nd edn, Paris, 1864), IV, p. 425, quoted in 1902b, p. 27: tr. 1933b, p. 63 (S.L.).

13. 1902b, p. 26: tr. p. 62 (S.L.).

14. *Cours*, IV, pp. 428–9, quoted in 1902b, p. 348: tr. p. 357 (S.L.).

15. ibid.; tr. pp. 357–8 (S.L.).

16. *Cours*, IV, p. 429, quoted in 1902b, pp. 348–9: tr. p. 358 (S.L.). Durkheim quotes Espinas to the same effect: 'Division . . . is dispersion' (ibid.).

'sufficiently to contain and so far as possible arrest this fatal disposition to the fundamental dispersion of ideas, sentiments and interests'; it would have to 'intervene appropriately in the daily performance of all the various functions of the social economy, to sustain continuously the idea of the whole and the sentiment of common solidarity'.[17] Government was, properly speaking, 'the reaction . . . of the whole upon the parts', and it naturally gained and required an authority, not only 'material' but also 'intellectual and moral', which was to be provided by the positivist philosophy.

Spencer took a quite opposite view. He held that industrial societies naturally cohered as a result of the unhindered play of individual interests and required neither conformity to shared beliefs and norms, nor state regulation; indeed these would seriously undermine their equilibrium. As Durkheim saw it, social harmony in Spencer's 'industrial societies' 'essentially derived from the division of labour' and consisted in 'a co-operation which occurs automatically simply because each individual pursues his own interests'.[18] This co-operation consisted in universal free exchange of goods and services: as industrialism progressed, 'the sole link which remains between men is absolutely free exchange'.[19]

On Spencer's view there had been a progressive decline in the regulation of individual behaviour in all spheres of life – and especially the economic – as societies had advanced from the militant to the industrial type, and this development would continue as societies became ever more purely industrial. The role of the State was in decline and would finally be merely

17. *Cours*, IV, pp. 430–31, quoted in 1902b, p. 349: tr. pp. 358–9 (S.L.).
18. 1902b, p. 177: tr. p. 200 (S.L.). See Spencer, H., *The Principles of Sociology*, vol III (London, 1896), pt VIII, for Spencer's fullest treatment of industrialism. (Cf. Burrow, J. W., *Evolution and Society*, Cambridge, 1966, ch. 6, especially pp. 225–6.) In fact, Spencer's view is more complex than Durkheim claimed, for he saw industrial men's economic self-interest as itself dependent on the growth of 'altruism' and 'sympathy' (see *Social Statics* and *The Principles of Psychology*). For Spencer, industrialism increasingly reconciled self-interest and altruism. I am grateful to John Peel for stressing this point to me. See Peel, J. D. Y., *Herbert Spencer: The Evolution of a Sociologist* (London, 1971), ch. 8.
19. ibid., p. 178: tr. p. 201 (S.L.).

administrative. Social solidarity would, in Durkheim's words, eventually be

> nothing other than the spontaneous accord of individual interests, an accord for which contracts are the natural expression. The typical social relation would be the economic, stripped of all regulation and resulting from the entirely free initiative of the parties. In a word, society would be merely the bringing together of individuals who exchange the products of their labour, without any genuinely social influence coming to regulate that exchange.[20]

Spencer's pure industrial society was a vast system of bargaining and exchange – and the assumption that it would be a system as opposed to a chaos was merely Spencer's inheritance from Adam Smith and the Manchester School.

Tönnies's *Gesellschaft* was in some ways very close to Spencer's industrial society: contract had replaced status, competing individual interests operated freely, traditional beliefs were succeeded by freedom of thought, common by individual property, and commerce, large-scale industry, free exchange and cosmopolitanism had grown apace. In the *Gesellschaft*, as opposed to the *Gemeinschaft*,

> we find no actions that can be derived from an *a priori* and necessarily existing unity; no actions, therefore, which manifest the will and the spirit of the unity ... On the contrary here everybody is by himself and isolated, and there exists a condition of tension against all others ... nobody wants to grant and produce anything for another individual, nor will he be inclined to give ungrudgingly to another individual, if it be not in exchange for a gift or labour equivalent that he considers at least equal to what he has given.[21]

Durkheim interpreted Tönnies as maintaining that if the *Gemeinschaft* was organic, the *Gesellschaft* was mechanical, an aggregate resulting from the juxtaposition of its parts.[22]

20. ibid., p. 180: tr. p. 203 (S.L.).

21. Tönnies, F., *Gemeinschaft und Gesellschaft* (Leipzig, 1887), pp. 46, 47: tr. as *Community and Society* by Loomis, C. P. (Harper Torchbook edn, 1963), p. 65, quoted in 1889b, p. 419.

22. Tönnies objected to Durkheim's interpretation of his ideas (Tönnies, 1929, pp. 215–17) and in particular on this point. In return, he characterized 'Durkheim's whole sociology' as 'a modification of Spencer's' (ibid., p. 216).

Yet, unlike Spencer, Tönnies painted a sombre picture of capitalism, borrowing, in Durkheim's view, from Marx and Lassalle. Like them he held that it required a very strong state 'to ensure that particular agreements are carried out, to back ... contractual law with sanctions, to prevent all that might harm the general interests of society'.[23] The State needed to be strong 'to keep within bounds all those particular wills, all those individual interests that are no longer connected with one another, all this unchained greed'.[24] But such a social and political system, a form of State-regulated capitalism which was Tönnies's version of socialism, could not endure; rather, it was the prelude to a final dissolution. As Durkheim, interpreting Tönnies, wrote,

By an altogether artificial coercion, [the State] can for a time hold in check all the internal contradictions, all the destructive conflicts which beset the society, but sooner or later these will eventually tear it asunder. The State has no real power except in so far as it represents common ideas and common interests. Now, as the *Gemeinschaft* regresses, the number of these ideas and the importance of these interests progressively declines. The state of war which society conceals in its bosom must some day come to a head, bringing with it its natural consequences, namely, the breaking of all social bonds and the decomposition of the social body.[25]

Durkheim took exception to all three views. Comte's view, in so far as it entailed the need for a detailed regulation of economic life by the State, took, he argued, no account of the naturally achieved solidarity of an independently functioning system of activities: that 'spontaneous *consensus* of the parts', that 'internal solidarity which not only is as indispensable as the controlling influence of higher centres, but is even a necessary condition for their operation'[26] (this being true both of 'organized societies' and of organisms). Even more important, in so far as the Comtean view stressed the need for moral consensus in industrial societies, it was anachronistic: such a uniformity 'cannot be maintained by force and against the

23. 1889b, p. 420.
24. ibid.
25. ibid., pp. 420–21.
26. 1902b, p. 351: tr. p. 360 (S.L.).

nature of things'.[27] Functional diversity 'entails an inevitable moral diversity'[28]; and

> Collective sentiments thus become more and more powerless to contain the centrifugal tendencies which, it is claimed, the division of labour engenders, since these tendencies increase as labour is more divided, while at the same time the collective sentiments themselves grow weaker.[29]

The Spencerian view was rejected on very different grounds. In the first place, Durkheim argued, the free play of individual interests could not be a sufficient explanation for social solidarity in industrial societies. Indeed it would produce instability, for interest only relates men momentarily and externally: in the process of exchange, men are 'only in superficial contact; they do not interpenetrate, nor do they adhere strongly to one another'.[30] More generally, every so-called 'harmony of interests' turns out to 'conceal a latent or merely deferred conflict',[31] for

> where interest alone holds sway, since there is nothing to curb men's egoism, each individual finds himself on a footing of war with every other, and any truce in this eternal antagonism could not last long.[32]

Thus, far from being a social cement, interest could 'only give rise to transient relations and passing associations'.[33]

The second argument against Spencer was an appeal to empirical evidence to show that, far from the social regulation of individual behaviour having declined with the growth of industrialism, it was rather the case that, as social and economic life had become differentiated and specialized, and grown in complexity and volume, so had the laws and rules governing its operation grown in complexity and volume. Finally, Durkheim argued, Spencer's account of the typical social relationship of industrialism, contract, was misleading: even

27. ibid., p. 352: tr. p. 361.
28. ibid. (S.L.).
29. ibid., pp. 352–3 (S.L.).
30. ibid., p. 181: tr. p. 203 (S.L.).
31. ibid. (S.L.).
32. ibid.: tr. p. 204 (S.L.).
33. ibid.

so seemingly private and individual a thing as contract was a product of society, which gives it binding force and defines the conditions of its operation. These non-contractual elements in the contract must form part of any satisfactory sociological account of contractual relations.

The case against Tönnies was that his theory of *Gesellschaft* accounted for social solidarity in terms of a temporary and artificial mechanism: the controlling influence of the State. Durkheim agreed with Tönnies's classification of societies into two great types and he agreed that the *Gemeinschaft* was historically prior; he also accepted (at least in 1889) 'in its general lines the analysis and description he gives of *Gemein-schaft*'.[34] Tönnies's *Gesellschaft*, however,

would essentially be a mechanical aggregate; the only truly collective life remaining in it would result, not from any internal spontaneity, but from the entirely external impulsion of the State. In a word . . . it is society as imagined by Bentham. Now, I hold that the life of the great social agglomerations is just as natural as that of small aggregates. It is neither less organic nor less internal. Apart from purely individual movements, there is in our contemporary societies a genuinely collective activity which is just as natural as that of the less extended societies of earlier times. It is certainly distinct; it constitutes a different type. But between these two species of a single genus, however diverse they may be, there is no difference of kind. To prove this would need a book . . .[35]

That book became *The Division of Labour*.[36] It sought to develop an explanation of social solidarity in industrial or 'organized' societies that was consistent with Durkheim's

34. 1889b, p. 421.

35. ibid.

36. For illuminating discussions of it, see Bouglé, 1903, Sorokin, 1928 (pp. 479–80 fn.), Merton, 1934, Parsons, 1937 and 1960, Alpert, 1939, Friedmann, 1955, Schnore, 1958, Aimard, 1962, Pizzorno, 1963, Nisbet, 1965, and Barnes, 1966; and also Cohen, P. S., *Modern Social Theory* (London, 1968), pp. 35–7 and 224–32, Fox, A., and Flanders, A., 'The Reform of Collective Bargaining: From Donovan to Durkheim', *British Journal of Industrial Relations*, 7 (1969), pp. 151–80, Goldthorpe, J. H., 'Social Inequality and Social Integration in Modern Britain', *Advancement of Science* (December 1969), pp. 1–13, Bernstein, B., 'Open Schools, Open

objections to Comte, Spencer and Tönnies: that is, an explanation which did not, like Comte, exaggerate the role of consensus and conformity, of shared beliefs and sentiments,[37] and of uniform patterns imposed on individual behaviour, and which allowed for increasing differentiation of occupation, beliefs and behaviour; an explanation, secondly, which did not, like Spencer, assume a harmony of interests, but postulated a complex social regulation of individual behaviour; and an explanation, finally, which, unlike Tönnies and also Comte, detached such regulation from the State, linking it rather to the 'internal' functioning of society, and to the processes of social differentiation.

Durkheim's central thesis was that 'the division of labour', by which (like Comte) he primarily meant occupational specialization, 'is more and more filling the role that was once filled by the *conscience commune*; it is this that mainly holds together social aggregates of the more advanced type'[38]; the division of labour was 'the sole process which enables the necessities of social cohesion to be reconciled with the principle of individuation'.[39] Thus the argument, quite logically, divided into three sections: an analysis of how the *conscience commune* and the division of labour contributed to mechanical and organic solidarity respectively; an explanation of the historical development from the one to the other; and an examination of the respects in which contemporary European societies diverged from the 'normal' condition, or ideal type, of organic solidarity.

MECHANICAL AND ORGANIC SOLIDARITY

In contrasting organic to mechanical solidarity, Durkheim was consciously reversing the dichotomy between modern and

Society', *New Society*, no. 259, 14 September 1967, pp. 351–3, and Gibbs, J. P., and Martin, W. T., 'Urbanization, Technology and the Division of Labour', *ASR*, 27 (1962), pp. 667–77.

37. This aspect of Durkheim's argument in *The Division of Labour* is stressed in Gouldner, 1958.

38. 1902b, p. 148: tr. 1933b, p. 173 (S.L.).

39. 1904a (3).

traditional societies characteristic of German social thought, and Tönnies (as he read him) in particular. His own distinction was partly a way of stressing the social differentiation of 'organized' societies, involving interdependent and multiplying specialized roles, beliefs and sentiments as opposed to the undifferentiated unity of uniform activities, beliefs and sentiments and rigid social control found in 'segmental' societies.[40] 'Mechanical' and 'organic' referred, none too seriously, to an analogy – that of 'the cohesion which unites the elements of an inanimate body, as opposed to that which makes a unity out of the elements of a living body': in mechanical solidarity, 'the social molecules . , . could only operate in harmony in so far as they do not operate independently', whereas, in organic solidarity, 'society becomes more capable of operating in harmony, in so far as each of its elements operates more independently'. In the one case, the individual's *conscience* is a 'simple appendage of the collective type, following it in all its movements'; in the other, 'the unity of the organism increases as this individuation of the parts is more marked'.[41] More revealingly perhaps, organic solidarity can be seen as an echo of the Saint-Simonian notion of organic periods, of which emergent, *organized* industralism was to be the next example.

It will be useful to set out the features which Durkheim held to characterize societies integrated by mechanical and organic solidarity respectively (and to say something about the empirical adequacy of these ideal types[42]). We can then see what explanatory relations he postulated between these features

40. Durkheim's broadly evolutionary classification of social *structures* (as opposed to his distinction between types of solidarity) was strongly influenced by Spencer's similar scheme. Cf. Rumney, 1934 (especially p. 87).

41. ibid., pp. 100, 101: tr. pp. 130, 131.

42. That they are intended as ideal types rather than concrete descriptions can be seen from various remarks in the book, for example: 'These two societies . . . are two aspects of one and the same reality, but none the less they must be distinguished'; 'If [the organized] social type is nowhere observable in a state of absolute purity, just as organic solidarity is nowhere found wholly alone, at least it becomes increasingly pure as it becomes more and more preponderant' (1902b, pp. 99, 166: tr. pp. 129, 190 – S.L.).

in each case (thus revealing certain theoretical difficulties concerning organic solidarity, which he left unresolved).

Consider first mechanical solidarity. Durkheim saw this as 'a solidarity *sui generis* which, born of resemblances, directly links the individual with society'[43]; it 'arises from the fact that a number of states of consciousness (*conscience*) are common to all the members of the same society'.[44] It can be strong

only to the extent that the ideas and dispositions common to all the members of the society exceed in number and intensity those which pertain personally to each of them. The greater this excess, the stronger it is. Now, personality consists in each of us having his own characteristic qualities, which distinguish him from others. Thus this solidarity can only grow in inverse proportion to personality. There are in each of our *consciences* ... two *consciences*: one which we share with our entire group, which, in consequence, is not ourselves, but society living and acting within us; the other which, on the contrary, represents only that which is personal and distinctive to each of us, which makes him an individual. The solidarity which derives from resemblances is at its *maximum* when the *conscience collective* is exactly co-extensive with [the individual's] entire *conscience* and coincides at all points with it: but at this moment his individuality is non-existent.[45]

'There is', Durkheim maintained, 'a social structure of a determinate nature to which mechanical solidarity corresponds. It can be characterized as a system of homogeneous segments that are similar to one another,'[46] the segments themselves comprising 'in their turn only homogeneous elements'.[47] Society is thus 'divided into quite small compartments which completely envelop the individual'.[48] Originally, the segmental type of society had a clan base, this type being 'almost the most widespread among the less advanced societies',[49] but at a

43. ibid., p. 74: tr. p. 106.
44. ibid., p. 78: tr. p. 109 (S.L.).
45. ibid., p. 99: tr. pp. 129–30 (S.L.).
46. ibid., p. 157: tr. p. 181 (S.L.).
47. ibid., p. 152: tr. p. 176–7 (S.L.).
48. ibid., p. 287: tr. p. 300 (S.L.).
49. ibid., p. 152: tr. p. 177 (S.L.). 'In saying of one social type that it is more advanced than another', Durkheim wrote, 'we do not mean that the

later stage in evolution, 'the segments are no longer familial aggregates but territorial districts' and the 'mass of the population is no longer divided according to relations of consanguinity, real or fictitious, but according to territorial divisions'.[50] (And, as organic solidarity grows, division by territory ceases to approximate to 'the real and moral division of the population' and becomes a merely 'arbitrary and conventional combination'.)[51] Segmental social structures were further characterized by a low degree of interdependence: '. . . what occurs in one [segment] is less likely to affect the others to the degree that the segmental organization is strong'.[52] Finally, segmental social structures had a relatively low volume and (material and moral) density: 'less advanced societies are scattered over immense areas relative to the number of individuals that compose them'.[53]

What sort of norms characteristically regulate behaviour in conditions of mechanical solidarity? 'The similitude of *consciences*', Durkheim wrote, 'gives rise to legal rules which, under the threat of repressive measures, impose uniform beliefs and practices upon all; the more pronounced it is, the more completely is social life blended with religious life and the nearer are its economic institutions to communism.'[54]

---

different social types are ranged in a single ascending linear series, more or less elevated at different moments in history. It is, on the contrary, certain that, if the genealogical table of social types could be completely drawn up, it would rather take the form of a tufted tree, with a single trunk, to be sure, but with divergent branches. But, despite this tendency, the distance between two types is measurable; they are higher or lower. One has certainly the right to say of one type that it is above another when it began with the form of the latter and has gone beyond it. It then certainly belongs to a higher branch or bough' (ibid., pp. 112–13 fn.: tr. pp. 141–2 – S.L.). It is interesting to note that Spencer also often used the analogy of a tree to symbolize evolution.

50. ibid., p. 161: tr. p. 185 (S.L.).
51. ibid., p. 166: tr. p. 190 (S.L.).
52. ibid., p. 202: tr. p. 223 (S.L.). Also, the bonds, both between individuals and segments, are relatively weak, and can be broken or created relatively easily (ibid., pp. 120 ff: tr. pp. 148 ff.).
53. ibid., p. 238: tr. p. 257 (S.L.).
54. ibid., pp. 205–6: tr. p. 226 (S.L.).

Penal or 'repressive' law[55] 'materially represents'[56] the incidence of mechanical solidarity: the number of social relations
controlled by the *conscience commune* is 'itself proportional to that
of repressive rules; in determining what fraction of the legal
system penal law represents, we at the same time measure the
relative importance of this solidarity'[57] (abstracting from the
sub-legal norms of custom and opinion, which vary in the
same proportion[58]). Punishment not only expresses the incidence of mechanical solidarity; it maintains that solidarity by
reinforcing collective sentiments and values.[59]

Finally, at the cultural or ideational level, what of the
conscience collective under mechanical solidarity? Durkheim
defined 'the *conscience collective* or *commune*' as follows: 'the set
of beliefs and sentiments common to the average members of a
single society [which] forms a determinate system that has its
own life': it is 'by definition diffused throughout the whole
society, but it none the less has specific features which make it a
distinct reality'.[60] One can distinguish (though Durkheim did
not) between those features relating to its form and those
relating to its content.

With respect to the former, Durkheim held that the strength
of the social bonds characteristic of mechanical solidarity is a
function of three variables: (1) 'The relation between the
volume of the *conscience commune* and that of the individual
conscience. They are stronger to the degree that the former is
more completely co-extensive with the latter'; (2) 'The average
intensity of states of the *conscience collective*', and (3) 'The
greater or lesser determinateness of those same states. In other
words, the more defined beliefs and practices are, the less
room they leave for individual divergences.'[61] Thus where
mechanical solidarity predominates, the *conscience collective* is

55. For a definition of repressive law, see ibid., p. 33: tr. p. 69.
56. ibid., p. 78: tr. p. 109.
57. ibid. (S.L.). Elsewhere Durkheim speaks of measuring it by the
number of types of crime (ibid., p. 126 ff.: tr. pp. 153 ff.).
58. See ibid., pp. 119–20: tr. pp. 147–8.
59. See the discussion of Durkheim's theory of crime and punishment
below.
60. 1902b, p. 46: tr. pp. 79–80 (S.L.).
61. ibid., pp. 124–5: tr. p. 152 (S.L.).

'extensive and strong'[62] and 'harmonizes men's movements in detail'.[63] In these conditions, 'the individual *conscience* is scarcely distinguishable from the *conscience collective*' and 'collective authority' is 'absolute', whether it is diffused throughout the community or incarnated in its chiefs.[64]

The *content* of the *conscience collective* under mechanical solidarity has a number of distinguishing features. It is preeminently religious: 'religion pervades the whole of social life, but this is because social life consists almost exclusively in common beliefs and practices which derive from unanimous adherence a very special intensity'.[65] Durkheim here foreshadowed his future theory of religion, arguing that ·

It is, indeed, a constant fact that when a somewhat strong conviction is shared by a single community of men, it inevitably acquires a religious character; it inspires in their *consciences* the same reverential respect as properly religious beliefs. It is thus infinitely probable . . . that religion corresponds to a region that is equally very central to the *conscience commune*.[66]

Indeed, at the beginning 'religion pervades everything; all that is social is religious; the two words are synonymous'.[67] Society had a 'religious and, so to speak, superhuman character', whose 'source lies in the constitution of the *conscience commune*'[68] (and which can be transmitted to its chief), and social organization was deemed to have 'a transcendental character which placed it as if in a sphere superior to human interests'[69] and 'beyond the pale of discussion'.[70] Furthermore, the states of the *conscience collective* were 'essentially concrete',[71] being linked to 'local circumstances, to ethnic and climatic

62. ibid., p. 118: tr. p. 146.
63. ibid., p. 74: tr. p. 106 (S.L.). 'In less advanced societies, even the external form of conduct is predetermined down to its details' (ibid., p. 274: tr. p. 289 – S.L.).
64. ibid., pp. 170–72: tr. pp. 194–5 (S.L.).
65. ibid., p. 154: tr. p. 178 (S.L.).
66. ibid., p. 143: tr. p. 169 (S.L.).
67. ibid. (S.L.).
68. ibid., p. 156: tr. p. 181 (S.L.).
69. ibid., p. 374: tr. p. 380 (S.L.).
70. ibid., p. 208: tr. p. 228.
71. ibid., p. 272: tr. p. 287.

particularities, etc.',[72] relating to 'precise objects, such as this animal, this tree, this plant, this natural force, etc. Then, since everyone is similarly situated in relation to these phenomena, they affect all *consciences* in the same way ... The collective impressions resulting from the fusion of all these individual impressions are thus determined in their form as well as in their objects and, in consequence, the *conscience commune* has a definite character.'[73]

If these are the defining features of the ideal type corresponding to mechanical solidarity, what of that corresponding to organic solidarity? Durkheim saw the division of labour as the 'essential condition'[74] of organic solidarity, which is '*sui generis* and gradually replaces that engendered by social likenesses'.[75] Here the individual 'depends upon society because he depends upon the parts which compose it', while society is 'a system of different and special functions united by definite relations'.[76] It presupposes that individuals 'differ one from another' and is only possible to the extent that

each has a sphere of action that is specific to him, and in consequence a personality. Thus the *conscience collective* must leave free a part of the individual *conscience*, so that special functions may be established there which it cannot control; and the greater this area the stronger the cohesion which results from this solidarity. Thus, on the one hand, each depends more intimately on society as labour is more divided, while, on the other hand, the activity of each is more personal as it becomes more specialized. Of course, however limited it may be, it is never entirely original; even in our occupational activity we conform to practices and ways of acting that we share with our whole corporation. But even here, the yoke we submit to is infinitely less heavy than when the entire society weighs on us, and it leaves much more room for the free play of our initiative.[77]

The 'structure of societies where organic solidarity is preponderant' is 'organized' as opposed to 'segmental' – 'a

72. ibid., p. 274: tr. p. 289 (S.L.).
73. ibid., p. 272: tr. p. 287 (S.L.).
74. ibid., p. 395: tr. p. 400.
75. ibid., p. 356: tr. p. 364 (S.L.).
76. ibid., p. 99: tr. p. 129 (S.L.).
77. ibid., p. 101: tr. p. 131 (S.L.).

system of different organs each of which has a special role and which are themselves formed of differentiated parts' and which are 'co-ordinated and subordinated to one another around a single central organ which exercises a moderating influence over the rest of the organism'.[78] The 'fusion of segments becomes more complete' and the individual 'forms relations with distant regions, [relations] which multiply as the process of concentration advances', so that 'the centre of his life and preoccupation is no longer so completely confined to the place where he lives'[79]: the fusion of segments also 'involves the [fusion] of markets in a single market which embraces virtually the whole society'[80] (and beyond) and society itself comes to 'resemble a great city which contains the entire population within its walls'.[81] Individuals 'are here grouped, no longer according to their lineage, but according to the particular nature of the social activity to which they devote themselves. Their natural and necessary environment is no longer the place of birth but the place where they work.'[82] Organized social structures are characterized by a high degree of interdependence: the scale of industry increases and, 'as the progress of the division of labour determines a greater concentration of the social mass ... changes arising at one point are rapidly transmitted to others'.[83] (Hence the growing need for state intervention and legal regulation.) Finally, organized social structures have a relatively high volume and (material and moral) density: 'societies are generally more voluminous to the degree that they are more advanced and, in consequence, that labour is more divided' and 'among more advanced peoples, the population becomes ever more concentrated'.[84]

78. ibid., p. 157: tr. p. 181 (S.L.).

79. ibid., pp. 286–7: tr. p. 300 (S.L.).

80. ibid., p. 361: tr. p. 369 (S.L.).

81. ibid., p. 286: tr. p. 300 (S.L.).

82. ibid., p. 158: tr. p. 182 (S.L.).

83. ibid., p. 203: tr. p. 224 (S.L.). Also, the bonds, both between individuals and functional units, are relatively strong, and can only be broken or created with difficulty (ibid., pp. 120 ff.: tr. pp. 148 ff.).

84. ibid., pp. 242, 238: tr. pp. 260, 257 (S.L.).

As for the social norms corresponding to organic solidarity, 'the division of labour gives rise to legal rules which determine the nature and the relations between divided functions, but whose violation only entails restitutive measures without any expiatory character'.[85] Law with sanctions of the restitutive type, or 'co-operative law' (involving merely 'the restoration of troubled relations to their normal state'[86]), is an index of the incidence of organic solidarity: it consists of 'civil law, commercial law, procedural law, administrative and constitutional law, abstracting from the penal rules that are found there'.[87] Here, as with penal law and mechanical solidarity, the extent of co-operative law is proportional to 'that part of social life' which consists in 'the bonds engendered by the division of labour', and one can reasonably discount all 'those relations of mutual dependence linking the divided functions' which are 'regulated only by customs'.[88] These rules, legal and customary, are needed to maintain organic solidarity, since 'for organic solidarity to exist . . . it is necessary that the way in which organs should co-operate, if not in every encounter, at least in the most frequent circumstances, be predetermined'. Thus, for instance, 'a contract is not self-sufficient, but presupposes a regulation that is as extensive and complicated as contractual life itself'.[89]

What *form* does the *conscience collective* take in conditions of organic solidarity? Concerning its volume, intensity and determinateness, Durkheim argued that the first had at the most

85. ibid., p. 206: tr. p. 226 (S.L.). For a definition of restitutive law, see ibid., pp. 33–4: tr. p. 69.

86. ibid., p. 34: tr. p. 69 (S.L.).

87. ibid. (S.L.). Though developed in a different context and for different purposes, Durkheim's dichotomy between types of law is, in some ways, similar to H. L. A. Hart's distinction between primary and secondary rules: the former are 'rules of obligation', they 'impose duties' and they are used to justify 'demands for conformity, social pressure and punishment'; the latter are 'rules of recognition, change and adjudication', they 'confer powers, public or private' and they involve such concepts as 'legislation, jurisdiction, validity and generally . . . legal powers, private and public' (Hart, H. L. A., *The Concept of Law*, Oxford, 1961, ch. v: 'Law as the Union of Primary and Secondary Rules').

88. ibid., p. 119: tr. p. 147 (S.L.).

89. ibid., pp. 356–7: tr. p. 365.

remained constant but probably diminished, while the latter two had certainly declined: the *conscience collective* is 'only a very restricted part' of advanced societies,[90] and 'the average intensity and the average degree of determinateness of collective states have ... diminished',[91] so that 'the *conscience collective* became weaker and vaguer as the division of labour developed'.[92] It is composed of 'weak impulsions and has only a weak power to carry the individual in a collective direction', and 'the rules of conduct and those of thought are general and indeterminate', so that 'individual reflexion must intervene to apply them to particular cases'.[93]

The *content* of the *conscience collective* under organic solidarity becomes increasingly secular, human-oriented (as opposed to transcendent) and rational, and ceases to attach supreme value to society and collective interests. The 'domain of religion contracts more and more' and 'there is an ever decreasing number of collective beliefs and sentiments that are both collective enough and strong enough to take on a religious character'[94] (thus making way for science, first natural, now social).[95] Social organization increasingly loses 'the transcendent character which placed it as if in a sphere superior to human interests'[96]; indeed,

There is an area in which [the *conscience commune*] becomes stronger and more precise: that is, the way in which it regards the individual. As all the other beliefs and all the other practices take on an increasingly less religious character, the individual becomes the object of a sort of religion. We have a cult of personal dignity ... if it is common in being shared throughout the community, it is individual in its object. If it turns all wills towards a single end, that end is not social. It thus has an altogether exceptional place in the *conscience collective*. It is still from society that it derives all its force, but it is not to society that it attaches us: it is to ourselves.[97]

90. ibid., p. 46: tr. p. 80.
91. ibid., p. 125: tr. p. 152 (S.L.).
92. ibid., p. 267: tr. p. 283.
93. ibid., pp. 124–5: tr. p. 152 (S.L.).
94. ibid., p. 144: tr. pp. 169–70 (S.L.).
95. See ibid., pp. 269–70: tr. pp. 285–6.
96. ibid., p. 374: tr. p. 380 (S.L.).
97. ibid., p. 147: tr. p. 172 (S.L.).

Durkheim saw this belief system, which he took to be characteristic of the modern *conscience collective*, as placing a supreme value not only on individual dignity, but also (and as a corollary) on equality of opportunity, a highly developed work ethic and social justice. 'If one recalls', he wrote,

that the *conscience collective* increasingly reduces itself to the cult of the individual, one will see that what characterizes the morality of advanced societies, compared to that of segmental societies, is that it is more human, and therefore more rational. It does not attach our activity to ends which do not concern us directly; it does not make us into servants of imaginary powers of a nature other than our own, which go their own ways without considering the interests of men. It simply requires that we be kind to one another and be just, that we perform our duty well, and that we work to achieve a situation in which everyone will be called to the function that he can best perform, and receive a just price for his efforts.[98]

Finally, there is a further respect in which the content of the *conscience collective* is transformed: 'its nature changes as societies become more voluminous. Because these latter are spread over a vaster surface, it is itself compelled to rise above all local diversities, to range over a greater area, and in consequence to become more abstract,'[99] for

when civilization develops over a vaster field of action, when it applies to more people and things, general ideas necessarily appear and become predominant. The idea of man, for example, in law, in morality and in religion replaces that of the Roman, which, being more concrete, is more refractory to science. It is the growth in volume of societies and their greater condensation that explain this great transformation.[1]

In brief, our morality becomes universalized: our 'collective ideal is that of humanity as a whole', since it has 'become sufficiently abstract and general to seem appropriate to all men without distinction', though 'each people adheres to a particular conception of this would-be human [ideal] which relates to its specific character'.[2]

98. ibid., pp. 403–4: tr. p. 407 (S.L.).
99. ibid., p. 272: tr. p. 287 (S.L.).
 1. ibid., p. 275: tr. p. 290 (S.L.).
 2. ibid., p. 392: tr. pp. 396–7 (S.L.).

The foregoing account of Durkheim's ideal types may be summarized in the following table:

MECHANICAL AND ORGANIC SOLIDARITY

	MECHANICAL SOLIDARITY based on resemblances (predominant in less advanced societies)	ORGANIC SOLIDARITY based on division of labour (predominant in more advanced societies)
(1) Morphological (structural) basis[3]	Segmental type (first clan-based, later territorial) Little interdependence (Social bonds relatively weak) Relatively low volume of population Relatively low material and moral density	Organized type (fusion of markets and growth of cities) Much interdependence (Social bonds relatively strong) Relatively high volume of population Relatively high material and moral density
(2) Type of norms (typified by law)	Rules with repressive sanctions Prevalence of penal law	Rules with restitutive sanctions Prevalence of co-operative law (civil, commercial, procedural, administrative and constitutional law)
(3) (a) Formal features of *conscience collective*	High volume High intensity High determinateness Collective authority absolute	Low volume Low intensity Low determinateness More room for individual initiative and reflexion
(3) (b) Content of *conscience collective*	Highly religious Transcendental (Superior to human interests and beyond discussion) Attaching supreme value to society and interests of society as a whole Concrete and specific	Increasingly secular Human-oriented (Concerned with human interests and open to discussion) Attaching supreme value to individual dignity, equality of opportunity, work ethic and social justice Abstract and general

3. In our discussion and in the above table, we have followed Durkheim's implied classification of social phenomena (in the first

Of the empirical criticisms that may be made of Durkheim's ideal types in application to pre-industrial and industrial societies, perhaps the most important are twofold. First, Durkheim vastly understated the degree of interdependence and reciprocity in pre-industrial societies, constituted by ties of kinship, ritual participation and political alliance, linking both groups and individuals.[4] In this he was overinfluenced by Spencer's characterization of the social structures of simpler societies as homogeneous and loosely articulated.

Second, he vastly overstated the role of repressive law in pre-industrial societies,[5] and its insignificance in industrial societies. He had no knowledge (nor was much available) of the manifold ways in which the principle of restitution operates in primitive societies, and indeed, his evidence for the prevalance of penal law in less advanced societies was largely drawn from his knowledge of Hebrew law, Roman law and the law of early European Christian societies. At this stage of his career, he had not yet come upon the growing body of ethnographic literature that was to transform his ideas and dominate his later work. Furthermore, he had at this stage no feel for the historical variability of penal law, and in particular for its independent relationship to political power[6]: hence his unidimensional thesis of its progressive decline in industrial

---

chapter of *The Rules*) along a continuum ranging from the morphological (the most 'crystallized') through institutionalized norms (legal and sublegal) to *représentations collectives* and, at the extreme, 'those free currents of social life that have not yet taken a distinct form' (1901c, p. 19: tr. 1938b, p. 12 – S.L.). For further discussion, see Introduction, above, and Chapter 10, below. (Also cf. Mauss, 1927b, especially ch. 3, and Halbwachs, 1938b.)

4. Cf. Mauss's later work, especially Mauss, 1925b and 1932. See also Cohen, op. cit., p. 227, Barnes, 1966, and Fürer-Haimendorf, C. von, *Morals and Merit* (London, 1967).

5. Cf. Merton, 1934, and Barnes, 1966, p. 168: '... the ethnographic evidence shows that, in general, primitive societies are not characterized by repressive laws'.

6. See below, Chapter 13. Cf. Barnes, 1966, p. 169: '... the ethnographic record shows that it is governmental action that is typically repressive, and redress by self-help that is restitutive'.

societies.[7] In general, he nowhere satisfactorily justified his sweeping claim that 'in order to know the respective importance in a given social type [of the two sorts of solidarity], it is enough to compare the respective extent of the two sorts of law which express them, since law always varies in proportion to the social relations which it regulates'.[8]

This leads us to consider what explanatory relations Durkheim postulated between the features, or variables, combined in his opposed ideal types. 'Just as social resemblances give rise to a law and a morality which protect them,' he wrote, 'so the division of labour gives rise to rules which ensure the peaceful and regular co-operation of divided functions.'[9] How did he suppose these processes operate in each case?

First, Durkheim explained how 'mechanical solidarity is linked to the existence of the segmental type [of social structure]' as follows: 'It is because this special structure allows society to enclose the individual more tightly – attaching him more strongly to his domestic environment and, in consequence, to traditions – and, further, by helping to narrow his social horizon, it contributes to rendering it concrete and defined.'[10] This amounts to a 'morphological' explanation in terms of the structural preconditions of mechanical solidarity; but Durkheim also offered a 'physiological' explanation of its functioning, of the mechanism maintaining it, and protecting it against breakdown – namely, the institution of punishment. It was in this context that Durkheim began to elaborate his sociological (and much attacked) theory of crime and punishment.[11] He defined crime as an act which 'offends strong and definite states of the *conscience collective*',[12] though he

7. Cf. Cohen, op. cit., p. 228: 'It is quite possible for advanced industrialization to be accompanied by increasing centralization of power and an extension of the idea of criminality: for example, in a state-controlled economy, actions which were previously considered in breach of contract might become criminal offences.'

8. 1902b, pp. 101–2: tr. p. 132 (S.L.).

9. ibid., p. 403: tr. p. 406 (S.L.).

10. ibid., p. 288: tr. pp. 301–2 (S.L.).

11. For the attacks (and Durkheim's defence), see Chapter 16, below.

12. 1902b, p. 47: tr. p. 80 (S.L.). Cf. 1895a (1901c), ch. III, 1895c, 1897a, bk 3, ch. 3, and 1925a, chs. 11, 12 and 13.

had not yet come to see crime (as long as it does not exceed 'normal' levels) as 'a factor in public health, an integral part of every healthy society', 'bound up with the fundamental conditions of all social life', and even playing 'a useful role' in the 'normal evolution of morality and of law', sometimes helping to predetermine necessary changes by providing 'an anticipation of the morality of the future' (as the crime of Socrates did for the Athenians).[13] He at this stage still saw crime as essentially parasitic and 'the very negation of solidarity'.[14]

He defined punishment as 'a passionate reaction, of graduated intensity, which society exercises, through the agency of a constituted body, upon those of its members who have violated certain rules of conduct'.[15] Punishment, he argued, maintains the functioning of mechanical solidarity by reacting against those acts which offend strong and defined common sentiments (or else the organ of the *conscience commune*, the State) by violating important social values, but the very process of punishment itself reinforces those sentiments and reaffirms the values. Hence the 'true function' of punishment is 'to maintain social cohesion intact by maintaining the *conscience commune* in all its vitality'.[16] He later described this as a striking instance of the interdependence of cause and effect in social life (punishment deriving from intense collective sentiments and having the function of maintaining those sentiments at the same degree of intensity),[17] but its significance with respect to mechanical solidarity was that it was the mechanism by means of which the *conscience commune*, conceived of as a force acting upon individuals, maintains their solidarity. Criminal acts could offend it either directly, or indirectly by offending the State. In either case, that force

which is shocked by the crime and which suppresses it is . . . one and the same; it is a product of the most essential social conformity [*similitudes*] and it has the effect of maintaining the social cohesion

13. 1901c, pp. 83, 87, 88, 87, 88: tr. pp. 67, 70, 71, 70, 71 (S.L.).

14. 1902b, pp. 343–4: tr. pp. 353–4. See the footnote pointing out this change in his views in 1901c, p. 89: tr. 1938b, p. 72.

15. 1902b, p. 64: tr. p. 96 (S.L.).

16. ibid., p. 76: tr. p. 108 (S.L.).

17. 1901c, p. 118: tr. 1938b, p. 96.

which results from that conformity. It is this force which penal law protects from being weakened, by simultaneously requiring from each of us a minimum of conformity without which the individual would threaten the unity of the social body, while imposing on us a respect for the symbol which expresses and sums up that conformity at the same time that it guarantees it.[18]

Thus, punishment 'does not serve, or only serves very secondarily, to reform the guilty or to deter his possible imitators: from this double point of view, its efficacy may justifiably be doubted': in fact, it is 'intended above all to act upon honest persons' since it 'serves to heal the wounds done to collective sentiments'.[19]

Durkheim was here proposing both a functional sociological explanation of punishment and a general justification of its practice. But with respect to the latter, it is important to see that he was only offering a general justifying aim for punishment, not a specific doctrine endorsing any particular penal practice, for, as he wrote:

In saying that punishment, as it exists, has a *raison d'être*, we do not mean that it is perfect and incapable of improvement. On the contrary, it is only too evident that, being the product of causes that are in large part entirely mechanical, it cannot fail to be very imperfectly adjusted to its role. It is only a matter of a justification in general.[20]

Of course, this whole account of punishment rested on the crucial empirical assumptions that (mechanical) social solidarity would be threatened if the community did not react collectively to crime,[21] and that the infliction of punishment is the only effective form such a reaction can take. Thus Durkheim wrote that in the face of crime, the *conscience commune*

18. 1902b, p. 75: tr. p. 106 (S.L.).

19. ibid., p. 77: tr. p. 108 (S.L.). This perspective seems surprisingly absent from discussions of punishment among contemporary Anglo-Saxon philosophers and legal theorists. But cf. Moberly, Sir W., *The Ethics of Punishment* (London, 1968), especially ch. 8.

20. ibid., pp. 77–8 fn.: tr. p. 109 (S.L.).

21. This is a version of what Prof. H. L. A. Hart has called 'the disintegration thesis' in Hart, 1967, which contains an illuminating discussion of this and related issues.

would necessarily lose its strength (*énergie*) if an emotional reaction of the community did not come to compensate this loss and a slackening of social solidarity would ensue. It is therefore necessary that it assert itself forcibly at the moment it is contradicted, and its only means of self-assertion is to express the unanimous aversion which the crime continues to inspire, by an authentic act that can only consist in suffering inflicted on the agent ... That is why it is right to say that the criminal must suffer in proportion to his crime, and why theories which deny that punishment has any expiatory character seem to so many people to be subversive of the social order.[22]

Unfortunately, Durkheim nowhere sought to verify the empirical assumptions underpinning his theory of punishment, or to indicate what would *count* as such a verification.[23] On the other hand, he did, as we shall see, carry further his inquiry into the relation between types of punishment and the maintenance of a community's values.[24]

What explanatory relations did Durkheim propose between the variables associated with organic solidarity? As with mechanical solidarity, he offered a 'morphological' account in terms of its structural preconditions: with the 'effacement of the segmental type', and the growth of the 'organized' type, and the corresponding growth of the division of labour, 'the individual regains consciousness of his dependence on society; from it come the forces which keep him in check and restrain him ... the division of labour becomes the chief source of social solidarity ...'[25] However, his account of the process involved here is rather inexplicit:

... in the normal state, these rules [determining the mutual relations of functions] themselves arise out of the division of labour; they are, as it were, an extension of it. Certainly, if it only brought together individuals who co-operate for a few moments in order to

22. 1902b, pp. 76–7: tr. p. 108 (S.L.). With respect to the first assumption, Durkheim argued that the collective sentiments in question must 'unite to give mutual evidence that they remain common' and that 'the sole means for this is a collective reaction' (ibid., p. 71: tr. p. 103 – S.L.). Behind this argument lies a rudimentary crowd psychology, of which he was to make further use in *The Elementary Forms* (see Chapter 23, below).

23. See Hart, 1967.

24. See Chapter 13, below.

25. 1902b, p. 396: tr. p. 401 (S.L.).

exchange personal services, it could not give rise to any regulating influence. But what it brings face to face are functions, that is determinate ways of acting, which are repeated, in an identical form, in given circumstances, since they relate to general and constant conditions of social life. The relations which form between these functions cannot therefore fail to attain the same degree of fixity and regularity. There are certain ways in which they react on one another, which, being more in accordance with the nature of things, are repeated more often and become habits; then the habits, as they acquire force, are transformed into rules of conduct. The past predetermines the future. In other words, a certain selection of rights and duties is made by habitual practice (*usage*) and these end up by becoming obligatory.[26]

The meaning of this passage is not very clear. It seems to imply a kind of technological determinism, whereby functionally interdependent activities 'in accordance with the nature of things' give rise to regulative norms (rather as traffic gives rise to traffic regulations) – though, of course, Durkheim's notion of the division of labour extended very much wider than the system of production, encompassing the 'division of labour in the family',[27] commerce, administration and government. What, at any rate, is clear is that Durkheim saw the legal and sub-legal norms regulating organic solidarity as (to borrow a term from a different theoretical system) part of the *superstructure*.

But this leads us to ask: how did Durkheim explain the *functioning* of organic solidarity; what was the mechanism maintaining it and protecting it against breakdown? This question is deeply problematic. The first step to answering it is to consider his claim that, in the first two parts of his book, he had 'studied the division of labour as a normal phenomenon', arguing that 'normally, the division of labour produces social solidarity'; on the other hand, it 'sometimes happens that it has altogether different and even opposite consequences',[28] in particular anomie and class exploitation – consequences discussed as 'Abnormal Forms' in the third part. In face of the existence of these in contemporary industrial

26. ibid., pp. 357–8: tr. pp. 365–6 (S.L.). Neyer suggests that Durkheim's argument here derives from Schmoller: see Neyer, 1960, p. 69.
27. ibid., p. 92: tr. p. 123 (S.L.).
28. ibid., p. 343: tr. p. 353 (S.L.).

societies, he reasoned that if 'in certain cases, organic solidarity is not all that it should be, ... this is because all the conditions for [its] existence have not been realized'.[29] He thus treated organic solidarity as 'normal' relative to the 'organized' or modern industrial type of society (a social phenomenon being normal, on his definition, *in relation to a given social type, at a given phase of its development, when it is present in the average of the societies of that type at the corresponding phase of their evolution*[30]). Yet all the existing societies of this type available for observation were undergoing a 'severe crisis':

Profound changes have occurred in the structure of our societies in a very short time. They have become free of the segmental type with a rapidity and in proportions that are without historical parallel. As a result, the morality which corresponds to that social type has regressed, but without the other developing fast enough to fill the ground the first left vacant in our *consciences*. Our faith has been disturbed; tradition has lost its sway; individual judgement has become free of collective judgement. But, on the other hand, the functions that have been dissociated in the course of the upheaval have not had the time to adjust to one another, the new life that has emerged as if suddenly has not been able to become completely organized, and above all it has not been organized in such a way as to satisfy the need for justice that has become more intense in our hearts.[31]

The social type (in relation to which normality could alone be assessed) had not yet passed through the course of its evolution; 'all of its traits have not been formed ... disordered at certain points by a transitional crisis, it is itself in process of development'.[32] The conditions for the functioning of organic solidarity could therefore only be postulated in the form of a prediction about the conditions for a *future* state of social normality and health.

29. ibid., p. 356: tr. pp. 364–5 (S.L.).
30. 1901c, p. 80: tr. 1938b, p. 64 (S.L.). Durkheim first worked out this definition in the introduction to the first edition of *The Division of Labour* (1893b, pp. 33 ff.: tr. 1933b, pp. 431 ff.).
31. 1902b, p. 405: tr. pp. 408–9 (S.L.).
32. 1893b, p. 36: tr. 1933b, p. 434. Cf. his argument in *The Rules* that where '*a social type has not yet undergone the entire course of its evolution*', one can establish normality only on the basis of '*the general conditions of collective life in the social type considered*' (1901c, p. 80: tr. 1938b, p. 64 – S.L.).

In making this prediction, Durkheim was (understandably) indecisive. On the one hand, the *conscience commune* was not 'in danger of disappearing altogether'; indeed, in the way in which it regards the individual, it 'becomes stronger and more precise'.[33] On the other hand, this cult of personal dignity 'does not constitute a genuine social bond'[34] – 'what a small thing this is, especially when one thinks of the ever-growing extent of social life'[35]; and, in general, 'the weakening of the *conscience collective* is a normal phenomenon',[36] the 'role of the *conscience collective* becomes smaller as labour is divided',[37] collective sentiments are no longer integrative,[38] and 'rules with restitutive sanctions are alien to the *conscience commune*'.[39] As for those rules, on the one hand they arise naturally out of interdependent functions, whose relations they then regulate; on the other hand, they need to be developed, especially in the economic sphere, in the form of 'an occupational morality for each occupation'.[40]

The Division of Labour was thus inconclusive with respect, first, to the place of the *conscience collective* in organic solidarity, and, second, to the source and nature of the norms regulating its functioning. On both these matters, Durkheim's thought was to develop. He came to distinguish between the formal features of the *conscience collective* and its content, and to argue, in effect, that it would retain, or rather regain, its strength, intensity and determinateness, but change in content. Thus, far from the cult of the individual failing to constitute 'a genuine social bond', he came to see it as 'the sole link which binds us one to another', the 'only system of beliefs which can ensure the moral unity of the country' – a new religion which has 'for its first dogma the autonomy of reason and for its first rite freedom of thought', and which 'has all that is required to speak to its believers in a tone that is no less imperative than the

33. 1902b, pp. 146–7: tr. p. 172 (S.L.).
34. ibid. (S.L.).
35. ibid., p. 396: tr. p. 400 (S.L.).
36. ibid., p. 356: tr. p. 364 (S.L.).
37. ibid., p. 356: tr. p. 364.
38. ibid., 352–3: tr. p. 361.
39. ibid., p. 83: tr. p. 115 (S.L.).
40. ibid., p. 206: tr. p. 227 (S.L.).

religions it replaces'.[41] Hence his passionate defence of the morality and 'religion' of individualism during the Dreyfus Affair and his argument that the collective sentiments it represented would be weakened at the cost of social dissolution.[42] Hence also his eventual commitment to the morally regenerative side of socialism. These changes went with a new sense of the independent role of collective beliefs and sentiments in social life[43]; the explanatory role given to these was henceforth to loom greater and greater in the course of his intellectual development.

He likewise soon discarded the rather naïve evolutionary optimism that allowed him to believe that in due course organic solidarity would become self-regulating, that in time the division of labour would 'give rise to rules which ensure the peaceful and regular co-operation of divided functions'.[44] He soon abandoned this position for one which stressed the need to *introduce* new norms of behaviour, above all in the industrial sphere, in the context of occupation associations, and as part of an extensive reconstruction of the economy.[45]

THE THEORY OF SOCIAL CHANGE

The theory of social change advanced in *The Division of Labour* has been much misunderstood.[46] It is primarily a sociological

41. 1898c, pp. 12, 10, 9: tr. 1969d, pp. 27, 25, 24, 23.

42. See 1898c and Chapter 17, below.

43. This, as we shall see, can be dated from the mid-nineties, when he turned to the study of religion (see Chapter 11, below). Cf., for example, the relatively shallow account of the change from repressive to co-operative law offered in *The Division of Labour* with the much more penetrating analysis of the evolution of penal law in 1901a(i), which precisely seeks to relate that evolution to changes in 'collective beliefs and sentiments' (see Chapter 13, below).

44. ibid., p. 403: tr. p. 406 (S.L.).

45. See, for example, the introduction to the second edition of *The Division of Labour* (1902b). The argument was first advanced in the lectures on socialism and repeated in *Suicide*. For discussion of it, see Chapters 13 and 26, below.

46. As Schnore has quite correctly observed, 'a whole generation of American sociologists have been given an essentially incorrect image of one of Durkheim's most important theoretical contributions': Schnore,

explanation of the growth of differentiation.[47] Having disposed (by his characteristic method of argument by elimination[48]) of individualistic and psychological attempts to explain the progress of the division of labour by men's unceasing desire to increase their happiness,[49] or by their need to relieve boredom, he proceeded to advance his own sociological explanation. That explanation (again *pace* a number of influential commentators) appealed to a number of causal factors, all of them social, the key explanatory variables being morphological, namely, 'certain variations of the social environment (*milieu*)'.[50]

His central thesis was that the 'division of labour develops ... as there are more individuals sufficiently in contact to be able to interact with one another. If we agree to call this coming together and the active intercourse resulting from it "dynamic or moral density", then we can say that the progress of the division of labour is in direct ratio to the moral or dynamic density of society.'[51] But to what could one attribute

1958, p. 626, which gives, passim, a clear and largely accurate exegesis and critique of Durkheim's argument. Despite his criticisms, Schnore concludes that 'Durkheim provided a highly useful framework for the analysis of social structure and particularly for the examination of changes in structure' (ibid., pp. 628–9), while Herskovitz has described it as carrying 'a considerable validity' (cited in Barnes, 1966, p. 169).

47. As opposed to an allegedly 'biologistic' one. Cf. for examples of this mistaken interpretation: Sorokin, 1928, p. 480; Parsons, 1937 (1949), p. 323; Alpert, 1939, p. 91; Benoît-Smullyan, 1948, p. 508, etc. This interpretation not only misdescribes Durkheim's own argument, but seems to rest on the curious assumption that demographic change is a purely 'biological' process (though Durkheim himself stresses, for instance, the role of migration).

48. See Introduction, above, and Alpert, 1939, pp. 87–8.

49. He saw this theory as 'classic in political economy' (1902b, p. 212: tr. p. 234). His arguments against it (in bk 2, ch. 1) constitute a powerful attack on some central positions in utilitarianism (see his distinction between pleasure and happiness). His own central positive claims were that the conditions of happiness are culturally defined and historically relative, and that all the available evidence (for example, rising suicide rates) argues against a progressive increase in happiness with advancing civilization.

50. 1902b, p. 237: tr. p. 256 (S.L.).

51. ibid., p. 238: tr. p. 257 (S.L.). In *The Division of Labour*, he takes material density to be an index of moral density, but renounces this procedure in *The Rules*.

this heightened social interaction? Durkheim offered two general explanations for the 'progressive condensation of societies in the course of historical development',[52] one demographic, the other technological. In the first place, there was the concentration of populations, particularly through the growth of cities (especially via immigration). Secondly, there 'are the number and rapidity of means of communication and transportation. By suppressing or diminishing the spaces separating social segments, they increase the density of society.'[53] Thus the prime causal factor determining the growth of the division of labour was the increasing (moral) density of society (though the effect could react on its cause, increasing in turn the condensation of society).

Durkheim proposed a second, and essentially permissive (though not, as Schnore writes, necessary[54]) causal factor, namely, population size, or 'social volume', arguing that population growth could substantially reinforce the effects of increased social interaction. On its own, high social volume was compatible with an undeveloped division of labour and the survival of the segmental type (as in China and Russia); it was 'not sufficient that society has many members, but they must also be in sufficiently intimate contact to interact'.[55]

Hence Durkheim derived his general hypothesis that the '*division of labour varies in direct proportion to the volume and the density of societies, and, if it progresses in a continuous manner in the course of social development, this is because societies become regularly more dense and generally more voluminous.*'[56] He saw the whole process as occurring 'mechanically' ('*Tout se passe mécaniquement*'[57]) – that is, determined by social causes independent of individual men's wills. Indeed, he even described his general hypothesis as stating a 'law of gravitation of the social world', arguing, further, that

52. ibid. (S.L.).
53. ibid., p. 241: tr. pp. 259–60 (S.L.).
54. art. cit., p. 622.
55. 1902b, p. 243: tr. p. 262 (S.L.).
56. ibid., p. 244: tr. p. 262 (S.L.). He justly observed that Comte had proposed a very similar theory, likewise stressing the crucial causal role of increased social density (ibid.).
57. ibid., p. 253: tr. p. 270.

The partitions which separate the different parts of society are gradually worn away by the force of things, as the result of a sort of natural attrition, whose effect can be further reinforced by the influence of violent causes. Population movements thus become more numerous and more rapid, and paths of migration are sunk along which those movements take place: these are the channels of communication. They are especially active at those points where several of these paths cross: these are the towns. Hence the growth in social density. As for the growth in volume, it is due to causes of the same type. The barriers which separate peoples are analogous to those which separate the various cells of a single society and disappear in the same way.[58]

If 'everything occurs mechanically', what, then, was the mechanism? *How* did increased (moral) density, generally reinforced by population increase, produce increased social differentiation, or a growth in the division of labour? Durkheim's answer was: 'because the struggle for existence is more acute'.[59] Appealing to Darwin's theory that the more alike two organisms are, if resources are scarce, the more severe is the competition between them, he reasoned that, given scarce resources, increased contact between undifferentiated individuals or communities would entail heightened competition between them – which is resolved by the division of labour. Thus in 'the same city, different occupations can coexist without being forced to harm one another, for they pursue different objects',[60] while throughout society, 'similar occupations situated at different points in the territory are more keenly in competition the more alike they are, so long as the difficulty of communication and transport does not restrict their sphere of influence'[61]; as communications improve and the market extends (and population grows), they 'are put in contact, competing and seeking to supplant one another', which 'cannot fail to lead to advances in specialization'.[62] Hence,

58. ibid., p. 330 fn.: tr. p. 339 fn.
59. ibid., p. 248: tr. p. 266 (S.L.).
60. ibid., p. 249: tr. p. 267 (S.L.).
61. ibid., p. 250: tr. p. 268 (S.L.).
62. ibid., p. 252: tr. p. 269 (S.L.).

The division of labour is . . . a result of the struggle for existence:
but it is a mitigated resolution. Indeed, because of it, rivals are not
forced to eliminate one another, but can coexist. Moreover, in
proportion to its development, it provides the means of maintenance
and survival to a greater number of individuals who in more
homogeneous societies would be condemned to disappear.[63]

Durkheim assumed that this 'mitigated resolution' of
heightened competition would occur (as opposed to the other
possible resolutions, whether demographic, technological or
organizational – only some of which he saw[64]); he merely
appealed to 'secondary', cultural, factors as helping to facilitate
this particular result. His central, morphological explanation
of structural differentiation is incomplete and largely speculative, saying very little about exactly how competition is
resolved and virtually ignoring (unlike Spencer's theory) the
vital permissive influence of features of the physical environment. Nonetheless, Schnore has written that it

provides, though only in outline, a framework for studying one of
the most salient aspects of social organization, viz., the degree of
structural differentiation. It can be applied to static, cross-sectional
analysis as well as to dynamic, longitudinal study. Although it
stands in need of certain modifications, his morphological theory
seems particularly useful in approaching the problem of structural
differentiation within and between areally based aggregates, i.e.,
communities.[65]

Alongside that theory, Durkheim sought to identify the
'secondary factors' conducive to the growth of the division of

63. ibid., p. 253: tr. p. 270 (S.L.).
64. '. . . specialization is not the sole posssible solution to the struggle for
existence: there are also emigration, colonization, resignation to a precarious and more competitive existence, and finally the total elimination
of the weakest, by suicide or otherwise' (ibid., pp. 270–71: tr. p. 286 –
S.L.). See Schnore, 1958, for a more systematic consideration of the
alternatives, which essentially reduce to (1) elimination of excess numbers,
(2) expansion of the resource base, and (3) functional differentiation, or
some combination of these changes.
65. Schnore, 1958, p. 629. Schnore further discusses the contribution
of Durkheim's theory to human ecology in America, from Park onwards,
on which he claims its 'stamp is clearly imprinted' (p. 631). Cf. Halbwachs,
1938b.

labour. Taken together, these form a broad account of the preconditions for industrialization: among the factors specified were the 'progressive indeterminacy of the *conscience commune*'[66]; secularization and the rise of science; the weakening authority of age, tradition and custom and the increasing 'rationality of law, morality and civilization in general'[67]; the declining significance of heredity in the allocation of individuals to social roles; and, in general, the decline of the pressure of society on the individual and the emergence of the autonomous individual personality.

ABNORMAL FORMS

The third section of *The Division of Labour* is devoted to the examination of 'abnormal forms', where the division of labour can be seen to 'deviate from its natural course'[68]; namely, the production of organic solidarity. Here we have Durkheim's all too brief diagnosis of the ills of capitalism, under three heads: anomie, inequality and inadequate organization.

This, his first account of anomie was in terms of the absence of 'a body of rules' governing 'the relations ... between social functions'.[69] It was to be seen in 'industrial or commercial crises' and in the 'conflict between labour and capital'.[70] There were, he argued, 'no longer today any rules which fix the number of economic enterprises, and in each branch of industry production is not regulated in such a way as to remain exactly level with consumption', while the 'relations between labour and capital have, up to the present, remained in the same state of legal indetermination'.[71] The resulting economic anarchy and industrial conflict were largely due, he claimed, to the rapidity with which industrialization had occurred (but also, as we shall see below, to inequality of

---

66. 1902b, p. 267: tr. p. 283 (S.L.).

67. ibid., p. 413: tr. p. xx (S.L.).

68. ibid., p. 343: tr. p. 353.

69. ibid., p. 360: tr. p. 368. It was not until *Suicide* that the concept attained its full socio-psychological status (see below).

70. ibid., pp. 344–5: tr. p. 354.

71. ibid., pp. 358, 359: tr. pp. 366, 367 (S.L.).

opportunity). Thus, with the growth of the market economy,

production becomes unchecked and unregulated; it can only proceed by taking risks, and in the course of doing so, it is inevitable that calculations will go wrong, sometimes in one direction, sometimes in the other. Hence the crises that periodically disturb economic functions.[72]

Likewise,

As the market extends, large-scale industry appears. It has the effect of transforming the relations between employers and workers. A greater fatigue of the nervous system, combined with the contagious influence of large agglomerations of men, increases the needs of the workers. Machines replace men; manufacturing replaces small workshops. The worker is regimented, separated from his family throughout the day; his life is ever more separate from that of his employer, etc. These new conditions of industrial life naturally require a new organization; but since these transformations have been accomplished with an extreme rapidity, the interests in conflict have not yet had time to achieve equilibrium.[73]

It is worth noticing that Durkheim's notion of anomie, here as elsewhere, can be understood only against the background of the 'normal' or 'natural' condition from which it is held to be a pathological deviation. The crucial 'normal' factors with which it is here contrasted are extensive economic planning and the normative regulation of industrial relations, and also (interestingly) a work situation which renders work meaningful by acquainting the worker of his role in the entire work process, for

normally, the operation of each special function requires that the individual does not become narrowly enclosed within it, but rather maintains constant relations with adjoining functions, and takes note of their requirements, the changes they undergo, etc. The division of labour presupposes that the worker, far from remaining bent over his job, does not lose sight of his collaborators and interacts with them. Thus he is not a machine repeating movements without knowing their meaning, but he knows they lead somewhere, towards

72. ibid., p. 362: tr. p. 370 (S.L.).
73. ibid. (S.L.).

an end that he perceives more or less distinctly. He feels that he is serving something.[74]

The only trouble with this account of anomie was that, although it pinpointed the central ills of capitalism – unregulated competition; class conflict; routinized, degrading, meaningless work – it characterized them all as 'abnormal'.[75] This procedure tended to hinder any full-scale investigation of their causes (which were assumed not to be endemic), especially given the evolutionary optimism Durkheim espoused at this stage. They were to be explained by the temporary and transitional lack of the appropriate economic controls, the appropriate norms governing industrial relations and the appropriate forms of work organization – a lack that would in due course be remedied by allowing the operation of interdependent functions to produce its natural consequences.

Durkheim did, however, go beyond this unsatisfactory position, in the chapter on 'The Constrained Division of Labour', where he argued that inequality was a further abnormal form of the division of labour with consequences deviating from organic solidarity.[76] All 'external inequality', he wrote, 'endangers organic solidarity', indeed the latter is 'only possible' on condition of its elimination, for the 'achievement of justice will become ever more complete, as the organized type develops'.[77]

74. ibid., p. 365: tr. p. 372 (S.L.).

75. Friedmann has justly observed that had he lived, Durkheim 'would have been obliged to consider "abnormal" most of the forms taken by labour in modern society both in industry and in administration, and even more recently in commerce...' (Friedmann, 1955 (1961), p. 75). As Friedmann clearly shows, his most unrealistic assumption was that *technical* specialization and interdependence naturally create organic solidarity in industry. Durkheim had, moreover, nothing to say about the other forms of solidarity to be found there, which could, in his own terms, be called 'mechanical', since they are based on common consciousness and shared sentiments (especially class and trade union solidarity, but also work-group solidarities and the sort of 'solidarity' engendered by 'Human Relations').

76. Friedmann mistakenly says that Durkheim failed to take the absence of equality into account (ibid.).

77. 1902b, p. 372, 373: tr. pp. 379, 380–81 (S.L.). By 'external' here, Durkheim means external to the division of labour.

Durkheim conceived of inequality in two broad ways: first, as the misallocation of individuals to social roles, and second, as a lack of reciprocity or equivalence in the exchange of goods and services.

In the first place, he argued that class or caste societies failed to produce solidarity because 'the distribution of social functions . . . does not correspond, or rather no longer corresponds, to the distribution of natural talents',[78] and 'within one whole region of society the agreement between individuals' aptitudes and the kinds of activity assigned to them is broken; constraint alone, more or less violent and more or less direct, binds them to their functions; in consequence, only an imperfect and troubled solidarity is possible'[79] (hence class warfare, in which the lower classes 'aspire to functions closed to them and seek to dispossess those who exercise them'[80]). By 'constraint' here Durkheim meant more than mere regulation: constraint 'only begins when regulation, no longer corresponding to the true nature of things and, accordingly, no longer having any basis in social practices (*mœurs*), can only be maintained by force'.[81]

In the second place, Durkheim observed that the 'public *conscience*' found unjust every exchange in which the price of the object bears no relation to the labour it costs or the services it renders'.[82] Thus, in particular, in contemporary industrial societies, unjust contracts were prevalent, in which services were exchanged without 'equivalent social value' because the contracting parties were not 'placed in conditions externally equal'.[83] If

one social class is obliged, in order to live, to offer its services at any price, while the other can do without them, thanks to the resources at its disposal, which are not however necessarily due to any social

78. ibid., p. 368: tr. p. 375 (S.L.).
79. ibid., p. 369: tr. p. 376 (S.L.).
80. ibid., p. 367: tr. p. 374 (S.L.).
81. ibid., p. 370: tr. p. 377 (S.L.). It is noteworthy that the meaning of 'constraint' in *The Rules* is quite different, being used to characterize social facts in general. Cf. Pizzorno, 1963, pp. 5 ff.
82. ibid., p. 376: tr. pp. 382–3 (S.L.).
83. ibid., pp. 376, 377: tr. p. 383.

superiority, the second unjustly dominates the first. In other words, there cannot be rich and poor at birth without there being unjust contracts.[84]

These injustices became increasingly intolerable as societies advanced, and common morality severely condemned 'every kind of leonine contract, in which one of the parties is exploited by the other, because it is weaker and does not receive the just price for its labour'.[85] In this case too, constraint was in evidence, subjecting men's wills to pressure, direct or indirect, 'and this pressure constitutes violence'.[86]

It is, again, necessary to interpret Durkheim's notion of inequality or injustice against the background of what he saw as the 'normal' condition of equality and justice. He saw this, first, as a perfect meritocracy:

... the division of labour only produces solidarity when it is spontaneous and in so far as it is spontaneous. But by spontaneity we mean the absence, not simply of all overt and formal violence, but of all that can hinder, even indirectly, the free deployment of the social force which everyone carries within him. It supposes, not only that individuals are not relegated by force to determinate functions, but also that no obstacle, of whatever nature, prevents them from occupying the place in the social framework that is compatible with their faculties. In short, labour is only divided spontaneously when society is constituted in such a way that social inequalities exactly express natural inequalities ... Perfect spontaneity is ... only a consequence of ... absolute equality in the external conditions of the struggle.[87]

Society was moving towards this ideal and increasingly felt obliged to 'give free scope to all merit and recognizes as unjust any inferiority that is not personally merited'.[88] Secondly, Durkheim envisaged equality and justice in terms of 'an exact reciprocity in the services exchanged',[89] that is, where they

84. ibid., p. 378: tr. p. 384 (S.L.).
85. ibid., p. 379: tr. p. 386 (S.L.).
86. ibid., p. 377: tr. p. 383 (S.L.).
87. ibid., pp. 370–71: tr. p. 377 (S.L.). Durkheim conceded that this perfect spontaneity was 'nowhere to be found in reality' (ibid., p. 371: tr. p. 378 – S.L.).
88. ibid., p. 372: tr. p. 379 (S.L.).
89. ibid., p. 380: tr. p. 386.

have 'an equivalent social value',[90] social value being 'the quantity of useful labour' contained in 'each object of exchange', that is, that part of the labour 'capable of producing useful social effects, i.e. which respond to normal needs'.[91]

Here again, Durkheim assumed an identity between the 'normal', the ideal and the about-to-happen. He did not consider a number of crucial difficulties latent in his ideal picture of social equality (let alone the formidable obstacles to realizing it). How are 'individual aptitudes' to be identified, how can 'natural' talents be distinguished from their socialized forms? (Here Durkheim was insufficiently Durkheimian.) How, in any case, could 'social inequalities' express 'natural inequalities'? Why assume a pure meritocracy would engender solidarity? What are 'normal needs'? If they are specified by norms, why assume that there is one set of these for the whole society, rather than a number of different, perhaps incompatible normative systems?[92] To these and other such questions Durkheim gave no answer; and, unfortunately, he never subsequently returned to them.

The third 'abnormal form' of the division of labour existed where the functional activity of each worker is insufficient because of a lack of co-ordination. Thus, 'in an organization where each employee is not sufficiently occupied, movements are poorly adjusted to one another, operations proceed without unity; in short, solidarity breaks down, and incoherence and disorder appear'.[93]

The 'normal' system of production, on the contrary, would be one in which an 'intelligent and experienced manager' would take care to 'suppress useless jobs, to distribute the work so that each individual is sufficiently occupied, thereby increasing the functional activity of each worker'.[94] Furthermore, Durkheim reasoned (in a most *a priori* fashion, using organic analogies) that increased functional activity is rendered possible by functions becoming more continuous and

90. ibid., p. 376: tr. p. 383.
91. ibid., p. 376: tr. p. 382 (S.L.).
92. For a discussion of these and related points, see Pizzorno, 1963.
93. 1902b, p. 383: tr. p. 389 (S.L.).
94. ibid., pp. 383–4: tr. p. 389 (S.L.).

co-ordinated and solidarity is thereby increased, as well as the skill of the worker.

However, as Georges Friedmann has remarked, this proposition has been falsified by the actual development of industrial work in the twentieth century.[95] It is not only that Scientific Management since Taylor and all forms of mass production have shown that continuous and co-ordinated work can be incompatible with organic solidarity. There are also no empirical grounds for supposing that as 'the division of labour tends of itself to render functions more active and continuous',[96] the worker's skill increases: quite the contrary; in Friedmann's words, 'the intensity and continuity so generally characteristic of rationalized production today are often accompanied by a debasement of the functional activity of the worker considered as an individual'.[97] Here, as elsewhere, Durkheim focused on identifying the ways in which the realities of his time deviated from a future, ideal state of 'normality', rather than applying his mind to the study of 'the concrete facts of industry, administration and commerce'.[98] He preferred to see them as transitional and remediable phenomena. However, as we have seen, he was soon to move toward a more activist view of the remedy, and would no longer count on the naturally emergent consequences of the division of labour. This change was crucial to the development of his ideas about moral education and his move towards socialism.

95. Friedmann, 1955 (1961), p. 73.
96. 1902b, p. 387: tr. p. 393 (S.L.).
97. Friedman, 1955 (1961), p. 74.
98. ibid. Hence perhaps the striking prevalence of organic analogies, especially in bk III, where the concrete evidence should be.

Chapter 8

The Family and Kinship

DURKHEIM's second public lecture-course in sociology at Bordeaux was on the family, and it was repeated several times at Bordeaux and later at Paris.[1] According to Mauss, it was, together with his courses on Morality (which we will consider below), his most cherished work. Indeed, the manuscript of 1890–92 was 'so full of facts and ideas and so precious that Durkheim himself treated these pages with respect and for several years kept them with him even when travelling'.[2] He always intended to take the subject up again systematically in his later years. He intended to devote the latter part of his life to a historical and comparative history of the family and marriage up to the present, and planned to spend several years of research on it with Mauss.[3] Throughout his life, he always followed the course of research and writing on this subject very closely, as can be seen from his many reviews in all twelve volumes of the *Année sociologique*, in which he always edited the section on 'Domestic Organization'. Unfortunately, his early death prevented his work on the family from ever reaching completion.

He approached the subject from the evolutionary, historical and comparative perspective common to such contemporary writers on the family as Morgan, Westermarck, Maine,

1. 1888–9, 1890–92, 1895–6 (?) (Bordeaux) and 1905–6 (?), 1907–8, 1909–10 (Paris): see Appendix A, below. Durkheim's work on the family is seriously under-represented in his published works. Apart from his introductory lecture of 1888 (1888c) and the concluding lecture of the 1891–2 lecture course (1921a: tr. 1965a) his researches were never published and although his manuscripts survived him, they no longer exist. It is a pity that Mauss never followed up his half-promise to contravene Durkheim's wish that they should not be published posthumously. However, see Davy's study based on these lectures (Davy, 1925).

2. Mauss, 1925a, p. 13.

3. See ibid.

Bachofen and others. In the opening lecture of the course, he stressed the need to establish the principal family-types and ascertain the causes for their appearance and their survival, using the comparative method as a form of indirect experiment. By studying the whole historical development of the family, one would be in a position to understand the modern family, for, as he subsequently wrote,

> In order properly to understand a practice or an institution, a legal or a moral rule, it is necessary to trace it back as near as possible to its origins; for there is a close relation between what it is now and what it was in the past. Doubtless, since it has been transformed in the course of its development, the causal conditions on which it originally depended have themselves altered; but these transformations in turn depend on what the point of departure was.[4]

Initially he saw the most suitable method as being the historical study of laws and customs, for these represented what was common and constant in individuals' behaviour in any given society; as in *The Division of Labour*, he thought of them as the best indices of changes in social structures, since, in a sense, they constituted those structures. He also, from the beginning, saw the value of statistical, especially demographic, study in relation to the contemporary family.[5] But it was not until after he had come upon the English and American ethnographic work on religion in the mid-nineties that he grasped the relevance of ethnography to the study of the family.[6] From that time on, he immersed himself in the writings

4. 1898a (ii), p. 1: tr. 1963a, p. 12 (S.L.). Cf: '. . . as soon as it is a question of explanation, the genetic method imposes itself on the sociologist – namely, that which, in order to explain the facts, begins by indicating their place in the course of development. For an institution is always, in part, the product of the past . . .' (1898a (iv) (2), p. 327); also 1901c, p. 169: tr. 1938b, p. 139.

5. See 1888c, p. 271.

6. In the opening lecture he had been scathing about the biased accounts of visitors and natives, and in 1894 he contrasted 'the confused, hastily made observations of travellers' with 'the precise texts of history' (1901c, p. 163: tr. 1938b, p. 133 – S.L.) – still, it would seem, under the influence of Fustel de Coulanges. The sociologist, he continued, should 'take as the principal material for his inductions societies whose beliefs, traditions, customs and laws have taken shape in written and authentic

of ethnographers and came to see very clearly both the possibility and the theoretical importance of applying a rigorous interpretation to their findings. Although he never finally and definitively threw off his evolutionary preconceptions, he came increasingly near to doing so[7]; and the theoretical contributions he made to the understanding of kinship systems result in large part from features of his approach that were independent of his evolutionism. Conversely, as one writer has put it, it is 'not fanciful ... to suppose that Durkheim might have pioneered the formal analysis of relationship-systems had he not been sidetracked by his pseudo-evolutionary theorizing'.[8]

His starting-point was a firm assertion of the view that the family and marriage are social institutions, and that there is a definite relation between these and other forms of social organization.[9] He did not accept Westermarck's view that monogamy was the first form of marriage and was rooted in the nuclear family, which was universal and based on instinctual

---

documents. To be sure, he will not spurn the information offered by ethnography (there are no facts which may be disdained by the scientist), but he will put them in their true place. Instead of making them the centre of gravity of his researches, he will in general use them only to complement historical data, or, at least, he will seek to confirm them by the latter' (ibid., pp. 163–4: tr. pp. 133–4 – S.L.). Cf., however, the following statements from *The Elementary Forms of the Religious Life*: 'the observations of ethnographers have often been veritable revelations, which have renewed the study of human institutions'; and '. . . nothing is more unjust than the disdain with which too many historians still regard the work of ethnographers. On the contrary, it is certain that ethnography has very often brought about the most fruitful revolutions in the different branches of sociology' (1912a, pp. 8, 9: tr. 1915d, pp. 6, 7 – S.L.). On the significance of this change in Durkheim's attitude to ethnography, see Lévi-Strauss, 1960.

7. The nearest he came to doing so was in the introduction to *The Elementary Forms*: 'Primitive civilizations constitute . . . privileged cases, because they are simple cases'; they offer us 'a means of discerning the ever-present causes upon which the most essential forms of religious thought and practice depend' (1912a, pp. 8, 11; tr. 1915d, pp. 6, 8 – S.L.). See Chapter 23, below.

8. Maybury-Lewis, 1965, p. 259.

9. See 1895d, p. 622.

needs[10]; nor did he accept the prevalent picture of kinship as based on consanguinity. He concentrated instead on the socio-logical character of these institutions and relationships, defining them as systems of rights and obligations, themselves ordered by systems of terminology. For there to be a family, he wrote

it is not necessary that there should be cohabitation and it is not sufficient that there should be consanguinity. But in addition there must be . . . rights and duties, sanctioned by society and unifying the members of which the family is composed. In other words, the family only exists in so far as it is a social institution, at once legal and moral, placed under the protection of the surrounding collec-tivity . . . when one seeks to trace the history of the human family, it is with the family as a social instititution that one is concerned.[11]

THE HISTORY OF THE FAMILY

In seeking to trace that history, Durkheim elaborated an evolutionary scheme ranging from the amorphous, exogamous clan to the contemporary conjugal family. It was, he held,

through laborious and complex transformations that, little by little, from the midst of the confused and unorganized clan there emerged families more and more restricted in extent, along definite genea-logical branches and with an ever greater degree of organization.[12]

The clan, based, he maintained, on totemism, was thus the primitive family, united by mystical beliefs: to be a member it was 'necessary and sufficient to have in oneself something of

---

10. See ibid. Durkheim saw Westermarck as proposing a pure and simple return to the biblical account of the origin of the family which he saw as a 'veritable and regrettable setback for sociology' (ibid., p. 621). On the contrary, he stressed the infinitely varied forms taken by the family, which he contrasted with Westermarck's simplistic psychological appeal to instincts – which he thought were as non-explanatory as Molière's *virtus dormitiva*. He also criticized Westermarck for relying on 'a too easy Darwinism' (ibid., p. 611) and for using data from ethnography rather than history, for 'history brings ethnography more light than it receives from it' (ibid., p. 609).

11. 1898a (iv) (2), pp. 329–30.

12. ibid., p. 331.

the totemic being, that is, of the deified object which serves as a collective emblem for the group'.[13] Not only were all the members considered as descended from a single ancestor but 'the relations which they maintain with one another are identical to those which, in all times, have been regarded as characteristic of kinship'.[14] From this original politico-familial group, a process of contraction could be traced:

As it becomes settled on the ground, the totem loses its primitive character; it ends by becoming no more than a collective emblem, a particularly venerated name. The clan becomes a village; that is to say that its character as a domestic society is no longer anything more than a memory.[15]

There developed, in the context of a more stable political organization, an extended, largely consanguineous family, of which the community of patrimony was the essential bond (that is, Maine's 'joint-family' of the 'zadruga' type, with agnatic or uterine descent and several collateral branches). Thence there derived a still narrower zone of kinship: the patriarchal family (of which the Roman was the most perfect example); here the absolute and monarchical paternal authority was the unifying bond.[16] A separate process of development, Durkheim argued, occurred within Germanic and Christian civilizations leading to the so-called 'paternal' or 'cognate' family, in which paternal and maternal descent were put on the same footing and in which there was a kind of fusion of kin and of patrimony.[17] Finally, out of the patriarchal and paternal families there emerged the modern conjugal family, based on

13. 1898a (iv) (1), p. 317. The connection between totemism and exogamy had been propounded by Sir James Frazer. In 1886, Lucien Herr, the Librarian at the École Normale, directed Durkheim's attention to Frazer's article on 'Totemism' (Mauss, 1927a, p. 9). Frazer, however, unlike Durkheim, subsequently abandoned this hypothesis.

14. 1898a (ii), p. 9.

15. 1898a (iv) (2), p. 331.

16. Davy describes the account of this family-type as 'without doubt, one of Durkheim's most original insights' (Davy, 1925, in Davy, 1931 (1950 edn), p. 112).

17. See 1905a (ii) (18), p. 429.

marriage and consisting of husband and wife together with minor and unmarried children.[18]

THE CONJUGAL FAMILY

The conjugal family, though essentially consisting of this 'zone' or central circle of kinship, was also surrounded by 'secondary' zones, which Durkheim described as survivals of earlier stages. As the final stage of the process of contraction, it represented only the vestiges of family communism (that is, co-ownership of property) and an ever-growing freedom for its members, since 'the same causes that led to the contraction of the family circle are responsible for the emergence of the personalities of family members ... Each person takes on more of an individual physiognomy, a personal manner of feeling and thinking'.[19] Whereas originally the solidarity of the family had primarily derived from things rather than persons, it now became 'completely personal. We are attached to our family only because we are attached to our father, our mother, our wife, our children.'[20] Accordingly, rights of succession had been increasingly curtailed and eventually all rights of hereditary transmission would be abolished: just as offices and status could no longer be so transmitted, hereditary wealth would also disappear, for this 'injustice, which strikes us as increasingly intolerable, is becoming increasingly irreconcilable with the conditions for existence of our present-day societies'.[21]

In general, whereas the family had formerly 'kept most of its members within its orbit from birth to death and formed a compact mass, indivisible and endowed with a quality of permanence',[22] it was becoming increasingly short-lived: apart from the period of child-rearing, it was reduced to the married couple alone. The 'hereditary name, together with all the memories it recalled, the family house, the ancestral domain,

18. See 1921a: tr. 1965a.
19. ibid., p. 8: tr. p. 533 (S.L.).
20. ibid., p. 9: tr. p. 533.
21. ibid., p. 10: tr. p. 534.
22. 1897a, p. 433: tr. 1951a, p. 577.

the traditional situation and reputation'[23] – all this was disappearing. Yet men needed to have collective ends relevant to their daily activities; personal ends were not a sufficient motivation for work, since 'our work has meaning only in so far as it serves something beyond ourselves' and indeed, 'when [the individual] takes himself as his end he falls into a state of moral misery which leads him to suicide'.[24] Thus there was a need for a functional alternative to the family: something 'other than personal and domestic interest must stimulate us to work' deriving from 'some other group outside the family, more circumscribed than political society, nearer to us and touching us more closely'.[25] Marriage was too impermanent to provide such an object of attachment, since it was dissolved by death in each generation. The only group which could perform this function was the occupational or professional group:

> Only this group, in my view, is able to perform the economic and moral functions which the family has become increasingly incapable of performing ... Men must gradually become attached to their occupational or professional life. Strong groups relative thereto must be developed. In the hearts of men professional duty must take over the place formerly occupied by domestic duty.[26]

On the other hand, the family, though it 'plays a smaller role in life',[27] would continue to be an important centre of morality, a basis for moral education, a centre of moral security and a source of attachment and regulation for the individual.[28] Indeed, since the conjugal family was based on marriage, extra-marital sexual unions became all the more

23. ibid. (S.L.).
24. 1921a, p. 11: tr. 1965a, p. 534.
25. ibid.: tr. pp. 534–5.
26. ibid., p. 13: tr. pp. 535–6.
27. 1897a, p. 433: tr. 1951a, p. 377.
28. 'It is not only the framework which socially sustains the individual and constitutes the organized defence of certain of his interests. It is also the moral environment where his inclinations are disciplined and where his aspirations towards the ideal are born, begin to expand and continue to be maintained. In presenting him with domestic duties and affections ... which ... are obligatory like moral imperatives; in showing him the continuous operation of ... an altruism dictated as much by necessity

serious: where they existed, the children reared in such environments showed 'moral defects ... A child cannot have a moral upbringing unless he lives in a society whose every member feels his obligations toward every other member.'[29] Moreover, the bonds of kinship became more and more indissoluble in the conjugal family, protected by the state which intervened more and more in determining and enforcing domestic rights and obligations. Thus the family, while becoming more concentrated and individualized, and while its centrality declined as the contexts of social interaction widened and multiplied, retained an essential role in modern societies.

Durkheim's subsequent work on kinship took a somewhat different turn, chiefly as a result of his immersion in ethnography. He became involved in and made notable contributions to debates on ethnological issues – such as the interpretation of marriage-systems and the various rights and duties they involve[30] (stressing a view of marriage as a contract[31]), on the position of women[32] (questioning the assumption that matriliny necessarily grows out of or otherwise implies matriarchy[33]) and, above all, on incest and exogamy[34] and on Australian section systems.[35]

---

as by instinct; in offering husband and wife the most propitious opportunity for the most intimate physical and moral union which is also the most permanent; ... in providing a place of refreshment where effort may be relaxed and the will reinvigorated; in giving this will and effort... an end going beyond egoistic and momentary enjoyments; in forming, finally, a refuge where the wounds of life may find their consolation and errors their pardon, the family is a source (*foyer*) of morality, energy and kindness, a school of duty, love and work – in a word, a school of life which cannot lose its role' (Davy, 1925, in Davy, 1931 (1950 edn), p. 119). Cf. Bellah, 1959, in Nisbet, 1965, pp. 162–3. Also cf. the account of the modern family in Parsons, T., and Bales, R. F., *Family, Socialization and Interaction Process* (New York, 1955), ch. 1.

29. 1921a, p. 14: tr. 1965a, p. 536.
30. 1899a (iv) (19) and (22); and 1908a (ii) (12) and (13).
31. 1901a (iii) (25).
32. 1899a (iv) (7).
33. 1899a (iv) (23).
34. 1898a (ii). For discussion, see Lévi-Strauss, 1949, ch. ii.
35. 1902a (i) and 1905a (i); also see 1903a (i), pp. 7–21: tr. 1963b, pp. 10–26. For a brief discussion of some of this work on kinship, see Maybury-Lewis, 1965.

INCEST

Durkheim's study of incest was a curious mixture of evolutionary speculation and incisive analysis, which Lévi-Strauss describes as 'the most conscientious and systematic interpretation [of it] from purely social causes'.[36] Seeing the connection between incest-prohibition and rules of exogamy, he sought to account for it by going back 'to the very origins of this evolution, as far as the most primitive form which the repression of incest has historically taken: namely, the law of exogamy'.[37] What, then, was the nature of exogamy? He saw it as intimately linked to the nature of the clan[38] – of which Durkheim's account has been well described as postulating a 'sort of *Ur*-group, omnipresent in the early history of every society'.[39] From its original elementary form in the uterine clan, the rule of exogamy thereafter changed in its scope of application in accordance with the evolution of the family. But it was itself to be explained in terms of 'the religious beliefs of lower societies'[40]; indeed, it was 'merely a particular case of a much more general religious institution, found at the basis of all primitive religions, and indeed, in a sense, of all religions – namely, *taboo*'.[41] This was Durkheim's alternative to the various conjectural explanations of incest of McLennan, Lubbock, Spencer and Morgan and the prevalent 'instinctive aversion' types of explanation, such as that of Westermarck (which really amounted, Durkheim wrote, to a refusal to explain[42]). Durkheim argued that the totemic beliefs underlying exogamy imparted a 'sentiment of religious horror'[43] to blood, which was closely related to the totem, itself immanent in the clan, and that this sentiment naturally extended to woman, who 'so to speak, passes a part of her life in blood',[44]

36. Lévi-Strauss, 1949 (1969), p. 20.
37. 1898a (ii), p. 2: tr. 1963a, p. 14 (S.L.).
38. ibid., p. 9: tr. p. 25.
39. Maybury-Lewis, 1965, p. 257.
40. 1898a (ii), p. 39: tr. 1963a, p. 69.
41. ibid.: tr. pp. 69–70 (S.L.).
42. See ibid., p. 38: tr. p. 68.
43. ibid., p. 44: tr. 76 (S.L.).
44. ibid., p. 53: tr. p. 89.

and thence to sexual relations with her. The relation of this account to exogamy was that sexual prohibitions applied exclusively to members of the clan, since 'the totem, in effect, is only sacred for its followers'.[45] Hence the rule of inter-clan marriage alongside the prohibition of marriage within the clan.

He went further, relating contemporary rules concerning incest to these original exogamous practices, which had contracted in scope, while the family continued to inspire a kind of religious respect ('it is always the Ark of the Covenant which it is forbidden to touch, precisely because it is the school of respect and respect is the religious sentiment par excellence'[46]). Although the original beliefs justifying the sentiments and practices relating to incest had long disappeared, these latter had entered into the mores and survived as a crucial element of our morality. Indeed Durkheim advanced the bold hypothesis that this explained a whole set of contemporary beliefs and practices relating to women, as well as the dichotomy between sensuality and familial morality, and, more generally, that between sex and morality[47]; he can even be seen as offering a sociological, or cultural, account, as opposed to Freud's bio-psychological account, of 'the eternal antithesis between passion and duty'.[48]

Lévi-Strauss has well summarized the structure of Durkheim's argument as follows:

by proceeding analytically, we see that for Durkheim the prohibition of incest is a remnant of exogamy, that this exogamy is explicable in terms of the special prohibitions relating to women, that these prohibitions originate in the fear of menstrual blood, that this fear is only a particular case of the general fear of blood, and finally, that this fear merely expresses certain feelings deriving from the belief in the consubstantiality of the individual clan member and his totem.[49]

45. ibid., p. 54: tr. p. 90.
46. ibid., p. 60: tr. p. 101 (S.L.).
47. Cf. 'Love ... excludes all idea of obligation and rule. It is the domain of freedom, where the imagination moves unhindered, where the interests of the parties and their gratification are almost the dominant law' (ibid., pp. 60–61: tr. p. 101 – S.L.).
48. ibid., p. 67: tr. p. 112. This antithesis might, he consistently argued, have taken a different form (ibid.).
49. Lévi-Strauss, 1949 (1969), p. 21.

But despite its boldness and capacity to systematize a wide range of different and seemingly unintelligible phenomena, this explanation is, as Lévi-Strauss shows,[50] subject to a crucial set of criticisms. Leaving aside the assumed universality and primitiveness of totemism, it is clear that the links between the various stages identified above are extremely weak: indeed, 'there is nothing more arbitrary than this succession of transitions'.[51] Why should totemic substantiality preclude intra-clan marriage and sexual relations? Why should the horror of menstrual blood be extended only to women of the clan? Why should prejudices relating to menstrual blood lead to rules of exogamy (rather than, say, merely to the prohibition of sexual relations with the wife during her menses)? And how could the universality and vitality of the incest prohibition be explained if it were merely a historical survival of exogamy? Durkheim's interpretation of incest was in the end just another attempt (analogous to those of McLennan, Lubbock and Spencer, which he attacked) to explain a universal institution by appealing to a speculative, if·complex, historical sequence.

SECTION SYSTEMS

Durkheim's work on Australian section systems was more technical in character; indeed, its interest and importance largely reside in the method employed.[52] *Sur le totémisme*[53] was an analysis of the material presented in Spencer and Gillen's *The Native Tribes of Central Australia*,[54] in opposition to

50. ibid., pp. 21 ff.
51. ibid., p. 23.
52. Rodney Needham has observed that 'Durkheim's writings on "marriage class" or section systems in Australia have a clarity, command of ethnographic sources, and theoretical interest which gives them a sustained and even classical interest today. In particular, his radical analysis of the four-section system (in "La Prohibition de l'inceste et ses origines"), though invalidated in the event by precisely the type of evidence that he himself had said was to be looked for, became the mainstay of the theories of Radcliffe-Brown (*The Social Organization of Australian Tribes*, Melbourne, 1931) and Lévi-Strauss (*Les Structures élémentaires de la parenté*, Paris, 1949)'. (Personal communication.)
53. 1902a (i).
54. London, 1899 (cf. 1900a (8)).

Frazer's second theory of totemism,[55] which sought to deny that matrimonial (and alimentary) prohibitions were essential to it. The kernel of Durkheim's argument was an attempt to show that the Arunta, in which such prohibitions were lacking and which Frazer thought of as primitive, had in fact developed out of an originally exogamous clan. In particular, he argued that the Arunta's eight-section system could be explained in terms of a shift from matriliny to patriliny[56]; and in a subsequent article[57] he added the further hypothesis of the joint operation of the principles of territoriality and descent. Quite apart from the question of empirical evidence for this case,[58] the significant thing was the formal character of the argument, pursuing the internal logic of the system.[59] Durkheim's approach was, in this respect, distinctly modern, foreshadowing, for example, the kind of analysis to be found in Lévi-Strauss's *Les Structures élémentaires de la parenté*.[60] Indeed, Durkheim wrote in conclusion to his article on Australian matrimonial organization:

one cannot but be struck by the remarkable logic with which the ideas that are at the basis of this matrimonial organization develop across the various circumstances of history. In fact, one can, by a simple calculation, construct the system of classes of a tribe as a function of the mode of descent which is in practice there ... It is as though we were following the discussion of a mathematical problem ... Is this not one more proof that these classes and phratries are not simply social categories (*cadres*), but also logical categories, subject, no doubt, to a special logic, different from ours, but which nonetheless has its own definite rules.[61]

55. Expounded in his 'The Origins of Totemism', *Fortnightly Review*, April and May 1899.

56. As Maybury-Lewis points out, he went on to over-generalize from this, using this shift to explain too much: see, for example, 1904a (14); 1905a (ii) (4); 1907a (11) and (12); and 1913a (ii) (18), (19) and (22). See Maybury-Lewis, 1965, p. 258.

57. 1905a (i).

58. See below, p. 528, for Durkheim's correspondence with Radcliffe-Brown on this question. Cf. Maybury-Lewis, 1965, p. 258.

59. For an illuminating discussion of this, see Peristiany, 1960.

60. Lévi-Strauss, 1949.

61. 1905a (i), p. 147. Cf. 1903a (i): tr. 1963b.

Chapter 9

Suicide

CLOSELY connected with his ideas concerning the moral functions of the modern family was Durkheim's intensive work on suicide. This began with an article on suicide and the birth rate[1] and was followed by a whole year's lecture-course on suicide – the third public course in sociology of 1889–90.[2] He continued to work on the subject for the next seven years, collecting and interpreting statistics,[3] in which task he was greatly helped by his nephew Marcel Mauss, who came to Bordeaux to study under him in the early 1890s. The final result of all this work was *Suicide*, published in 1897.[4]

Why did Durkheim turn to the study of suicide? The suicide of his very close friend at the École, Victor Hommay, clearly affected him deeply and may well have influenced not only his interest in suicide but also his very explanation of it, at least in its 'egoistic' form.[5] But there were also at least five less personal explanations for his interest.

For two centuries suicide had been a subject of widespread and continuing debate.[6] Having originally been treated largely as a moral problem in the eighteenth century,[7] it came to be regarded in the nineteenth as a growing social problem requiring explanation. Statistical and interpretative work on variations in the suicide rate multiplied in France, Belgium,

1. 1888d.

2. See Appendix A, below.

3. He contributed a statistical map of suicides in France to the International Exhibition held at Bordeaux in 1895, along with a phylogenetic schema of the evolution of the family (Lacroze, 1960a, pp. 4–5).

4. 1897a: tr. 1951a.

5. See Chapter 2, above, and 1887d.

6. See Giddens, 1965, and Douglas, 1967.

7. See Crocker, L. G., 'The Discussion of Suicide in the Eighteenth Century', *Journal of the History of Ideas*, 13 (1952), pp. 47–52.

Germany and Italy.[8] A number of statistical correlations were established and hypotheses advanced relating differential suicide rates to social factors, such as occupation, urbanization, religion and the rate of social change, and to non-social factors, such as heredity, race and climate; and there was an unresolved dispute as to whether or not suicide was related to mental disorder. There was also general agreement that the overall rise in suicide rates was due to the passing of the traditional social order and the growth of industrialism. Here, then, was a subject peculiarly rich in systematically recorded and comparative evidence, in explanatory hypotheses, and in wide-ranging implications. Indeed, Durkheim's *Suicide* can be seen as a culmination of the moral statistics tradition, as 'primarily an attempt at a theoretical synthesis of the many earlier ideas and findings concerning suicide as a social phenomenon'.[9]

Secondly, it was a subject which seemed concrete and specific, offering the researcher 'groups of facts clearly circumscribed, capable of ready definition, with definite limits'.[10] This, in Durkheim's view, was the kind of front on which sociology should advance. As he wrote in the preface to *Suicide*:

Suicide has been chosen as [the present work's] subject . . . because, since there are few that are more precisely delimitable, it seemed to us peculiarly timely . . . by such concentration, real laws are discoverable which demonstrate the possibility of sociology better than any dialectical argument.[11]

Moreover, it was a subject which, though restricted, was directly related to the institutions and the general features of the wider society (in particular, marriage, widowhood, family life and religion).

Thirdly, as he observed in the same preface, it offered an excellent opportunity for demonstrating the principles set out in *The Rules of Sociological Method*.[12] In particular, he claimed that

8. Cf. Durkheim's own bibliography in 1897a, pp. 16–17: tr. 1951a, pp. 52–3; and Giddens, 1965.

9. Douglas, 1967, p. 152; see also pp. 15 ff.

10. 1897a, p. vii: tr. 1951a, p. 36.

11. ibid., p. viii: tr. p. 37.

12. 1894a: repr. 1895a, to be considered in the next chapter.

Suicide vindicated social realism ('There is no principle for which we have received more criticism'), proving the existence of 'realities external to the individual' and 'as definite and substantial as those of the psychologist or the biologist'.[13] The existence of these social realities became evident when

> each people is seen to have its own suicide rate, more constant than that of general mortality, that its growth is in accordance with a coefficient of acceleration characteristic of each society; when it appears that the variations through which it passes at different times of the day, month, year, merely reflect the rhythm of social life; and that marriage, divorce, the family, religious society, the army, etc., affect it in accordance with definite laws, some of which may even be numerically expressed. . .[14]

The relevant explanatory variables were 'real, living, active forces which, because of the way they determine the individual, prove their independence of him': although 'the individual enters as an element in the combination whence these forces ensue', they 'control him once they are formed'.[15]

Fourthly, since the essence of Durkheim's diagnosis of the ills of his own society was an analysis of the differential strength and impact of those forces, the study of suicide offered a means of approaching 'the causes of the general malaise currently being undergone by European societies', since it was 'one of the forms through which the collective malady from which we suffer is transmitted'. And it even led to suggestions 'concerning remedies which may relieve it'.[16]

Finally, and perhaps most significantly, suicide was peculiarly well suited to the task of establishing Durkheim's claims

13. 1897a, pp. ix, xi: tr. pp. 37–8, 39. As he wrote to Bouglé (letter dated 16 May 1896): 'I stopped lecturing in April so as to devote myself fully to the book I am preparing on Suicide. I hope that when it appears people will have a better understanding of that reality of social phenomena about which they disagree with me, for what I study there is the social disposition to suicide (*le courant social au suicide*), the tendency to suicide of social groups, isolated from its individual manifestations (by abstraction certainly, but no science isolates its object in any other way).' On the criticisms of his social realism, referred to here, see Chapter 16, below.

14. ibid., pp. x–xi: tr. pp. 38–9.

15. ibid., p. xi: tr. p. 39.

16. ibid., p. viii–ix: tr. p. 37 (S.L.).

for sociology, for two further reasons. In the first place, it was, on the face of it, the most private of acts – 'an individual action affecting the individual only', which 'must seemingly depend exclusively on individual factors, thus belonging to psychology alone'.[17] Explaining it, or, more precisely, explaining differential suicide rates sociologically, would be a singular triumph.[18] In the second place, it had the most direct bearing on the initial question of Durkheim's sociological work – 'what are the bonds which unite men one with another?' – for it offered the clearest case of the dissolution of those bonds.

The early article on suicide and the birth rate reveals how strong was Durkheim's sense of the contemporary social 'malaise' and of the role of sociology as in part social pathology (for, as he had learnt from the philosopher-psychologist, Théodule Ribot, explaining the pathological is a means of explaining the normal). Beginning from the assumption that the suicide rate is an index of social health or illness, he advanced the hypothesis that the birth rate is a function of the suicide rate and that in any given society there is a normal zone for the birth rate, such that, if it is too low (or too high), there is a rise in suicides, indicating a deeper social malaise.

The decline in the birth rate (which was, in fact, only temporary) was a matter of widespread concern in France at this period. It was discussed and lamented by philosophers, statisticians, economists and novelists, crusaded against by conservatives and Catholics, who were joined by many liberals, Radicals and socialists, and there were vast numbers of publications on the subject, from the scientific to the popular; there was even a large organization, the Alliance pour l'Accroissement de la Population Française, founded to alleviate this

17. ibid., p. 8: tr. p. 46.
18. Though, as Douglas observes, the idea that social conditions predetermine differential suicide (and other crime) rates had long been commonplace among the moral statisticians, being particularly clear, for example, in the work of Adolphe Quételet (Douglas, 1967, p. 16). (Durkheim, however, was very critical of Quételet's explanation in terms of the intervening variable of the average man, or personality type: see 1897a, pp. 337 ff.: tr. 1951a, pp. 300 ff.)

alleged symptom of national decadence.[19] Durkheim offered a characteristic explanation: the high and rising suicide rate and the low and falling birth rate were both to be attributed to the nature of the 'social milieu'.[20] They both resulted from a regression of 'domestic sentiments': when men lose 'the taste and habit of domestic solidarity' and when 'families move' (in particular from the countryside to the towns) and 'individuals are less close', then the 'cold wind of egoism freezes their hearts and weakens their spirits'.[21]

Suicide[22] was a systematic generalization of these preliminary insights: it generalized them by seeking to identify the areas and growing points of social dissolution in contemporary societies, and it was systematic in doing so within a general theoretical framework.

THE THEME OF SOCIAL DISSOLUTION

The theme of social dissolution was a pervasive one in nineteenth-century French thought.[23] Deriving from the

19. See Swart, K. W., *The Sense of Decadence in Nineteenth-Century France* (The Hague, 1964). pp. 172–8.

20. It is worth noting that in this article, written five years before *The Division of Labour*, Durkheim explicitly argued that the birth rate depends on social practices and ideas ('*mœurs et idées*'), offering a further proof of the error of seeing his account of demographic change as 'biological' (see Chapter 7, above).

21. 1888d, p. 463. This article also advanced the distinction between two types of suicide, 'absurd' and 'rational' suicide, the fomer due to an 'organic fault', the latter to social causes.

22. For useful discussions of *Suicide*, see above all Halbwachs, 1930, especially the Introduction and Conclusion; Fauconnet, 1898, Tosti, 1898b, Bayet, 1922, Blondel, 1933, Parsons, 1937, Gold, 1958, Selvin, 1958 in Nisbet, 1965, Dohrenwend, 1959, Madge, 1962, Johnson, 1965, Giddens, 1965 and 1966, and Douglas, 1966 and 1967; also see Gibbs, J. P., chapter on suicide in Merton, R. K., and Nisbet, R. A., *Contemporary Social Problems* (New York, 1961, rev. edn 1966), Gibbs, J. P. (ed.), *Suicide* (New York, 1968), Gibbs, J. P., and Martin, W. T., *Status Integration and Suicide* (Eugene, Oregon, 1964), Wilson, 1963, Weiss, 1964, Pierce, A., 'The Economic Cycle and the Social Suicide Rate', *ASR*, 32 (1967), pp. 457–62, Sainsbury, P., *Suicide in London* (London, 1955), and Henry, A. F., and Short, J. F., *Suicide and Homicide* (Glencoe, 1954).

23. Cf. Swart, K. W., ' "Individualism" in the Mid-Nineteenth Century (1826–1860)', *Journal of the History of Ideas*, 23 (1962), pp. 77–90;

counter-revolutionary reaction of the early nineteenth century, it was taken up, with differing emphases, by conservatives, Catholics, Saint-Simonians, Positivists, liberals, and socialists. All agreed in condemning '*l'odieux individualisme*' – the social, moral and political isolation of self-interested individuals, unattached to social ideals and unamenable to social control; and they saw it as spelling the breakdown of social solidarity. For some it resided in dangerous ideas, for others it was social or economic anarchy, a lack of the requisite institutions and norms, for yet others it was the prevalence of self-interested attitudes among individuals. It was variously traced to the Reformation, the Renaissance, the intellectual anarchy consequent on the 'negative' thought of the Enlightenment, the Revolution, to the decline of the aristocracy or the Church or traditional religion, to the Industrial Revolution, to the growth of capitalism or democracy. Almost all, however, agreed in seeing it as a threat to social order – whether that order was conceived of in a traditionalist and hierarchical manner, or as an organized technocracy, or as essentially liberal and pluralist, or, as the socialists envisaged it, as an ideal co-operative order of 'association' and 'harmony'.

Horror of it dominated the thought of the French theocrats, such as de Maistre and de Bonald, while Lamennais saw 'individualism' as that 'which destroys the very idea of obedience and of duty, thereby destroying both power and law; and what then remains but a terrifying confusion of interests, passions and diverse opinions?'[24] Louis Veuillot, the militant Catholic propagandist, saw it as the 'evil which plagues France', observing that it was

---

and two articles by the present writer: 'The Meanings of "Individualism"', *Journal of the History of Ideas*, 32 (1971), pp. 45–66, and 'Individualism' in *Dictionary of the History of Ideas*, ed. Wiener, P. P. (New York, 1973). (These articles form the basis for a forthcoming book on the subject.)

24. Lamennais, F. de, *Des progrès de la révolution et de la guerre contre l'église* (1829), ch. 1 in *Œuvres complètes* (Paris, 1836–7), vol. IX, pp. 17–18. For Lamennais, 'the same doctrine which produces anarchy in men's minds further produces an irremediable political anarchy, and overturns the very bases of human society' (ibid.).

not difficult to see that a country where individualism reigns is no
longer in the normal conditions of society, since society is the
union of minds and interests, and individualism is division carried
to the infinite degree.[25]

(And, as we shall see, during the Dreyfus Affair, Durkheim was
to cross swords with Ferdinand Brunetière, the strongly
traditionalist anti-Dreyfusard, who defended the army and the
social order against the menace of 'individualism' and
'anarchy'.)[26] Both Saint-Simon and Comte sought to combat it
by means of social organization and the establishment of
secular religions; the Saint-Simonians proclaimed against the
'disorder, atheism, individualism and egoism' of the modern
epoch, and saw 'the doctrine of individualism' as leading to
'one political result: opposition to any attempt at organization
from a source of direction for the moral interests of mankind . . .'[27] Liberal thinkers were no less appalled by its
dangers: Benjamin Constant believed that 'when all are
isolated by egoism, there is nothing but dust, and at the advent
of a storm, nothing but mire',[28] while it was Alexis de Tocqueville who gave '*individualisme*' its most distinctive and influential liberal meaning in France. For Tocqueville it meant the
apathetic withdrawal of individuals from public life into a
private sphere and their isolation from one another, with a
consequent and dangerous weakening of social bonds: individualism was

a deliberate and peaceful sentiment which disposes each citizen to
isolate himself from the mass of his fellows . . . [which] at first saps
only the virtues of public life, but, in the long run, . . . attacks and
destroys all others and is eventually absorbed into pure egoism.[29]

25. Veuillot, L., 'Lettre à M. Villemain' (1843), in *Mélanges religieux,
historiques, politiques et littéraires (1842–56)* (Paris, 1856–60), 1ère série,
vol. 1, pp. 132–3.

26. See Chapter 17, below.

27. *The Doctrine of Saint-Simon: An Exposition, First Year 1828–9*, tr.
Iggers, G. (Boston, 1958), pp. 247, 182.

28. Quoted in Marion, H., 'Individualisme', in *La Grande Encyclopédie*
(Paris, n.d.), vol. xx.

29. Tocqueville, A. de, *De la démocratie en Amérique*, bk II, pt II, ch
11 in *Œuvres complètes*, ed. Mayer, J. P. (Paris, 1951–), t. I, pt II, p. 105.

And among French socialists, it referred to the doctrine of *laissez-faire* and to the anarchy, social atomization and exploitation produced by industrial capitalism. For Pierre Leroux, it was the principle, proclaimed by political economy, of 'everyone for himself, and . . . all for riches, nothing for the poor', which atomized society and made men into 'rapacious wolves', as opposed to the era of 'association' that was to come[30]; and for the Utopian, Étienne Cabet,

Two great systems have divided and polarized Humanity ever since the beginning of the world: that of Individualism (or egoism, or personal interest), and that of Communism (or association, or the general interest, or the public interest).[31]

Likewise, the conspirational revolutionary, Auguste Blanqui, asserted that 'Communism is the protector of the individual, individualism his extermination'.[32]

In short, Durkheim's notions of 'egoism' and 'anomie' were rooted in a broad and all-pervasive tradition of discussion concerning the causes of imminent social disintegration and the practical measures needed to avoid it – a tradition ranging from the far right to the far left.[33] His own approach was distinctive. As we shall see, he saw egoism and anomie as deriving in part from 'the same state of disaggregation',[34] in which the 'meshes' of 'the social fabric . . . are so dangerously slack'.[35] Egoism existed where 'society is not sufficiently integrated at all points to keep all its members dependent upon it' and increased because 'society, disordered and weakened, lets too many people escape its influence too completely'[36]; while anomie 'springs from the lack of collective forces at

30. Quoted in Arieli, Y., *Individualism and Nationalism in American Ideology* (Cambridge, Mass., 1964), p. 233.

31. Quoted in Dubois, J., *Le Vocabulaire politique et sociale en France de 1869 à 1872* (Paris, 1962), p. 322.

32. Quoted in ibid., p. 267.

33. This, incidentally, shows how inadequate is the view that Durkheim's sociology is primarily to be seen in the context of French conservatism (cf. Nisbet, 1952, 1965 and 1966).

34. 1897a, p. 440: tr. 1951a, p. 382.

35. ibid., p. 438: tr. p. 381 (S.L.).

36. ibid., p. 428: tr. p. 373 (S.L.).

certain points in society; that is, of groups established for the regulation of social life'.[37] The remedy lay neither in outdated traditionalist beliefs and institutions, nor in speculative and utopian social schemes; the only way to solve 'the difficulties of these critical times'[38] was the scientific way.[39] And he concluded from his sociological diagnosis that the only remedy was to restore the vitality of intermediary groups in society, above all in the industrial world – to 'render social groups sufficiently established so that they have a firmer hold on the individual and he adheres to them'.[40] Moreover, whereas it had been a commonplace of nineteenth-century French thought to equate 'individualism' with incipient social dissolution, Durkheim maintained that a new set of values had become institutionalized in modern societies, rendering the individual sacred, attaching moral value to individual autonomy, and justifying individual freedom and rights – and it was this which he chose to call 'individualism'. His case was that it was possible, indeed necessary, to find a remedy to the dissolution of social bonds within a social context shaped by liberal and humane values.

Perhaps the best way to approach Durkheim's *Suicide* will be to consider, first, what he sought to explain; second, the explanations he rejected as unsatisfactory; third, the explanatory theory he advanced; fourth, the exact nature of the explanation he proposed; and finally, his application of his theory to the diagnosis of the ills of his society and his suggestions about remedying them.

THE EXPLANANDUM

He sought to discover 'from which diverse tributaries (*confluents*) suicide considered as a collective phenomenon results' and claimed that to do this 'one must first consider it through

---

37. ibid., p. 440: tr. p. 382.
38. ibid., p. 171: tr. p. 169.
39. 'Once the social instinct is weakened, intelligence is the only guide that remains and we must remake a *conscience* for ourselves by its means' (ibid., p. 171: tr. p. 169 – S.L.).
40. ibid., p. 429: tr. p. 373 (S.L.).

statistical data. It is the social rate that one must take directly as the object of analysis.'[41] The suicide rate, he argued,

constitutes a single and determinate order of facts – as is shown both by its permanence and its variability. For that permanence would be inexplicable if it were not related to a cluster of distinct characteristics, associated with one another, and simultaneously effective despite different attendant circumstances; and the variability proves the concrete and individual nature of those same characteristics, since they vary with the society's individual character. In short, what these statistical data express is the tendency to suicide with which each society is collectively afflicted.[42]

Durkheim's justification for this approach is interesting and highly characteristic of his style of argument. He began with a definition of suicide ('*every case of death which results directly or indirectly from a positive or negative act, accomplished by the victim himself which he knows must produce this result*') – a definition without reference to the agent's intention, since intentions are hard to identify, and 'an act cannot be defined by the end sought by the agent, for the same set of movements can, without changing their nature, be adapted to too many different ends'.[43] In short, the defining feature of suicide for Durkheim was the conscious renunciation of existence. Now, given this starting-point, one might, he argued, in principle proceed by observing the largest possible number of individual suicides, classify them 'morphologically' into types according to their resemblances and differences, and then seek to determine their causes. But such a classification of suicides was impracticable, given the almost total lack of the requisite evidence. However,

41. ibid., p. 143: tr. p. 148 (S.L.).
42. ibid., p. 14: tr. p. 51 (S.L.).
43. ibid., pp. 5, 4: tr. pp. 44, 43 (S.L.). For discussions of Durkheim's definition of suicide, see Halbwachs, 1930, especially pp. 451 ff., and Douglas, 1967, Appendix 11. Durkheim's doctrine of the irrelevance of intention to the definition of actions is philosophically unacceptable; Halbwachs' procedure of incorporating in the definition of suicide both the agent's intention and 'the attitude of society and the different judgements it makes of acts externally similar' is much more satisfactory (Halbwachs, 1930, p. 480).

we can achieve our objective by another route. It will be sufficient to reverse the order of our investigation. In fact, there can only be different types of suicide insofar as the causes on which they depend themselves differ. For each of them to have its own distinctive character, it must also have conditions of existence that are peculiar to it. A single antecedent or a single set of antecedents cannot sometimes produce one consequence and sometimes another, for then the difference between the two would itself be without cause, which would be to deny the principle of causality. Every specific difference that is established between causes thus implies a similar difference between effects. Consequently, we can establish the social types of suicide, not by classifying them directly according to their preliminarily described characteristics, but by classifying the causes which produce them. Without bothering to discover why they differ from one another, we will look at once for the social conditions on which they depend; then we will group these conditions according to their differences and resemblances into a number of separate classes, and we can be certain that to each of these classes there corresponds a determinate type of suicide.[44]

Indeed, Durkheim continued, not only is this method dictated by practical considerations: 'one penetrates much more deeply into the nature of a phenomenon when one knows its cause than when one only knows its characteristics, however essential they may be'. Subsequently, 'once the causes are known, we can try to deduce from them the nature of the effects', namely, individual suicides, which 'will thus be both characterized and classified merely by being attributed to their respective sources'. Here, such meagre data as existed about individual suicides could be used to guide and check the deduction. In this way, 'we will return from causes to effects and our aetiological classification will be completed by a morphological one which will serve to verify the former, and vice versa'.[45]

The *petitio principii* involved here is only too apparent: Durkheim's so-called 'aetiological classification' of suicides already presupposes that his causal explanations of suicide are true. In other words, he began with a causal theory which he

44. ibid., p. 141: tr. pp. 146–7 (S.L.).
45. ibid., pp. 141–2: tr. pp. 147–8 (S.L.).

assumed to be true and sought to verify this theory by establishing that suicide rates 'vary as a function of several social concomitants',[46] which represent 'the states of . . . different social environments (religious confessions, family, political society, professional groups, etc.)', placing these latter into categories of social causes specified by the causal theory. Having done this, 'returning to individuals', he considered 'how these general causes become individualized in order to produce the homicidal effects they imply'.[47] In short, he *identified* types of suicide by means of their alleged causes. This procedure had two unfortunate consequences: it precluded consideration of the possibilities (i) that there might be other typologics of suicide that fit the suicide data better, and (ii) that there might be other causal factors at work. (On the other hand, this procedure greatly reinforces the book's persuasive force, to the extent that the reader is also induced not to consider these possibilities.) An 'aetiological classification' would, indeed, be both logically and methodologically acceptable *if* the causal theory advanced were true and exhaustive of the explananda; otherwise it will be both restrictive and misleading.

However, given that Durkheim's classification presupposes and is governed by his theory, it is not in itself an argument against the latter to maintain, as Douglas does, that it is 'a realist theory – that is, an explanation of events in nature by the applications of ideas that are not abstractions from other events, but, rather, ideas merely assumed, intuited, or derived from we know not where'.[48] (In fact, as we shall see, the ideas derive from Durkheim's theory of morality and its implications for social solidarity.) What matters is not where the explanation comes from, but rather whether it is superior to all other available explanations; and whether it fits the facts and renders them intelligible.[49] To Durkheim's considerations of these matters we may now turn.

---

46. 1897a, p. 456: no tr.
47. ibid., p. 148: tr. p. 151 (S.L.).   48. Douglas, 1967, p. 33.
49. Of course, there is much room for dispute about what the facts *are* (into which we cannot enter here). For valuable correctives to some of Durkheim's evidence, see Halbwachs, 1930, and for a highly sceptical discussion of the reliability of official suicide statistics, see Douglas, 1967.

REJECTED EXPLANATIONS

Pursuing his characteristic method of argument by elimination, he systematically considered and rejected the 'principal extra-social factors liable to have an influence on the social suicide rate',[50] namely (i) 'organico-psychic dispositions'[51] internal to individuals, both abnormal and normal; (ii) features of the physical environment; and (iii) the process of imitation. His method was a combination of statistical proof and dialectical argument.

First, he argued that suicide was neither a distinct form of insanity, or monomania (on clinical and psychological grounds), nor a specific symptom of insanity (since suicide is by definition both deliberate and based on non-hallucinatory sense-impressions), nor correlated with the various forms of nervous disorder (since, assuming nervous disorders vary with insanity, there is no positive correlation between suicide and insanity, testing for sex, religion, age, country and degree of civilization) – which lack of correlation he explained by pointing to the indeterminateness of the symptoms of nervous disorders, which differ according to different (socially determined) conditions. Finally, there was no correlation between suicide rates and alcoholism (more specifically between suicide rates and the geographical distribution of offences and mental illnesses associated with alcoholism, and of alcohol consumption). In short, 'there is no pathological psychological condition that has a regular and indisputable relation to suicide', though such a condition provides 'an eminently suitable psychological field for the influence of causes which can determine a man to kill himself'.[52]

Second, with respect to 'normal' organico-psychic factors, Durkheim argued (in particular against Wagner and Morselli) that race was a highly ambiguous and non-operational concept, that Morselli's evidence was highly dubious and that differences in the geographical distribution of suicide were better explained by social factors, and finally that there was no evidence that suicide is hereditary (especially since it is less prevalent

50. 1897a, p. 453: no tr.
51. ibid., p. 19: tr. p. 57 (S.L.).   52. ibid., pp. 52–3: tr. p. 81 (S.L.).

among women and becomes more probable with the advance of age).

As for features of the physical environment, Durkheim argued, first, that there was no correlation (as the Italian criminologists supposed) between suicide rates and either climate or temperature, and, second, that the only positive correlation was that between the monthly variations of suicide and the length of day. Durkheim explained this, together with the fact that most suicides occurred during the daytime, by arguing that 'the daytime favours suicide because it is the time when business is most active, when human relations cross and intercross, when social life is most intense'[53] (an explanation he sought to confirm by noting a lower variation in cities where the intensity of social life is less dependent on the length of day). Thus, he concluded, the monthly and seasonal variations of suicide could be attributed to social causes.

Finally, he dismissed the view, then popular, that the distribution of suicide could be explained by the 'purely psychological phenomenon' of imitation.[54] (This, in effect, was part of Durkheim's wide-ranging battle with Tarde, though the latter is scarcely mentioned in this chapter.[55]) Imitation, Durkheim argued, was an elastic and inadequately defined concept, but if it were seen as a purely automatic process, there was no evidence of its influence, either in the geographical distribution of suicides or in their relation to the statistics of newspaper reading. Once more, Durkheim concluded that the evidence pointed rather to the inescapable conclusion that 'suicide depends essentially on certain states of the social environment'.[56]

53. ibid., p. 99: tr. p. 117 (S.L.).
54. ibid., p. 107: tr. p. 123.
55. See Chapter 16, below. Durkheim was clearly thinking of Tarde in declaring himself amazed 'that it is still necessary to discuss a hypothesis which, despite the grave objections to which it is subject, has never even begun to receive experimental proof . . . sociology can only claim to be considered as a science when it is no longer permissible for those who cultivate it to dogmatize in this fashion, so patently eluding the regular obligations of proof' (ibid., pp. 137–8: tr. p. 142 – S.L.).
56. ibid., p. 129: tr. p. 138.

THE EXPLANATION OFFERED

Durkheim's own explanation was really a systematic attempt to answer the question: what explanatory relations are there between forms of social life and individual acts of abandoning it? Though the attempt was only partly successful, it has had an immense influence, both within (sociological) suicide theory and beyond. As one writer has observed,

Advance in suicide theory since Durkheim published *Le Suicide* has been limited indeed: writers have offered substitute terms to embody, often in less precise formulation, Durkheim's major concepts; but little has been added in extension of his theory.[57]

More widely, since the basic theme of *Suicide* is the ways in which social bonds become weakened and ultimately break down in modern societies, the work has had an immediate and continuing relevance to the study of deviance and the whole field of social pathology; indeed, it is scarcely too much to describe it as 'one of the seminal works in the formation of the academic discipline of sociology'.[58] Moreover, the scrupulous way in which Durkheim tested his explanation against the available data has been much admired – though, as Halbwachs observed, it is not always clear whether one is being persuaded by dialectical argument or by statistical proof.[59] His principal methodological advance over previous scholars was his handling of various factors affecting suicide rates, not one by one, but rather as jointly operative and mutually interrelated. Valid criticisms have been made of specific mistakes in interpretation and invalid inferences (in particular his constant resort to the ecological fallacy)[60]; on the other hand, he was among the first to use multivariate analysis, as well as internal and external replications, and many of his

57. Giddens, 1965, p. 12.
58. Douglas, 1967, p. 79, which contains (passim) a critique of the Durkheimian approach on the grounds that it fails to investigate how individuals themselves construct the meanings of their actions. It is true that Durkheim did not explore this crucial aspect of suicidal actions; he saw suicide rather as the ultimate response of the psychologically vulnerable to certain socially structured situations.
59. Halbwachs, 1930, p. 3.
60. See, for example, Selvin, 1958, in Nisbet, 1965.

results have been broadly confirmed by subsequent research. One contemporary mathematical sociologist has written that

> Few, if any, later works can match the clarity and power with which Durkheim marshalled his facts to test and refine his theory. The stature of this work is even more impressive when one remembers that Durkheim lacked even so rudimentary a tool as the correlation coefficient. Yet the methodology of *Suicide* is important to those now engaged in empirical research, not merely to historians of sociology. Durkheim recognized and solved many of the problems that beset present-day research.[61]

The essence of Durkheim's explanatory theory was its specification of three, theoretically interrelated, types of 'social cause', each type representing what he held to be common to a particular set of social factors associated with relatively high or rising suicide rates. The theoretical framework relating these types of social cause – egoism, altruism and anomie – derived from his conception of morality and its relation to social solidarity. He saw suicide as the individual antithesis of social solidarity, and a high suicide rate as an index of the inadequate effectiveness of social bonds. He saw social bonds essentially as relating the individual to a group or to 'society', in two ways: attaching him to socially given purposes and ideals, and regulating his individual desires and aspirations. Egoism and its opposite altruism pick out that which ties an individual to socially given ideals and purposes; anomie (and its curiously shadowy opposite, fatalism[62]) pick out that which holds an individual's desires in check, regulating and moderating them.

Thus, in the case of egoism 'the bond attaching man to life slackens because the bond which attaches him to society is itself slack'[63]; the 'individual is isolated because the bonds uniting him to other beings are slackened or broken, because society is not sufficiently integrated at the points at which he is in contact with it'.[64] Altruism, on the other hand, exists where

61. ibid., p. 113.
62. Durkheim said very little indeed about fatalism, deeming it to be of 'little contemporary importance' (1897a, p. 311: tr. p. 276).
63. ibid., p. 230: tr. pp. 214–15 (S.L.).
64. ibid., p. 317: tr. p. 281 (S.L.).

the individual is 'too strongly integrated' into society,[65] where 'the self is not autonomous, where it is fused into something other than itself, where the goal (*le pôle*) of its behaviour is situated outside it, that is in one of the groups of which it forms part'.[66] Anomie differs from egoism and altruism in that it depends not on how individuals are attached to society,

but on how it regulates them. Egoistic suicide occurs because men no longer see any justification for life; altruistic suicide because that justification seems to them to be beyond life itself; [anomic] suicide . . . because their activity lacks regulation and they therefore suffer.

Thus both egoism and anomie mark 'society's insufficient presence in individuals', the one involving a lack of 'object and meaning' in 'genuinely collective activity', the other leaving 'individual passions . . . without a curb to regulate them'.[67] (And fatalism, the converse of anomie, consists in 'an excess of regulation' and is found among 'subjects whose future is relentlessly blocked, whose passions are violently repressed by an oppressive discipline'; it identifies the 'unavoidable and inflexible character of a rule over which one is powerless'.[68]) In brief, the two dimensions of anomie-fatalism and egoism-altruism represent the two sides of the notion of the 'social bond', equivalent, it will immediately be seen, to Durkheim's first two elements of morality: the 'spirit of discipline' and 'attachment to social groups'.[69]

Durkheim used the categories of egoism, altruism and anomie to distinguish distinct 'suicidogenic currents', affecting different groups and classes in society and corresponding to 'the states of the different social environments . . . as a function of which suicide varies'.[70]

65. ibid., p. 233: tr. p. 217 (S.L.). 66. ibid., p. 238: tr. p. 221 (S.L.).
67. ibid., p. 288: tr. p. 258 (S.L.). Cf. Mawson, 1970, which usefully explores the distinction between egoism and anomie, arguing (against Durkheim) that they in fact represent different kinds of normlessness: thus egoism is the breakdown of social attachments *constituting* the breakdown of the self; anomie is the breakdown of constraining legal and moral norms.
68. ibid., p. 311 fn.: tr. p. 276 fn. (S.L.).
69. See Chapter 6, above. 70. 1897a, p. 148: tr. p. 151 (S.L.).

Accordingly, he associated egoism with Protestantism, with the prevalence of a high value placed on acquiring knowledge (measured by the extent of popular and general education) and the highly educated liberal professions and intellectual elites, and with unmarried men and persons without families. He likewise identified a range of preservatives against egoistic suicide: Catholicism and Judaism, the Anglican church, marriage (slightly and only for men), and, to a lesser degree, widowhood, the family in proportion to its density and degree of integration, and national political crises.

He reasoned, first, that Protestantism, because it allowed greater freedom to individual thought and judgement, had 'fewer common beliefs and practices' and was 'a less strongly integrated church than the Catholic church',[71] while the Jews lived in small, highly cohesive communities and Judaism consisted in 'a body of practices minutely governing all the details of life and leaving little free room to individual judgement'[72] (the Anglican church, however, was 'far more powerfully integrated than other Protestant churches'[73]). As for education, its significance in this context was that it was associated with 'the weakening of traditional beliefs and . . . the state of moral individualism resulting from this'.[74] Thus 'Protestants are better educated and commit suicide more than Catholics',[75] while the fact that Jews were relatively highly educated but had a low suicide rate could be explained in terms of the particular significance of education for the Jew: he 'seeks to learn, not to replace his collective prejudices by ideas based on reflection, but simply to be better armed for the struggle. It is for him a means of compensating for the unfavourable position imposed on him by opinion and sometimes by law . . . he superimposes this intellectual life on his customary activity without the one encroaching on the other.'[76]

71. ibid., pp. 158–9: tr. p. 159.
72. ibid., pp. 159–60: tr. p. 160 (S.L.).   73. ibid., p. 160: tr. p. 160.
74. ibid., p. 170: tr. p. 168.   75. ibid., p. 165: tr. p. 164.
76. ibid., pp. 169–70: tr. p. 168 (S.L.). Thus, Durkheim wrote, the Jew 'combined the advantages of the severe discipline characteristic of the small groups of former times with the benefits of the intense culture enjoyed by our contemporary large-scale societies. He has all the intelligence of modern man without sharing his despair' (ibid. – S.L.).

Secondly, Durkheim argued that though marriage was somewhat advantageous to men as a preservative against egoistic suicide and quite disadvantageous to women (because of their low status and relative exclusion from social life), it was the family (in proportion to its density) which accounted for nearly all the immunity of husbands and all that of wives; and he explained this in terms of the strength of 'collective sentiments', and the 'state of integration' reflecting the 'intensity of collective life'.[77]

Finally, he reasoned in parallel fashion with respect to political crises:

great social disturbances and great popular wars rouse collective sentiments, stimulate partisan spirit and patriotism, political faith and national faith alike, and, focusing activities on a single end, produce, at least for a time, a stronger integration of society.

As men 'come together to face the common danger, the individual thinks less of himself and more of the common cause'.[78]

In sum, Durkheim identified the 'degree of integration' as the variable that was decisive in all these cases and concluded that 'suicide varies inversely with the degree of integration of the social groups of which the individual forms a part.'[79] Egoistic suicide resulted from 'excessive individuation'[80]: as the individual became alienated from religion, family and community', he became 'a mystery to himself, unable to escape the exasperating and agonizing question: to what purpose?'[81]

Altruistic suicides, on the other hand, were those which resulted from 'insufficient individuation'.[82] Durkheim brought under this heading suicide in 'less advanced societies' (though, of course, he had no systematic data for these, least of all concerning rates) – whether they were obligatory, 'optional' (for instance where honour is involved), or performed in order to achieve a 'higher' existence.[83] Secondly, he labelled 'altruistic' the suicides found in modern European armies (where in

77. ibid., pp. 213, 214: tr. pp. 201–2.   78. ibid., p. 222: tr. p. 208 (S.L.).
79. ibid., p. 223: tr. p. 209.   80. ibid. (S.L.).
81. ibid., p. 228: tr. p. 212.   82. ibid., p. 233: tr. p. 217.
83. Cf. Halbwachs' convincing observations about the important differences between sacrifice and suicide (Halbwachs, 1930, pp. 451 ff).

certain respects 'primitive morality' still survived[84]), which he saw as due not to the rigours of military service but to the altruistic character of the military spirit, according to which the soldier 'must be drilled to set little value on his person', so that his 'principle of action is outside him'.[85]

Durkheim inferred from his evidence two kinds of anomie: economic and conjugal. Observing a positive correlation between suicide and economic crises, whether they were booms or slumps, he interpreted it as indicating the breakdown of an established and accepted normative framework, fixing 'with relative precision the maximum standard of living which each social class may legitimately seek to attain'.[86] Such a framework, though subject to change, insured that men were 'content with their lot while stimulating them moderately to improve it'.[87] In the case of economic disasters,

a kind of *déclassement* occurs, suddenly thrusting certain individuals into a situation inferior to the one they occupied hitherto. They must therefore lower their demands, restrain their wants, learn greater self-control . . . they are not adjusted to the condition imposed on them and find its very prospect intolerable; thus they experience sufferings which detach them from a reduced existence even before they have tried it out.[88]

On the other hand, crises of prosperity had a no less disequilibrating effect:

The scale [regulating needs] is upset; but a new scale cannot be improvised. . . One no longer knows what is possible and what is not, what is just and what is unjust, which claims and expectations are legitimate and which are immoderate. As a result, there is no limit to men's aspirations . . . appetites, no longer restrained by a disoriented public opinion, no longer know where to stop. . .

84. 1897a, p. 260: tr. p. 238.
85. ibid., p. 254: tr. p. 234 (S.L.). Durkheim saw this explanation as confirmed by the statistical distribution of military suicides which were higher among populations with a lower tendency to egoistic suicide, at a maximum among elite troops, and declined in proportion to the rise in egoistic suicide.
86. ibid., p. 276: tr. p. 249 (S.L.).
87. ibid., p. 277: tr. p. 250.
88. ibid., p. 280: tr. p. 252 (S.L.).

[Moreover] because prosperity has increased, desires are heightened. . . But their very demands make it impossible to satisfy them. Overexcited ambitions always exceed the results obtained, whatever they may be; for they are not warned that they must go no further. Nothing, therefore, satisfies them and all this agitation is perpetually maintained without abatement. Above all, since this race toward an unattainable goal can afford no other pleasure than the race itself, if pleasure it is, once it is interrupted, one is left quite empty-handed. At the same time, the struggle grows more violent and painful, both because it is less regulated and because the competition is more keen. All classes are set against one another because there is no longer any established classification. Effort grows just when it becomes least productive. How, in these conditions, can the will to live not weaken?[89]

Durkheim further claimed that in contemporary societies, economic anomie was chronic in the industrial and commercial world (correlating with a high suicide rate), probably located to a greater degree among employers than workers. Indeed, economic anomie was 'a regular and specific factor in suicide in our modern societies',[90] resulting from the decline of religious, political and occupational controls, the growth of ideologies sanctifying industrial progress for its own sake, and 'the very development of industry and the almost infinite extension of the market'[91]:

From top to bottom of the scale, greed is aroused unable to find ultimate foothold. Nothing could calm it, since its goal is infinitely beyond all it can attain. . . Men thirst for novelties, unknown pleasures, nameless sensations, which lose all their savour once experienced. Henceforth, men have no strength to withstand the least reverse. . . [while this] passion for the infinite is daily presented as a mark of moral distinction, whereas it can only appear within unregulated *consciences* which elevate to a rule the lack of rule from which they suffer.[92]

Finally, conjugal anomie (resulting in the suicides of men, divorced and married, in populations where divorce is frequent) was also, Durkheim claimed, relatively chronic and

89. ibid., pp. 280–81: tr. p. 253 (S.L.).
90. ibid., p. 288: tr. p. 258.
91. ibid., p. 284: tr. p. 255.
92. ibid., pp. 285–7: tr. pp. 256, 257 (S.L.).

could be traced to 'a weakening of matrimonial regulation'.[93] In such conditions, the 'restraint [marriage] placed on desire is less firm; since it is more easily disturbed and substituted for, it controls passions less effectively and these tend in consequence to expand beyond it'. The 'calm and moral tranquillity which were the husband's strength' are 'to some extent replaced by a state of unease preventing him from being content with what he has'.[94] Hence the parallel development of divorces and suicides and the special suicide-proneness of divorced men (while, conversely, '*from the standpoint of suicide, marriage is more favourable to the wife the more widely practised divorce is*; *and vice versa*'[95]). Here too anomie resulted from the weakening of an established and accepted normative framework, a weakening of which divorce was both an expression and a powerful contributory cause.[96]

Finally, returning 'from causes to effects', following 'the various suicidogenic currents to their individual manifestations',[97] Durkheim made an attempt to 'complete' and 'verify' his aetiological classification of suicides by a morphological classification of their individual forms. Proceeding deductively (on the assumption that the 'social and general causes . . . must imprint the suicides they determine with a distinctive character', despite their individual differences[98]) and citing literary, historical and clinical cases to support his reasoning, he argued that egoistic suicide was associated with apathy (whether melancholic and self-indulgent or sceptical and disillusioned), altruistic suicide with passionate or deliberate determination (expressing a calm sense of duty, or a mystical

93. ibid., p. 307: tr. p. 273.

94. ibid., p. 305: tr. p. 271 (S.L.).

95. ibid., p. 302: tr. p. 269.

96. For completeness, one might mention fatalism, which Durkheim held to characterize 'the suicides of very young husbands and of childless wives' (and also perhaps 'the suicides of slaves' and all those attributable to 'the excesses of material or moral despotism') (ibid., p. 311: tr. p. 276 – S.L.).

97. ibid., p. 312: tr. p. 277 (S.L.).

98. ibid., p. 313: tr. p. 278 (S.L.). Thus the types of suicide are like 'the prolongation of these causes within individuals' (ibid., p. 324: tr. p. 287 – S.L.).

enthusiasm, or a quiet courage) and anomic suicide with irritation and disgust (accompanied by violent recriminations against life in general, or against some particular person).[99] For the egoistic suicide, life 'seems empty' because 'thought, by becoming self-absorbed, no longer has an object'[1]; the altruistic suicide abandons himself to 'enthusiasm, religious, moral or political faith ... [or] the military virtues', and 'almost by definition, sacrifices himself'[2]; while for the anomic suicide, 'lost ... in the infinity of desire', 'passion, no longer recognizing any bounds, no longer has any aim'.[3] Finally, there were 'mixed types' of suicide, resulting from converging social causes – egoistic-anomic (these two having 'a special affinity for one another,' being generally 'merely two different aspects of a single social state'[4]), anomic-altruistic and (oddly enough) egoistic-altruistic, with correspondingly mixed individual symptoms.

THE NATURE OF THE EXPLANATION

Many commentators and sociologists have had difficulty with Durkheim's theory of suicide: how does it relate to his methodological pronouncements, in particular his social realism? what is the precise nature of the *explanans*? does it involve a social psychology? It is therefore worth asking exactly what his explanation amounts to, what difficulties it raises and where its limitations lie.

We have seen that Durkheim sought to explain differential suicide rates in terms of 'social causes', 'real, living, active forces', 'suicidogenic currents'. He assumed a radical disjunction to exist between these social causes, on the one hand, and the individual's psychological characteristics, his 'motives and ideas' and his particular circumstances on the other. He

99. See ibid., p. 332: tr. p. 293.
  1. ibid., pp. 321, 324: tr. pp. 285, 287 (S.L.).
  2. ibid., p. 321: tr. pp. 284, 285.
  3. ibid., p. 324: tr. p. 287 (S.L.).
  4. ibid., p. 325: tr. p. 288 (S.L.). On the relation between egoism and anomie, see Johnson, 1965, which argues (unsuccessfully in the present writer's opinion) that they are 'identical conceptually as well as empirically' (art. cit., p. 884).

assumed that only the former are determining (that 'there is no individual state except insanity which may be considered a determining factor of suicide'[5]) since they alone can account for the variations and the stability of the rates. The currents impinge from outside on suicide-prone individuals at their 'weak points'[6]; and in any given population there is assumed to be a given distribution of such individuals ready to succumb to the impact of the currents, in proportion to the latter's strength. Thus the currents predetermine the rate of suicide but not who will commit it. Moreover, the 'currents' of egoism, altruism and anomie represent 'three currents of opinion', necessary to all societies, 'which incline men in three divergent, even contradictory directions' – namely, the opinions that 'the individual has a certain personality'; that 'he is ready if the community requires, to abandon it'; and that 'he is in some measure open to ideas of progress'. Where these currents of opinion 'mutually moderate one another, the moral agent is in a state of equilibrium which shelters him against any thought of suicide. But let one of them come to exceed a certain degree of intensity to the detriment of the others, and, for the reasons given, it becomes suicidogenic as it is individualized.'[7]

What, then, *are* the social causes, or currents, generating suicide? In the course of the book, Durkheim presents them in a wide variety of ways. They are variously described as, among other things: 'states of the various social environments',[8] 'what is most deeply constitutional in each national temperament',[9] 'the nature of . . . civilization, . . . the manner of its distribution among the different countries',[10] the 'moral state [or] temperament [or] constitution' of 'society' or 'groups',[11] 'ideas and sentiments',[12] 'common ideas, beliefs,

5. 1897a, p. 365: tr. p. 322.
6. ibid., p. 147: tr. p. 151.
7. ibid., p. 363: tr. p. 321.
8. ibid., p. 148: tr. p. 151.
9. ibid., p. 13: tr. p. 50.
10. ibid., p. 84: tr. p. 105.
11. ibid., pp. 136, 142, 307, 336, 343: tr. pp. 141, 147 (S.L.), 273, 299–300, 305.
12. ibid., p. 84: tr. p. 106.

customs and tendencies',[13] 'currents of opinion',[14] 'the weakening of traditional beliefs and ... the state of moral individualism',[15] 'the loss of cohesion in ... religious society',[16] 'excessive individuation',[17] 'currents of depression and disenchantment ... expressing society's state of disaggregation [and] the slackening of social bonds',[18] 'the set of states, acquired habits or natural predispositions making up the military spirit',[19] 'traditionalism [when] it exceeds a certain degree of intensity',[20] 'crises, that is, disturbances of the collective order',[21] 'a moral constitution *sui generis*, itself resulting from a weakening of matrimonial regulation',[22] 'pessimistic currents',[23] 'a state of crisis and perturbation',[24] a 'state of disaggregation'[25] and 'the state of deep disturbance from which all civilized societies are suffering'.[26]

In identifying all these as 'causes', Durkheim was, in effect, seeking to specify all those social factors which can impair the psychological health of the individual by rendering social bonds inadequately or excessively effective (thereby reducing his immunity to suicide). He was, in other words, by implication proposing a social-psychological theory about the social conditions for individual psychological health – a fact partially concealed by his use of the language of 'forces' and 'currents'.[27] He used this distinctly inappropriate analogical language as a weapon in the battle to win recognition for

13. ibid., p. 339: tr. p. 302.
14. ibid., p. 363: tr. p. 321.
15. ibid., p. 170: tr. p. 168.
16. ibid., p. 171: tr. p. 169.
17. ibid., p. 223: tr. p. 209.
18. ibid., p. 230: tr. p. 214 (S.L.).
19. ibid., p. 254: tr. p. 234.
20. ibid., p. 257: tr. p. 236.
21. ibid., p. 271: tr. p. 246.
22. ibid., p. 307: tr. p. 273.
23. ibid., p. 367: tr. p. 324.
24. ibid., p. 423: tr. p. 369.
25. ibid., p. 440: tr. p. 382.
26. ibid., p. 450: tr. p. 391.
27. 'There is ... for each people a collective force of a determinate amount of energy, impelling men to self-destruction' (ibid., p. 336: tr. p. 299).

sociology's scientific status. Thus he sought to demonstrate that 'collective tendencies ... are forces as real as cosmic forces, albeit of a different nature; they likewise act on the individual from without, though through other channels'. The important thing was

> to recognize their reality and conceive them as a set of forces which determine our behaviour from without, just like the physico-chemical forces to whose influence we are subject. So truly are they phenomena (*choses*) *sui generis*, and not verbal entities, that one can measure them and compare their relative magnitude, as one does the strength of electric currents or of sources of light. Thus, this fundamental proposition that social facts are objective, a proposition that we have had occasion to establish in another work, and which we consider to be the principle of sociological method, finds a new and particularly decisive proof in moral statistics and especially in those of suicide.[28]

This aggressively sociologistic language, implying that individuals merely responded differentially to external collective forces, was at odds with the central social-psychological theory advanced in *Suicide* – namely, that only in certain social conditions, where social bonds are neither too lax nor too oppressive, that is socially given goals and rules are neither too ineffective nor too demanding, can the individual achieve psychological or moral health and equilibrium. The language of 'currents' and 'forces' acting on individuals and 'mutually moderating one another' was altogether less suited to what he wished to say than the language of 'social bonds', attaching individuals to social goals and regulating their desires. Essentially, he wished to advance three social-psychological propositions: first, that the individual needs to be attached to a social goal, since social man

> necessarily presupposes a society that he expresses and serves ... our activity needs an objective transcending it ... [such an objective] is implicit in our moral constitution and it cannot disappear, even in part, without the latter to the same degree losing its reasons for existence;[29]

28. ibid., pp. 348–9: tr. pp. 309–10 (S.L.).
29. ibid., p. 228: tr. p. 213 (S.L.).

second, that he must not be so committed to such a transcendent goal that he loses all personal autonomy[30]; and third, that his desires and passions need to be regulated (though not to excess, as in fatalism), since this relative limitation and moderation

makes men contented with their lot while stimulating them moderately to improve it; and it is this average contentment which gives rise to that sentiment of calm and active happiness, that pleasure in existing and living which characterizes health for societies as well as for individuals. Everyone, at least in general, is then in harmony with his condition and only desires what he can legitimately expect as the normal reward for his activity . . . loving what he has, rather than applying all his passion to seeking what he lacks, new satisfactions to which he may aspire can fall short of his desires and expectations without leaving him totally destitute. He retains what is essential. The equilibrium of his happiness is stable because it is defined and a few disappointments are not enough to destroy it.[31]

Durkheim's theory of suicide therefore amounts to this: that under adverse social conditions, when men's social context fails to provide them with the requisite sources of attachment and/or regulation, at the appropriate level of intensity, then their psychological or moral health is impaired, and a certain number of vulnerable, suicide-prone individuals respond by committing suicide. There are, needless to say, a number of difficulties with this theory.

(i) In the first place, Durkheim's characterization of the adverse social conditions is problematic. He saw them entirely in terms of the relative absence or excessive influence of social goals and rules; he never saw the importance in this context of discriminating between different types of goals and of rules. He never clearly conceived of the possibility that there might be socially given goals that are non-integrative, and social rules or norms that do not lead, in general, to social harmony and individual contentment (though he did, of course, also argue that modern industrial societies 'normally' require a particular set of goals and rules). Hence his basic view of

30. Cf. the third element of morality: see Chapter 6, above.
31. 1897a, p. 277: tr. p. 250 (S.L.).

egoism and anomie as signifying the relative *absence* of social goals and social regulation. It is true that he also saw egoism and anomie as themselves products of modern forms of society and modern belief systems (protestantism, *laissez-faire*, etc.); thus the ideology of individualism (a social product) is 'not necessarily egoism, but it comes close to it',[32] and 'every morality of progress and perfection is ... inseparable from a certain amount of anomie'.[33] But he never conceptualized egoism and anomie as themselves consisting in socially-given goals and norms. This is clearest in the case of anomie. He failed to realize that anomie can itself be seen as a norm, culturally prescribed and accepted, rather than 'a state of normlessness. His model of the operation of norms was that of external and constraining rules curbing the individual's limitless (organico-psychic) desires. He did not picture these desires as themselves resulting from social or cultural influences, or envisage that there could be internally-accepted norms, to which men willingly conform, with results that are socially anarchic and psychologically harmful.

(ii) Secondly, there is the difficulty of identifying psychological or moral health. What are its distinguishing features? And, most importantly, are they culturally variable? If they *are*, then, of course, the theory becomes more complex, since what is to count as psychological disequilibrium will itself have to be determined for each given society. (How?) Durkheim does not provide answers to these questions. Presumably, to be truly Durkheimian, he should have argued that what counts as psychological or moral health is socially-determined and therefore variable. On the other hand, his statements on this issue are framed in completely general terms (and indeed his account of altruistic suicide implies that the need for a degree of personal autonomy exists even in pre-modern, pre-individualist societies – which seems to contradict the theory of mechanical solidarity). He appears, in short, to have ignored the difficulties in postulating a non-relative standard of psychological health, while failing to explore those of postulating a relative standard.

32. ibid., p. 416: tr. p. 364.
33. ibid., p. 417: tr. p. 364 (S.L.).

(iii) Thirdly, his account of why certain individuals are suicide-prone is indecisive. On the one hand he suggests that they are random: on this view, randomly given organico-psychic features of individuals render a certain proportion of them vulnerable when a suicidogenic current of a certain strength 'insinuates itself' into them at their 'weak points'.[34] On the other hand, he argues that

the causes determining the social currents act simultaneously on individuals and predispose them to submit to the collective influence. There is a natural affinity between these two orders of factors, for the very reason that they depend on a single cause and express it: that is why they combine and are adapted to one another. The hypercivilization giving rise to the anomic tendency and to the egoistic tendency also has the effect of rendering men's nervous systems sensitive and excessively delicate . . . for this very reason they are more susceptible to violent irritation and exaggerated depression.[35]

But this is precisely to admit that 'psychological' states of the individual are at least in part subject to social influences – that, say, certain social environments are more conducive to neuroses than others. Durkheim never pursued this insight. He did not see the implication that taking it seriously would have for his theory of suicide – namely, the need to supplement it with a social-psychological theory of suicide-proneness. More generally, Durkheim did not see the wider implications of this insight for his own thought as a whole, pushing back the boundary between the 'organico-psychic' and the 'social'.[36]

(iv) A fourth difficulty lies in the very connection postulated between psychological malaise or disequilibrium and suicide. Two questions arise here. First, why should psychological disequilibrium lead to *suicide*? And second, why assume that suicide is always or usually the result of psychological disequilibrium?

Durkheim reasoned that suicide is the ultimate, most extreme response to socially-induced psychological disequilibrium.

34. ibid., p. 147: tr. p. 151 (S.L.).
35. ibid., pp. 365–6: tr. p. 323 (S.L.).
36. For Mauss's development of this theme, see Mauss, 1924; cf. Lévi-Strauss, 1950 (1966), pp. xv ff.

But psychological disequilibrium (assuming it could be identified) could be shown to have other consequences, and these may themselves be explicable sociologically. Suicide may be shown to be a response arising out of certain social contexts and not others: explaining individuals' resort to that response will involve, among other things, investigating the meaning of suicide to them and to others by whom they are influenced or whom, perhaps, they hope to influence (and this will further involve looking, for instance, at their beliefs about death). Conversely, Durkheim's assumption that suicide results from psychological disequilibrium may be questionable on the grounds that it or types of it result from other causes and are explicable in other ways – in particular that it may be an entirely rational response to certain situations.

(v) Finally, the most fundamental (and most fruitful) criticism of Durkheim's theory of suicide is that it is incomplete. This can be shown most clearly by drawing two distinctions. First, in seeking to identify factors explanatory of suicide one can distinguish between those that are external (or objective) and those that are internal (or subjective) to those that commit it. Thus among the external factors facing suicidal individuals are the nature and strength of the sources of attachment and regulation in their social environment and the particular circumstances in which they find themselves. Among internal, or subjective, factors are their perception of, or attitudes towards, the goals and norms of their society, their definition or perception of their particular circumstances, and the interpretation they give to the suicidal act. The second distinction to be drawn is that between factors that are general throughout a given society and those that are relatively personal or specific to a given individual or individuals.[37]

Now, in conformity with his general methodological principles, Durkheim thought it necessary to confine sociological explanation to the external and the general. His picture was one of social (external and general) social causes producing a certain number of extreme individual responses. But here his radical dichotomy between social and individual factors

37. These distinctions may be represented graphically as shown opposite:

(reinforced by his purportedly 'scientific' vocabulary) badly misled him.[38] It led him to ignore what he conceptualized as 'individual' factors – namely, both particular circumstances and internal or subjective factors ('motives and ideas'). This was unfortunate for two reasons.

In the first place, it is incoherent to claim that particular circumstances and 'motives and ideas' are irrelevant to the explanation of suicide (or indeed of any human action). For these cannot be simply abstracted from actions as though they were merely contingently related to them. Indeed, the actions cannot even be identified independently of them. In general, suicide precisely *is* a motivated act arising out of, and perhaps intended to affect, a particular situation. To put it baldly, explaining suicide – and explaining suicide rates – must involve explaining why people commit it.

	External to suicidal individuals		*Internal to suicidal individuals*	
General	Durkheim's social causes of suicide	*State of goals and norms* Inadequate regulation (anomie) Inadequate integration (egoism) Excessive integration (altruism) Excessive regulation (fatalism)	Perception of attitudes towards	social norms and goals
Personal or Specific		Particular circumstances	Definition of Perception of	particular circumstances
			Interpretation of suicidal act	

38. Cf. the Introduction to the present work.

In the second place, Durkheim failed to see that both particular (objective) circumstances and men's subjective perceptions, beliefs, attitudes and motives are all eminently amenable to sociological inquiry and explanation. As Halbwachs put it, 'circumstances and motives are certainly related to the organization of society'; indeed he saw himself as going 'further than Durkheim along the path he was himself pursuing, since we would explain by social causes not only the great forces which avert suicide, but even the particular events that serve, not as pretexts, but as motives for suicide'.[39] Again, how men perceive and interpret the prevalent goals and norms of their society is of crucial importance to any fully articulated sociological theory of suicide, as are their definitions of their particular situations, and their conceptions of the meaning of suicide itself.[40] Nonetheless, Durkheim's theory, with its isolation of the external and general social preconditions for suicide – despite its difficulties and obscurities – represented a major advance in suicide studies, which still dominates the field and the implications of which have still to be fully explored.

We have argued that *Suicide* advances a theory concerning the social conditions for psychological health; but it also advances a theory of social health, and to this we may finally and briefly turn.

DIAGNOSIS AND REMEDY

Claiming that what 'is morbid for individuals may be normal for society',[41] Durkheim argued that a certain rate of suicide (as of crime) can be considered normal for any given social type. Thus where the individual is subordinated to the group, a certain rate of altruistic suicide is inevitable; where the morality of individualism exists, there will be some egoistic suicides[42]; and some anomic suicides are bound to accompany

39. Halbwachs, 1930, pp. 13, 513.
40. Cf. Douglas, 1966 and 1967.
41. 1897a, p. 418 fn.: tr. p. 365 fn.
42. 'Individualism, of course, is not necessarily egoism, but it comes close to it; the one cannot be stimulated without the other being increased' (ibid., p. 416: tr. p. 364 – S.L.).

social change and economic progress.[43] Durkheim's grounds for asserting this were that

In every society there are particular environments into which collective states only penetrate by being modified; they are, in different cases, either reinforced or weakened. In order that a current should have a certain intensity throughout the country, it must therefore exceed or fall short of it at certain points.[44]

And he further argued that such environmental variations are functional for the whole society, preserving forms of activity that can be useful to it (such as 'a relentless spirit of criticism and free inquiry' in intellectual circles, or 'the old religion of authority' in the army[45]): they enable it to adapt to different situations and are important factors in its development.

· He concluded that 'the spirit of renunciation, the passion for progress and the desire for individuation have their place in every kind of society, and ... cannot exist without generating suicides at certain points', but he held that 'it is necessary that they only do so to a certain extent, varying according to different societies'.[46] Not surprisingly (though with flimsy evidence and poor arguments) he maintained that the suicide rates of contemporary European societies were abnormally high, arguing that 'the enormous increase in the number of voluntary deaths during the last century' must be regarded as 'a pathological phenomenon which becomes more menacing every day'.[47]

In citing evidence for this 'enormous increase', he failed to allow for the increase in population.[48] But even granting the

43. 'Every morality of progress and of perfection is ... inseparable from a certain degree of anomie' (ibid., p. 417: tr. p. 364 – S.L.).

44. ibid. (S.L.).   45. ibid., p. 418: tr. p. 365 (S.L.).

46. ibid., p. 420: tr. p. 366 (S.L.).   47. ibid., p. 424: tr. p. 370 (S.L.).

48. This could just have been a slip, since Durkheim's whole argument is elsewhere couched in terms of suicide *rates*. On the other hand, I am grateful to Andrew Scull for pointing out to me a source of possible error connected with the rise of population, which even the use of gross rates per 100,000 would fail to correct for. This derives from the fact that all forms of deviance (including suicide) are *age-specific* (as Durkheim himself shows with respect to suicide). We know that the increase in population during the nineteenth century led to changes in the age-distribution – much of this change resulting from increased average life-expectancy. As *Suicide* shows, the rate of suicide increases directly with

plausible assumption of a considerable increase during the nineteenth century, his 'proofs' that it should be seen as a pathological phenomenon are far from overwhelming. He compared nineteenth-century Europe with Rome at the height of the Empire when, he claimed, there occurred 'a veritable hecatomb of voluntary deaths',[49] but, as Bayet remarked,[50] there is no evidence whatever for such an assertion (nor, indeed, for his claim that subsequent Christian societies until the eighteenth century had low suicide rates). No more convincing is his argument (a typical instance of *petitio principii*) that the vast and rapid social changes of the nineteenth century must be 'morbid; for a society cannot change its structure so suddenly' and that 'the changes underlying contemporary suicide statistics cannot therefore be normal' but

result, not from a regular evolution, but from an unhealthy disturbance which has succeeded in uprooting the institutions of the past but put nothing in their place; for the achievement of centuries cannot be rebuilt in a few years. Yet, if the cause is abnormal, the effect cannot fail to be so too.[51]

Again, his citing of anarchism, aestheticism, mysticism and revolutionary socialism as evidence of an abnormal 'sense of hatred or disgust for what exists' and 'need to destroy reality or escape it'[52] was no more conclusive. Finally, his argument that contemporary suicide rates were abnormal suffered from the same defect as his presentation of the 'abnormal forms' of the division of labour: it implied that all existing industrial societies were abnormal and deviated from some future, ideal state of 'normality'. As Halbwachs wrote, noting the relatively high suicide rates found in all advanced societies and all advanced sectors within societies:

---

age. Hence reliance on suicide rates of the general population uncorrected for the bias caused by that changing age-composition is likely to prove misleading. In addition to this, there is also the more obvious point, stressed by Douglas, that record-keeping practices markedly improved during this period, so that actual suicides were almost certainly rising more slowly than reported suicides.

49. ibid., p. 421: tr. p. 367.   50. Bayet, 1922, p. 290.
51. 1897a, p. 423: tr. p. 369 (S.L.).   52. ibid., p. 424: tr. p. 370 S.L.).

When the same phenomenon is found, not only in a great number of societies, but even within each of them for . . . a prolonged time period, one can say that it is general both in space and in time. Are all European societies unhealthy? Can a single society remain in a pathological state for three-quarters of a century?[53]

Durkheim's diagnosis of the 'state of crisis and perturbation'[54] he saw was to trace it to the sources of 'the chief suicidogenic currents', egoism and anomie (altruism having 'no role in the current growth of suicides'[55]). These were, in his view, the growing points of social dissolution in modern societies. Neither repressive legislation, nor education, nor the revival of political loyalties or religion or the role of the family were effective or feasible solutions. The only practicable remedies, he maintained, were to organize economic life around occupational groups, which would 'tighten and strengthen' the 'social fabric',[56] providing individuals with centres of attachment and regulation; and to make the conjugal family more indissoluble, while enhancing the status of women, so as to increase the moral benefits they derived from marriage. The proposed remedies followed from the diagnosis, and the diagnosis from his interpretation of the data.

53. Halbwachs, 1930, p. 484.
54. 1897a, p. 423: tr. p. 369.
55. ibid., p. 428: tr. p. 373 (S.L.).
56. ibid., p. 438: tr. p. 381.

Chapter 10

The Method and Subject-Matter of Sociology

IF Durkheim saw *Suicide* as the best kind of proof of sociology's distinctive, even exclusive, power to explain, he still felt the need to provide arguments to defend this claim and to support his own view of what the explanations should look like. He felt this need for a number of reasons. First, there was the rationalist, and indeed philosophical, tendency in his own intellectual temperament: if something was to be proved, it could and should be argued for; and the argument should systematically explore the presuppositions and implications of the position adopted – that is, it should be philosophical. Secondly, he had a strong desire to persuade the hostile and the sceptical (whose reactions we will consider below[1]); he was not content to pursue his own path independent of the views of others, since he was ready to see such views, where they were resistant to the claims of social science, as irresponsible and sometimes dangerous. He always had the sense of living through a period of social crisis, and he saw the enemies of social science as real obstacles to its alleviation. Thirdly, he wished to found a school: a body of scholars engaged in co-operative research, who would engage in specialist studies in a way that would ultimately transform all the specialized social sciences into the systematically organized branches of a unified social science. For this purpose, one needed a programmatic set of principles providing guidelines for future research. Accordingly, *The Rules of Sociological Method* was at once a treatise in the philosophy of social science, a polemic and a manifesto.[2]

1. In Chapter 16, below.
2. 1894a, repr. as 1895a; 2nd edn 1901c: tr. 1938b. Among the numerous discussions of this book, and of Durkheim's methodology generally, see Mauss and Fauconnet, 1901, Bayet, 1907, Davy, 1911a, Deploige, 1911, Gehlke, 1915, Bureau, 1923, Bouglé, 1924, Lacombe,

The arguments advanced in *The Rules* partly concern the method and partly the subject-matter of sociology, and Durkheim obviously thought of the method he proposed as 'adapted to the particular nature of social phenomena'.[3] Yet, though he saw all his rules of method as dependent on 'our fundamental principle: the objective reality of social facts' (for 'in the end, it is on this principle that all else is based, and everything comes back to it'[4]), it was precisely in its treatment of the nature of social phenomena that *The Rules* was least probing and decisive. The reason for this is that, written between *The Division of Labour* and the first lecture-course on religion, it marked a transitional point in Durkheim's intellectual development. He had formulated the basic problem of his sociology: the nature of social solidarity. He had determined his central theoretical interest: the social role and historical development of morality, in its widest sense. He had focused on a range of empirical concerns: changes in social structure and the corresponding changes in institutions, practices and beliefs. He had developed a method: asking functional questions within a broadly evolutionary framework. The step yet to be taken was one that was implicit in what had gone before, and indeed in *The Rules* itself, but was only to become fully explicit in 1898: namely, the analytical separation of socially given ideas, concepts, values and beliefs – or 'collective *représentations*' – as a crucial and relatively independent set of explanatory variables.

In *The Rules* Durkheim formulated procedures to be followed in the collection and interpretation of evidence, in the construction of explanatory hypotheses and in their validation. These procedures – for the elimination of bias, the construction of initial definitions and the choice of indicators; for the specification of normality relative to social type, the construction of a typology of societies and the identification of social

---

1925 and 1926 (which contains an especially rewarding discussion), Essertier, 1927b, Parsons, 1937 (ch. IX) and 1960, Gurvitch, 1938, Alpert, 1939a, b and c, Benoît-Smullyan, 1948, Gisbert, 1959, and Aimard, 1962. See also the Introduction to the present work.

3. 1901c, p. 3: tr. 1938b, p. lx (S.L.).
4. ibid., p. xxiii: tr. p. lvii (S.L.).

causes and functions; and for the use of the comparative method, in particular that of concomitant variation, whether within a single society, within different societies of a single type or across different types – all these, in Durkheim's view, presupposed the specificity of the 'social' element in social phenomena. Indeed – and here the polemical nature of the argument influenced its content – Durkheim took the specificity of the social to entail the exclusiveness of sociology, and the irrelevance of psychology.[5] Very many of his critics, both contemporary and posthumous, have regarded this exclusion of psychology as his major theoretical failing; and it certainly led him to rely all too often upon unexamined psychological assumptions.[6] Yet it could equally well be argued that it sprang from a sound instinct, since it enabled him to concentrate on a level of explanation hitherto virtually unexploited.

The position of *The Rules* concerning the nature of social phenomena was indecisive in at least two respects. In the first place, their supposedly identifying characteristics of 'exteriority' and 'constraint' were, as we have seen, highly ambiguous.[7] In the second place, the argument of *The Rules* was noticeably inconclusive concerning explanatory priorities. If social phenomena ranged from the most 'crystallized', or morphological, phenomena of social structure through laws to moral maxims and thence to 'currents of opinion' (those 'free currents of social life which have not yet taken any definite form'[8]), where were sociological explanations in general to stop? At first sight, Durkheim seemed to give a clear answer: 'the facts of social morphology . . . play a preponderant role in collective life and, in consequence, in sociological explanations . . . The first origin of every social process of any importance must be sought in the constitution

5. See Introduction, above.

6. For example, in *Suicide* and *The Elementary Forms* (cf. regarding the latter, Lévi-Strauss, 1962a (1964), pp. 70–1).

7. In the Introduction, above. Cf. Lacombe, 1926, for an excellent discussion of these ambiguities, especially pp. 28 ff. For a passage in which the meaning of 'constraint' perceptibly changes, see 1901c, pp. 6–7: tr. 1938b, pp. 2–3.

8. 1901c, pp. 18, 19: tr. 1938b, pp. 11, 12 (S.L.).

of the internal social environment'.[9] In particular, Durkheim alluded to his own explanation, in *The Division of Labour*, in terms of 'the number of social units or, as we have also called it, the volume of society, and the degree of concentration of the mass, or what we have called dynamic density'.[10] While disclaiming 'having found all the features of the social environment which are able to play a role in the explanation of social facts', he remarked that 'these are the only ones we have discerned and we have not been led to seek others'.[11]

He hastened to add that this explanatory priority did not imply that one should see the social environment as 'a sort of ultimate and absolute fact beyond which one cannot go'[12]: it should rather be seen as primary simply because

it is general enough to explain a great number of other facts ... the changes which occur within it, whatever their causes, have repercussions in all directions throughout the social organism and cannot fail to affect in some degree all its functions.[13]

Yet, even on this qualified interpretation, it is not at all clear that Durkheim could justifiably claim to have identified a set of social facts with explanatory priority. For, earlier in the same book, he had argued that morphological phenomena were 'of the same nature'[14] as other social facts, that the political divisions of a society were essentially 'moral', that a society's organization was determined by 'public law' and that if 'the population crowds into our towns instead of dispersing into the countryside, it is because there is a current of opinion, a collective pressure which imposes this concentration on individuals'.[15]

Thus *The Rules* stood at a point of transition. Previously to it, Durkheim had been tempted in the direction of singling out a subset of social facts, characteristic of the structure or 'milieu' of a given society, as basic. Although, since his return from Germany, he had never explicitly *excluded* ideas

9. ibid., pp. 137–8: tr. pp. 112–13 (S.L.).
10. ibid., p. 139: tr. p. 113 (S.L.).
11. ibid., p. 141: tr. p. 115 (S.L.).
12. ibid., p. 142: tr. p. 116 (S.L.).
13. ibid. (S.L.).
14. ibid., p. 19: tr. p. 13.
15. ibid., pp. 17–18: tr. p. 11 (S.L.).

and beliefs from that subset,[16] he nevertheless tended to consider them as, in a broad sense, derivative and without any major independent explanatory significance. After *The Rules* he was to give them greater and greater significance – so that by 1914 he was writing of the 'ideas and sentiments that are elaborated by a collectivity' as having 'an ascendancy and an authority that cause the particular individuals who think them and believe in them to represent them in the form of moral forces that dominate them and sustain them', and of 'states of consciousness' which 'come to us from society, . . . transfer society into us and connect us with something that surpasses us'.[17]

Here was a remarkable development, the principal stages of which may briefly be noted. *The Rules* already marked an advance from *The Division of Labour* with respect to 'material' and 'moral' density: *The Division of Labour* had represented the former as an exact expression of the latter, whereas *The Rules* made it clear that the latter was defined 'as a function of the number of individuals who are effectively related not merely commercially but morally; that is, who not only exchange services and engage in competition, but live a common life'.[18] Again, in *The Division of Labour* Durkheim had written, in criticism of Fustel de Coulanges, that 'it is [social arrangements] that explain the power and nature of the religious idea', arguing that Fustel had 'mistaken the cause for the effect'[19];

16. See Chapter 4, above.

17. 1914a: tr. 1960c, pp. 335, 337.

18. 1901c, p. 139: tr. 1938b, p. 114 (S.L.). (See especially the footnote to p. 140: tr. p. 115.)

19. '. . . M. Fustel de Coulanges has discovered that the primitive organization of societies was of a familial nature and that, on the other hand, the constitution of the primitive family had religion for its basis. However, he has mistaken the cause for the effect. Having postulated the religious idea, without deriving it from anything, he has deduced from it the social arrangements he observed, while, on the contrary, it is these latter that explain the power and nature of the religious idea' (1902b, p. 154: tr. 1933b, p. 179 – S.L.). Fustel's *La Cité antique* concludes with the words: 'We have written the history of a belief. It was established and human society was constituted. It was modified, and society underwent a series of revolutions. It disappeared and society changed its character. Such was the law of ancient times' (*The Ancient City*, p. 396).

subsequently he was to adopt a less unilateral view. In *Suicide* he was already maintaining that 'essentially social life is made up of *représentations*',[20] yet he was also still arguing that

> a people's mental system is a system of definite mental forces ... [which] is related to the way in which the social elements are grouped and organized. Given a people, consisting of a certain number of individuals arranged in a certain way, there results a determinate set of collective ideas and practices, that remain constant so long as the conditions on which they depend are themselves unchanged. In fact, according to whether the parts composing it are more or less numerous and structured in this or that way, the nature of collective life (*l'être collectif*) necessarily varies and, in consequence, so do its ways of thinking and acting; but these latter cannot be changed without its changing, and it cannot be changed without its anatomical constitution being modified.[21]

In the same year that *Suicide* was published, in a review of a Marxist work on historical materialism, Durkheim expressed himself as follows:

> We regard as fruitful this idea that social life must be explained, not by the conception of it held by those who participate in it, but by profound causes which escape consciousness; and we also think that these causes must be sought chiefly in the way in which the associated individuals are grouped. We even think that it is on this condition, and on this condition alone, that history can become a science and sociology in consequence exist. For, in order that collective *représentations* should be intelligible, they must come from something and, since they cannot form a circle closed upon itself, the source whence they derive must be found outside them. Either the *conscience collective* floats in the void, like a sort of inconceivable absolute, or it is connected with the rest of the world through the intermediary of a substratum on which, in consequence, it depends. On the other hand, of what can this substratum be composed if not of the members of society as they are socially combined?[22]

He distinguished this position from economic materialism ('we reached it before knowing Marx, by whom we have in no

20. 1897a, p. 352: tr. 1951a, p. 312.
21. ibid., p. 446: tr. p. 387 (S.L.).
22. 1897e, p. 648. For a discussion of this passage, see Winch, P., *The Idea of a Social Science* (London, 1958), pp. 23 ff.

way been influenced'[23]). Historians and psychologists had long
been aware that one had to look elsewhere for explanations
than to ideas held by individuals, and it was natural to extend
this to collective ideas, but he could not see 'what part the
sad conflict of classes that we are currently witnessing can have
had in the elaboration or development of this idea' and he
denied that the causes of social phenomena 'come back, in the
last analysis, to the state of industrial technique and that the
economic factor is the motive-force of progress'.[24] Economic
materialism pretended to be the key to history, but it had not
begun to be systematically verified; quite the contrary:

> Sociologists and historians tend more and more to agree in the
> common view that religion is the most primitive of all social
> phenomena. It was the source, through successive transformations,
> of all other manifestations of collective activity: law, morality, art,
> science, political forms, etc. In the beginning, all is religious.[25]

Indeed, so far was anyone from showing how religion could
be reduced to economic causes, that it seemed altogether more
likely that the latter depended on religion. However, he
added, this anti-Marxist case should not be pushed too far:
if the 'different forms of collective activity' derived in the last
instance from their 'substratum', they then became 'in their
turn, original sources of influence', with 'an efficacity of their
own', and they 'react upon the very causes on which they
depend'.[26] Thus the economic factor was far from an epiphenomenon: it had 'an influence that is special to it; it can
partially modify the very substratum from which it results'.
Nonetheless, everything led one to the view that it was
'secondary and derivative'.[27]

23. ibid., p. 649.
24. ibid.
25. ibid., p. 650.
26. ibid., p. 651.
27. ibid. This review is the only place in which Durkheim explicitly
states his theoretical position *vis-à-vis* Marxism (but see also 1902f.). Cf.
Engels' letter to Bloch: 'The economic situation is the basis, but the
various elements of the superstructure ... also exercise their influence
upon the course of the historical struggles and in many cases preponderate
in determining their *form*' (Marx and Engels, *Selected Works*, Moscow,
1962, vol. ii, p. 488).

This new view of the preponderance of religion, and of the partial autonomy of the 'different forms of collective activity' relative to their 'substratum' formed the basis for the subsequent development of his thought – with an ever-growing explanatory role for religion and an ever-growing autonomy for the 'collective *représentations*'. As we have seen, he claimed in *Suicide* that 'essentially social life is made up of *représentations*', adding that 'these collective *représentations* are of quite another character from those of the individual',[28] and illustrating the point by reference to religion – 'Religion is, in a word, the system of symbols by means of which society becomes conscious of itself; it is the way of thinking characteristic of collective existence'.[29] The point was taken up and systematically argued for the following year in the article on 'Individual and Collective *Représentations*'.[30] Here Durkheim sought to demonstrate the relative autonomy of the latter *vis-à-vis* their social substratum (relying on a parallel though shaky argument concerning the relative autonomy of mental phenomena *vis-à-vis* the brain).[31] Thus, though initially dependent on 'the number of social elements, the way in which they are grouped and distributed, etc.', collective *représentations* became 'partially autonomous realities which live their own life'.[32] They had 'the power to attract and repel each other and to form amongst themselves various syntheses, which are determined by their natural affinities, and not by the state of the environment in the midst of which they evolve': *représentations* were caused by others, and not by 'this or that characteristic of the social structure'.[33] The evolution of

28. 1897a, p. 352: tr. 1951a, p. 312.

29. ibid. (S.L.).

30. 1898b: repr. 1924a: tr. 1953b.

31. He also used (from about this period onwards) a number of arguments by analogy to support this position, especially the argument from the origin of life (existing in the cell, but not in its component elements – see, for example, 1901c, p. xv: tr. 1938b, pp. xlvii; 1925a, p. 303: tr. 1961a, p. 264) and the argument from chemical synthesis (for example 1901c, p. xvi: tr. 1938b, p. xlviii; 1900b, p. 649). This all went back to Boutroux's conception of different levels of nature. See the Introduction above.

32. 1924a (1951 edn), p. 43: tr. 1953b, p. 31.

33. ibid.

religion, he observed, gave 'the most striking examples of this phenomenon':

It is perhaps impossible to understand how the Greek or Roman Pantheon came into existence unless we go into the constitution of the city, the way in which the primitive clans slowly merged, the organization of the patriarchal family, etc. Nevertheless the luxuriant growth of myths and legends, theogonic and cosmological systems, etc., which grow out of religious thought, is not directly related to the particular features of the social structure.[34]

The article ended by asserting the 'hyper-spirituality' of social life – so that 'collective psychology is the whole of sociology'.[35]

34. ibid. (S.L.). Greek mythology posed a problem for Marx, and it is interesting to note that he treated it, in the *Grundrisse*, in a way that is closer to Durkheim's (and Fustel de Coulanges') account than to the stricter, and cruder, versions of historical materialism: 'It is a well-known fact that Greek mythology was not only the arsenal of Greek art, but also the very ground from which it had sprung. Is the view of nature and of social relations which shaped Greek imagination and Greek [art] possible in the age of automatic machinery, and railways, and locomotives, and electric telegraphs? ... All mythology masters and dominates and shapes the forces of nature in and through the imagination; hence it disappears as soon as man gains mastery over the forces of nature ... Greek art presupposes the existence of Greek mythology, i.e. that nature and even the form of society are wrought up in popular fancy in an unconsciously artistic fashion' (Marx, *Introduction to the Critique of Political Economy* (1857) in *A Contribution to the Critique of Political Economy*, tr. Stone, N. I., Chicago, 1913, pp. 310–11). See the discussion of this passage in Kamenka, E., *The Ethical Foundations of Marxism* (London, 1962), pp. 135 ff. Kamenka rightly observes that Marx's view here is that the 'existence of Greek social organization ... [is] *necessary* for Greek art and mythology, but *not sufficient*' (p. 135).

35. ibid., p. 47: tr. p. 34 (S.L.). Cf. 1898a (ii), p. 69: tr. 1963a, p. 114 (S.L.): 'One cannot repeat too often that everything which is social consists of *représentations*, and therefore is a product of *représentations*.' At this same period Durkhiem was writing to Bouglé that he had 'never dreamt of saying that one could do sociology without any psychological background, or that sociology is anything other than a form of psychology; but merely that collective psychology cannot be deduced directly from individual psychology, because a new factor has intervened which has transformed the psychic material, a factor which is the source of all that is different and new, namely association. A phenomenon of individual psychology has an individual *conscience* for its substratum, a phenomenon of collective psychology a group of individual *consciences*' (letter undated).

And we may note that, by 1899, his view of the relative explanatory position of social morphology had changed accordingly from a primary, determining cause to something more like a precondition: 'the constitution of [the] substratum affects, directly or indirectly all social phenomena, just as all psychological phenomena are, directly or indirectly, connected to the state of the brain'.[36]

The rest of Durkheim's career consisted of pursuing the implications of this new position, notably in the study of primitive classification and *The Elementary Forms of the Religious Life*. His methodological writings on the way echoed this preoccupation – in particular, the preface to the second edition of *The Rules*[37] (stressing the 'representational' aspect of sociology's subject-matter), the essay on 'Value Judgements and Judgements of Reality' ('The principal social phenomena, religion, morality, law, economics and aesthetics, are nothing more than systems of values and hence of ideals. Sociology moves from the beginning in the field of ideals. The ideal is in fact its peculiar field of study ... It ... accepts them as given facts, as objects of study, and it tries to analyse and explain them'[38]) and the essay on 'The Dualism of Human Nature' (in which the individual is pictured as split between two conflicting 'states of consciousness': 'the sensations and sensual appetites, on the one hand, and the intellectual and moral life, on the other' – the latter being 'social and nothing but an extension of society'[39]). From the initial position in *The Division of Labour*, where he had been tempted to write that 'everything occurs mechanically',[40] Durkheim had by the time of his latest writings come very close to maintaining that symbolic thought is a condition of and explains society.[41] In place of the

36. 1899a (iii), p. 520.
37. 1901b.
38. 1911b: repr. 1924a (1951 edn), pp. 140–1: tr. 1953b, p. 96.
39. 1914a: tr. 1960c, pp. 338, 337.
40. 1902b, p. 253: tr. 1933b, p. 270.
41. Cf. Lévi-Strauss, 1945, p. 518: 'Society cannot exist without symbolism, but instead of showing how the appearance of symbolic thought makes social life altogether possible and necessary, Durkheim tries the reverse, i.e. to make symbolism grow out of society.' I think that Durkheim in fact did both. M. Lévi-Strauss apparently now also takes

original concentration upon structural determinants, he could write that a 'society cannot be constituted without creating ideals. These ideals are simply the ideas in terms of which a society sees itself . . . To see society only as an organized body of vital functions is to diminish it, for this body has a soul (*âme*) which is the composition of collective ideals.[42] Yet, throughout this development, and despite this major change in emphasis, he always remained alive to the interaction between social structure and consciousness.

---

this view. He has recently written that Durkheim ('at his best') admitted that 'all social life, even elementary, presupposes an intellectual activity in man of which the formal properties, consequently, cannot be a reflection of the concrete organisation of the society' (Lévi-Strauss, 1962a (1964), p. 96). He notes that the theme of *The Elementary Forms*, together with the preface to the second edition of *The Rules* and the essay on *Primitive Classification*, 'shows the contradiction inherent in the contrary view, which is only too often adopted by Durkheim when he affirms the primacy of the social over the intellect'. In short, Durkheim's thought was 'torn between two contradictory claims' (p. 97).

42. 1911b: repr. 1924a (1951 edn), pp. 135–6; tr. 1953b, p. 93. Durkheim used 'ideals' in a very wide sense, including 'concepts' as a sub-class (this is the gist of 1911b): in the case of judgements of reality, 'the ideal is a symbol of the thing so as to render it assimilable to thought'; in the case of value-judgements, 'the thing is a symbol for the ideal, representing it to different minds' (ibid., p. 140: tr. pp. 95–6 – S.L.). In 1912 he wrote to Bouglé that *The Elementary Forms* showed that sociology had 'the ideal for its domain'; and he concluded that 'Ultimately this is what is essential in sociology' (letter dated 13 October, 1912).

Chapter 11

The Sociology of Religion – I

DURKHEIM recognized the importance in his intellectual development of the 1894–5 lecture-course on religion:

it was not until 1895 that I achieved a clear view of the essential role played by religion in social life. It was in that year that, for the first time, I found the means of tackling the study of religion sociologically. This was a revelation to me. That course of 1895 marked a dividing line in the development of my thought, to such an extent that all my previous researches had to be taken up afresh in order to be made to harmonize with these new insights... [This re-orientation] was entirely due to the studies of religious history which I had just undertaken, and notably to the reading of the works of Robertson Smith and his school.[1]

And this is corroborated by another of his rare autobiographical passages (written in rebuttal of Deploige's 'accusation' that his thought was essentially German in inspiration):

1. 1907b; repr. in Deploige, 1911, pp. 402–3. These studies made him see old problems in a new light: 'Religion contains in itself from the very beginning, even in an indistinct state, all the elements which in dissociating themselves from it, articulating themselves, and combining with one another in a thousand ways, have given rise to the various manifestations of collective life. From myths and legends have issued forth science and poetry; from religious ornamentations and cult ceremonials have come the plastic arts; from ritual practice was born law and morals. One cannot understand our perception of the world, our philosophical conceptions of the soul, of immortality, of life, if one does not know the religious beliefs which are their primordial forms. Kinship started out as an essentially religious tie; punishment, contract, gift and homage are transformations of expiatory, contractual, communal, honorary sacrifices and so on. At most one may ask whether economic organization is an exception and derives from another source; although we do not think so, we grant that the question must be kept in abeyance. At any rate, a great number of problems change their aspects completely as soon as their connections with the sociology of religion are recognized' (1899a (i) pp. iv–v: tr. 1960c, pp. 350–51).

it is known what a preponderant place the study of religious phenomena has taken in our researches. Now, the science of religions is essentially English and American: not at all German. It is to give a systematically mutilated 'genesis' of our thought to neglect all that we owe to Robertson Smith and to the works of the ethnographers of England and America.[2]

I have not been able to discover any extant account of the 1894–5 course, but one may suppose that it included a discussion of Robertson Smith's theory of the clan cult of totemism as the earliest and most elementary form of religion, necessarily linked to societies with the simplest form of social structure, the clan segmentary system. Smith's theory (which was influenced by Fustel de Coulanges' *La Cité antique*, via Smith's friend J. F. McLennan) presented religion as a social phenomenon, maintaining the values of the group and consisting in the idealization, indeed divinization of the clan, which was seen as composed of men, animals and gods bound together by ties of blood and was symbolized by the totem. Hence the communion meal as the most ancient form of sacrifice which renewed this bond; from it there developed property rights, the idea of taboo and further forms of sacrifice. That this theory must have been a considerable revelation to Durkheim can be judged from the thinness and inconclusiveness of his previous observations on religion. In 1886 he had written of religion as having, together with law and morality, the role of assuring the equilibrium of society and adapting it to external conditions and of its being a 'form of social discipline', merely a form of custom; he also saw the idea of divinity as serving to 'symbolize traditions, cultures, collective needs' and argued that the sociologist must look at 'what the symbol conceals and translates'.[3] By 1887 he was writing of religion as springing from the sentiment 'attaching the individual to the whole social being', still emphasizing its essentially moral character, and calling the primitive gods social rather than personal.[4] In 1893, in *The Division of Labour*, there

2. 1913(a) (ii)(15), p. 326. On Robertson Smith, see 1912a, pp. 126–7: tr. 1915d, pp. 89–90.

3. 1886a, pp. 68, 66.

4. 1887b, pp. 309–11.

was a general identification of repressive law and religious law in primitive societies ('offences against the gods are offences against society'[5]) and of primitive religion and mechanical solidarity ('religious *consciences* are identical there . . .'[6]), and there was also an inconclusive and un-pursued definition of religion in terms of the high intensity of shared sentiments producing a sort of 'reverential respect' for certain beliefs and rules.[7] It can easily be seen that with these half-formulated ideas, together with the notion that religion was best studied in its 'primitive' forms, for 'religion tends to embrace a smaller and smaller portion of social life' whereas 'Originally, it pervaded everything',[8] he was likely to be deeply impressed by Robertson Smith's sociological theory of the religion of the Semitic societies of ancient Arabia[9] – especially its emphasis on the social functions of totemic rituals and its central idea of the divinization of the community.

The work of Robertson Smith and his school offered Durkheim an overall perspective on religion, which he then transformed in the light of his own theoretical preoccupations. As Malinowski observed, Smith was one of the first to see that religion should be accounted for in terms of its social nature,[10] and, in particular, this meant concentrating on ritual practices: in Smith's words, early religions 'consisted entirely of institutions and practices'.[11] The attractiveness of this approach for Durkheim can be appreciated if it is set beside the profusion of psychological theories of religion, especially primitive religion, that was characteristic of the time – illusionist theories, especially animism, as propounded by Spencer, Tylor and Frazer; nature-myth theories, typified by the work of Max Müller; and theories, such as Lang's, deriving religion from

5. 1902b, p. 60: tr. 1933b, p. 93.

6. ibid., p. 105: tr. p. 135.

7. ibid., pp. 142–4: tr. pp. 168–70.

8. ibid., p. 143: tr. p. 169.

9. See Robertson Smith, W., *Lectures on the Religion of the Semites: First Series* (Edinburgh, 1889; 3rd edn, London, 1927).

10. Cited in Kardiner and Preble, 1961, p. 82.

11. op cit., p. 16 (cited in Evans-Pritchard, 1965, p. 53).

the idea of God.[12] In this intellectual climate, religion was a peculiarly challenging subject for Durkheim: how was religion to be explained sociologically?

There are really two stages in Durkheim's development of an answer to this question, marked respectively by the essay 'On the Definition of Religious Phenomena'[13] and by *The Elementary Forms of the Religious Life*. The first stage (to be considered in this chapter) was largely pre-ethnographic; Durkheim had not yet become 'saturated'[14] with the technical and first-hand literature, and in particular he was not yet, as he later became, 'a veteran in Australian ethnology'[15] (albeit a veteran at a distance, since he never visited Australia). Indeed, the great period of Australian ethnographic work, which attracted an immense amount of interest among European scholars, really dated from the late 1890s.[16] At this early stage, Durkheim's approach was largely formal and rather simpliste: he worked out a number of hypotheses about the nature of religion and its role in social life, and he set out a range of questions for the sociology of religion to confront. Subsequently, his treatment of religion was to be considerably more nuanced and complex, and in contact with a rich and detailed mass of empirical material; he then tested, modified and extended his hypotheses and, further, sought to generalize his conclusions to give sociological answers to the most fundamental philosophical questions concerning the bases of morality and knowledge.

'On the Definition of Religious Phenomena' was a first, rather groping attempt to see religion as a social phenomenon, indeed, *the* primitive social phenomenon, from which others subsequently emerged. Characteristically, Durkheim saw the first step as the construction of a definition, to 'delimit the circle of facts on which research will concentrate'.[17] Again

12. For Durkheim's extensive critiques of these various types of theories, see 1899a(ii), pt II, and 1912a: tr. 1915d, bk I, chs. 2 and 3.

13. 1899a (ii).

14. Lowie, 1937, p. 211 (cited in Stanner, 1967, p. 217).

15. Goldenweiser, 1915, p. 719 (cited in ibid.).

16. In particular, there were the publications of Roth, Spencer and Gillen, and Howitt.

17. 1899a (ii), p. 1.

characteristically, he sought that definition, not in the content (which was infinitely variable and waiting to be explored), but in 'the exterior and apparent form of religious phenomena'.[18] Following Robertson Smith, he turned first to the cult, which consisted of 'practices, that is of definite ways of acting'.[19] What was the general distinguishing criterion marking out those that are religious rather than moral and legal? Being obligatory was clearly not enough; and a supernatural reference would not do, since there were cults without gods. Interestingly, Durkheim at this stage also ruled out reference to sacred things as an identifying criterion (observing that, since the sacred was the religious, this was to beg the question at issue). The answer he proposed was in terms of the obligatory character of the beliefs lying behind the practices ('Not only does the Israelite believe that Jehovah is God, that He is the only God, the creator of the world, the revealer of the Law; but he must believe it'[20]). There was 'a pressure exercised by a society on its members to prevent them from deviating from the common faith'.[21] Indeed, 'the more religious [the beliefs], the more they are obligatory'.[22] In short, 'Religious phenomena consist of obligatory beliefs united with definite practices which relate to the objects given in the beliefs.' Religion was 'a more or less organized and systematized collection of phenomena of this sort'.[23]

Durkheim saw this definition as achieving a number of aims. First, he took it as marking off religion from law and morality (obligatory practices without obligatory beliefs), from science (in which it was sensible but not obligatory to believe) and from collective beliefs of a modern, secular sort, such as those in progress and democracy (obligatory beliefs which 'while exercising a very general influence on conduct, are not tied to definite ways of acting, which express them'[24]). There were,

18. ibid., p. 16.
19. ibid.
20. ibid., p. 17.
21. ibid., p. 18.
22. ibid.
23. ibid., pp. 22–3.
24. ibid., p. 22.

of course, half-way cases, such as beliefs relating to 'the flag, the country, this or that political organization, or hero, or historical event'; these were 'to some degree indistinguishable from properly religious beliefs'.[25] What characterized religion was the inseparable unity of thought and action: it corresponded to 'a stage of social development at which these two functions are not yet dissociated and established apart from one another, but are still so confused with one another that it is impossible to mark a very clear dividing-line between them'.[26]

In the second place, Durkheim pursued what he saw as a number of assumptions and implications of this definition. Religious beliefs and practices were obligatory; 'all that is obligatory is of social origin', and conformity to religious rules involved the individual's deference to the moral power of society:

> The state of perpetual dependence in which we are towards [society] inspires us with a sentiment of religious respect for it. It is therefore it which prescribes to the believer the dogmas he must believe and the rites he must observe; and if this is so, it is because the rites and dogmas are its creation.[27]

Moreover, it followed from this that the determining cause of religious phenomena lay in 'the nature of the societies to which they relate, and if they have evolved in the course of history it is because social organization has itself been transformed'.[28] On the other hand, Durkheim wrote of religious '*représentations*' as the work of the 'collective mind' ('the manner *sui generis* in which men think when they think collectively') and subject to 'laws of collective ideation',[29] yet to be discovered. Hence the distinction between sacred and profane – here rather crudely expressed as that between what is collectively conceived and of general interest, on the one hand, and what is individually conceived (constructed out of 'quite naked individual impressions'[30]) and the result of empirical observation,

25. ibid., p. 20.
26. ibid., p. 22.
27. ibid., p. 23.
28. ibid., p. 24.
29. ibid., p. 25.
30. ibid., p. 26.

on the other. And he went on to link this with the distinctions between spiritual and temporal, social and individual, sociology and psychology (so that, historically, socialization was for long accompanied by 'initiation into sacred things'[31]). Finally, he argued that individual, private religions were secondary and derivative from collective, public ones: they were merely the 'subjective aspect of the external, impersonal and public religion'.[32]

Durkheim saw this definition as giving the science of religions a determinate direction and enabling it to become 'truly sociological'.[33] In particular, the sociology of religion should examine the 'social forces' dominating the believer – forces which were the 'direct product of collective sentiments which have taken on a material form'.[34] It should investigate:

What are these sentiments, what are the social causes that have awakened them and have determined their expression in this or that form, to what social ends does the social organization which thus arises respond?

In short the sociologist of religion must observe 'the conditions of collective existence'.[35]

For the next thirteen years Durkheim delved into these questions.[36] He eventually came to regard this initial definition of subject-matter, not as inaccurate but as 'too formal' and neglecting 'the contents of the religious *représentations* too much'.[37] Moreover, he observed that while their 'imperative character is really a distinctive trait of religious beliefs, it allows of an infinite number of degrees; consequently, there

31. ibid.
32. ibid., p. 28.
33. ibid., p. 23.
34. ibid., p. 24.
35. ibid.
36. He lectured on 'The Elementary Forms of Religion' in 1900–1901 (Bordeaux) and subsequently as 'Religion: Origins' in 1906–7 (Paris): see Appendix A, below. He contributed numerous reviews of ethnographic studies and writings on primitive cults in the volumes of the *Année*. In addition, he encouraged Mauss to take up the study of primitive religion (see Lukes, 1968a).
37. 1912a, p. 66: tr. 1915d, p. 47.

are even cases where it is not easily perceptible'.[38] Just as he had gradually abandoned constraint as a criterion for social facts, he similarly dropped obligatoriness from the definition of religious facts; these developments coincided with a deepening interest in the operation of 'collective *représentations*', in particular values and ideals, in social life.

In the context of the sociology of religion, that interest took the form of marrying a particular view of totemism to the growing mass of Australian material. As Frazer put it, the central Australian tribes appeared to be 'humanity in the chrysalis stage', which he assumed to be identical with 'the totem stage';[39] in particular, the *Intichiuma* ceremony (in which the totemic animal is eaten) seemed to Frazer, as to Durkheim, to be 'the actual observance of that totem sacrament which Robertson Smith, with the intuition of genius, divined years ago, but of which positive examples have hitherto been wanting'.[40] Frazer later abandoned this view, but Durkheim did not. It has been well said that Durkheim was 'clearly captivated by what seemed an extraordinary primitivity'.[41] He took a position in the current debate on totemism – an extreme position at odds with many of his contemporaries[42] – and he interpreted, with considerable plausibility, a certain specific range of central Australian ethnographic material on that basis. He wanted to find an instance of an extremely primitive group united by the same name and emblem and participating in the same cult. He thought he had found it among the aboriginal tribes of central Australia, and that these constituted the crucial experiment which validated his theory of religion, to be considered below.[43]

38. ibid.

39. Frazer, J. G., 'The Origin of Totemism', *The Fortnightly Review*, April-May, 1899, p. 838 (cited in Stanner, 1967, p. 219).

40. ibid. Cf. Durkheim, 1912a, p. 485: tr. 1915d, p. 339: 'By an intuition of genius, Smith had an intuition of all this [i.e. the Intichiuma], though he was not acquainted with the facts.'

41. Stanner, 1967, p. 219.

42. See Van Gennep, 1920. According to Van Gennep, 'no ethnographer would have dared go as far in the theory of the religious nature of the totem and totemism as M. Durkheim . . .' (ibid., p. 40).

43. See Chapter 23, below.

Chapter 12

The History of Socialism[1]

IN 1895-6 Durkheim gave a lecture-course on the history of socialism. In formulating his diagnosis of the ills of contemporary European societies and in proposing remedies, he was naturally concerned to make his position clear in relation to the various sorts of socialism that were current. As we have seen, the original title of his doctoral thesis had been 'The Relations between Individualism and Socialism' and throughout his early writings up to the mid-nineties, although he had abandoned the direct study of socialism, one can discern a constant concern to distil what he saw as acceptable in socialism from what he saw as unacceptable. He had emerged from the École Normale an ardent republican, pre-occupied with 'social questions'; indeed, Mauss reports that it was Durkheim who 'turned [Jaurès] away from the political formalism and the shallow philosophy of the Radicals'.[2] But he did not just become a socialist: none of the available varieties of socialism in France in the eighties seems to have attracted him – neither Vaillant and the *Blanquistes*, nor the *Guesdistes*, nor the *Possibilistes*, nor the workers' movements, mostly in favour of direct action, nor, above all, the anarchists. His attention was turned rather towards Germany, where the theoretical level of socialist thinking was, in any case, much higher.[3] He particularly admired Albert Schaeffle's *Die Quintessenz des Sozialismus*[4] (already familiar in France through Benoît Malon's translation), which advocated the rational planning of production and

1. For a fuller discussion of Durkheim's attitude to contemporary socialism, see below, Chapter 17, and pp. 542-6.
2. Mauss, 1928, p. viii: tr. Durkheim, 1958b, p. 3.
3. See Lichtheim, G., *Marxism in Modern France* (New York and London, 1966), ch. 1.
4. Gotha, 1875.

which he saw as 'revealing the social side of economic questions'.[5] He approved of Schaeffle's approach, as formulated in the question: 'Until now economic life has only been a collection of reflexes; what would it become if it were attached to the conscious centres of the social organism?' and he endorsed Schaeffle's view of the state as 'an organ which concentrates and expresses the whole of social life'.[6] In 1888 he corresponded with Schaeffle and even wrote an article praising and defending Schaeffle's socialism against the charges of 'collectivism' and pro-bureaucratic authoritarianism. He valued this version of socialism chiefly because of its attempt to 'combat . . . the dispersive tendencies engendered by the practice of individualism', and he called it 'organized socialism, that is to say, where the industrial forces are grouped around centres of influence which regulate their co-operation'.[7] He had studied Marx (on the advice of a Finnish friend, Neiglick, during his stay at Leipzig[8]), but he preferred the ideas of Schaeffle which, he held, freed socialism from internal contradictions. Even the idea of occupational groups is to be found in Schaeffle, but Durkheim did not seriously take this up until the mid-nineties.

In 1893 he published a 'Note on the Definition of Socialism' in which he argued that all socialist doctrines had in common an attitude of protest against the existing economic situation and the aim of organizing, regulating and unifying economic life, in a society where labour is very divided, thereby introducing morality into the economic sphere. Socialism, which he distinguished sharply from 'communism', always involved the claim that the moral transformation depended on a prior transformation in economic organization. By eliminating unorganized competition and the unregulated distribution of economic functions, one would be able to 'socialize' economic forces and introduce a 'higher morality'. Thus, his definition of socialism was 'a tendency to make the economic

5. 1886a, p. 77.
6. ibid., pp. 76, 79.
7. 1888b, pp. 4–5.
8. See Mauss, 1928, p. viii: tr. Durkheim, 1958b, p. 3. He was evidently somewhat familiar with *Das Kapital*: see, for example, 1902b, p. 388: tr. 1933b, p. 393, and 1928a, pp. 5–6: tr. 1958b, pp. 6–7.

functions, which are in a diffuse state ... develop, suddenly or gradually, into an organized state'.[9] This definition impressed both Guesde and Jaurès, who declared themselves to be in agreement with Durkheim, but he, as we shall see, remained uncommitted to socialism as a movement. As Mauss put it, 'all his life he was loath to adhere to socialism in the true sense only because of certain features it possessed: its violent character, its class character – more or less purely working-class – and also its political, even politician-like tone'.[10]

He felt the need to examine the causes giving rise to socialism and the needs to which it offered (preliminary) solutions. Thus, in 1895, at a time when it was undergoing a considerable revival in France, with some of his most brilliant students turning to socialism of the Marxist, even Guesdist variety,[11] he began what he intended to be a comprehensive course on the history of socialism, treating it as an ideology requiring sociological explanation. He examined it, Mauss wrote, 'from a purely scientific point of view, as a fact which the scholar should look upon coldly, without prejudice and without taking sides'. To do this it was necessary to 'analyse the social pressures which caused men like Saint-Simon and Fourier, Owen and Marx to develop new principles of morality and of political and economic action'.[12] This first course of 1895–6, which had great success, was, in Mauss's words, 'a model of the application of a sociological and historical method to the analysis of the causes of an idea'.[13] By giving it, Durkheim 'satisfied at the same time the demands of both his moral and his scientific thought. He wished to take a stand and to justify it'.[14] Indeed,

9. 1893c, p. 511.

10. Mauss, 1928, p. viii: tr. Durkheim, 1958b, p. 3 (S.L.).

11. See ibid., p. viii: tr. pp. 2–3. These students formed a Circle of Social Studies, where Marx's *Capital* was discussed in the way that others discussed Spinoza. According to Mauss, Durkheim sensed their hostility to liberalism and bourgeois individualism. In a lecture in 1893, organized by this Circle and the Workers' Party, Jaurès enthused about Durkheim's work (ibid.).

12. ibid., p. vii: tr. p. 2 (S.L.).

13. ibid. (S.L.).

14. ibid. (S.L.).

he took up these studies to 'justify himself in his own eyes, in those of his students, and one day in the eyes of the world'.[15] That he felt this need is indicative both of the contentious political climate of the time and of his personal sense of intellectual responsibility.

The 1895-6 lectures developed and explored the implications of the definition already reached, and discussed the origins of socialism from the eighteenth century through Sismondi and Saint-Simon to the Saint-Simonians.[16] He had prepared a course for 1896-7 on Fourier and Proudhon (whose works he had studied), and he intended to devote a third year to Lassalle, of whom he knew little at that time, and to Marx, and German socialism (with which he was very familiar).[17] But he abandoned these projects and in 1896 'returned to pure science'[18] by founding the *Année sociologique*. Mauss records that Durkheim 'always regretted his inability to continue or resume' his 'History of Socialism'.[19]

Durkheim aimed to study socialism 'as a reality',[20] as 'an unknown phenomenon, yet to be explored',[21] seeking 'to determine what it consists of, when it began, through what transformations it has passed and what determined those transformations' – studying it 'in the same way that we studied suicide, the family, marriage, crime, punishment, responsibility and religion'.[22] He approached it, not as a scientific theory or a 'sociology in miniature'[23] to be evaluated for its

15. See ibid., p. ix.: tr. p. 3.

16. For useful discussions referring to this course (1928a: tr. 1958b), see Gouldner, 1958, Cuvillier, 1959b, Neyer, 1960, Aron, 1962, Filloux, 1963 and 1971, Birnbaum, 1969 and 1971, and Giddens, 1971b. It has been unduly neglected, probably because of the seemingly idiosyncratic definition of socialism Durkheim used. In fact, as a study of the technocratic strand in socialist thought, it is of both historical and contemporary interest.

17. See Mauss, 1928, p. ix: tr. p. 3. None of this material survives.

18. ibid.

19. ibid.

20. 1928a, p. 11: tr. 1958b, p. 10.

21. ibid., p. 26: tr. p. 20 (S.L.).

22. ibid., p. 11: tr. p. 10. For a discussion of his work on crime, punishment and responsibility, see Chapter 13, below.

23. ibid., p. 6: tr. p. 7.

truth or plausibility, but rather as a 'practical' doctrine, a 'plan for the reconstruction of present-day societies'[24] and a 'cry of anguish, and, sometimes, of anger, uttered by the men who most keenly feel our collective malaise'.[25]

Durkheim's definition of socialism was a bold attempt to seize the essential of a historically specific ideology:

We define as 'socialist' every doctrine which calls for the connection of all economic functions, or of certain among them which are currently diffuse, to the directing and conscious centres of society... Secondly, we also define as 'socialist' theories which, while not relating directly to the economic order, are nonetheless linked with theories of the preceding type.[26]

He stressed that 'connection' did not mean 'subordination' ('Socialists do not demand that economic life be put into the hands of the state, but rather into contact with it'[27]) and also that his definition referred neither to the class war nor to bettering the workers' lot: the latter was 'only one of the results socialism hopes for from the economic reorganization it demands, just as the class war is only one of the means by which this concentration may result'.[28] Socialism as a response to industrialism, demanding that it be *organized* – this was Durkheim's working definition, which he used to encompass both 'workers' socialism', coming 'from below' and 'State socialism', coming from 'the higher regions of society'.[29] It was 'bound up with a particular state of society', revealing itself from the beginning 'in the form of a social and enduring current' and expressing sentiments which were 'general' and 'manifest themselves simultaneously at differing points in society and assert themselves persistently so long as the conditions which created them have not disappeared'.[30] In particular,

24. ibid., p. 4: tr. p. 5 (S.L.).
25. ibid., p. 6: tr. p. 7 (S.L.).
26. ibid., pp. 25, 37: tr. pp. 19, 28 (S.L.).
27. ibid., p. 28: tr. p. 21 (S.L.).
28. ibid., p. 31: tr. p. 23 (S.L.).
29. ibid., p. 35: tr. p. 26 (S.L.). Socialism, he wrote, 'is essentially a movement to organize' (ibid., p. 30: tr. p. 23).
30. ibid., p. 53: tr. p. 39 (S.L.).

it arose out of three sets of pre-conditions: first, industrialization and secularization, especially of social institutions ('it was
necessary, on the one hand, that economic functions acquire
greater social importance, and, on the other, that social functions acquire a more human character . . . that commerce and
industry become more essential wheels of the collective
machine, and that society cease to be regarded as a transcendent being, towering high above men . . .'[31]); second, a sufficient development in the influence of the state for its further
extension into the economy to be conceivable; and third, a
sufficient growth of industrial concentration ('the regime of
big industry must be established'[32]). Socialism, in short, was
'essentially a process of economic concentration and centralization'.[33]

This clear-cut view of socialism allowed Durkheim to
distinguish it from classical economics: both assuming industrialism, deriving from the same source and corresponding to
the same state of society, which they expressed differently,
the one sought to organize economic interests, while the other,
illogically, refused 'to submit them to any collective control',
believing that 'they can order and harmonize themselves
henceforth without any prior reorganization'.[34] Likewise,
he contrasted socialism, thus defined, with 'communism', by
which he meant utopianism – radical demands for justice or
equality, occurring sporadically throughout history, and typified by Plato, More and Campanella. Communism was anti-
industrial (putting 'industrial life outside the state'[35]), in favour
of private production and communal consumption, ascetically
opposed to all wealth and abundance, and in favour of small-
scale, homogeneous societies in which desires are few and
horizons narrow. All that socialism and communism had in
common was a shared hostility to the exaltation of private interest: both opposed 'radical and intransigent individualism'.[36]

31. ibid., p. 57: tr. p. 41 (S.L.).
32. ibid., p. 58: tr. p. 42 (S.L.).
33. ibid., p. 74: tr. p. 54.
34. ibid., p. 285: tr. p. 196 (S.L.).
35. ibid., p. 42: tr. p. 32.
36. ibid., p. 55: tr. p. 40. Cf. Marx's and Engels's discussions of
utopianism in the *Communist Manifesto* and *Anti-Duhring*.

Durkheim first examined the pre-history of socialism in the eighteenth century. Beginning with the 'communist' systems of Morelly, Mably and Rousseau, he emphasized the 'positive efflorescence'[37] of such systems during this period, as well as their new and distinctive tone: they were more morally imperative, more saddened, disturbed and discouraged by their own societies and they betrayed a stronger and more generalized concern for social justice. Here was a historical link with socialism: 'though born under quite other influences and responding to quite different needs, socialism, just because it naturally came to take an interest in the working classes, found itself quite naturally and especially susceptible to these feelings of pity and fraternity . . .'[38] He traced a development of concern with economic realities and industrial life, through Linguet, Necker and Graslin; always, however, the conclusions were, in his view, timid and conservative – 'a hope for a more just social order and an idea of the rights of the State, which, together, are the seeds of socialism, but which were limited at the time to only rudimentary wishes – that is all we find in the eighteenth century'.[39] These were the principles of 1789, but 'in order for these factors to produce their social or socialist consequences they had first to produce their political consequences'.[40]

After considering the ideas of Sismondi, as identifying disequilibrium in the economy and expressing 'the need for a more regular and stable industrial life',[41] Durkheim turned to a detailed examination of Saint-Simon and *Saint-Simonisme*. Given Durkheim's definition of socialism, it is clear that Saint-Simon would be bound to take a central place in his socialist tradition – Saint Simon, the half-mad prophet of a

37. ibid., p. 68: tr. p. 49 (S.L.).
38. ibid., p. 76: tr. p. 55 (S.L.). Durkheim also observed that socialism by no means met the problem posed by communism: 'Should the socialization of economic forces be an accomplished fact tomorrow, [the sentiments to which communism responds] will be opposed to the excessive inequalities that will obtain then as now' (ibid. – S.L.).
39. ibid., p. 91: tr. p. 65 (S.L.).
40. ibid., p. 96: tr. p. 68.
41. ibid., p. 114: tr. p. 81 (S.L.).

planned industrial society and the first organization theorist,[42] of whom Engels wrote that almost all the ideas of later socialism were 'contained in his works in embryo'.[43] Durkheim presented Saint-Simon, first, as the real founder of positivism (and thus of sociology); second as the historian and 'apostle of industrialism',[44] who foresaw 'the coming of a new form of collective life, the first attempts at a social organization resting on an economic base',[45] and argued that 'modern societies will finally be in equilibrium only when completely organized on a purely industrial basis'.[46] Thirdly, he showed Saint-Simon in his latter, quasi-religious phase, concerned about impending social dissolution and propounding his pantheistic 'New Christianity'. Durkheim argued that these three sides of Saint-Simon were linked. They 'only express the same social state in varied ways' and contained 'the germ of all the great intellectual currents produced during the nineteenth century'[47]; the science of history and the positivist philosophy; socialism; and 'those aspirations for a religious revival which, in spite of periods of apathy, never remained completely foreign to the spirit of the century'.[48] All these flowed from what Saint-Simon called the principle of industrialism. Saint-Simon epitomized the spirit of his time, but the substance of his thought was too rich to continue within the confines of a single, unified system, and his legacy was fragmented.

Durkheim's critique of Saint-Simon's thought marks an important stage in the development of his own. Saint-Simon's error, he argued, 'consisted in wishing to construct a stable society on a purely economic base'.[49] He had commented approvingly on Saint-Simon's view of industrialism, in the course of his exposition, as follows:

42. See the author's chapter on Saint-Simon in *Founding Fathers of Social Science*, London, 1969.
43. Cited in ibid.
44. 1928a, p. 197: tr. 1958b, p. 137.
45. ibid., p. 181: tr. p. 127 (S.L.).
46. ibid., p. 188: tr. p. 131 (S.L.).
47. ibid., pp. 280–81: tr. p. 193 (S.L.).
48. ibid.
49. ibid., p. 336: tr. p. 230.

in our great contemporary societies, where economic relations form the basis of common life, social unity is above all the result of the solidarity of interests; it is therefore due to internal causes, to the bonds of interdependence which unite the various parts of society ... Each people today forms a cohesive whole ... because it is a system of functions, inseparable from one another and mutually complementing each other.[50]

This, of course, is organic solidarity, as in *The Division of Labour*, seemingly without any *conscience collective*, half-seen as operating without unifying beliefs and norms. However, when Durkheim subsequently turned, later in the argument, to criticism of Saint-Simon, he argued that 'economic functions cannot co-operate harmoniously nor be maintained in a state of equilibrium unless subjected to moral forces which surpass, contain and regulate them'.[51] Saint-Simon had made the mistake of supposing that 'the way to realize social peace is to free economic appetites of all restraint on the one hand, and on the other to satisfy them by fulfilling them'.[52] Such an enterprise was contradictory; appetites could only be appeased by being limited, by being 'subordinated to some end which surpasses them'.[53] Otherwise, even in conditions of maximum and universal abundance, men's potentially unlimited and competitive desires would lead, then as now, to individual torment and social disorder.

Saint-Simon, Durkheim maintained, in arguing that 'industry should be organized without subordinating it to anything',[54] had been mistaken 'about what, in the present situation, is the cause of the malaise, and in proposing, as a remedy, an aggravation of the sickness'.[55] Saint-Simon's latter-day, somewhat artificial religiosity, and the posthumous degeneration of his doctrine into 'a mystical sensualism, an apotheosis of comfort, a consecration of excess'[56] – Durkheim took all

50. ibid., p. 214: tr. p. 148 (S.L.).
51. ibid., p. 287: tr. p. 197.
52. ibid., p. 290: tr. p. 199.
53. ibid.
54. ibid., p. 295: tr. p. 202.
55. ibid. (S.L.).
56. ibid., p. 344: tr. p. 235 (S.L.).

this as confirmation of the validity of his criticism. What was needed if social order was to reign in contemporary industrial societies was 'that the generality of men be content with their lot'[57]; this required 'social forces, moral authorities, which must exercise this regulating influence, without which appetites become deranged and economic order disorganized'.[58] Where were these contemporary moral forces to be found that would be capable of 'establishing, making acceptable and maintaining the necessary discipline?'[59] As we have seen, Durkheim's answer was occupational groups, which were in touch with industrial life, close to individuals' interests and capable of acting as moral forces. He developed that answer most fully in his lectures on professional ethics, which formed part of the general course on law and social norms, to which we now turn.

57. ibid., p. 291: tr. p. 200 (S.L.).
58. ibid., p. 293: tr. p. 201 (S.L.).
59. ibid., p. 296: tr. p. 203.

Chapter 13

The Sociology of Law and Politics

'THE essential thing', Durkheim wrote in 1899, 'is to get [pupils in lycées] to reflect upon the nature of society, the family, the State, upon the principal legal and moral obligations, and upon the ways in which these different social phenomena are formed ... I began here, in about 1896, a course entitled 'Physique Générale du Droit et des Mœurs'[1] ... in which all these questions are treated sociologically'.[2] This was the content and purpose of the public lectures in sociology that Durkheim delivered twice at Bordeaux between 1896 and 1900. The future teachers of philosophy who attended them would acquire a 'sociological training' and would then be able to 'treat all the questions of sociology to which it is suitable to initiate pupils'.[3] The old philosophical questions, the problems of ethics, would come to be seen in a new light, as largely empirical questions amenable to scientific inquiry. Durkheim's lecture-course even followed 'exactly, or almost so, the classical divisions of lycée courses' in moral philosophy.[4] Mauss describes the 1898–1900 version as a 'complete Ethics ("Morale")'.[5] It was divided into two parts, following the 'classical' division of French philosophy teaching. The first

1. By '*mœurs*' Durkheim meant, quite generally, norms governing behaviour.
2. 1899c, p. 679.
3. ibid.
4. ibid.
5. Mauss, 1925a, p. 11. Mauss adds that the 1898–1900 draft was 'the definitive draft of this series of lectures' (ibid). This is the draft subsequently published, *in part*, as 1937a and 1950a: tr. 1957a. The information which follows, concerning the remaining, unpublished parts of the course (the manuscripts of which have not survived), comes from Mauss, 1925a, and Mauss, 1937. The course had first been given at Bordeaux in 1890–91 (of which the manuscript has disappeared). The content of that early version, according to Mauss, went into *The Division of Labour* (ibid.).

year of the course corresponded, in Mauss's words, 'to what is improperly called "Theoretical Ethics" ("Morale théorique")'. Durkheim, 'operating in the concrete', preferred to call it 'Theory of Obligation, Sanction and Morality'. The second year, according to Mauss, corresponded to 'what is popularly and quite improperly called "Practical Ethics" ("Morale pratique")'.[6] The first concerned questions relating to society as a whole ('Morale de la société') and the second those bearing on particular contexts within the wider society ('Morale des groupes spéciaux de la société').[7] In sum, Mauss described the whole course as providing 'a complete picture of all moral phenomena'. Durkheim had established the *Science des mœurs* for his students – 'that science on which so many philosophers still discourse, and of which he not only provided the idea but also began to fill out the framework with content'.[8]

The first part, dealing with 'moral facts in general',[9] was concerned with both law and morality. It examined the nature of moral and legal rules and the classification of these, breaches of them, criminality, repression, responsibility, morality, suicide and anomie.[10] It began with a definition of moral facts, which was followed by what Mauss described as 'two capital parts of the work; two essential pieces of Durkheim's system'[11]: the first being the theory of moral obligations and of moral obligation in general, together with a classification of obligations; and the second, Durkheim's theory of sanctions, with a classification of these. All this corresponded to the 'general physiological study of law and social practices',[12] concentrating on the 'functioning' of these within the total society. All these lectures remained unpublished and no longer exist. For this reason, and because Durkheim's sociology of morality underwent considerable development during his years in Paris,

6. ibid.
7. ibid., p. 12, but see below.
8. ibid., pp. 12–13.
9. Mauss, 1937, p. 528.
10. ibid.
11. Mauss, 1925a, p. 12.
12. ibid.

we will leave the consideration of his ideas on this subject until a later stage.[13]

The first part of the course continued with two special studies of the operation of social norms ('*mœurs*'). The first of these was a study of their infringement and the nature of crime, which included some statistical work, subsequently abandoned, that was, according to Mauss, comparable to that in *Suicide*. In the course of this work, Durkheim made a point of drawing the distinction, then unfamiliar, between violent crime, against persons (found among 'backward classes and peoples'), and 'mild' crime, against property, such as swindling and breach of confidence (to be found among 'the commercial classes, and urban and civilized populations').[14] However, having made this promising start in criminology, Durkheim left the work to be continued by his students; none of his empirical work in this area survives. On the other hand, his sociological theory of crime was firmly and clearly expressed in *The Rules of Sociological Method*[15] and it was one of the chief points at issue in Durkheim's sharp polemical exchanges with the sociological statistician Gabriel Tarde, in particular his claim that a certain crime rate should be seen as normal for a given society, rather than as intrinsically pathological.[16]

THE EVOLUTION OF PUNISHMENT

Finally, concluding the first year's lectures, there was a study of the genesis and evolution of punishment, which developed into an article written for the fourth volume of the *Année*

13. See Chapter 21, below. It can reasonably be assumed that Durkheim's discussion of morality in the *Moral Education* course, considered above in Chapter 6, represents an accurate summary of his views at this period (see Mauss, 1937, p. 528).

14. Mauss, 1925a, p. 12. Cf., for instance, Sutherland, E. H., *White Collar Crime* (New York, 1949).

15. See especially 1901c, pp. vi. 45, 81–91: tr. 1938b, pp. xxxviii, 35–6, 65–74.

16. See below, Chapter 16, which contains an account of Durkheim's theory of crime.

sociologique on 'Two Laws of Penal Evolution'.[17] That article advanced two important arguments – important both in themselves and in the context of Durkheim's thought. The first implied that political power has a certain independence of the social structure. In *The Division of Labour*, Durkheim had argued that 'governmental power [is] an emanation of the life inherent in the *conscience collective*' and that 'the power of authoritarian governments does not come from themselves but derives from the very structure of society'.[18] *The Division of Labour* had claimed that penal law, and generally the degree of repression, had progressively declined with the recession of mechanical and the advance of organic solidarity; and that this decline was a function of the growth in social complexity, organization, administration, specialization and individual autonomy, and an increasing respect for justice, equality of opportunity and individual dignity. Durkheim now argued that the 'intensity' of punishment, or the quantity of severe punishments, '*is greater in so far as societies belong to a less advanced type – in so far as the central power has a more absolute character*'.[19] Thus the initial hypothesis of *The Division of Labour* was qualified: governmental power was an independent variable in determining the intensity of punishment. The concentration or 'hypercentralization' of power, with no countervailing power 'regularly organized in order to moderate it',[20] was a historically contingent phenomenon and was not dependent on this or that social type. The influence of governmental organization could neutralize that of social organization. Durkheim provided a broad comparative survey of societies, beginning with Ancient Egypt and ending with

17. 1901a (i). It also formed the basis for Paul Fauconnet's subsequent work on responsibility (Fauconnet, 1920). All these ideas on crime and punishment presumably developed out of Durkheim's lectures on criminal sociology given between 1892 and 1894: see Appendix A, below. It is striking that these ideas, and in particular the study of penal evolution, have been universally ignored by later sociologists and writers on Durkheim (but see Richter, 1960, and Tiryakian, 1964b).

18. 1902b, pp. 172–3, 172: tr. 1933b, p. 195 (S.L.). I have translated '*force*' by 'power' in this quotation.

19 1901a (i), p. 65.

20. ibid., pp. 68, 67.

his own, to verify this qualified law of evolution. It was a suggestive qualification with rich possibilities. As one writer has observed, it might 'have led him to consider the possibility of authoritarianism in modern society'.[21] As we shall see, he did consider this possibility much later, in reaction to the thought of Treitschke and the condition of Germany at the time of the First World War.[22] However, it remains broadly true to say that, in this respect, this first law of penal evolution remained 'an unexploited insight'.[23]

The second important argument in this article implied the crucial relevance of collective sentiments and beliefs to the explanation of social practices. How was one to explain the two laws of penal evolution, of which the second was that the *'deprivation of liberty and of liberty alone, for periods of time varying according to the gravity of the crime, tends increasingly to become the normal type of repression'*?[24] Durkheim maintained that the second law depended in part on the first, since the 'various modalities of detention' gradually replaced, and were indeed 'the natural and necessary substitutes for', the other harsher penalties that were disappearing[25]; and they obeyed the same law of declining intensity. The question therefore reduced to explaining 'how it is that punishments become milder as one goes from less to more advanced societies' (since Durkheim assumed that the factor of political power played 'the less important role' and could provisionally be abstracted).[26] The key to his answer lay in his view of the relation between punishment and crime; 'Since punishment results from crime and expresses the manner in which it affects the public *conscience*, it is in the evolution of crime that one must seek the cause determining the evolution of punishment'.[27]

The argument rested on the claim that 'the manner in which collective sentiments react against crime has changed, because

21. Richter, 1960, p. 193.
22. See Chapter 27, below.
23. Richter, 1960, p. 193.
24. 1901a (i), p. 78.
25. ibid., p. 84.
26. ibid., p. 85.
27. ibid., p. 86.

these sentiments have changed'.[28] Durkheim classified crimes into two fundamental categories: those directed against 'collective things',[29] such as the public authority and its representatives, customs and traditions, and religion; and those only injuring individuals, such as murder, theft, violence, and frauds of all kinds. The first category he labelled 'religious criminality', since 'offences against religion are the most essential part of it and . . . crimes against traditions or heads of state always have a more or less religious character'[30]; the second he called 'human criminality'. The first, he argued, covered almost the whole of the penal law of less advanced societies, but they regressed as one advanced in evolution, while offences against the human person gradually took their place. The crimes characteristic of less advanced societies had the character of sacrilege: they offended sentiments that were directed towards transcendent and superhuman beings, inspiring reverential fear. Such crimes were seen as 'exceptionally odious',[31] and pity for the criminal could not 'serve as an effective counterweight to the indignation aroused by the sacrilegious act, nor, in consequence, appreciably moderate the punishment'. The two sentiments were too unequal: what was 'an individual's suffering when it is a question of appeasing a god'?[32] However, the case was quite otherwise with the collective sentiments which had the individual as object. Durkheim here gave the fullest and clearest account available in his writings of the collective psychological forces underlying 'individualism'. The 'sentiments protecting human dignity',[33] leading us to 'respect the life and property of our fellows', arose, not out of calculations of individual advantage, but out of 'the sympathy we have for man in general'.[34] They recalled Kant rather than the utilitarians: the object of the sentiments was *general*, involving an abstraction of 'the

28. ibid., p. 92.
29. ibid., p. 86.
30. ibid.
31. ibid., p. 88.
32. ibid.
33. ibid.
34. ibid., pp. 88, 89.

concrete and diverse forms under which it offers itself to observation'.[35] However, that object was closely related to real men: it offered 'the model of which we are the varied specimens'.[36] It was an ideal whose transcendence was much less marked; each person realized it in part. It remained essentially human and to some degree immanent.

The nub of the argument concerned the difference between the beliefs accompanying the two types of sentiment. In the latter case, pity for the criminal and for his victim were of the same *sort*:

That which tempers the collective anger which is the soul of punishment is the sympathy we feel for every man who suffers, the horror which all destructive violence produces in us; now, this is the same sympathy and the same horror which incites that very anger. Thus, here, the very cause which sets in motion the repressive apparatus tends to halt it. The same mental state drives us to punish and to moderate the punishment. Hence, an attenuating influence cannot fail to make itself felt ... there is a real and irremediable contradiction in avenging the human dignity offended in the person of the victim by violating it in the person of the criminal. The only way, not of removing the antinomy (for it is strictly insoluble), but of alleviating it, is to alleviate the punishment as much as possible.[37]

Thus, as crime became more human and less religious, punishment became generally less severe. This was not simply an explanation in terms of increasing human sympathy: that would lead rather to increased severity toward crimes against persons. The point was that 'the compassion of which the victim is the object is no longer overborne by contrary sentiments that do not allow it to exercise its influence'.[38]

Durkheim held that this broad explanation in terms of the gradual replacement of religious by human criminality applied

35. ibid., p. 89.
36. ibid.
37. ibid., p. 90. This *type of explanation*, in terms of the *logic* of a set of beliefs modifying social practices, is strongly reminiscent of Max Weber's account of the relation between puritan beliefs and capitalist practice: see *Die protestantische Ethik und der 'Geist' des Kapitalismus* in *Archiv für Sozialwissenschaft und Sozialpolitik*, xx-xxi (1904-5): tr. as *The Protestant Ethic and the Spirit of Capitalism* by Parsons, T. (London, 1930).
38. 1901a (i), p. 91.

to all types of crime, including those against collectivities ('We no longer hypostasize the family or society as transcendent or mystical entities'[39]). Moreover, this transformation was useful, 'in harmony' with the conditions of modern societies, as collective coercion diminished and grew less exclusive of free thought, giving greater room for individual spontaneity, initiative and reflection. Finally, Durkheim turned to the independent variable of political power. He sought to assimilate this to his general explanation by claiming that, as governments became more absolute, so they became invested with a kind of religiosity: where absolute governments existed, political offences were seen as sacrilegious and were violently repressed, and all offences tended to become political and to be seen as attacks on the sovereign. Thus 'the gravity of most crimes is raised by several degrees; as a result the average intensity of punishments is very greatly strengthened.'[40] This, one might say, was Durkheim's theory of charisma, and the nearest he came to developing a theory of totalitarianism.

Durkheim's study of penal evolution thus explained a transformation in social practices or institutions in terms of a transformation in collective sentiments and beliefs; this is true despite his claim that the former had been 'produced mechanically' by 'new forces' which had 'come into play'.[41] It followed, importantly, that punishment was not destined to disappear, as many believed (and continue to believe): the penal system was ultimately a function of the moral beliefs of society, and it was fair to predict that the list of human crimes would lengthen, and that they would be punished less severely, but punished nonetheless. The penal law of all civilized peoples was in a state of crisis:

> We have arrived at a point where the penal institutions of the past have either disappeared or only survive through the force of custom, without others being born which respond better to the new aspirations of the moral *conscience*.[42]

39. ibid., p. 92.
40. ibid., p. 94.
41. ibid., p. 92.
42. ibid., p. 95.

The second part of the lecture-course on law and social practices covered a number of areas, of gradually increasing scope. It appears to have been organized as follows. First, there were lectures on 'the moral and legal rules applying to the relations of the individual with himself',[43] followed by a set of lectures devoted to 'domestic organization and domestic ethics',[44] which was, according to Mauss, 'a more popular and moralistic version of his work on the family'.[45] Then there followed three lectures on occupational ethics, six on civic ethics, and, finally, nine on 'Duties in General', independent of any particular social grouping, covering homicide, property and contract.[46] These latter constituted the 'culminating part' and the 'highest point' of ethics, concerning the relations men had to one another solely in virtue of being men.[47] The other

43. 1950a, p. 52: tr. p. 42. Durkheim described these rules as having the function of 'fixing in the individual's conscience the fundamental and general bases of all morality' (ibid., p. 8: tr. p. 3 – S.L.). (The text of these lectures has disappeared.)

44. See Mauss, 1925a, p. 11. Mauss places these lectures in the *second* part of the second year, but that is contradicted by what Durkheim wrote, in 1950a, p. 8: tr. 1957a, p. 4, where they are referred to as having been delivered *before* those on occupational ethics (and indeed in the first year). However Mauss makes clear that they were separate from the first, theoretical part of the course (Mauss, 1937, p. 528), and this accords with the available texts.

45. Mauss, 1925a, p. 13. Before his death, Durkheim gave instructions that only this form of his work on the family should be published (ibid.), but it never was. (The manuscript does not survive.) It probably fell half-way between the lectures considered above in Chapter 8 and the lecture on the family reproduced in Appendix C of Lukes, 1968b (the Lenoir manuscripts).

46. This set of eighteen lectures is reproduced in 1950a: tr. 1957a. (This is the complete version of this part of the course.) For discussions, see Davy, 1950, Cuvillier, 1954, König, 1956, Richter, 1960, Nisbet, 1965, Allardt, 1968, and Giddens, 1971c; also Bendix, R., 'Social Stratification and Political Community', *European Journal of Sociology*, 1, 2 (1960), pp. 181–210: reprinted in Laslett, P., and Runciman, W. G. (eds.), *Philosophy, Politics and Society: Second Series* (Oxford, 1962) and Bendix, R. and Lipset, S. M. (eds.), *Class, Status and Power* (2nd edn, New York, 1966). Durkheim repeated them at the Sorbonne between 1903–5, 1909–11 and 1914–16. Cuvillier recalls that Durkheim 'made them the basis of all his teaching of ethics' (Cuvillier, 1954 (1956), p. 238).

47. 1950a, p. 8: tr. 1957a, p. 3 (S.L.).

categories of ethics (apart from the first) were dependent on particular types of institution or grouping, this 'moral particularism' being at a maximum in the case of occupational ethics.[48]

In these lectures Durkheim turned to a range of traditional questions in moral, political and legal philosophy, to which he sought distinctively sociological answers: to the question of the nature and limits of men's obligations with respect to various social groups, from the family to the state; to the issue, previously treated by Montesquieu and Tocqueville, of secondary groups, or *corps intermédiaires*, in society; to the definition of the state, the relation of the state to the individual, and the nature of and justifications for democracy; to the so-called natural rights, and their correlative duties, protecting life and property; and to the nature of contract, its rights and obligations. While approaching all these questions in a new way, his discussion of them is also within an old, indeed venerable, tradition of discourse.

The novelty of Durkheim's approach lay in his recasting of the old, seemingly timeless and *a priori* problems of ethics, political theory and jurisprudence into a set of hypotheses about the presence or absence in particular social contexts of operative rules and ideals, or (to use a more modern idiom) of norms and values. As he later observed, concerning the whole of this second part of the course, his aim was to conduct a careful review of 'the details of moral rules (domestic, occupational, civic, contractual)' and to show 'both the causes which have given rise to them and the functions which they fulfil'.[49] Yet, despite these strictly descriptive and explanatory aims, his argument incorporates the central features characterizing much of traditional social and political theory, from Aristotle and Plato to his fellow nineteenth-century liberals,

48. ibid., p. 10: tr. p. 5. It will thus be seen that only the middle sections of this second part of the course are strictly consistent with Mauss's description of it as concerning 'Morale des groupes spéciaux de la société'.

49. 1924a (1951 edn), p. 55: tr. 1953b, p. 39 (S.L.). Cf. 1950a, p. 5: tr. 1957a, p. 1 (ff.), where he observes that comparative history and ethnography are relevant to the genesis of the rules, and comparative statistics to their functioning.

J. S. Mill and T. H. Green: a predilection for large themes (justice, liberty, obligation, order) and abstract definitions, an underlying view of human nature and of the relation of man to society and of both to the state, and a concern to specify the nature and pre-conditions of the good society and, in general, to draw prescriptive conclusions relevant to the times'.[50]

DOMESTIC AND OCCUPATIONAL ETHICS

In the lectures on domestic organization and ethics, Durkheim traced the history of the family's declining role and the causes of that decline in terms of social differentiation and industrialization. He also outlined its present reduced but essential functions in maintaining social stability and as an agent of socialization: a source of moral life, of regulation and attachment, for individuals.[51] It was in the lectures on occupational ethics that he explored the implications of his view that the economic life of an industrial society needs to be organized around occupational groups or corporations. These would take over some of the moral functions once performed by the family and 'moralise economic life',[52] specifying the rights and duties of individuals' working lives and providing a continuous collective and relevant focus for their loyalties, while at the same time playing a central role at the national level in the operation of a planned and organized socialist economy.[53] In this way Durkheim sought to provide practical solutions to the problem of anomie identified in *The Division of Labour* and

50. Cf. Wolin, 1960, for an outstanding recent study of that tradition: also Lukes, 1967a (especially pt IV) for an account of Durkheim's place within it. Mauss describes Durkheim's approach in these lectures as pragmatic, in the aristotelian sense of the word, seeking answers to practical problems by 'starting from solutions to general and theoretical problems' (Mauss, 1937, p. 530).

51. See Chapter 8, above.

52. 1950a, p. 37: tr. 1957a, p. 29 (S.L.).

53. For a discussion of how Durkheim envisaged the structure and functions of these corporations, see Chapter 26. Apart from the lectures of this course, he also discussed them in the course on socialism (1928a, pp. 296–7: tr. 1958b, pp. 203–4); in the conclusion to *Suicide* (1897a, pp. 434–51: tr. 1951a, pp. 378–92); and in the preface to the second edition of *The Division of Labour* (1902b, pp. i–xxxvi: tr. 1933b, pp. 1–31).

Suicide – solutions which went beyond the purely materialistic perspective considered in the lectures on socialism.

Durkheim's strategy here was, first, to identify the morbid state of anomie among the 'economic functions, both industry and trade'.[54] There were no rules, let alone obligations enforced by sanctions, determining 'the relations between the employee and his employer, the worker and the boss of the company, between manufacturers in competition with one another, and between them and the public'.[55] The result was an anarchic state of disequilibrium in which 'nothing remains but individual appetites, and since they are by nature boundless and insatiable, if there is nothing to control them they will not be able to control themselves'[56]: the unchaining of economic interests had been accompanied by a decline in public morality, so that 'the manufacturer, the businessman, the worker, the employee, in carrying out his occupation, is subject to no influence set above him which contains his egoism, nor to any moral discipline, and, as a result, he dispenses with all discipline of this kind'.[57] Such a situation, Durkheim argued, was abnormal, for 'It is not possible for a social function to exist without moral discipline'.[58] Moreover, he advanced a further, normative argument against those classical economists who celebrated this anarchic state of *laissez-faire* and for whom 'productive output seemed to be the sole and essential aim of all industrial activity'.[59] It might indeed appear that 'from certain points of view, production, to be intensive, does not require to be regulated; that, on the contrary, it is best to leave individual initiatives and particular interests to stimulate and inflame one another, rather than try to contain and moderate them'.[60] However,

production is not all, and if industry can only bring its output to this point by maintaining a state of chronic warfare and perpetual

54. 1950a, p. 14: tr. 1957a, p. 9.
55. ibid., p. 15: tr. p. 9 (S.L.).
56. ibid., p. 16: tr. p. 11.
57. ibid., p. 18: tr. p. 12 (S.L.).
58. ibid., p. 16: tr. pp. 10–11.
59. ibid., p. 22: tr. p. 15.
60. ibid.: tr. pp. 15–16.

discontent among the producers, there is nothing to balance the evil it does. Even from a purely utilitarian point of view, what is the use of increasing abundance, if it does not succeed in calming the desires of the greatest number, but, on the contrary, only serves to arouse their impatience. It is forgotten that economic functions are not their own justification; they are only a means to an end; they constitute one of the organs of social life, and that social life is above all a harmonious community of endeavours, a communion of minds and wills working toward the same end. Society has no *raison d'être* if it does not bring men a little peace, peace in their hearts and peace in their mutual relations. If industry can only be productive by disturbing that peace and by unleashing warfare, then it is not worth the cost.[61]

Durkheim next turned to a historical study of the role of occupational groups in other societies, in particular Ancient Rome and medieval Europe. He argued that if 'from the origins of the City until the height of the Empire, and from the birth of the Christian societies until the French Revolution they have been necessary, this is probably because they respond to some permanent and profound need'.[62] Their 'radical suppression' at the time of the Revolution had itself been a 'morbid phenomenon'[63] and resulted from the fact that the guilds, being local and municipal institutions, had failed to adjust to the demands of large-scale industrialization. The guild had been 'too slow in transforming itself, so as to adjust to these new needs, and that is why it was destroyed ... by the eve of the Revolution the craft guild had become a sort of dead substance or foreign body, which only survived in our social organism by the force of inertia. And thus a point came when it was violently ejected.'[64] Then, finally, Durkheim spelt out his own image of a future in which 'the guild will be restored, but in an entirely new form',[65] in order to play its

61. ibid.: tr. p. 16. The Galbraithian echoes of this argument are remarkable: see, for example, Galbraith, J. K., *The Affluent Society* (Boston, 1958), especially ch. IX, and Veblen, T., *The Theory of the Leisure Class* (New York, 1899).
62. ibid., p. 26: tr. p. 19 (S.L.).
63. ibid.
64. ibid., p. 46: tr. pp. 36–7 (S.L.)
65. ibid., p. 47: tr. p. 37 (S.L.). See Chapter 26, below.

role 'in the present conditions of collective existence'.⁶⁶ There
is no hint of Fascist corporatism about that image, as some have
suggested,⁶⁷ nor is it merely an expression of medieval nos-
talgia.⁶⁸ Indeed, both the critique of the ills of capitalism and
the kind of centralized guild socialism proposed as their remedy
are, at almost every point, strikingly similar to the arguments
of R. H. Tawney – another socialist thinker within a quite
different, but equally moralistic, tradition.⁶⁹

CIVIC ETHICS: THE STATE, DEMOCRACY AND POLITICAL OBLIGATION

Durkheim identified the area of civic ethics as that of 'political
society', which he defined as 'a society formed by the union of
a more or less considerable number of secondary social groups,
subject to a single authority which is not itself under the
jurisdiction of any other superior authority properly constituted'.⁷⁰ The operative rules, or norms, to be studied here were
'those determining the relations of individuals with this
sovereign authority, to whose influence they are subject'.⁷¹

66. ibid., p. 35: tr. p. 27.

67. See, for example, the review of 1950a in *CIS* 14 (1953), p. 181, fn.

68. See, for example, Nisbet, 1965 and 1966.

69. Cf. *The Acquisitive Society* (London, 1921; Fontana Books edn,
1961): e.g.: 'It is because the purpose of industry, which is the conquest
of nature for the service of man, is neither adequately expressed in its
organization nor present to the minds of those engaged in it, because it is
not regarded as a function but as an opportunity for personal gain or
advancement or display, that the economic life of modern societies is in a
perpetual state of morbid irritation' (ibid., p. 177). (For an account of the
intellectual tradition from which Tawney's thought stemmed, see
Williams, R., *Culture and Society, 1780–1950*, London, 1959.) The parallel-
ism between these two thinkers' views of capitalism and socialism even
extends to their imagery (sickness and health) and their broad conceptions
of economic history. There was one respect, however, in which Durkheim
was nearer to solidarism than to Tawney and guild socialism: his attitude
to the employers. They would continue to play a crucial part and would be
represented separately in the industrial corporations (see Chapters 17 and
26, below, and Barnes, 1920, p. 251).

70. 1950a, p. 55: tr. 1957a, p. 45 (S.L.).

71. ibid., p. 58: tr. p. 47 (S.L.).

In particular, if the 'State' referred to 'the agents of the sovereign authority' and 'political society' to 'the complex group of which the State is the eminent organ', then 'the principal duties of civic ethics are clearly those which the citizens have to the State, and, reciprocally, those which the State has to individuals'.[72]

Durkheim's definition of the State was in terms, not of authority or power, nor of ethical purposes, but rather of function: the State was a collection of special groups 'qualified to think and to act instead of and on behalf of society'.[73] Government and parliament constituted an organizing centre of thought and decision, sometimes influenced but not determined by public opinion in the wider society. The State was 'a group of officials of a special kind, within which ideas and decisions are evolved which involve the whole society without being the creation of society'.[74] Thus it was essentially deliberative (this being true both of the executive and legislative branches); execution was, strictly speaking, the task of administrative agencies of all sorts. The difference between the latter and the State was analogous to 'that between the muscular system and the central nervous system'.[75] In brief, the state was 'the very organ of social thought'.[76]

As to the purposes of the State, Durkheim approached this time-honoured question of political theory with care: he wished to pose it as a sociological and not as a philosophical question. Thus he put it as follows: 'what end does the State normally pursue, and in consequence ought it to pursue, in the social conditions of the present time?'[77] He answered this

72. ibid., p. 59: tr. p. 48 (S.L.).

73. ibid., p. 60: tr. p. 48. The English translation of 1950a, pp. 59–60, is completely misleading; at certain points the English states the reverse of the French.

74. ibid., p. 61: tr. pp. 49–50 (S.L.).

75. ibid., p. 62: tr. p. 51. There is a very close but seemingly unwitting, parallel between this view of government (and, indeed, Durkheim's account of democracy), on the one hand, and the very similar ideas of Karl Deutsch and his followers, on the other: cf., for instance, Deutsch, K., *The Nerves of Government* (New York, 1963).

76. ibid.

77. ibid., p. 63: tr. p. 51 (S.L.).

in two ways. First, and negatively, he examined and rejected two traditional theories of the State. The first of these, the liberal-individualist view (found in Spencer and the classical economists, on the one hand, and in Kant, Rousseau and the Idealists, on the other), accorded the State a decreasing and ideally minimal role of safeguarding individual rights; but this was contradicted by the uninterrupted historical growth in the functions of the State. The second traditional theory was what he called the 'mystical solution',[78] which he associated with Hegel. This argued that the State should pursue a truly social end, peculiar to each society, which did not concern individuals and of which they were the mere instruments; the individual must work for the glory, grandeur and wealth of society, and in return he would receive 'some of the rays of that glory', which would be sufficient recompense for his pains.[79] Durkheim observed (it was at the height of the Dreyfus Affair) that this doctrine, 'profiting from the present confusion of ideas',[80] was about to undergo a kind of rebirth: France, which had hitherto been hostile to it, seemed ready to welcome it.

The positive answer Durkheim offered to the question of the proper ends of the State was in terms of the specific requirements of modern societies, which he saw as largely dictated by the values normally characteristic of those societies. Thus the modern State existed alongside the modern cult of the individual; indeed the growth of the former coincided with and partly explained that of the latter. Durkheim argued that the individual was 'in certain respects, the very product of the State, since the activity of the State [is] essentially liberating for the individual'.[81] The historical evidence allowed one to accept 'this relation of cause and effect between the advance of abmoral individualism and the advance of the State'.[82] Except in abnormal cases, 'the stronger the State, the more the individual is respected'.[83]

78. ibid., p. 66: tr. p. 54.
79. ibid.
80. ibid.
81. ibid., p. 71: tr. p. 57 (S.L.).
82. ibid. (S.L.).
83. ibid.

Durkheim's pursuit of the implications of this idea led him to develop a liberal political theory that was reminiscent both of T. H. Green and of Alexis de Tocqueville, with a strongly interventionist State offset by a plurality of countervailing secondary groups. It was the State which 'creates and organizes and makes a reality' of the individual's 'natural rights',[84] indeed its 'essential function' was to 'liberate individual personalities',[85] by offsetting the pressure on them of local, domestic, ecclesiastical, occupational and other secondary groups; the latter, on the other hand, offset the potential tyranny of the State. It was 'out of this conflict of social forces that individual liberties are born'.[86] Hence, in a society characterized by social pluralism and individualist values, the State had 'the right and the duty to play the widest possible role in all spheres of collective life, without, however, becoming a *mystique*'.[87]

This theory entailed an incisive critique of the view of the State, held by utilitarian and Kantian individualism, as confined to 'the functions of a supreme arbiter, of the administrator of a totally negative justice'[88]; on the contrary, Durkheim held that the State 'must deploy energies proportionate to those it must counterbalance'.[89] Likewise, it implied a critique of theories of natural rights: the right of an individual depended not on the notion of the individual as such, but on 'the way in which society puts [the right] into practice, conceives it, and appraises it'.[90] Social beliefs were progressively expanding the scope of these rights and everything 'leads one to foresee that we will become more alive to what concerns the human personality'.[91] Accordingly, the 'fundamental duty of the State' was, as for Green, essentially moral, not to say religious: it was to 'progressively call the individual

84. ibid., p. 74: tr. p. 60.
85. ibid., p. 77: tr. p. 62 (S.L.).
86. ibid., p. 78: tr. p. 63.
87. ibid.: tr. p. 64 (S.L.).
88. ibid., p. 79: tr. p. 65 (S.L.).
89. ibid. (S.L.).
90. ibid., p. 81: tr. p. 67 (S.L.).
91. ibid., p. 83: tr. p. 68 (S.L.).

into moral existence', to maintain the religious cult of the individual, 'to organize the cult, to watch over it, to ensure its regular functioning and development'.[92] In particular and in practice, this meant

planning the social environment so that the individual may realize himself more fully, controlling the social machine so that it will bear less heavily on individuals, guaranteeing the peaceful exchange of services and the co-operation of all men of good will aiming at an ideal which they pursue peacefully and in common. . .[93]

The state had special responsibility to impose rules of justice on economic exchanges, to ensure that 'each is treated as he deserves, that he is freed of all unjust and humiliating dependence, that he is joined to his fellows and to the group without abandoning his personality to them'.[94] The State was 'above all, the organ *par excellence* of moral discipline'.[95]

Durkheim continued the argument by examining the relations between State, society and individual under democracy. He took democracy to be the ideal, and normal, form of State within a modern industrial society – that is, the form normally most appropriate to its collective beliefs and sentiments. His contribution to democratic theory lay both in his definition and in his justification of democracy. Rejecting as unhelpful Montesquieu's definition in terms of the numbers of those governing, and as 'primitive' the view of democracy as 'the political form of a society governing itself, where the government is spread throughout the *milieu* of the nation',[96] he chose rather to classify political systems along a continuum ranging from one extreme at which 'the governmental consciousness (*conscience*) is as isolated as possible from the rest of society, and has a minimum range' to the other at which the extent of this consciousness and the degree of communication between state and society are at a maximum. The latter point represented the maximization of democracy; in general, the defining

92. ibid., p. 84: tr. pp. 69–70 (S.L.).
93. ibid., p. 86: tr. p. 71 (S.L.).
94. ibid., p. 87: tr. p. 72 (S.L.).
95. ibid. (S.L.).
96. ibid., p. 99: tr. p. 82.

characteristics of democracy were '(1) the greatest extension of governmental consciousness; (2) the closest communication between this consciousness and the mass of individuals'.[97] From the first of these there resulted a diminution of traditionalism and of resistance to change: matters that were formerly obscure 'increasingly reach the clear region of the social consciousness, namely the governmental consciousness'.[98] Democracy thus appeared as

the political form by which society arrives at the purest consciousness of itself. A people is more democratic in so far as deliberation, reflection and the critical spirit play a more considerable role in the conduct of public affairs. It is less democratic in so far as unawareness, unconsidered practices, obscure sentiments and, in brief, unexamined prejudices are predominant.[99]

Thus Durkheim argued for the 'moral superiority' of democracy in contemporary societies: it was 'a system based on reflection, it allows the citizen to accept the laws of his country with more understanding, and thus with less passivity'[1]; and, further, it was 'the political system that conforms best to our present-day notion of the individual'.[2]

From these arguments Durkheim derived a critique of the mandate theory ('The role of the State . . . is not to express and sum up the unreflective thought of the mass of the people but to superimpose on this unreflective thought a more considered thought . . .'[3]), which he traced back to Rousseau and which he believed to be partly responsible for the degeneracy of Third Republic politics: the idea that 'the government is only the translator of general wills' was 'current among us' and, with certain qualifications, lay 'at the basis of our parliamentary practices'.[4] Thus he concluded with a number of practical proposals whose aim was to interpose 'secondary

97. ibid., pp. 101, 107: tr. pp. 84, 88 (S.L.).
98. ibid., p. 106: tr. p. 87 (S.L.).
99. ibid., pp. 107-8: tr. p. 89 (S.L.).
 1. ibid., p. 110: tr. p. 91 (S.L.).
 2. ibid., p. 109: tr. p. 90.
 3. ibid., p. 111: tr. p. 92.
 4. ibid., p. 114: tr. p. 94 (S.L.).

cadres ... between the individual and the State'. Such bodies (regional and, hopefully, occupational) would increase the autonomy of the government, while preserving 'continuous communication between it and all the other social organs'.[5] Ultimately there might be two-stage elections, with the revived occupational groups serving as the intermediary electoral units.

Finally, Durkheim drew from this account of democracy a new set of justifications for political obligation. The obligation to respect the law did not follow from having willed it (here Durkheim echoed Hume); what was crucial was rather

the way in which [the law] is made, the competence of those whose function it is to make it and the nature of the specific organization rendering possible their execution of that function. Respect for the law depends on the value of the legislators and the value of the political system. The particular advantage of democracy in this respect is that, thanks to the communication established between government and citizens, the latter are in a position to judge the way in which the former fulfils its role and, knowing the facts more fully, are able to give or withhold their confidence.[6]

The duty to vote in present conditions was a real duty, though the time might come when appointments to public bodies might result from the pressure of opinion in other ways. As it was, in the present abnormal situation in which it was 'on the mass of individuals that the whole weight of the society rests',[7] each citizen had 'to some extent to turn into a statesman'.[8] As things were, the only agents of public life were 'the multitude of individual forces'.[9] The urgent task and 'primary duty' was to bring this anomic and disorganized state to an end, by 'creating those secondary organs which, as they take shape, will at the same time liberate the individual from the State and the State from the individual, while increasingly dispensing the latter from a task for which he is not fitted'.[10]

5. ibid., p. 121: tr. p. 101 (S.L.).
6. ibid., p. 129: tr. p. 108 (S.L.).
7. ibid., p. 130: tr. p. 108.
8. ibid.
9. ibid.
10. ibid. (S.L.).

HOMICIDE, PROPERTY AND CONTRACT

The remaining lectures of the course, concerning 'Duties in General', consisted, in effect, of comparative historical surveys relating changing norms of behaviour to changing systems of values, and of studies of the contemporary functioning of those norms. Thus rules prohibiting homicide were a function of collective ideas and sentiments concerning the value of human life; with the progressive divinization of the latter, the former had become more rigorous. In examining the contemporary functioning of these rules, Durkheim rather questionably argued that the statistical evidence showed a downward trend in the rate of mortality by homicide in civilized countries (except during wars, which were a reversion to a more primitive type of collective state). His consideration of the rules protecting property began with a critique of the influential theories of Locke and Mill, deriving property from the labour of the individual ('To derive property from labour is to accept that the value of things results from objective and impersonal causes, independent of all evaluation. But this is not so. Value depends upon opinion and is a matter of opinion'[11]); and he went on to attack the equally *a priori* theories of Kant and Rousseau. He advanced instead a theory of property which assumed that it was 'the opinion of each society which makes certain objects susceptible to appropriation, and others not'.[12] His explanation of the origins of property rules was in terms of primitive religious beliefs and an original link between property and taboo. The moral and legal bond between owner and thing possessed had originally been a collective, religious bond specifying the sacred possessions of the group (sacrifices had been the first taxes). Originally, property had been primarily related to land and associated with mystic beliefs; it had become progressively individualized and secularized[13] and was becoming increasingly dependent on

11. ibid., p. 149: tr. p. 125 (S.L.). 12. ibid., p. 164: tr. p. 138 (S.L.).

13. '...the individualisation of property occurred because landed property lost its sacrosanct quality, which was absorbed by man, and because other forms of property which did not themselves have this quality developed sufficiently to establish a distinct and separate set of legal rules' (ibid., p. 199: tr. p. 168 – S.L.).

contract rather than inheritance. Finally, in his discussion of
the rules of contract, he sought to account for the changing
nature of these rules in different societies by looking at the
changing 'non-contractual element in the contract' – in
particular, the beliefs characteristic of those societies, which
were themselves partly to be explained by relating them to
features of the social structure. Thus, blood covenants and
communion rites, incorporating individuals to social groups
in certain ways, were to be explained in terms of sacred beliefs
relating to kinship and clan structure. Real contracts were to
be explained in terms of (changing) beliefs about property.
Consensual contracts were to be explained in terms of beliefs
about the rights and freedom of individuals, that were themselves related to the contemporary stage of industrial society,
in which the economy was not yet subject to moral rules. And,
finally, what Durkheim called contracts of equity, which he
saw as increasingly in evidence (implying a 'whole recasting of
the rules of property'[14]) were to be accounted for in terms of
emerging ideas about justice and equality. ('It is not·sufficient
that the contract be consented to; it must be just . . .'[15]) These
ideas were linked to the social order which he believed to be
emerging and which needed to be brought into being in the
face of the anarchic forces of unregulated capitalism – an order
that was, in the ways we have considered, at once socialist,
liberal and democratic.

14. ibid., p. 252: tr. p. 215.
15. ibid., p. 243: tr. p. 207 (S.L.).

Chapter 14
The History of Sociology

THE last public course in sociology which Durkheim delivered at Bordeaux was entitled 'History of Sociological Doctrines'.[1] He valued these lectures, seeing them virtually as a kind of homage to his scientific ancestors.[2] On the other hand, the relatively meagre published evidence of his work in this field[3] indicates a tough-minded and critical approach to the social and political theories of the past – an approach determined by the single desire to specify and appraise the ideas they contained that were of sociological significance.

Mauss wrote in 1925 that there then existed manuscripts of series of lectures on Hobbes, on Rousseau (whose 'sociological spirit' he had discovered, a 'spirit very different from the anarchism ordinarily said to originate with Rousseau'), on Condorcet (for whom he had a 'keen admiration', whose writings he 'knew thoroughly' and whose influence on Saint-Simon and Comte he noted), on Saint-Simon and Comte themselves, and finally a manuscript of lectures of a much earlier date on 'The Sociology and Ethics of Spencer'.[4] According to Mauss, Durkheim intended to publish most of this material in a volume under the title *The Origins of Sociology*. In 1925 Mauss wrote, 'We will endeavour to realize this wish'.[5] But he never did, and the manuscripts no longer exist.

Durkheim's interest in the history of sociology was constant throughout his life, though his interpretations of that history

1. 1901–2: see Appendix A, below. All that survives of this course is 1918b: repr. 1953a: tr. 1960b. See below.

2. See Mauss, 1925a, p. 15.

3. For example, 1890a, 1892a, 1895e, 1900b, 1903c, 1915a, 1918b and 1925b.

4. Mauss, 1925a, p. 15. The lectures on Comte were taken up again at the Sorbonne in 1915–16 (see Appendix A, below), but no manuscript survives of that course.

5. ibid.

changed, even while at Bordeaux. In 1886 he had written of sociology's always having existed in a 'latent and diffuse' form and of the 'simplistic' conceptions of Rousseau and the classical economists that the state is artificially conjoined to society, rather than emanating from it.[6] Two years later, in his inaugural lecture, he summed up his account of the history of sociology by observing that the subject had been 'born with the economists, established with Comte, consolidated with Spencer, delimited with Schaeffle and led to specialize with the German economists and jurists'.[7] In 1892 he wrote that it was 'Montesquieu who first laid down the fundamental principles of social science'[8]; and, as we have seen, his attention increasingly turned to the history of the subject in France, so that by 1900 he was writing:

To determine the part played by France in the development of sociology during the nineteenth century is, in large measure, to write the history of that science; for it is amongst us and during that century that it was born, and it has remained an essentially French science.[9]

And he continued that same article by tracing the theoretical development from Montesquieu and Condorcet (whose efforts remained 'brilliant personal works', which were 'unable to serve as the point of departure for a scientific tradition'[10]) through Saint-Simon (the 'first to have formulated' the 'idea of social science'[11]), Comte (with whom 'the great project conceived by Saint-Simon began to become a reality'[12]) and Cournot (whose work, however, remained an eclectic 'philosophy of history'[13]) to Espinas (who found in society 'an organization of ideas' and showed that 'sociology's essential object is to discover how collective *représentations* form and

6. 1886a, pp. 77–8.
7. 1888a, p. 41.
8. 1953a, p. 110: tr. 1960b, p. 61.
9. 1900b, p. 609.
10. ibid., p. 610.
11. ibid.
12. ibid., p. 611.
13. ibid., p. 613.

combine'[14]) and thence to his own work and that of his colleagues and contemporaries.[15]

The only two studies in depth in this area which survive relate to the pre-history rather than the history of sociology, though they both concern thinkers who may be considered as French. The first, the study of Montesquieu, was Durkheim's Latin thesis of 1892[16]; the second, the study of Rousseau's *Social Contract*, was the manuscript of Durkheim's lectures on Rousseau in 1901–2, published posthumously by Xavier Léon.[17] Both advance original and still controversial interpretations of their subjects.

MONTESQUIEU

It was entirely natural that, in his search for sociological ancestors, Durkheim should turn to the author of *The Spirit of the Laws*, with his keen sense of the variability, complexity and interdependence of social phenomena, his conservative view of the link between the scientific understanding of society and the danger of seeking its radical reconstruction, and his sensitivity to the diversity of societies. Above all, Montesquieu had a feeling for the specificity of social phenomena; as Durkheim put it, he 'understood with a wonderful lucidity that the nature of societies is no less stable and consistent than that of man and that it is no easier to modify the types of a society than the species of an animal'.[18]

Durkheim offered both an exegesis and a critique of Montesquieu's sociologically relevant ideas.[19] His general view was

14. ibid., p. 648.
15. See Chapter 20, below.
16. 1892a: tr. into French 1937b and 1953a: tr. into English 1960b.
17. 1918b: repr. 1953a: tr. 1960b.
18. 1953a, p. 52: tr. 1960b, p. 21.
19. A contemporary authority on Montesquieu has written that 'much of what Durkheim said about Montesquieu was cogent and still remains among the best analyses of one great practitioner by another' (Melvin Richter, 'Comparative Political Analysis in Montesquieu and Tocqueville', *Comparative Politics*, 1, 1969, p. 156). That analysis can, however, be challenged for its failure to see that Montesquieu's types were ideal types, and that he saw politics as relatively autonomous (ibid.).

that Montesquieu had made social science 'aware of its subject matter, its nature and its method' and laid the 'groundwork' on which it was to be established; indeed, no one had 'perceived so clearly the conditions necessary for [its] establishment'.[20] He singled out two ideas, implicit in Montesquieu's thought, as crucial: the notions of *type* as applied to societies and of *law* as applied to social phenomena. Concerning the first, he admired Montesquieu's own typology, regarding it as expressing 'not without some truth the real division of things',[21] but he criticized its political emphasis (for 'the nature of the supreme power can be modified, while that of society remains unchanged, or conversely it can remain identical in societies which differ in the extreme'[22]) as well as his inconsistent view that the despotic type was intrinsically abnormal. He regarded Montesquieu's conception of law as recognizing a 'fixed and necessary order' in social phenomena and denying that 'societies are organized according to man's caprice and that their history depends on accidents'[23]; but he criticized its teleological character and his tendency to apply it to 'relations between ideas rather than between things'.[24] More generally, Durkheim criticized Montesquieu for confusing laws concerning efficient causes, according to which 'social institutions follow from the nature of things',[25] with laws relating to final causes, which 'can only exist by being established through the special will of a legislator'.[26] To this conceptual ambiguity he traced what he saw as a fundamental

20. 1953a, p. 28: tr. p. 2.
21. ibid., p. 111: tr. p. 62 (S.L.).
22. ibid., p. 69: tr. p. 33 (S.L.).
23. ibid., p. 112: tr. p. 63 (S.L.).
24. ibid.
25. ibid., p. 81: tr. p. 40.
26. ibid., p. 82: tr. p. 41 (S.L.). 'In Montesquieu's work . . . the lawgiver emerges as the indispensable maker of the laws . . . If we assume, however, that the laws are produced by efficient causes of which men may often be unaware, the function of the lawgiver is reduced . . . Laws are not devices that the lawgiver thinks up because they seem to be in harmony with the nature of the society. They spring most often from causes which engender them by a kind of physical necessity' (ibid., pp. 81, 84, 84–5: tr. pp. 40, 42, 43).

ambiguity in Montesquieu's method between deduction and induction: Montesquieu's method was essentially deductive, and he used evidence merely to illustrate its conclusions. In addition, Durkheim criticized Montesquieu for being blind to the idea of progress: he 'does not suspect that these different kinds of society [Republic, Monarchy, Despotism, and the democracy of barbaric peoples] descend from the same origin and succeed one another'[27] and he failed to see that

a society contains within it conflicting forces, because it is gradually emerging from a previous form and is also gradually tending towards another to which it will give birth. He fails to recognize the continuous process by which a society, while remaining true to its nature, constantly becomes something new.[28]

Thus he overstressed the role of concomitant environmental conditions and ignored the dynamic of history – the '*vis a tergo* that drives societies forward'.[29] This criticism, which was the opposite to that which he advanced against Comte, was later to be advanced, with some justice, against Durkheim's own method as set out in *The Rules*.

Durkheim found much else of sociological value in Montesquieu's ideas. While himself drawing a sharp distinction between 'science' and practice, or 'art' ('The sharper the distinction between science and art, the more useful science can be to art'[30]), and criticizing Montesquieu for failing to do so, he clearly approved of Montesquieu's approach to the problem of practice:

Since, for each social body, *salus populi* is the supreme law, and since society cannot survive without taking care to safeguard its specific nature, it suffices to describe that nature to be in a position to determine what should be aimed at and what avoided: for sickness must be avoided at all costs and health is always desirable.[31]

27. ibid., pp. 106–7: tr. p. 58. Durkheim qualifies this evolutionism by denying its unilinearity, preferring the image of 'a tree with branches spreading in different directions' (ibid., p. 106: tr. p. 58).
28. ibid., pp. 107–8: tr. p. 59 (S.L.).
29. ibid., p. 108: tr. p. 59. Cf. Davy, 1949.
30. ibid., p. 34: tr. p. 7 (S.L.).
31. ibid., p. 46: tr. p. 17.

He further approved of Montesquieu's relativism ('Montesquieu understands that the rules of life vary with the conditions of life ... What monarchy should seek, democracy should avoid'[32]), though he rightly discerned in Montesquieu a residual belief in natural law. He approved of his classification of societies as being based, not merely on political factors, but also on 'the number, arrangement and cohesion of their elements'[33]; indeed, he saw mechanical solidarity in Montesquieu's republic and organic solidarity in his monarchy (in which the famous 'separation of powers' was merely a particular form of the division of labour, preserving freedom through mutual balance[34]). Durkheim even attributed to Montesquieu what he currently saw as the crucial determining role of the volume of society, on the grounds that the principle peculiar to each of Montesquieu's types 'ceases to operate if the population increases or diminishes excessively'[35] (though Montesquieu had failed to see the importance of dynamic density). Finally, he endorsed Montesquieu's use of the comparative method and his emphasis on 'the reciprocal relations between social phenomena'.[36] Without drawing the conclusions implied by his own principles, Montesquieu had, in Durkheim's view, 'paved the way for his successors'.[37]

ROUSSEAU

Durkheim's interest in Rousseau is no more surprising than that in Montesquieu. Cuvillier records that he was 'fully

32. ibid., pp. 47–8: tr. p. 18 (S.L.).

33. ibid., p. 58: tr. p. 26 (S.L.).

34. Thus, there was unity, homogeneity, equality and no division of labour in republics: the 'social spirit' existed in the minds of all, and there was little individuality. In monarchies, however, the division of labour was at its maximum, inequalities and personal interests developed, but the 'very diversity of the component parts makes for cohesion' (ibid., p. 65: tr. p. 30). Hence (social) *virtue* characterized the former and (individual) *honour* the latter. Cf. Richter, art. cit., p. 157.

35. ibid., p. 78: tr. p. 38.

36. ibid., p. 104: tr. p. 57 (S.L.). 'Montesquieu, however, saw quite clearly that all these elements form a whole and that if taken separately, without reference to the others, they cannot be understood' (ibid., p. 103: tr. p. 56).

37. ibid., p. 105: tr. p. 57.

aware of having been influenced by Rousseau, who was one of his favourite authors',[38] and, indeed, it has been suggested by a recent writer that his work contains the 'purest restatement of Rousseau' and that 'Durkheim has been the medium, so to speak, by which Rousseau has left his mark on modern social science'.[39] This is too strong: the continuities between the two thinkers are balanced by their equally suggestive divergences.

Durkheim's ideas are certainly close to Rousseau's at a number of points. He shared Rousseau's concern to counteract the individual's 'particular will', his potentially anarchic egoistic desires, by placing him securely within the context of a group and a system of impersonal and rationally justifiable rules; these rules would induce internal satisfaction by providing the individual with an external, and just, framework of order. For Durkheim, as for Rousseau, the multiplication of self-interested desires was psychologically and socially harmful; the remedy for both thinkers lay in the internalization of norms accepted as rational and just.[40] Secondly, there is an obvious parallel between the *conscience collective* and the General Will; they are both collective in source, impersonal in form and authoritative with respect to individuals. Like the General Will, the *conscience collective* was the 'work of the community'[41]

38. ibid., p. 121: tr. p. 143 (fn.). See Chapter 6, above.

39. Wolin, 1960, p. 372.

40. Wolin is, however, mistaken to argue that Durkheim postulated a society in which 'As in Rousseau's community, no tension existed between self and society; there was only the *moi commun* of perfect identification' (op. cit., p. 372). In fact, as we have seen, Durkheim regarded some degree of anomie as indispensable to industrial societies and came to express a view close to Freud's of the painful (and growing) personal consequences of social repression. Cf.: 'We must . . . do violence to certain of our strongest inclinations. Therefore, since the role of the social being in our single selves will grow ever more important as history moves ahead, it is wholly improbable that there will ever be an era in which man is required to resist himself to a lesser degree, an era in which he can live a life that is easier and less full of tension. To the contrary, all evidence compels us to expect our effort in the struggle between the two beings within us to increase with the growth of civilization' (1914a: tr. 1960c, pp. 338–9).

41. 1887c, p. 119.

embodying 'something other than the totality of individuals composing it'.[42] Thirdly, Durkheim's social realism was, in part, foreshadowed in Rousseau, who at one point wrote of society as 'a moral entity having specific qualities distinct from those of the individual beings who compose it, somewhat as chemical compounds have properties that they owe to none of their elements'.[43] Durkheim saw this 'remarkable passage' as showing that 'Rousseau was keenly aware of the specificity of the social order. He conceived it clearly as an order of facts different from purely individual facts.'[44]

Fourthly, Durkheim and Rousseau were alike in seeing an analogy between the satisfaction of man's organic needs through an equilibrium in the natural environment (Rousseau's state of nature) and the satisfaction of his moral needs through an equilibrium in the social environment. In Rousseau's state of nature, as Durkheim wrote, 'so long as man has relations only with the physical environment, instinct and sensation suffice for all his needs',[45] while in the ideal society specified in the *Social Contract*, 'civil man, though differing profoundly from natural man, maintains the same relation to society as natural man to physical nature'.[46] One might compare this most plausible interpretation of Rousseau with the following passage from *Suicide*, concerning the overcoming of anomie:

A regulative force must play the same role for moral needs which the organism plays for physical needs. This means that the force can only be moral. The awakening of conscience interrupted the state of equilibrium of the animal's dormant existence; only conscience, therefore, can furnish the means to re-establish it.[47]

Finally, there is a close similarity between Durkheim's and Rousseau's conceptions of liberty (recalling that of Kant, which was influenced by Rousseau and influenced Durkheim). Rousseau's man was free through collective and impersonal

42. 1924a (1951 edn), p. 73: tr. 1953b, p. 51.
43. Cited in 1953a, p. 136: tr. 1960b, p. 82.
44. ibid.: tr. p. 83.
45. ibid., pp. 127–8: tr. p. 75.
46. ibid., p. 149: tr. p. 93 (S.L.).
47. 1897a, p. 275: tr. 1951a, p. 248.

forces liberating him both from personal dependency on others and from his own imperious desires: 'The truly free man desires only what is possible and does as he pleases.'[48] For Rousseau and Durkheim, man 'is free only when a superior force compels his recognition, provided, however, that he accepts this superiority and that his submission is not won by lies and artifice. He is free if he is held in check.'[49] As Durkheim frequently said, 'liberty is the fruit of regulation'.[50]

Against these points of convergence, however, one must set their differences, marked by Durkheim's criticisms of Rousseau. First, Rousseau used an essentially individualistic method of explanation: his natural man was 'simply man without what he owes to society',[51] and he held that since 'nature ends with the individual, then everything that goes beyond the individual is bound to be artificial'.[52] The state of nature was a 'methodological device', the product of a sort of Cartesian intellectual purge, which misconstrued the entirely natural character of social phenomena and social causation.[53] Secondly, and closely related to this, Durkheim saw a contradiction in Rousseau between 'the conception of society as a product of reason and the conception of society as an organism'.[54] Rousseau had, Durkheim thought, been led to this contradiction by failing to see that society, while being 'superior' to individuals, was external to them. He had failed to make the intellectual leap necessary in order to 'widen the circle of natural phenomena'.[55] Thirdly, Durkheim pointed

48. Quotation from Rousseau, cited in 1953a, p. 144: tr. 1960b, p. 88.
49. ibid., p. 144: tr. p. 88.
50. 1925a, p. 62: tr. 1961a, p. 54.
51. 1953a, p. 116: tr. 1960b, p. 66.
52. ibid., p. 117: tr. 66.
53. On the other hand, it can be seen as making an important sociological point: as Robert Derathé has put it, Rousseau 'showed that the intellectual and moral development of man is a result of social life' (*Jean-Jacques Rousseau et la science politique de son temps*, Paris, 1950, p. 379, cited in ibid., p. 121: tr. p. 143 – S.L.). Cf. Durkheim's observation that the 'great difference between man and the animal, that is the superior development of man's mental life, can be reduced to man's greater sociability' (1902b, p. 338: tr. 1933b, p. 347 – S.L.).
54. 1953a, p. 138: tr. p. 84.
55. ibid., p. 139: tr. p. 85.

to the individualist character of Rousseau's account of obligation, authority and sovereignty. Despite his awareness that
'the individual is dependent on society', he saw 'society as a
mere instrument for the use of the individual'.[56] Rousseau
thus found himself unable to give a sociological account of
obligation.[57] Fourthly, and in consequence, the General Will
was entirely closed in upon itself, moving within a realm of
universals, unable to express itself concretely, because 'Rousseau sees only two poles of human reality, the abstract, general
individual who is the agent and objective of social existence,
and the concrete empirical individual who is the antagonist of
all collective existence. He fails to see that, though in a sense
these two poles are irreconcilable, the first without the second
is no more than a logical fiction.'[58] Finally, Durkheim observed
how precarious was Rousseau's social cohesion, both with
respect to actual, historical societies and to the ideal society he
wished to establish:

just as he fails to explain how social life, even in its imperfect
historical forms, could come into being, he has great difficulty in
showing how it can possibly cast off its imperfections and establish
itself on an ideal basis. So unstable is its foundation in the nature of
things that it cannot but appear to us as a tottering structure whose
delicate balance can be established and maintained only by an almost
miraculous conjunction of circumstances.[59]

Rousseau's problem had been 'to find a form of association
... whose laws can be superimposed upon the fundamental
laws inherent in the *state of nature* without doing violence to
them'.[60] He had succeeded in showing that such a form of
association was conceivable, and that in this sense social life

56. ibid., p. 166: tr. p. 108.
57. Cf.: 'the Rousseauist conception of obligation is unrelated to
Durkheim's: it is rigorously individualist. Political authority has its basis
in the act by which the individual commits himself to obeying the general
will. The primary source of sovereignty is the individual himself'
(Derathé, op. cit., p. 239, cited in ibid., pp. 165: not translated in 1960b).
58. 1953a, p. 191: tr. p. 131.
59. ibid., pp. 197–8: tr. pp. 137–8 (S.L.).
60. ibid., p. 115: tr. p. 65.

was not in principle 'contrary to the natural order': what he had failed to show, Durkheim argued, was 'how it is possible'.[61]

To show this was, as we have seen, the first and fundamental problem of Durkheim's sociology from the time of his first lecture-course on 'Social Solidarity', which had begun by asking 'what are the social bonds which unite men one with another?'[62] His reflections on the pre-history of sociology led him to a very clear perception of the inadequacy of non-sociological approaches to the problem. He saw that for Hobbes the explanation of social order was entirely individualist: for Hobbes it was

an act of will which gives rise to social order and an act of will, that is constantly renewed, which maintains it. Societies are formed because men desire, in order to escape the horrors of the state of war, to submit themselves to an absolute sovereign; and societies are maintained because that sovereign prevents them from breaking up. It is he who makes the law, and it is men's submission to his sovereign will that constitutes the entire social bond. They must obey him because he commands. Of course, they consent to this dependence because it is in their interests, but those interests do not explain all the details of social organization. Once the State is established, it is the head of the State who makes the law, accepting no check to his power.[63]

He regarded Montesquieu's explanation as no less inadequate: it could only account for the relation of 'appropriateness' between specified social conditions and the laws appropriate to them. The laws were instituted by the legislator – a picture as individualist as that of Hobbes. What Montesquieu saw was that there were certain laws which were required by 'the conditions prevailing in society'.[64] He did not explain the genesis and operation of actual laws and social practices, whether appropriate or not. Rousseau, Durkheim thought, was even less concerned to provide such an explanation. His conception was of an (ideal) society in which the 'social system is based on

61. ibid., p. 197: tr. p. 137.
62. See chapter 7, above.
63. 1953a, pp. 195–6: tr. p. 136 (S.L.).
64. ibid., p. 196: tr. p. 136.

an objective harmony of interests and on the state of public opinion, mores and customs, and the law can only express this state of affairs'.[65] Rather than providing empirical explanations, his aim was to 'shape men's minds in such a way that resistance [to the sovereign] does not occur'.[66] Durkheim's interpretation of Hobbes, Montesquieu and Rousseau clearly implied that it was only within a sociological perspective, first fully articulated by Saint-Simon and Comte and first put to work by himself and his colleagues, that the problem of social solidarity could appear as an empirical problem amenable to the procedures of science.

65. ibid.: tr. pp. 136–7 (S.L.).
66. ibid., pp. 196–7: tr. p. 137.

Chapter 15

The *Année sociologique*

THE range of Durkheim's teaching at Bordeaux implied a view of the scope of sociology that was neither modest nor unambitious. Yet the many-sidedness of his scientific work contrasts with a cardinal principle he often expressed: that in modern societies, work, including intellectual work, must become more and more specialized, while remaining an organic part of a total system.[1] What was needed was a massive programme of collaboration, based on an intellectual division of labour. Therefore in 1896, instead of continuing his work on socialism, he decided to establish, along with a small number of colleagues and pupils, a new journal, the *Année sociologique*, that would not only provide an annual survey of the strictly sociological literature, but also, to quote the Preface to the first volume (1896–7; published 1898), 'regular information concerning studies which are being carried on in the special sciences – the histories of law, culture and religion; moral statistics; economics; and so on – for it is these special sciences that offer the materials out of which sociology must be built'.[2] In addition, there would be original papers (*Mémoires originaux*) that would contribute directly to this task of construction.[3]

1. '. . . in advanced societies, our duty is not to extend the area of our activity, but to concentrate and specialize it'; 'as [the different sciences] become specialized, these grand syntheses can no longer be anything more than premature generalizations, for it becomes increasingly impossible for one human mind to gain a sufficiently exact knowledge of this immense mass of phenomena, laws and hypotheses which they must contain' (1902b, pp. 396, 353: tr. 1933b, pp. 401, 362 – S.L.).

2. 1898a (i), p. 1: tr. 1960c, p. 341.

3. From vol. XI (1906–9; publ. 1910) the *Mémoires originaux* were published separately (see 1910a (i)). For a discussion of the organizing principles of the *Année* see Bouglé, 1907, appendix ('Note sur *l'Année sociologique*'). Davy has described the *Année* as 'the laboratory in which [Durkheim's] method was made precise, flexible and broad' (Davy, 1919, p. 196). See also Mauss, 1927b.

Durkheim and his fellow editors[4] thus treated the business of reviewing and, indeed the very organizing of their material under classifications, as a creative task; one of the chief purposes of the *Année* was 'gradually to work out the natural divisions of sociology'.[5] Durkheim wrote to Bouglé in 1897:

As regards the special branches of sociology, we could not be complete; it is also not a good thing that we should be too complete to begin with. One must leave some scope for future progress... Our *Année* must provide people with a picture of what genuinely sociological production there has been, of its intensity as well as its quality. For this reason, the mediocre products must be noted; they form an element of the whole, in their fashion ... [but] if everything must find a place in our *Année*, the place must be very different [in different cases]. We must concentrate on what is important, fruitful or that can be made fruitful ... it is the more or less important residue that can be extracted from the book, whether it takes the form of data (*choses*) or ideas, which should determine the length of the analysis ... We must, don't you think, reject the current methods of criticism, which are too concerned with seeing the author behind the work, and with ranking talents instead of noting results and their importance. In matters of science, shouldn't the ranking of men be a simple consequence of ranking what one owes them, whether it be insights or information?[6]

And, in the Preface to the first volume of the *Année*, he wrote:

Our role as critics must be to extract from the works we study the objective residue, that is, the suggestive facts and the fruitful insights – whether they be interesting for their intrinsic value or because of the discussions they evoke. The critic must be the collaborator of the author, his grateful collaborator; for whatever little remains of a book after critical evaluation, that much is gained for science... Since many of [the works with which we have to deal] are not explicitly sociological, we could not be satisfied with giving their contents, with merely expounding, as it were, the materials they contain; as far as was possible, we had to submit them to a preliminary elaboration which would indicate to the reader what information contained in them is useful to the sociologist ... all analyses of works which refer to the same question have been

4. See Appendix C, below.
5. 1901a (ii) (1), p. 433.
6. Letter dated 20 June 1897.

grouped together in such a way that they complement and illuminate each other. By themselves, these groupings already constitute comparisons which may be useful.[7]

The classifications used underwent significant changes during the first five years of the *Année*.[8] As Bouglé put it, the fundamental task of the *Année* was 'to develop lasting frameworks for future analyses and syntheses, which follow the essential relations between social phenomena, the truths accumulated by the historical sciences, and thus to organize the latter, no longer from outside, imposing on them the conclusions of detached speculations, but from within by assimilating their conquests'.[9] Thus to trace the changes in the organization of the various sections of the *Année* is at the same time to trace the development in theoretical grasp of the various areas in question. For example within the first few volumes, the economic sociology section (edited by François Simiand) progressed from a chronological classification to an analytical one[10]; and the religious sociology section (edited by Mauss and Henri Hubert), which in the first volume had divided up the field into 'general treatises', 'primitive religions in general', 'domestic cults', 'beliefs and practices concerning the dead', 'popular cults in general, especially agrarian', 'ritual', 'myths', 'organization of the cult' and 'various notices on the great religions in general', had by the twelfth volume recast the study of religious phenomena into the following categories (themselves subdivided): 'general treatises – religious philosophy', 'religious systems of lower societies', 'national religious systems', 'universalist religious systems', 'religious systems of secondary groups', 'special cults', 'beliefs and practices called popular', 'beliefs and practices

7. 1898a (i), pp. vi–vii: tr. 1960c, pp. 346–7 (S.L.).

8. See especially Durkheim's notes; 1898a (iii), 1899a (iii), 1901a (ii) (1) and (2), 1902a (ii), 1903a (ii) (1) and (2), 1910a (ii) and 1913a (i) (1), (2), (3) and (4). See also Bouglé, op. cit.

9. op. cit., p. 166.

10. One, incidentally, which distinguished between '*régimes*' and '*formes*' of production, thus implying, as Bouglé points out, a criticism of the Marxist notion of the 'mode' of production, which does not distinguish between the technical and legal aspects of economic phenomena (see Bouglé, op. cit.).

concerning the dead', 'magic', 'ritual', 'objects and places of
the cult', 'religious *représentations*', and 'religious societies,
their law and morality'.[11] Moreover, from the second volume
onwards, a section on social morphology was included, dealing
with the 'exterior form of societies' (their 'material substratum') which poached on geography, history and demo-
graphy.[12]

Durkheim's founding of the *Année* was a new departure on
the organizational as well as the theoretical level. It was the
first example in France (apart from that of the Le Playists)
of systematic collaborative work in social science, and here
the German influence must have been strong, particularly that
of Wundt, whose psychological laboratory in Leipzig had
impressed him.[13] As he wrote to Bouglé shortly before the
publication of the first volume: 'for the first time one will see
a group of sociologists devoting themselves to a single task
and working together towards a single end'[14]; while in
another letter he wrote: 'First of all, the *Année sociologique*
must be a society of mutual assistance for the collaborators.'[15]

From the beginning he recruited promising young students
(usually philosophers) to the group.[16] It was, as Lewis Coser
has justly observed, 'probably the most brilliant ever gathered

11. Cf. 1899a (ii), and Mauss, 1968–9, I, pp. 89–106.

12. Bouglé, op. cit., p. 170. Cf. 1899a (iii), pp. 520–1: 'It is, we believe,
worth drawing these fragmentary sciences out of their isolation and
putting them in contact by reuniting them under one rubric: they will
thus achieve a sense of their unity'. Cf. Mauss and Fauconnet, 1901,
pp. 175–6.

13. See 1887a, pt II, especially p. 433. Cf. Bouglé, 1930b, p. 283:
'. . . what I was able to see of German intellectual organization made me
clearly understand the degree to which a collective effort could benefit
French sociology, an effort in groups that Durkheim would guide. I was
thus fully prepared to offer him my collaboration, to recruit collaborators
for him, in order to swell the ranks of the "*École de Bordeaux*" that he had
formed.' (For Durkheim's attitude to Bouglé, see Davy, 1967.)

14. Letter undated.

15. Letter to Bouglé dated 25 October 1897.

16. Of the Durkheimian school Hubert Bourgin (a member of it for a
time) wrote: 'it had a great power of capturing and keeping [recruits]
and it firmly retained those it had seized; moreover, it chose them well'
(*Cinquante Ans d'expérience démocratique (1874–1924)*, Paris, 1925, p. 45).

in the history of the discipline', and, compared with the other
two schools that have appeared in sociology, was much
more unified than the Chicago School, and much more comprehensive in its scope than Znaniecki's Polish school.[17] Durkheim always encouraged his collaborators to specialize across
a wide range, within the framework of the methodological
principles laid down in *The Rules*, and elaborated in Mauss and
Fauconnet's celebrated encyclopaedia article on sociology[18]
and in various methodological notes in the volumes of the
Année. He regarded these principles as specifying the conditions for scientific and impersonal achievements. Hitherto
sociology had been 'closely related to the personalities of
particular scholars', yet 'science, because it is objective, is an
essentially impersonal affair and cannot progress except
through collective labour'.[19] Thus when a hostile reviewer of
the *Année* in the *Revue de métaphysique et de morale* singled out
Durkheim's methodological views for criticism, Durkheim
wrote a very angry letter to Xavier Léon, the editor of the
Revue, protesting that '"*my sociologism*", "*my method*" are
presented as impediments of which my colleagues are invited to
disembarrass themselves'. 'What I deplore', he continued, 'is
precisely that [your reviewer] should have thought it necessary to give a personal character to the criticism of a work that
is essentially collective and impersonal and which I try to keep
as impersonal as possible.'[20]

On the other hand, Durkheim kept a firm control over the
editorship of the journal and formed a focus for the intellectual integration of the group, many of whose members were
dispersed throughout France in provincial lycées. He revised
almost all the copy and even supervised the setting up in
proofs.[21] Davy has recorded that he would send back even the

17. Coser, 1971, p. 165.
18. Mauss and Fauconnet, 1901.
19. 1898a (i) p. vii: tr. 1960c, p. 347.
20. Letter dated 21 September 1902. Durkheim took this matter so
seriously that he temporarily refused to allow Léon to publish his inaugural
lecture at Paris (1903b).
21. Davy, 1960b, p. 11.

smallest reviews to their authors, with suggestions for revision and that he 'insisted on examining everything in the smallest detail'.[22] (Durkheim wrote to Lévy-Bruhl in 1900. 'The *Année sociologique* takes up all my time'.[23]) Davy also writes of 'the clan of the *Année sociologique*', whose unifying spirit Durkheim 'created and maintained . . . without the least tyranny, leaving to each his entire liberty. He exerted influence only through the immense superiority of his mind and his method. Everyone liked to go and see him and, while receiving his advice, experience the affectionate interest he had for all. But there were no committee meetings, no gatherings, no watchword.'[24] As Durkheim himself wrote to Bouglé: 'it is neither necessary nor desirable that everyone should adopt exactly the same formula'.[25]

On this last issue there was, it is clear, a certain amount of disagreement about policy among the collaborators. It is also clear that Durkheim's own inclination was anti-eclectic, if not dogmatic. If there was no single 'formula' adopted by all, it was evident that Durkheim wished to maximize the degree of

22. Davy, 1957, p. viii. This is borne out in the letters to Bouglé and Simiand.

23. 1969b.

24. Davy, 1919, p. 195. Cf. Faublée, 1964, p. 69; and Le Bras, 1966, p. 53: '. . . a perfect liberty of thought permitted diversity of opinions'. Espinas, however, had, from the outside, a different view: he saw the Durkheimians as a 'militia' and a 'secret society' which used 'its mysteries to conceal its ambitions' and operated with 'its police, its reports, its admissions, its white and black lists' (quoted in Bourgin, 1938, p. 91). Bourgin himself later described his former colleagues thus: '[Durkheim] had been able to gather round him a group of workers – of whom many were first-rate – devoted to the work, convinced of its importance and intelligently compliant to his direction . . . He had the right to think that he would achieve what he had resolved he would achieve: a positive sociology, gradually extending to all the forms and manifestations of social life. But thinking this, and knowing that this work was to be his, he experienced and indeed cultivated the strong and exalted feeling of the obligations this work imposed – obligations of honesty, of precision, of critical judgement, of reason, which he, for his part, assumed. He also had to inspire his colleagues to observe them, though they were sometimes less punctual, less active, less rigorous than they should have been' (ibid., pp. 217–18).

25. Letter undated.

intellectual unity among his colleagues; and to a remarkable extent he succeeded. Certainly, the *Année* became more Durkheimian and less eclectic (the first issue had published Simmel and the third Ratzel) over the years. Durkheim's attitude is well brought out in a letter to Simiand, in which he discussed this very issue of policy and referred to the suggestion that the *Année sociologique mémoires* should be 'our work or the work of people still entirely in agreement with us'. 'This last principle', Durkheim told Simiand,

seems to me altogether excellent. I have no need to tell you how much it has cost me to publish certain things. I did it in the first place because in the beginning I did not dare to hope for the friendly homogeneity that has been established amongst us, and because I only thought of making the *Année* a collection, for entry into which the only qualification would be scientific honesty. I acted in this way because there was no means of acting otherwise. But it is clear that this eclecticism, however limited it may have been, harms the impression of the whole. I might add that in what has been published, it is only what comes from us that is of value.[26]

This characteristic and self-confident identification of Durkheimian sociology with the scientifically valuable was a major element in the considerable *élan* generated among the Durkheimians; but, needless to say, it also contributed greatly to the enmity of those beyond the pale.

26. Letter to Simiand dated 15 February 1902.

Chapter 16

The Reception of Durkheim's Ideas

DURKHEIM'S aggressive claims for sociology and their implied, and usually explicit, criticisms of existing disciplines and scholars were not calculated to endear him to the wider academic establishment. Davy has written of 'the militant period of the early days when [Durkheim] was the target of so many arrows and his imperious doctrine was passionately denounced by many'.[1] It is worth examining the hostilities and polemics of the Bordeaux period in some detail, because they formed part of the intellectual context within which Durkheim's thought developed, and because they were themselves a contributing factor to that development.

'THE DIVISION OF LABOUR'

The reception of his doctoral theses by the Sorbonne philosophers at his oral defence gave some indication of future hostilities. According to Bouglé, Boutroux accepted Durkheim's dedication of *The Division of Labour* to himself with a grimace and Paul Janet at one point smote the table and invoked the name of God.[2]

One observer of the defence described Durkheim's appearance and manner thus:

M. Durckheim [*sic*], tall, thin and fair, is already bald ... His voice at the start was feeble and subdued, but gradually, under the pressure of the ideas he was expressing, it rose and grew animated and warm, until it seemed capable of filling a vast vessel.[3]

He was questioned first about his Latin thesis on Montesquieu, the examiners paying tribute to its 'probing study of the

1. Davy, 1967, p. 8.
2. Bouglé, 1930b, p. 281.
3. Report to the Recteur from a M. Perreur dated 11 March 1893 in Durkheim's dossier, Archives Nationales.

texts, the excellence of its method and the clarity of its exposition' but questioning his own 'personal, ingenious and bold views'.[4] The Doyen's report records that 'the candidate defended himself with much vigour and the jury was unanimous in admiring the precision of his ideas, the sureness of his speech, and the sincerity and the convinced ardour which he manifested throughout'.[5]

On being asked to give an account of *The Division of Labour*,[6] Durkheim emphasized that he had not departed from an absolute 'mechanicism', or determinism, and that he had discovered a constant index of the division of labour in the legal system: his was a 'purely scientific thesis'. Marion remarked that Durkheim should have ignored morality altogether, saying, 'Your thesis is not acute enough to reach morality. It is a thesis on the *physique des mœurs*.' To this Durkheim replied by justifying his moral starting-point by a 'historical argument' (he had begun from the insufficiency of existing moral codes) and by a 'polemical argument' (moralists attacked sociology and it was necessary to put them right). Paul Janet took up Marion's objection, arguing that Durkheim had substituted *function* for *duty*. Durkheim replied that for the modern and informed *conscience*, to specialize was a duty: 'to be more of a man today is to consent to be an organ'. Waddington then said, 'You bring us nothing that is new: we are in the lower realm of morality ... You ignore liberty and you do not believe in Duty in general.' To this Durkheim replied, 'That was not my subject. Why ask me questions with which my thesis is not concerned?'

Hitherto the discussion had borne entirely on the relation of Durkheim's work to systems of formal ethics and not at all on its scientific claims; but this, as the writer of the account we are following observed, was in part Durkheim's own fault, 'considering the moral importance which he himself attributes to his researches'. Boutroux, however, then turned to this

4. Doyen's report, 8 March 1893, in ibid.
5. ibid.
6. The main account I have used here is to be found in the *Revue universitaire*, 2ᵉ année, t.1 (1893), pp. 440–43. (It is, very partially, summarized in Alpert, 1939a, pp. 45–6.)

aspect and asked Durkheim whether his use of indices ('the signs of realities') did not detract from the value of his work, making its results less certain. Durkheim replied as follows: ' 1. The signs are brought ever closer to living reality: there is a continuous approximation; 2. consequently, concerning the division of labour, we have every day new and more veridical signs; 3. and, as each sign encompasses less and less, we see through them more and more'. Boutroux then observed, concerning the law that the increase in the division of labour is a direct result of the increasing density and volume of population, that the increasing division of labour was not the only possible solution to the problem. 'I did not wish', 'replied Durkheim, 'to show that my law was the only possible consequence, but rather that it was a necessary consequence. There are others, but they are secondary and weak.' Brochard then returned to the earlier theme and remarked, 'Your main argument against the systems of formal ethics is that none of them can explain charity. How do you yourself explain it? You explain solidarity, not charity.' To this Durkheim replied, 'I do not see the distinction. I define charity as the attachment of a man to something other than himself. Solidarity and charity are related as motion is to force. I am a scientist: I study motion.' Then after a factual objection concerning the law of the division of labour, to which Durkheim briefly replied, Séailles ended by expanding on 'interior morality' and on the latent idealism of Reason.

Durkheim, according to this account, showed throughout, though somewhat impatiently, 'a simple and sincere eloquence'. This was a thesis-defence in which 'the upper hand was almost constantly taken by the candidate'. And according to another observer of the proceedings,

Unprecedented applause broke out more than once. The oratorical powers of our candidate were not a sham. His responses – and this is indeed rare! – were often very successful, never ending in evasions or in a cowardly or prudent capitulation. One can certainly say that in this joust he was the equal of his examiners and indeed often had the advantage over them.[7]

7. M. Perreur's report, loc. cit.

In his official report, the Doyen referred to the 'rare distinction' with which Durkheim had defended the propositions in his thesis, and concluded:

M. Durkheim had reflected on them for too long not to have foreseen all the objections to which they could and should give rise. He replied to these with a sureness of thought, a breadth of knowledge and a firmness of speech that were as striking to the public as to the members of the Faculty. A certain nervousness and quivering in his voice – which in no way detracted from the precision of his replies and never became declamatory – added further to the sincerity of his tone and consequently to the authority of his thought. We were agreed in considering M. Durkheim one of the best successful doctoral candidates we have announced for a long time. Needless to add, we were unanimous.[8]

The defence was widely reported and acclaimed: it was taken to indicate a victory for the new science of sociology over the traditionalists at the Sorbonne, who had been compelled, despite their views, to grant a doctorate with unanimity because of the quality of the candidate. *La Petite Gironde* in Bordeaux carried the following report of Durkheim's 'brilliant success':

... we are happy to state that, thanks to M. Durkheim, sociology has finally won the right to be mentioned at the Sorbonne. It was received with great favour by the eminent professors charged with judging M. Durkheim's work and, it may be said, with enthusiasm by the many members of the public who had the good fortune to hear the explanations exchanged in the course of the defence. It was indeed an event of great importance. It could not fail to concern both those interested in the progress of social science and those who are concerned for the good name of our University of Bordeaux, of which M. Durkheim is one of the most hard-working and distinguished members.[9]

The Division of Labour was widely discussed by the students.[10] The early 1890s were a time of widespread unease in France: young men actively sought ideals, whether these were religious,

8. Doyen's report, ibid.
9. From Durkheim's dossier, Bordeaux.
10. Bouglé, *Les Pages libres*, 5 October 1897, quoted in Lasserre, 1913, pp. 186–7.

secular-religious or political. Durkheim, like T. H. Green at Oxford, offered them an ideal that claimed to be both spiritually appealing and socially relevant, though many found it deeply objectionable. It was not surprising that 'appearing in this context of moral uneasiness, the initial impact of *The Division of Labour* was one of shock'.[11] Its message was striking; as Bouglé put it:

'The origin of your malaise', the author seemed to say, 'is elsewhere than at the bottom of your hearts. To restore equilibrium you must establish new social relations. Encourage the normal effects of specialization. Equalize the conditions of competition between individuals. We must rebuild anew professional groups. Salvation lies without and this is how it may be achieved.'[12]

Both Durkheim's method and his solution struck many as disconcerting. Bouglé writes of one student, who was something of an aesthetic individualist, 'walking off his indignation in the corridors of the Sorbonne, denouncing such formulae of Durkheim's as "Man must be taught to play his role as an organ"'.[13] But others were strongly attracted – Bouglé himself, Simiand, Fauconnet and the others who were to form the select band of disciples grouped around the *Année sociologique*. Of them Bouglé writes that 'obsessed ... by the problem of national reconstruction, of secular emancipation, of economic and social organization, and seeking, on the other hand, a path equidistant from over-abstract speculation and over-minute erudition, [they] chose to take their stand with him, and work under his direction to advance the scientific understanding of societies.'[14]

The opposition of the Sorbonne moral philosophers was largely due to Durkheim's own hostility to the purely *a priori* discussion of moral questions. From an early date, as has been seen, he opposed the methods of 'the large majority of contemporary French moralists and economists': they began 'from the abstract, autonomous individual, depending only on

11. ibid.
12. ibid.
13. ibid. (The student was Henri Vaugeois.)
14. Bouglé, 1938, p. 35.

himself, without historical antecedents or social context' and thence deduced 'how he is able to conduct himself, whether in his economic relations or in his moral life'.[15] And indeed, Mauss states that it was the opposition of moralists and economists that kept him away from Paris for so long.[16]

The Division of Labour caused 'a great noise in the philosophical world',[17] but it was with the publication of *The Rules* in 1894 that the polemics really began. The boldness and intransigence of Durkheim's style, evident in both works, led many of his first readers to react strongly against what they saw as his hypostasization of the group and his emphasis on what seemed to be mechanical and *sui generis* social forces that could only be known externally by their effects, of which individuals were unaware and before which they were powerless. As he wrote in the preface to the second edition of *The Rules* in 1901:

When this book appeared for the first time, it aroused lively controversy. Current ideas, disconcerted, at first resisted so fiercely that for a time it was impossible to make ourselves understood. On the very points on which we had expressed ourselves most explicitly, views were freely attributed to us which had nothing in common with our own, and we were held to be refuted when they were refuted. Although we had repeatedly asserted that the *conscience*, both individual and social, was for us in no way substantial, but only a more or less systematized collection of phenomena *sui generis*, we were charged with realism and ontologism. Although we had expressly stated and abundantly repeated that social life is constituted wholly of *représentations*, we have been accused of eliminating the mental element from sociology.[18]

15. 1890a, p. 451. Cf. 1902b, p. 380: tr. 1933b, p. 386.
16. He resented his exile from Paris. After being passed over for an appointment at the Collège de France, he wrote to Léon of his great regret at 'seeing myself separated *sine die* from Paris, where I would find resources and means of action that I do not have at Bordeaux' (letter dated 19 August 1897). (The appointment was a chair in Social Philosophy and the successful candidate Jean Izoulet: see *Journal officiel*, 4 August 1897.)
17. Sorel, 1895, p. 1. It also commanded much admiration. Lucien Herr, for example, wrote that it denoted 'an understanding that is as yet rare of the social realities of our time' (Herr, 1893).
18. 1901c, p. ix: tr. 1938b, p. li (S.L.).

Such interpretations of his thought were evidently offensive, especially to moralists and philosophers in the neo-Kantian philosophical atmosphere of the time. He was quite widely regarded as an obscurantist and an anti-individualist.

THE DEBATE WITH TARDE

The most notable and persistent of these attacks came from Gabriel Tarde, a magistrate, criminologist, statistician and sociologist, who was from 1894 director of the criminal statistics office of the Ministry of Justice (and in that capacity the provider of some of the statistical data for *Suicide*). Tarde had for twenty years been engaged in a one-man campaign against the various forms of biologism in sociology – Darwinism, organicism, transformism – that he found in the work of such writers as Spencer, Espinas, Worms (whom he actually converted), de Greef, Gumplowicz, Novicow, Lombroso, Lilienfeld and Roberty. At the same time he had been developing his own system of sociology, founded entirely on psychology, or, as he was later to call it, 'Interpsychology', and, in particular, on the notion of imitation. Within this elastic concept Tarde proposed to encompass the whole of social behaviour, analysed at a microscopic level. For Tarde, it has rightly been said that 'Everything in the social world is explained in terms of beliefs and desires that are imitated, spread and susceptible of increasing and diminishing, and these rises and falls are measured by statistics'.[19] All is reduced to the 'elementary social fact' of imitation, supplemented by spontaneous, and unexplained, 'inventions', random products of

19. Essertier, 1930, p. 204. On Tarde, see Clark, T. N. (ed.), *Gabriel Tarde: On Communication and Social Influence* (Chicago and London, 1969); the sections on him in Essertier, op. cit., and Barnes and Becker, 1938; Davis, M. M., *Gabriel Tarde* (New York, 1906); Parodi, 1919, pp. 117–19; Bouglé, C., 'Un Sociologue individualiste: Gabriel Tarde', *Revue de Paris*, 15 May 1905; Worms, R., 'La Philosophie sociale de Gabriel Tarde', *RP*, 1906; Hughes, E. C., 'Tarde's "Psychologie économique"': An Unknown Classic by a Forgotten Sociologist', *AJS*, 1961; and Milet, J., *Gabriel Tarde et la philosophie de l'histoire* (Paris, 1970). On Tarde *versus* Durkheim, see Essertier, 1930, Barnes and Becker, 1938, Benoît-Smullyan, 1937, pp. 488–510, Blondel, 1928, and Milet, op. cit., pp. 247–57.

genius (the 'supreme accident') to supply the *deus ex machina* of
social change. Despite the poverty and superficiality of his
explanatory framework, and despite the fact that he did not
attempt a psychology of imitation but rather took it as his
starting point, Tarde's work is full of striking and suggestive
observations and had (it is worth adding) a notable influence in
America.[20] Tarde's sociological system reached its maturest
expression[21] at precisely the time that Durkheim's first original
writings were appearing, and it is not surprising that, given
Durkheim's methodological views, Tarde should have reacted
strongly against them, as he had previously reacted against
biologism, and that he should have waged a protracted and
highly polemical battle against them. Tarde wrote as a methodological individualist: everything in society could be reduced
to and explained in terms of individuals. As Bouglé wrote of
Tarde, 'In his eyes, everything stemmed from the individual,
and everything came back to him: the individual is the first
and last piece of the edifice; he is the alpha and omega of the
system.'[22]

Durkheim defended his views against Tarde with considerable vigour and indeed his formulation of them was to some
extent determined by the terms of the debate laid down by
Tarde. He did not, however, enjoy these polemics. Characteristically, but not entirely unjustifiably, he held that Tarde misconstrued his thought.[23] Thus he wrote to Léon in 1898,
asking him to publish his article 'Représentations individuelles
et représentations collectives'[24] as quickly as possible because
'Tarde has announced to me his intention of attacking me
again, but I have definitely decided not to reply any more,

20. In particular on E. A. Ross, J. M. Baldwin, C. H. Cooley and
F. H. Giddings; and also on the sociologists of the Chicago school, as
well as on many American anthropologists, especially Franz Boas.

21. See, for instance, *Les Lois de l'imitation* (Paris, 1890), Tarde, 1895a,
L'Opposition universelle (Paris, 1897), Tarde, 1898a, and Tarde, 1898b.

22. art. cit., p. 313. Cf. Lukes, 1968c.

23. According to Davy, '. . . he viewed with . . . genuine suffering
certain criticisms relying on a distortion of his thought' (Davy, 1960a,
pp. 17–18).

24. 1898b.

judging that this debate has lasted long enough. I would therefore have preferred that the little work I am sending you
should not appear after the attack, so that it would not look
like a reply.'[25] Moreover, certain personal factors no doubt
aggravated the controversy. Tarde was something of a dilettante, who dabbled in literary activities and frequented
Parisian *salons*; he was also hostile to socialism and in favour of
an intellectual aristocracy. Greatly influenced by Renan, he
followed the latter's belief that 'truth lies in the nuance'; his
purportedly scientific writing was often fanciful and epigram-
matic and his intellectual activity was far from single-minded
and systematic. Indeed, when Tarde was appointed to the
chair in modern philosophy at the Collège de France, Durkheim wrote to Léon in the following acid tones: 'I deeply
regret, for the sake of both sociology and philosophy, both
of which have an equal interest in remaining distinct, a confusion which shows that many good minds still fail to understand what each should be.'[26]

The first shot was fired by Tarde in a generous and respectful
review of *The Division of Labour*[27] (a 'remarkable and profound
study'), which he criticized on three counts. First, its account
of social evolution left out 'wars, massacres and brutal annexations',[28] considering only intra-national and not international
relations. Changes in social structure were rather the result of
annexations and conquests, which were caused by 'ambition,
cupidity, love of glory, proselytizing fanaticism'.[29] Second, the
division of labour was 'the daughter of genius', resulting, not
from the increasing volume and density of societies, but from
the presence of inventiveness, creating new branches of
activity. Thus Durkheim 'took too little account' of 'the
accidental, the irrational, . . . the accident of genius'.[30] Third,
and most interestingly, he questioned Durkheim's opposition
of mechanical and organic solidarity, arguing that the division

25. Letter undated.
26. Letter dated 7 February 1900.
27. Tarde, 1893, reprinted in Tarde, 1895d.
28. ibid., p. 187.
29. ibid., p. 190.
30. ibid., p. 187.

of labour as such could neither socialize nor moralize men, and that in fact it merely 'has the constant effect of developing and strengthening, under new forms, [the] intellectual and moral community [of beliefs and sentiments] by multiplying the objects of this common fund and notably facilitating their diffusion'.[31] Differentiation presupposed community.

There followed an attack on Tarde by Durkheim in the first chapter of *The Rules*, where, after defining a social fact in terms of its power of external coercion and observing that if it is general, that is, common to members of a society, it is only so 'because it is collective (that is, more or less obligatory)', he remarked in a footnote how remote his definition was from that which was at 'the basis of M. Tarde's ingenious system'. His researches, he wrote, did not support Tarde's view of the preponderant influence of imitation in the genesis of collective facts, and, in any case, the diffusion of social facts, which the notion of imitation purported to explain, was itself the consequence of their obligatory character. ('No doubt, every social fact is imitated ... but that is because it is social, i.e. obligatory'). He added that 'one may wonder whether the word 'imitation' is indeed fitted to refer to a propagation due to a coercive influence. Under this single term one is confusing very different phenomena which need to be distinguished'.[32]

Tarde reacted strongly to Durkheim's definition of social facts, with a number of arguments[33]: the externality of the social fact does not apply to all individuals taken together; he could not make sense of Durkheim's notion of the social fact as being 'external to its individual manifestations'; social phenomena *are* transmitted from individual to individual (Durkheim admitted it); and the defining notion of constraint is based on a narrow analogy that led Durkheim to recognize as social bonds 'only the relations of master to subject, professor to student, parents to children, without having any regard to free relations among equals' and imitation arising from

31. ibid., p. 193.

32. 1901c, pp. 14–16: tr. 1938b, pp. 9–11 (S.L.). Cf. Durkheim's critique of Tarde's use of 'imitation' in *Suicide*, ch. 4.

33. In Tarde, 1894; repr. in Tarde, 1898a, pp. 63–94; also Tarde 1895a, pp. vi–vii, and Tarde, 1895c, passim.

spontaneous interaction.[34] He accused Durkheim of reifying the social group ('Are we going to return to the realism of the Middle Ages?'[35]) and argued that the social whole was an illusion and that Durkheim's 'social realism' was counter-factual, mystical, metaphysical and incompatible with posi-tivism. Social phenomena were immanent in the conscious-nesses and memories of the associated individuals and were no more exterior to them than was the wave to the drops of water which composed it.[36] The source of Durkheim's illusion, wrote Tarde, was his assumption (derived, as we have seen, from Boutroux) that there were distinct levels of reality. Ultimately, Tarde consistently believed, everything would be explained in terms of '... cells ... molecules ... atoms'; Durkheim's 'postulate that the simple relation of several beings could itself become a new being superior to others' was 'a chimerical conception'.[37] To Durkheim's slogan: 'every time that a social phenomenon is directly explained by a psycho-logical phenomenon, we may be sure the explanation is false',[38] Tarde replied, 'in social matters, every clear explana-tion must necessarily be erroneous'.[39] To Durkheim's prin-ciple that psychological explanations left out the specifically social element, Tarde replied: 'yes, if one wants to account for collective phenomena by the psychology and logic of indi-viduals alone, and only of existing individuals; but not if one has regard also for the psychology and logic of masses and of the dead' (*sic*).[40] To Durkheim's objection that psychology could not explain the evolution of societies, Tarde replied that this could be reduced to the imitation of ideas of genius.[41]

34. Tarde, 1895a, p. vi: cf. Tarde 1898a, pp. 71–2. This objection resembles that of Piaget, 1932.

35. ibid., cf.: 'M. Durkheim confronts us like a scholastic. Sociology does not mean ontology' (ibid.). According to Albert Thibaudet, this charge against Durkheim of scholasticism was to become a commonplace at the Sorbonne in the early 1900s (*La République des professeurs*, Paris, 1927, p. 223).

36. Tarde, 1898a, p. 73.

37. ibid., p. 76.

38. 1901c, p. 128: tr. 1938b, p. 104.

39. ibid., p. 77.

40. ibid.

41. ibid., pp. 77–8.

Against Durkheim's view that social phenomena could be isolated and methodically observed, he wrote that 'in sociology we have, through a rare privilege, intimate knowledge both of that element which is our individual *conscience* and of that compound which is the sum of individual *consciences*'; and to Durkheim's maxim: 'remove individuals and society remains'[42] he countered: 'remove the individual and nothing remains of the social'.[43] To these latter two statements of Tarde, Durkheim responded in *Suicide*. To the first he replied that mental phenomena are not directly knowable and must be reached 'little by little by devious and complex procedures like those used by the sciences of the external world'; to the second, which he called 'arbitrary', he replied that 'proofs supporting this statement are lacking and discussion is therefore impossible', but that it would be only too easy to oppose to it the feeling of many that society is not a 'form spontaneously assumed by individual nature as it expands outwards, but . . . an antagonistic force restricting individual natures and resisted by them'. Moreover, if Tarde were right, if 'we had really only to open our eyes and take a good look to perceive at once the laws of the social world, sociology would be useless or at least very simple'.[44] But the evidence here was against Tarde; distinctively social causes could not just be directly observed, but they could be discovered by the use of scientific procedures. As we have seen, Durkheim saw no point in continuing this dispute with Tarde; but the 1898 article and the second preface to *The Rules* (1901) are to be seen as comprehensive replies to Tarde and Durkheim's other critics, discussed below.

He crossed swords with Tarde in a much more acrimonious fashion in connection with his own views about the normality of crime ('a factor in public health, an integral part of all healthy societies'[45]), views which were regarded by many

42. 1895a: tr. in 1938b, p. 102 (S.L.).

43. Quoted in 1897a, pp. 350–51: tr. 1951a, p. 311 (S.L.), from Tarde 1895c, repr. in Tarde, 1898a, p. 75. Cf. Tarde, 1895a, p. vi. 'Remove the professors and I do not see what remains of the university.'

44. ibid. (S.L.).

45. 1901c, p. 83: tr. 1938b, p. 67. Cf. 'Crime . . . must no longer be conceived as an evil that cannot be too much suppressed' ibid., p. 89: tr. p. 72).

contemporaries as both startling and offensive. As George Sorel put it, Durkheim's principle that 'it is normal that there should be criminality, so long as this attains and does not exceed a certain level' scandalized 'moral persons'[46] and Durkheim himself observed that 'this affirmation has ... disconcerted certain persons and may have seemed, on superficial examination, to shake the foundations of morality'.[47] Tarde disputed[48] that it might be justifiable to seek to suppress what does good, and that the normal may be defined in terms of the general (the morbid is most often the general, while the normal is the highest state a given being can attain, which for society is 'the ideal ... peace in justice and light, ... the complete extermination of crime, vice, ignorance, poverty, corruption'[49]), and he also disputed that human ideals can be determined by means of science which was, in the hands of Durkheim ('*mon subtil contradicteur*'), the 'cold product of abstract reason, alien, by hypothesis, to every inspiration of the conscience and the heart'.[50] More specifically, Tarde disputed the following propositions which he attributed to Durkheim: (1) that the contemporary increase in crime was normal; (2) that crime was useful because it prevented the moral conscience from being too severe on insignificant acts; (3) that if certain crimes became rarer, the corresponding punishments would increase; (4) that crime and genius were two aspects of the same mental state; and (5) that one should be exclusively concerned with 'low and rampant crime, that is hated and condemned'.

Durkheim's reply, 'Crime and Social Health',[51] was sharp and bitter. First, he denied that he had asserted any of these

46. Sorel, 1895, p. 176. Compare the view of Menachem Horovitz, the sociologist who heads Israel's probation service, according to whom, 'the normalization of the Jewish people in their own State has brought a normal crime rate. Crime is a normal phenomenon' (reprinted in the *Sunday Times*, 9 May 1971).

47. 1897a, p. 413: tr. 1951a, p. 361 (S.L.).

48. Tarde, 1895b.

49. Tarde, 1895b, p. 160. 'What,' said Tarde, 'about the old distinction between good and evil?' (ibid.).

50. ibid., p. 161.

51. 1895c.

five propositions and agreed with Tarde ('*mon éminent critique*') in judging them false. He then restated his views on crime, arguing that crime was normal because it was 'linked to the fundamental conditions of all social life', for in all societies some individuals must diverge from the collective type, among which divergences some must be criminal; and that the existence of crime was generally useful, either indirectly or directly: indirectly (as in most cases) because it 'could only cease to exist if the *conscience collective* dominated individual *consciences* with such an ineluctable authority that all moral change would be rendered impossible'[52]; and directly (and rarely) when the criminal was an innovator, the precursor of a new morality. Tarde was too preoccupied with contemporary morality; in a wider view the normality of crime seemed less paradoxical and was a condition of changes in morality. Moreover, Durkheim argued, morality was a social function and, for the sake of social equilibrium, must be limited in influence (for instance, *too much* respect for individual dignity rendered military discipline impossible). Finally, Durkheim disposed of two minor arguments of Tarde ('*mon ingénieux contradicteur*') against his definition of normality: to the objection that illness is general, he replied that illnesses vary, and it is a limited resistance to illness that is general; and to the objection that an inferior society composed of inferior people could not survive but would have to be called healthy, he replied that such a society would itself be abnormal, that 'it is socially normal that in every society there should be psychologically abnormal individuals' and that the normality of crime is only a particular instance of this general truth. The conditions of individual and social health were very different, even contrary to one another. This, he observed, followed from his own position that there was 'a deep dividing line between the social and the psychological',[53] but it could also be seen in the simple fact that the succession of generations implied the death of individuals.

In conclusion, Durkheim turned to the origin of the dispute between Tarde and himself. It sprang, he wrote, 'above all

52. ibid., p. 321.
53. ibid., p. 323.

from the fact that I believe in science and M. Tarde does not'.[54] Tarde wished to 'reduce it to being nothing more than an intellectual amusement, at best capable of showing us what is possible and impossible, but incapable of use for the positive regulation of conduct. If it has no other practical utility [than this], it is not worth the trouble it costs.' Tarde gave too many hostages to the enemies of science and thus allowed there to be placed above reason 'sensation, instinct, passion, all the base and obscure parts of ourselves'. To condone this was mysticism – 'the rule of anarchy in the practical order, because it is the reign of fantasy in the intellectual order'.[55]

Tarde replied to this,[56] insisting that Durkheim ('*le savant professeur*') had no objective basis for deciding what was a *normal* crime-rate and arguing that Durkheim's identification of crime and deviance was an *a priori* dogma. He reacted to Durkheim's bitter charge that he did not believe in science, by insisting on the distinction between science and the intellect, on the one hand, and moral character and the heart, on the other. Scientific knowledge, he wrote, 'enlightens both the good and the wicked and serves all ends, good and bad' and 'if mysticism consists in not giving science and reason their due – and I am certainly not guilty of this – the anti-mysticism, calling itself positivist but scorned by Auguste Comte under the name of "pedantocracy", anti-mysticism which consists in not giving their due to the heart, to love, to national loyalties, and also to imagination, the source of hypotheses and theories as well as of poetry and art, that is more disastrous still. And indeed, what can my eminent adversary have in mind but this personified abstraction of Science, pure Science?'[57] He was himself, Tarde added, too well disposed towards science and reason to adore them.

The hostilities continued, with particularly strong attacks by Durkheim on Tarde in the course of *Suicide* and in the second of the 1900 articles on the history of French sociology, in which he repeated the charge that Tarde's work was unscientific,

54. ibid.
55. ibid.
56. Tarde, 1898a, pp. 158–61.
57. ibid., p. 160.

putting chance and contingency at the centre of social life, and being rather 'a very particular form of speculation in which imagination plays the preponderant role and thought does not regard itself as constrained by the regular obligations of proof or the control of facts ... caprice ... is permitted to thought'.[58] In 1901, Tarde published an article on 'Social Reality',[59] arguing that there was indeed a social reality, but it was composed of psychological states and that sociology should concern itself with 'belief, desire and imitation'.[60] He rejected the charges of 'caprice and the negation of science', arguing that sociology 'must show the emptiness of sham formulas, of sham historical laws which would place insurmountable obstacles in the way of individual wills'[61] and he once more rejected Durkheim's account of the external and constraining character of social phenomena (such as a religion, language or custom), insisting that they were rather to be seen in terms of 'the similarity and simultaneity of multiple central imprints produced by an accumulation and a consolidation of individual actions'.[62] Tarde added, in a sly footnote, that he was glad to see that 'the learned professor of sociology' had, since the foundation of the *Année*, come much nearer to the psychological conception of social facts.[63]

This drew a reply from Durkheim, in the form of a letter to the editor of the *Revue philosophique*.[64] If Tarde meant by this

---

58. 1900b, p. 650. Cf. also 1906a (1), where Durkheim offers a brief and incisive critique of Tarde's system, arguing that Tarde's notion of 'interpsychology' was 'arbitrary and confused', that the study of individual interactions must lead to a search for some means of observing them objectively and discovering the conditions of their variation, and that Tarde's thought moved within a vicious circle: 'imitation, the source of social life, itself depends on social factors; it presupposes what it produces'. Thus: 'One imitates superiors, but superiority is already a social institution, so that "imitation" is empty and non-explanatory. One must know why men imitate; and the causes which lead men to imitate and obey are already social' (pp. 134–5).

59. Tarde, 1901.
60. ibid., p. 468.
61. ibid., p. 464.
62. ibid., p. 461.
63. ibid., p. 460.
64. 1901d.

last suggestion that he shared the view that social phenomena could be immediately explained by individual mental states, not a line of his supported it: 'I always see the same dividing-line between *individual* psychology and sociology, and the numerous facts we have had to catalogue every year in the *Année sociologique* only confirm me in this view.' If, however, Tarde meant that social life was 'a system of *représentation* of mental states, providing it is understood that these *représentations* are *sui generis*, different in nature from those which constitute the mental life of the individual, and subject to their own laws which individual psychology could not predict', then this was indeed his view, and always had been. Sociology was 'a special psychology, with its own object and a distinctive method'.[65]

The final confrontation between Tarde and Durkheim came in 1903–4 at the École des Hautes Études Sociales, when Durkheim and Tarde each gave a lecture on 'Sociology and the Social Sciences' and, at a third meeting, debated with each other, maintaining, according to the published report, 'with much heat their respective theses'.[66] Durkheim's lecture argued that sociology was the daughter of philosophy ('born in the womb of the Comtist philosophy, of which it is the logical completion'[67]) but must now specialize in studies of complex, concrete phenomena, rather than seeking abstract, general laws. Special disciplines must become truly sociological sciences, becoming infused with the ideas evolved by social philosophy. Tarde's lecture argued that the study of social phenomena had to refer to 'elementary acts' studied by 'intermental psychology', or 'elementary sociology', which was presupposed by, and an indispensable guide for, the special social sciences. Elementary sociology, thus understood, was both general and central: the special social sciences would become objective as they were 'psychologized'.[68]

65. This, as we have seen, was the view set out in the article on 'Individual and Collective *Représentations*' (1898b) and had, in fact, been fully developed only *after* the first edition of *The Rules*.

66. 1904b, p. 86.

67. ibid., p. 83.

68. ibid., pp. 85–6.

In their joint discussion, Tarde began by admitting the value of deriving general laws by means of the comparative method, but insisted on the importance of the microscopic study of intermental psychology. Durkheim replied that general sociology could only be the synthesis of the results of particular sciences and as yet one could not prejudge these results, nor whether they would be obtained by intermental psychology. He went on,

M. Tarde claims that sociology will arrive at such and such results; but we are not able to say what the elementary social fact is, in the present state of our knowledge. We know too little, and the construction of the elementary social fact in these conditions can only be arbitrary. Whatever the value of this intermental psychology, it is unacceptable that it should exert a sort of directing influence over the special disciplines of which it must be the product.

Tarde replied that laws could be formulated without sciences being definitively constituted. The social sciences did not owe their progress to certain rules of objective method, but to the extent to which they had moved in the direction of psychology. Tarde then proceeded to repeat that there was nothing in social life except acts between individuals. Did M. Durkheim think otherwise?

If you do think so [Tarde continued], I understand your method: it is pure ontology. The debate between us is that of nominalism and scholastic realism. I am a nominalist. There can only be individual actions and interactions. The rest is nothing but a metaphysical entity, and mysticism.

Durkheim retorted that M. Tarde was confusing two different questions and refused to say anything about a problem which he had not touched on and which, moreover, had nothing to do with the discussion.[69]

OTHER CRITICISMS

We have covered the Durkheim–Tarde debate[70] in some detail, not only for its intrinsic interest and importance, but

69. 1904b, p. 86–7. Tarde died in 1904. Eleven years later, Durkheim could be more generous: see 1915a: tr. in 1960c.

70. This has nowhere been fully reconstructed hitherto (though Benoît-Smullyan, 1937 and 1938, and Milet, op. cit., offer partial summaries).

also because Tarde's reactions to Durkheim's ideas were identical to those of many of the first readers of *The Rules*. Thus, for example, among early reactions, the socialist historian of German thought, Charles Andler, objected to Durkheim's social realism (calling it 'mysticism'), observing that it was just a sociological version of the mistaken economic *'chosisme'* of Marx,[71] and declaring himself quite unconvinced by Durkheim's claims for sociology; Marcel Bernès also disputed Durkheim's account of social reality, and in particular his emphasis on externality and constraint, arguing that he should have considered the beliefs and desires of individuals[72]; James Tufts and Gustavo Tosti, in the United States, argued similarly,[73] the former quoting John Stuart Mill against Durkheim ('Men are not, when brought together, converted into another kind of substance'[74]); Alfred Fouillée observed that 'the concept of society as existing outside individuals is pure metaphysics'[75]; while Sorel criticized Durkheim's 'mysterious alchemy'.[76] Even Durkheim's fellow editor of the *Année*, François Simiand, offered a mild criticism of his 'sociological metaphysics'.[77] Another critic wrote that 'this pursuit of pure ontology, despite its avoidance of hypostasizing

71. Andler, 1896a, especially p. 258. But see Durkheim, 1896a, where 'without wishing to prolong the discussion', he 'rejects absolutely the ideas which M. Andler attributes to me'. See also Bouglé's defence of Durkheim (Bouglé, 1896b and c), for which Durkheim thanked Bouglé, stressing the need to separate oneself from the charlatans who had exploited the vogue of sociology and were discrediting it (letter dated 27 March 1897).

72. Bernès, 1895, especially p. 239.

73. Tufts, 1896, and Tosti, 1898a and 1898b. Cf. Durkheim's reply (1898d) to Tosti's charge that he had not realized that 'a compound is explained both by the character of its elements and the law of their combination': 'I do not at all deny that individual natures are the components of the social fact. It is only a question of knowing if, in combining . . . they are not transformed by the very fact of the combination.'

74. *A System of Logic* (9th edn London, 1875), vol. II, p. 469.

75. *Le Mouvement positiviste et la conception sociologique du monde* (Paris, 1896), p. 248.

76. Sorel, 1895, p. 19.

77. Simiand, 1898. Cf. Gaston Richard (at this time still a Durkheimian), in the first volume of the *Année*: 'Let us beware of sociological metaphors' (p. 405).

the social, personifies it none the less ...'[78] In Germany, Ferdinand Tönnies observed that Tarde, while he was mistaken in failing to recognize that social phenomena must have features independent of individual *consciences*, was right in criticizing Durkheim for constructing sociological concepts without psychological foundations.[79]

Lucien Herr, the eminent and immensely influential socialist librarian of the École Normale (who in 1886 had brought an article by Sir James Frazer on Totemism to Durkheim's notice[80]), summed up the substance of all these criticisms in a magisterial review of *The Rules* in the *Revue universitaire*. He began by insisting on his profound admiration for Durkheim's sincerity, character and mind and on the extent to which he agreed with Durkheim's critique of contemporary sociology, with his scientific aims for sociology and his view of methodology, but he then continued:

when he goes on to define the elementary social fact, when he discerns in it a reality exterior and superior to individuals because exterior and anterior to *one* individual, when he attributes to rules, that is to generalized abstractions, to signs or symbols, that is to conventions between individuals, an imperative and coercive power, when he affirms that an emotion common to a collectivity of individuals has for its substratum not the sum of these individuals taken one by one, but the collectivity of those individuals, when he poses as a principle of this new science ways of acting, thinking and feeling external to the individual, that is to say to all individuals, and when he provides sociology with the subject-matter of social facts thus defined, then not only do I no longer give my support, but I no longer understand, and I refuse to recognize as scientific anything that will be built on this basis, with these materials. I am certain that M. Durkheim will himself be horrified by the phantom of the old realist metaphysics, the day he clearly perceives it behind his formulas and images.[81]

These sorts of criticism were frequently to be advanced,

78. Mazel, 1899, p. 677.
79. Tönnies, 1898 (1929), p. 275.
80. Mauss, 'Notice biographique: Lucien Herr', *AS*, n.s., 2 (1927), p. 9.
81. Herr 1894, p. 487.

throughout Durkheim's career and subsequently.[82] Moreover, Durkheim brought the best out of his critics. As one writer has justly observed, 'It is from the individualists that the most acute and cogent criticisms of the Durkheim school have come. In fact, the best statements of the individualistic position are to be found in the large literature of Durkheim criticism in France.'[83]

As we have seen, Durkheim saw his *Suicide* as triumphantly vindicating his claims for sociology, his methodology, and, in particular, his social realism. His attitude to the hostility he knew it was bound to bring forth is interestingly revealed in a letter to Bouglé written in 1897. Bouglé had suggested that the extreme way in which Durkheim presented his thesis might antagonize some of his readers. Durkheim replied:

There is much truth in your remarks. It would perhaps have been more politic not to present things in this form. But what can I do? It is in my nature to present ideas by the point rather than by the hilt (*par la pointe plutôt que par la poignée*). What is more, it seems to me impossible that, if your pursue your ideas to their conclusion, you will not arrive at a formula more or less like mine. If society is something other than the individual, it has a different basis (*substrat*) from the individual, though it could not exist without individuals. That seems to me a truism. It is not in any one individual that society is to be found, but in all the individuals associated in a determinate manner. It is not, therefore, by analysing the individual *conscience* that one can do sociology. Now, in the first place, isn't it necessary to pursue one's ideas to their conclusion? Besides being necessary, it also turns out to be desirable, for method thereby rests on a more solid foundation. It is not only as part of a necessary technique (*artifice*) and in order to avoid the danger of substituting one's own opinions for realities that one should consider social phenomena from the outside; but because they really extend beyond the individual. Is it not then of some interest to show that morality is in part external to individuals? In this way many phenomena are explained. But as you say, however basically simple the proposition may be, it is natural that it should be resisted to begin with.

82. See Essertier, 1927b, and Lukes, 1968c, for references. There is a broad anti-social-realist tradition stretching from Tarde to Popper and Homans.

83. Benoît-Smullyan, 1938 p. 51.

Since Hobbes, at least, the idea is latent in all attempts at sociology; but what a delay and what difficulties have attended its emergence, while it is evident that thinkers were conscious of its necessity!'[84]

In addition, Durkheim's views on crime met, as we have seen, with strong opposition.[85] His general scientific aims also came under attack from a number of quarters; some objected to the implied determinism, others to the extent of his scientific ambitions. Still others, such as Gustave Belot,[86] objected to the narrowness of his characterization of morality. *Suicide* and the first volumes of the *Année* provoked many such criticisms, though they also induced widespread admiration in France (and much incomprehension abroad).[87]

In the pages of the *Revue socialiste*, Charles Péguy advanced a characteristic and distinctively socialist critique of *Suicide*, which is of both historical and intrinsic interest. After criticizing Durkheim for writing of theft without considering 'the unceasing theft of surplus labour committed by the majority of employers', Péguy referred to Durkheim's assertion that egoistic suicide, seen as a social sickness, had been greatly aggravated in 'our western civilization' since the beginning of the nineteenth century. Durkheim's remedy was to reconstitute society, and, wrote Péguy,

doubtless he regards it as sufficient to reconstitute corporate groups into true communities. M. Durkheim forgets that it is not in vain that men have acquired the taste for universal harmony and lost the taste for more particular harmonies. In order that the baker of today should desire to form a close association with his neighbouring bakers, it is necessary that he sense, above his single

84. Letter dated 6 July 1897.

85. In addition to Tarde's critique, see that of the Italian criminologist, Enrico Ferri, in *Sociologia criminale* (Turin, 1900; 5th edn 1929), vol. 1, pp. 157–8 and 193–202; and *L'omicida* (Turin, 1895; 5th edn 1925), pp. 445–7.

86. Belot, 1894, pp. 414–15.

87. See especially Small, 1898, 1899, 1900, 1902a, 1902b, etc., Hinkle, 1960, and the reactions to Durkheim's views from scholars from many countries to be found in *Sociological Papers* (The Sociological Society: Macmillan, London, 1905), pp. 204–56 (in response to Durkheim, 1905c). (For list of these scholars see p. 578, fn.). Cf. Chapter 25, below.

corporation, the single and harmonious City of which his corporation will merely be an organic part. The time is past when one could hope to build out of particular justices and harmonies what is, in the end, a total injustice.[88]

Finally, another socialist critic of Durkheim is worth special mention: Péguy's friend, Georges Sorel, who published a long study of *The Rules* in 1895 in his socialist journal *Le Devenir social*. Sorel was at this time a self-proclaimed though unorthodox marxist and his criticisms of Durkheim from this perspective have much interest.

Socialism, wrote Sorel, had in M. Durkheim an adversary of the first order: the forces of conservative democracy had found a 'theoretician who is, at the same time, a metaphysician of a rare subtlety and a scholar fully armed for the struggle'.[89] Sorel first criticized Durkheim's view of science as being too ambitious in aiming at determinate solutions: all sociology could hope to establish was the patterns of the principal social changes and one should be sceptical of deriving generalizations from statistical regularities. Secondly, Durkheim's account of social facts was not sufficiently mechanistic, for the notion of constraint was itself in part psychological. Thirdly, Sorel approved of Durkheim's account of the development of the division of labour in terms of a struggle for existence, but he pointed out that Durkheim left classes out of the picture – if he had included them his account would have been more historically concrete, instead of being purely logical and schematic. Next, Durkheim's use of the notion of the social milieu came under attack as being non-explanatory: it should be 'defined in a materialist manner and viewed as a field of forces'.[90] Fifthly, Durkheim's principles of classification were attacked as insufficiently materialist, and as deriving ultimately from an idealist theory of progress. Sixthly, Durkheim's morphological explanations, in particular the notions of volume and density, were criticized as being unduly *simpliste*, and as leaving differential class relations out of account (groups, their

88. Péguy, 1897, p. 636.
89. Sorel, 1895, p. 2.
90. ibid., p. 181.

tendencies, the general character of their movements'[91]), so that there was an undue emphasis on the growth of modern states and a failure to 'penetrate the principle of the political state'.[92] Seventhly, Durkheim's account of normality in terms of 'the general conditions of collective existence', misdescribed the latter by 'stop[ping] before the marxist philosophy'.[93] Lastly, Sorel argued that if one was to seek to satisfy Durkheim's aim of aiding the statesman by indicating to him where he should yield to the pressure of circumstances, it was necessary to abandon the theories of classical sociology and turn to socialism for its theory of the class struggle; the statesman would then yield to revolutionary forces. Sorel concluded by observing that Durkheim had pushed his investigations as far as he could without entering into socialism, and by asking whether he would advance further and pass through 'the frontier which separates him from us'. If he did that, Sorel proclaimed that he himself would be 'the first to acclaim him as my master', for 'No thinker is as well prepared as he to introduce the theories of Karl Marx into higher education'.[94] But in this connection, as in most others, Sorel's hopes were to remain unfulfilled.

91. ibid., p. 168.
92. ibid., p. 171.
93. ibid., p. 177.
94. ibid., pp. 179–80. Sorel's opinion of Durkheim was to grow much more hostile.

Chapter 17

Socialism, the Dreyfus Affair and Secular Education

SOREL was right to see Durkheim as an enemy on the left, but quite mistaken to see him as a potential ally. Durkheim was for him the theoretician of the 'new ideas of conservative democracy, establishing more justice in economic relations, favouring the intellectual and moral development of the people, encouraging industry to develop in more scientific directions', who was 'for the intervention of the State and for organization'.[1] This description was broadly accurate.

Indeed, Durkheim was in his sympathies a late-nineteenth-century French socialist closer to Jaurès than to Guesde, and to German Socialism of the Chair than to any form of marxism or revolutionary syndicalism. He was also a liberal, a passionate Dreyfusard and an anti-clerical. His views about the political, ideological and educational issues of his time, together with his conception of his own role in relation to those issues, form a fascinating object of inquiry. He viewed these issues in a single, coherent perspective; they were all for him, in a sense, parts of the same issue. His socialism formed the general perspective for his views about the reform of his society; the Dreyfus Affair provided the principal context in which those views were worked out and applied; and his attitude to education (and his role as an educator) determined the nature of his own practical concerns and activities.

SOCIALISM

Durkheim, as all those who knew him testify, was always, above all, a moralist. As Hubert Bourgin wrote, 'sociology was for him the means, unique and certain, of reconstructing morality',[2] and, in consequence, politics also. Bourgin recalls

1. ibid., p. 2.
2. Bourgin, 1938, p. 218. Cf. Bouglé, 1938, p. 32: '... behind the scientist, there was always the moralist...'

that one day Durkheim told him 'with a moving simplicity how, at a certain moment of his spiritual life, he had had to admit to himself that he was a socialist'[3]:

> While meditating on the state of his research, his science and his practical influence, he had one day arrived at a new understanding and had become aware of the new obligations which this revelation imposed upon him, with an emotion which I could sense on the occasion when, in his serious and subdued voice, he recounted this memory to me. He considered that a society transformed by the methods and practical applications of the sciences, including his own, was ripe for a great legal reconstruction, responding to its moral regeneration, and it was this reconstruction, proceeding from science, carried out with a method as rigorous and prudent as that of scientific research, which he called socialism.[4]

At the height of the First World War he was to write to Léon of the 'rich vitality' in the country and the powerful feeling which united it. When peace came, he wrote, this moral enthusiasm should be maintained. This would not be easy, for 'all these mediocre parties will want to throw themselves on their prey. Our salvation lies in socialism discarding its out-of-date slogans or in the formation of a new Socialism which goes back to the French tradition. I see so clearly what this might be!'[5]

In consequence, his socialism was of a peculiarly idealistic and non-political variety: he embraced the ends of socialism, conceived, in a manner that was characteristic of him, in terms of society as a whole, but he never pre-occupied himself with short-term questions of political means. Furthermore, he had little interest in the economics of socialism – a weakness then characteristic of French socialists in general. In Bourgin's view, he 'desired the advent of a socialist government, meaning by socialism what he meant by it . . . He constructed his political and social edifices with the materials of the mind, and not with

3. Bourgin, 1942, p. 75.
4. Bourgin, 1938, pp. 219–20. It must be stressed that Bourgin's memoirs, of which the present work makes extensive use, should be viewed with caution; by the time he wrote them, Bourgin had become an extreme right-wing and anti-semitic polemicist. (Another Durkheimian who was to move to the extreme right was Marcel Déat.)
5. Letter dated 30 March 1915.

those of actual, living humanity.'[6] Yet this very aloofness freed him from some political illusions characteristic of the time. He had faith neither in the activities of politicians in parliament nor in the possibilities of a proletarian revolution; least of all did he believe in the internationalism of the working class. He was, as Mauss put it,

deeply opposed to all war whether of classes or of nations; he desired change only for the benefit of society as a whole and not that of any one of its parts, even if the latter had numbers and force. He regarded political revolutions and parliamentary developments as superficial, costly and more theatrical than serious. He therefore always resisted the idea of submitting himself to a party and its political discipline, above all an international one. Even the social and moral crisis of the Dreyfus Affair, in which he took a great part, did not change his opinion. Even during the [First World] War, he was among those who put no hope in the so-called internationally organized working class. Thus he always remained on the middle ground; he 'sympathized', as they now say, with the socialists, with Jaurès, with socialism. He never gave himself to it.[7]

None the less, Bourgin records that

he did not hide his active sympathy for the socialist party, and, more particularly, for certain of its leaders, such as Jaurès. By public acts, he was not afraid to exhibit this sympathy...[8] He did not think that his science, which he kept sheltered from political influences, condemned him to neutrality and abstention. He appeared, therefore, in the political field, as a certain kind of socialist, with a particular allegiance, that of the Jaurèsian reformists ... [yet] he retained full freedom of thought and action with regard to the party that he honoured with this sort of pragmatic confidence; and, if he showed himself favourable to projects of reform that were analogous to those advocated in Germany by professors of the school of Schmoller and Wagner, he was energetically hostile to demagogic activities and to revolutionary struggles. At the time of the events

6. Bourgin, 1938, p. 220.

7. Mauss, 1928, p. viii: tr. Durkheim, 1958b, p. 3 (S.L. – the English translation omits part of this passage, from 'Even' to 'class').

8. For example, Durkheim made a point of openly carrying a copy of the socialist paper *L'Humanité* under his arm at his Sorbonne lectures (M. A. Cuvillier: personal communication). He wrote in socialist journals and, in general, moved in socialist circles.

that resulted from such activities, and struggles, I remember having heard him say, with force, but without emphasis, these simple words: 'I fear a reaction'.[9]

Durkheim's socialism was strongly reformist and revisionist. He was opposed to agitation which 'disturbs without improving', and above all to social changes which 'destroy without replacing'.[10] He applauded the efforts of those socialists, especially in Germany, Belgium and Italy, who were seeking to 'renew and extend the formulae of which they have for too long been the prisoners'.[11] In particular he cited 'the doctrine of economic materialism, the marxist theory of value, the iron law [of wages], [and] the pre-eminent importance attributed to class conflict'.[12] These 'disputable and out-of-date hypotheses', though they still served as propaganda for the party, in fact compromised the idea of socialism. Moreover, 'anyone who is familiar with the present state of the sciences and their orientation cannot easily rest content with them'.[13] More generally, he held that it would, above all,

be a mark of considerable progress, from which everyone would benefit, if socialism finally ceased to confuse the social question with the working-class question. The first includes the second but goes beyond it. The malaise from which we suffer is not located in a particular class; it is general throughout the whole of society. It affects employers as well as workers, though it takes different forms in the two cases: an anxious and painful restlessness in the case of the capitalist, discontent and irritation in that of the worker. The problem is thus immeasurably greater than that of the conflicting material interests of the classes; it is not simply a question of diminishing the share of some so as to increase that of others, but rather of remaking the moral constitution of society. This way of putting the problem is not only truer to the facts: it should have the advantage of divesting socialism of its aggressive and malevolent character with which it has often, and rightly, been reproached. Socialism

9. Bourgin, 1942, pp. 75–6.
10. Fauconnet, 1922, p. 14: tr. Durkheim, 1956a, p. 39.
11. 1899e, p. 433. It can probably be inferred that Durkheim, unlike Jaurès, sided with Bernstein against Kautsky.
12. ibid.
13. ibid.

would then appeal, not to those feelings of anger that the less-favoured class nourishes against the other, but to those feelings of pity for this society which is suffering in all its classes and all its organs.[14]

In addition, Durkheim was opposed to what he called 'unilateral solutions' to the problem of realizing socialism, holding that 'it is quite certain that the societies of the future, whatever their nature, will not rest on a single principle: the old social forms always survive beneath the new ...'[15] After all, the former responded to social needs which could scarcely suddenly disappear without trace; the new needs could only relegate them to second place, not 'eliminate them radically'. Thus,

However future society is organized, it will contain alongside one another the most diverse forms of economic management. There will be a place for all.[16]

On one issue, however, he was quite clear: the role of the state would be very great. As societies advance, 'its functions become more numerous and increasingly permeate all other social functions which it thereby concentrates and unifies'.[17] The state was not as such antagonistic to the individual (a view common to orthodox economists, and anarchists): it was 'rather the liberator of the individual', for

it is the state which, as it has grown in strength, has freed the individual from the particular and local groups which tended to absorb him – family, city, corporation, etc. . . . Not that the state may not become despotic and oppressive . . . the social force which it contains must be neutralized by other, counteracting social forces. If the secondary groups can easily become tyrannical when their influence is not moderated by that of the state, conversely that of the State, if it is to remain normal, also needs to be moderated in its turn. To arrive at this result, there should exist in society, outside the State but subject to its influence, groups that are more restricted ... but strongly constituted and possessing an individuality and an

14. ibid., pp. 437–8.
15. ibid., p. 438. •
16. ibid.
17. ibid.

autonomy sufficient to permit opposition to the encroachments of the central power. What liberates the individual is not the elimination of a controlling centre, but rather the multiplication of such centres, provided that they are co-ordinated and subordinated one to another.[18]

Thus the 'anarchist tendency which has impaired the thought of [socialisms's] greatest thinkers' was for Durkheim quite unacceptable – 'a veritable sociological heresy',[19] which quite misunderstood 'the true nature and role of social discipline', the 'very core of collective life'.[20] It would be impossible to arrive at 'a more perfect and more complex justice' in society without an ever more powerful and active, though greatly transformed, state.

Durkheim, as we have seen, made a sharp distinction between the existing varieties of socialism, on the one hand, and sociology, on the other. His general view was that, ideally, socialism could in the future become the application of the remedies proposed by sociology. It would then become 'the social and political art which complemented the social and political science constituted by sociology'.[21] But as things were, while recognizing how the history of socialism 'blends with the very history of sociology',[22] he firmly held that '[of] socialism, viewed as a theory of social facts, the sociologist can say but one thing: from the point of view of method and consistency he must refuse to see it as a scientific enterprise'.[23] On the other hand, sociology must take socialism very seriously, for it 'expresses a state of society. It does not express this accurately . . . Socialism is above all the manner in which certain sections of society, particularly subject to collective sufferings, represent these to themselves. But it at least bears witness to the existence of a social malaise, and although not an adequate expression of it, it can help us to understand it

18. ibid., p. 439.
19. ibid., p. 438.
20. ibid., p. 439.
21. Bourgin, 1942, p. 73. Cf. Aron, 1960, p. 31: '. . . He conceived sociology as the scientific counterpart of socialism.'
22. 1928a, p. 4: tr. 1958b, p. 6.
23. 1897d, p. 204.

since it derives from it ... its formulae are symbols'.[24] It was by means of sociology alone that one could 'look at the needs to which it responds', although 'the [political] parties have ready answers to the problem'.[25] Socialism, in its historical and existing forms, embodied a sort of primitive and pre-scientific sociology. Durkheim's diagnosis of the malaise, and his remedy, arrived at by the methods of sociology, have already been considered. His principal concern was with economic anarchy and injustice, and anomie in the industrial and commercial sphere, where 'latent or acute, the state of war is necessarily chronic',[26] and his principal remedy, developed in the mid-nineties, was the economic and moral reorganization of industry through the systematic re-creation of occupational groups, supervised by but independent of the state (for 'Anomie ... springs from the lack of collective forces at certain points in society; that is, of groups established for the regulation of social life'[27]). More generally, he wished to 'complete, organize and extend individualism',[28] to establish

24. ibid., p. 205. Cf. Chapter 12, above, and especially 1928a, p. 6: tr. 1958b, p. 7.

25. ibid. 'One would not ask a sick man about his ailments to discover their causes, nature and remedy ... we need research, information, methodical comparisons in which the confused and passionate intuitions of the common *conscience* should have no place' (ibid.).

26. 1902b, p. iii: tr. 1933b, p. 3. (S.L.).

27. 1897a, p. 440: tr. 1951a, p. 382. Mauss refers to this as the '*idée maîtresse* of Durkheim's specifically moral and political work', entailing that 'a part of the ancient political and property rights formerly held by domestic groups must be transferred to the occupational group, if the individual is not to be alone in face of the State and live a life alternating between anarchy and servitude'. Mauss adds that this idea was influential: Sorel (whose 'mind was penetrating, if not learned or just, whom we knew since 1893') took it up in some articles in *Le Devenir social*, and later 'revolutionary syndicalism was in part nourished by it'; 'we were', Mauss continues, 'some of us at least, more than observers in this connection between 1893 and 1906' (Mauss, 1928, pp. vi-vii: tr. Durkheim, 1958b, p. 2 – S.L.). For a brief discussion of Durkheim's influence on Sorel, see Goriely, G., *Le Pluralisme dramatique de Georges Sorel* (Paris, 1962), especially p. 187. For Durkheim's attitude to syndicalism, see Chapter 26, below.

28. Cf. Jaurès: 'socialism is the logical completion of individualism' ('Socialisme et Liberté', *Revue de Paris*, XXIII, December 1898, p. 499). Cf.

absolute equality of opportunity for all,[29] 'to organize economic life and introduce more justice into contractual relations', and 'to alleviate the functioning of the social machine, that is still so harsh to individuals, to put within their reach all possible means of developing their faculties without hindrance, to strive to make a reality of the famous precept: "to each according to his work" '[30]

If Durkheim's attitude to socialism was sympathetic but politically somewhat aloof, that of his disciples, the group of the *Année*, tended to be much more *engagé*. As Bouglé has recorded,

the majority, indeed almost all, of the contributors to the *Année sociologique* . . . great friends of the famous librarian of the École Normale . . . Lucien Herr, were members of the Socialist party and more than one was a contributor to *L'Humanité*.[31]

Indeed, Mauss and Simiand, together with Lucien Lévy-Bruhl (who was very close to the Durkheimians but not one of the inner group) were among that paper's founders. Many of the Durkheimians (such as Mauss, Simiand, Fauconnet and Emmanuel Lévy) lectured to workers in the *École socialiste*, in which they 'sought a basis for socialism in sociology'[32]; and most of them 'used up whatever time and energy their teaching

---

also Noland, A., 'Individualism in Jean Jaurès' Socialist Thought', *Journal of the History of Ideas*, 22 (1961), pp. 63–80, in which this passage is quoted (p. 74).

29. '. . . there cannot be rich and poor at birth without there being unjust contracts . . .': 1902b, p. 378: tr. 1933b, p. 384 (cf. bk III, ch. II passim).

30. 1898c, p. 13.

31. Bouglé, 1938, p. 34. 'Herr had begun his thirty-eight-year directorship of the library of the École Normale in 1888. Equipped with a staggering mastery of sources and endowed with great personal warmth, Herr, who had become socialist by 1889, directed successive generations of *normaliens* to the important treatises on socialist theory. "Here was the man, whom the public did not know", Léon Blum once exclaimed, "yet under whom the socialist *universitaires* were formed . . ." ' (Goldberg, H., *The Life of Jean Jaurès*, Madison, 1962, p. 62). Mauss wrote of Herr that he was always 'for all of us a constant and welcome advisor' (*AS*, n.s., 2 (1927), p. 9).

32. Andler, *Vie de Lucien Herr*, p. 163.

and research left them in the ... *Universités populaires* ...
[while] others, like Mauss, devoted themselves to the organization of co-operatives'.[33] They took part in strikes and election
campaigns and they published their sociological work in
abridged and popularized form in socialist tracts.[34] During the
Dreyfus Affair, many of them campaigned with Péguy and
Herr, organizing Dreyfusard agitation on the Left Bank,
circulating petitions and writing political pamphlets.[35] In
particular, a notable group formed around Herr, which for a
few years ran a socialist publishing house.[36] The group consisted of Herr, Simiand, Hubert Bourgin, Mario Rocques and
Léon Blum, and it called on the aid of many others including
most of the young Durkheimians. (It was founded as a

33. Bouglé, *Les Pages Libres*, 5 October 1907, quoted in Lasserre, 1913,
p. 179. On the people's universities, see Hayward, J. E. S., 'The Co-
operative Origins, Rise and Collapse of the "Universités Populaires"',
Archives internationales de sociologie de la co-opération, XI (1961), pp. 3–17.
The first was founded in 1898 and for a few years the movement flourished,
bringing together workers and Radical and socialist intellectuals. Cf.
Goldberg, op. cit., pp. 269–70, and Jackson, J. Hampden, *Jean Jaurès*
(London, 1943), pp. 94–5.

34. See Bourgin, 1938 and 1942, passim. The socialist tracts were in a
series called *Cahiers du socialiste*, founded a few years before the First
World War by François Simiand, Robert Hertz and Hubert Bourgin
(Bourgin, 1942, pp. 127–9). Also, between 1900 and 1906, Simiand, with
Herr's help, published a journal called *Notes critiques – sciences sociales*, a
sort of socialists' *Année sociologique*, to which Durkheim occasionally
contributed (see bibliography). The following were contributors to
Notes critiques: Charles Andler, Léon Blum, Hubert Bourgin, Durkheim,
Paul Fauconnet, M. Ostrogorski, Charles Rist, Charles Seignobos,
François Simiand, Lucien Lévy-Bruhl, Georges Bourgin, M. Lazard,
Albert Thomas, Louis Gernet, Robert Hertz, Maurice Halbwachs and
Arnold van Gennep. In 1903 Lucien Herr wrote, 'I know of no collective
enterprise that gives so strong an impression as this does of vigour, of
certainty, of bold and prudent firmness' (*NC*, IV, p. 262). Cf. Andler, op.
cit., pp. 159–60. The slim but inaccessible volumes of the *Notes critiques*
are indeed full of interesting and valuable reviews and notes, many of
them well worth republishing.

35. See Goldberg, op. cit., p. 478.

36. This was Péguy's Librairie Georges Bellais, which, on being rescued
by Herr and the others, became La Société Nouvelle de Librairie et
d'Édition. For various versions of the story, see Andler, op. cit., pp. 151–
67, Bourgin, 1942, pp. 110–16, and Péguy, C., *Pour moi* in *Œuvres en
prose* (Paris, 1959), I, pp. 126 ff.

rescue-operation for an earlier venture of Péguy's that had gone bankrupt – but Péguy soon quarrelled violently with the new regime and left to found the *Cahiers de la quinzaine*.) This group formed a real centre for socialist intellectual activity. Bourgin records that Durkheim's attitude to this publishing venture was critical:

From the heights of his doctrine, the theoretician of the Division of Labour, the moralist of professional specialization, had declared that it would collapse,[37] for it contravened the laws of industrial and commercial organization, which did not permit professors suddenly to become publishers; and he deplored the fact that so much energy was swallowed up in this way, and was thus lost to scientific work and achievement, which was their true occupation and function.[38]

The socialism of the Durkheimians was abstract, intellectual, evolutionary, reformist, optimistic, inspired by large ideals of co-operation and organization with an over-riding respect for social science. They believed that the critical and constructive tasks of socialism demanded 'precise scientific data, investigations, statistics, comparative studies of history and geography . . .'[39] As Bourgin recalled,

. . . most of those amongst us who adhered to socialism, to bring about the transformation not only of the relations between 'capital' and 'labour', but the total reform of the State, considered economic phenomena to be the most important: philosophers, historians, students of literature and language, turned themselves, so as to be better and more useful socialists, into economists and sociologists . . . First, there was to be the organization of producers: the regulation and harmonization of the relations between workers and bosses, employees and employers, businessmen, entrepreneurs and financiers . . . wishing to solve [what others called 'the social question'] with the double aim of saving humanity from slavery and bondage

37. As indeed, it very soon did, in 1902, when the business manager absconded to America with all the funds (Andler, op. cit., p. 165).

38. Bourgin, 1938, p. 117. An instance of this same attitude occurs in a letter to Hamelin where Durkheim wrote of the sympathy he felt towards his future colleague and disciple Robert Hertz, but expressed the hope that 'practical politics will not take this excellent mind away from us! There lies the danger. But he should have a sufficiently firm scientific temperament to resist the temptation' (Letter dated 11 September 1904).

39. Challaye, F., *Péguy socialiste* (Paris, 1954), p. 97.

and protecting industry against disorder, anarchy, idleness, parasitism, paralysis, we sought our method in a combination of positivism, applied to take account of all existing forms of organization, and democratism, determined to discover and develop, in a society troubled and weakened by disorder, the possibilities of consciousness and action. Also it was necessary to organize the consumers. That form of society, which ... would manage commercial and financial interests, saving, mutual insurance, even production itself, adapted to the positive needs of consumption, and developing, so it seemed, before our very eyes, in all sectors of urban and rural life – this vision had a great, seductive power over us.[40]

Bourgin wrote (sourly) of their ideals as follows:

In a society transformed by the division of labour, specialization, large-scale production and the anonymous management of enterprises, where the old status-system of employer, artisan and wage-earner had broken up, bringing the ruin of the system of professional ethics that was linked to it, new types of group were necessary which could, with the infinitely fragmented and atomized working-population, rebuild *'consciences communes'*, *'âmes collectives'* that were indispensable to the mobilizing of efforts and to output. In face of the weakening of old beliefs and of the 'secularization' of most institutions, it was the morality of work, of the vocation, of the professional association, in accordance with the absolute law of the division of tasks and the hierarchy of functions, that seemed to offer a means of salvation: it seemed that this form of organization, as yet in chaos and confusion, could bring about a world we imagined ourselves capable of controlling.[41]

THE ACADEMIC AND POLITICS

Durkheim shared his disciples' aims and ideals, but he did not share their commitment to practical party politics. Apart from his role in the Dreyfus Affair, during which 'Durkheim and the sociologists were everywhere in the mêlée',[42] it was his pedagogy lectures to future schoolteachers and his efforts to

40. Bourgin, H., *Cinquante Ans d'expérience démocratique* (Paris, 1925), pp. 51–2.
41. ibid., p. 55.
42. Besse, 1913, p. 238.

develop a national system of secular education (which we will consider below) that constituted his only direct contribution to the social regeneration he wished to bring about. He considered day-to-day political activity to be an unsuitable, even a harmful, pursuit for academics, above all participation in party and parliamentary politics. Certainly writers and scholars had, as citizens, a 'strict duty to participate in public life[43]; the question was what form this participation should take. As 'men of thought and imagination', they were not generally suited to a political career, which 'demands above all the qualities of men of action'.[44] Great physiologists were generally poor clinicians and the sociologist was likely to make a poor statesman. Intellectuals should be represented in parliament, to provide information and 'defend the interests of art and science',[45] but they need not be numerous. Besides, with rare exceptions (Durkheim was perhaps thinking of Jaurès), it was doubtful whether a politician could remain a scholar. It was, he wrote,

by means of books, lectures and contributing to popular education that our influence should be exercised. Before all else we should be *advisers* and *educators*. Our function is to help our contemporaries to understand themselves through their ideas and their feelings, rather than to govern them; and in the state of mental confusion in which we live is there any role which is more useful? Moreover we will perform it much more satisfactorily if we limit our ambitions in this way. We will gain popular confidence much more easily if we are suspected less of ulterior motives. The lecturer of today must not be seen as the candidate of tomorrow.[46]

His conception of the political role of the academic bears a certain resemblance to that of Max Weber.[47] The academic had a right, indeed a duty, to take a stand on major political issues,

43. 1904e, p. 705.
44. ibid.
45. ibid.
46. ibid., pp. 705–6. According to M. Henri Durkheim, his uncle never wished to enter active politics (personal communication).
47. Weber, M., *Wissenschaft als Beruf* (Munich, 1919), tr. as 'Science as a Vocation' in *From Max Weber: Essays in Sociology*, tr. and ed. Gerth, H. H., and Mills, C. W. (London and New York, 1946). Cf.: 'It is said, and I agree, that politics is out of place in the lecture-room ... the true

but he must not use his academic authority for political ends. He was later to say, in this connection:

I consider that a professor who, even outside the context of his teaching, seeks to exercise any political influence over his students thereby often puts himself in a delicate position. For he is making use of the authority which is inherent in his post for purposes that are foreign to it. That authority is not his personal property: he cannot just use it as he pleases.[48]

There was a certain ambiguity here. Much of Durkheim's teaching presupposed and entailed evaluations that were political in the widest sense – even if he himself saw such evaluations as scientifically justified. Moreover, twice in his life, when issues that seemed to transcend ordinary politics were in question, during the Dreyfus Affair and the First World War, Durkheim became an intensely active partisan. The key to his attitude lies in his (justifiably) low estimation of current politics as a superficial game of parties and personalities. In such circumstances, the academic should without question abstain from taking part in political campaigns and contro- versies. Only when great moral and social questions were matters of public debate, and above all when the very ideals of the Republic were threatened, should his voice be raised. When this happened he should come into the political arena to 'advise' and 'educate' his contemporaries. In brief, the aca- demic could be an ideologist, but not a mere activist. He should propagate ideas which he held to be true and important, leaving the practice of politics to others.

THE DREYFUS AFFAIR

A revealing instance of Durkheim's practical interpretation of this principle occurred during the course of the Dreyfus

---

teacher will beware of imposing from the platform any political position upon the student, whether it is expressed or suggested . . . the prophet and the demagogue do not belong on the academic platform' (*From Max Weber*, pp. 145–6). On the other hand, Weber differed sharply from Durkheim in his view of the academic's political role outside the university – and indeed in his attitude to politics.

48. 1907d, pp. 142–3.

Affair.[49] In January 1898, after the publication of Émile Zola's famous letter headed '*J'accuse*' addressed to the President of the Republic, a local Bordeaux paper carried the following news item:

We are told that two professors, MM. Durkheim and Waitz, have written to M. Zola a letter of warm congratulations and have asked their students to countersign the letter.

There subsequently appeared in the same journal the following report:

MM. Durkheim and Waitz declare that they have never written to Zola, still less urged their students to do so. M. Durkheim has explained that, on the 21st January, two of his students came to him to ask his advice. He told them that 'personally he thought that one ought to protest against the grave illegalities that appeared to have been committed during the trial of 1894, *but that he explicitly refused to offer them the slightest advice on what their conduct should be*'. He even added that, on principle, he preferred to see students abstaining from these sorts of demonstration, whatever their import.

For their part, a delegation of students brought to the *Nouvelliste* [the paper concerned] a letter in which they protested and made it clear that their two professors had in no way solicited their signatures.[50]

Durkheim's attitude to the Dreyfus Affair itself was entirely consistent with his general view of politics. Like Péguy, he regarded it as '*un moment de la conscience humaine*' and saw it as introducing into political life a new degree of moral seriousness and public participation. In 1904, in the long shadow cast by the Affair and in the midst of the Combist anticlerical crusade which so disillusioned Péguy, he compared the intense activity of the intellectuals provoked by the Dreyfus Affair with their pronounced political apathy during the first twenty years of the Third Republic. The latter had been due, he held, to the fact that no 'great moral and social problem' had been presented before the country. Politics had been

49. It is worth noting that both Georges Davy and Henri Durkheim agree that Durkheim's attitude to the *Affaire* was 'moral', rather than 'narrowly political'; nor did he see it explicitly as a Jew (see Filloux, 1970, p. 257).

50. Durkheim's dossier, Bordeaux (emphasis in dossier).

pitifully engulfed in questions of personalities. Divisions were about who should have power. But there was no great impersonal cause to which one could devote oneself, no elevated end to which men's wills could adhere ... But, as soon as a grave question of principle was raised, one saw the scientists leave their laboratories and the scholars their studies, and they drew near to the crowd, took part in its life; and experience has shown that they knew how to make themselves heard.[51]

Durkheim held that this 'moral agitation' was necessary and that it should continue. The apathy that had previously existed was 'abnormal' and dangerous. Like the Saint-Simonians, he saw the period since the fall of the *Ancien Régime* as a 'Critical Period' which had not ended: 'The hour of rest has not sounded for us.' There was

too much to do for it not to be indispensable that we should keep our social energies, as it were, permanently mobilized. That is why I believe the politics of these last four years preferable to that which preceded it. For it has succeeded in maintaining a constant flow of collective activity, at a certain pitch of intensity. Of course, I am far from thinking that anticlericalism is enough; I long to see society adhering to more objective ends. But it is essential not to let ourselves relapse into our previous state of prolonged moral stagnation.[52]

Durkheim's was the authentic attitude of the Dreyfusard 'intellectual'. It was precisely this high-minded attitude on the part of many of the academic supporters of Dreyfus that so incensed the anti-Dreyfusards, from the hooligans who broke up their lectures to sophisticated men of letters who scorned them in print. Catholic polemicists pilloried the 'ignoble race of these academics ... who spend their lives teaching error and in corrupting souls, and, in due course, society as a whole'.[53] They were the 'atheistic educators of the young, agents of social harm ... the main source of evil, the true enemies of social order'.[54] For Maurice Barrès

51. 1904e, p. 706.
52. ibid.
53. Renaud, *La Conquête protestante*, p. 378, cited in Soltau, R., *French Political Thought in the Nineteenth Century* (New York, 1959), pp. 354–5.
54. ibid.

The great culprits, who should be punished, are the 'intellectuals', the 'anarchists of the lecture-platform', the 'metaphysicians of sociology'. A band of arrogant madmen. Men who take a criminal self-satisfaction in their intelligence, who treat our generals as idiots, our social institutions as absurd and our traditions as unhealthy . . .[55]

To Ferdinand Brunetière, the literary historian and critic, and one of the immortals of the strongly anti-Dreyfusard Académie Française, the very word 'intellectual' proclaimed 'one of the most ridiculous eccentricities of our time – I mean the pretension of raising writers, scientists, professors and philologists to the rank of supermen'.[56]

Indeed, early in 1898, Brunetière published an article entitled 'Après le procès'[57] in which he defended the army and the social order, threatened by 'individualism' and 'anarchy', and poured scorn on 'various intellectuals' who had presumed to doubt the justice of Dreyfus's trial. After Zola's '*J'accuse*' (indicting Esterhazy's judges, the officers who had directed the investigation of Dreyfus, the chiefs of the general staff, the handwriting experts and various departments of the War Ministry) the intellectuals had publicly declared themselves – artists, men of letters, scientists, lawyers and professors. The 'Manifesto of the Intellectuals' published in *L'Aurore* the day after '*J'accuse*' stated:

55. Barrès, M., *Scènes et doctrines de nationalisme* (Paris, 1902), Livre 2ᵉ, pp. 209–10. Barrès defined an intellectual as 'an individual who persuades himself that society must be based on logic and who fails to recognize that it rests in fact on necessities that are anterior and perhaps foreign to the reason of the individual' (ibid., p. 45).

56. Paléologue, M., *Journal de l'affaire Dreyfus* (Paris, 1966), pp. 90–1. For further discussions of the Dreyfusard 'intellectuals' and attacks on them, see Brombert, V., *The Intellectual Hero 1880–1955* (London, 1962), ch. 2; Coser, L. A., *Men of Ideas* (New York, 1965), pp. 207–26; Gauthier, R., *Dreyfusards* (Paris, 1965); Kayser, J., *The Dreyfus Affair* (tr. London, 1931) (see p. 183 for a useful list of the leading Dreyfusard intellectuals); and Curtis, M., *Three Against the Republic: Sorel, Barrès and Maurras* (Princeton, N.J., 1959), ch. vii.

57. *Revue des deux mondes*, 4ᵉ période, t.146, 67ᵉ année (15 March 1898), pp. 428–46.

We the undersigned protest against the violation of judicial procedure and against the mystery surrounding the Esterhazy affair and
persist in demanding Revision.[58]

A few days later, various members of the Institut presented a
petition to the Chamber of Deputies in support of Zola.
The second, ultimately victorious, phase of the Dreyfusard
campaign had begun. Brunetière took up the battle with the
intellectuals with enthusiasm.

He addressed himself to three questions: the causes of anti-
semitism, the place of the army in a democracy, and the claims
of the 'intellectuals'. Concerning the first, he advanced the
remarkable argument that it was science, or rather pseudo-
science, that had first given rise to anti-semitism by postulating
the inequality of races: anthropologists, ethnographers,
linguists, historians and critics had lent their authority to this
hypothesis which had then passed into the popular imagination. He argued, further, that the prejudice against Freemasons,
Protestants and Jews was a natural and legitimate reaction to
their 'domination' in the spheres of politics, law, education and
administration, and that the Jews themselves were partly
responsible for anti-semitism.

Secondly, Brunetière argued that the army was vital for
French security, prosperity and democracy. It was incompatible only with individualism and anarchy, such as that
advanced by Herbert Spencer, who argued that the military
profession was an anachronistic survival of barbarism in the
age of industry and commerce. On the contrary, war and
diplomacy were still 'the keystone of social equilibrium'.[59]
The mass of the people had rightly sensed during Dreyfus's
trial that 'the army of France, today as of old, is France herself . . . our armies have made us what we are . . . it is in their
blood . . . that national unity has been formed, cemented and
consolidated'.[60] Its composition was truly national, its spirit
honourable and its discipline humane; with national service it
had even become a 'school of equality'.[61]

58. 14 January 1898.
59. art. cit., p. 437.
60. ibid., p. 440.
61. ibid., p. 441.

The individualism and anarchy which threatened the army and all that it represented were primarily to be found among 'various intellectuals' – persons who, in virtue of some specialized knowledge, were assumed to have some special authority in all matters, including 'the most delicate questions concerning human morality, the life of nations and the interests of society'.[62] Such an assumption was unfounded and dangerous, and the danger was only increased by their appeal to 'science' to support their purely individual opinions. Grand phrases like 'the scientific method, aristocracy of intelligence, respect for truth' only served to conceal the pretensions of 'Individualism', which was

the great sickness of the present time . . . Each of us has confidence only in himself, sets himself up as the sovereign judge of everything and does not even allow his opinion to be discussed. Don't tell this biologist that human affairs are not amenable to his scientific 'methods'; he will laugh at you! Don't confront this palaeographer with the judgement of three court-martials; he knows what the justice of men is, and, anyway, is he not the director of the École Nationale de Chartes? And this man, the first person in the world to scan the verses of Plautus, how can you expect him to bend his 'logic' at the word of an army general? One does not spend one's life in studies of that importance in order to think 'like everyone else'; and the true intellectual could not behave like just anyone. He is Nietzsche's 'superman' or 'the enemy of laws' who was not made for laws but rather to rise above them; and we others, mediocre as we are, have only to admire and be grateful! I am merely pointing out that when intellectualism and individualism reach this degree of self-infatuation, one must expect them to be or become nothing other than *anarchy*; – perhaps we are not yet at this point, but we are rapidly approaching it.[63]

For the past hundred years, the intellectuals had caused a great deal of harm and they were 'capable of causing us still more'.[64] Moreover, recent events had shown 'the ways in which their self-satisfaction is truly anti-social'.[65]

62. ibid., p. 444.
63. ibid., p. 445.
64. ibid., p. 446.
65. ibid.

Durkheim replied to Brunetière in an article entitled 'Individualism and the Intellectuals',[66] in which he took up the issue of principle: 'the state of mind of the "intellectuals", the fundamental ideas to which they adhere'.[67] They had refused to 'bend their logic at the word of an army general'; they were 'putting their own reason above authority, and the rights of the individual appear to them to be imprescriptible'.[68] 'Let us', he wrote, 'forget the Affair itself and the melancholy scenes we have witnessed. The problem confronting us goes infinitely beyond the current events and must be disengaged from them'.[69] Durkheim's article is of considerable interest. It offers a conclusive refutation of a certain interpretation of him as fundamentally anti-liberal and anti-individualistic, as a right-wing nationalist, a spiritual ally of Charles Maurras and a forerunner of twentieth-century nationalism,[70] even fascism[71] – an interpretation that relied on a selective misreading of certain

66. 1898c: tr. 1969d. Cf. Lukes, 1969a. For other discussions, see Neyer, 1960, Richter, 1960, and Filloux, 1970. Durkheim wrote to Bouglé on 28 March 1898: 'I had also been thinking of writing a sociological article on the question and Brunetière's vapid article makes me itch to reply.' Émile Duclaux, the distinguished scientist and member of the Académie Française also replied to Brunetière's article, calling his reply 'Avant le procès', and accusing Brunetière of selective evidence and inconsistent arguments.

67. ibid., p. 7: tr. p. 19.

68. ibid.: tr. p. 20.

69. ibid.

70. Cf., for example, Parodi, 1909 and 1919, pp. 149–50; Benda, J., *La Trahison des clercs* (Paris, 1927), 3, 3; and Mitchell, 1931. In Hayes, C. J. H., *A Generation of Materialism* (New York and London, 1941), Durkheim is described as one of a number of 'sources . . . of totalitarian nationalism' (p. 247). For the contrasts between Durkheim and Maurras, see Fonsegrive, G., *De Taine à Péguy: l'évolution des idées dans la France contemporaine* (Paris, 1920); e.g.: '. . . having started from the same principles, M. Durkheim and M. Maurras reach very different conclusions: M. Durkheim is a loyal supporter of the present Republic; M. Maurras sees no solution for France except through the restoration of the monarchy, and what he calls "integral nationalism" ' (p. 287).

71. In Ranulf, 1939, the author argues that Durkheim was a forerunner of Fascism (along with Tönnies and Comte). He includes two quotations of the greatest interest from letters to the author from Marcel Mauss written in 1936 and 1939. Mauss wrote: 'Durkheim, and after him, the rest of us are, I believe, those who founded the theory of the authority

of his writings and, in some cases, a mistaken importation into his centralized guild socialism of the connotations of fascist corporatism. Here, in effect, is a Dreyfusiste manifesto and an eloquent defence of liberalism, stated in the categories of Durkheim's sociological theory. It was an attempt to give a sociological account of 'individualism' as a set of operative ideals, moral beliefs and practices, indeed as a religion in which the human person becomes a sacred object. This attempt sheds considerable light on Durkheim's thought in two respects. In the first place, it shows how he came to conceive of the *conscience collective* in a modern industrial society. Such a society required a 'religion', in the sense of a 'system of collective beliefs and practices that have a special authority';[72] this religion, deriving from Christianity, sanctified the values of liberalism and pointed towards socialism. In the second place, Durkheim's sociological account of individualism is the clearest instance of the way in which he saw sociology, or the science of ethics, as going beyond the philosophical ethics of the past, by treating moral beliefs and practices as social facts. Individualism was

itself a social product, like all moralities and all religions. The individual receives from society even the moral beliefs which deify him. This is what Kant and Rousseau did not understand. They

---

of the collective *représentation*. One thing that, fundamentally, we never foresaw was how many large modern societies, that have more or less emerged from the Middle Ages in other respects, could be hypnotized like Australians are by their dances, and set in motion like a children's roundabout. This return to the primitive had not been the object of our thoughts. We contented ourselves with several allusions to crowd situations, while it was a question of something quite different. We also contented ourselves with proving that it was in the collective mind [*dans l'esprit collectif*] that the individual could find the basis and sustenance for his liberty, his independence, his personality and his criticism [*critique*]. Basically, we never allowed for the extraordinary new possibilities ... I believe that all this is a real tragedy for us, too powerful a verification of things that we had indicated and the proof that we should have expected this verification through evil rather than a verification through goodness [*le bien*]' (ibid., p. 32). M. Aron recalls that, at the same period, Léon Brunschvicg said to him: 'Nuremberg is religion according to Durkheim, society adoring itself' (personal communication).

72. 1898c, p. 10: tr. p. 25.

wished to deduce their individualist ethics not from society, but from the notion of the isolated individual.[73]

Thus, Durkheim maintained, it was 'possible, without contradiction, to be an individualist while asserting that the individual is a product of society, rather than its cause'.[74]

He began by drawing a sharp distinction between 'the narrow utilitarianism and utilitarian egoism of Spencer and the economists ... that narrow commercialism which reduces society to nothing more than a vast apparatus of production and exchange' and 'another individualism', that of 'Kant and Rousseau, that of the *spiritualistes*, that which the Declaration of the Rights of Man sought, more or less successfully, to translate into formulae, that which is currently taught in our schools and which has become the basis of our moral catechism'.[75] Utilitarian individualism was indeed anarchical (an 'apotheosis of comfort and private interest, [an] egoistic cult of the self'[76]) though it was fast losing adherents. The other individualism, however, saw personal motives as the very source of evil and held that 'the only ways of acting that are moral are those which are fitting for all men equally, that is to say, which are implied in the notion of man in general'.[77] Indeed, it pointed towards an ideal that went

so far beyond the limit of utilitarian ends that it appears to those who aspire to it as marked with a religious character. The human person, whose definition serves as the touchstone according to which good must be distinguished from evil, is considered as sacred, in what one might call the ritual sense of the word. It has something of that transcendental majesty which the churches of all times have given to their Gods. It is conceived as being invested with that mysterious property which creates an empty space around holy objects, which keeps them away from profane contacts and which draws them away from ordinary life. And it is exactly this feature which induces the respect of which it is the object. Whoever makes an attempt on a man's life, on a man's liberty, on a man's honour

73. ibid., p. 12 fn.: tr. p. 28 fn.
74. ibid.
75. ibid., pp. 7–8: tr. pp. 20–21.
76. ibid., p. 8: tr. p. 21.
77. ibid.

inspires us with a feeling of horror in every way analogous to that which the believer experiences when he sees his idol profaned. Such a morality is therefore not simply a hygienic discipline or a wise principle of economy. It is a religion of which man is, at the same time, both believer and God.[78]

This individualism was uncompromising in its defence of the rights of man: there was 'no reason of State which can excuse an outrage against the person when the rights of the person are placed above the State'.[79]

It was, however, far from anti-social: the cult of which man was both object and follower addressed itself to 'the human person, wherever it is to be found, and in whatever form it is incarnated'.[80] Such an end was 'impersonal and anonymous', placed above particular consciences and able to serve as a 'rallying-point' for them.[81] All that societies require in order to hold together, Durkheim argued (in contrast to the argument of *The Division of Labour*) is that 'their members fix their eyes on the same end and come together in a single faith'.[82] The object of that faith need not be remote and unconnected with individual persons. Individualism thus understood was 'the glorification, not of the self, but of the individual in general' and its motive force was 'not egoism but sympathy for all that is human, a wider pity for all sufferings, for all human miseries, a more ardent desire to combat and alleviate them, a greater thirst for justice'.[83]

This 'cult of man' had 'for its first dogma the autonomy of reason and for its first rite freedom of thought'.[84] What then of the argument that intellectual and moral anarchy was the inevitable consequence of liberalism? Durkheim answered this argument, 'which the perennial adversaries of reason take up periodically',[85] by observing that liberty of thought (the

78. ibid.: tr. pp. 21–2.
79. ibid., pp. 8–9: tr. p. 22.
80. ibid., p. 9: tr. p. 23.
81. ibid.
82. ibid.
83. ibid.: tr. p. 24.
84. ibid., p. 10: tr. p. 24.
85. ibid.

'first of liberties') was compatible with respect for authority where that authority was rationally grounded: reasons had always to be given to show why one opinion was more competent than another. The case of Dreyfus was one where submission could not be justified in this way: it was 'one of those questions which pertain, by definition, to the common judgement of men', for 'in order to know whether a court of justice can be allowed to condemn an accused man without having heard his defence, there is no need for any special expertise. It is a problem of practical morality concerning which every man of good sense is competent and about which no one ought to be indifferent.'[86] The intellectuals had refused to assent to the legally suspect judgement of Dreyfus, not because they claimed any special expertise or privileges, but because they were exercising their rights as men, and because, accustomed to withhold judgement when not fully aware of the facts, they were inclined to 'give in less readily to the enthusiasm of the crowd and to the prestige of authority'.[87]

At this point in the argument, Durkheim executed an ingenious and effective inversion of the characteristic anti-Dreyfusard argument that the unity, indeed the very survival, of the nation were being threatened for the sake of one individual's rights. Individualism, he argued, was 'henceforth the only system of beliefs which can ensure the moral unity of the country'.[88] As societies grew in volume and spread over vaster territories, traditions and practices adapted to social change by becoming more plastic and unstable; social and cultural differentiation had developed almost to a point at which the members of a single society retained only their humanity in common. The 'idea of the human person', given different emphases in accordance with the diversity of national temperaments, is therefore the 'sole idea that survives, immutable and impersonal, above the changing tides of particular opinions'.[89] The communion of minds could no longer form around 'particular rites and prejudices'; individualism was 'the doctrine

86. ibid.: tr. p. 25.
87. ibid.
88. ibid.
89. ibid., p. 11: tr. p. 26.

that is currently necessary'.[90] In order to hold back its progress,

we would have to prevent men from becoming increasingly differentiated from one another, reduce their personalities to a single level, bring them back to the old conformism of former times and arrest, in consequence, the tendency of societies to become ever more extended and centralized, and stem the unceasing growth of the division of labour. Such an undertaking, whether desirable or not, infinitely surpasses all human powers.[91]

Individualist morality was the natural successor to Christian morality, out of which it had grown. In these circumstances, outrages against the rights of an individual

cannot rest unpunished without putting national existence in jeopardy. It is indeed impossible that they should be freely allowed to occur without weakening the sentiments they violate; and as these sentiments are all that we still have in common, they cannot be weakened without disturbing the cohesion of society. A religion which tolerates acts of sacrilege abdicates any sway over men's minds. The religion of the individual can therefore allow itself to be flouted without resistance, only on penalty of ruining its credit; since it is the sole link which binds us one to another, such a weakening cannot take place without the onset of social dissolution. Thus the individualist, who defends the rights of the individual, defends at the same time, the vital interests of society . . .[92]

It was thus the anti-Dreyfusards who were threatening the nation with moral anarchy by seeking to destroy individualism, which had 'penetrated our institutions and our customs' and become 'part of our whole life'.[93] But that individualism itself needed to be completed, organized and extended. Durkheim argued, in a fashion reminiscent of Marx, that its eighteenth-century form had expressed only its most negative aspect, and must be 'enlarged and completed'[94]: freeing the individual from political fetters was only the pre-condition for subsequent progress. It was vital that political liberties be put

90. ibid.
91. ibid.
92. ibid. pp. 11–12: tr. p. 27.
93. ibid., p. 9: tr. p. 22.
94. ibid., p. 12: tr. p. 28.

to use by working towards economic and social justice. Liberty was a delicate instrument the use of which must be learnt; 'all moral education should be directed to this end'.[95] Above all, it would be senseless to renounce objectives already attained so as to pursue the new ones more easily.

The most immediate task, however, was 'that of saving our moral patrimony'.[96] Already there were 'initiatives awakening within the country, men of good will seeking one another out. Let someone [Jaurès?] appear who can combine them and lead them into the struggle: perhaps victory will then not be long in coming.'[97] Durkheim concluded on an optimistic note: the anti-Dreyfusards were strong only by virtue of their opponents' weakness. They had 'neither that deep faith nor those generous enthusiasms which sweep people irresistibly to great reactions as well as to great revolutions', they were 'neither apostles who allow themselves to be overwhelmed by their anger or their enthusiasm, nor are they scientists who bring us the product of their research and their deliberations'.[98] They were 'literary men seduced by an interesting theme'; and it therefore seemed 'impossible that these games of dilettantes should succeed in keeping hold of the masses for very long, provided that we know how to act'.[99] His optimism, though not perhaps his reasons for it, soon proved justified.

In the following year, Durkheim published two replies to surveys of opinion which dealt with the other principal issues raised in Brunetière's article: militarism[1] and anti-semitism.[2] Concerning militarism, he held that it 'no longer has, or should not have, a moral value', and that its present recrudescence was abnormal, due to temporary circumstances and the exorbitant prestige of the army. Contemporary France needed 'qualities of another sort – those of the scientist, the engineer, the doctor, the *industriel*', and Frenchmen should

95. ibid., p. 13: tr. p. 29.
96. ibid.: tr. p. 30.
97. ibid.
98. ibid.
99. ibid.
 1. 1899b.
 2. 1899d.

pursue other goals: 'respect for the law, love of liberty, a proper concern for duties and responsibilities, whether they derive from individuals or society, and the desire for a more equitable distributive justice'. One major need was to reform the system of public education.

Concerning contemporary anti-semitism in France, Durkheim, unlike Theodore Herzl, who attributed it to the fundamental racialism of the French people,[3] saw it as 'the consequence and the superficial symptom of a state of social *malaise*'[4]:

> When society undergoes suffering, it feels the need to find someone whom it can hold responsible for its sickness, on whom it can avenge its misfortunes: and those against whom public opinion already discriminates are naturally designated for this role. These are the pariahs who serve as expiatory victims. What confirms me in this interpretation is the way in which the result of Dreyfus's trial was greeted in 1894. There was a surge of joy on the boulevards. People celebrated as a triumph what should have been a cause for public mourning. At last they knew whom to blame for the economic troubles and moral distress in which they lived. The trouble came from the Jews. The charge had been officially proved. By this very fact alone, things already seemed to be getting better and people felt consoled.[5]

There were, of course, secondary causes: certain vaguely religious aspirations that had recently appeared had been able to profit from this movement of opinion, and certain faults of the Jewish race could be invoked to justify it. But these same faults were counterbalanced by undoubted virtues, and,

3. See *L'Affaire Dreyfus* (Fédération Sioniste de France, n.d.); cf. Kedward, R., *The Dreyfus Affair* (London, 1965), pp. 65–8.

4. 1899d, p. 60. Durkheim distinguished here between two sorts of anti-semitism: that of Germany and Russia, which was 'chronic and traditional', and 'our own', constituting 'an acute crisis, due to passing circumstances'. The former had 'an aristocratic character', it consists of disdain and arrogance'; the latter was 'inspired by violent, destructive passions which seek to express themselves by any means' (ibid.). This view of anti-semitism as basically un-French was common to many Jewish writers of the period: see Marrus, M. R., *The Politics of Assimilation: A Study of the French Jewish Community at the Time of the Dreyfus Affair* (Oxford, 1971), p. 99.

5. ibid., p. 61.

besides, 'the Jews are losing their ethnic character with an extreme rapidity. In two generations the process will be complete.'[6] (Compare this view with that of the leading Dreyfusard and Zionist, Bernard Lazare, who wrote that 'it is because [the Jews] are a nation that anti-semitism exists . . . and what are the effects of this anti-semitism? To make this nationality more tangible for the Jews, to strengthen their realization that they are a people').[7] Also, Durkheim argued, the primary causes could not be of a religious order, for religious faith had been no less intense twenty or thirty years before, yet anti-semitism did not then exist as it existed now.

It was, in fact, 'one of many indices by which the grave moral disturbance from which we are suffering is revealed'.[8] Thus the real way to check it was to 'put an end to this state of disorder; but that is not the work of a day'. None the less, there was 'something that was immediately possible and urgent that could be done'.[9] If the sickness could not be attacked at its source, at least the special manifestations which aggravated it could be combated, for 'one does not let a sick man avenge his sufferings on himself by tearing himself apart with his own hands':

> To achieve this result, it would be necessary, first of all, to repress severely every incitement to hatred by some citizens against others. Doubtless, on their own, repressive measures cannot convert people's minds; all the same, they would remind public opinion what it is forgetting, namely, how odious such a crime is. It would, secondly, be necessary that one should not, while condemning anti-semitism in theory, provide it with genuine satisfactions that encourage it; that the government should take it upon itself to show the masses how they are being misled and not allow itself to be suspected of seeking allies within the party of intolerance.[10]

Finally, Durkheim concluded, it would be necessary for 'all men of good sense', instead of contenting themselves with

6. ibid.
7. *Le Nationalisme juif*, 6 March 1897, quoted in Kedward, op. cit., p. 51.
8. 1899d, p. 62.
9. ibid.
10. ibid.

'platonic disapproval', to 'have the courage to proclaim aloud what they think, and to unite together in order to achieve victory in the struggle against public madness'.[11]

What form of action did Durkheim himself adopt? He seems to have been a Dreyfusard from a relatively early date. According to his nephew, M. Henri Durkheim,[12] he was instrumental in persuading Jaurès to take up the cause of Dreyfus. I have been able to discover no independent confirmation of this, though it is perfectly possible that he added his voice to that of Herr, Lucien Lévy-Bruhl and the others who convinced Jaurès that principles of liberty and justice were at stake. Again according to M. Durkheim, his uncle had, as early as 1896, made an outspoken Dreyfusiste speech at the tomb of a recently deceased colleague at Bordeaux, which caused something of a sensation.[13] (However, his signature does not appear in the 'Manifesto of the Intellectuals' published in *L'Aurore* on 14–16 January 1898.) In 1898 he became an active member of the Ligue pour la Défense des Droits de l'Homme, founded (partly on his suggestion) on 20 February between the twelfth and thirteenth hearings of the Zola trial by Senator Ludovic Trarieux and a number of his political and academic friends. The Ligue, which has been called 'the most effective and durable creation of all this Dreyfusiste agitation',[14] was committed to the view that Dreyfus's conviction, Esterhazy's acquittal and the proceedings against Zola were all a travesty of republican justice and a victory for the forces of reaction. By May it had over 800 supporters in Paris and the provinces, and by the end of 1898 it claimed over 4,500. It appealed primarily to teachers and intellectuals; and although basically liberal in its theory, it became intensely anticlerical in practice.[15] It held meetings and in general acted as a pressure-group in the cause of revision, in

11. ibid., pp. 62–3.
12. Personal communication.
13. Personal communication. M. Durkheim was living with his uncle at Bordeaux for some of this period.
14. Miquel, P., *L'Affaire Dreyfus* (Paris, 1961), p. 51.
15. See Kedward, op. cit., pp. 31–2, and Gauthier, R., *Dreyfusards* (Paris, 1965), p. 133.

contrast to the anti-Dreyfusard Ligue de la Patrie Française, founded in December 1898 (and to which Brunetière belonged).

Durkheim was a very active participant in the Ligue des Droits de l'Homme. Indeed, as he wrote to Bouglé early in 1898,

> I was a member of the Ligue in advance; I was part of it before it existed. During the Zola trial, the result of which could not be in doubt, I wrote to Hubert asking him to suggest to certain well-known people he had occasion to see the idea of a permanent organization with the aims of showing that we were not abdicating, of forestalling the consequences of moral ostracism, and preparing for the future. Reinach had thought of something similar. Duclaux was spoken to, and I wrote to him directly; and that is how, a fortnight ago on Sunday, the statutes were drawn up. But recruitment will be a laborious business. What meanness and what cowardice one encounters! This has the advantage of unmasking those people whose courage and decency is a sham, who, in ordinary times, speak of nothing but their disinterestedness, and today, while thinking as we do, find miserable pretexts for not saying so aloud. But those who are united must stand together all the more. Let there be, at least, this moral benefit from the situation![16]

Durkheim organized and became secretary of the Bordeaux branch of the Ligue.[17] As he wrote to Bouglé early in 1899,

> . . . I have organized here a section of the Ligue. This has been rather hard because the Bordeaux temperament is so lazy. But at last things are moving. We now have between 180 and 190 [members]; in December there were about 60.[18]

A report in a local newspaper gives an account of a meeting of the Ligue on 6 June 1900, in which homage was paid to the activity of the Bordeaux committee. M. Stapfer (Honorary Dean of the Faculty of Letters at Bordeaux) was, we are told,

16. Letter dated 28 March 1898.
17. See the *Bulletin* of the Ligue. Durkheim was also elected honorary president of the Eynesse branch.
18. Letter dated 13 March 1899. The letters to Bouglé contain a number of observations on the course of the Affair.

no less applauded when he spoke of M. Durkheim, professor at the Faculty of Letters at Bordeaux, whose fiery speeches bring supporters to the Ligue from far and wide.[19]

The Ligue did not confine its activities to the cause of Dreyfus: it was concerned also to extend its republican and anticlerical outlook to discussions of the condition and future of the country as a whole. Indeed, the Bordeaux committee broadened its focus to include international issues. As Durkheim wrote in a letter to Louis Havet, one of the Ligue's founders and leaders, inviting him to give a lecture at Bordeaux:

After your lecture the statutory General Assembly of our section will – very briefly – take place. At that Assembly we are planning to put to the vote a motion concerning the war between England and the Boers. In the few words that I shall say in proposing it, I will take care to specify that we are not yielding to any feeling of Anglophobia, but that we are merely claiming the right of every man to protect his country as his family. As the motion is not unrelated to the subject you will be dealing with, I thought it might be useful to let you know about this. As to the reason which has led us to propose it, it is not, of course, that we expect any practical result, but rather that we have been reproached with having aroused Europe on behalf of one man's fate while remaining indifferent to that of a whole people.[20]

19. Durkheim's dossier, Bordeaux. The Rector of Bordeaux, however, took a very different view of Durkheim's activities. In 1899, he sent the Minister of Public Instruction a newspaper report of a speech given by Durkheim at a public banquet. 'I consider', he wrote to the Minister, 'that whatever the position taken by teachers of the University of Bordeaux in their speechifying at militant meetings, they never do good: for they make their divisions more and more palpable to the entire population and above all to the students, to whom one should preach concord and unity, and who are led into demonstrating themselves, in the steps of, and in imitation of, several overexcited professors, under opposed flags and in committed groups' (letter dated 16 July 1899 in Durkheim's dossier, Archives Nationales).

20. Letter dated 4 February 1901. Later that year Durkheim extended a similar invitation to Havet, whose subject then was 'The Idea of the Fraternity of Peoples' (letter dated 22 October 1901).

DURKHEIM AND SOLIDARISM

In the previous year, Durkheim had given an address to a different and more influential audience on the theme of 'Patriotism and Cosmopolitanism'.[21] This was a subject on which he had fairly constant views, which were very close to those of Jaurès: national loyalties were real and valuable, but they should not be exclusive and they should be extended in an internationalist direction. He was to observe on another occasion,

Doubtless, we have towards the country in its present form, and of which we in fact form part, obligations that we do not have the right to cast off. But beyond this country, there is another in the process of formation, enveloping our national country: that of Europe, or humanity.[22]

Durkheim's speech on this subject was delivered to the Congrès International de l'Éducation Sociale, held in Paris under the auspices of the government as part of the Exposition Universelle of 1900.[23] The aim of this Congress, which gathered together the most prominent adherents of solidarism, was to discuss the concept of *solidarité* and to consider ways and means of diffusing it through the educational system. The audience consisted of many leaders of the Radical and Radical Socialist Party, Senators, Deputies, teachers, magistrates, industrialists, and representatives of trade unions and co-operatives. Other speakers included the Radical Léon Bourgeois, the aptly named philosopher-politician of *solidarité* and ex-Prime Minister; Alexandre Millerand, the reformist Socialist Minister of Commerce; the historian Charles Seignobos; the economist Charles Gide; the republican educational administrator and theorist Ferdinand Buisson; and Gustave Geffroy, the Radical journalist and associate of Clemenceau. The Congress concluded with a resolution stating the meaning

21. Letter to Léon dated 7 February 1900.
22. At a meeting of the Société Française de Philosophie: 1908a (i), p. 45. Cf. 1925a, pp. 87–90: tr. 1961a, pp. 77–9; and, for a development of Durkheim's ideas on this subject, see Mauss, 1968–9, vol. III, Annexe: 'Sociologie politique: la nation et l'internationalisme'.
23. For details of the Congress, see Scott, op. cit., pp. 179–81.

and implications of the notion of *solidarité* – the idea of justice as the repayment of a 'social debt' by the privileged to the underprivileged, assuming mutual interdependence and quasi-contractual obligations between all citizens and implying a programme of public education, social insurance, and labour and welfare legislation.[24]

However, despite his attendance at this Congress, and a number of common ideas with the solidarists (organic solidarity as conflict-free interdependence based on justice, the emphasis on just contracts, on secular education and on applying the principles of 1789 in the social and economic spheres), Durkheim was not in the main stream of solidarism, though he certainly came within its general *ambiance* and used its terminology. Its advocacy of state intervention, social legislation and voluntary associations, seeking a 'middle way' between *laissez-faire* liberalism and revolutionary socialism, between 'individualism' and 'collectivism', made it well suited to become virtually the official ideology of the Third Republic in the two decades before the First World War. By 1900 it could be said that 'Today, anyone who wishes to receive a sympathetic hearing or even receive professional advancement must speak of solidarity'.[25] Its ideological role was as central and pervasive as that of 'individualism' in the very different conditions of late-nineteenth-century America. Solidarism, in effect, 'provided a formula for the amelioration of glaring social abuses while maintaining untouched the existing bases of existing capitalist society in private property and freedom of

24. On solidarism generally, see Scott, op. cit., pt 1 ch. 11, and the following articles by Hayward, J. E. S.: 'Solidarity: The Social History of an Idea in Nineteenth Century France', *International Review of Social History*, IV (1959), pp. 261–84; 'The Official Social Philosophy of the French Third Republic: Léon Bourgeois and Solidarism', ibid., VI (1961), pp. 19–48; and 'Educational Pressure Groups and the Indoctrination of the Radical Ideology of Solidarism, 1895–1914', ibid., VIII (1963), pp. 1–17. On Durkheim and Solidarism, see Scott, op. cit., pp. 183–4, Alpert, 1941, and Hayward, 1960.

25. D'Haussonville, Comte, 'Assistance publique et bienfaisance privée', *Revue des deux mondes* (1900), p. 777, quoted in Hayward, 'Léon Bourgeois and Solidarism', p. 25.

business enterprise'.[26] It was a kind of moralistic French equivalent of Benthamite utilitarianism, a reformist doctrine 'opposed alike to liberal economism, Marxist collectivism, Catholic corporativism, and anarchist syndicalism',[27] which in no way challenged the existing social structure or the security of property, but had the immediate practical consequence of a stream of welfare legislation.[28] Its natural home was the Radical party and its classic expression Bourgeois's well-known book *La Solidarité*,[29] which provided an eclectic and ambiguous theoretical basis for left-wing Radicalism, invoking science and morality in support of social justice. The aim was to 'redress the injustice of . . . natural solidarity by the application of the principles of justice to the exchange of services between men',[30] to 'transform the involuntary, blind and unequal interdependence that is the result of the antiquated social policy of the past, into a free and rational interdependence based upon equal respect for the equal rights of all.'[31]

Its theoretical basis was (usefully) ambiguous because it provided no criterion for distinguishing solidarism from socialism. It was a conciliatory and reformist doctrine which proclaimed grand and generous ideals of equality and justice, but did not go beyond seeking to deal with the symptoms of injustice. As Félix Rauh observed, its principles led logically beyond the measures of social assistance with which it remained content, beyond the alleviation of existing injustices to the prevention of future ones.[32] It was friendly to socialism but opposed to social reconstruction. Indeed, Bourgeois proclaimed himself a 'liberal socialist, the most liberal of

26. Scott, op. cit., p. 178.

27. Hayward, 'Léon Bourgeois and Solidarism', p. 20.

28. See ibid. and Henderson, C. R., 'Social Solidarity in France', *AJS*, XI (1903), pp. 168–82.

29. First published in *La Nouvelle Revue* in 1895, reissued as a book in 1896.

30. ibid. (7th edn, 1912), p. 120, quoted in Hayward, loc. cit., p. 27.

31. Bourgeois, L., *La Politique de la prévoyance sociale* (Paris, 1914), vol. I, p. 21, quoted in Hayward, loc. cit., p. 33.

32. In his contribution to *Essai d'une philosopie de la solidarité: conférences et discussions* (Paris, 1902).

socialists'[33] and, at the parliamentary level, coined and followed that tactical slogan of the Third Republic '*pas d'ennemis
à gauche*', yet at the same time implicitly denied the need for
socialism by concealing the facts of class conflict behind the
elevated and seductive formulae of 'solidarity' and 'co-operation'. Solidarism sought to embrace socialism in theory, so as
to neutralize it in practice. As Parodi justly observed:

... the idea of contract loses, in M. Bourgeois' theory, all its legal
precision: in the absence of any definite obligation, it comes down
to the vague idea of a debt towards the collectivity: we owe to
society whatever seems just, at a given moment and in a given
civilization, to attribute to it. In this way, any radical distinction
between solidarism and socialism becomes arbitrary. . .[34]

Durkheim was less timid and more consistent than the
solidarists. At the most basic level, he shared their social
pacifism and desire for social solidarity through reconciliation,
believing that class warfare was not worth the cost. He did not,
however, share their commitment to private property, or their
faith in legislative reformism. He believed, partly as a result of
his studies of religion in the mid-nineties, in the prior and
crucial importance of what he called 'moral beliefs': it was only
by ending the current 'dissolution of our moral beliefs' that
the preconditions for resolving the social crisis could be laid.[35]
He saw that crisis as resulting

above all from the disarray in which men's consciences find themselves and in the extreme confusion of ideas. The most diverse and
the most contradictory conceptions clash with one another in men's
minds, cancelling one another out. How could our legislators fail to
be impotent when the country is to this degree uncertain about what
it should aim at?
  What it seems to me above all to need is to learn to know itself
across the opposing tendencies which agitate it and to see into itself
with a little clarity.[36]

Thus he was distinctly cool towards the parliamentary focus of
the leading solidarists, and he went beyond their zeal for

33. Bourgeois, L., in ibid., p. 34.
34. Parodi, D., Review of ibid. in *AS*, vii (1904), p. 388.
35. 1901a (iii) (45), p. 444.
36. 1908e, p. 397.

voluntary associations, such as co-operatives and friendly societies, though he supported the educational reforms pursued by Buisson and advocated by the numerous solidarist-inspired educational pressure-groups of the period. His sympathies basically lay with the regenerative aspects of socialism rather than with the piecemeal and practical reformism of the solidarists. As he wrote in criticism of the leading solidarist social philosopher Alfred Fouillée, the latter's practical proposals could not fill 'the void in our moral *conscience*':

> How could mere legislative measures have such an effect? They cannot provide us with new ends to desire and become attached to. Besides, is it not the case that the faults of the magistrates and the legislators only express, indeed reinforce, the prevailing lack of direction, and that we must first put an end to the latter if we want to cure the former?

Fouillée merely sought to 'consolidate what can be conserved of the existing discipline, rather than attempt to identify the direction that must resolutely be pursued'.[37]

SECULAR EDUCATION

The central practical issue was, therefore, first, to discover and clarify those beliefs which were uniquely appropriate to a modern industrial society, and France in particular, and uniquely capable of assuring its integration; and second, the systematic dissemination of those beliefs throughout the schools of the nation. Durkheim believed that

> the present malaise derives essentially from a dissolution of our moral beliefs. The ends to which our fathers were attached have lost their authority and their appeal, without our seeing clearly, or

37. 1901a (iii), pp. 444–5. On Fouillée, see Hayward, J. E. S., ' "Solidarity" and the Reformist Sociology of Alfred Fouillée', *American Journal of Economics and Sociology*, 22 (1963), pp. 205–22 and 305–12. Hayward emphasizes Fouillée's attempt to synthesize the thought of Kant and Comte (an attempt Durkheim also made), social contractualism and social organicism, and 'the greatest individuality of each member' of society with 'the greatest solidarity of all members'. But Fouillée, like Bourgeois and unlike Durkheim, disagreed with the socialists over the sanctity of private property.

at least with the necessary unanimity, where to find those that must be pursued in future.[38]

The task of the sociologist was to discover these ends. As to their realization, the preconditions could be prepared by means of the school:

> We have here a unique and irreplaceable opportunity to take hold of the child at a time when the gaps in our social organization have not yet been able to alter his nature profoundly, or to arouse in him feelings which make him partially unamenable to common life. This is virgin territory in which we can sow seeds that, once taken root, will grow by themselves. Of course, I do not mean that education alone can remedy the evil – that institutions are not needed which will need legislative action. But that action can only be fruitful if it is rooted in a state of opinion, if it is an answer to needs that are really felt ... today because of the critical situation in which we find ourselves, the services that the school can render are of incomparable importance.[39]

None the less, if education was to have these beneficial consequences, there would have to be a massive programme of educating the educators:

> the schoolmasters must be shown what new ideal they should pursue and encourage their pupils to pursue, for that is the great *desideratum* of our moral situation.[40]

In his belief in national reintegration through (secular) education, Durkheim was within a tradition reaching back, in particular, to the Kantian Renouvier and the Comtian Jules Ferry, who had written that 'the principles of 1789 are the basis of modern French society: the teaching of them must be ensured'.[41] There was, Ferry believed, a need to maintain 'a certain morality of the State, certain doctrines of the State which are important for its conservation'.[42] And indeed,

38. ibid., p. 444.

39. 1925a, p. 270: tr. 1961a, p. 236 (S.L.).

40. 1901a (iii) (45), p. 445.

41. Cited in Weill, G., *Histoire de l'idée laïque en France au XIXe siècle* (Paris, 1925), p. 270, which contains an extremely illuminating discussion of this tradition.

42. Cited in Nizan, P., *Les Chiens de garde* (Paris, 1932: new edn, Petite Collection Maspero, 1971), p. 145.

from 1880 onwards that morality was spelt out and those doctrines developed by a whole body of thinkers, among whom the philosophers were pre-eminent, and they were disseminated throughout the highly centralized French education system. As the Marxist writer Paul Nizan observed in 1932:

the philosophers multiplied radical textbooks and university courses, in the service of the class morality for which the ministers asked them for justifications. The great speciality of French philosophy was pedagogy: hence all those names in the service of secular majorities – names such as Marion, Espinas, Dauriac, Egger, Thamin, Durkheim and Fauconnet.

These philosophers, Nizan wrote,

placed at the summit of the university hierarchy, produce bodies of ideas. This is the raw material on which the University sets to work. The ideas pass through a series of workshops where they are fashioned, polished, simplified and become public and popular at the hands of those skilled artisans, the professors and makers of textbooks. One saw the development of this manufacturing-process, at work on the material of morality, one of the great objectives of the Third Republic. When the University presumed to look for a morality, it took, where it could find them, the quite threadbare elements the past had left at its disposal. It manufactured a morality with the debris of Kantian moralism and ancient spiritualism. A certain atmosphere of benevolent science still floated around these dusty maxims. A secular ethics had been developed, though quite inadequately. It required Durkheim for the bourgeois University to acquire a suitable doctrine.

Durkheim, according to Nizan, provided the required 'strengthening of the spiritual situation', the 'passage from vagueness to dogma, from obscurity to clarity'.[43]

Durkheim's aim was, indeed, to develop a new republican ideology that was both scientifically grounded and pedagogically effective; what he produced amounted to a distinctive form of liberal and reformist socialism framed in solidarist terms. The need for a scientific grounding was widely felt by contemporaries: as one wrote, 'the ideas of justice and reason, in order to have a practical value, must correspond to

43. ibid., pp. 146, 96±7.

the very laws of reality', deriving from 'profound necessities which come from nature, from realities ... necessities which peoples will understand the more rational and the freer they are. A firm basis is thus given to the law and such a theory will find no sceptics.'[44] And indeed, its pedagogical effectiveness seems to have been considerable: as one historian of education has put it, 'the sociology of Durkheim was triumphantly to invade the *écoles normales*, sweeping out the ideology with which the bourgeois security of Ferry was naïvely satisfied'.[45] Nizan's (highly Marxist) view of Durkheim's influence is worth quoting at length:

... in reality everything occurred as though the founder of French sociology had written *The Division of Labour* in order to permit obscure administrators to draw up an education destined for school-teachers. The introduction of Sociology into the Écoles Normales consecrated the administrative victory of this official morality. These were the years when Durkheim was engaged in building up his work and propagating his teaching, with great obstinacy and great authoritarian rigour, while giving that work the venerable appearance of science. In the name of that appearance, in the name of that science, teachers taught children to respect the French nation, to justify class collaboration, to accept everything, to join in the cult of the Flag and bourgeois Democracy.

And Nizan cites the textbooks and writings of Hesse and Gleyze, Bouglé, Cuvillier, Déat and Fauconnet as manifesting 'the ability to spread of this doctrine of obedience, of conformism, of social respect that has with the years acquired such

44. Mabilleau, *L'Instruction civique*, pp. 13–14, cited in ibid., p. 148.

45. Duveau, G., *Les Instituteurs* (Paris, 1957), p. 120. Cf. Bouglé and Déat, 1921. We still await an investigation into the influence of Durkheimian sociology on French education (see Bouglé, 1938, pp. 35 ff.). A key figure in this connection was Paul Lapie, who became a Durkheimian partly as a result of Bouglé's influence, contributing to all but one of the volumes of the *Année* (see Appendix C, below). As Director of Primary Education in France, Lapie introduced sociology into the syllabus of the *écoles normales primaires* and made it a requirement for competitive entry to the higher grades of teaching and administration in primary education. He aimed to combine the long course of Civil Ethics and Political Economy with a number of sociological ideas. This measure was for long bitterly opposed; its consequences await study. On Lapie, see obituary in *AS*, n.s., 2(1927), pp. 7–8.

immense credit, such a vast audience'. Durkheim, he concludes, 'finally accomplished and perfected in his death the task of bourgeois conservation he had undertaken during his life ... Durkheim's success consists precisely in the moral propaganda he was capable of establishing, in the measures of social defence he was the first to provide so securely.'[46]

One key element in his success was certainly his aggressive secularism, his desire to establish and inculcate a doctrine that would replace, and not compromise with, religion. Certainly, his view of existing religious beliefs did not allow him to favour any kind of eclectic compromise between the religious and the secular (such as that attempted by his old teacher Boutroux or his rival Bergson), or any attempt to secularize or modernize the teachings of the Church. Like his equally rationalist colleague and close friend, Octave Hamelin, he held that 'in a rational morality God could not intervene as the source of obligation'.[47]

At the height of the Dreyfus Affair, which did so much to encourage the diffusion of the *esprit laïque*, Durkheim and Hamelin founded at Bordeaux an association of university teachers and students called 'La Jeunesse Laïque'.[48] Such associations were being founded at this time in many cities and were federated on a national basis in 1902. At Bordeaux meetings were held once a week, mostly in cafés, with about twenty-five members present. Political and ideological rather than strictly religious issues were discussed,[49] and the movement as a whole became increasingly more political in character, tending in a socialist and anti-militarist direction.[50]

A record survives of an address by Durkheim to one of these meetings on 22 May 1901, on the subject of 'Religion and

46. Nizan, op. cit., pp. 97–8.
47. Hamelin's words, cited in Weill, op. cit., p. 333. This rationalism was common to all those, including Durkheim, who were grouped around Xavier Léon's *Revue de metaphysique et de morale*. Other members of this group included the philosophers Léon Brunschvicg and Louis Weber, and the historian Élie Halévy.
48. M. Henri Durkheim, personal communication.
49. ibid.
50. Cf. Weill, op. cit., p. 318.

Freedom of Thought',[51] in which he made very clear his view of the incompatibility of religion and science and the ability of the latter not only to offer superior explanations of the world but also to discover superior and more suitable moral ends for contemporary society to pursue. In general, religion, like socialism, should then be seen as responding blindly to needs which science would uncover, and the educators of the future would seek explicitly to satisfy:

The speaker proposed to treat the problem scientifically. He declared that while he predicted the triumph of science, he realized that one could not eliminate religion with a stroke of the pen. One had to satisfy the needs to which it had responded for so long. It was no use whatever seeking a compromise whereby these two enemies would live in peace, each in its own sphere: giving Science the world of appearances and Religion the inner depths and the mystery of things. This so-called mysterious world was, in reality, that which was not understood. 'What, then, is the essential difference between Religion and Science? It·is that religious belief is obligatory, while scientific opinion is free. The scientist has the right and even the duty always to be self-critical and sceptical of his theories; the believer is immured in his dogma.' The only possible reconciliation between Science and Religion consisted in discovering within Science itself moral ends. 'Science – indeed science above all – must discover ends which transcend the individual; it must have an ideal, that is, make a reality of what is outside us: Justice, the welfare of others.'[52]

Durkheim believed that the relation of the science of sociology to education was that of theory to practice; and, in this respect, it would become a rational substitute for traditional religion. Teachers should be imbued with the 'sociological point of view' and children should be made to think about 'the nature of society, the family, the State, the principal legal and moral obligations, the way in which these different social

51. 1901h.

52. Durkheim's dossier, Bordeaux. The same source indicates that in February 1899 Durkheim addressed the 'Patronage Laïque de Nansouty', expressing 'in an eloquent and brilliant impromptu speech his devotion to the cause of education' and his belief in 'the solidarity of the three parts of the education system'. In February 1902 he again addressed the Bordeaux Jeunesse Laïque on 'Individualism'.

phenomena are formed'.[53] With these views, and this mission, it was entirely appropriate that in 1902 he should be appointed as *chargé d'un cours* in the Science of Education at the Sorbonne to replace Ferdinand Buisson, who, as Director of Primary Education at the Ministry of Public Instruction from 1879 to 1896, had been the man most responsible for the practical implementation of the Ferry Laws, the central objective of which was to establish a national system of free, secular education that would secure the moral foundations of the Third Republic.

53. 1899c. Durkheim also proposed that lessons on the history of religions should replace those on the history of philosophy, which are 'customary and of little use' (ibid.).

Part Three

Paris: 1902-17

Chapter 18

Durkheim at the Sorbonne

WHEN Durkheim arrived in Paris in 1902, he already had a reputation as a formidable intellectual figure armed with a doctrine, and he was not without some enemies. These enemies multiplied. There were those among his future critics – including writers, such as Charles Péguy,[1] Daniel Halévy and Romain Rolland (all devotees of Bergson); philosophers, such as Félix Rauh[2]; Catholic priests, such as Dom Besse[3] and Simon Deploige[4]; and opponents of the 'New Sorbonne' and of sociology in particular, including such figures of the far right as Agathon[5] and Pierre Lasserre[6] – who were to speak and write about him with an abusiveness and a vehemence that seem to require explanation. This is partly to be sought in his aggressive combination of rationalism and positivism. All problems worth considering could be approached scientifically; all else was dilettantism, mysticism, irrationalism. In particular, religion, to the study of which Durkheim's years at Paris

1. See Péguy, 1906 (see *Situations*, Paris, 1940, pp. 161 ff.). Péguy pictured Durkheim as one of the Inquisitors of Joan of Arc.

2. Rauh spoke (according to Henri Massis) of the logical tendency of Durkheim's methods as 'the intellectual form of brutality', quoted in Massis, H., *Évocations: souvenirs (1905–1911)* (Paris, 1931), p. 146. Cf. Rauh, 1904. Rauh, was, however, a personal friend of Durkheim's. On Rauh's death, Durkheim wrote to Léon, 'It is difficult for me to speak only as Rauh's colleague. I shall speak *also* as a friend . . .' (letter undated).

3. See Besse, 1913.

4. See Deploige, 1911.

5. A joint pseudonym for Henri Massis and Alfred de Tarde, son of Gabriel Tarde, two young men (also influenced by Bergson – but mainly by Sorel and Péguy) who wrote highly polemical pamphlets attacking the new, positivist and anti-classical spirit of the Sorbonne; see *L'Esprit de la Nouvelle Sorbonne* (Paris, 1911). For details of their collaboration, see Massis, op. cit., passim.

6. See Lasserre, 1913. Both Lasserre and Massis were members of the Action Française.

were primarily devoted, could be seen as both irrational, in so far as it consisted of beliefs that were imprecise, illogical, untestable and counterfactual, and also scientifically explicable as the symbolic agent of social cohesion. Since, in addition to this militant intellectual standpoint, Durkheim was responsible for the education of successive generations of schoolteachers whom he sought to imbue with the elements of a rationalist secular morality (some said a dogmatic secular religion), it is not surprising that his enemies were passionate and numerous: as one Catholic writer observed 'the obligation of teaching the sociology of M. Durkheim in the 200 *écoles normales* of France is the gravest national peril our country has known for a long time'.[7]

One of the charges that his future opponents were to make has a certain plausibility. This was that his reception into the Sorbonne was not entirely free of extra-academic considerations. In Daniel Halévy's view, Durkheim was appointed to the Sorbonne by 'Herr and his friends' in order to

furnish them with a doctrine to propound. The word *socialist* was unsuitable. The more prudent word *sociology* was chosen. A keen enthusiast, with limited powers of thought but good organizing ability, a man called Durkheim, had started using it ten years ago, and Herr and his friends had at first disapproved but now made use of the word, the theories and the man.[8]

Halévy's charge is polemically put, yet its substance seems to be echoed by Bouglé – hardly an unsympathetic witness:

Politics was not unconnected with this change of mind [i.e., on the part of the academic establishment, from a position of hostility towards sociology to one of sympathy]. There was the crisis of the [Dreyfus] Affair. Sociologists and anti-sociologists, one found them all on the same side. Suddenly there were better things to do than pursue internal quarrels, and one saw more clearly, in face of the

7. The phrase was Jean Izoulet's: cited in Goyau, M., *Comment juger la 'sociologie' contemporaine* (Marseilles, 1934), p. 184, and in Bouglé, 1938, p. 37.

8. *Péguy and Les Cahiers de la quinzaine*, tr. R. Bethell (London, 1946), p. 93. By 'Herr and his friends' Halévy doubtless meant, among others, Jaurès and Lucien Lévy-Bruhl. For similar attacks, see Lasserre, 1913, pp. 178 ff., and Besse, 1913, pp. 237 ff.

common adversary, that all served the same ideal. The *Année sociologique* group did not spare its efforts. Old and young, in Paris and in the provinces, all did their duty – that of the 'intellectual' citizen. All were concerned to show, in the aftermath of the Affair itself, that they had perceived the dimensions of the problem that it raised and had envisaged the reconstruction that would be necessary ... By their political attitudes the collaborators on the *Année* had given proof of their integrity. In addition, their books were all favourable to democracy ... there is no doubt that moral and political sympathies served the cause of social science: they laid a soft carpet beneath its feet.[9]

Yet, while Bouglé's observations about the relation between *Dreyfusisme* and the acceptance of sociology may be treated as broadly true, Halévy's specific charge concerning Durkheim's appointment is at best unsubstantiated. The most that can be said with certainty is that his *Dreyfusisme* was no barrier to his advancement. He himself viewed the appointment with considerable misgivings. When the question arose in 1902 of applying to the Sorbonne to replace Ferdinand Buisson, who held the chair in the 'Science of Education' and had just been elected to the Chamber of Deputies, it needed all the insistence and diplomacy of Durkheim's friends to prevail on him to let his candidature go forward. In a letter written at this time to Lucien Lévy-Bruhl, he marshalled all the arguments against his own cause. As a specialist in sociology, how could he be a candidate for a chair in education?

I will give the impression of someone who seeks to use any expedient in order to insinuate himself into Paris. I find the idea of giving such an impression repulsive, especially since it does not correspond at all with my state of mind.[10]

9. *Les Pages libres*, 5 October 1907, cited in Lasserre, 1913, pp. 178–9. Cf. Weber, E., *The Nationalist Revival in France* (Berkeley, California, 1959), p. 79: 'The *Dreyfusard* victory led to the rise of Dreyfusards to leading functions in an institution [i.e. the Sorbonne], whose appointments were as politically motivated as those of any ministry'; and Goriely, op. cit., pp. 176–7; '... Durkheimian sociology seemed to constitute the major arm of this "*parti intellectuel*", which, thanks to *Dreyfusisme*, had conquered certain high university posts ...'

10. Cited in Saraillh, 1960, p. 8.

But, above all, he was afraid that he would not have sufficient competence for the task:

> It would be alright so long as I had to deal with moral education, the teaching of morality. There I feel at home. For this I would have enough material to fill my lectures adequately for two or three years. But after that it would be different.[11]

And he ended his letter by observing that he was 'a poor politician' and far from an expert in the art of selling himself.

In fact, the Council of the Faculty of Letters in Paris, after seeking the opinions of Boutroux, Victor Brochard and Buisson (the first two of whom were, as we have seen, largely unsympathetic to Durkheim's sociology), decided by a very large majority to appoint him as Buisson's replacement, and when, four years later, he was himself given the title of professor, that majority became unanimity.[12] (It was not until 1913 that his chair was renamed 'Science of Education and Sociology'.)

His move to Paris was, it seems, very distressing to him. He wrote to his friend Hamelin of a 'bad period' following his move, when he underwent a 'lamentable depression' which he largely attributed to 'the sense of a certain moral diminution, due to the fact that I had renounced, without any absolutely overriding reason, the severe life that I led together with you'. Though that life had, 'in certain aspects, lacked excitement', he had been attached to it: therefore, 'it is not surprising that the change has been distressing. Now that I have redrawn a plan of existence – at least for four years – I have regained my equilibrium.'[13] And he subsequently wrote of the 'partial change of my moral personality' and the 'bad moments I had to undergo – partly because of my own imagination', but that he had realized that 'I had to come, or else remain Bordelais for ever'.[14]

We will subsequently consider in detail the specific charges that were to be made against Durkheim's ideas and their

---

11. ibid. See also his letter to Simiand of 28 June 1902.
12. For the material in the last two paragraphs, see ibid., pp. 8–9.
13. Letter to Hamelin dated 21 October 1902.
14. Letter to Hamelin dated 8 August 1903.

supposed practical consequences.[15] But at this point it may be useful to construct some kind of picture of the man himself and the nature of his influence through the recollections of those who knew him, both sympathetic and hostile.

Hubert Bourgin (at the time sympathetic but subsequently hostile) provides a vivid description of Durkheim in his last years at Bordeaux:

> ... having been proposed by [François Simiand], the director of the economic section, I was accepted as a collaborator on the *Année sociologique* by the master whom I respected, indeed already venerated, but whom I had never seen. He received me in his study, which was vast and simple, lacking any adornment or evidence of artistic preoccupations. His long, thin body was enveloped by a large dressing-gown, a cassock of flannel, which concealed his bony and muscular frame, the fragile support for his thought. The face emerged, pale and ascetic, with its high forehead bare, a short beard, a thick moustache, the pronounced nose of a rabbi, but this whole austere and severe face magnificently illuminated by two deep-set eyes that had an intense and gentle power, so that he commanded respect, attention, even submission, while at the same time compelling one to be serious and speak plainly with absolute sincerity, as one saw those imperious eyes before one, and one thus gained confidence. One felt oneself before the judgement and already under the authority of a man who was devoted, entirely devoted, to his task, to his mission, and who, by admitting you to his side, along with his colleagues, delegated to you a part of the responsibilities he had assumed.[16]

He was, on all accounts, a man of considerable presence, with an '*air terrible*'[17] who 'always dominated the situation'.[18] In his daily life he spoke little and was 'forbidding and serious'.[19] It was often said of him that he rejected friendship. Davy denies this, stressing another side to his character; he

15. See Chapter 25, below
16. Bourgin, 1938, pp. 216–17.
17. M. Davy, personal communication.
18. M. Henri Durkheim, personal communication. Davy writes that he inspired both 'the enthusiasm of fascinated listeners [and] the terror of candidates who had been reduced to extremities': Davy, 1960a, p. 14 (cf. Appendix B, below).
19. M. E. Halphen, personal communication.

writes of 'that mixture of severe authority and anxious affection which seems to me the basis of Durkheim's temperament'.[20] It was, in Davy's words,

in friendship that Durkheim's feelings were most evident; his
loyalty, his subtlety, his anxious expressions of concern add warmth
to his correspondence with his friends. When they had the slightest
trouble, such as worry about their own health or that of their
families, Durkheim was on the watch for news which he demanded
frequently. If he thought he detected some hesitation or agitation,
some brief change in the look of your handwriting, he took alarm
and was ready to comfort you with sympathetic words. Even in the
letters of scientific direction and advice, one feels the affection to be
present.[21]

It seems that he had an enormous impact on students in Paris.
Dominique Parodi wrote that it was

important above all to emphasize how great Émile Durkheim's
influence was just before the War and to point out that a great
number of students of philosophy turned to him. What they found
was a mind that was firm, imperious and sure of itself, and, above
all, a positive programme of work opening up large horizons of
future research. They also found a method that appeared rigorous
and afforded the certainty that the work to be undertaken would be

20. Davy, 1960b, p. 8.
21. Davy, 1960a, p. 18. The letters to Léon, Hamelin and Bouglé
abundantly confirm this picture. To cite just two examples: 'Dear friend,
I was very glad to receive your good news. The fact that you can work is
the best indication that your recovery is complete. But when you are in
Heidelberg, please protect your stomach against the combination of
German cooking and warm weather' (letter to Léon dated 24 July 1908);
'My dear friend, I learned from *Le Temps* of your bereavement . . . I do
not know what place your uncle had in your life; and I know from experience how these things vary. But in any case, it is a part of your past
that has disappeared and that leaves a painful void. And one cannot avoid
a somewhat egoistic heaviness of heart at seeing a clearing of the ranks
of those around us' (letter to Léon dated 28 September 1911). As an
instance of Durkheim's loyalty to his friends, one might mention the
assiduous care he took, together with Rodier, to publish his dead friend
Hamelin's manuscripts (see 1907e and 1911d). When Rodier was at one
point reluctant to continue with this work, Durkheim wrote to Léon:
'I have already told him that we had in this regard duties which we could
not escape . . .' (letter dated 22 August 1908).

both original and truly scientific. At the same time attempts to achieve wider syntheses were not ruled out, provided that they rested on a clearly sociological basis.[22]

One of his students later wrote that 'those who wished to escape his influence had to flee his lectures'.[23] Bourgin gives the following account:

... he appeared, thin and pale, in his grey jacket, with an immense head and sombre eyes, on the platform of the amphitheatre where there waited, crowded on the benches, male and female students. He took up his lecture at the point where he had stopped, picking up the thread with a brief résumé. Without the affectation of rhetoric or art, but with a concentrated argument, punctuated with references, he pursued his demonstration – and there always was one – concerning marriage, the family, morality, education. His grave manner never brightened; nonetheless, his speech, always somewhat subdued at the most significant moments, was not without charm; and one felt it turning into a sort of incantation.[24]

Félix Pécaut wrote of his influence on primary school-teachers, as well as on university students, as being not merely great: 'he did not just have pupils, but rather disciples. He forged their understandings; he armed them with new categories ...' He fired them with a 'veritable moral faith' and gave them the 'certainty of duty'.[25] Pécaut sought to explain this ascendancy in terms of 'ardent intellectual passion, imperious eloquence, a dialectic that was so rapid and so decisive that it compelled conviction and paralyzed objections' and, behind this, the existence of 'a doctrine and a faith. He was a philosophical innovator and there was in him something of the apostle'.[26] This explanation is advanced by many others. Davy wrote of him as an 'orator without equal', whose 'faith communicated to his thought and speech an enthusiastic and

22. Parodi, 1919, p. 150.

23. Maublanc, 1930, p. 297.

24. Bourgin, 1938, pp. 222–3.

25. Pécaut, 1918, p. 1. Bourgin (ibid., p. 224) writes of his ascendancy as 'unique', adding that 'it seemed to us that Durkheim gave us scientific and political aims that were equally sound' and seemed to 'protect one against error'.

26. ibid., p. 2.

commanding – one is tempted to say an inspired – character, giving those who heard him the impression that this was the· prophet of a new religion'.[27] Xavier Léon, similarly, wrote as follows:

What explains his influence is not only the dominating power of his philosophical thought, the richness of the fields of research that the novelty of his method opened up to the curiosity and activity of his disciples; it was this face and body of an ascetic, those flashes of light in his face, the metallic tone of that voice that expressed an ardent faith which, in this latter-day prophet, burned to mould and force the convictions of his hearers.[28]

Indeed, the analogy to which these explanations appeal was not unfamiliar to Durkheim himself, who one day said to Bouglé, as they were passing Notre Dame, 'It is from a chair like that that I should have spoken.'[29]

Others, however, were less impressed and far from persuaded. This was especially true of those under the contrasting, but no less overwhelming, influence of Bergson, one of whom writes that it was scarcely exaggerating to compare

the impressive gravity of [Durkheim's] face ... to that of a death's head on which a macabre fantasy had adjusted a professor's spectacles and spread a fluffy beard. This master suited his thin and gaunt body, his severe appearance, his cold voice whose mechanical accents revealed a perfect gramophone-record. One immediately saw him

27. Davy, 1919, p. 194. Davy adds that they were 'astonished at first by so warm a speech from one who seemed so cold', but were then 'seduced, conquered, mastered' (ibid.). Léon described the impression Durkheim made at the International Congress of Philosophy at Bologna in 1911, when he delivered his paper on judgements of value and of reality (1911b). Those who were there would 'never forget the sight of that assembly suddenly dominated, then spontaneously arising and crowding round his chair, straining towards the speaker as if drawn to him' (Léon, 1917, p. 749).

28. Léon, 1917, p. 749. Cf. Maublanc, 1930, p. 299: 'A believer in reason, he confessed his faith with the same intransigence and the same passion as his ancestors, the prophets of Israel, had confessed their faith in Jehovah.' Another of his students has written of 'the words of a biblical prophet conveyed to us in his muffled, passionate and sober tone of voice' (Mme L. Prenant, personal communication).

29. Bouglé, 1930b, p. 280.

as a sort of automaton of super-human creation, destined endlessly to preach a new Reform, and who concealed within some vital organ, perhaps the brain ... a perpetual system of unanswerable arguments. His eloquence, truly comparable to that of a running tap, was inexhaustible and ice-cold: it would not have profaned the inside of a mortuary; indeed it would have substantially assisted the refrigeration of the corpses. And to be acquainted with Durkheim's appearance and his speech was virtually equivalent to grasping his system. For any given question, it contained the answer, classified, set down in its proper place, ranged in an immutable order which evoked not the shelves of a grocer's shop, but niches for epitaphs distributed under the galleries that surround crematoria.

Family, country, institutions ... were preserved by his efforts and confined within his system, but preserved and confined like mummies in a necropolis.[30]

The most offensive features, for Durkheim's critics, of his teaching were its aggressive moralism and its apparent lack of respect for established religious beliefs. As Henri Massis wrote, 'he declared to his terrified audience that the teaching of morality was in a state of atrophy, that morality was no longer discussed, that what passed for it was no more than an insipid mixture of old Kantian and Idealist doctrines and that he no longer wished to find such obsolete ideas in examination answers'.[31] As to religion, Massis recalls a student button-holing him in front of the statue of Auguste Comte, in order to explain to him that we had entered definitively into the 'era of the social'. The student said:

Until Durkheim, my friend, the religions were an embarrassment to science and the scientists, I grant you. The fact of the religious mind existed – primordial and irreducible ... It was an open door to all insanities and obscurantisms; and it was this that allowed the Jameses and Bergsons of two continents to scorn rationalism. The irreducible had to be reduced, the primordial subordinated. Then

---

30. Maire, G., *Bergson, mon maître* (Paris, 1935), p. 140. This passage is, in part, an expression of the rivalry between Bergson, at the Collège de France, and Durkheim, at the Sorbonne. Cf.: 'A majestic evolutionism [was expressed] in the militant dogmatism of the French School of Sociology of which the great rival of Bergson, Durkheim, was the pope' (Rolland, *Péguy*, Paris, 1944, I, p. 35).

31. *Évocations*, p. 60.

came Durkheim, and this soon happened . . . The religious, he said, is quite simply the social. And whoosh! the ground was cleared . . . The first element is the existence of the social *conscience*. The religious is none other than the social personified, hypostasized, substantified, made absolute . . . You see, everything resides in the totem. The totem is the symbol of the social soul – and there is no other soul but that . . . the individual isn't interesting! What does the individual matter to us sociologists ?[32]

Durkheim came to be an extremely influential figure at the Sorbonne, both as a lecturer and as an administrator. Lasserre wrote in 1913 that 'among the chapels of science of the university, Durkheimian sociology is rising up like a cathedral whose primacy is recognized by all'[33]; and Massis was later to observe that 'the students of today [1931] can no longer conceive how great Durkheim's dominance was at that time [*c.* 1910], nor the extent of the power and the authority that sociology exercised over certain people'.[34] Durkheim's education lecture-courses were the only compulsory courses at the Sorbonne, being obligatory for all students seeking teaching degrees in philosophy, history, literature and languages. He lectured at the École Normale Supérieure and at the École des Hautes Études Sociales. In his administrative capacity, he sat on the Council of the University, as well as on numerous other councils and committees in the University and at the Ministry of Public Instruction.

His critics complained of his power and what they saw as his misuse of it. Lasserre noted that he 'soon became a great political and administrative power in the university',[35] while Agathon bitterly observed that the Rector Liard had

given [Durkheim] his entire confidence and had him appointed, first to the Council of the University of Paris, then to the Comité

32. ibid., p. 78. The students at the École Normale devised various jingles about Durkheim, such as the following: 'Adorons le totem, le grand manitou/que le Maître Durkheim prêcha parmi nous' (Mme Kennedy, personal communication). See Peyrefitte, A., *Rue d'Ulm* (Paris, new edn, 1963), p. 99, fn.

33. Lasserre, 1913, p. 183.

34. *Évocations*, p. 78.

35. Lasserre, 1913, p. 180.

Consultatif, which allows M. Durkheim to survey all appointments within the field of higher education.[36]

Durkheim represented 'a victory of the new spirit':

Endowed with university pomp, he is the regent of the Sorbonne, the all-powerful master, and it is known that the professors in the philosophy section, reduced to the role of humble functionaries, carry out his every order, dominated by his authority ... M. Durkheim has firmly established his intellectual despotism. He has made of his teaching an instrument of domination.[37]

He was often accused of managing appointments. According to Rolland, chairs in sociology were 'created in all the universities in order to propagate the Durkheimism of the State'[38] and Dom Besse claimed that the advancement of careers 'came to depend on absorbing and propagating the definitions of the master'.[39] Massis remarked in his memoirs that

to be a sociologist at that time was to have one's career made. A sociologist never had to wait. Immediately he was given a doctorate, immediately he was provided for: if there was no chair available, one was created, as for Mauss, as for Hubert. And the ambitious young men ... became imbued with the new dogma ... a whole eager clergy was formed by the words of the master·who received his deacons, every Sunday, in his austere cell in the rue St Jacques, at the corner of the boulevard Arago![40]

The use of ecclesiastical imagery was as frequent among his opponents as among his admirers, though the particular images chosen differed significantly in the two cases. To friends he was a prophet and an apostle, but to enemies he was a secular pope. Lasserre wrote of the 'scholarly papacy which the State and its agents, rectors, inspectors and deans ... have established in Durkheim'.[41] Rolland likewise wrote of

36. *L'Esprit de la Nouvelle Sorbonne*, p. 98.
37. ibid.
38. *Péguy*, I, p. 138.
39. Besse, 1913, p. 237.
40. *Évocations*, p. 77.
41. Lasserre, 1913, p. 214.

'the tyrannical encroachment of socialism . . . with its sociological Sacred College, issuing by decree its *Syllabus* of secular
and obligatory reason, and its catechism of the State',[42] and
Péguy asked,

> Will this World without God that we are building inevitably
> become in its turn, by a regression that we did not anticipate, a new
> governmental catechism, taught by the gendarmes, with the benev-
> olent collaboration of the police?[43]

According to Rolland, Péguy held that the danger was en-
hanced by what he saw as Durkheim's inverted mysticism
'insinuated in his myth of the *conscience collective*'. It was, in
effect, 'a revival of the authoritarian dogma of the Church,
through the official freedom of thought, the opposite of true
freedom of thought'.[44]

As to the interests served by Durkheim's ascendancy, these
were commonly held by his enemies to be political. To Massis,
his doctrine was 'an ideology of the State, a metaphysic of the
social',[45] while to Rolland he was the 'anti-Bergson . . . who
tyrannized over the ideology of the Sorbonne and – reaching
beyond this – the ideology of the Combist and Jaurèsiste
State'.[46] According to Besse, Durkheim was

> the agent, in our official education system, of the oligarchy which
> imposes its wishes on French democracy. This influence is not
> confined to the Sorbonne and the direction of higher and secondary
> education; it extends as far as the Confédération Générale du
> Travail.[47]

Indeed, it became common to attack Durkheim as the agent of
the anti-clerical governments of the 1900s: as Daniel Halévy
put it, 'Durkheim's lecture-course was the sign of the insolent
capture by a doctrinaire group of the teaching of the State'.[48]
Lasserre cited as the final proof of this charge a debate in the

42. *Péguy*, I, p. 138.
43. Péguy, 1906, cited in ibid., pp. 138–9.
44. *Péguy*, I. p. 139.
45. *Évocations*, p. 77.
46. *Péguy*, I. pp. 137–8.
47. Besse, 1913, p. 231.
48. Cited in Rolland, *Péguy*, I, p. 138.

Chamber of Deputies in February 1910 on education, when, after a speech by Maurice Barrès which described sociology as the latest example of the secular moralities propagated over the previous thirty years, a deputy, later to become Minister of Public Instruction, 'glorified the new dogma' and 'recited passages from *The Division of Labour* at the *tribune*'.[49]

The chief charge of all these critics of Durkheim was that he and his followers were seeking a unique and pernicious domination over the minds of the young. Lasserre regarded Durkheim's education course as a carefully devised plot to make 'the new generation of the university' listen to Durkheim 'in order to make sociology, as presented by Durkheim, their religion'.[50] The charge and its implications were stated most clearly by Rolland:

> The French sociological school, inspired by [Durkheim's] imperious doctrine, with a fanatical docility, was no longer content with thinking and philosophizing for themselves; it sought, by the application of positive methods to social and moral facts, studied from the outside and treated 'like things', to 'act upon them', methodically to transform institutions and ways of behaving. A chair of pedagogy had been created at the Sorbonne, and the teaching, obligatory for candidates for teaching degrees, had been entrusted to Durkheim who, unequivocally, had declared that he was concerned, not to accumulate the lessons of the past, but rather to develop and mould the man of tomorrow.[51]

And Albert Thibaudet described the subsequent introduction of the teaching of sociology into the *écoles normales* by Lapie as a very important date in the calendar of the republican spirit:

> By this, the State provided in its schools to the teachers what the Church provided in its seminaries to the teachers' adversaries, namely, a theology. Lapie imagined that the teachers would react to this teaching critically. Not at all: they reacted theologically.[52]

There was exaggeration and caricature in these views, but they did have a certain validity. Durkheim did come to have

49. Lasserre, 1913, p. 184.
50. ibid., p. 182.
51. *Péguy*, 1, p. 138.
52. Thibaudet, A., *La République des professeurs* (Paris, 1927), pp. 222–3, cited in Nizan, P., *Les Chiens de garde* (Paris, 1932; 1971 edn), p. 145.

considerable authority and influence within the University and the French education system as a whole; and his purpose was indeed, as we have seen, to 'develop and mould the man of tomorrow'. M. Georges Friedmann has written:

Towards the end of the Combes ministry, and even more in the years which followed, Durkheimian sociology established itself, alongside secular morality, in the official ideology of the Third Republic, through the various grades of teaching, and in particular through the écoles normales. It possessed considerable power and influence.[53]

Such influence was only strengthened by the impersonality and highmindedness of Durkheim's aims. The suggestion that he was influenced by politicians, or merely political motives is, however, implausible.

He certainly numbered influential politicians among his friends. Apart from Jaurès, with whom he kept on very good terms[54] (Jaurès was guest of honour at the dinner to celebrate the tenth anniversary of the *Année*),[55] he moved within circles frequented by both the academic and political worlds. For example, he often used to attend large parties given by Gustave Lanson, Henri Berr and, above all, his good friend, Xavier Léon, which were attended both by the professors of the Sorbonne and by politicians such as Millerand, Poincaré and Painlevé.[56] These parties, according to Bourgin, were

of a scientific and academic nature, at times more spiritual, at others more temporal, and political too, for politics was represented by those great academics-turned-politicians, and by others who desired to be so, and by yet others who kept on the margin ... In the crowded *salon*, boudoirs and buffet are found Henri Poincaré, deformed, distracted, and awkward and strikingly odd in manner, Painlevé, bird-like with his nose in the air, Émil Borel, like a butter-

---

53. *La Crise du progrès* (Paris, 1936), pp. 33–4. Cf. Guitton, 1968, p. 116: 'Durkheim's thought became the official thought of France, since the study of sociology figured after the war in the syllabus of the *écoles normales*, thus contributing to the formation of the teachers of contemporary French youth' (written in 1943).

54. M. Henri Durkheim, personal communication.

55. Bourgin, 1938, p. 192.

56. ibid., p. 223.

fly, Jean Perrin, joking and laughing, Gustave Lanson and Lévy-Bruhl, deep in a conversation apart, and generation after generation of professors, mostly philosophers, of beginners and even aspirants, summoned or admitted to the contemplation and conversation of their masters. In this crowd, which already contributed to spreading the reputation of sociology, Durkheim, erect and thin with brilliant and bright eyes, moved, stopped, conversed, said a few words and, without affectation, pursued his mission.[57]

Davy writes that Durkheim was made use of by 'several ministers'.[58] Yet, as we have shown, he was temperamentally averse to political activity and always retained a somewhat haughty contempt for the general run of politicians and for the political parties. He himself, apart from his active support of the Dreyfusard cause and his subsequent whole-hearted participation in the war effort, always avoided all direct political involvements. Many of his colleagues at the Sorbonne, such as Lucien Lévy-Bruhl[59] and Gabriel Séailles, were much more politically committed than he.

It was his commitment to a cause that transcended both party politics and personal self-advancement that was a major source of his influence over others. As Bourgin wrote,

He had in him, alongside the philosopher, moralist and priest, something of the politician and the negotiator ... He was capable of adroitly moving the pawns on a political chess board, albeit one confined to the dimensions of the Sorbonne, and to pursue strategies, as in a game. His adversaries, his enemies, not taking sufficient account of his personal disinterestedness, considered him, and sometimes treated him, as ambitious and as an intriguer. What an error of judgement! His ends were noble and went beyond personal rewards, and I believe that all the steps he took, when they related to getting people jobs – advancing some, and thwarting and excluding others – had the single objective of the interest of science and the community.[60]

This lack of personal ambition is borne out by his refusal in 1908, at the early age of fifty, to let his name be put forward

57. ibid., pp. 223–4.
58. Davy, 1919, p. 190.
59. See Cazeneuve, J., *Lucien Lévy-Bruhl* (Paris, 1963), pp. 5 ff.
60. Bourgin, 1938, p. 221.

for admission to the Institut, though strongly pressed to do so by the Rector Liard, Théodule Ribot and Lucien Lévy-Bruhl. Considering the candidature of a philosopher much older than himself to be more worthy, he responded to the flattering insistence of which he was the object by writing, 'The idea that I might appear to bar the way to this man who has come to the end of his career and almost of his life was intolerable to me.'[61]

61. Davy, 1960a, p. 18. The philosopher in question was Evellin (M. Davy, personal communication.) Though not admitted to the Institut, he received the Légion d'Honneur in 1907 (Durkheim's dossier, Bordeaux).

Chapter 19

The History of Education in France

THE compulsory education course that was the occasion for so much rancour had been established by Liard as the theoretical part of the training of teachers in secondary education. Durkheim was persuaded by Liard, much against his will,[1] to give this course, intended for all students at the University of Paris seeking *agrégations* in sciences and in letters; he delivered it annually at the École Normale Supérieure from 1904 to 1913.[2] Durkheim interpreted his task as giving the future teacher 'a full consciousness of his function'.[3] For this, he believed, historical understanding was indispensable, for 'only history can penetrate under the surface of our present educational system; only history can analyze it; only history can show us of what elements it is formed, on what conditions each of them depends, how they are inter-related; only history, in a word, can bring us to the long chain of causes and effects of which it is the result'.[4] He therefore chose to lecture on the

1. Davy, personal communication.
2. See Appendix A, below. The inaugural lecture of the 1905–6 course was published as 1906c: repr. in 1922a: tr. 1956a. The whole course was published posthumously in two volumes with an introduction by Halbwachs (1938a). It has been almost completely ignored by writers on Durkheim and on the history and sociology of education, though it is unquestionably a major work that deserves to be translated. For very brief discussions, see Fauconnet, 1922; Halbwachs, 1938a; Bellah, 1959; and Floud, 1965. Halbwachs justly calls it 'a vast and bold fresco covering ten centuries of history . . a sort of continuous discourse on the progress of the human mind in France' (loc. cit., not paginated) and Fauconnet describes it as 'one of [Durkheim's] finest courses . . . an incomparable model of what the application of sociological method to education can give' (loc. cit., pp. 27, 28: tr. 1956a, pp. 51, 52).
3. 1922a, p. 135: tr. 1956a, p. 135 (S.L.).
4. ibid., pp. 157–8: tr. pp. 152–3. Halbwachs notes (loc. cit.) that Durkheim's knowledge of 'modern historical methods' could be traced back to Fustel de Coulanges; that he went back to the original sources,

'Formation and Development of Secondary Education in France' from its origins in the Primitive Church to the confused situation of his own time.

That confusion was fundamental and prolonged. Durkheim observed that 'secondary education has for more than half a century been undergoing a grave crisis that is not yet, and is indeed far from being, resolved. Everyone feels it cannot remain what it is, but no one can yet see clearly what it is required to become.'[5] French secondary education was essentially education for the elite and it was centralized to an extreme degree. Its content thus formed the focus for perpetual social and political conflict. What kind of elite was desirable? Where should the balance be struck between the requirements of an industrializing society and a common cultural tradition? And what was the nature of that tradition: classical or modern, religious or secular? Throughout the nineteenth century there had been a succession of officially prescribed and often politically induced changes in syllabus, oscillating between a total monopoly of classical, literary studies and varying degrees of incorporation of the sciences, and between an exclusive emphasis on general culture and a sporadic recognition of the need for specialization.

Durkheim's aim was to help to bring an end to this 'intellectual disarray',[6] to contribute to the elaboration of a new 'pedagogical faith' to succeed the 'old faith in the persistent virtue of classics'.[7] Studying the history of education, relating educational change to wider cultural, social and economic changes, would enable one to 'anticipate the future and understand the present'.[8] As Mauss commented, Durkheim

always used the same method: both historical and sociological to begin with, and then inductive and normative. This enabled him to

---

reading Alcuin, for instance, in the original; and that most of the lectures included bibliographies (not repr. in 1938a) testifying to 'vast reading'. Yet, according to Fauconnet, he was unsatisfied at several points with his research and documentation, to which he had devoted 'hardly more than one or two years of work' (loc. cit., p. 28: tr. 1956a, p. 52).

5. 1938a, 1, p. 10.
6. ibid., 1, p. 12.
7. ibid.
8. ibid., 1, p. 13.

make intelligible the practice followed up to our own time, on the one hand, and to guide the young teachers, on the other, towards a better appreciation of that practice, towards a better application of their powers and, eventually, towards the consideration of carefully presented reforms.[9]

Durkheim's method was 'historical and sociological' in that it went beyond the analysis of successive educational institutions and practices, and the exposition of educational doctrines: he continually sought to explain why particular ideas and ideals, practices and institutions arose, survived during certain periods, disappeared, and, in some cases, reappeared. His explanatory scheme was neither monocausal nor one-sided; the explanations advanced were always complex and stressed different explanatory factors at different points. Sometimes the main factors were cultural, or 'representational'; at others geographical, or political, or economic. Here we can refer only summarily to the rich diversity of historical detail and explanatory argument which this work contains.

Durkheim began by relating the concentration and co-ordination of teaching in a single place and the notion of the school as a 'morally unified environment closely enveloping the child and acting upon his entire nature'[10] to the religious idealism of early Christianity, seeking to act upon 'the depths of the soul'[11]; but he also pointed to a 'sort of contradiction' in the teaching of the early Church between 'the religious element, the Christian doctrine' and 'Ancient Civilization, and all the borrowings the Church had to make from it, that is, the profane element'.[12] On the other hand, he attributed the growth of the school system under Charlemagne to a primarily political development: the 'energetic movement of concentration' which occurred at this time, bringing together 'the intellectual forces of the country at a small number of points', so that they 'could mutually reinforce one another by virtue of their association'.[13] He then discussed the teaching of grammar

9. Mauss, 1925a, p. 19.
10. 1938a, 1, p. 39.
11. ibid., 1, p. 38.
12. ibid., 1, pp. 32, 33.
13. ibid., 1, pp. 49, 50.

during the Carolingian period, as 'the origin and basis of all the other arts',[14] arguing that it was a kind of preliminary form of the study of logic and that the 'age of grammar' led naturally to the Scholastic age of logic and dialectic. This whole development was, in effect, the 'very slow and very gradual development of one and the same idea',[15] involving the focusing of education on thought, in its most formal and abstract aspect, and it was 'attached by deep roots to the intellectual structure of European countries, that is Christian countries'.[16]

The explanation Durkheim offered of the origins of the universities in the eleventh and early twelfth centuries appealed to a number of factors: a 'general stimulation of the intellectual activity throughout Europe',[17] the 'extreme mobility of men of all classes and professions',[18] a 'double concentration of this [heightened] activity: first at a number of dispersed points, then at a single but stable point'[19] and finally (and of subsidiary importance), the personal influence of Abelard. In discussing the early development of the University of Paris, Durkheim traced the growth of its internal organization, with the grouping of masters in a corporation (following the medieval corporative pattern), their struggles with the Chancellor of Notre Dame and their alliance with the Pope; but he also stressed the cultural preconditions – 'a conception *sui generis* of education and teaching characteristic of Christian societies, a conception which existed prior to the function of a teaching corporation, but which found in the latter the means of realizing itself in the most active manner that it could conceive'.[20] After examining the development of tutorial organization in Faculties and Nations (the Faculty of Arts corresponding to secondary education) and the rise of the colleges, he sought to account for the system of '*internat*' in the latter, and a

14. ibid., 1, p. 70.
15. ibid., 2, p. 7.
16. ibid., 1, p. 81.
17. ibid., 1, p. 90.
18. ibid., 1, p. 86.
19. ibid., 1, p. 90.
20. ibid., 1, p. 120.

general bureaucratization of the university which set in in the fifteenth century, in terms of a wider process of 'morbid' and 'excessive' centralization and 'moral and political unification'[21] beginning in France at this period, having deep cultural roots and wide-ranging consequences.

The next three lectures consisted of a penetrating inquiry into the framework and content of teaching, including a striking discussion of the role of dialectic as a means of coping with the world of experience within a pre-scientific cultural tradition innocent of the experimental method.[22] In this context, Durkheim argued, a respect for books and texts and for the words of wise men was entirely natural, and not, as the men of the Renaissance argued, a mark of intellectual servility.

In examining the educational changes wrought by the Renaissance, Durkheim offered an account of the latter that was in the first place economic, invoking 'a whole set of changes in the economic order'.[23] The growth of order and security, with a better organized administration, the development of markets and of consumers' demands, the multiplication of towns and the growth of population, the discovery of America and the route to the Indies – all this galvanized economic activity and led to a growth of consumption and a change in manners, especially in Italy and thence to France. Durkheim argued that this growing wealth was accompanied by a declining social distance between social classes, and an increasing emulation of aristocratic styles of life, with a consequent change in the conception of education, for 'the teaching destined to produce a good bachelor of arts, skilled in all the secrets of the syllogism and the *disputatio*, could not serve to form an elegant and eloquent gentleman, able to hold his place in a salon, expert at all the arts of society'.[24] In the second place, Durkheim pointed to the consolidation of 'the great European nationalities',[25] breaking up the old unity of Christendom, with the resulting diversification in the interpretation of

21. ibid., 1, p. 158.
22. See ibid., 1, pp. 192 ff.
23. ibid., 1, p. 216.
24. ibid., 1, p. 218.
25. ibid.

fundamental dogmas, entailing the right to diverge from received beliefs, a limited right of schism and of freedom of thought, and, in general, a growing 'movement of individualization and differentiation ... within the homogeneous mass of Europe'[26] (a process for which Scholasticism had paved the way and which was also bound to affect religiously determined conceptions of education).

In the education of the Renaissance Durkheim discerned two great currents of opinion: the 'encyclopaedic' or scholarly current represented by Rabelais, stressing the cognitive faculties and the unlimited acquisition of knowledge; and the humanist current, represented by Erasmus, emphasizing the arts of expression and the cultivation of taste. Durkheim explored the differences and similarities between the ideas of these two thinkers and between the cultural tendencies they expressed, relating them both to the formation of a polite society, to a general relaxation of moral sentiment and of the traditional Christian appeal to duty, to an increasing stress upon personal emulation and honour, and to a growth in dilettantism and essentially aristocratic values. Montaigne's 'pedagogical nihilism'[27] only expressed the logical conclusions of his predecessors' ideas. In general, the sixteenth century was 'an epoch of educational and moral crisis':

Under the influence of changes within the economic and social order, a new education had become necessary. But the thinkers of the time only conceived of it in the form of an aristocratic and, directly or indirectly, aesthetic education ... Although a scientific education, such as Rabelais envisaged, was certainly superior to the purely literary education recommended by Erasmus, it also had the grave defect of remaining unrelated to the demands of serious life, and of only occupying minds in a noble game.[28]

It fell to the Jesuits to put these prevailing ideas into practice; and Durkheim's account of their acquisition of a sort of hegemony in French education, of their essentially ambiguous role, combining humanism and faith, employing paganism for the glorification and propagation of Christian morality,

26. ibid., 1, p. 219.
27. ibid., 2, p. 65.
28. ibid., 2, p. 67.

and of their immense influence on the growth of French classical culture constitutes a real *tour de force*. Essentially, Durkheim argued that the Jesuits were able, by deferring to the tastes and ideas of the time, to direct their development and, in consequence, both to mutilate and impoverish the educational ideal of the Renaissance and to bring about a 'retrograde movement which put back our educational organization by several centuries'.[29] On the other hand, their discipline, based on the two principles of close personal supervision and extreme rivalry and emulation between students, had its roots in the 'moral constitution of society',[30] in particular the development of the individual personality:

At the time of the Renaissance, the individual begins to become conscious of himself; he is no longer, at least in enlightened regions, a simple aliquot fraction of a whole, he is already a whole in a sense, a person with his own physiognomy, who has and who experiences at the very least the need to develop his own ways of thinking and feeling ... as *consciences* become individualized, so education itself must become individualized...[31]

Durkheim's discussion of the cultural consequences of the education inaugurated at the time of the Renaissance, and propagated primarily by the Jesuits, laid stress upon 'some of the most distinctive features of our national spirit',[32] implanted during the classical era. He instanced the marked and exclusive taste of seventeenth-century literature for general and impersonal types, abstracted from all social context in space and time, and traced it to the system of education which explicitly taught men to conceive of human nature as 'a sort of eternal reality, immutable, invariable, independent of time and space...'[33] This conception of human nature was, he argued, not merely a distinctive trait of French literature; it affected 'our whole intellectual and moral temperament',[34] leading to a sort of 'constitutional

29. ibid., 2, p. 78.
30. ibid., 2, p. 115.
31. ibid.
32. ibid., 2, p. 126.
33. ibid., 2, p. 128.
34. ibid., 2, p. 129.

cosmopolitanism', to an over-abstract and *simpliste* rationalism and, in particular, to the abstract individualism of the eighteenth century.

The remaining historical lectures covered the development of scientific teaching, relating it to Protestantism in Germany and to a growing civic consciousness in eighteenth-century France; the abortive educational reforms of the French Revolution; and, finally, the extraordinary see-saw of educational reforms in the nineteenth century, which he attributed to a wider social and intellectual crisis, as well as to more immediate political interests, with the traditionalists (religious, social and political) defending the inheritance of humanism against the claims of science.

It is evident from this extremely selective summary that Durkheim's method was 'historical and sociological'. If there is an explanatory bias, it is perhaps in the direction of the cultural: the factors he tended to find especially fruitful in the explanation of educational developments were collective aspirations, values, beliefs and ideals. Conversely, he had an ingrained distrust of an appeal to purely personal factors. Thus, when writing about the origin of the university, he observed that, far from it being 'possible, as some historians have done, to attribute it to the personal influence of several men of genius, we have seen that it was the product of general causes . . .'[35] Similarly, as we have seen, he regarded particular educational doctrines as 'nothing other than the expression of currents of opinion which agitate . . . the social environment in which they arose', registering 'prevailing aspirations' with particular force and clarity.[36]

Durkheim's method was, in Mauss's words, also 'inductive and normative'. He aimed both to generalize from the explanations he had arrived at and to derive practical conclusions from them. It is worth looking, first at his generalizations, and, finally, at his normative conclusions.

He made a systematic attempt to identify broad historical continuities, interpreting them as evidence of cultural traits or as answering fundamental social needs. Thus one can trace

35. ibid., 1, p. 113.
36. ibid., 2, pp. 9–10.

a number of recurring themes: the continuity of 'formalism'
('To the grammatical formalism of the Carolingian epoch and
to the dialectical formalism of the Scholastic age there succeeded a new kind of formalism: literary formalism')[37]; the
continual re-appearance of encyclopaedic ambitions, under
different forms (among the grammarians and then the Scholastics, in Rabelais, and, above all, in the eighteenth century); the
gradual, but for long retarded, growth of secularism and
reason within education to an ultimate position of dominance[38];
the extremely prolonged educational monopoly of studies
relating to man,[39] only lately matched by an equal concern for
the rest of nature; the continuity of educational organization,
reaching back to the Middle Ages ('universities, faculties,
colleges, grades, examinations, all come from that period'[40]);
indeed, the very existence of secondary education itself, whose
objective Durkheim defined as 'awakening the reflective
faculties, exercising and strengthening them in a general way
and without employing them in any occupational pursuit',[41]

37. ibid., 2, p. 38.

38. The nominalist-realist controversy was 'a first and powerful effort
to confront faith with reason'; the Scholastics allowed 'the enemy within
the gates'. They 'introduced reason into dogma, while refusing to deny
dogma', trying to hold an equal balance. It was not until the seventeenth
and eighteenth centuries that the harvest sown by these ideas was reaped
(ibid., 1, p. 95).

39. Durkheim attributed this in part to a central feature of Christianity
(as opposed to the religions of Antiquity): 'For Christianity .. it is the
mind, the *conscience* of man which is sacred and incomparable; for the
soul . . . is a direct emanation of divinity. The world is defined as matter,
and matter is profane, vile, degrading, the source of evil and sin. Between
mind and matter there is the whole distance separating the spiritual from
the temporal . . . with Christianity the world loses the confused unity it
had primitively, and divides into two parts, into two halves of unequal
value; there is, on the one hand, the world of thought, of the conscience,
of morality, of religion; and, on the other, the world of matter, unthinking,
amoral and areligious. Now, religious, moral, intellectual activity, these
are what is truly human and characteristic of man. Since . . . education
has above all the aim of developing in the child the germs of humanity
to be found there, the idea could not even arise that nature and the sciences
of nature might serve this end' (ibid., 2, p. 140).

40. ibid., 2, p. 133.

41. ibid., 2, p. 183.

the differences between different periods consisting only in *which* form of reflection appeared to be most important at any given time.

He was also concerned to generalize about historical discontinuities, to postulate a hypothetical 'norm' of historical development from which the actual historical process might at times diverge. In general, a kind of natural selection operated and it was 'the most apt' ideas which survived, but it was possible, in 'the course of the struggles and conflicts which have arisen between contrary ideas', for valuable ideas to founder.[42] It could happen that 'elements of the past disappear which could and should have become normal elements of the present and the future'.[43] Thus,

> The Renaissance followed upon Scholasticism; the men of the Renaissance began by thinking it obvious that there was nothing worth preserving in the Scholastic system. It is for us to ask whether the result of this revolutionary attitude was not that the educational ideal we have inherited contains lacunae. Thus the historical study of education, while enabling us to gain a better understanding of the present, [offers] us the chance to revise the past itself and to bring to light the errors of which it is important that we become aware, since we have inherited them.[44]

From his generalizations about educational ideas and practices in the past, or the consequences of their absence, and from his assessment of the present and future needs of industrial societies, Durkheim concluded by drawing a number of prescriptive conclusions, in answer to the question: 'what should [secondary education] become henceforth?'[45] It was these conclusions – pro-scientific and anti-literary, uncompromisingly secular and anti-classicist – that so upset Durkheim's traditionalist critics.[46]

42. ibid., 1, p. 18. 'Here, as elsewhere, the struggle for survival produces only rough and approximate results' (ibid.).

43. ibid., 1, p. 22.

44. ibid., 1, pp. 22–3.

45. ibid., 2, p. 181.

46. See Chapter 18, above.

The formalism of earlier periods had been one way of achieving the objective of secondary education, as he defined it, but it had always sought to form the mind by applying it to purely abstract and conceptual matter – 'to the abstract forms of pure understanding . . . to the subjects of literature, to the general aspirations of the human mind and heart'.[47] He proposed instead that contemporary education should direct reflection to 'solid, firm, resistant objects, to objects from which we have much to learn, of which the mind needs to take account and on the understanding of which it needs to be formed . . .'[48] There were two categories of such objects: 'human' and 'natural'.

How should the former be studied at the level of secondary education? In answering this, Durkheim argued that humanism 'no longer responds to the real demands of today, and . . . must in consequence be transformed'.[49] In place of its twin basic principles that human nature is unchanging and that ancient literature, above all Latin, is 'the best possible school of humanity',[50] it was clear that 'another conception of man is necessary today, along with other methods to teach it'.[51] The humanists' human nature was an arbitrary construction of the mind, a product of the fusion of the Christian ideal with those of Rome and Greece, part of a particular historical context. What was currently needed was to convey to the pupil 'not only what is constant, but also what is irreducibly diverse in humanity'.[52] He needed to become aware of different moralities and mentalities, and to appreciate, for example, the very complex mental processes of primitive peoples; he should acquire a conception of man 'not as a system of definite and countable elements, but as an infinitely flexible and proteiform force, capable of assuming the most diverse aspects under the pressure of endlessly varied circumstances'.[53] Such a new

47. ibid., 2, p. 187.
48. ibid., 2, pp. 187–8.
49. ibid., 2, p. 190.
50. ibid., 2, p. 192.
51. ibid., 2, p. 193.
52. ibid., 2, p. 198.
53. ibid., 2, p. 199.

conception would influence attitudes, making men less hostile to change on the grounds of the supposed inflexibility of human nature, showing them that, at any given point in history, we contain 'a multitude of unrealized possibilities',[54] while giving them a healthy appreciation of social complexity. Given the currently rudimentary state of the psychological and social sciences, Durkheim proposed history in depth as the most effective discipline to achieve these ends,[55] using literature as a means of understanding civilizations and revealing the variability of human nature and its extreme complexity (thus adapting the work of the humanists to contemporary ends).

As to the teaching of the natural sciences, Durkheim advocated it as essential for the formation of a complete mind. Not only was man part of nature, so that it was essential to grasp his place within it, but science was itself a human product, at least equal in importance to literature: its development and procedures, its methods of thinking and reasoning were of incomparable educational value. Teaching pupils to think scientifically was an 'invaluable instrument of logical training',[56] the way to fill the educational lacuna that had been left by the demise of Scholasticism. In any case, Durkheim argued that ultimately the gap between the study of the physical and human worlds would disappear; scientific culture was becoming an indispensable part of human culture. Finally, he advanced the case for studying language and logic as a means of training the mind. In general, he characterized his educational ideal as encyclopaedic in the sense, not of aiming to produce the 'complete scholar', but rather the 'complete reason'. True to his most basic intellectual principle, he sought to form 'men who are concerned to have clear ideas',

54. ibid.

55. He proposed the history of 'various peoples, chosen carefully among those which differ from [peoples] of whom we have immediate experience', in particular Greek and Italian history and that of those primitive societies whose cultures could be related to those of Ancient Greece and Rome (ibid.).

56. ibid., 2, p. 216.

rationalists of a new type, who know that things, whether human or physical, are of an irreducible complexity and who know how to confront that complexity directly and without faltering.[57]

57. ibid., 2, p. 225. He elsewhere applied this principle to higher education, complaining that the syllabus for the *agrégation* was such that it did not allow candidates to 'acquire definite knowledge [or] to develop ideas, on a number of problems, that are equally definite (though provisional)'; what achieved success was 'neither knowledge, nor firmness and solidity of thought . . . but a talent that is entirely formal and of doubtful value' (1909b, p. 160).

Chapter 20

Durkheimian Sociology: Its Context and Relation to Other Disciplines

THE CONTEXT

By the turn of the century the idea of sociology had acquired a new popularity throughout Europe and the United States. As Durkheim wrote in 1900,

> our science came into being only yesterday. It must not be forgotten, especially in view of the favourable reception that sociology is given now, that, properly speaking, Europe did not have as many as ten sociologists fifteen years ago.[1]

A major precipitating factor in this development was the enormous influence of Herbert Spencer. *The Study of Sociology* won widespread recognition between 1870 and 1890 and *The Principles of Sociology* was likewise extensively studied, particularly in German and American universities.[2] In France Spencer's influence was especially notable: he was widely seen as the true scientific descendant of Comte, free from the later quasi-religious excesses of Comte himself and his contending disciples. As William Graham Sumner said, he 'rescued social science from the dominion of cranks'.[3] Durkheim wrote that in the history of sociology Spencer was 'Comte's immediate successor' who, in the course of applying the evolutionary hypothesis to the social world, 'found himself compelled, on a number of points, correspondingly to complete or rectify the generalization of the Comtist sociology'.[4]

Following upon Spencer, there arose, in Durkheim's words,

1. 1900c: tr. 1960c, p. 354. Cf. 1895e.
2. Charles Horton Cooley wrote that in the United States *The Study of Sociology* 'probably did more to arouse interest in the subject than any other publication before or since' ('Reflections upon the Sociology of Herbert Spencer', *AJS*, 26 (1920), p. 129).
3. Cited in Carneiro, R. L., 'Herbert Spencer', *IESS*.
4. 1905d, pp. 262–3.

'a whole legion of workers, a few in every country, but most especially in France, who applied themselves to [sociological] studies. Sociology has now emerged from the heroic age.'[5] And indeed, there was a remarkable growth of studies of a sociological character in the 1890s and 1900s.[6] This growth was evident in the establishment of chairs and lectureships and of new institutions, as well as in the publication of books and new sociological journals. In France the lectures and writings of Tarde, of the neo-Comtean Eugène de Roberty, and, above all, of Durkheim himself and his colleagues were of particular significance. The mid-nineties also saw the founding by René Worms of the Institut International de Sociologie, the Société Sociologique de Paris, the *Revue internationale de sociologie*, and the prolific *Bibliothèque internationale de sociologie*. Worms, who was a brilliant organizer, saw his and sociology's primary task as co-ordinating and synthesizing the various social sciences, and the truths and insights to be found in the one-sided theories of others. (Like Tarde, he opposed Durkheim's 'social realism', and he was strongly, though increasingly less, attached to social organicism.[7]) Worms formed the focus for an alternative sociological tradition to the Durkheimian. He gathered around him a large number of scholars, professional and amateur, both in France and abroad, among them Tarde, and others such as the Russian émigrés Maxim Kovalevsky, Jacques Novicow and de Roberty[8] – and eventually (from 1907 or so) the apostate Durkheimian Gaston Richard, who inherited Worms's position on his death in 1926. The *Revue internationale* has justly been called the 'chief organ of expression of the anti-Durkheimian sociologists in France',[9]

5. 1909e (3rd edn, 1914), p. 317.

6. Cf. Branford, V. V., 'On the Origin and Use of the Word "Sociology"', *Sociological Papers*, 1 (1905), especially pp. 8–9.

7. On Worms, see Essertier, 1930, pp. 232 ff.; Benoît-Smullyan, 1938, pp. 861–2; Simon, 1963, pp. 147–9; and Clark, T. N., 'René Worms', *IESS*. For Worms's attitude to Durkheim, see Worms, 1907, 1917 and 1921. Cf. Clark, T. N., 'Marginality, Eclecticism and Innovation: René Worms and the Revue Internationale de Sociologie from 1893 to 1914', *RIS*, ser. 11, 3 (1967), pp. 3–18.

8. Cf. Sorokin, 1928.

9. Benoît-Smullyan, 1938, p. 861.

though these latter differed widely among themselves. Equally productive, but without influence in the academic world, which resolutely ignored them, were the Catholic and upper-class Le Playists, who produced a number of remarkable monographs concerning family types and industrial organization, as well as community studies and work in 'social geography'. They were divided between a highly ideological, conservative and largely anti-industrial group centred on the journal *La Réforme sociale* and a much more empirically productive group around *La Science sociale*.[10]

In addition to these various groups, there were many other individual scholars who saw themselves, and were seen, as pursuing sociological studies, such as the versatile Espinas, in Paris since 1894, the demographic sociologist Adolphe Coste, the anti-individualist Catholic Jean Izoulet at the Collège de France, and Charles Letourneau at the École d'Anthropologie. Various institutions fostered a wide range of sociological work, among them the Institut International de Sociologie, the École des Hautes Études Sociales, the Collège Libre des Sciences Sociales, the École d'Anthropologie, and the École Socialiste. Finally, though many specialists in particular disciplines remained hostile or indifferent, others became increasingly well disposed to sociology, many of them to the Durkheimian variety. Chief among these were the historians grouped around Henri Berr's *Revue de synthèse historique*, founded in 1900, which sought to bring together all the various kinds of history and the human sciences, especially sociology. Indeed, there developed close links between the schools of Durkheim and Berr, and wide areas of agreement, both in substantive interests and methodological views.[11] There were the human geographers, especially Paul Vidal de la

10. See Davy, 1926, Chulliat, 1956, Essertier, 1930, pp. 284 ff., and Pitts, J. R., 'Frédéric Le Play,' *IESS*.

11. See Faublée, 1964, where it is argued that the divergences between the two groups were evident but unimportant. (For Durkheim's attitude to Berr, see 1913a (ii) (4)). Cf. Hughes, H. S., *The Obstructed Path: French Social Thought in the Years of Desperation 1930–1960* (New York and Evanston, 1968), ch. 2 (1): 'From Michelet via Durkheim to Henri Berr'.

Blache, who became more and more sociological, and some of them eventually Durkheimian, despite some violent territorial disputes.[12] The legal theorists Léon Duguit and Maurice Hauriou and the economist Charles Gide were very impressed by the value of sociological perspectives. The statisticians, from Adolphe Quételet to Tarde and Jacques Bertillon (who was on the editorial board of the *Revue internationale de sociologie*), were increasingly preoccupied with sociological problems and explanations, though mostly critical of the Durkheimians. The psychologist-philosopher Théodule Ribot's work became increasingly sociological in character; he became impressed by the thought that psychology had confined itself to studying the white, adult, civilized man and by the corresponding need to study different social 'milieux'. As Durkheim noted with pleasure, Ribot's *La Logique des sentiments* demonstrated that 'psychology, once it had arrived at a certain stage in its development, becomes inseparable from sociology'.[13] Moreover, from 1894 onwards, Ribot's *Revue philosophique* included a section entitled 'Sociologie' and carried frequent sociological articles and reviews, many of them by Durkheim and his associates. As to the philosophers, though there were many who found sociology in general, and Durkheimian sociology in particular, intellectually and morally repugnant, there were others who were its varyingly enthusiastic supporters, especially among the growing number sympathetic to rationalism and the claims of science. Among these were Xavier Léon, who opened up the pages of his *Revue de métaphysique et de morale* to the Durkheimians, Lucien Lévy-Bruhl, whose whole subsequent intellectual career consisted in a tireless pursuit of the philosophical implications of (mainly Durkheimian) sociological ideas and ethnographic evidence, and, as we have seen, some of the most promising young agrégés; equally, there were other philosophers, such as Gustave Belot, who, while favour-

12. See Essertier, 1930, pp. 369 ff.; for the disputes, see, for instance, Simiand, F., review in *AS*, XI (1910), especially p. 727, and Febvre, L., *La Terre et l'évolution humaine* (Paris, 1922), p. 76; also see 1913a (ii) (37). One member of this school, Albert Demangeon, was an editor of volume 12 of the *Année*.

13. 1906a(8), p. 158.

able to sociology in general, were hostile to Durkheimism in particular.[14]

By 1900, Durkheim noted, in France

the word ['sociology'] is on everyone's lips, and it is even used abusively; the thing has become popular. People's eyes are fixed on the new science and they expect much from it. There has thus emerged at the end of the century an intellectual movement altogether analogous to that which we have noticed at its beginning [including Saint-Simonism, Fourierism, Comtism and, in general, the birth of sociology] which, moreover, results from the same causes.[15]

These causes came down to a condition of acute social disorder, bringing with it a fundamental questioning of the bases of social order. Durkheim dated the new intellectual awakening from that year of disaster, 1870:

The shock of those events was the stimulus which re-animated men's minds. The country found itself confronting the same question as at the beginning of the century. The system of organization that constituted the imperial system, which was in any case nothing but a façade, had just collapsed; it was a matter of rebuilding another, or rather of building one that could survive otherwise than by means of administrative gimmicks, that is to say, a system with a real basis in the nature of things. For this purpose it was necessary to know what that nature of things was. In consequence, the urgency of establishing a science of societies did not delay in making itself felt.[16]

Sociology made comparable progress elsewhere in the 1890s and 1900s. In Italy, the *Rivista italiana di sociologia* was founded in 1897 and there was a considerable growth of sociological teaching in the universities and of publications. In Belgium there was the foundation of the Université Nouvelle by Guillaume de Greef on a specifically sociological basis and of the Institut de Sociologie Solvay. In Germany there were the sociology courses of Georg Simmel in Berlin, of Ferdinand

14. See Chapter 16, above, and Chapter 25, below.

15. 1900b, p. 651. Cf. Espinas' judgement: 'Social science has become a fashionable novelty in Paris, where it has its museum and its colleges' ('Être ou ne pas être, ou du Postulat de la sociologie', *RP*, 51 (1901), p. 451).

16. ibid., p. 647.

Tönnies in Kiel and of Paul Barth in Leipzig, the founding in 1904 of the journal *Archiv für Sozialwissenschaft und Sozial-politik* and the existence of long-standing sociological approaches and sympathies on the part of specialists in a wide variety of fields. In the United States there was a widespread development of sociological courses in universities, colleges and theological seminaries and the publication in Chicago of the *American Journal of Sociology* (of which Durkheim was an advisory editor until the War) from 1895 onwards. Even in Britain a Sociological Society was founded in 1903, at the third meeting of which, on 20 June 1904, Durkheim's views were very extensively discussed[17]; and in 1903 sociological teaching was begun at the University of London by Patrick Geddes, Edward Westermarck, A. C. Haddon and L. T. Hobhouse.[18]

In general, however, these developments tended to follow their separate national courses. There were of course certain specific cross-national influences, such as that of some of the Germans and of Gabriel Tarde in the United States, of the Le Playists in England and Scotland, and of Social Darwinism generally, but national sociological traditions tended to crystallize and become increasingly isolated from one another. This was especially true of France and Germany and is symbolized in the total lack of interest in each other's work shown by Durkheim and Weber.[19] Durkheim had, as we have seen, been strongly influenced in his youth by German historians and social scientists, but by 1902 he was writing:

I have the very distinct impression that, for some time now, Germany has not been able to renew its formulae. Its scholarly production continues to be abundant, more abundant than ours. But I do not see any evidence of a new impetus in the field of the social sciences. Sociological studies, which are currently almost too fashionable amongst us, have scarcely any representatives. This fact

17. See 1905d (for details see bibliography, below).
18. Branford, art. cit., p. 9 fn.
19. Cf. Tiryakian, 1966; and Bendix, 1971, for a plausible set of conjectures to explain this lack of interest. (Tiryakian is mistaken to say that Durkheim nowhere refers to Weber: see 1913a (ii) (3), p. 26). M. Davy confirms that Durkheim '*connaissait très mal les œuvres de Weber*' (personal communication).

seems to me all the more remarkable since, when I first began my present studies some eighteen to twenty years ago, it was from Germany that I sought enlightenment.[20]

Germany, he thought, was becoming intellectually parochial and stagnant, displaying 'a certain lack of curiosity, a sort of falling back on its own resources, an intellectual surfeit hostile to new developments'.[21] (Durkheim himself had scarcely any influence in Germany, though a German translation of *Les Règles* appeared in 1904.)[22]

France, on the other hand, Durkheim thought of as on the intellectual frontiers in the social sciences and above all in sociology. He attributed this to the decline of traditionalism, and to the native rationalism of 'the country of Descartes' – to that 'cult of distinct ideas, which is at the very root of the French spirit, as it is the basis of all science'.[23] He even went so far as to call sociology 'an essentially French science'.[24] From the late nineties onwards Durkheim exhibited to the full an assertive and self-confident cultural patriotism that was, however, in no way parochial (as the reviews in the *Année* abundantly confirm). Indeed its encyclopaedic range was matched only by its claims to universal scientific validity.

DURKHEIM'S SOCIOLOGICAL IMPERIALISM

Yet in Durkheim's case the assertiveness was more an expression of his intellectual imperialism on behalf of sociology than of satisfaction in its being French. This imperialism was radical, even subversive in character. The aim of sociology was to transform existing specialisms, which it was 'bound to imbue . . . with a new spirit'.[25] The very word 'sociology'

20. 1902d.
21. ibid.
22. For the beginnings of an explanation of this lack of influence, see Maus, H., 'Simmel in German Sociology', in *Essays in Sociology, Philosophy and Aesthetics by Georg Simmel et al.*, ed. Wolff, K. H. (New York, 1965), pp. 189 ff.
23. 1900b, p. 651.
24. ibid., p. 609.
25. 1899a (i) p. i: tr. 1960c, p. 348.

sums up and implies a whole new order of ideas: namely that social facts are indissolubly linked together, and, above all, must be treated as natural phenomena governed by invariable laws. To say that the various social sciences should be particular branches of sociology is therefore to state that they should be positive sciences themselves; that they should be developed in the same spirit as the other sciences of nature, and inspired by the methods which these employ, while keeping their own individualities . . . Integrating them into sociology is not simply imposing a new generic name on them; it is claiming that they must be orientated in a new direction. This conception of natural law, which it is Comte's glory to have extended to the social kingdom in general, must be applied to detailed facts, and found a home among these special researches from which it was originally absent, and into which it cannot be introduced without accomplishing an entire revolution in them.[26]

This, he wrote, was 'the task of the sociologist of today and the true way of continuing the work of Comte and Spencer'. It 'maintains their fundamental principle, but gives it its true value by applying it no longer to a restricted category of social phenomena, more or less arbitrarily chosen, but to the whole area of social life'.[27]

The entire work of the Durkheimians can be seen as an attempt to effect this revolution in 'the various social sciences'. The extent to which that attempt succeeded has yet to be definitively assessed.[28] What is clear is that, quite apart from direct influences on particular scholars,[29] the Durkheimian

26. 1903c: tr. 1905d, p. 268.

27. ibid., pp. 268–9.

28. See, however, Essertier, 1930; Bouglé, 1935; Benoît-Smullyan, 1937, 1938 and 1948; Cunnison, 1948; Hinkle, 1960; Honigsheim, 1960a; Gugler, 1961; and Wilson, 1963.

29. For examples within France, see below. Among examples outside France are the anthropologist A. R. Radcliffe-Brown (see Chapter 25, below) and the classical scholars Francis Cornford and Jane Harrison. On the latter's reaction to Durkheim's ideas, see Stewart, J. G., *Jane Ellen Harrison: A Portrait from Letters* (London, 1959): Jane Harrison wrote that Durkheim had 'formulated perhaps the greatest discovery yet made in the scientific study of religion, its social origin' (quoted in ibid., p. 85). During the war, she wrote an article in the *New Statesman* which began: 'I learn two things: my duty towards God and my duty towards my neighbour. É. Durkheim tells us they are one.' Shortly afterwards she wrote to Gilbert Murray: 'I had a delightful letter from old Durkheim

influence ramified (and continues to ramify) across an enormous range, from ethnology to social psychology and from the sociology of deviance to sinology. The immediate gains, as they appeared to Durkheim and his colleagues, were clear. Durkheimian sociology implied the dissolution of arbitrary barriers between subjects and a new perspective on their subject-matter. Who, asked Durkheim, could until quite recently have supposed 'that there are relationships between economic and religious phenomena, between demographic adaptations and moral ideas, between geographic forms and collective manifestations, and so on?'[30] His own studies of the relationship between social structure and forms of religious practice and belief and, most importantly, systems of classification are a striking example of the kind of inquiry that the Durkheimians opened up.

Their general principle was that when describing or explaining 'religious, juridical, moral and economic facts,'

one must relate them to a particular social milieu, to a definite type of society; and it is in the constitutive characteristics of this type that one must search for the determining causes of the phenomenon under consideration.[31]

They carried this principle very far, delving into areas at first sight recalcitrant to sociological inquiry. Thus Mauss (whom Durkheim once described as '*un peu mon alter ego*'[32]) investigated reciprocity in the form of gift-giving in relation to 'the manner in which sub-groups within segmentary societies of an

---

about my article in the *New Statesman*. He said I had understood him absolutely and seemed so pleased – but he is fearfully depressed about the war and says he can do nothing at his own work' (quoted in ibid., p. 162). Cornford's *From Religion to Philosophy* (London, 1912) and Harrison's *Themis* (Cambridge, 1912) were both highly Durkheimian works and were reviewed sympathetically but critically by Maxim David in the *Année*, vol. 12, pp. 41–4 and 254–60 (see Humphreys, 1971). Among examples of Durkheimian influence in the United States perhaps the most notable are Elton Mayo, W. Lloyd Warner, Talcott Parsons and Robert Merton.

30. 1900c: tr. 1960c, p. 371.
31. 1899a (ii), p. ii: tr. 1960c, p. 348.
32. Letter to Bouglé dated 27 March 1896.

archaic type are constantly embroiled with and feel themselves in debt to each other'[33]; he also explored (among many other subjects) the social determinants of sacrifice,[34] magic,[35] and prayer,[36] of seemingly natural, inconsequential bodily movements[37] and of the very notion of the person or 'self'.[38] Maurice Halbwachs not only extended Durkheim's sociological theory of suicide[39]; he also, daringly, investigated 'the social framework of memory'[40] and explored the social determinants of differential standards of living and variable definitions of 'needs', in relation to social classes, and of budgets and consumption patterns.[41] Célestin Bouglé studied the social preconditions for the growth of egalitarian ideas,[42] and for the evolution of values generally,[43] as well as the Indian caste system.[44] Paul Fauconnet studied forms of responsibility as socially determined, analyzing 'its conditions, its nature and its function'.[45] François Simiand, the economist of the group,

---

33. Mauss, 1925b, repr. in Mauss, 1950 (1966), p. 194: tr. p. 31.

34. Hubert and Mauss, 1899.

35. Hubert and Mauss, 1904.

36. Mauss, 1909. Cf.: 'Prayer is social not only in its content, but also in its form. Its forms are of an exclusively social origin. It does not exist outside a ritual . . . The individual . . . merely appropriates to his personal sentiments a language he has in no way made. Ritual remains the very basis of the most individual prayer' (ibid., repr. in Mauss, 1968–9, vol. 1, pp. 378–9).

37. 'Les Techniques du corps' (1935), repr. in Mauss, 1950 (1966).

38. 'Une Catégorie de l'esprit humain: la notion de personne, celle de "moi", un plan de travail' (1938), repr. in Mauss, 1950 (1966). On Mauss, see Karady, 1968, and Lukes, 1968a.

39. Halbwachs, 1930.

40. Halbwachs, 1925 and 1950.

41. For example, Halbwachs, 1913 and 1933. Cf. also his celebrated work on social morphology (Halbwachs, 1938b). On Halbwachs, see Friedmann, 1968.

42. Bouglé, 1899.

43. Bouglé, 1922.

44. Bouglé, 1901 and 1908.

45. Fauconnet, 1920, p. 23. Cf. ibid., Preface: 'Émile Durkheim treated responsibility in four lectures of his course on the Theory of Sanctions delivered at the Faculty of Letters at Bordeaux in 1894. When he proposed to me that I should take up this subject again, he gave me the manuscript of his lectures.'

investigated the determinants of wages and prices,[46] of economic fluctuations,[47] and of the value of money and the origin, evolution and role of money in social life,[48] as well as writing extensively about the methodology of the social sciences.[49] Henri Hubert collaborated with Mauss in the studies of sacrifice and magic, worked intensively on Celtic archaeology,[50] and wrote a remarkable study of the conception of time in religion and magic.[51] Henri Beuchat, who worked in American archaeology and philology, also collaborated with Mauss on their important study of the impact of 'social morphology' on the seasonally varying legal, moral, domestic and religious life of the Eskimos.[52] Georges Davy studied the social conditions within which the institution of contract arose and evolved,[53] and also wrote, with the Egyptologist Alexandre Moret, a study of the origins of Egyptian civilization 'from clans to empires'.[54] And Robert Hertz investigated the collective conception of death in primitive societies,[55] and the religious polarity represented by the pre-eminence of the right hand,[56] as well as the Alpine cult of Saint-Besse, and folklore gathered from infantrymen at the front during the First World War.[57]

That war was a shattering blow to the Durkheimians. At its outbreak they formed 'a sort of society in full vigour of mind and heart. A mass of work and of ideas were being developed

46. Simiand, 1932a.

47. Simiand, 1932b.

48. Simiand, 1934.

49. For example, Simiand, 1903, 1912 and 1922. Cf. Simiand's journal *Notes critiques – sciences sociales*, to which he contributed many methodological notes. On Simiand, see Dalamas, B. V., *L'Œuvre scientifique de François Simiand* (Paris, 1943), Lazard, M., *François Simiand* (Paris, 1936) and Bouglé, 1936.

50. Hubert, 1932.

51. Hubert, 1905.

52. Mauss and Beuchat, 1906 (see Jaszi, 1906).

53. Davy, 1922.

54. Davy and Moret, 1923. On Davy, see Gugler, 1968.

55. Hertz, 1907.

56. Hertz, 1909.

57. 'Saint-Besse. Étude d'un culte alpestre' (1913) and 'Contes et dictions recueillis sur le front, parmi les poilus de la Mayenne et d'ailleurs' (1917), repr. in Hertz, 1928. See Durkheim's obituary of Hertz: 1916b.

within it,' but the war came to 'decimate it, almost to destroy it', killing many of its outstanding young scholars (including Durkheim's son) whose promise was still unrealized.[58] But apart from these, many scholars who had been part of, or close to, the group continued to apply and develop Durkheimian ideas within their various specialist fields. Among them were the great comparative linguist Antoine Meillet,[59] the eminent sinologist Marcel Granet,[60] the jurists Emmanuel Lévy and Paul Huvelin and the pioneering scholar of Ancient Greek law Louis Gernet,[61] the arabist Edmond Doutté, the historians Georges Bourgin, Marc Bloch, Georges Lefebvre, Albert Mathiez and Lucien Febvre,[62] the psychologists Charles Blondel, Georges Dumas and Henri Wallon, the economic and social geographer Albert Demangeon, the philosopher-sociologist Lucien Lévy-Bruhl and a whole generation of French ethnologists taught by Marcel Mauss.[63]

One crucial element in the Durkheimians' attempt to revolutionize the social sciences was their rigorous insistence on a rationally defensible method that was comparative in its use of evidence and sought to arrive at general laws that ranged over social types. Durkheim was devastating in criticism of what he saw as inadequate method, as can be seen in very many of the reviews in the *Année* and in his ruthless criticisms of doctoral candidates.[64] M. Davy tells the story of Durkheim examining a candidate, whom he had terrorized by his peremptory manner, and saying:

58. Mauss, 1925a, p. 7, q.v. passim, and Mauss, 1927a.

59. See Meillet, 1906.

60. On Granet, see Levy, M. 'Marcel Granet' in *IESS*, and C. Wright Mills, 'The Language and Ideas of Ancient China: Marcel Granet's Contribution to the Sociology of Knowledge' in *Power, Politics and People: The Collected Papers of C. Wright Mills* (New York, 1963).

61. See Humphreys, 1971.

62. According to Charles Morazé, Febvre 'recognized in Durkheim his master' ('The Application of the Social Sciences to History', *Journal of Contemporary History*, 3, (1968) p. 208). Cf. Hughes, H. S., *The Obstructed Path*, op. cit., ch. 2.

63. See Lévi-Strauss, 1950..

64. See Appendix B, below.

Monsieur, you could either have a method, which is not mine but which I understand; or else you could use my method, and then I would be satisfied; or else, thirdly, you could, as is the case, use no method at all, so that I do not understand you at all.[65]

He was particularly critical of historians, whom he saw as over-inclined to describe rather than seeking to explain; he thought of the historical method as an 'indispensable auxiliary to sociology'.[66] History played, or should play, 'in the order of social realities, a role analogous to that of the microscope in the order of physical realities'.[67] History provided the principal mode of access to data for the sociologist in his search for general relations and laws verifiable in different societies. Durkheim had no time for any conception of history as humanistic and non-scientific, and least of all as an alternative mode of synthesizing the social sciences.

He offered abundant argumentative refutations of general sociological approaches and methods that differed from his own – such as those of Marx,[68] J. S. Mill,[69] Espinas,[70] Tarde,[71] Simmel,[72] Franklin H. Giddings,[73] Albion Small,[74] Ludwig

65. Personal communication.

66. 1928a, p. 348: tr. 1958b, p. 238. For the disputes between the Durkheimians and the historians, see the *Bulletin de la Société française de philosophie* for 30 May 1906, 30 May 1907 and 28 May 1908. Cf. also Durkheim, 1902a(iii) (1) and 1903a(iii) (1)–(3).

67. 1909e (3rd edn, 1914), p. 328. He was, however, 'convinced that [sociology and history] are destined to become ever more intimate and that a day will come when the historical approach and the sociological approach will no longer differ by any more than nuances' (ibid., pp. 330–1).

68. 1897e.

69. 1903c, pp. 473–6.

70. 1902a (iii) (3).

71. See Chapter 16, above.

72. 1900c, 1901e, 1902a (iii) (6), 1903c, pp. 479 ff, and 1904a (29) and (30) Durkheim himself translated Simmel's article 'Comment les formes sociales se maintiennent' for the first volume of the *Année*, observing to Bouglé that 'the complexity of the phrasing is not proportionate to the complexity of the thought which is, on the contrary, quite simple' (letter dated 25 October 1897). He further wrote to Bouglé, concerning this article, that Simmel had 'a sense of the specificity of social facts' but did not 'pursue his ideas to their conclusion' and remained 'wedded to

Gumplowicz,[75] Alfred Vierkandt,[76] Gaston Richard[77] and very many others – in fact those of all his major contemporaries (with the exception of Max Weber[78]). He was above all contemptuous of sociological theorizing that operated in a philosophical void, did not connect with the detail of the facts and failed to generate empirical hypotheses. A characteristic passage is the following, in criticism of Jankelevitch:

Here is yet another book of philosophical generalities about the nature of society, and of generalities through which it is difficult to sense a very intimate and familiar practical acquaintance with social reality. Nowhere does the author give the impression that he has entered into direct contact with the facts of which he speaks, for the general ideas he develops do not appear to be illustrated by a single concrete example nor applied to a single determinate and precise sociological problem. However great the dialectical and literary talent of authors may be, one cannot protest enough against the scandal of a method which offends as much as this book does against all our scientific practices and which is still, none the less, often employed. We no longer today allow that one can speculate on the nature of life without being first introduced to the techniques of biology. By what privilege is the philosopher to be permitted to speculate about society, without entering into commerce with the detail of social facts?[79]

---

generalities', though the article was 'lively, agreeable to read and certainly in the general spirit of the *Année*' (letters dated 6 July and 13 September 1897).

73. 1903c, pp. 476–9.
74. 1902a (iii) (4).
75. 1902a (iii) (7).
76. 1903a (iii) (4).
77. 1913a (ii) (1).
78. See Tiryakian, 1966, Bendix, 1971, and above. He saw (the early) Pareto as seeking 'to justify the old abstract and ideological method or political economy and wanting to make it the general method of all the social sciences' (1900a(3)). For a brief comparative discussion of Durkheim, Simmel and Pareto, see Lukes, 1966.
79. 1907a (1), p. 171. Cf. his remarks about Gustave Belot in a letter to Bouglé: 'It is not tolerable that one should spend one's life in this way, dogmatizing about social phenomena without entering into contact with any of them. Besides, I have little taste for his prolix and formal dialectics' (letter dated 25 July 1897).

SOCIOLOGY AND PHILOSOPHY

Yet, despite his imperialistic positivism, Durkheim retained a fundamental respect for philosophy. In 1911 Georges Davy published a small book of extracts from Durkheim's writings,[80] with a long introduction which laid emphasis on the philosophical side of Durkheim's thought. Durkheim wrote Davy a letter in which he commented on its 'rigour to which an old systematizer like me is particularly sympathetic', adding the following observation:

Certain of our friends will criticize you for having presented me in the more philosophical aspect. But there is no doubt that my thought tends in that direction. Having started out from philosophy, I am tending to return to it, or rather I have naturally been led back to it by the nature of the questions which I found on my way.[81]

It will be recalled that, when at the École Normale, Durkheim had been known by the nickname 'the Metaphysician',[82] and throughout his life, while engaged in the most detailed empirical work, he never lost sight of its philosophical assumptions and ultimate implications. Moreover, he retained a keen interest in current philosophical debates. In 1908, for example, he wrote to Léon:

I have just read Boutroux's book.[83] It would be really interesting if on Tuesday you could raise at the Société de Philosophie the question of the relations between philosophy and religion. There is a question which hovers over all the recent discussions which I have attended and which this book raises once again, namely, whether there are two types of reason, the one relating to science, the other to philosophy and religion.[84]

Durkheim was a regular attender and contributor at the meetings of the Société Française de Philosophie and in 1906 presented a paper on 'The Determination of Moral Facts'.[85]

80. Davy, 1911.
81. Davy, 1960b, p. 10.
82. ibid., p. 9.
83. This must have been *Science et religion dans la philosophie contemporaine* (Paris, 1908).
84. Letter dated 8 May 1908. For a report of the meeting, see 1909a(i).
85. 1906b.

Again, in 1911 he gave his paper on 'Judgements of Value and Judgements of Reality'[86] to the fourth International Congress of Philosophy at Bologna, which caused a considerable stir.[87] In 1913–14 he gave a philosophical course on Pragmatism and Sociology.[88] He planned a major work on *La Morale*, but he never got further than the introduction, written during the last weeks of his life.[89] In addition, at Paris he voluntarily undertook the teaching of general philosophy to candidates for the *agrégation*,[90] lecturing on such subjects as infinity, matter, teleology and so on.[91] As Davy has observed, there was always a philosophical exigency in his temperament.[92]

Indeed, not only did his sociological work presuppose well-defined epistemological and ethical positions; it had, as we shall see, the long-term aim of providing an empirically based account of the nature of morality and of perception and knowledge.[93] He never achieved a fully worked-out sociology of morality, which was his greatest ambition, but his work on the sociology of knowledge is to be found in the essay on primitive classification[94] and in *The Elementary Forms of the Religious Life*[95] and was carried further by a number of his disciples.[96] A letter to Léon written in 1908 shows very clearly where his preoccupations lay. He could, he wrote, offer Léon the introduction to the book he then proposed to call '*Les Formes élémentaires de la pensée et de la pratique religieuse*', for publication in his *Revue*. This would be

a short exposition in which I will indicate the object of the work, from the double point of view of the nature and the genesis of religious thought, and more generally of the genesis and nature of

86. 1911b.
87. Léon, 1917, p. 749.
88. 1955a: see Chapter 24, below.
89. 1920a: see Chapter 21, below.
90. Davy, 1960b, p. 9.
91. Davy, 1919, p. 194.
92. Davy, 1958.
93. See Chapters 21, 22 and 23, below.
94. 1903a (i).
95. 1912a.
96. By, for example, Hubert, Halbwachs and Granet.

thought. I intend to indicate, in effect, in passing, in the course of the book, some of the social elements which have helped to constitute certain of our categories. (Time, causality, the notion of force, the notion of personality.) This question, which has preoccupied me for a long time, and which I do not dare for the time being to approach directly, can, I think, be tackled from this perspective of religious thought.[97]

The introduction as published in the *Revue de metaphysique et de morale*[98] included, interestingly, a whole section which did not appear in *The Elementary Forms*.[99] This dealt, in part, with the relations between sociology and philosophy. He had felt it necessary, he wrote, to remove sociology from 'a philosophical tutelage that could only prevent it from constituting itself as a positive science'[1]; and, as a result, he had been suspected of being hostile to philosophy, or at least sympathetic to a narrow empiricism (that is, bad philosophy). In fact, his view was that sociology could help to renew perennial metaphysical problems. By focusing on the *conscience collective*, it fixed on man's representation of the world, a 'true microcosm',[2] for 'it is in the totality formed by [a civilization's] religion, its science, its language, its morality, that one finds realized the integral system of human *représentations* at a given time'.[3] Moreover, the study of the categories, the fundamental and universal forms of thought, provided access to the 'synthetic expression of the human mind'[4]: there was 'no more suitable object for philosophical thought.'[5] By studying these empirically, how they were formed and what elements entered into them,

[sociology] is destined, we believe, to furnish to philosophy, the bases which are indispensable to it and which it currently lacks.

97. Letter dated 24 July 1908.
98. 1909d.
99. For a contemporary study which makes extensive use of this omitted section, see Needham, R., 'Terminology and Alliance', *Sociologus*, 17 (1966), pp. 141–57, and 18 (1967), pp. 39–53.
   1. ibid., p. 755.
   2. ibid., p. 756.
   3. ibid., pp. 756–7.
   4. ibid., p. 757.
   5. ibid.

One can even say that sociological reflexion needs to extend itself naturally and spontaneously in the form of philosophical reflexion ...[6]

(One may suppose that he excluded this pasage from the book because it gave too many hostages to the philosophers: it was still important to avoid their tutelage.)

Ultimately Durkheim thought of sociology as 'destined to open a new way to the science of man'.[7] By finding empirical answers to questions that had hitherto seemed purely philosophical because non-empirical, he hoped that the social sciences would 'restore to philosophy, with interest, what they had borrowed from it'.[8] This hope was central to his sociology of morality, of knowledge and of religion, to which we will now turn.

6. ibid., p. 758.
7. 1912a, p. 637: tr. 1915d, p. 447.
8. 1903c: tr. 1905d, p. 280.

Chapter 21

The Sociology of Morality

DURKHEIM'S thought about morality operated at a number of different levels. In effect, he proposed a complex system of interdefined concepts with which he sought, first, to describe and explain empirical data – the genesis and functioning of particular moral codes in particular social contexts; second, to make evaluative judgements about such data – about whether and how they should be reformed; and third, to provide solutions to fundamental philosophical questions – such as the nature of evaluation and moral judgement, the autonomy of morals, and the 'dualism of human nature'. In our consideration of these ideas, and the development they underwent, it will be useful to begin by examining the conceptual scheme, and its progressive development, and then to look at its application to Durkheim's explanatory, evaluative and philosophical purposes.

The chief difficulty in pursuing such an inquiry is that Durkheim never synthesized his work on morality. We have already discussed his early interest in the 'positive science of morality' which he discovered among the Germans.[1] We have seen how he gradually deepened his view of morality as a social phenomenon, moving from an exclusive concentration on moral rules and their obligatory character ('all moral phenomena consist in rules of sanctioned conduct',[2] differing from laws in that sanctions were diffuse rather than organized)[3] to the more complex ideas set out in the course on moral

---

1. See Chapter 4, above.

2. 1893b, p. 24: tr. 1933b, p. 425 (S.L.). This definition occurs in that part of the introduction to *The Division of Labour* which was omitted from the second edition (1902b) and subsequent editions.

3. Cf.: 'the external sign of morality ... consists in a diffuse repressive sanction, that is, blame on the part of public opinion ...' (1901c, p. 52: tr. 1938b, p. 41).

education, analyzing morality as combining the imperative and the desirable, the 'spirit of discipline' and 'attachment to social groups', with the progressive introduction of autonomy through rational understanding.[4] We have also discussed Durkheim's early empirical work in the sociology of morality, which includes *The Division of Labour*, *Suicide* and the course on law and social norms (*physique du droit et des mœurs*).[5]

However, during his years in Paris, Durkheim never ceased to think about morality and his ideas about it evolved during successive Sorbonne lecture-courses.[6] His book on morality was 'the work Durkheim wanted to write' and he 'awaited an opportunity ... to recast his whole theory'.[7] Unfortunately, the opportunity never came; he got no further with his *Morale* than the beginning of its theoretical introduction.[8] All that he published were two short papers on morality, both delivered to philosophical audiences.[9] It is partly for this reason that a number of critics have complained that in this

4. See Chapter 6, above.

5. See Chapter 13, above.

6. See Mauss, 1925a, p. 12. These lectures were delivered in 1902–5, 1908–12 and 1914–16: see Appendix A, below.

7. ibid. M. Davy has confirmed this, pointing out that Durkheim intended his projected book to *replace* his existing publications on morality (personal communication).

8. 1920a. Mauss gives (in Mauss, 1920, p. 80) the following summary of the projected contents of the first, introductory book of Durkheim's *La Morale* (based on notes Durkheim had gathered together, deriving mainly from his 1914–15 lectures): 'Object of course – traditional conception of morality (1920a); critique of traditional ethics; critique of the conception that morality is entirely subjective; critique of Tarde's theory; the problem and the Kantian solution; critique of Kantian ethics; value judgement and ideal (sociological idealism); the individual moral conscience and objective morality (morality and moral conscience); objective and subjective point of view (sentiment of justice, idea of justice); the relation between public morality and individual morality (autonomy and the Kantian solution); collective type and average type; unity of the two elements (ideal and duty); how can we attach ourselves to society?' Mauss reports that Durkheim was also proposing to use material from: 'Introductory lecture to the course on domestic morality; and lectures on divorce, the three zones of kinship, property – the Kantian theory, and the consensual contract and sanctions'.

9. 1906b and 1911b: repr. in 1924a; tr. 1953b.

area Durkheim's work was more philosophical than sociological.[10] In trying to give a more rounded account, it will be
necessary to draw on various different sources in Durkheim's
work, as well as on the notes taken by MM. Davy and Cuvillier
at the Sorbonne lectures.[11] Hopefully, this account will suggest
where Durkheim's thought was tending and something of
what it might have yielded.

THE CONCEPTUAL FRAMEWORK

In his paper 'Determination of the Moral Fact',[12] delivered to
the Société de Philosophie in 1906, Durkheim offered the
clearest formulation of his conceptual scheme, which he saw as
the theoretical framework for his sociology of morality.
This formulation re-stated and extended that offered in the
moral education course. In accordance with his third rule of
sociological method,[13] he began with an 'initial, provisional
definition' in order subsequently to discover 'the intrinsic
differences between . . . moral rules and other rules by beginning with their apparent and exterior differences'.[14] The observable difference between moral and technical rules lay in the
obligatory character of the former. This was shown by the
existence of 'sanctions', whether negative (punishment and

10. For example, Ginsberg, 1951 (1956), p. 52, and Gurvitch, 1937
(1950). Gurvitch argues that 'instead of working on the sociology of
morality, or on the *science des mœurs*, Durkheim wished to derive from
sociology a moral philosophy based on the metaphysical and dogmatic
equation between Supreme Good, *Conscience Collective* and Spirit, from
which he was never able to detach himself' (ibid., p. 553). Cf. Gurvitch,
G., *Morale théorique et science des mœurs* (Paris, 1937), pp. 96–103.

11. Reproduced in Lukes, 1968b, Appendix D (1) and (2). Cf. Richard,
1911; Bouglé, 1922; Bayet, 1925; Bouglé, 1935, last chapter; Gurvitch,
1937; Parsons, 1937, ch. x; Ginsberg, 1951; Ladd, 1957; Indan, 1960;
and Aron, 1962 (1967), pt II, ch. 6; also Chapter 25, below, and the references therein.

12. 1906b: repr. 1924a: tr. 1953b.

13. '*The subject matter of every sociological study should comprise a group of
phenomena defined in advance by certain common external characteristics, and all
phenomena so defined should be included within this group*' (1901c, p. 45: tr.
1938b, p. 35).

14. 1924a (1951 edn), pp. 58, 60: tr. 1953b, pp. 41, 42 (S.L.).

blame) or positive (honour and praise), which were consequences 'synthetically' related to an action, that is, in virtue
of a pre-existing rule; as opposed to consequences that were
'analytically', or causally, related to the action.[15] To his
Kantian, anti-utilitarian account of the obligatory aspect of
morality, Durkheim added what he saw as the anti-Kantian
proposition that 'moral ends must be desired and desirable'.[16]

He went beyond the discussion in *Moral Education* by
elaborating on the relations between these two characteristics.
His distinction between them was an analytical one: 'moral
reality always presents simultaneously these two aspects which
cannot be isolated empirically'.[17] Thus 'No act has ever been
performed as a result of duty alone; it has always been necessary for it to appear in some respect as good'.[18] On the other
hand, 'Something of the nature of. duty is found in the desirability of morality'.[19] They were combined in different proportions within different actions, different personalities and different civilizations.[20] Neither could be derived from or reduced
to the other; this would be artificially to simplify moral
reality.[21] Finally, Durkheim compared morality, thus defined,
with sacredness, which he saw as similarly dual ('The sacred
being is in a sense the forbidden being, that one dares not
violate; but it is also good, loved and sought after'[22]), concluding that morality and religion were closely related: for
centuries they had been 'intimately linked and even completely

15. Durkheim recognized (elsewhere) that there were borderline cases
between technical, or practical, rules and moral rules: '. . . the moral order
is not isolated. It is tied to experience. One can move without interruption
from ordinary practical rules to moral rules' (Lukes 1968b, Appendix
D (2)).

16. ibid., p. 63: tr. p. 45 (S.L.).

17. ibid., p. 64: tr. p. 45 (S.L.).

18. ibid., pp. 64–5: tr. p. 45.

19. ibid., p. 51: tr. p. 36.

20. Durkheim argued that the morality of Ancient Greece and Rome
was primarily eudemonistic: cf. 1938a, 2, p. 47.

21. He saw the utilitarians as reducing duty to good, and Kant as
reducing good to duty: see Appendix D(2) in Lukes, 1968b.

22. 1924a (1951 edn), p. 51: tr. 1953b, p. 36 (S.L.).

fused'[23] and there were always elements of morality in religion and of religion in morality.[24]

Thus far Durkheim had proposed a set of inter-related definitions to be used in analyzing moral rules and behaviour and in situating such rules and behaviour in relation to other spheres of social life. He next asked an ambiguous question to which he gave a deeply ambiguous answer. How was one to 'explain' these characteristics of moral reality? This question could be construed as asking for an empirical study of a wide variety of moral codes, their causes and functioning, leading to 'some idea of the general causes upon which depend those essential characteristics that they have in common'.[25] Alternatively, it could be seen as asking for a 'purely dialectical argument'[26] to support the system of concepts already presented.

In pursuing the latter, Durkheim showed himself to be a poor philosopher. His aim was to determine the necessary conditions for calling an act 'moral', and his method was to 'question the common moral *conscience*'.[27] Beginning from the postulate that 'we have no duties except in relation to *consciences* ... to moral persons, or thinking beings'[28] and that an act can only have two sorts of end, myself and beings other than myself, he argued as follows:

(i) The qualification 'moral' has never been given to an act which has individual interests, or the perfection of the individual from a purely egoistic point of view, as its object; (ii) if I as an individual do not constitute an end having *in itself* a moral character, this is necessarily also true of other individuals, who are the same as myself, differing only in degree; (iii) from which we conclude that, *if a morality exists*, it can only have as an objective the group

23. ibid., p. 69: tr. p. 48.
24. As he remarked in his lectures, in morality 'the feature of sacredness is less clearcut. Dogmas and myths do not exist here ... The emphasis is upon acts. The difference is nonetheless entirely one of degree' (Lukes, 1968b, Appendix D (2). Cf. 1912a, pp. 295–9: tr. 1915d, pp. 206–9).
25. 1924a (1951 edn), p. 70: tr. 1953b, p. 49. He explained that he followed this method in his teaching, but was unable to do so here.
26. ibid., p. 55: tr. p. 39.
27. ibid., p. 71: tr. p. 50.
28. ibid.: tr. p. 49 (S.L.).

formed by a plurality of associated individuals – that is to say, society, *but on condition that society be considered as a personality qualitatively different from the individual personalities who compose it.*[29]

In reaching this conclusion, Durkheim assumed that the 'object' of moral activity must have 'moral value'. Morality, he argued, 'according to common opinion, begins where disinterestedness and devotion begin', but 'disinterestedness only makes sense when that to which we subordinate ourselves has a higher moral value than we have as individuals. In the world of experience I know of only one being that possesses a richer and more complex reality than our own, and that is the collectivity,'[30] as opposed to any, some or all of its separate elements. Thus, when 'acts directed towards others or myself' had moral value, 'they are oriented towards a higher end ... the morality which is recognized in them must derive from a higher source',[31] namely, society as a *sui generis* moral being.

Durkheim compared the structure of this argument with Kant's argument (as he read it) for the existence of God:

Kant postulates God, since without this hypothesis morality is unintelligible. We postulate a society specifically distinct from individuals, since otherwise morality has no object and duty no roots. Let us add that this postulate is easily verified by experience.[32]

As Durkheim saw it, 'One must choose between God and society'.[33] There were coherent reasons militating in favour of each solution, but he was 'quite indifferent to this choice, since I see in divinity only society transfigured and conceived symbolically'.[34]

Durkheim thought it possible to use the conclusion of this argument to 'explain' (a) the characteristics of desirability and obligatoriness into which he had analyzed morality, as well as (b) their unity, and (c) the close relation between morality and

29. ibid., pp. 52–3: tr. p. 37 (S.L.). This argument derives from Wundt's *Ethik*. Cf. Chapter 4, above; and 1887c, p. 130, where Durkheim first adopted it.
30. ibid., p. 74: tr. p. 52 (S.L.).
31. ibid., p. 73: tr. p. 51 (S.L.).
32. ibid., p. 74: tr. pp. 51–2.
33. ibid., pp. 74–5: tr. p. 52 (S.L.).
34. ibid., p. 75: tr. p. 52 (S.L.).

sacredness. Thus, 'society is good and desirable for the individual who cannot exist without it or deny it without denying himself, and . . . because society surpasses the individual, he cannot desire it without to a certain extent violating his nature as an individual'.[35] Likewise, society 'has all that is necessary for the transference to certain rules of that very imperative character which is distinctive of moral obligation'.[36] As to the unity of the two aspects, society 'commands us because it is exterior and superior to us . . . [but it is also] internalized within us and *is* us, we love and desire it, albeit with a *sui generis* desire since, whatever we do, society can never be ours in more than a part and dominates us infinitely'.[37] Finally, 'the sacred character which marks and has always marked moral things'[38] was to be similarly explained: sacred things were things given an incommensurable value by collective opinion and to which *sui generis* collective sentiments were attached, sentiments which 'speak to us from a higher level and [which] by reason of their origin . . . have a force and an ascendancy peculiarly their own'[39] (witness the socially determined 'sacredness with which the human being is now invested'[40]).

This argument is a typical instance of Durkheim's characteristic mode of argument by elimination: he sought to prove his definition of morality was correct by eliminating its competitors – having laid down the rules of the competition. Moreover the conclusion he drew from it relied on a confusion between various different relations between 'society' and 'morality'.[41] He failed altogether to see that there were a

---

35. ibid., p. 53: tr. p. 37. Thus society 'is at once the source and the guardian of civilization, the channel by which it reaches us . . . a reality from which everything that matters to us flows . . .' (ibid., p. 78: tr. p. 54).

36. ibid., p. 80: tr. p. 56 (S.L.).

37. ibid., p. 82: tr. p. 57 (S.L.).

38. ibid.

39. ibid., p. 84: tr. p. 58.

40. ibid.

41. It relies, among other things, on a confusion between 'end', 'objective' or 'object'; 'interest'; 'motive'; 'ideal'; 'precondition'; and 'cause'.

number of importantly different relations involved here. We have already cited Morris Ginsberg's observation that 'in general, "la société" had an intoxicating effect on his mind',[42] hindering further analysis. This confusion is a good example, though one might plausibly argue that it was a fertile confusion, leading Durkheim to insights he might not otherwise have attained.

He believed he had discovered in society 'the end and the source of morality'.[43] This statement, and the whole course of his argument, here and elsewhere, imply at least five distinct ways of relating the 'social' and the 'moral'. Durkheim can be seen as advancing

(i) a definition of 'moral' according to which an action is moral if and only if it is aimed at a *social* or impersonal, rather than individual or personal, *end* or *object* or *interest* – more specifically, at securing the *common good*, rather than the good of a particular individual or individuals[44];

(ii) a definition of 'moral' according to which an action is moral if and only if it is *motivated* by *social*, or altruistic, *sentiments*, rather than egoistic ones[45];

(iii) a definition of 'moral' according to which an action is moral if and only if it is *socially prescribed* and/or in accordance with a society's *ideals* and *values*[46];

42. Ginsberg, 1951 (1956), p. 51, cited in the Introduction, above.
43. 1924a (1951 edn), p. 84: tr. 1953b, p. 59 (S.L.).
44. When actions have a moral value, 'they are oriented towards a higher end than the individual himself or other individuals' (ibid., p. 73: tr. p. 51); 'Man ... acts morally only when he takes a collectivity as the goal of his conduct' (1925a, p. 294: tr. 1961a, p. 256 – S.L.). 'To act morally is to act with a view to a collective interest' (ibid., p. 68: tr. p. 59 – S.L.).
45. 'Sensibility ... inclines us towards ends that are individual, egoistic, irrational, immoral' (ibid., p. 128: tr. p. 112 – S.L.); 'The basis of the moral life is the sentiment that man does not belong to himself alone ...' (1938a, 2, p. 54).
46. Thus, when 'the ideal of society is a particular form of the human ideal, when the model of the citizen is in large part identical with the generic model of man, it is to men as such that we find ourselves attached. This is what accounts for the moral character attributed to sentiments of sympathy between individuals, and to the actions which they inspire' (1924a (1951 edn), p. 76: tr. 1953b, p. 53 – S.L.).

(iv) the claim that society, or rather a *social context*, is a pre-condition for the existence of morality. This claim could be either

(a) philosophical, or conceptual – i.e.: 'we could not make sense of morality unless . . .'[47]; or

(b) empirical – i.e.: 'certain initial conditions must exist if . . .'[48];

(v) the empirical hypothesis that adherence to particular moral codes,[49] involving deference to a particular moral authority[50] and the attribution of particular moral values,[51] is socially determined; and, as a corollary, the methodological precept that it can be sociologically explained.[52]

---

47. 'Morality begins with life in the group, since it is only there that disinterestedness and devotion become meaningful' (ibid., p. 74: tr. p. 54); 'Let all social life disappear, and moral life will disappear with it, since it would no longer have any objective . . . Morality, in all its forms, is never met with except in society' (1902b, pp. 394–5: tr. 1933b, p. 399).

48. 'Society is the field of an intense intellectual and moral life with a wide range of influence. From the actions and reactions between its individuals arises an entirely new mental life which lifts our minds into a world of which we could have not the faintest idea had we lived in isolation' (1924a (1951 edn), p. 85: tr. 1953b, p. 59).

49. 'Up to the present I have not found in my researches a single moral rule that is not the product of particular social factors . . . all moral systems practised by peoples are a function of the social organization of these peoples, are bound to their social structures and vary with them . . . Individual morality . . . does not escape this law, for it is social to the highest degree. What it makes us try to realize is the ideal man as the society conceives him, and each society conceives the ideal in its own image' (ibid., pp. 56–7: tr. p. 81).

50. 'society . . . by manifesting itself in certain precepts particularly important to it, confers upon them an obligatory character' (ibid., p. 53: tr. p. 38).

51. '. . . the human being is becoming the primary focus for the social conscience of European peoples and has acquired an incomparable value. It is society that has consecrated him' (ibid., p. 84: tr. p. 58 – S.L.).

52. 'The diversity of individual moral consciences shows how impossible it is to make use of them to arrive at an understanding of morality itself. Research into the conditions that determine these individual variations would no doubt be an interesting psychological study, but would not help us to reach our particular goal' (ibid., p. 57: tr. p. 40); '. . . it is in their social form that [moral facts] must above all attract scientific research . . .' (1920a, p. 97).

It was the fifth of these connections between morality and society that was potentially the most fruitful, and it was here that Durkheim's ideas gradually evolved. In the earlier part of his career, though morality was always the 'centre and end of his work',[53] he tended to see it primarily as a system of constraining rules, as a kind of informal analogue to law – 'a system of rules of action that predetermine conduct . . . so many moulds, with given structures, which serve to shape our behaviour'.[54] Even in 1907 he was writing that the sociology of morality must begin by studying 'rules of conduct, the judgements which imperatively enunciate the way in which the members of a given social group must behave in the different circumstances of life',[55] and must subsequently seek the causes on which they depend. But the focus of his attention was gradually shifting from the obligatory to the 'desirability' aspect of morality, and from the rules people follow to the moral beliefs expressed by the rules. Largely as a result of his preoccupation with religion, he became more and more interested in the sphere of beliefs and ideals, and in the sociological explanation of the attribution of moral values.

Already in 1906 he characterized society as 'above all a composition of ideas, beliefs and sentiments of all sorts which realize themselves through individuals. Foremost of these ideas is the moral ideal which is its principal *raison d'être*.'[56] Pursuing the analogy between the moral and the sacred, he postulated the existence of incommensurable secular values, a 'separate world of *sui generis représentations*', endowing certain things and ways of acting with a 'sacred quality which effects a solution of continuity between morality and economic and industrial techniques, etc. . . .'[57] The ideal, he liked to say, was part of the real world and could be studied as such.[58] In

53. Davy, 1920, p. 71; see Chapter 4, above.

54. 1925a, pp. 27, 30: tr. 1961a, pp. 24, 26 (S.L.); see Chapter 6, above. Cf., especially, *The Division of Labour*.

55. 1907a (10), p. 386. Cf.: 'Morality appears everywhere to the observer as a code of duties . . . the idea of duty expresses its fundamental characteristic . . .' (1906a (11), p. 325).

56. 1924a (1951 edn), p. 85: tr. 1953b, p. 59.

57. ibid., p. 104: tr. p. 71.

58. See Appendix D (2) in Lukes, 1968b.

'Value Judgements and Judgements of Reality'[59] he described values as '*sui generis* realities'[60] corresponding to 'ideals' which were 'essentially dynamic, for behind them are . . . collective forces – that is, natural but at the same time moral forces . . . The ideal itself is a force of this type and therefore subject to scientific investigation.'[61]

He took two further steps along this road in his last work, the unfinished introduction to *La Morale*. In the first place, he began to draw out the connections between the sociology of morality and the sociology of knowledge, arguing that 'the manner in which man situates himself in the world, the way in which he conceives his relations with other beings and with his fellows varies according to the conditions of time and place. Now, the moral ideal is always strictly dependent upon the conception that men have of themselves and of their place in the universe.'[62] Secondly, he made a new distinction, between '*morale*' and '*mœurs*', which amounted to that between ideals, values and norms, on the one hand, and practices, or rule-governed behaviour, on the other. His last theoretical statement on the sociology of morality was the announcement of a firm, anti-behaviourist predilection for the study of the former:

Doubtless the morality (*morale*] of the time is to be found in social practices (*mœurs*), but in a degraded form, reduced to the level of human mediocrity. What they express is the way in which the average man applies moral rules, and he never applies them without compromising and making reservations. The motives on which he acts are mixed: some are noble and pure, but others are vulgar and base. Contrary to this, the science whose scope we are outlining, seeks to attain moral precepts in their purity and their impersonality. It has as its subject-matter morality itself, ideal morality, over and above human behaviour, not the deformations it undergoes in being incarnated in current practices which can express it only imperfectly. How it is to confront this subject-matter is something we will have to consider. However, it should be appropriately named, and we therefore propose to call it the 'science of morality' or

59. 1911b.
60. ibid.: repr. in 1924a (1951 edn), p. 119: tr. 1953b, p. 81.
61. ibid., p. 136: tr. p. 93.
62. 1920a, p. 89.

'science of moral facts', meaning by this that it treats of moral phenomena, of moral reality, as it appears to observation, whether in the present or in the past, just as physics or physiology treat their data . . .[63]

EXPLANATION

Durkheim never abandoned this intransigently positivist (or, as he preferred to say, rationalist) position. Morality was a subject for science, a 'system of realized facts',[64] indeed (as he increasingly came to describe it) 'a system of forces, not physical forces, certainly, but mental, moral forces, forces which draw all their power of action from *représentations*, from states of mind (*états de conscience*)'.[65] He always saw morality as essentially social, as opposed to individual (that is, organically based, personal, spontaneous, private and egoistic), as irreducibly dual,[66] and as set apart from the rest of life. What gradually changed was the focus of his interest, moving from the study of constraining and obligatory rules or norms to the ideals and values, and the beliefs, underlying them.

One can only guess at the use to which Durkheim would have put his conceptual scheme in his projected science of morality.[67] It is most likely that, while continuing his work on such areas as the family, property and contract, he would have given much attention to the sociological explanation of both the genesis and the functioning of moral ideals. He would probably have attempted the former along two separate lines: first, by seeking the long-term origins and historical development of a set of beliefs (as in his tracing of the respect for the

63. ibid., p. 96. According to Mauss, in Durkheim's last lecture-courses on the subject in 1915 and 1916, 'The principal ideas of the *Morale Générale*, those concerning the relations between the average, the normal and the ideal had been . . . clarified in lectures to which he . . . attached much importance' (Mauss, 1925a, p. 9).

64. 1902b, p. xli: tr. 1933b, p. 35.

65. 1910b, p. 60. Cf. Lukes, 1968b, Appendix D (1): 'The ideal is a system of forces, which can be studied and made the object of a science.'

66. Cf. the rule of method recommended in his 1908–9 lectures: 'One must explain the two aspects of each moral rule' (Lukes, 1968b, Appendix D (2)).

67. For the plan drawn up in 1908–9, see Lukes, 1968b, Appendix D (2).

human person and the sacrilegious character of homicide to the notion of the soul and the derivation of this latter from totemic beliefs gradually becoming individualized)[68]; and second, by looking for those 'moments of effervescence', those 'periods of creation and renewal' when 'men are brought into more intimate relations with one another, when meetings and assemblies are more frequent, relationships more solid and the exchange of ideas more active'.[69] As examples of such creative moments, Durkheim cited 'the great crisis of Christendom, the movement of collective enthusiasm which, in the twelfth and thirteenth centuries, bringing together in Paris the scholars of Europe, gave birth to Scholasticism ... the Reformation and Renaissance, the Revolutionary period and the great Socialist upheavals of the nineteenth century'.[70] The explanation he offered here was in terms of what one might call collective psychology. At such moments there is an intense and exclusive mental exaltation, eliminating all egoistic and commonplace concerns, when men believe that 'the time is close when the ideal will be realized and the Kingdom of God established on earth'.[71] Then the crisis passes and social life returns to its ordinary level; 'all that has been said, done, thought and felt during the period of fertile upheaval survives only as a memory ... an idea, a set of ideas',[72] that is, as ideals, distinct from ordinary experience. These, to survive, must be periodically revived by means of 'festivities and public ceremonies, whether religious or secular, by oratory and preaching of all kinds, in the Church or in the schools, by dramatic representations, artistic displays – in a word, everything that brings men together and makes them communicate in the same intellectual and moral life'.[73] But such revivals are only partial and have only a temporary effect.

As to the study of the functioning or operation of moral

68. See ibid., Appendix D (1). Cf. the discussions of homicide, property and contract in 1950a: tr. 1957a (see Chapter 13, above).

69. 1924a (1951 edn), p. 134: tr. 1953b, p. 91 (S.L.).

70. ibid., p. 134: tr. pp. 91–2 (S.L.).

71. ibid.: tr. p. 92.

72. ibid., pp. 134–5: tr. p. 92 (S.L.).

73. ibid., p. 135: tr. p. 92 (S.L.).

ideals, there are a number of clues which suggest what kind of investigation Durkheim might have undertaken. In the first place, he continued to see value in the study of statistical rates as indices, albeit crude and approximate, of collective beliefs and sentiments.[74] Secondly, he spoke of the importance of consulting 'popular beliefs' and observing people's reactions when such beliefs were contravened in practice.[75] There were

a considerable number of moral ideas and maxims that are easily accessible: those that are written down, condensed in legal formulas. In law the greater part of domestic morality, contractual morality, the morality of obligations, all the ideas relating to the great fundamental duties are expressed and reflected ... When we have broken this new ground we will pass on to another ... Proverbs, popular maxims and non-codified customs are no less sources of information. Literary works, the conceptions of philosophers and moralists ... direct our attention to aspirations that are only in the process of becoming conscious, enabling us to go more deeply into the analysis of the common *conscience*, to reach those depths where these obscure and still half-conscious currents are elaborated.[76]

Such data would enable one to 'cut broad avenues that may bring in some light to this virgin forest of moral and, more generally, social facts'.[77]

Thirdly, Durkheim began to develop a theory of symbolism, which has a markedly modern ring. Collective ideals, he argued, 'can only become manifest and conscious by being concretely realized in objects that can be seen by all, understood by all and represented to all minds: figurative designs, emblems of all kinds, written or spoken formulas, animate or inanimate objects'.[78] The actual objects serving as such symbols came to do so as the result of 'all sorts of contingent

74. See ibid., pp. 130–31: tr. p. 89: '[The sentiment of respect for human dignity] is at the root of the moral ideal of contemporary societies. Now, as it is more or less intense, the number of criminal assaults against the person is low or high. Likewise, the number of adulteries, divorces and separations expresses the relative force with which the conjugal ideal makes itself felt.' Cf. Lukes, 1968b, Appendix D (2).

75. See Lukes, 1968b, Appendix D (1).

76. 1924a (1951 edn); p. 114: tr. 1953b, p. 77 (S.L.).

77. ibid.

78. ibid., pp. 137–8: tr. p. 94 (S.L.).

circumstances' but, once selected, they acquired a unique prestige: thus 'a rag of cloth becomes invested with sanctity and a tiny piece of paper can become a very precious thing'.[79] In his lectures Durkheim offered a preliminary list of such symbols: things (emblems), places (e.g. in pilgrimages), days and dates (e.g. anniversaries and religious and national holidays), words (e.g. political formulas – such formulas being 'impersonal, rhythmic and imperative'), and men (not only great men, but also, e.g., priests and magistrates – the 'functionaries of society'). He remarked on the considerable role of emblems in 'religious moral life', observing that the fact that the flag was virtually the only emblem in modern secular life was an indication that the latter was undergoing a period of transition and crisis. Likewise, the absence of public festivities (*fêtes*) showed that 'we have not established a new ideal'.[80]

The most modern and suggestive aspect of these ideas is to be found in Durkheim's speculation on the general significance of such symbolism:

In this way collective thought transforms everything it touches. It fuses natural orders and combines contraries; it reverses what one might regard as the natural hierarchy of being, it eliminates differences and differentiates between what is similar. In a word, it substitutes for the world revealed to us by the senses, a quite different world which is nothing other than the projection of the ideals it constructs.[81]

EVALUATION

Durkheim never abandoned his explicit concern to derive value judgements from the scientific study of morality, though he was equally concerned to avoid the contamination of the latter by such judgements; indeed, he saw its pursuit as rigorously separated from 'art', but a rational art could then

79. ibid., p. 138: tr. p. 94 (S.L.).

80. Appendix D (1) and (2) in Lukes, 1968b.

81. 1924a (1951 edn), p. 138: tr. 1953b, pp. 94–5 (S.L.). Cf. the more recent writings of Claude Lévi-Strauss, especially Lévi-Strauss, 1962a and b.

be derived from science. Like Lucien Lévy-Bruhl, he believed in the 'necessity of clearly separating, in all speculation relative to morals, science and the practical applications that can be made of it'.[82] In order that 'we should be in a position, not merely to gain a scientific understanding, but to make an objective evaluation of moral practices, we must have considered them in an entirely free spirit'.[83] On the other hand his 'constant preoccupation' was that sociology 'might have practical results'.[84] As he wrote in reply to a critic,

We wonder . . . how anyone could think that we refuse to evaluate the morality of our contemporaries, when the first work of any importance that we published had precisely as its declared object the making of an evaluation of this kind.[85]

In the sphere of morality as elsewhere, 'the science of reality puts us in a position to modify what exists and to control it'. Thus, the 'science of moral opinion provides us with the means to evaluate moral opinion and, where necessary, to rectify it'.[86]

What kind of evaluations did Durkheim believe could be derived from the sociology of morality? He was clear that the latter afforded no basis for judging *between* societies, no general criterion, no 'formula for the universal moral ideal'[87]: the 'anarchist will prefer pure diversity; the authoritarian absolute unity. Rousseau preferred small societies where a strong moral

---

82. 1906a (11), p. 325. Cf. Lévy-Bruhl, 1903; and Durkheim, 1904a (5).

83. 1907a (3,4,5), p. 355. Cf. 'The role of sociology . . . must properly consist in emancipating us from all parties, not so much by opposing a doctrine to other doctrines, but by enabling the mind to acquire, in relation to these [practical] questions, a special attitude that science alone can provide through its direct contact with realities' (1901c, p. 175: tr. 1938b, p. 143 – S.L.).

84. 1901c, p. 174: tr. p. 143.

85. 1907a (3,4,5), p. 355. Durkheim here goes on to observe that 'in *The Division of Labour*, we evaluate the old ideal of humanist morality, the moral ideal of the cultivated man, we show how it can be regarded today as increasingly anachronistic, how a new ideal is forming and developing as the result of the increasing specialization of social functions' (ibid., fn.).

86. 1924a (1951 edn), p. 86: tr. 1953b, p. 60.

87. 1906a (10), p. 324.

homogeneity prevented individual dissent; how could one show him to be wrong?'[88] On the other hand, only the sociology of morality 'can help us in solving these practical problems'.[89] How? Durkheim's answer is very revealing:

Each moral institution must be studied separately, in its genesis and in its functioning, in its relations with the environment; and it is in accordance with its past that we can conjecture its future.[90]

In other words, Durkheim believed that, in the last analysis, evaluation was strictly determined by explanation; that, in any given situation, only one set of moral judgements was rationally possible in face of a fully scientific understanding of the present and foreseeable future: 'it is never possible to desire a morality other than that required by the social conditions of a given time. To wish for a morality other than that implied in the nature of society is to deny the latter and, consequently, oneself.'[91] He recognized an ultimate value premise here, which he did not think needed to be discussed: that 'we are right in wishing to live'.[92] This was to imply that only one set of moral judgements was consistent with social and consequently individual, survival. Thus Durkheim could write of the 'state of society' as providing 'an objective standard to which our evaluations must always be brought back'.[93] The sociologist could do no more than 'enlighten [society] about the value, the true significance of the needs it experiences'.[94]

88. ibid.
89. ibid.
90. ibid.
91. 1924a (1951 edn), p. 54: tr. 1953b, p. 38 (S.L.). Cf.: 'Our whole thesis can be summarized as follows: in order to be able to determine what morality should be at a given point in time, one must first know what morality is, how to distinguish what is moral from what is not, and one cannot answer that question unless one has previously studied moral phenomena in themselves and for themselves. We cannot choose a criterion by an act of decision: we can only observe it and derive it from the facts' (1913a (ii) (15), p. 327).
92. ibid. On this point, see Cuvillier, 1955, p. 17.
93. ibid., p. 88: tr. p. 61 (S.L.).
94. 1907a (3,4,5), p. 368. Cf.: '... the role of reflexion has always more or less consisted in helping contemporaries to become aware of themselves, their needs and their sentiments. The science of morality, as I understand

Perhaps it was because of the all-purpose relationship that he sought to establish between society and morality that Durkheim could suppose that this position followed inexorably from a sociological view of morality. To support it, he argued that the 'reason' employed in making such evaluations was not individual and personal, but relied on 'knowledge, as methodically elaborated as possible, of ... social reality. Morality depends on society, not on the individual.'[95] Instead of merely arguing that rational evaluation must be based on adequate knowledge[96] and that in any given situation certain possibilities of change can in the light of such knowledge be precluded,[97] he concluded that scientific knowledge would show there to be only one possible path of development and that, consequently, no other could rationally be preferred.[98]

Yet this arch-historicist and deterministic position does not adequately characterize Durkheim's thought, and even less his practice: he found a number of ways of avoiding its implications. In the first place, he argued that the nascent science of morality was not yet 'in a condition to act as the sovereign guide of conduct'; in the meantime, one must make '*reasoned evaluations*' on as informed and scientific a basis as possible.[99] Secondly, he freely interpreted his position in such a way as to allow for the possibility of *critical* value judgements of a reformist, even radical character. He explicitly acknowledged two main possibilities. First, it could happen that, 'under the influence of passing circumstances, certain principles that are even essential to the existing morality, should be for a time

---

it, is only a more methodical application of reflection put to the service of the same end' (1924a (1951 edn), p. 93: tr. p. 64 – S.L.).

95. 1924a (1951 edn), p. 88: tr. p. 81 (S.L.).

96. 'in order to ratiocinate about morality, one must first know what it is, and ... to know what it is, one must observe it' (1907a (3,4,5), p. 368).

97. 'There can be no question of assigning ends to a society that are quite alien to it, of which it has no idea, and for which it feels no need' (ibid.).

98. '... how can one choose between the diverse tendencies active [in a society], and decide which are well-founded (*fondées*) and which are not, except by taking as a guide-line the nature of that society?' (ibid.).

99. 1924a (1951 edn), p. 89: tr. 1953b, p. 62.

rejected into the unconscious and be, thenceforth, as though they did not exist'.[1] The sociologist could then, by contrasting their previous permanence with their present absence, cast 'rational doubts' on the legitimacy of their denial; and he could further seek to show their relation to the 'essential and ever-present conditions of our social organization and our collective mentality'.[2] Secondly, new tendencies emerged out of the existing moral order and the '*science des mœurs*' enabled the sociologist to opt for those which were 'in relation with changes that have occurred within the conditions of collective existence and required by those changes'.[3] It could therefore happen that 'we judge it our duty to combat moral ideas that we know to be out of date and nothing more than survivals, and that the most effective way of doing this may appear to be the denial of these ideas, not only theoretically, but also in action'.[4]

Of course, the crucial difficulty here was that of determining which tendencies and ideas were 'essential' to a given social and cultural system and, again, which were 'required' by changing conditions. The assumption that there were, in principle, unique and scientifically ascertainable answers to these questions never seems to have caused Durkheim any intellectual discomfort; and it never occurred to him to doubt that such answers were all that was ultimately needed for the solution of 'practical' moral questions.[5]

He therefore never felt the need to ask the question: how can we justify adhering (or not adhering) to the single morality

1. ibid., p. 54: tr. p. 38 (S.L.).

2. ibid., pp. 86, 87: tr. p. 60 (S.L.). As an example, Durkheim cites society's losing sight of 'the sacred rights of the individual' (ibid.). He appealed to this argument during the Dreyfus Affair (see 1898c and Chapter 17, above).

3. ibid., p. 87: tr. p. 61 (S.L.).

4. ibid., p. 88: tr. p. 61 (S.L.). This, in Durkheim's view was the historical role of Christ and Socrates: see 1901c, p. 88: tr. 1938b, p. 71; 1924a (1951 edn), pp. 93–4: tr. pp. 64–5; 1925a, pp. 60–61, 103: tr. 1961a, pp. 53, 90.

5. But see 1938a, I, pp. 197–8, for the hint of a doubt whether science will ever be able to banish controversy over legal, moral and political questions.

allegedly determined and required by society (other than to suggest that the answer lay in the desire to live)? A similar difficulty arises in the thought of Lévy-Bruhl, who argued, in parallel fashion, that morality could become a 'rational art', 'comparable to mechanics and medicine', which would 'use the knowledge of sociological and psychological laws for the amelioration of existing practices and institutions'.[6] There is a crucial passage in Lévy-Bruhl's book, where he asks himself the question: 'Ameliorate, you say? But what sense can this term have in a doctrine such as yours?'[7] His answer is simple:

the sociologist can ascertain in current social reality such and such an 'imperfection', without thereby having recourse to any principle independent of experience. It is enough for him to show that a given belief, for instance, or a given institution is out of date, obsolete and that they are true *impedimenta* to social life. M. Durkheim has made this point perfectly clear.[8]

It eventually turns out that 'amelioration' for Lévy-Bruhl involves the elimination of 'useless, barbaric and injurious practices, and the inhuman sentiments associated with them'.[9] A humane, liberal ethic was assumed to be built into 'current social reality'.

Durkheim enthusiastically endorsed Lévy-Bruhl's book and its arguments,[10] and for a long time he offered an account very similar to Lévy-Bruhl's of the application of the science of morality. In the *Introduction à la morale*, however, the ground shifts slightly. The applied sciences, he argued,

take [their] ends as given, assume that men attach value to them, and are solely concerned with the most suitable and effective techniques of attaining them. It is different with morality. Morality consists, above all, in proposing ends; it prescribes to man the goals he should pursue, and, in this respect, is distinct from the applied sciences properly so called.[11]

6. Lévy-Bruhl, 1903 (1953 edn), p. 256.
7. ibid., p. 272.
8. ibid., p. 273.
9. ibid., p. 291.
10. 1904a (5).
11. 1920a, p. 85. He can be seen to be moving towards this position in the Sorbonne lectures (Lukes, 1968b, Appendix D (2)), where he

But he never drew from this the conclusion that the choice of ends might itself be problematic and beyond the reach of science.[12]

In 1900 Durkheim reviewed an article about the relation between the science and practice of morality, which he criticized in terms that can be applied precisely to his own ideas on this subject. The solution offered by the author to 'the great difficulty of the problem' was, he wrote, 'rather too summary':

How should one establish the standard according to which these [reforms of the functioning of morality] will be carried out? Can one take the prevailing morality to fulfil this role? Yes, in general; but it is never all that it should be. It therefore must itself be reformed at certain points. But the author does not make clear how these points are to be identified and according to what standard the reforms are to be made. He is content to invoke the principle of adaptation to social needs. But which are normal needs and which are not, and when are the former at normal intensity?[13]

This was indeed the great difficulty of the problem. By assuming that the needs of society could ultimately be specified by scientific inquiry alone, and that adaptation to them required no further justification (other than the 'desire to live'), Durkheim failed to confront it – and, therefore, to see the crucial role of evaluation within the structure of his own thought.

APPLICATION TO PHILOSOPHY

Durkheim attempted to use his account of morality to solve some fundamental questions of moral philosophy – the nature of value judgements, the autonomy of morals and the dualism of human nature. This attempt relied on the ambiguous relationship he posited between the 'moral' and the 'social'.

In 'Value Judgements and Judgements of Reality', he aimed 'to show by a specific example how sociology can help to

---

argues that morality is more analogous to 'therapeutics, hygiene and medicine', because these are related to 'theoretical sciences that have the object of determining what is health: normal and pathological physiology'.

12. Contrast Max Weber's absolutely opposite position.

13. 1900a (7).

resolve a problem of philosophy'.[14] The problem was no less than to offer an explanation of evaluation, to 'understand how value judgements are possible'[15] (and by this he chiefly meant moral judgements). After dismissing various forms of utilitarianism (for failing to account for the content of actual, especially moral, judgements) and philosophical idealism and 'the theological hypothesis' (for postulating trans-empirical ideals which themselves required explanation, and for failing to account for the diversity of moralities), Durkheim argued that it was 'not enough to postulate a certain number of ideals; they must themselves be accounted for, by showing where they come from, how they relate to experience while transcending it, and the nature of their objectivity'.[16] By suggesting 'society' as the solution, he was, without realizing it, appealing to all the relations between society and morality distinguished above. Thus, value (and, in particular, moral) judgements are 'transcendent' and 'objective' with respect to an individual insofar as they are defined as 'social' in ways (i) – (iii) (especially (iii)). They are made 'possible' by society insofar as a social context can be shown to be a pre-condition for morality ((iv)). Finally, they 'come from' society and relate to 'social' experience insofar as their content and adherence to them can be shown to be socially determined ((v)).

Such arguments are of interest, but they do not amount to the solution of the philosophical problem of the nature of evaluation and the justification of moral judgements. Definitions (i) – (iii) are simply (different) stipulative definitions of 'moral', in themselves neither valid nor invalid, and fitting some empirical cases better than others. The argument relying on relation (iv) (in both its forms) is plausible and interesting, but, at the most, it proves only what it claims to prove. As to the hypothesis of (v), this is a fruitful basis for empirical inquiry, but not the solution to a philosophical problem.

As to the autonomy of morals, Durkheim added to the Kantian notion of obligation the idea of essentially social moral goals, according to definitions (i) – (iii). In relating the

14. 1911b: repr. 1924a (1951 edn), p. 117: tr. 1953b, p. 80.
15. ibid.
16. ibid.

latter to the notion of 'sacredness', he thereby (perhaps deliberately) failed clearly to distinguish morality from religion, but he hoped that he had distinguished it from other areas of judgement and activity (for instance, from 'economic and industrial techniques, etc.'[17]). Unfortunately, the arbitrariness and indiscriminateness of the definitions (and his failure to distinguish between them) renders his attempt to account for the autonomy of morals a good deal less than plausible. In any case, this could hardly be achieved by definitions alone. On the other hand, his analysis of the relations between moral rules, ideals and values and the hypothesis of their social determination ((v)) remain useful, as a basis for empirical inquiry, as does his hypothesis that morality is *sui generis*, forming 'a distinct sphere of social life'.[18] It would indeed be of great interest to discover whether 'this word "moral", which is found in various forms in all languages, connotes phenomena that are distinct from all other human phenomena in virtue of definite and homogeneous characteristics'.[19]

In seeking to account for the 'dualism of human nature', Durkheim discussed a basic theme of philosophy and religion.[20] For many philosophers, man was essentially double, split, as Pascal said, between 'angel and beast', between mind and body, reason and sensation; and in religious thought, the opposition of soul and body represented a particular case of

17. ibid., p. 104: tr. p. 70.

18. ibid., p. 105: tr. p. 72 (S.L.).

19. 1920a, p. 93. It is astonishing how little attention has been given to such questions in twentieth-century sociology and social anthropology. Indeed, it is not an exaggeration to say that the sociology of morality is the great void in contemporary social science (though the current growth of interest in deviance is highly relevant to it). Among the very few contemporary studies in this (largely untilled) field, see Ladd, 1957, Brandt, R. B., *Hopi Ethics* (Chicago, 1954), Fürer-Haimendorf, C. von, *Morals and Merit* (London, 1967), and Ossowska, Maria, *Social Determinants of Moral Ideas* (London, 1971). (It is interesting to note that Professor Ossowska, who has worked extensively in this field but most of whose writings are available only in Polish, was in direct contact with the Durkheimians in Paris in the early 1920s.) A very valuable bibliography of works on the sociology of morality appeared in the *Cahiers internationaux de sociologie*, XXXVI (1964), pp. 133–84.

20. See 1914a: tr. 1960c, pp. 325–40. Cf. 1913b and Introduction, above.

that between the sacred and the profane. For Durkheim, this traditional theme expressed a real 'constitutional duality'[21] within the individual 'at the very heart of [his] inner life',[22] a 'double existence ... the one purely individual and rooted in our organisms, the other social and nothing but an extension of society'.[23] In identifying the former with 'sensations and the sensual appetites' and the latter with 'the intellectual and moral life',[24] he was in part relying on definitions (i) – (iii) (especially (ii)) of 'moral', arguing that conceptual thought and moral activity 'by definition [*sic*] ... pursue impersonal ends'.[25] Thus, 'Morality begins with disinterest, with attachment to something other than ourselves', as opposed to the 'sensual appetites' which were 'necessarily egoistic'.[26] So far, this is simply to restate three different (and arguable) definitions of morality. However, Durkheim's account of the duality of human nature can also be read as the assertion in a bold form of the empirical hypothesis (v) concerning the (unique) social determination of moral beliefs and behaviour (as well as of concepts and categories).

Durkheim deepened and extended that hypothesis, towards the end of his life, in a way that is sharply reminiscent of the thought of the later Freud.[27] He argued that the 'painful character of the dualism of human nature is explained by this hypothesis',[28] that there is in man a permanent tension between the demands of social life and those of his individual, organic nature, a tension which will increase with the advance of civilization: for society's

requirements are quite different from those of our nature as individuals ... Therefore, society cannot be formed or maintained

21. ibid., p. 326.

22. ibid.

23. ibid., p. 337. 'The old formula *homo duplex* is therefore verified by the facts' (ibid., p. 328).

24. ibid., p. 338.

25. ibid., p. 327.

26. ibid.

27. Cf., especially, *Civilisation and Its Discontents* (London and New York, 1930, 8th impression 1957). There is no evidence that Durkheim knew of Freud's work.

28. 1960c, p. 338.

without our being required to make perpetual and costly sacrifices ...
We must ... do violence to certain of our strongest inclinations.
Therefore, since the role of the social being in our single selves will
grow ever more important as history moves ahead, it is wholly
improbable that there will ever be an era in which man is required
to resist himself to a lesser degree, an era in which he can live a life
that is easier and less full of tension. To the contrary, all evidence
compels us to expect our effort in the struggle between the two
beings within us to increase with the growth of civilization.[29]

29. ibid., pp. 338–9. Cf. Freud: 'Culture has to call up every possible
reinforcement in order to erect barriers against the aggressive instincts of
men and hold their manifestations in check by reaction formations in
men's minds'; 'The fateful question of the human species seems to me to
be whether and to what extent the cultural process developed in it will
succeed in mastering the derangements of communal life caused by the
human instinct of aggression and self-destruction' (op. cit., pp. 86,
143–4).

Chapter 22

The Sociology of Knowledge

DURKHEIM'S conception of human nature as dual involved, as we have seen, two parallel oppositions: between sensual appetites and moral rules, and between sensations and concepts. The Kantian nature of this conception is unmistakable and corresponded to the predominant philosophical ideas of the time, which he had absorbed, first through the major formative influence of Renouvier,[1] and later from the more specifically epistemological thinking of Hamelin.[2] However, in epistemology as in ethics, he found the Kantian and neo-Kantian solutions unsatisfactory because question-begging. If Humean empiricism could not account for the function of classification and 'what philosophers since Aristotle have called the categories of the understanding: ideas of time, space, class, number, cause, substance, personality, etc.',[3] Kantian apriorism, while recognizing the mind's power to organize the data of immediate experience, could not explain it, for 'it is no explanation to say that it is inherent in the nature of the human intellect'.[4] Classical empiricism sought to

1. See Chapter 2, above. As Bouglé observed, 'Kantianism, through the intermediary of Renouvier, was as if reawakened in France after 1870', and a kind of idealist rationalism, combining the influences of Kant and Descartes, prevailed, in various forms, between 1880 and 1920 (Bouglé, 1938, pp. 53, 54).

2. See especially *Essai sur les éléments principaux de la représentation* (Paris, 1907).

3. 1912a, pp. 12–13: tr. 1915d, p. 9. Following Hamelin (op. cit.), Durkheim did not accept the Kantian distinction between the forms of intuition (*Anschauungen*) and the categories; he called all these ideas 'categories', arguing that they played the same role in intellectual life. In particular, he accepted Hamelin's argument (op. cit., pp. 75 ff.) that space was not, as Kant thought, indeterminate and homogeneous but was 'divided and differentiated' (1912a, p. 16: tr. p. 11).

4. ibid., p. 20: tr. p. 14. Moreover, postulating a transcendent divine reason (as Hamelin did: see op. cit., 2nd edn, 1925, p. 348) was not only

dissolve reason into individual experience; apriorism placed it outside nature and science. The solution lay in restating the old epistemological questions in sociological terms. The 'genesis, and consequently the functioning, of logical operations'[5] could then be related to social conditions and the categories could be considered as 'essentially collective *représentations*', which 'depend upon the way in which [the group] is founded and organized, upon its morphology, upon its religious, moral and economic institutions, etc.'.[6] A 'sociological theory of knowledge' could, Durkheim believed, unite the opposing advantages of the two rival philosophical theories: it 'leaves the reason its specific power, but it accounts for it and does so without leaving the world of observable phenomena'.[7]

In fact, Durkheim's sociology of knowledge[8] advanced six different claims which he did not constantly and clearly distinguish one from another. In so far as he did distinguish them, he none the less assumed, mistakenly, that they were logically related, and that arguments and evidence in favour of one therefore lent support to others.

THE CLAIMS ADVANCED

The first was the claim that 'concepts are collective *représentations*'.[9] In part, this can be seen as equivalent to the simple but

unscientific; it failed to account for the 'incessant variability' of the categories in different places and times (ibid., p. 21: tr. p. 15).

5. 1903a (i), p. 72: tr. 1963b, p. 88.
6. 1912a, p. 22: tr. 1915d, pp. 15–16.
7. ibid., p. 27: tr. p. 19.
8. This is to be found in 1903a(i): tr. 1963b, and 1912a, pp. 12–28, 203–22, 290–2, 336–42, 386–90, 459–64, 508–28, 616–35: tr. 1915d, pp. 9–20, 141–56, 203–4, 234–9, 269–72, 321–5, 355–69, 431–45. Cf. also 1910a (ii) (1) and (iii) (2), and 1913a (ii) (6) and (7). For discussions, see Gehlke, 1915, Schaub, 1920, Brunschvicg, 1922, Sorokin, 1928, Benoît–Smullyan, 1937 and 1948, Parsons, 1937, Worsley, 1956, and Needham, 1963; cf. also Chapter 25, below. Of course, much of Durkheim's other work, e.g. the discussions of the *conscience collective* in *The Division of Labour*, the history of education in France, and the history of socialism, can be seen as contributions in the broad sense to the sociology of knowledge.
9. 1912a, p. 621: tr. 1915d, p. 435. See especially ibid., pp. 616–27: tr. pp. 431–9. Cf. 1955a, pp. 203–5.

fertile idea, rediscovered half a century later by Wittgenstein, that concepts operate within forms of social life, according to rules. At the very least, this idea suggests that concepts are to be observed in use and as part of a wider system, but, at the philosophical level, it can easily be interpreted as leading to conventionalism and extreme relativism.[10] Durkheim met this problem by arguing that, although concepts, including the categories ('the pre-eminent concepts, which have a preponderating part in our knowledge'[11]), are imposed by social pressure on individuals, so that their authority is 'the very authority of society'[12]; although 'each civilization has its organized system of concepts which characterizes it'[13]; and although even the 'methods of scientific thought' should be seen as 'veritable social institutions'[14] – none the less, the validity of the categories and of science remained intact. Two somewhat different arguments for this conclusion can be found in his work. The first is a rather metaphysical appeal to the unity of nature, and a consequent isomorphism between thought and the world (foreshadowing both Lévi-Strauss and the early Wittgenstein of the *Tractatus*):

The social realm is a natural realm, which differs from the others only by its greater complexity. Now it is impossible that nature should differ radically from itself, in the one case and the other, in regard to its most essential features. The fundamental relations that exist between things – just that which it is the function of the categories to express – cannot be essentially dissimilar in the different realms ... If a sort of artificiality enters into them from the mere

10. Cf. the use made of Wittgenstein by P. Winch in *The Idea of a Social Science* (London, 1958) and 'Understanding a Primitive Society', *American Philosophical Quarterly*, 1 (1964), pp. 307–24. For a critique of Winch's arguments, see Lukes, 1967b and 1973.

11. 1912a, p. 628: tr. 1915d, p. 440.

12. ibid., p. 24: tr. p. 17. It is 'a special sort of moral necessity which is to the intellectual life what moral obligation is to the will' (ibid., p. 25: tr. p. 18).

13. ibid., p. 622: tr. p. 435.

14. 1903a (i), p. 2: tr. 1963b, p. 3. These were 'the work of tradition and are imposed on the [scientific] worker with an authority comparable to that with which the rules of law and morality are invested. They are veritable institutions concerning thought, just as legal and political institutions are obligatory methods of action' (1910a (iii) (2), p. 44).

fact that they are constructed concepts, it is an artificiality which follows nature very closely and which is constantly approaching it ever more closely.[15]

The second argument is an attempt to reconcile the social determination of thought with non-context-dependent criteria of rationality and truth:

If logical thought tends to rid itself more and more of the subjective and personal elements which still encumber it at its origin, it is ... because social life of a new sort is developing. It is this international life which has already resulted in universalizing religious beliefs. As it extends, the collective horizon enlarges; the society ceases to appear as the only whole, to become part of a much vaster one, with indeterminate frontiers capable of advancing indefinitely. Consequently things can no longer be contained in the social moulds according to which they were primitively classified; they demand to be organized according to principles which are their own and, therefore, logical organization becomes differentiated from social organization and becomes autonomous.[16]

On the other hand, Durkheim came to oppose Lévy-Bruhl's extreme antithesis of the pre-logical and mystical character of primitive and religious mentality to the rational procedures of modern thought[17]: they were but 'two moments of a single

15. 1912a, pp. 25–6: tr. 1915d, pp. 18–19 (S.L.). As illustrations, Durkheim cites, with respect to time, the 'rhythm of social life' and 'another in the life of the individual, and more generally in that of the universe'; likewise, there are natural classes and species, as well as human groups (ibid., fn.). Cf. 1910a (iii) (2), p. 45, where he describes society as 'the highest form of nature', adding that 'it is nature as a whole which becomes conscious of itself to the highest degree in and through society'.

16. ibid., pp. 634–5: tr. p. 445 (S.L.). Cf. 'The concept which was first held as true because it was collective tends to be no longer collective except on condition of being held as true: we demand its credentials of it before according it our confidence' (ibid., p. 624: tr. p. 437). But Worsley is right to say of *The Elementary Forms* that 'the distinction between objectivity in the sense of social authority or consensus, and objectivity as correspondence with nature counts for little in the total argument' (Worsley, 1956, p. 50).

17. See Lévy-Bruhl, 1910, and also 1922, 1927, 1931, 1935 and 1938 (but cf. Lévy-Bruhl, 1949, where Lévy-Bruhl retracts, moving closer to Durkheim's view). In *Primitive Classification*, Durkheim appears nearer to Lévy-Bruhl's conception of the 'pre-logical' and the initial confusion of the primitive mind (see 1903a(i), pp. 2–5: tr. 1963b, pp. 4–7).

evolution'.[18] Not only, Durkheim argued, were the categories 'elaborated in the very womb of religion',[19] but

> while the primitive is inclined to confusions, he is equally led to make sharp oppositions and often applies the principle of contradiction in an extreme fashion. Conversely, the law of participation is not peculiar to him: our ideas, today as formerly, participate in one another. This is the very condition of all logical thought. The difference lies above all in the way in which those participations are established.[20]

Hence,

> The explanations of contemporary science are surer of being objective because they are more methodical and because they rest on more rigorously controlled observations, but they do not differ in nature from those which satisfy primitive thought. Today, as formerly, to explain is to show how one thing participates in one or several others. It has been said [by Lévy-Bruhl] that the participations postulated by mythologies violate the principle of contradiction and are, for that reason, opposed to those implied by scientific explanations. Is not the statement that a man is a kangaroo, or that the sun is a bird, equal to identifying the two with each other? But our mode of thinking is no different when we characterize heat as movement, or light as a vibration of the ether, etc. Whenever we unite heterogeneous terms by an internal bond, we necessarily identify contraries. Of course the terms we unite in this way are not those which the Australian [aborigine] connects together; we select them according to other criteria and for other reasons; but there is no essential difference in the process by which the mind relates them.[21]

As Durkheim wrote to Lévy-Bruhl in 1909: 'There is no thought (*mentalité*) before logical thought. Is there not some positive term which would express your conception of this

18. 1913a(ii) (6,7), p. 35.

19. ibid.

20. ibid., p. 37. Lévy-Bruhl's 'law of participation' is as follows: 'In the collective *représentations* of primitive mentality, objects, beings, phenomena can, in a way that is incomprehensible to us, be at once both themselves and something other than themselves. In a manner that is no less incomprehensible, they emit and receive forces, virtues, qualities, mystical influences which are felt outside them, while remaining within them' (Lévy-Bruhl, 1910, p. 77). Cf. 1912a, 336–42: tr. 1915d, pp. 234–9.

21. 1912a, pp. 340–1: tr. p. 238 (S.L.).

thought without it being necessary to define it in relation to so-called logical thought?'[22] In short Durkheim saw clearly that there are criteria of truth and 'objective' explanation, as well as principles of logic, which are non-relative and non-context-dependent; and he further saw that these principles of logic are fundamental and universal to all cultures. As a firm rationalist, he did not succumb to the temptations of relativism. (He was to turn to this basic issue of the relation between the sociology of knowledge and the justification of canons of validity and truth in one of his last lecture-courses, on Pragmatism and Sociology, which will be considered below.[23])

Durkheim's first claim, then, was simply the heuristic idea that concepts, including the categories, are collective *représentations*, that (as opposed to sensations and images) they are 'common and communicable', that they are the means by which 'minds communicate'.[24] He drew from this idea the invalid inference that there was a causal relation between the social order and the conceptual order.[25] This constitutes his second claim. It is, however, ambiguous, since Durkheim gave different meanings to 'society'. In so far as this is *defined* in cultural terms as the *conscience collective*, consisting of ideas or *représentations* held in common,[26] it adds little to the first claim. But in so far as it refers to structural, or morphological, and institutional factors, it offers the basis for a number of bold and ambitious empirical hypotheses. Thus the central argument of *Primitive Classification* is that men 'classified things *because* they were divided by clans',[27] it was 'because men were organized that they have been able to organize things, for in classifying these latter, they limited themselves to giving them

22. 1970b, p. 164.

23. In Chapter 24. For a discussion of this issue, and of the respective positions of Durkheim and Lévy-Bruhl, see Lukes, 1971, and Horton, 1971.

24. 1913a (ii) (6, 7), p. 36.

25. 'Now a *représentation* cannot be common to all the men of a single group unless it has been elaborated in common by them, unless it is the creation (*l'œuvre*) of the community' (ibid.).

26. See especially 1911b: repr. 1924a: tr. 1953b.

27. 1903a (i), p. 67: tr. 1963b, p. 82 (my emphasis).

places in the groups they formed themselves'.[28] The categories, Durkheim argued, were 'the product of social factors'.[29] There were 'societies in Australia and North America where space is conceived in the form of an immense circle, *because* the camp has a circular form ... There are as many regions distinguished as there are clans in the tribe, and it is the place occupied by the clans inside the encampment which has *determined* the orientation of these regions'.[30] Likewise the divisions 'in relation to which all things are temporally located, are taken from social life'[31] and the category of causality 'depends upon social causes',[32] arising out of 'collective force objectified and projected into things', together with the practice of imitative rites.[33] Moreover, 'if the totality of things is conceived as a single system, this is *because* society itself is seen in the same way. It is a whole, or rather it is *the* unique whole to which everything is related.'[34] In general, 'logical life has its first source in society'.[35]

Durkheim saw this second claim – that specific classifications and conceptual orderings were caused by specific forms of society – as equivalent to a third: that these classifications and orderings were 'modelled' on, or (more precisely) structurally similar to, specific forms of society. Thus, in *Primitive Classification* it is claimed that among the Australian tribes '*the classification of things reproduces* [the] *classification of men*',[36] and that their classificatory systems, and those of the Zuñi and the Sioux,

merely express under different aspects the very societies within which they were elaborated; one was modelled on the jural and religious organization of the tribe, the other on its morphological organization ... In one case, the framework was furnished by the

28. 1912a, p. 206: tr. 1915d, p. 145.
29. ibid.
30. ibid., p. 16: tr. 1915d, pp. 11–12 (my emphases).
31. ibid., pp. 14–15: tr. p. 10.
32. ibid., p. 519: tr. p. 363.
33. ibid. et seq.
34. 1903a (i), p. 68: tr. 1963b, p. 83 (first emphasis mine).
35. 1913a (ii) (6, 7), p. 36.
36. 1903a (i), p. 8: tr. 1963b, p. 11.

clan itself, in the other by the material mark made on the ground by the clan.[37]

Durkheim took *Primitive Classification* to show that 'these classifications were modelled on the closest and most fundamental form of social organization'.[38] He believed he had shown there and in *The Elementary Forms* that the categories themselves were 'made in the image of social phenomena'[39]:

Cosmic space was primitively constructed on the model of social space, that is, on the territory occupied by society and as society conceives it; time expresses the rhythm of collective life; the notion of class was at first no more than another aspect of the notion of a human group; collective force and its power over men's minds served as prototypes for the notion of force and causality, etc.[40]

The very 'unity of these first logical systems merely reproduces the unity of the society'.[41] The classifications and categories observed in primitive societies took 'from society the models upon which they have been constructed'.[42]

Distinct from this claim is a fourth: that the categories are *functional* to society. Durkheim argued that if

men did not agree upon these essential ideas at every moment, if they did not have the same conception of time, space, cause, number, etc., all contact between their minds would be impossible, and with that, all life together.[43]

37. ibid., p. 55: tr. p. 66. The next sentence reads 'But both forms are of social origin'.

38. ibid., p. 67: tr. p. 82.

39. 1913a (ii) (6, 7), p. 36. Cf.: '... the social organization has been a model for the spatial organization ...'; 'the divisions into days, weeks, months, years, etc., correspond to the periodical recurrence of rites, feasts and public ceremonies'; '[these systematic classifications] have taken the forms of society as their framework'; 'the idea of power ... does not come without those of ascendancy, mastership and domination, and their corollaries, dependence and subordination; now the relations expressed by all these ideas are eminently social' (1912a, pp. 17, 15, 206, 522: tr. 1915d, pp. 12, 10, 145, 366).

40. 1913a (ii) (6, 7), p. 36.

41. 1912a, p. 206: tr. p. 145.

42. ibid., p. 628: tr. p. 440.

43. ibid., pp. 23–4: tr. p. 17.

A minimum of logical conformity was as indispensable as a minimum of moral conformity and society used 'all its authority' to ensure it; 'logical discipline' was a 'special aspect of social discipline'.[44] (This explained 'the exceptional authority which is inherent in the reason and which makes us accept its suggestions with confidence'.[45]) Thus, for example, the calendar not only expresses the rhythm of collective activities; 'its function is to assure their regularity'.[46] Likewise, the category of causality was 'made to fulfil the exigencies of life in common'.[47] In general, society was

possible only when the individuals and things which compose it are divided into certain groups, that is to say, classified, and when these groups are classified in relation to each other ... To avoid all collisions, it is necessary that ... space in general be divided, differentiated, arranged and that these divisions and arrangements be known to everybody. On the other hand, every summons to a celebration, a hunt or a military expedition implies fixed and established dates, and consequently that a common time is agreed upon, which everybody conceives in the same fashion. Finally, the co-operation of many persons with the same end in view is possible only when they are in agreement as to the relation which exists between this end and the means of attaining it, that is to say, when the same causal relation is admitted by all the co-operators in the enterprise.[48]

The fifth claim which Durkheim can be seen to have advanced is that belief-systems, and in particular primitive religions, can in part be seen as cosmologies; indeed, he asserted that there 'is no religion that is not a cosmology at the same time that it is a speculation upon divine things'.[49] Systems of primitive classification aimed 'to make intelligible the relations which exist between things ... to connect ideas, to unify knowledge' and could be said to constitute 'a first philosophy of nature'.[50] Thus, totemism could be shown to

44. ibid., p. 24: tr. p. 17.
45. ibid.
46. ibid., p. 15: tr. p. 11.
47. ibid., p. 526: tr. p. 368.
48. ibid., pp. 443–4: tr. pp. 632–3.
49. ibid., p. 9: tr. p. 12.
50. 1903a, (i) p. 66: tr. 1963b, p. 81.

'offer us a conception of the universe'[51] and it was through primitive religion 'that a first explanation of the world has been made possible'[52]; indeed, the 'great service that the religions have rendered to thought is that they have constructed a first representation of what [the] intelligible relationships between things might be'.[53] Accordingly, the Mount Gambier tribe divided the entire world into ten classes, each with its special totem, which when brought together, 'make up a complete and systematic representation of the world; and this representation is religious, for religious notions furnish its basis ... like the Greek religion, it puts the divine everywhere'.[54] Again 'the wakan plays the same role in the world, as the Sioux conceives it, as the one played by the forces with which science explains the diverse phenomena of nature'[55]; and when

the Iroquois says that the life of all nature is the product of the conflicts aroused between the unequally intense orenda of the different beings, he only expresses, in his own language, this modern idea that the world is a system of forces limiting and containing each other and making an equilibrium.[56]

As to the beliefs underlying imitative rites and magical techniques, they constituted 'a concrete statement of the law of causality', for a 'full conception of the causal relation is implied in the power thus attributed to the like to produce the like'.[57]

Finally, a sixth claim can be distinguished, which is evolutionary in character: that 'the fundamental notions of science are of a religious origin'.[58] *Primitive Classification* was about 'the genesis of the classificatory function in general' and sought to 'throw some light on the origins of the logical procedure

51. 1912a, p. 203: tr. 1915d, p. 141. Cf. ibid., bk II, ch. III, passim.
52. ibid., p. 339: tr. p. 237 (S.L.).
53. ibid., p. 340: tr. p. 237 (S.L.).
54. ibid., pp. 219–20: tr. p. 154.
55. ibid., p. 290: tr. p. 203.
56. ibid., p. 291: tr. pp. 203–4.
57. ibid., p. 518: tr. p. 363.
58. ibid., p. 616: tr. p. 431. Science, he maintained, 'puts to work the notions which dominate all thought and in which the whole of civilization is, so to speak, condensed: these are the categories' (1910a(iii) (2), p. 44).

which is the basis of scientific classifications'.[59] Durkheim claimed to have shown in *The Elementary Forms* that

the most essential notions of the human mind, notions of time, of space, of genus and species, of force and causality, of personality, those, in a word, which the philosophers have labelled categories and which dominate the whole of logical thought, have been elaborated in the very womb of religion. It is from religion that science has taken them.[60]

He sought to catch these ideas 'at their very birth'[61] and to show how 'Religion opened up the way for [science and philosophy]'[62] – thereby taking up in a new form the old Comtean theme of mankind's evolution from theology through metaphysics to science. Thus for example, 'the idea of force is of religious origin. It is from religion that it has been borrowed, first by philosophy, then by the sciences'[63]; and the 'idea of the personality' derived from 'the spiritual principle serving as the soul of the group' which gradually became individualized.[64] Conceptual thought was, in general, 'rich in all the experience and all the science which the collectivity has accumulated in the course of centuries'.[65]

THEIR EMPIRICAL BASIS
AND THEORETICAL SIGNIFICANCE

The empirical basis of Durkheim's sociology of knowledge must be distinguished, as far as possible, from its theoretical significance. The former is certainly open to a number of very

---

59. 1903a (i), pp. 66–7: tr. 1953b, p. 82. He argued that 'the history of scientific classification is, in the last analysis, the history of the stages by which [the] element of social affectivity has progressively weakened, leaving more and more room for the reflective thought of individuals' (ibid., p. 72: tr. p. 88).

60. 1913a (ii) (6, 7), pp. 35–6.

61. 1912a, p. 28: tr. 1915d, p. 20.

62. ibid., p. 340: tr. p. 237.

63. ibid., p. 292: tr. p. 204.

64. ibid., pp. 386–7: tr. p. 270.

65. 1913a (ii) (6, 7), p. 36.

serious objections.[66] In the first place, some crucial evidence appears to have been faulty: serious doubt has been cast on the accuracy of Cushing's account of the Zuñi clans and, in consequence, on the postulated correspondence between their classificatory system and their social organization, as well as on the hypothesis that they were or ever had been totemic in the Durkheimian, or any other, sense.[67] Secondly, *Primitive Classification* failed in many cases to establish the postulated correspondence between form of classification and form of society.[68] Thirdly, Durkheim and Mauss failed to test the evidence rigorously by concomitant variation and constantly tried to explain away counter-instances and deviant cases (as conjectural late developments or in various other ways). Fourthly, they wrongly assumed that, at any given stage, each society has only one system of classification and set of categories, and they did not distinguish (except very cursorily) between totemic and other kinds of classification. Fifthly, they constantly postulated, indeed took as established, evolutionary sequences for which there was and is no evidence, in order to harmonize with their preconceptions about the evolution of totemism from moieties to clans to sub-clans, and from classification by clans to that by regions, as well as from totemism itself to 'later' belief-systems. Finally, they never considered the diverse ways in which totems become attached to groups, nor the diversity of those groups (that is, other than clans), nor other available *sociological* explanations of classification (for example, on the basis of use and interest, and as a result of men's interaction with their natural environment[69]).

In addition to these criticisms of Durkheim's evidence and his interpretation of it, a more general point must be made with respect to the vaunting ambition of his sociology of knowledge, before considering its theoretical significance.

66. For fuller discussions of these, see Needham, 1963, Cazeneuve, 1958, and Worsley, 1956.

67. See Cazeneuve, 1958, and Kroeber, A. L., *Zuñi Kin and Clan* (New York, 1917).

68. See Needham, 1963.

69. See Worsley, 1956, for a discussion of such alternative interpretations.

It is one thing to investigate the relationships between forms of thought and forms of society; it is another to seek to account for the fundamental conditions to which all thought is subject. Kant wrote that there 'can be no doubt that all our knowledge begins with experience . . . but it does not follow that it all arises out of experience'.[70] Durkheim argued otherwise; he believed that sociology made it 'no longer necessary to place [man's distinctive attributes] beyond experience'.[71] In arguing thus, he went too far, since the operations of the mind and the laws of logic are not determined by, or given in, experience, even in social experience. No account of relations between features of a society and the ideas and beliefs of its members could ever explain the faculty, or ability, of the latter to think spatially and temporally, to classify material objects and to individuate persons, to think causally and, in general, to reason; nor could it ever show that the necessity, or indispensability, of doing all these things was simply an aspect of social authority. For, in the first place, the very relations established must always presuppose the prior existence of these very abilities; the aboriginal must have the concept of class in order even to recognize the classifications of his society, let alone extend them to the universe, and the putative Zuñi must likewise have the concept of space, and so on. In the second place, the very necessity of these conditions of thought makes the hypothesis of their causal determination unstatable, since the hypothesis to be empirical must be falsifiable. We cannot postulate a hypothetical situation in which individuals do *not* in general think by means of space, time, class, person, cause and according to the rules of logic, since this is what thinking *is*.[72]

Durkheim's failure to see this, and his consequent belief that sociology could solve the Kantian problem, by giving an empirical answer to a philosophical question, stemmed from his

70. *Critique of Pure Reason*, tr. Kemp Smith, N. (New York, 1950), p. 41.
71. 1912a, p. 638: tr. 1915d, p. 447 (S.L.).
72. This is not to say that there are not specific, and specialized types of thinking which do without some of these categories (e.g. mathematical thinking) or which violate some of the laws of logic (e.g. mythical or mystical thinking), but these are only possible within the context of ordinary thinking.

seeing the categories as concepts and concepts as collective *représentations*. As Gehlke wrote, he saw the categories as 'a content of mind rather than as a capacity of mind'[73]; he did not distinguish between the faculty of thinking spatially, temporally, causally, etc. and criteria for dividing space and time and identifying causes, or between the faculty of classification and specific classificatory criteria. It is as an attempt to throw light on these latter that the theoretical significance of his sociology of knowledge is best considered.

His first (heuristic) claim, whatever its philosophical importance, is a crucial first step in the sociology of knowledge, since it is only by seeing concepts as rule-governed elements within cultural systems that sociological questions can even be asked. The second (causal) claim is, however, extremely problematic. No convincing evidence is offered in *Primitive Classification* or *The Elementary Forms* to show that particular morphological or organizational features of particular societies *cause* particular classificatory or conceptual systems; indeed, the evident lack of a correspondence in many of the cases cited is especially damaging to this claim. Moreover, Durkheim's only attempt to specify this postulated causal mechanism ('the forces . . . which induced men to divide things as they did between the classes'[74]) is in terms of sentiments and affective values; yet the 'sentiments which are the basis of domestic, social and other kinds of organization' and 'emotional value' are not sufficient to establish a causal connection.[75] The fourth (functionalist) claim is, if interpreted generally,

73. Gehlke, 1915, p. 53. Cf. Dennes, 1924, p. 39, Sorokin, 1928, p. 477, Benoît-Smullyan, 1937, ch. III, pt iii, and 1948 (1966), pp. 240–41, and Needham, 1963, pp. xxvi–xxix. Durkheim does, in fact (inconsistently) grant that the individual, before he is socialized, is capable of distinguishing right from left, past from present, and that 'this resembles that, this accompanies that' – i.e., that he already possesses the essential categories (see 1903a (i), p. 5: tr. 1963b, p. 7, and 1912a, p. 206: tr. 1915d, p. 145). He also speaks of 'technological classifications . . . closely linked to practical concerns', but does not relate them to those he considers or realize that they refute his sociological explanation of the categories (see 1903a (i), p. 66 fn.: tr. 1963b, pp. 81–2 fn.).

74. 1903a (i), p. 69: tr. 1963b, pp. 84–5.

75. ibid., pp. 69, 70: tr. pp. 85, 86. As Needham has commented, 'there is neither truth nor use in such an assertion as that space is differentially

likewise open to objection: shared concepts are part of the very definition of society. On the other hand, the role played in particular societies by particular sets of concepts and classifications is a central area of sociological and anthropological inquiry.[76] Durkheim's sixth (evolutionist) claim is also of little use if interpreted generally, as a hypothesis about the intellectual evolution of mankind. On the other hand, the hypothesis that primitive and traditional religions contain the germs of scientific thinking is, in many ways, both challenging and plausible.[77]

This leads one directly to Durkheim's fifth claim, that belief-systems, including primitive religions, should be treated as cosmologies. This claim has proved immensely fruitful, both within the Durkheimian tradition and outside it[78]; and Durkheim's own analyses in this connection have continued to serve as a model for work in this area.[79] Perhaps their most theoretically significant aspect derives from the implications of his third (structuralist) claim: that there are structural correspondences between symbolic classification and social organization,[80] and quite generally between different orders of social facts.

conceived "because each region has its own affective value" ' (Needham, 1963, p. xxiv).

76. Cf. much of the work of the Durkheimians, especially that of Mauss, Hubert and Hertz. See especially Hubert's 'La Représentation de temps dans la religion' in Hubert and Mauss, 1909.

77. Cf. Horton, R., 'African Traditional Thought and Western Science', *Africa*, XXXVII (1967), pp. 50–71 and 155–87; Goody, 1961; and Lukes, 1967b and 1973, and Horton, 1973.

78. Cf., for example, Sir. E. E. Evans-Pritchard's *Nuer Religion* (Oxford, 1956), especially pp. 314–15, on the need to study 'primitive philosophies'. Cf. also Mary Douglas's Durkheimian work, *Natural Symbols: Explorations in Cosmology* (London, 1970).

79. Marcel Granet wrote that the pages on China in *Primitive Classification* 'mark a date in the history of sinological studies' (*La Pensée chinoise*, Paris, 1934, p. 29, fn.); though see Needham, 1963, p. xxii.

80. As Needham has written, 'in systems of prescriptive alliance [which are typical of Australia] there is such a concordance between the symbolic forms and social organization that these two orders of facts may be regarded as aspects of one conceptual order, one mode of classification. This concordance need not be a formal correspondence, such as Durkheim and Mauss supposed, but may subsist in a structural sense, institutions of different forms being seen as based on the same mode of relation' (Needham, 1963, p. xxxvii).

Chapter 23

The Sociology of Religion — II

INFLUENCES

DURKHEIM'S sociology of religion was, as we have seen, by his own testimony indebted both to 'Robertson Smith and his school' and to 'the ethnographers of England and America'.[1]

His debt to the former was multiple. To Smith himself it was both general and specific. He accepted Smith's sociological view of religion ('Religion . . . is a relation of all the members of a community to the power that has the good of the community at heart'; there was 'Solidarity of the gods and their worshippers as part of one organic society'[2]); his conception of its regulative and stimulative functions; his contrast between religion as within the communion of the church and magic as outside it and residual; even his association of religion and political structure. More specifically, as we have seen, he accepted Smith's interpretation of clan totemism as the earliest known form of religion, involving the idealization and divinization of the clan, personified by the god and materially represented by the totemic animal. He also accepted (in part) Smith's analysis of sacrifice as originally a sacramental meal creating social bonds of the same nature as kinship. The clan, according to Smith, periodically expressed its unity, binding its members to each other and to their god, and revitalized itself at this communal sacrifice 'in which the god and his worshippers unite by partaking together of the flesh and blood of a sacred victim'. In this way, 'commensality can be thought

---

1. See above, p. 238. There was, of course, the long-term influence of Fustel de Coulanges (see above, pp. 58–63). Fustel influenced Durkheim directly, and also indirectly *via* Robertson Smith.

2. *Lectures on the Religion of the Semites* (Edinburgh, 1889; 3rd edn London, 1927), pp. 55, 32. Cf.: 'Religion did not exist for the saving of souls but for the preservation and welfare of society' (ibid.).

of (1) as confirming or even (2) as constituting kinship in a very real sense'.[3]

Of Robertson Smith and Frazer, Durkheim wrote that they had 'contributed, more than anyone, to giving the sense of the extreme complexity of religious facts, the deep-lying causes on which they depend, and the partly unconscious evolution from which they result'.[4] On the other hand, he sternly opposed Frazer's third, 'conceptual' theory of totemism (which appealed to the fancies of the mother, ignorant of the causes of childbirth) as 'a particular case of the belief in miraculous births', describing it as 'the fruit of a sort of Voltairianism whose presence is astonishing in the development of our science and in M. Frazer himself'.[5] He adopted the same critical attitude to the explanations of the 'English school of religious anthropology' as a whole, the virtues and defects of which he characterized as follows, taking Crawley's *The Mystic Rose* as exhibiting them in an extreme form:

One certainly finds interesting insights there … But, to a rare degree, the method lacks a critical and discriminating character. In order to prove an assertion, the author does not hesitate to gather together, without distinguishing between them, facts borrowed from the most heterogeneous societies. All the continents are scoured without order or discrimination … The impression emerging from this whirling confusion of facts is itself confused and indeterminate. At the same time, the extreme facility with which all evidence serving to confirm the theses advanced is accepted without prior examination detracts from the authority of the conclusions. Finally, the theories offered to account for the facts are of a simplism that is truly intrepid.[6]

---

3. Smith, op. cit., pp. 227 and 274. Durkheim, however, maintained that the Australian evidence disproved Smith's thesis that 'the idea of oblation was foreign to the sacrificial institution and later upset its natural arrangement. The thesis of Smith must be revised on this point. Of course, the sacrifice is partly a communion; but it is also, and no less essentially, a gift and an act of renouncement' (1912a, p. 490: tr. 1915d, p. 343). Cf. Hubert and Mauss, 1899.

4. 1913a (ii) (11), p. 95.

5. ibid. Cf. 1912a: tr. 1915d, bk II, ch. v (III).

6. 1903a (iii) (32), p. 352.

The 'anthropological school', of which Frazer was typical, 'does not seek to locate religions in the social environments of which they are a part, and to differentiate them according to the different environments to which they are thus connected'[7]; rather,

all those who pass as being not too far removed from the origins, and who are confusedly lumped together under the rather imprecise rubric of *savages*, are put on the same plane and consulted indifferently. Since from this point of view, facts have an interest only in proportion to their generality, they consider themselves obliged to collect as large a number as possible of them; the circle of comparison could not become too wide.[8]

Durkheim, on the contrary, thought that the 'essential thing is to assemble, not a large number of facts, but facts that are at once *typical* and *well studied*. Rather than extending indefinitely the field of comparison (which compels one to rest content with poorly established data), one must limit it with discrimination and method.'[9]

Here lay the overwhelming importance he, and his followers, attached to the English and American ethnographers – above all to Spencer and Gillen, Howitt, Matthews (and the German missionary Strehlow) in Australia[10]; and also to Dall, Krause, Boas, Swanton, Hill Tout, Dorsey, Mindleff, Mrs Stevenson and Cushing in America. The Australian material, especially,

7. He saw Frazer's *Totemism and Exogamy*, however, as marking a methodological advance, since it sought to link domestic and religious institutions to their geographical and social conditions (see 1912a, p. 132: tr. 1915d, p. 93; and 1913a (ii) (11)).

8. 1912a, pp. 132–3: tr. 1915d, pp. 93–4. Cf., for instance, a similar criticism of Hartland: 1913a (ii) (28), p. 414.

9. 1901a (iii) (17), p. 341.

10. According to Stanner 'We have now lost a full sense of the impact [these ethnographic studies] made. Nothing since the explorers' journals had attracted such intellectual attention to Australia.' And, in Elkin's words, Spencer and Gillen's work especially 'fascinated the anthropological world' (Stanner, 1967, p. 218). In a review in the *Année*, Mauss described Spencer and Gillen's *The Native Tribes of Central Australia* as 'one of the most important books of ethnography and descriptive sociology of which we know'; the 'picture they give us of social and religious organization is one of the most complete with which anthropology has provided us' (*AS*, 3 (1900), pp. 205, 205–6).

seemed to furnish the evidential basis for a systematic theory of religion relying on the comparative method applied to 'so limited a number of societies that each of them can be studied with sufficient precision' and concentrating on 'one clearly determined type'.[11] The Australian tribal societies, he wrote, all belonged to one common type. Also,

> Australian totemism is the variety for which our documents are the most complete.[12] Finally, that which we propose to study in this work is the most primitive and simple religion which it is possible to find. It is therefore natural that to discover it we address ourselves to societies as slightly evolved as possible, for it is evidently there that we have the greatest chance of finding it and studying it well.[13]

The American evidence he used in a supplementary way, 'to illuminate and lend precision to the Australian facts'[14]: for, though the American Indians' civilization was 'more advanced', the 'essential lines of the social structure remain the same as those in Australia; it is always the organization on a basis of clans'. Here were not two different social types but 'two varieties of a single type, which are still very close to each other' representing 'two successive moments of a single evolution'. Moreover, 'certain aspects of their common social organization' were more easily studied among the American Indians; totemism was 'much more visible there'; their organization had 'a greater stability and more clearly defined contours'; and it was useful to trace the evolution of totemism, thereby revealing the historical place of the Australian variety. But it was the latter that constituted 'the real and immediate object of our researches'.[15]

---

11. 1912a, p. 134: tr. 1915d, pp. 95, 94.
12. Cf. the retrospective assessment of Evans-Pritchard: 'Durkheim's choice of that region for his experiment was unfortunate, for the literature on its aboriginals was, by modern standards, poor and confused, and it still is' (Evans-Pritchard, 1965, p. 58). Cf. also van Gennep, 1913 and 1920.
13. 1912a, p. 135: tr. 1915d, pp. 95–6.
14. 1913a (ii) (12), p. 96. But see below, pp. 479–80.
15. 1912a, pp. 136–8: tr. pp. 96–7 (S.L.).

DURKHEIM'S VIEW OF TOTEMISM

It must be said that Durkheim's view of totemism looked more to the past than to the future. In common with Smith, the early Frazer and Jevons, as well as Wundt and Freud, he accepted the view, going back to McLennan, that totemism was the most primitive form of religion and was its evolutionary origin, or at least its earliest known form. His imprisonment in this view can be gauged by looking at his reaction to Goldenweiser's (forward-looking) critique of contemporary ideas on the subject,[16] which adduced evidence from different societies to show that none of the supposedly essential traits of totemism (exogamy, totemic taboos, the use of totemic emblems, religious attitudes and practices concerning the totem, belief in descent from the totem) were invariable features of totemic societies. Durkheim wrote that Goldenweiser had no difficulty in showing that none of these traits was truly universal; his method could lead to no other result, for he

brings together forms of totemism that are quite heterogeneous, situated at moments of evolution far distant from one another: some pertain to primitives, others to societies where totemism is no longer any more than a shadow of itself. It is quite natural that no determinate institution can be found in an identical form in all instances; but that is not to say that none among them is closely linked to what is truly essential in totemism.[17]

This appeal to evolution to save a hypothesis was how Durkheim often used to get out of tight corners, or rather to avoid seeing they were tight. This passage also offers yet another example of *petitio principii*: in arguing against Goldenweiser, Durkheim assumes he has determined 'what is truly essential in totemism'.[18]

16. Goldenweiser, A. A., 'Totemism, an Analytical Study', *Journal of American Folk-lore*, 23 (1910), pp. 179–293. Cf. Chapter 25, below. For the subsequent development of the study of totemism, see van Gennep, 1920, and Lévi-Strauss, 1962a.

17. 1913a (ii) (13), p. 101.

18. On these characteristic forms of argument, see the Introduction, above.

Durkheim never doubted that totemism was a real social institution with distinctive characteristics. It was, moreover, 'the most primitive and simple religion which it is possible to find',[19] found in its purest form among societies 'as close as possible to the origins of evolution', with 'the most rudimentary techniques' and 'the most primitive and simple organization known', namely organization on a clan basis.[20] Indeed, it

seems as though the clan could not exist, in the form it has taken in a great number of Australian societies, without the totem. For the members of a single clan are not united to each other either by a common habitat or by common blood, since they are not necessarily consanguineous and are frequently scattered over different parts of the tribal territory. Their unity thus comes solely from their having the same name and the same emblem, from their belief that they have the same relations with the same categories of things, from the fact that they practise the same rites – in a word, from their participation in the same totemic cult. Thus totemism and the clan mutually imply each other, in so far, at least, as the latter is not confused with the local group. Now, organization on a clan basis is the simplest we know. It exists, in fact, with all its essential elements, from the moment that society includes two primary clans; hence there can be none more rudimentary, until a society reduced to a single clan has been discovered, and, up to now, no traces of such a society appear to have been found. A religion so closely related to a social system surpassing all others in simplicity can be regarded as the most elementary religion we can possibly know.[21]

METHODOLOGICAL ASSUMPTIONS

In focusing on totemism conceived in this way, Durkheim was making what he saw as a single methodological assumption – which, in fact, can be analyzed into two, importantly different, assumptions. The assumption he made was that 'all the essential elements of religious thought and life ought to be found, at least in germ, in the most primitive religions'.[22]

19. 1912a, p. 135: tr. p. 95.
20. ibid., p. 136: tr. p. 96 (S.L.).
21. ibid., pp. 238–9: tr. pp. 167–8 (S.L.).
22. ibid., p. 450: tr. p. 315.

The ambiguity lies in the crucial word 'primitive'. The 'most primitive' religion could either be the *simplest* religion, or the *earliest* religion. The first interpretation represents Durkheim's residual evolutionism; the second his inclination to study relatively undifferentiated, small-scale and closed societies. The first points backwards to the pervasive evolutionism of the nineteenth century; the second points forwards to modern social anthropology.

This ambiguity (and Durkheim's failure to perceive its significance) is evident in the opening paragraph of the book, where he defines 'the most primitive religion' as (1) that found in societies with the simplest social organization (he further assumed, mistakenly, that the simplest religion was to be found in the simplest form of society); and (2) that which can be explained without reference to a previous religion.[23] The ambiguity, and his blindness to it, are also revealed in his claim to be 'taking up again, *but under new conditions*, the old problem of the origin of religion', meaning by 'origin' not 'an absolute beginning, but the most simple social state that is currently known, that beyond which we cannot go at present', so as to discover 'the ever-present causes on which the most essential forms of religious thought and practice depend'.[24] He simply took it as axiomatic that there is an identity between (cultural and structural) simplicity and evolutionary priority. Durkheim never really shed his evolutionism, with its talk of 'origins', 'prototypes' and 'stages'. On the other hand, the enormous interest and importance of *The Elementary Forms* is largely independent of its

23. ibid., p. 1: tr. p. 1.

24. 1912a, pp. 10–11: tr. p. 8. For notably evolutionary passages in *The Elementary Forms*, see 1912a, pp. 4–5, 10–12, 123–4, 135–6, 238–9, 254–5, 272–3, 290, 422–3, 465: tr. pp. 3–4, 8, 87–8, 95–6, 167–8, 178, 191, 203, 295, 326. On the other hand, Durkheim had absolutely no interest in the evolutionary speculation characteristic of the period; he dubbed it 'subjective and arbitrary' (ibid., p. 11: tr. p. 8). Cf. his criticism of Andrew Lang in a review in the *Année*: 'his dominating preoccupation is to reconstitute the way in which men lived before they reached the most rudimentary social state that we can currently know by observation. This, on the contrary, is a question we avoid as much as possible, since we judge it now insoluble and somewhat vain' (1907a (16), p. 401).

evolutionism; and it is better seen as a classic of social anthropology than as a remote exercise in religious history using the data of ethnography – though Durkheim saw it, inseparably, as both.

In making this methodological assumption, he was powerfully influenced by an analogy taken from the natural sciences. He argued that, while 'an extended verification may add to the authority of a theory . . . it is equally true that when a law has been proved by one well-done experiment, this proof is valid universally'.[25] As examples he instanced the physicist simplifying phenomena in his experiments[26] and – gesturing again towards evolutionism – the biologist 'finding out the secret of life of even the most protoplasmic creature . . .'[27] Essentially, he saw the new Australian ethnography as having made possible a crucial experiment that would 'prove' the general theory of religion he had developed, in offering an exhaustive account of the simplest known instance. This analogy of one experiment proving a law can, of course, be seen as a 'piece of special pleading which [is] little more than the ignoring of instances which contradict the so-called law'.[28] On the other hand, it led him to develop and test a body of general ideas against a limited range of strictly comparable phenomena which he interpreted in a detailed and thoroughgoing way. It is, in passing, very interesting to contrast his concentration on what he saw as the simplest case with Max Weber's sociology of religion. The latter explicitly ignores ethnographic data and addresses itself to the great world religions, focusing on the most complex of them, Christianity. Indeed for Weber, Christianity was the most differentiated of the world religions, both internally and from other institutional spheres of society, and thereby provided a kind of natural experiment in which aspects of religion that are undifferentiated in other systems, are found separate and visible. In this way he could focus on the specific nature and effects of faith, on the differences

25. 1912a, p. 593: tr. p. 415 (S.L.).
26. See ibid., p. 11: tr. p. 8.
27. ibid., pp. 593–4: tr. p. 415.
28. Evans-Pritchard, 1965, p. 58.

between cult and morality, or church and state, and on their respective relations to other aspects of society.[29]

By contrast, Durkheim regarded 'the study of a very simple religion' as 'particularly instructive'. When, as we shall see, he was asked this very question – would it not be better to study the most advanced forms of religion? – he replied that

a science in its infancy must pose problems in their simplest form, and only later make them gradually more complicated. When we have understood very elementary religions, we will be able to move on to others.[30]

'Primitive civilizations', he believed, 'offer privileged cases . . . because they are simple cases'[31]: the constituent elements of primitive religion were especially visible and, 'Since the facts there are simpler, the relations between them are more apparent'.[32] Durkheim hoped by a close study of totemism to develop hypotheses about 'what religion is, of what elements it is made up, from what causes it results, and what functions it fulfils'.[33] Indeed, he went so far as boldly to claim that at 'the foundation of all systems of [religious] beliefs and of all cults there ought necessarily to be a certain number of *représentations* or conceptions and of ritual attitudes which, in spite of the diversity of forms which they have taken, have the same objective significance and fulfil the same functions everywhere'.[34] The simplest case would reveal 'the most essential elements of the religious life'.[35]

The Elementary Forms can be seen in a number of ways – as a study of Australian (and American) totemism, as a completely general theory of religion, as an incisive critique of other

29. Cf. Swanson, G. E., review in *History and Theory*, x (1971), pp. 260–61.

30. 1919b, pp. 142–3. See Chapter 25, below.

31. 1912a, p. 8: tr. p. 6. But cf. Mauss, 1909 in Mauss, 1968–9, vol. 1, p. 396: '. . . the most elementary forms are in no measure simpler than the more developed forms. Their complexity is merely of a different nature.'

32. 1912a, p. 9: tr. p. 7.

33. ibid., p. 65: tr. p. 47.

34. ibid., p. 6: tr. p. 5.

35. ibid., p. 450: tr. p. 315.

theories of totemism[36] and of religion,[37] and as we have seen, as a contribution to the sociology of knowledge (indeed, as we have also seen, the title of the work was originally to be 'The Elementary Forms of Thought and Religious Practice'[38]). Despite the many criticisms that have been justifiably advanced against this work – both ethnographic, methodological, logical and theoretical – it remains a major and profound contribution to the sociology of religion, and, more generally, to the sociology of ideas and of ideologies.[39] Here it will perhaps be most useful to consider, first, its general explanatory approach and, second, the general hypotheses it can be seen to have advanced. We will then conclude with some observations concerning the value and the limitations of Durkheim's sociology of religion.

THE EXPLANATORY APPROACH

'Our entire study', Durkheim wrote, 'rests upon this postulate that the unanimous sentiments of the believers of all times cannot be purely illusory.'[40] This postulate allowed him on the one hand to reject all those theories which presented religion

36. See bk II, ch. v.
37. See bk I, chs. II and III.
38. See above, p. 407.
39. Cf. Stanner's judgement that *The Elementary Forms* 'for all its faults remains indispensable to the philosophical, sociological, and – let us not fail to say – the ethnographic education of any anthropologist' (Stanner, 1967, p. 227). For helpful discussions relating to it, see, among many others, Webb, 1916, Goldenweiser, 1917 and 1923, Van Gennep, 1920, Richard, 1923, Lowie, 1924 and 1937, Malinowski, 1925, Parsons, 1937 and 1960, Radcliffe-Brown, 1952, Goody, 1961, König, 1962, Lévi-Strauss, 1962a, Evans-Pritchard, 1965, Stanner, 1967, Desroches, 1969 and Runciman, 1969; also see the discussion of Durkheim's critics in Seger, 1957, and Chapter 25, below. Apart from *The Elementary Forms*, Durkheim lectured once in Paris on 'Religion: Origins' in 1906–7 (see Appendix A, below; also see 1907f). His most relevant reviews were 1898a (iv) (1), 1900a (8) and (9), 1903a (iii) (33), 1904a (8) (9) and 1903d (cf. 1904d), 1906a (19), 1907a (16), 1910a (iii) (3) and 1913a (ii) (11), (12), (13) and (31). Also see the reviews in the 'Religious Sociology' section of the *Année*, by Mauss and Hubert, passim.
40. 1912a, p. 596: tr. p. 417.

as 'made up of a tissue of illusions', an 'inexplicable hallucination' based on 'some sort of a deep-rooted error'.[41] Thus he rejected animist and naturist theories, according to which man has superimposed on observable reality 'an unreal world, made up entirely of the fantastic images which excite his mind during a dream, or of the aberrations, often monstrous, allegedly generated by the mythological imagination under the bewitching but deceiving influence of language'. It was, he argued, 'incomprehensible that humanity should throughout the ages have remained obstinate in errors of which experience would very soon have made it aware'.[42]

On the other hand, although Durkheim did not regard the 'unanimous sentiment of the believers' as '*purely* illusory', he clearly saw it as partly illusory, for he at no point accepted the explanations and justifications of their beliefs and practices offered by the faithful. As he put it, arguing against William James, 'from the fact that a "religious experience", if we choose to call it that, exists ... it does not follow that the reality which is its foundation conforms objectively to the idea which believers have of it'.[43]

The whole problem, in Durkheim's mind, was to attain that reality – to 'know how to go underneath the symbol to the reality which it represents and which gives it its true meaning'.[44] 'Primitive religions', he argued, 'relate to reality and express it'[45]; the task of the sociology of religion was to discover whence those 'realities' expressed by religion 'come and what has been able to make men represent them under this singular form which is peculiar to religious thought'.[46] It was in this rather special sense that he claimed that 'there are no religions which are false. All are true in their own fashion.'[47] They were true in the sense that they stated and expressed in a non-objective, symbolic or metaphorical form, truths about

41. ibid., pp. 98, 322, 3: tr. pp. 69, 225, 2.
42. ibid., p. 322: tr. p. 225 (S.L.).
43. ibid., p. 597: tr. p. 417 (S.L.).
44. ibid., p. 3: tr. p. 2.
45. ibid. (S.L.).
46. ibid., p. 98: tr. p. 70.
47. ibid., p. 3: tr. p. 3.

the 'reality' underlying them and giving them their 'true meaning'.

The 'reality' Durkheim discovered was, of course 'society'. The believer was 'not deceived when he believes in the existence of a moral power upon which he depends and from which he receives all that is best in himself: this power exists, it is society'. When the Australian aboriginal 'is transported outside himself, when he feels a life flowing within him, whose intensity surprises him, he is not the dupe of an illusion':

this exaltation is real and it is really the product of forces exterior and superior to the individual. It is true that he is mistaken in believing that this heightening of vitality is the work of a power in the form of an animal or a plant. But the error is merely in regard to the letter of the symbol by means of which this being is represented to men's minds and the external appearance in which the imagination has clothed it, and not in regard to the fact of its existence. Behind these figures and these metaphors, however crude or refined, there is a concrete and living reality. Religion thus acquires a meaning and a rationale which the most intransigent rationalist cannot fail to recognize. Its primary object is not to give man a representation of the physical world; for if that were its essential task, one could not understand how it has been able to survive, since, on this interpretation, it is scarcely more than a tissue of errors. Above all, it is a system of ideas by means of which individuals represent to themselves the society of which they are members, and the obscure but intimate relations which they have with it. Such is its primordial role; and though metaphorical and symbolic, this representation is not unfaithful.[48]

Likewise, the practices of the cult were not merely to be seen as ineffective gestures: while 'their apparent function is to strengthen the bonds attaching the believer to his god, they at the same time really strengthen the bonds attaching the individual to the society of which he is a member, since the god is only a figurative expression of the society'.[49]

In developing this explanatory approach, Durkheim did not rest content with simply postulating the essentially non-explanatory notions of symbol and metaphor, nor with the

48. ibid., pp. 322–3: tr. p. 225 (S.L.).
49. ibid., p. 323: tr. p. 226.

elementary truth that religious worship is in part a communion. He advanced, as we shall see, a number of fertile explanatory hypotheses which themselves appeal to different types of relation between social realities and religious phenomena. Durkheim himself was not explicit about, and probably not aware of, all the significant differences between these hypotheses and the distinct relations between society and religion they involve. In fact, he saw religion as social in at least three broad ways: as socially determined, as embodying representations (in two senses) of social realities, and as having functional social consequences. We can therefore – at the risk of separating what he saw as inseparable – distinguish the central hypotheses of *The Elementary Forms* into the causal, the interpretative and the functional.

THE CENTRAL HYPOTHESES

Causal

Crucial to Durkheim's theory of religion as socially determined was his claim that certain social situations, those of 'collective effervescence', generate and recreate religious beliefs and sentiments. In advancing it, Durkheim was doubtless affected by the crop of studies in crowd psychology that had appeared at the end of the nineteenth century,[50] by Scipio Sighele,[51] Gustave Le Bon[52] and, indeed, Gabriel Tarde[53] among others, but there is no evidence that he was specifically influenced by any of them[54]; and, unlike them, he did not see crowd behaviour as pathological, undesirable and an argument against

50. See Bramson, L., *The Political Context of Sociology* (New Jersey, 1961), pp. 52–7.

51. See *Psychologie des sectes* (Paris, 1895) and *La Foule criminelle* (Paris, 1901).

52. See *Psychologie des foules* (Paris, 1895).

53. See *L'Opinion et la foule* (Paris, 1901).

54. I can find no basis for Mary Douglas's suggestion that Durkheim 'seems to have freely drawn upon' Le Bon's theory of crowd psychology (*Purity and Danger*, London, 1966, p. 20): Durkheim would have been the last person to regard Le Bon as a serious social scientist. The only suggestion of a possible influence relating to crowd psychology occurs in a

democracy. On the contrary, he argued that it was 'out of this effervescence itself that the religious idea seems to be born',[55] that 'after a collective effervescence men believe themselves transported into an entirely different world from the one they have before their eyes',[56] that sacred beings, the creations of collective thought, 'attain their greatest intensity at the moment when the men are assembled together and are in immediate relations with one another, when they all partake of the same idea and the same sentiment'.[57] Moreover, the 'only way of renewing the collective *représentations* which relate to sacred beings is to retemper them in the very source of the religious life, that is to say, in the assembled groups'.[58] The nearest he came to accounting for the mechanism supposedly involved here was to postulate a change in the 'conditions of psychic activity', an enhancement, even creation, of energies, passions and sensations, and a resulting attribution to things with which men are in most direct contact of exceptional powers and virtues: men create an ideal world with 'a sort of higher dignity' than the real, profane world.[59] Durkheim tried to use this type of explanation to account for the exuberance of religious imagery and activity,[60] for the sentiments associated with mourning rites and the idea of the soul's survival,[61] indeed for the sentiments aroused by all the various kinds of rites, as well as the mythological interpretations developed to account for them.[62]

More generally, Durkheim's view of religion as socially determined led him to seek to establish causal connections

---

footnote reference in *The Elementary Forms* to Stoll's *Suggestion und Hypnotismus in der Völkerpsychologie* (1912a, p. 300 fn.: tr. 1915d, p. 210 fn.). An early influence here may have been Espinas (see 1902b, p. 67: tr. 1933b, p. 99).

55. 1912a, p. 313: tr. 1915d, pp. 218–19.
56. ibid., pp. 323–4: tr. p. 226.
57. ibid., p. 493: tr. p. 345.
58. ibid., p. 494: tr. p. 346.
59. ibid., p. 603: tr. p. 422.
60. See ibid., p. 545: tr. p. 381.
61. See ibid., pp. 570–75: tr. pp. 399–403.
62. Like Robertson Smith, Durkheim thought that the object of myths was 'to interpret existing rites' (ibid., p. 183: tr. p. 130).

between (morphological) features of the social structure and the content of religious beliefs and ritual practices – an attempt seen most clearly in his account of the alleged social determination of the fundamental categories and forms of classification, themselves essentially religious in origin, considered in the last chapter. Again, he presented religious forces among the Australians as 'localized in definite and distinct social contexts' and thus 'diversified and particularized in the image of the environments in which they are situated'.[63] In this way he explained the fact that the Australians did not generalize the totemic principle beyond the 'limited circle of the beings and things of a certain species' and see it more abstractly and generally as an 'anonymous and diffused force', such as the *mana* of the Melanesians, the *wakan* of the Sioux and the *orenda* of the Iroquois.[64] This 'particularism' was, he argued, due to 'the nature of the social environment':

as long as totemism remains at the basis of the cultural organization, the clan keeps an autonomy in the religious society which, though not absolute, is always very marked. Of course we can say that in one sense each totemic group is only a chapel of the tribal Church; but it is a chapel enjoying a large independence. The cult celebrated there, though not a self-sufficing whole, has only external relations with the others; they are juxtaposed without interpenetrating; the totem of a clan is only fully sacred for that clan. Consequently, the groups of things allotted to each clan, and which form part of it in the same way that men do, have the same individuality and the same autonomy. Each of them is represented as irreducible to similar groups, as separated from them by a break of continuity, as constituting a distinct realm. In these conditions, it would occur to no one that these heterogeneous worlds were just various manifestations of one and the same fundamental force; on the contrary, one might suppose that each of them corresponded to a specifically different *mana* whose influence could not extend beyond the clan and the circle of things attributed to it. The idea of a single and universal *mana* could be born only at the moment when a tribal religion developed over and above the clan cults and absorbed them more or less completely. It is with the sense of tribal unity that there awakens

63. ibid., p. 282: tr. p. 198 (S.L.).
64. ibid., p. 278: tr. pp. 195, 194.

the sense of the substantial unity of the world ... totemism is essentially a federative religion which cannot go beyond a certain degree of centralization without ceasing to be itself.[65]

Similarly, he argued that the 'great god' was 'the synthesis of all the totems' and 'the personification of tribal unity'[66]; and he traced the development of religious universalism to the growth of interchanges between tribes:

if sacred beings are formed which are connected to no geographically determinate society, that is not because they have an extra-social origin. It is because, above these geographical groupings, there are others whose contours are less clearly marked: they have no fixed frontiers, but include a number of neighbouring and related tribes. The very special social life thus created tends to spread itself over an area with no definite limits. Naturally, the mythological personages who correspond to it have the same character; their sphere of influence is not limited; they extend beyond the particular tribes and their territory. They are the great international gods.[67]

Interpretative

Durkheim's second set of hypotheses concerns religion as a special kind of representation of social realities. There were two distinct emphases here (corresponding to a second ambiguity latent in the word '*représentation*'[68] – also found in the English word 'representation'). On the one hand, religion could be seen as 'representing' society and social relationships in a cognitive sense, to the mind or intellect. In this sense religion afforded a means of comprehending or rendering intelligible social realities. On the other hand, it could be seen as 'representing' them in the sense of expressing, symbolizing or dramatizing social relationships. Therefore, Durkheim can be seen as offering a set of hypotheses which *interpret* the *meaning* of men's religious beliefs and practices – on the one hand, as a particular way of understanding their society and their relations with it; and, on the other, as a way of expressing and dramatizing these in a particular symbolic idiom.

65. ibid., pp. 280–1: tr. pp. 196–7 (S.L.).
66. ibid., p. 421: tr. p. 294.
67. ibid., p. 609: tr. p. 426 (S.L.).
68. Cf. Introduction, above.

He applied the former conception of religion both to totemic religion in general and to specific beliefs. In general, as we have seen, he saw religion as 'a system of ideas with which the individuals represent to themselves the society of which they are members, and the obscure but intimate relations which they have with it'[69]; 'the sacred principle', he maintained, 'is nothing more or less than society hypostasized and transfigured',[70] and he argued that religion 'reflects all [society's] aspects, even the most vulgar and the most repulsive. All is to be found there . . .'[71] He claimed that 'the totemic principle or god' was 'nothing else than the clan itself, personified and represented by the imagination under the visible form of the animal or vegetable which serves as totem'[72]; and that 'a society has all that is necessary to arouse the sensation of the divine in minds, merely by the power that it has over them; for to its members it is what a god is to his worshippers', instilling 'the sensation of a perpetual dependence', pursuing its own ends but demanding men's aid, making them into its 'servitors' and submitting them to 'every sort of inconvenience, privation and sacrifice, without which social life would be impossible', exercising 'moral authority' and inspiring 'a veritable respect',[73] but at the same time exercising a 'stimulating influence' acting as a 'perpetual sustenance for our moral nature', revealing 'the other aspect of society which, while being imperative, appears at the same time to be good and benevolent'.[74]

More specifically, Durkheim tried in this way to account for the antithesis of body and soul ('we are made up of two distinct parts, which are opposed to one another as the profane to the sacred, and we may say that in a certain sense there is divinity in us . . . those *représentations* whose flow constitutes our interior life are of two different species which are irreducible one into another. Some concern themselves with the external

69. 1912a, p. 323: tr. p. 225.
70. ibid., p. 495: tr. p. 347 (S.L.).
71. ibid., p. 601: tr. p. 421.
72. ibid., pp. 294–5: tr. p. 206.
73. ibid., pp. 295–6: tr. pp. 206–7 (S.L.).
74. ibid., pp. 302, 303: tr. pp. 211, 212 (S.L.).

and material world; others with an ideal world to which we attribute a moral supremacy over the first'[75]). Similarly, he argued that the idea of the immortal soul was 'useful in rendering intelligible the continuity of the collective life',[76] and that the individual totem and the protecting ancestor were to be interpreted as external projections of the individual soul, representing 'an outside power, superior to us, which gives us our law and judges us, but which also aids us and sustains us'.[77] Again, the great god (arising out of tribal, especially initiation, ceremonies) was, as we have seen, 'the synthesis of all the totems and consequently the personification of the tribal unity',[78] and, in general, religious forces were 'nothing else than objectified sentiments',[79] so that when 'a society is going through circumstances which sadden, perplex or irritate it',

men ... imagine that outside them there are evil beings whose hostility, whether constitutional or temporary, can be appeased only by human suffering. These beings are nothing other than collective states objectified; they are society itself seen under one of its aspects. But we also know that the benevolent powers are constituted in the same way; they too result from the collective life and express it; they too represent the society, but seen from a very different attitude, to wit, at the moment when it confidently affirms itself and ardently presses on towards the realization of the ends which it pursues.[80]

In so far as Durkheim conceived religion in this way – as a mode of comprehending social realities – he can be said to have seen it as a sort of mythological sociology. When one 'set aside the veil with which mythological imagination has covered them', one could see that religion 'seeks to translate these realities into an intelligible language which does not differ in nature from that employed by science: the attempt is made by both to connect things with one another, to establish internal relations between them, to classify and systematize them'. The difference was simply that scientific method brought

75. ibid., pp. 376, 377: tr. pp. 262, 263 (S.L.).
76. ibid., p. 385: tr. p. 269.
77. ibid., p. 401: tr. p. 280.
78. ibid., p. 421: tr. p. 294.
79. ibid., p. 599: tr. p. 419.
80. ibid., p. 590: tr. p. 412.

to bear 'a critical spirit unknown to religion' and systematic precautions to avoid 'passions, prejudices and all subjective influences'.[81]

It was in this sense, Durkheim argued, that religion had offered 'a first representation of what [the] intelligible relationships between things might be' and a 'first explanation of the world'[82] – including the social world. Thus the unobservable entities of religious thought – the totemic principle and impersonal forces such as *mana*, or *orenda* or *wakan*, and the spirits and gods – served (just like the unobservable forces and entities of modern science) to explain 'the world of experienced realities'[83] – that is, social realities. But why, one might ask, did primitive religion offer this explanation in mythological terms? Durkheim's answer was as follows:

Since social pressure operates in mental ways, it could not fail to give men the idea that outside themselves there exist one or several powers, both moral and, at the same time, efficacious, upon which they depend. They must think of these powers, at least in part, as outside themselves, for these address them in a tone of command and sometimes even order them to do violence to their most natural inclinations. It is undoubtedly true that if they were able to see that these influences which they feel emanate from society, then the mythological system of interpretations would never be born. But social influence follows ways that are too circuitous and obscure, and employs psychical mechanisms that are too complex to allow the ordinary observer to see whence it comes. As long as scientific analysis has not come to explain it to them, men know well that they are acted upon, but they do not know by what. So they must invent by themselves the idea of these powers with which they feel themselves in connection, and from this, we are able to catch a glimpse of the way by which they were led to represent them under forms that are really foreign to their nature and to transfigure them by thought.[84]

We have suggested that Durkheim also saw religion as a way of 'representing' in the sense of *expressing* social realities.

81. ibid., pp., 612–13: tr. p. 429 (S.L.).
82. ibid., pp. 339, 340: tr. p. 237 (S.L.).
83. ibid.: tr. p. 238.
84. ibid., pp. 298–9: tr. p. 209 (S.L.).

Thus, 'the totem is the flag of the clan',[85] constituting its 'rallying sign', by which its members 'mutually show one another that they are all members of the same moral community and they become conscious of the kinship uniting them'.[86] And in particular, the so-called 'representative' or 'commemorative' rites have the function of 'representing or imprinting [the past] more deeply in the mind'; they are ceremonies 'whose sole aim is to awaken certain ideas and sentiments, to attach the present to the past or the individual to the collectivity'.[87]

In a striking passage interpreting these ceremonies, Durkheim discussed the 'recreative and aesthetic element' of religion, comparing the rites to 'dramatic representations', and relating them to 'games and the principal forms of art'. Interestingly (and none of his interpreters or critics have noticed this), he seems to have seen this expressive aspect of religion as a by-product of its cognitive role:

Although, as we have established, religious thought is very far from a system of fictions, the realities to which it corresponds can still only be expressed in a religious form when transfigured by the imagination. Between society as it is objectively and the sacred things which represent it symbolically the distance is considerable. The impressions really experienced by men, which served as the raw material for this construction, had to be interpreted, elaborated and transformed until they became unrecognizable. So the world of religious things is a partially imaginary world, though only in its outward form, which therefore lends itself more readily to the free creations of the mind. Besides, since the intellectual forces which serve to form it are intense and tumultuous, the unique task of expressing what is real with the aid of appropriate symbols is not enough to occupy them. A surplus generally remains available which seeks to employ itself in supplementary and superfluous works of luxury, that is to say, in works of art. There are practices as well as beliefs of this sort. The state of effervescence in which the assembled faithful find themselves is necessarily outwardly expressed by

85. ibid., p. 315: tr. p. 220.
86. ibid., p. 511: tr. p. 358.
87. ibid., pp. 537, 541: tr. pp. 376, 378 (S.L.). Jane Harrison made much of this aspect of Durkheim's sociology of religion.

exuberant movements which cannot be easily subjected to ends that are too closely defined. They escape, in part, aimlessly, they display themselves for the mere joy of doing so, and take delight in all kinds of games.

Hence those gestures in the rites which 'have no purpose' but 'simply respond to the need of the believers to act, to move, to gesticulate'; so that one sees them 'jumping, whirling, dancing, crying and singing, though it may not always be possible to give a meaning to this agitation'.

Durkheim thus saw religion as necessarily giving a place to 'the free combinations of thought and activity, to play, to art, to all that recreates the tired spirit'. Art was 'not simply an external ornament'; the cult has 'in itself something aesthetic' and indeed 'there is a poetry inherent in all religion'. However, Durkheim characteristically qualified these assertions by observing that the importance of this aspect of religion should not be exaggerated. Rites were certainly not mere works of art, awakening 'vain images corresponding to nothing in reality': 'a rite is something different from a game: it is part of the serious life'. On the other hand,

it plays a role which is by no means negligible. It has its share in that feeling of comfort which the believer draws from the rite performed; for recreation is one of the forms of that moral remaking which is the principal object of the positive rite.[88]

Functional

This leads directly to the third, functional, set of hypotheses which concern religion's consequences – hypotheses which can be expressed macroscopically, in terms of its effects on society and social relationships; and microscopically, in terms of its effects on individuals. As Durkheim wrote, in his own review of

88. ibid., pp. 542–8: tr. pp. 379–83 (S.L.). In general, the whole of bk III of *The Elementary Forms* can be seen as exploring the expressive nature of ritual. He himself later wrote that, for each of the types of rite there considered, he had examined 'what are the collective states of mind expressed, maintained or restored' and thereby shown 'how the details of ritual life are linked to what is most essential in social life' (1913a (ii) (12), p. 98).

The Elementary Forms, 'religion thus understood appears as consisting above all of acts which have the object of perpetually making and remaking the soul (*l'âme*) of the collectivity and of individuals'.[89] Their function was to 'strengthen the bonds attaching the individual to the society of which he is a member'.[90] (As for the sense in which these consequences are 'functional', Durkheim clearly supposed that they served to maintain the indispensable conditions of social, and therefore individual life.)

We have suggested that the analysis of the consequences of religion in *The Elementary Forms* can be seen as operating both at the social and at the individual levels. At the social level, Durkheim examined, for example, the social functions of religious asceticism ('. . . society itself is possible only at this price'[91]), he elaborated on Smith's view of sacrifice as an 'alimentary communion',[92] bringing about a 'collective renovation',[93] and he characterized commemorative rites as serving to 'revivify the most essential elements of the collective consciousness', so that 'the group periodically renews the sentiment which it has of itself and of its unity'.[94] Similarly, he analysed mourning rites as strengthening social bonds and as consisting in a 'communion of minds' which 'raises the social vitality',[95] and he regarded piacular rites in general as having a 'stimulating power over the affective state of the group and individuals'; thus, for example, when, in punishing the neglect of a ritual act, 'the anger which it causes is affirmed ostensibly and energetically', and is 'acutely felt by all', the 'moral unity of the group is not endangered'.[96]

Durkheim saw religion as performing these social functions, both as a system of communication of ideas and sentiments, and as a means of specifying and regulating social relationships.

89. 1913a (ii) (12), p. 98.
90. 1912a, p. 323: tr. p. 226.
91. ibid., p. 452: tr. p. 316.
92. ibid., p. 481: tr. 337.
93. ibid., p. 498: tr. p. 349.
94. ibid., p. 536: tr. p. 375.
95. ibid., p. 574: tr. p. 401.
96. ibid., pp. 583–4: tr. p. 408.

Thus, in the first place, symbolism was 'necessary if society is to become conscious of itself' and 'no less indispensable for assuring the continuation of this consciousness'[97]; indeed, 'social life, in all its aspects and in every period of its history, is made possible only by a vast symbolism'.[98] The role of emblems was to perpetuate and recreate the 'social sentiments'[99] aroused by the rites; moreover, the rites themselves enabled social communication to 'become a real communion, that is to say, a fusion of all particular sentiments into one common sentiment',[1] and they not only expressed but served 'to support the beliefs upon which they are founded'.[2] Hence, the cult in general was both 'a system of signs by which the faith is outwardly translated' and 'a collection of the means by which this is created and recreated periodically'.[3] In the second place, Durkheim, as we have seen, saw totemism as essentially constitutive of aboriginal social organization: the totem identified the clan, whose members were bound by specific ties of kinship, so that 'the collective totem is part of the civil status of each individual'.[4] Indeed, a

clan is essentially a group of individuals who bear the same name and rally round the same sign. Take away the name and the sign which materializes it, and the clan is no longer representable. Since the group is possible only on this condition, both the institution of the emblem and the part it takes in the life of the group are thus explained.[5]

97. ibid., p. 331: tr. p. 231.

98. ibid. Cf. Lévi-Strauss's mistaken claim that Durkheim failed to show how 'the appearance of symbolic thought makes social life together possible and necessary' (Lévi-Strauss, 1945, p. 518, discussed in Chapter 10, above).

99. ibid., p. 330: tr. p. 231.

1. ibid., p. 329: tr. p. 230.

2. ibid., p. 511: tr. p. 358. Cf.: 'We must refrain from regarding these symbols as simple artifices, as sorts of labels attached to *représentations* already created ... they are an integral part of them' (ibid., p. 331: tr. p. 231 – S.L.).

3. ibid., p. 596: tr. p. 417.

4. ibid., pp. 229–30: tr. p. 161.

5. ibid., p. 334: tr. p. 233 (S.L.).

At the individual level, Durkheim wrote that the 'Arunta who has been properly rubbed with his churinga feels himself stronger; he is stronger',[6] and argued that, in general, the

> believer who has communicated with his god is not merely a man who sees new truths of which the unbeliever is ignorant; he is a man who is stronger (*un homme qui peut davantage*). He feels within him more force, either to endure the trials of existence, or to conquer them. It is as though he were raised above the miseries of the world, because he is raised above his condition as a mere man; he believes that he is saved from evil, under whatever form he may conceive this evil. The first article in every creed is salvation by faith.[7]

In generalizing thus, he appealed to the evidence of the general experience of believers: 'whoever has really practised a religion knows very well that it is the cult which gives rise to these impressions of joy, of interior peace, of serenity, of enthusiasm which are, for the believer, an experimental proof of his beliefs'.[8] Among the Australian aboriginals, he argued, the 'negative cult' was 'found to exercise a positive influence of the highest importance over the moral and religious nature of the individual', so that, for example, in the initiation rites certain pains were inflicted on the neophyte 'to modify his condition and to make him acquire the qualities characteristic of a man'[9]; and the belief was 'not without foundation' that 'suffering creates exceptional strength'.[10] Similarly, as a result of the sacrificial rites, men 'are more confident because they feel themselves stronger; and they really are stronger, because forces which were languishing are now reawakened in the consciousness'.[11] As to the 'imitative rites', which Frazer misleadingly thought of as sympathetic magic, their 'moral efficacy' was real and itself 'leads to the belief in [the rite's] physical efficacy, which is imaginary'; their 'true justification . . . does not lie in the apparent ends which they pursue, but rather in the invisible influence which they exercise over the

6. ibid., p. 326: tr. p. 228 (S.L.).
7. ibid., p. 595: tr. 416.
8. ibid., p. 596: tr. p. 417.
9. ibid., pp. 441, 447: tr. pp. 309, 313 (S.L.).
10. ibid., p. 451: tr. p. 315.
11. ibid., p. 494: tr. p. 346.

mind and in the way in which they affect our level of consciousness'.[12] Again, the commemorative rites 'give [men] a feeling of strength and confidence: a man is surer of his faith when he sees to how distant a past it goes back and what great things it has inspired'[13]; while the recreative element of ritual activity 'contributes to that feeling of comfort which the worshipper draws from the rite performed'.[14] In general, Durkheim concluded, the object of the religious life, in all its forms, was

to raise man above himself and to make him lead a life superior to that which he would lead if he followed only his spontaneous desires: beliefs express this life in *représentations*; rites organize it and regulate its functioning.[15]

The foregoing analysis of *The Elementary Forms* helps, among other things, to resolve an ambiguity inherent in all Durkheim's writings: was religion in decline, or was it a permanent feature of all societies? Was he basically in the camp of those like de Maistre and de Bonald who argued that religion was an indispensable basis for all possible societies; or was he in the camp of Saint-Simon and Comte, who sought to propagate functional alternatives to traditional religion – secular Religions of Humanity, based on Science and Reason; or was he rather in the camp of Max Weber, seeing the modern world as increasingly secularized, disenchanted and rationalized?

The answer is that he had a foot in all three camps.[16] All societies, he believed, generated belief-systems which held

12. ibid., pp. 513, 514: tr. pp. 359, 360 (S.L.).
13. ibid., pp. 536–7: tr. p. 375.
14. ibid., p. 547: tr. p. 382 (S.L.).
15. ibid., p. 592: tr. p. 414.
16. This applies to his later thought, subsequent to his 'discovery' of religion in the mid-1890s. Thus in *The Division of Labour* he wrote that throughout history 'religion tends to embrace a smaller and smaller portion of social life' (1902b, p. 143: tr. 1933b, p. 169). He was, indeed, still stressing this view in the lectures on socialism of 1895–6 (see 1928a, p. 329: tr. 1958b, pp. 225–6). By 1898, he was already writing that a religion was 'in a sense, indispensable' and that the religion of individualism was 'the only system of belief which can ensure the moral unity of the country' (1898c, p. 10: tr. 1969d, p. 25).

certain beings and activities to be sacred, and which prescribed certain ritual practices: to the extent that these beliefs and practices were indecisive, a society was undergoing a period of (transitional) moral crisis. Among modern forms taken by such beliefs and practices were 'the sacred character' accorded to 'princes, nobles and political leaders', the belief in progress and the commitment to free inquiry, which is itself 'untouchable, that is to say . . . sacred'[17] – and the 'cult of man [which] has for its first dogma the autonomy of reason and for its first rite freedom of thought'.[18] Furthermore, he seems to have regarded the *expressive* role of religion as indispensable: thus symbolic representations were 'as necessary for the well working of our moral life as our food is for the maintenance of our physical life, for it is through them that the group maintains and affirms itself, and we know to what extent this is indispensable for the individual'.[19] Moreover, the *functions* performed by religion were, he thought, common to all societies, and in this sense he claimed that 'there is something eternal in religion which is destined to survive all the particular symbols in which religious thought has successively enveloped itself'. There could, he maintained, be

no society which does not feel the need of upholding and reaffirming at regular intervals the collective sentiments and the collective ideas which make its unity and its personality. Now this moral remaking cannot be achieved except by the means of reunions, assemblies and meetings where the individuals, being closely united to one another, reaffirm in common their common sentiments . . .[20]

If one saw religion in these functional terms, it was 'in a sense, indispensable'[21] and universal. What mattered with respect to ceremonies was 'their object, the results which they produce, or the procedures employed to attain these results'.[22] 'What essential difference was there between an assembly of Christians celebrating the principal dates of the life of Christ,

17. 1912a, p. 305: tr. p. 213 (S.L.).
18. 1898c, p. 10: tr. 1969d, p. 24. Cf. Chapter 17, above.
19. 1912a, p. 546: tr. p. 382 (S.L.).
20. ibid., pp. 609–10, tr. p. 427.
21. 1898c, p. 10: tr. p. 25.
22. 1912a, p. 610: tr. p. 427 (S.L.).

or of Jews remembering the exodus from Egypt or the promulgation of the Decalogue, and a reunion of citizens commemorating the promulgation of a new moral or legal system or some great event in the national life?'[23] On the other hand, as a *cognitive* enterprise, religion was, if not quite defunct, certainly moribund. Sociology was its successor.

It was in this way that Durkheim could reconcile de Maistre, Comte and Weber; and his view of religion and its functions with his scientific rationalism. What was 'eternal in religion' was 'the cult and the faith'; and 'in so far as religion is action, and in so far as it is a means of making men live, science could not take its place'. On the other hand, in the cognitive sphere, where 'scientific thought is only a more perfect form of religious thought', it was entirely natural that science had progressively taken over the natural world, most recently the psychological realm; and now one could foresee that the final barrier would give way and science would establish herself in the social realm, as mistress even in the reserved region of the moral and religious life itself.

Thus Durkheim could foresee both a (secular) religious revival and the limitless progress of science. On the one hand, he could look forward to the coming of a day when

our societies will know again those hours of creative effervescence, in the course of which new ideas arise and new formulae are found which serve for a while as a guide to humanity; and once these hours have been lived through, men will spontaneously feel the need to relive them in thought, keeping alive their memory by means of celebrations which regularly reproduce their fruits.

On the other hand, he could also look forward, as we have abundantly seen, to the ever-increasing scientific understanding of the human world, under the aegis of sociology; here, it was clear that science 'denies religion, not its right to exist, but its right to dogmatize on the nature of things and the special competence it claims for knowing man and his world'. Indeed, Durkheim envisaged that in the future, religious faith would become increasingly subject to the influence and the authority of the sciences. Though faith, under the pressure of practical

23. ibid.

needs, always had to 'anticipate science and complete it prematurely', Durkheim prophesied that an increasingly rationalized and secularized religion would become ever more subject to the criticism and the control of science.[24]

DURKHEIM'S SOCIOLOGY OF RELIGION

Durkheim's sociology of religion, as set out in *The Elementary Forms*, was, as we shall see, subjected to a barrage of extremely wide-ranging and often probing criticisms by contemporaries, and by succeeding generations of scholars to this day. In this final section we shall first survey the work's shortcomings, which can (somewhat arbitrarily) be grouped into the ethnographic, the methodological, the logical and the theoretical. It is, needless to say, a measure of the book's stature that its considerable value survives these many valid criticisms.

The ethnographic case against *The Elementary Forms* is multiple. The following points, among others, have been urged against it.[25] First, among the Australian aboriginals, it is the horde and the tribe which are the corporate groups – and not the clans, which are widely dispersed and un-cohesive, lacking both chiefs and a common territory, so that it is not clear why stress should be laid on the maintenance of their solidarity. Second, Central Australian totemism, on which Durkheim based his entire theory, is highly atypical and specialized, even within Australia – so that, for instance, the *intichiuma* ceremonies have a very different significance or do not even exist elsewhere in the continent; and many of the features found in Central Australia, and which Durkheim presented as characteristic of totemism, are lacking in other totemic systems – such as concentrations, ceremonies, sacred objects, designs, etc.[26] Third, there is no evidence at all that

---

24. ibid., pp. 611–16: tr. pp. 427–31 (S.L.). For some further hints of how Durkheim envisaged the religion of the future, see below, pp. 516–17.

25. Here I rely mainly on Evans-Pritchard, 1965, pp. 64–7, Stanner, 1967, and van Gennep, 1920. For these and further ethnographic objections, see the final section of Chapter 25, below.

26. Durkheim, according to Stanner, was the victim of a 'freakish, passing state of affairs in Australian ethnography' (art. cit., p. 240).

Australian totemism is the earliest form of totemism (let alone of religion). Moreover, although the Australians are at a more primitive stage of technical development and social organization than the Indians of North America, this does not mean that their kinship system or their totemic organization is less developed. Indeed, quite the contrary: these had developed very far beyond the primitive stage postulated by Durkheim.[27] Fourth, there is evidence that totemism is not associated with the simplest forms of social organization and technology. There are societies which are simpler in these latter senses which have religious beliefs and rites but no totems, or indeed clans. Fifth, there is evidence against Durkheim's equation of totemism and the religion of the clan: that is, there are clans without totems and totems without clans. Indeed, the ethnographic evidence goes contrary to Durkheim's claim that the social organization of the Australians themselves is on a clan basis.[28] Sixth, Durkheim's emphasis on figured representations of the totems is questionable, since most of the totems are not so represented. Seventh, there is no evidence that the gods of Australia are syntheses of totems. Eighth, there is no ethnographic evidence that 'the ideas of *wakan* and of *mana* are derived [from] the notion of the totemic principle'.[29] Finally, and perhaps most importantly, there is the question of Durkheim's dichotomy between the sacred and the profane. We have already discussed this in relation to the other dichotomies which structure his thought.[30] Let it suffice here to recall Stanner's remark that it is 'unusable except at the cost of undue interference with the facts of observation'. The aboriginal universe is 'not divided in fact, and therefore should not be divided in theory, into two classes'.[31]

These, then are the main ethnographic criticisms of *The Elementary Forms*, and they amount to a powerful case. After making his ethnographic objections to the work, van Gennep wrote as follows:

27. Cf. van Gennep, 1920, p. 71.
28. See Goldenweiser, 1917.
29. 1912a, p. 290: tr. 1915d, p. 203.
30. In the Introduction, above.
31. Stanner, 1967, pp. 229, 230.

I will not deny the ingenuity of this whole construction, which in its breadth and simplicity, is the equal of the best constructions of the Hindu metaphysicians, the Muslim commentators and the scholastic Catholics, taken together. But as for recognizing in it any scientific reality and truth, that appears to me difficult, given, above all, that it is entirely based on analyses and interpretations whose accuracy ethnographers could not accept.[32]

On the other hand, it is worth citing Stanner's remark that, despite the inadequacies of the ethnography on which he relied, Durkheim's 'insight from afar was in many ways brilliantly penetrating',[33] as well as Elkin's judgement that

ever since it has been my good fortune to get to understand native life in Australia, I have been amazed at the remarkable manner in which Durkheim was able to penetrate that life through the medium of Spencer and Gillen, Strehlow and a few others. Durkheim's position cannot be completely held, but his work is an inspiration.[34]

The principal methodological criticism of *The Elementary Forms* concerns what we have called Durkheim's 'methodo-logical assumption' that he was engaged in a crucial experiment that would verify his theory. Not only is it highly dubious that he had found the simplest available case that contained in germ 'all the essential elements of religious thought and life'; this concentration on a very limited range of evidence served to shield him from uncomfortable evidence from elsewhere than Central Australia, and led him to make the boldest generalizations on the slim basis of his own theory-laden view of one very particular religion. Hence, for example, his neglect of the role of individuals, especially religious leaders and functionaries, such as prophets, magicians, sorcerers and shamans, and of religious elites; of social and religious conflict

32. Van Gennep, 1920, p. 49.
33. Stanner, 1967, p. 240.
34. Elkin, A. P., Review of W. Lloyd Warner's *A Black Civilisation* (New York, 1937) in *Oceania*, VIII (1937), p. 119. Elkin saw Warner's book as 'a successful attempt' to interpret the life of the aborigines (in fact, the Murngin tribe) 'in the light of Durkheim's sociological principles ... and although Professor Warner does not blindly follow Durkheim, his work shows that the latter's original interpretation of Aboriginal ceremonial life ... was sound' (ibid.).

and the non-integrative consequences of religion. Hence, in general, his failure to consider all other varieties of religious experience, belief and behaviour, and his rejection of all the alternative interpretations of mythology, symbolism and ritual excluded by his own narrowly based theory.[35] Furthermore, not only did his assumption of the crucial experiment limit his vision (rendering it, perhaps, the more intense); he also violated it in practice. He made use of the American evidence whenever the Australian data did not support his thesis. Apart from the arbitrariness of assuming that these were 'two varieties of a single type . . . still very close to each other' and representing 'two successive moments of a single evolution',[36] it was surely inconsistent to appeal to the American evidence on the grounds that in Australia social organization on a clan basis was 'in a state of fluctuating change and dissolution, which is in no way normal', but rather 'the result of a degeneration'.[37] In brief, not only did Durkheim implausibly rest his entire theory on his single experiment; he used data from outside that experiment whenever it failed to furnish him with the evidence he needed.

The logical failings of *The Elementary Forms* are those characteristic of Durkheim's thought as a whole – in particular, argument by elimination, special pleading to account for awkward evidence and, above all, *petitio principii*.[38] There is, for example, a passage which neatly combines both argument by elimination and *petitio principii*. Having dismissed animism and naturism as plausible theories of religion, he proceeded to draw one 'positive conclusion':

Since neither man nor nature have in themselves a sacred character, they must get it from another source. Apart from the human individual and the physical world, there must therefore be some other reality in relation to which this type of delirium in which all religion, in a sense, consists gains a significance and an objective value. In other words, beyond what has been called naturism and animism, there must be another cult, more fundamental and more

35. Cf. Chapter 25, below, passim.
36. 1912a, pp. 136–8: tr. pp. 96–7 (S.L.).
37. ibid., p. 157: tr. p. 112 (S.L.). Cf. van Gennep, 1920, pp. 45, 48.
38. See Introduction, above.

primitive, of which the former are probably only derived forms or particular aspects.

This cult exists, in fact; it is that to which ethnographers have given the name of totemism.[39]

This passage assumes, first, that animism, naturism and a third explanation in terms of 'some other reality' (guess which) are mutually exclusive and jointly exhaustive of the possible explanations of religion; and secondly, it assumes – indeed asserts – both that there must be a more fundamental and more primitive cult, and that this cult is totemism – which is, of course, exactly what is at issue. In fact, *petitio principii* is, in a sense, a feature of the book as a whole, for Durkheim begins it with his conclusion, building it into his very definition of religion and then seeking to prove it by finding examples.[40] As one of his critics observed, this meant that one could only get out of his analysis what had been put into it.[41]

This leads us, finally, to what he did put into it – namely, the theory he brought to bear. Here there is one single and central, valid criticism common to all Durkheim's critics. This is that his theory – despite the impressive coherence of its structure and its monumental sweep, and despite its brilliantly penetrating insights into certain dimensions of religious experience and practice – is altogether too unilateral. He was, indeed, quite obsessed by the vision of society as the unique and all-encompassing *fons et origo* of religion – as it also was of morality and of knowledge. Hence his effort, which we have analysed, to establish multiple explanatory relations between society and religion – seeing the former as causal determinant, cognitive and symbolic referent, and functional consequence of the latter. His 'sociocentric fixation' was, truly, 'all-consuming'.[42] For him, there could simply be no other basis of

39. 1912a, p. 124: tr. pp. 87–8 (S.L.).

40. Thus the two crucial elements of the definition are *sacredness* (which, as we have seen, Durkheim interpreted as signifying the social in contrast to the individual) and *the uniting of men into a single moral community*.

41. Wallis, 1914: see p. 513 below.

42. Stanner, 1967, p. 238. Stanner writes: 'There could be but one mould for everything: beliefs, rites, sentiments, social forms, categories of thought, schemes of classification, scientific concepts. It is this vision which explains the quality, a pervasive atmosphere of inevitability, that

explanation. Van Gennep was only repeating what countless other critics have said when he observed that Durkheim made of the totem a sort of social Logos.[43]

Yet the book remains a classic of its kind, which continues to afford intellectual excitement and inspiration to its readers. This is, perhaps, not so much because of the explanations it offers as because of the explanatory ideas it so richly suggests. It is to be read less as a study in Australian ethnology or even as a general theory of religion, but rather as a storehouse of ideas worth developing and refining, as well as criticizing.

There is, first, and perhaps most fundamentally, its challenging, and over-ambitious, contribution to the sociology of knowledge, which we have considered above. Second, there is its fertile, and complex, explanatory approach – seeking to avoid both the facile rationalism of the anti-religious and the explanations or justifications of the religious. His assumption that one should aim to go 'underneath the symbol to the reality which it represents and which gives it its true meaning' and that all religions 'answer, though in different ways, to the given conditions of human existence'[44] are potent, indeed invaluable working assumptions to anyone engaged on the sociology of religion – and on the sociology of thought in general.

Finally, there are the work's central explanatory hypotheses. These have, of course, been very influential, often without

---

every reader of *The Elementary Forms* must have noticed. It produces a sense, which grows always stronger, that the earnest stress on scientific method, the painstaking empiricism, the textual care, the dazzling erudition, the sinewy argument are superogatory, which is not in any way to say unauthentic, but merely that in the beginning was the end' (ibid., pp. 238–9).

43. Van Gennep, 1920, p. 50.

44. 'Among these given conditions,' writes Victor Turner (after quoting these words of Durkheim), 'the arrangement of society into structured groupings, discrepancies between the principles which organize these groupings, economic collaboration and competition, schism within groups and opposition between groups – in short, all those things with which the social aspect of ritual symbolism is concerned – are surely of at least equal importance with biopsychical drives and early conditioning in the elementary family' (Turner, V. W., 'Symbols in Ndembu Ritual', reprinted in Emmet, D., and MacIntyre, A., eds., *Sociological Theory and Philosophical Analysis*, London, 1970, p. 170).

knowledge of their authorship; and they retain all their power to stimulate ideas and theories, provided that one conceives of the social realities to which they relate religious phenomena in a much more complex and less unitary fashion than Durkheim did.[45] The hypothesis of religious belief and practice as (to whatever degree) socially determined remains at the centre of the sociological study of religion – though Durkheim's rather dated stress on crowd-psychology as the principal mechanism of such determination is no longer of such great interest. The idea that religious thought is to be seen as a cognitive enterprise, and that the non-empirical and supernatural beings that comprise it have a crucial role in rendering the human world intelligible, is an idea of considerable explanatory power and suggestiveness.[46] Again, the perhaps more familiar idea that religious thought and ritual express and dramatize social relationships is central to a whole and still living tradition of anthropological work,[47] as is the functionalist hypothesis relating religion in various ways to the

45. Cf. Max Gluckman's comment that 'What Durkheim missed when he derived "God" from the feeling of the presence of society at an Australian corroborree, was that the members of the "congregation", assembled in unity there, are enemies of one another in many other situations'. Gluckman, M., 'Les Rites de passage' in Gluckman, M. (ed.), *Essays on the Ritual of Social Relations* (Manchester, 1962, p. 40).

46. See especially the writings of Robin Horton and the so-called 'Neo-Tylorians': for example, Horton, R., 'Neo-Tylorianism: Sound Sense or Sinister Prejudice?', *Man*, 3 (1968), pp. 625–34; 'African Traditional Thought and Western Science', *Africa*, 37 (1967), pp. 50–71 and 155–87; 'Ritual Man in Africa', *Africa*, 34 (1964), pp. 85–103; also Horton, 1973. Also see Spiro, M. E., 'Religion: Problems of Definition and Explanation' in Banton, M. (ed.), *Anthropological Approaches to the Study of Religion* (London, 1966), and Goody, 1961.

47. Interestingly, Runciman calls this tradition 'Neo-Durkheimian', though the foregoing analysis suggests that, if anything, it is the stress on the cognitive role of religion that is central to Durkheim's thought. Chief among contemporary exponents of the symbolic-expressive-dramatic view of religion (and magic) are Edmund Leach, Raymond Firth and John Beattie. See, for example, Leach, E., *Political Systems in Highland Burma* (London, 1954); Firth, R., *Essays on Social Organisation and Values* (London, 1964); and Beattie, J., *Other Cultures* (London, 1964), chs. v and xii; 'Ritual and Social Change', *Man* (1966), pp. 60–74; and 'On Understanding Ritual' in Wilson, B. R. (ed.), *Rationality* (Oxford, 1970). For a critique see Lukes, 1967b, reprinted in ibid.

maintenance of social solidarity.[48] Finally, of course, the interest and suggestiveness of these hypotheses extends beyond the study of religion, pointing, for example, to ways of accounting for other forms of symbolism and ritual, and the complex ways in which societies are ideologically integrated.[49]

However, independently of the explanatory power of *The Elementary Forms*, there still remained a residual but philosophically fundamental problem contained in Durkheim's claim that all religions were 'true in their own fashion', a problem of central significance for his sociology of knowledge. It was to the consideration of this problem that he turned in the following year.

48. Here, of course, the main influence was Radcliffe-Brown.

49. There have been a number of what one might call 'neo-Durkheimian' attempts to account for political ritual as integrative in modern societies: for example, Warner, W. L., *The Living and the Dead: A Study of the Symbolic Life of Americans* (New Haven, 1959) and *American Life* (Chicago, 1962) on 'the sacred symbolic behaviour of Memorial Day'; Shils, E., and Young, M., 'The Meaning of the Coronation', *Sociological Review*. 1, n.s. (1953), pp. 63–81; Verba, S., 'The Kennedy Assassination and the Nature of Political Commitment', in Greenberg, B. S., and Parker, E. B. (eds.), *The Kennedy Assassination and the American Public* (Stanford, 1965) on the popular reaction to the President's death; and Bellah, R. N., 'Civil Religion in America' in McLoughlin, W. G., and Bellah, R. N. (eds.), *Religion in America* (Boston, 1968). For a valuable critique of Shils and Young, see Birnbaum, N., 'Monarchs and Sociologists', *Sociological Review*, 3, n.s. (1955), pp. 5–23; and of Verba, see Lipsitz, L., 'If, as Verba says, the state functions as a religion, What are we to do then to save our souls?', *American Political Science Review*, LXII (1968), pp. 527–35. The gist of these critiques of the neo-Durkheimian theory of political ritual is that such rituals are rather to be seen as agencies of mystification and the perpetuation of a conservative ideology. Cf. also Edelman, M., *The Symbolic Uses of Politics* (Urbana, Chicago and London, 1967), and Lukes, S., 'Political Ritual and Social Integration', *Sociology*, 7 (1973), forthcoming. Finally, for an interesting, critical discussion of the relevance of Durkheim's sociology of religion to the explanation of nationalism (and the use made of it by political scientists studying the formation of new states in Asia and Africa) see Smith, A. D., *Theories of Nationalism* (London, 1971), pp. 45 ff.

Chapter 24

Pragmatism and Sociology

IN 1913–14 Durkheim offered a new course of lectures, on 'Pragmatism and Sociology'. This course, of which we now fortunately have a published version derived from students' notes,[1] appeared to Mauss as 'the crowning achievement of Durkheim's philosophical work'.[2] Mauss recalled that

> The goal he set himself was to make known to his students that form of philosophical thought called 'Pragmatism' which was at that time still a novelty. He had especially intended this course for his son André Durkheim, who was now his pupil. He wished to fill a gap in the education of these young men. He seized the opportunity, not only to acquaint them with this philosophy, but also to specify the relations, the agreements and the disagreements which he held to exist between this system and the philosophical truths which appeared to him already to have emerged from a nascent sociology. He situated himself and his philosophy in relation to M. Bergson, to William James, to M. Dewey, and the other American pragmatists. Not only did he summarize their doctrine forcefully and faithfully; he also sifted from it what, from his own point of view, appeared to be worth preserving. He took especial account of M. Dewey, for whom he had a very strong admiration. This course was of great value and made a great impression on a very large public, and especially (which is all Durkheim wanted) on a number of young and good minds.[3]

It was also, as Cuvillier has observed, 'a complement and, so to speak, a continuation of the theory of knowledge outlined

1. 1955a. Surprisingly, the only published discussions of this are Cuvillier, 1955 and 1958, and de Gaudemar, 1969. It certainly deserves to be much more widely known, both for what it reveals about Durkheim's thought and for its pungent critique of ideas that are still, in various forms, current.
2. Mauss, 1925a, p. 10.
3. ibid.

in *The Elementary Forms of the Religious Life*,[4] for it tackled the issues, raised by Pragmatism and crucial for the sociology of knowledge, of the criterion, or criteria, of truth and its alleged relativity.

That relativity was proclaimed in its most extreme form by James, whose writings were beginning to find a ready public in France. The ground had been prepared by increasing attacks on neo-Kantianism and positivism from various quarters but most effectively from the pen of Bergson. James's *The Meaning of Truth* had just appeared in French translation, two years after a translation of his *Pragmatism*, with a preface by Bergson.[5] Through these and other writings, Jamesian Pragmatism was attracting interest, seeming to offer a philosophical, even para-scientific, rationale for the anti-intellectualist currents of the time.[6] As Durkheim observed, it offered 'almost the sole theory of truth currently existing'[7] and it shared with sociology 'a sense of *life* and *action*',[8] but its conclusions were part of a general 'assault upon Reason, a real armed struggle'.[9] Not surprisingly, Durkheim took up the struggle, seeing in 'this form of irrationalism which Pragmatism represents'[10] a threat that was both cultural ('A total negation of Rationalism . . . [which] would subvert our entire national culture'[11]) and philosophical. The whole philosophical tradition, with the exception of the Sophists, had been rationalist in the relevant sense that in all its forms, whether Rationalist or Empiricist, it recognized 'the obligatory and necessary

4. Cuvillier, 1955, p. 11. See Chapter 22, above.

5. *A Pluralistic Universe* was translated in 1910.

6. It was especially evident in the 'modernist' neo-religious movement, of which Édouard Le Roy was a leading figure (see 1955a, p. 41, and Chapter 25, below). Bergson himself seems to have been relatively uninfluenced by Pragmatism.

7. 1955a, p. 27: tr. 1960c, p. 386 (S.L.).

8. ibid. (S.L.).

9. ibid. (S. L.). As Cuvillier notes, Durkheim was here probably referring to James's statement: 'Against rationalism as a pretension and a method pragmatism is fully armed and militant' (*Pragmatism*, London, 1907, p. 54, cited in ibid.).

10. ibid., p. 28: tr. p. 386 (S.L.).

11. ibid. (S.L.).

character of certain truths'[12]; Pragmatism broke with this tradition by affirming that 'the mind remains free in the face of what is true'.[13] It thereby showed 'the necessity for renovating traditional rationalism',[14] so as to 'satisfy the demands of modern thought, and to take account of certain new points of view that have been introduced by contemporary science'.[15] The problem Durkheim set himself was 'to find a formula that will preserve the essence of rationalism, while answering the justified criticisms made of it by Pragmatism'.[16]

Durkheim concentrated on the ideas of James, together with the elaboration of them by the Oxford philosopher F. C. S. Schiller, their refinement and modification by Dewey, and a number of arguments gratefully borrowed by James from Bergson. These ideas and arguments posed the crucial question not yet directly confronted by Durkheim's sociology of knowledge: is truth itself variable, a function of human interests and purposes? The virtue of Pragmatism, he thought, was to have raised the question, but its answer was unacceptable. From the Pragmatist point of view, 'though the truth is certainly good, useful, "satisfying", it is nonetheless without any characteristic of logical necessity. It is we who make it and we make it thus to satisfy our needs. We are therefore entirely *free* in the process of its construction.'[17] Yet, as he repeatedly argued, 'Pragmatism offers no proof of the thesis it

12. ibid.: tr. p. 387.

13. ibid. Durkheim rightly distinguished this position from that of Nietzsche, for whom there was a 'higher' truth, and from that of Peirce, whose ideas were distorted by James; as Durkheim justly observed, Peirce 'does not repudiate rationalism', offering no theory of truth, indeed admitting its inescapability (ibid., pp. 29–36: tr. pp. 387–92). Cf. Perry's dictum that 'the philosophical movement known as Pragmatism is largely the result of James's misunderstanding of Peirce' (cited in Gallie, W. B., *Peirce and Pragmatism*, London, 1952, in which see ch. 1 and passim.).

14. 1955a, p. 27: tr. p. 386 (S.L.).

15. ibid., p. 29: tr. p. 387 (S.L.).

16. ibid. (S.L.). Cf. 1912a, p. 26 fn.: tr. 1915d, p. 19 fn. (S.L.), where Durkheim writes of the 'rationalism which is immanent in a sociological theory of knowledge'.

17. 1955a, p. 125.

advances, the thesis that truth is amorphous.'[18] He maintained, on the contrary, that truth 'is enriched, but it does not, properly speaking, change.'[19] The Pragmatist thesis 'has a certain basis', resting on 'certain facts which the Pragmatists sense only vaguely, but which must be given their true significance'[20] by being explained sociologically. The 'sociological point of view', he claimed, 'has the advantage of making it possible to apply analysis even to so august a thing as truth', while retaining the 'higher value' possessed by 'truth, together with reason and morality'.[21] As he had written in *The Elementary Forms*, to 'attribute social origins to logical thought is not to debase it or diminish its value or reduce it to nothing more than a system of artificial combinations'.[22]

Broadly speaking, Durkheim, while rejecting virtually all the Pragmatists' specific arguments,[23] found some value, first in their negative critique of 'rationalism' and, second, in their positive objectives.

The Pragmatists, in criticizing the 'Dogmatic Conception of Truth', according to which 'the truth is given, either in the world of sense-experience (as in Empiricism) or in an intelligible world – in an absolute thought or Reason (as in Rationalism)',[24] were really taking on virtually the whole of Western philosophy under the general heading of 'rationalism'. The Pragmatist objections to this basic conception of truth as 'objective, transcendent, impersonal' were, as Durkheim

18. ibid., p. 146: tr. 1960c, p. 432.
19. ibid., p. 144: tr. p. 431 (S.L.).
20. ibid., p. 146: tr. p. 432 (S.L.).
21. ibid., p. 144: tr. p. 430 (S.L.).
22. 1912a, p. 634: tr. 1915d, p. 444 (S.L.).
23. Apart from the Pragmatists' arguments against the correspondence theory of truth, Durkheim found equally unacceptable their identification of knowledge and existence, the instrumentalist conception of knowledge, their criterion of truth and James's empty appeal to 'satisfaction', their confusion of logical and existential questions, James's psychological and individualist explanation of religion, which showed 'much indulgence for mystical intuitions' (ibid., p. 133) and the contradiction in Pragmatism between epiphenomenalism and idealism. In general, Pragmatism lacked 'the fundamental characteristics one has the right to expect from a philosophical doctrine' (ibid., p. 140: tr. p. 427 – S.L.).
24. ibid., p. 46: tr. p. 400 (S.L.).

carefully set them out, manifold but largely unconvincing: the Pragmatists held that truth on this view was useless and redundant, unknowable, extra-human, unchanging, incommensurate with human diversity, conducive to intolerance and based on a static conception of reality. Even more unacceptable to Durkheim was the critique of conceptual thought itself, borrowed by James from Bergson,[25] according to which 'the principle of identity and the law of non-contradiction do not apply to reality'[26]; Durkheim rejected this hostile 'attitude to classical Rationalism' shared by both thinkers, their 'tendency to subordinate clear thought to the confused aspect of things' and their 'form of argument, which puts conceptual thought in the dock'.[27] On the other hand, it was true that 'classical Rationalism' conceived of truth as 'a simple, quasi-divine thing which would derive all its value from itself', which was 'placed above human life' and whose 'role is to let itself be contemplated'; and it likewise put 'reason outside scientific analysis'.[28]

Accordingly, in terms of Pragmatism's positive objectives, there was value in James's ambition to 'soften the truth', in so far as this meant removing from truth 'this absolute and almost sacrosanct character' and making it 'part of reality and life'.[29] It could then be seen as having

antecedents and consequences. It poses problems: one is entitled to ask where it derives from, what function it serves, and so on. It becomes an object of science. Here lies the interest of the Pragmatist enterprise: one can discern in it an effort to *understand* truth and reason themselves, to restore to them their human interest, to make of them human things that derive from temporal causes and engender temporal consequences. To 'soften' truth is to make it into something that can be analysed and explained.[30]

25. *A Pluralistic Universe*, ch. VI.
26. 1955a, pp. 79–80: tr. p. 425.
27. ibid., pp. 80–1: tr. p. 425 (S.L.).
28. ibid., p. 141: tr. p. 428 (S.L.).
29. ibid., pp. 141–2: tr. p. 429 (S.L.).
30. ibid., p. 142: tr. 429 (S.L.).

Unfortunately, it was also to 'free it ... from the discipline of logical thought'.[31] Thus, despite Pragmatism's commendable aim of seeking to 'link thought to existence and to life',[32] despite its 'very keen sense of the diversity of minds and of the variability of thought in time'[33] and despite its realization that 'thought, tied to action, in a sense creates reality itself',[34] none the less its arguments led it to impugn logic itself and to fail to account for the universally held conception that 'the truth ... imposes itself on us independently of the facts of sensibility and individual impulse'.[35]

Durkheim argued that the facts which Pragmatism vaguely sensed but failed to explain were that there was no 'unique system of categories and intellectual frameworks', that the 'frameworks which had their *raison d'être* in former civilizations do not have it today, though this in no way detracts from the value they had for their time'.[36] All that Pragmatism offered by way of explanation of this was an '*ideal* notion', an arbitrary definition without objective value, according to which the true is the useful[37]; yet, to establish this very claim, Durkheim argued, one would need an independent criterion of truth. He proposed instead an inquiry into the characteristics of 'recognized truths', examining 'what makes them accepted', just as with morality one should begin with the study of moral facts.[38] Pragmatism, which was a kind of 'logical utilitarianism', could explain neither the obligation to accept truths, nor their 'factual necessitating power' (indeed, the 'truth is often bitter'[39]) nor their impersonality; nor could it account for the speculative function of truth, the intellectual need to understand, the non-utilitarian desire for knowledge, evident not only in history, science and philosophy, but also in primitive mythology; indeed, it failed to see that 'seeking truth for

31. ibid., pp. 140–1: tr. p. 428.
32. ibid., p. 53: tr. p. 407 (S.L.).
33. ibid., p. 67: tr. p. 416 (S.L.).; cf. ibid., p. 59: tr. p. 411.
34. ibid., p. 65: tr. p. 415.
35. ibid., p. 143: tr. p. 430 (S.L.).
36. ibid., p. 149: tr. p. 434–5 (S.L.).
37. ibid., p. 150: tr. p. 435.
38. ibid. Cf. 1906b: repr. 1924a: tr. 1953b.
39. ibid., pp. 154, 155.

truth's sake is neither an isolated case, nor a pathological fact, nor a deviation of thought'[40] and that 'the exigencies of knowledge are fundamentally different from those of practice'.[41] An inquiry such as Durkheim proposed would, he claimed, show that 'a *représentation* is considered to be true when it is believed to represent reality',[42] whether this belief was justified or not. This pointed to the need to know 'the causes which have determined that men should believe that a *représentation* conforms to reality',[43] and here the various '*représentations* that have been recognized as true in the course of history have an equal interest for us'.[44] It was necessary to examine pre-scientific and non-scientific truths, as well as scientific truths. In distinguishing between different sorts of truths, Durkheim was therefore led to distinguish between different sorts of correspondence between *représentations* and reality.

At this point, Durkheim's argument took a characteristic turn. Complex questions were best approached through evidence from simpler societies. Beginning with mythological truths, he asked:

Now, what led men to consider these mythological propositions or beliefs as true? Was it because they had confronted them with a given reality, with spirits, for example, or with divinities of whom they had a real experience? Not at all: the world of mythical beings is not a real world, and yet men have believed in it. Mythological ideas have not been regarded as true because founded on an objective reality. It is, on the contrary, our ideas, our beliefs which confer on the objects of thought their reality.[45]

From this he generalized to arguing that these ideas were collective *représentations*, endowed 'in virtue of their very origin, with a prestige thanks to which they have the power to *impose* themselves', a superior 'psychological energy', in

40. ibid., p. 164.
41. ibid., p. 167.
42. ibid., p. 172.
43. ibid.
44. ibid.
45. ibid., pp. 172–3.

which the 'very force of truth resides'.[46] Thus one redis-covered, transposed to another level, the double Pragmatist thesis that '(1) the model and the copy are identical; (2) we are the co-authors of reality'[47]; the difference was that sociology explained 'that impression of resistance and that sentiment of something transcending the individual which we experience in the presence of the truth and which are the very condition of objectivity'.[48] Thus, 'it is thought which creates reality, and the pre-eminent role of collective *représentations* is to "make" that superior reality which is *society* itself'.[49]

What, then, was the distinction between the 'two types of truths which are opposed to one another in the history of human thought', namely, '*mythological truths* and *scientific truths*'?[50]

The former were accepted without verification or demon-stration because of collective pressure; moreover, they were 'the conditions of existence of the societies who have believed in them', in which 'common life ... supposes common ideas and intellectual unanimity'.[51] Yet this did not imply a kind of sociological pragmatism, according to which peoples, rather than individuals, would be 'free to create the truth according to their fantasy'[52]: 'ideas, *représentations*, in effect, cannot become collective if they respond to nothing in reality'.[53] In general,

Every collective *représentation* must, on the practical level, be of service to individuals, that is, it must engender actions which are adjusted to things, to the realities to which they correspond. Now, in order to engender these actions, the *représentation* must itself be adapted to those realities.[54]

46. ibid., p. 173.
47. ibid.
48. ibid., p. 174.
49. ibid.
50. ibid., p. 175.
51. ibid.
52. ibid., p. 176. Cf. Parodi, 1919 (3rd edn), p. 458, for such a criticism applied to Durkheim.
53. ibid.
54. ibid., pp. 176–7.

Mythological *représentations* expressed society, and what 'religion translates, in its *représentations*, its beliefs and its myths, are social realitities and the way they act on individuals'.[55] Things served as symbols for the self-expression of society and, in consequence, 'mythical *représentations* are false in relation to things, but they are true in relation to the subjects who think them'.[56] Hence, truth was, in a sense, variable, but the Pragmatists were wrong to say that truths were constantly being created and old truths abolished:

All the cosmologies immanent in mythological systems are different from one another and yet those different cosmologies can legitimately be regarded as equally true, because they have fulfilled the same functions in relation to the peoples who have believed in them, because they have had the same social role.[57]

Scientific truths, on the other hand, 'express the world as it is',[58] and yet, Durkheim argued, 'scientific *représentations* too are collective *représentations*', for 'scientific truth contributes to reinforcing the social *conscience*, just like mythological thought, but by other means'.[59] There were two types of communication between individual minds: 'by becoming fused one with another, so as to become a single collective mind' and 'by communicating with respect to a single object which is the same for all, each still retaining his personality, like Leibniz's monads each of which expresses the universe as a whole while preserving its individuality'. The first procedure was that of mythological thought, the second that of scientific thought. The very object of science was 'to represent things as though viewed by a purely objective understanding'.[60]

Durkheim next turned to an examination of the place of science and the 'survival of mythological *représentations*' in contemporary society, and thereby offered a further clue to his conception of ideology and its relation to science.[61] Comte

55. ibid., p. 177.
56. ibid.
57. ibid., p. 178.
58. ibid.
59. ibid.
60. ibid., p. 179.
61. ibid., pp. 183 ff. Cf. Chapter 12, above.

had been wrong to expect that science would put an end to mythology, that 'one would live on scientific, positive truths, that one could consider established, and that for the rest one would live in intellectual doubt'.[62] Though true of the physical world, this was untrue of the human and social world, where science was still rudimentary and direct experiment impossible; here 'notions which express social phenomena in a truly objective fashion are still very rare'.[63] Sociology itself could only offer fragmentary hypotheses which had so far had little influence on the popular mind. Yet it was necessary to act and to live, and society could not wait for its problems to be solved scientifically. Consequently,

in the absence of objective knowledge, it can only know itself from within and must seek to translate the sentiment it has of itself and be guided by it. In other words, it must be led by a *représentation* of the same nature as those which constitute mythological truths.[64]

These expressed 'a unanimous conception', which gave them 'a force, an authority which imposes them on individuals and removes them from control or doubt'.[65] Hence the existence of formulas 'that we do not see as religious, but which still have the character of dogmas and are not discussed' – notions such as 'democracy', 'progress' and 'the class struggle'.[66] Durkheim concluded:

There is, there will always be, in social life, a place for a form of truth which will be expressed perhaps in a very secular form, but which will still have a mythological and religious basis. For a long time yet, there will exist in all societies two tendencies: a tendency towards objective and scientific truth, and a tendency towards truth perceived from within, towards mythological truth. This is . . . one of the greatest obstacles to the progress of sociology.[67]

Finally, he sought to establish a link between mythological truth and conformism, on the one hand, and between scientific

62. ibid., p. 183.
63. ibid.
64. ibid., p. 184.
65. ibid.
66. ibid.
67. ibid.

truth and 'intellectual individualism', on the other. The latter was 'an indispensable factor in the establishment of scientific truth and the diversity of intellectual temperaments can come to serve an impersonal truth'.[68] Not only was scientific truth compatible with 'the diversity of minds'; it also went with social diversity ('as the complexity of social groups ceaselessly grows, it is impossible that society should have a single conception of itself...') and a growth in tolerance (which 'must henceforth rest on the idea of the complexity and the richness of reality, and consequently, on the diversity, at once necessary and effective, of opinions').[69]

It is clear that in all this Durkheim was really maintaining two different theses which he failed to separate from one another because he did not distinguish between the truth of a belief and the acceptance of a belief as true.[70] The first was the important philosophical thesis that there is a non-context-dependent or non-culture-dependent sense of truth (as correspondence to reality), such that, for example, primitive magical beliefs could be called 'false',[71] mythological ideas could be characterized as 'false in relation to things',[72] scientific truths could be said to 'express the world as it is'[73] and the Pragmatist claim that the truth is essentially variable could be denied. It was this thesis that Durkheim was advancing when, as against Bergson, he argued that the 'concept... expresses a reality: if it is distinct, this is because it expresses distinctions that are something quite other than a simple product of the mind' and that 'distinction is a need of conceptual thought; but it is already in things as it is in the mind. Likewise, continuity, communication is in the mind just as it is in things.'[74] Durkheim's second thesis, which he confused with the first, was a sociological one concerning beliefs (that is, propositions accepted as true) in different contexts and societies. This thesis

68. ibid., p. 186.
69. ibid., pp. 186–7.
70. Cf. de Gaudemar, 1969, p. 84.
71. See 1955a, p. 110.
72. ibid., p. 177.
73. ibid., p. 178.
74. ibid., pp. 194, 195.

had a number of component elements: first, that such beliefs (including scientific ones) have a social origin; second, that their *authority* comes from society ('*truth is a norm for thought as the moral ideal is a norm for conduct*'[75]); third, that they have social *functions* ('reinforcing the social *conscience*'; indeed, the expression of reality 'constitutes societies, though one might equally say that it derives from them')[76]; and fourth, that they are 'in no way arbitrary: they are modelled on realities, and in particular on the realities of social life'.[77] In this way, Durkheim's critique of Pragmatism can be seen as implying, first, a philosophical vindication of 'the essence of rationalism' (and with it the practice of sociology), and, second, a programme for the sociology of knowledge.[78]

75. ibid., p. 197.
76. ibid., p. 196.
77. ibid., p. 197.
78. For further discussion of this issue, see Lukes, 1973.

Chapter 25

Durkheim and His Critics

DURKHEIM'S ideas never ceased to be the centre of intense controversy. It was not merely that they were new, often extreme, and pungently and dogmatically expressed. They challenged academic and religious orthodoxies, disputing the methodologies of the former and discounting the supernatural justifications of the latter. Five areas in particular were especially productive of lively and worthwhile argument (in which Durkheim himself took an active part)[1]: his methodological principles, his critique of liberal economics, and his sociological treatment of morality, knowledge and religion.

SOCIAL REALISM

In the first place, Durkheim continued to be widely attacked for his so-called 'social realism'. Critics continued to characterize this (despite his repeated clarifications and disclaimers[2]) as dogmatic, scholastic, even mystical, as unverifiable and unscientific or alternatively as a denial of the freedom and uniqueness of the individual, and sometimes as immoral, entailing advocacy of the subordination of the individual to the group. Typical among these critics were, as we have seen, Tarde, Worms and (latterly) Richard; and also Alfred Fouillée, Andler, Belot, Bernès, Deploige, Leuba and Parodi.[3]

One of the most interesting expressions of this kind of criticism is to be found in the writings of the Nietzschean

1. For reasons of space, it seemed best in this chapter simply to convey the main lines of this argument, and to resist the temptation of commenting on, or engaging in, it.

2. See, for example, 1897a, pp. 14–15 fn.: tr. 1951a, p. 51 fn.; 1898d; 1901c, p. ix: tr. 1938b, p. xli; and many other places.

3. For references, see bibliography. Deploige's treatment is the most thorough, though very unscholarly (see 1913a (ii) (15)).

Georges Palante.[4] For Palante the antinomy between the individual and society was incapable of resolution; indeed one must
take sides and 'fight for the individual' and free him from social
constraint. Tarde, thought Palante, had been right in arguing
that 'the individual is not a simple product of biological and
social factors. He has at least the power to register in his own
way previous and present social influences, to react against
them and become a new centre of activity, the point of departure for a new social orientation.'[5] Palante took Durkheim to be
advocating a false methodology ('. . . it is to [individual
psychology] that one must always return. It remains – whether
one wishes it or not – the key which opens all doors'[6]) together
with a restrictive authoritarianism ('It seems to be Durkheim's
plan for sociology to take over the function previously
assumed by religion, namely, to restrain the individual in the
interests of society'[7]). Palante's alternative was to adopt
Tarde's methodology and to advocate a form of 'aristocratic'
individualism, encouraging the historical growth of individuality, and in particular the development of supermen who
would enhance social and cultural progress.

In general, however, the criticisms of Durkheim's social
realism did no more than repeat the observations of Tarde.
Durkheim offered a final defence against these charges in the
omitted section of the introduction to *The Elementary Forms*.[8]
He was not, he protested, indifferent to human beings, as his
critics claimed. In studying religious phenomena, his hope was

that this study will throw some light on the religious nature of man,
and it is to explain the *conscience morale* that is the ultimate aim of the
science des mœurs. In general, we hold that sociology has not completely achieved its task so long as it has not penetrated into the
mind (*le for intérieur*) of the individual in order to relate the institutions it seeks to explain to their psychological conditions. In truth –

4. See especially *Précis de sociologie* (2nd edn, Paris, 1903), *Combat
pour l'individu* (Paris, 1904), *La Sensibilité individualiste* (Paris, 1905) and
Les Antinomies entre l'individu et la société (Paris, 1913).

5. *Précis*, p. 60.

6. ibid., p. 3.

7. *Antinomies*, p. 280. For Durkheim's response to Palante, see 1901a
(iii) (2), 1902a (iii) (11) and 1902c.

8. 1909d. See above, pp. 408–9.

and this is doubtless what has given rise to the misunderstanding in question – man is for us less a point of departure than a point of arrival. We do not begin by postulating a certain conception of human nature so as to deduce from it a sociology: it is rather from sociology that we seek an increasing understanding of humanity.[9]

The general mental characteristics studied by psychology were universal and thus could not explain any particular social configuration. It was society that

informs our minds and wills in such a way as to put them in harmony with the institutions which express them. It is from here, in consequence, that sociology must begin.[10]

ECONOMICS AND SOCIOLOGY

The economists, still largely hostile to the intrusive claims of sociology, were equally critical of Durkheim's methodological views. At a meeting of the Société d'Économie Politique in 1908[11] Durkheim advanced his views concerning the nature of economic phenomena and the relation of economics to the other social sciences. It was clear, he argued, that the scientific study of morality, of law, of religion and of art were concerned with ideas. Was political economy different: did it deal with phenomena 'independent of opinion'?[12] He maintained that economic facts could also be considered as matters of opinion, though this did not mean that they did not operate according to laws.[13] The value of things depended not only on their objective properties but also on the opinion held concerning them. For example, religious opinion could affect the exchange value of certain goods, as could changes in taste. Again, wage-rates were a function of a basic minimum standard of living, but this standard itself varied from period to period as a

9. ibid., p. 755.
10. ibid.
11. 1908c (1).
12. ibid., p. 65.
13. Cf. 1924a, pp. 82–3: tr. 1953b, p. 57. See also Neyer, 1960, pp. 75–6. For a systematic exploration of this point of view, see the writings of François Simiand, passim., especially Simiand, 1912.

function of opinion.[14] And certain forms of production (for instance, co-operation) expanded not because of their objective productivity but because of certain moral virtues ascribed to them by opinion. Thus economics lost its preponderance and took its place beside the other social sciences and in close relation to them. The only primacy correctly attributable to economic factors resulted from those which 'profoundly affect the way in which a population is distributed, its density, the form of human groups, and thereby often exercise a profound influence on the various states of opinion'.[15] In reply, the economist Leroy-Beaulieu accused Durkheim of exaggerating the influence of opinion on the economy. Although it was doubtless a powerful factor in modifying certain economic forms, it would never transform the great immutable economic laws. A psychological factor did intervene in determining economic value but it was eternally subject to the eternal law of supply and demand.[16]

THE SOCIOLOGY OF MORALITY

Another favourite object of attack was Durkheim's theory of morality, especially on the part of philosophers. Many of his critics agreed with Henri Poincaré, who once remarked to Durkheim that from the scientific proposition 'A toadstool is a poisonous mushroom' one cannot derive the proposition 'Don't eat toadstools'.[17] Among the more notable published critiques were those of Richard,[18] who argued (among other things) that Durkheim made an illegitimate slide from the social fact of solidarity to a principle of moral obligation, from social pressures to moral rules, and in particular from the fact of organic solidarity to the demands of justice; that of Rauh,[19] who argued that Durkheim misdescribed the nature of moral

14. This idea formed the basis for Halbwach's work in this area: see for example, Halbwachs, 1913 and 1933.

15. ibid., p. 67.

16. ibid., p. 72.

17. Guitton, 1968, p. 140.

18. Richard, 1912 and 1923.

19. Rauh, 1904.

judgements, making them purely cognitive, and that he concentrated on the external, immobile shell of social life, missing its active and living reality; and that of Cantécor,[20] who objected that Durkheim missed the transcendent and subjective side of morality.

There were also three extended philosophical critiques of Durkheim's attempt to develop a sociology of morality by Landry, Fouillée and Belot,[21] which Durkheim in turn submitted to a lengthy examination in a review in the *Année*.[22] Landry argued that Durkheim was really a utilitarian in that he maintained that the generality of institutions would be inexplicable if they were not the most advantageous. To this Durkheim replied that he maintained no more than that institutions, especially moral institutions, fulfil useful functions; utilitarian explanations were one-sided and archaic, and at variance with the evidence of history and comparative ethnography. Far from his being a utilitarian himself, he laid chief stress on the 'contrary principle' of obligation in the Kantian sense.[23]

Fouillée argued (1) that Durkheim wished to eliminate the making of value judgements from speculation about morality and reduce this to mere 'descriptions'[24]; (2) that there was no need for 'long studies of history, of comparative jurisprudence, of comparative religion' to discover 'why we must not kill, steal, rape, etc.,' or what were the sources of 'brotherly affection, respect for children and their modesty, the keeping of promises'.[25] These were self-evident truths, perceived by intuition; and (3) that for Durkheim there was nothing either moral or immoral that was not social in origin. Durkheim replied (1) that he maintained only that the danger

20. Cantécor, 1904.
21. Landry, 1906; Fouillée, 1905; and Belot, 1905–6.
22. 1907a (3), (4) and (5).
23. ibid., p. 354.
24. op. cit., p. 234.
25. ibid., p. 247. This view was also Bergson's, who attributed the following dialogue to Durkheim: 'What is your morality? – I do not have one, he replies, but wait a fortnight and I will bring you one' (Chevalier, J., *Entretiens avec Bergson*, Paris, 1959, p. 98). Agathon reports the same dialogue.

of bias and prejudice in social science was particularly great; so far from his method making evaluation dispensable or impossible, it was a preliminary to it ('explanation opens the way to justification...'[26]) and scientific reflection could change morality by the very act of explaining it; (2) that in contrast to Fouillée's *'simpliste'* attitude, he was conscious of the extreme complexity of the ideas and sentiments that made up morality and the need to explain it in its rich and particular detail; and (3) that he did not hold the *a priori* and unscientific view that everything was social: he merely adopted 'the hypothesis, largely borne out by history, that morality at any given point in time depends closely – this being normal and legitimate – on the state of society', believing further that the 'individual and interior side is neither the whole nor the essential element of morality, and that is because moral facts are given to us in history as essentially social facts, varying as societies do'.[27]

Belot's critique amounted to the denial that a *science des mœurs* had any practical relevance (though it might be of academic interest). He offered two reasons: (1) that a purely historical inquiry into origins could not tell us what to do; the only sociological knowledge of any practical use was of the present social system, but even this was insufficient to provide moral reasons for action; and (2) that, consciousness being an active element in society, it always reacted upon and thereby modified its preconditions; thus a study of the latter could not tell us which ends deserved to be preferred. Durkheim answered that it was a truism that we only had a practical interest in the present; the point was that 'in order to analyse those extraordinarily complicated wholes which are social phenomena, we cannot do without historical analysis'.[28] In order to know how to act, one needed to know the actual and possible effects of given causes in the social world (did Belot deny the operation of the principle of causality in the social realm?); moreover the sociological study of morality could even provide us with ends to pursue. The sociologist must

26. 1907a (3)–(5), p. 356.
27. ibid., pp. 360–61.
28. ibid., p. 365.

identify 'the tendencies to movement, the germs of change, aspirations to a different form of society, ideals striving to be realized'[29]; the 'present prefigures the future . . . the future is already written for those who know how to read . . .'[30] There was no point in giving society ends which did not correspond to its needs: the sociologist could identify these and indicate the various tendencies operating in the present, showing which were well founded and which not.

There was also a lively discussion of Durkheim's views on morality at the Société de Philosophie in 1906, when he read his paper on 'The Determination of the Moral Fact'.[31] The most significant objections follow, with Durkheim's replies in brackets.

Parodi maintained that by concentrating on the *conscience collective*, Durkheim reduced the study of morality to the study of public opinion (but opinion was a major clue to the nature of society and its needs, and indeed part of it). Darlu argued that Durkheim allowed no scope for the individual's reason; what about the rebellion of the individual against traditional morality? In any case the individual's mind was richer than the most perfect and complex society (the point about reason was not that it was *individual* but rather that it was impersonal and scientific, and, like moral ideals, collective in source; rebellion could be justified only in terms of emerging forms of society; and with respect to the individual *conscience*, 'How much richer and more complex is the moral life of society, with all its complementary or conflicting aspirations of all kinds . . .'[32]; moreover, individual constructions were socially determined, refracting common ideals). Jacob objected to the analogy of the moral and the sacred and the association of morality with religion; this view was inconsistent with the application of reason to morality (but morality was historically associated with religion; there was an analogy between our horror at crime and the believer's reaction to sacrilege; both religion and morality involved 'a world, separate and apart, of *sui generis*

29. ibid., p. 368.
30. ibid.
31. 1906b: discussion partially reproduced in 1924a: tr. 1953b.
32. ibid. (1951 edn), p. 98: tr. 1953b, pp. 67–8 (S.L.).

représentations'[33]; and the point was to account for both in secular, rational terms). Brunschvicg argued that the progress of civilization consisted in its allowing more and more scope to the individual to regain his rights against the material structure of society (but those rights were the *product* of society; the progressive emancipation of the individual consists in the transformation not the weakening of social bonds). Malapert said that Durkheim saw society as a moral legislator and as ideally perfect (but society played the part of legislator because it was granted moral authority by its members' beliefs; Durkheim did not think of it as ideally perfect, just as a 'rich and complex moral reality'[34]). Louis Weber objected that philosophers not sociologists were the proper students of morality (but they were more concerned to develop their own systems, to argue as revolutionaries or iconoclasts; Durkheim was more concerned to discover morality as it was and had been, not as conceived by some philosopher). Finally, Rauh made a plea for the individual's inner moral life; for instance, he knew scholars and artists who considered some of their duties to be extra-social (so did most people, but the claim was that this picture of morality was mistaken; and as to the inner life, 'There is no individual *conscience* that exactly expresses the common moral *conscience* . . . each of us is immoral in some respects.'[35])

Durkheim attended two further sessions of the Société when morality was discussed, in 1908[36] and 1914,[37] at which his views were subjected to further criticisms. At the first, Belot developed the argument that 'one could never in fact arrive at moral ends or develop new rules if societies *could* be the object of a complete and definitive science'[38]: seeing social facts as 'dead *things*'[39] was incompatible with the very essence of morality – 'this need for improvement, this dissatisfaction with

33. ibid., p. 104: tr. p. 71 (S.L.).
34. ibid., p. 108: tr. p. 74.
35. ibid., p. 115: tr. p. 78 (S.L.).
36. 1908a (2).
37. 1914b.
38. 1908a (2), p. 195.
39. ibid.

the given',[40] in particular the fact that 'individual *consciences* rebel against collective imperatives, conceive new imperatives, develop new *practical hypotheses*'.[41] Durkheim agreed that reflection was increasingly becoming an element in morality, but he denied that it was a necessary element, as was its social character: 'The immense majority of men passively carry out moral imperatives, and even the most cultivated among them reflect on them only rarely. Certainly, reflection elevates and perfects morality, but it is not, in effect, its necessary condition.'[42]

At the second meeting, the Bergsonian Wilbois argued that duty could not be founded 'on rational principles or empirical data but was rather a primary reality which it is at once useless and impossible to prove'[43]; it could not be explained by 'relating it to what purports to be society considered as a thing'.[44] Indeed he denied 'not only the possibility of this attempt but even its intelligibility'.[45] Secondly, Wilbois characterized Durkheim's method as 'static', arguing that it missed out the internal '*élan*' of historical development. Durkheim replied that, on the first point, Wilbois simply asserted but had not proved that duty was inexplicable and that it could not be related to any synthesis of natural forces; and, on the second, that Wilbois' charge was without foundation: 'I do not understand how such a mistake could be made, nor do I see which text of mine could give rise to it.'[46] He added:

40. ibid., p. 194.
41. ibid., p. 195.
42. ibid., p. 197.
43. 1914b, p. 27.
44. ibid. Of Bergson's own views about Durkheim's account of morality we know little directly. However, in his *Souvenirs sur Henri Bergson* (Paris, 1942), I. Benrubi wrote that 'Bergson thinks that [Durkheim's] conception of morality is accurate with respect to the "closed morality", but not with respect to the "open morality". This opinion has only confirmed the impression I have had while reading *The Two Sources [of Morality and Religion]* that Bergson, in distinguishing closed from open morality, wished also to react against Durkheim and sociologism in general' (pp. 126–7).
45. ibid.
46. ibid., p. 35.

I believe and I have very often said that the novelties that are produced in the course of social evolution are not a legacy of the past. The past does not create; it can only transmit what has been created. Its creations can only be the work of associated and co-operative living persons, arising from contemporaries. Every new impulse in life can only emanate from beings who are alive and acting. It is even thanks to them, and to them alone, that the past continues to live. I have therefore devoted part of my effort to the study of these creative syntheses.[47]

THE SOCIOLOGY OF RELIGION AND KNOWLEDGE

It was, however, Durkheim's sociology of religion and of knowledge that came in for the most severe and sustained criticism from a number of quarters.[48] We have already considered some of its more personal and polemical forms.[49] Let us now look at the more intellectual, theoretical and empirical, criticisms that were characteristically advanced.

At a meeting of the Société de Philosophie in 1913 Durkheim read a paper on 'The Religious Problem and the Duality of Human Nature',[50] in which he presented what he took to be the main philosophical implications of his recently published *The Elementary Forms*. The 'religious problem' was one of explanation: whence came those 'forces *sui generis*, which elevate the individual above himself, which transport him into another world from that in which his profane existence is passed, affording him a life that is very different, more exalted and intense'.[51] Given that the source or sources of religious life were to be sought within nature, the sole moral forces superior to the individual that were to be found in the observable world were 'those which result from the grouping of individual forces, from their synthesis in and through society,

47. ibid.
48. Cf. Seger, 1957, and van Gennep, 1920, pp. 52 ff. We will consider these two areas together, since Durkheim's critics rightly saw them as intimately linked.
49. See Chapter 18, above.
50. 1913b.
51. ibid., p. 63.

that is, collective forces'.[52] He claimed to have shown with respect to one particular religion 'that collective forces can account for the characteristic effects which have at all times been attributed to religious forces.[53]

This conception of religion could also account for a perennial feature of religious and philosophical systems: a belief in the duality of human nature. Hence the division, indeed antithesis, between immediate sensation and conceptual thought, between egoistic appetites and religious and moral activity – expressed in religious thought as that between body and soul, and between profane and sacred. Philosophers had no genuine solution: empiricists, materialists and utilitarians, on the one hand, and absolute idealists, on the other, simply denied these antinomies without accounting for them; ontological dualists simply reaffirmed them without explaining them. 'A sociological explanation of religion', however, 'enables one to discern a new approach'[54]: it then becomes apparent that 'the duality of man is to be seen as the antithesis between the individual and the social'.[55] For,

simply because he is social, man is therefore double, and between the two beings that reside within him there is a solution of continuity, the very same which exists between the social and the individual, between the parts and the whole *sui generis* that results from the synthesis of those parts. From this perspective the duality of human nature becomes intelligible, without it being necessary to reduce it to no more than an appearance; for there really are two sources of life that are different and virtually antagonistic in which we participate simultaneously.[56]

To this position the psychologist Delacroix made a number of objections, prefacing his remarks with a fulsome tribute:

His doctrine, too narrow perhaps, still contains a part of the truth. He has shown, brilliantly, how in the study of religion, as of all

52. ibid., p. 64.
53. ibid.
54. ibid., p. 65.
55. ibid., p. 74.
56. ibid., p. 65.

spiritual phenomena, it is necessary to consider the role of society; this necessity henceforth imposes itself on all. I would add that his book seems to me masterly, and I am not generous with such praises.[57]

Delacroix offered four main objections. First, that religious beliefs purported to be true: 'religion is an interpretation of the world and a philosophy, quite as much as it is an active force'.[58] It could not be dismissed as 'the inadequate apprehension of the sentiment of power that participation in his society gives to a believer'.[59] Second, the social was not *ipso facto* religious; there were many collective phenomena, such as feasts and assemblies, that were in no way religious. Also social effervescence and collective over-excitement were necessary but not sufficient conditions of religion. They only released what originated within individuals. Third, the duality of man was between his intelligence and his will and was psychologically, not socially, given. Finally, Durkheim's dualism was itself metaphysical: the relation between society and the individual was unintelligible.

To these points Durkheim replied, first, that he not only agreed but had often indicated that religion was in part 'a certain representation of the world which the believer believes to be true'.[60] He had 'sought to show that religion contained within it the essential germs of reason, that it was in consequence rich in intellectual elements'.[61] Second, he had never said that everything social is necessarily religious. Some social relations were characterized by religion; others, such as those of exchange, were not. M. Delacroix offered no support for his hypothesis that 'the individual carried within himself ready-made the religious idea'.[62] Third, Delacroix's account of the duality of man was incoherent and he had no explanation for it. Finally, his own explanation was not metaphysical: 'Society is

57. ibid., p. 75.
58. ibid., p. 77.
59. ibid.
60. ibid., p. 82.
61. ibid., p. 83.
62. ibid., p. 84.

an observable phenomenon just like the individual',[63] and clearly required certain given individual predispositions.

Next, Darlu (after remarking on 'the force and beauty in the new and great work'[64] of Durkheim) asserted that there were two ideas in Durkheim's thesis which he confused: (1) that 'religious, moral and even logical concepts are of social origin'[65] and (2) that they were 'primitively and essentially concepts of social phenomena, formed on the model of social phenomena'.[66] Darlu accepted the first but not the second. Durkheim's only proof for it was that 'the social group has, in the eyes of the individual, a unique force, authority and majesty'.[67] This was insufficient to support an idea that 'went against the whole philosophical tradition'.[68] Moreover Durkheim's two ideas were contradictory: on the one hand, religious concepts were formed by cóllective, not individual thought; but on the other, they consisted of the impression of influence and authority that society caused individuals to experience.

Durkheim first denied any confusion, saying that he had made exactly this distinction in his book. Second, he rejected Darlu's purported summary of his 'proof' as far too simple and was not too bothered about his views being incompatible with a philosophical tradition. As to the contradiction, he denied it: religion was a collective force penetrating individual minds. It was a moral force, a system of ideas and sentiments elaborated by the collectivity and symbolizing it. It exercised a stimulating and imperative influence on individuals but was not formed by them.

Le Roy then sought to emphasize the personal and moral side of religion in contrast to what he saw as Durkheim's 'physical' point of view. Durkheim replied that the idea of moral influence pervaded his whole book and he could not understand the objection. Le Roy then made another: that

63. ibid., p. 86.
64. ibid., p. 87.
65. ibid.
66. ibid., p. 88.
67. ibid., p. 89.
68. ibid., p. 93.

Durkheim thought he could define and 'discover the essence of religion by analysing one of its most rudimentary, inferior and primitive forms'.[69] Religion evolved from period to period. Durkheim denied this charge. To define religion one must take account of both primitive and advanced religions. His reason for studying a very primitive religion was that 'religious phenomena there appear in a very simple form which facilitates their study'. He did assume there were 'permanent and fundamental elements of religion'[70] – that was his working assumption. Finally, Le Roy objected that Durkheim's theory of religion entailed that certain religious beliefs were illusory; but was not the believer's illusion the very essence of religion? In reply Durkheim said that his explanation gave a meaning and a *raison d'être* to religion. Religious rites served to 'discipline and fortify men's minds' and helped 'periodically to make and remake our moral life'.[71] M. Le Roy had not explained what he thought the true religious life consisted in.

At this point Durkheim rounded on his critics and observed:

Once more I must remark that in this debate, instead of grappling in detail with the facts and arguments by which I have tried to demonstrate my thesis, I am too often confronted with impressions, personal feelings, mental habits, in other words prejudices, and even acts of faith which do not easily lend themselves to discussion.[72]

Finally, the philosopher Lachelier engaged Durkheim in a prolonged and heated debate over whether religion was essentially individual or social. For Lachelier, religion (following Kant) consisted 'for a mind capable of it, in an individual and solitary effort to free itself and to cast off all that is external to it and all that is incompatible with its own freedom'.[73] The religious spirit operated far from, and often in opposition to, the social group. Durkheim was concerned with 'barbarian' religions and the 'adoration of gods in the streets'.[74]

69. ibid., p. 94.
70. ibid.
71. ibid., p. 95.
72. ibid.
73. ibid., p. 96.
74. ibid., pp. 96, 99.

Durkheim denied that religion was *essentially* a matter of individual and solitary effort, though one of its essential functions was indeed to lead the individual to 'free himself from his profane nature, to rise above and transcend himself'.[75] He knew of no gods – by which he meant those that had been a part of history – that had been born in solitude. Lachelier was concerned with what a few refined and unusual persons had done and believed; but he was concerned with the religion 'that has allowed the bulk of humanity to make existence supportable'.[76] Besides, it was likely that even Lachelier's religion could be explained sociologically: even his believer 'derived from society the very forces which allowed him to become free of the world and of society'.[77] It was 'not for religion to dogmatize about itself'[78]; only 'the science of religions, thanks to the methods of analysis and comparison at its disposal, is in a position gradually to explain religious phenomena'.[79]

Durkheim's theory of religion met with a number of other criticisms that are worth mentioning. Belot published an article[80] in which he made a number of incisive (and valid) objections. Durkheim, he argued, had confused the causes of religion, the value of the services it renders and the truth of what it affirms. His definition assumed a complete heterogeneity between the sacred and the profane which had not been demonstrated. He assumed there was a single, irreducible essence of religion manifest in all its forms, which was doubtful. Finally, there was a logical incompatibility between his religious sociology and religion itself: a secular, scientific

75. ibid., p. 96.
76. ibid., p. 100.
77. ibid.
78. ibid.

79. ibid. Sociology had 'taught us, or at least given us the sense that, beyond the world of the individual, a new world was disclosed, in which hitherto unsuspected forces operated which could explain many phenomena that had long been thought of as inexplicable. This discovery of a new realm, added to the other realms of nature, is destined to turn the science of man in new directions, to open up unknown horizons ...' (ibid., p. 98).

80. Belot, 1913.

investigation into the realm of the sacred challenged the very essence of religion.

Among the reviewers of *The Elementary Forms*, Matisse (in the *Revue des idées*) objected to Durkheim's account of man as *homo duplex* – 'that old aberration which, in deifying humanity, isolated it from the rest of creation'.[81] In general, religious critics objected to Durkheim's naturalism, arguing that it was impossible to preserve in relation to society, seen as a product of the laws of nature, sentiments that had been directed towards God, for the transcendental character of the deity thereby became illusory.[82] Goblet d'Alviella, in a largely favourable review,[83] protested against what he saw as Durkheim's too easy dismissal of animism and naturism; he also maintained that the notion of force was not, as Durkheim thought, social in origin and he argued that, while admitting the role of social pressure in forming religious sentiments, consideration must also be given to the 'part of individual reasoning in the origin and development of religion'.[84] Höffding,[85] on the other hand, saw *The Elementary Forms* as in effect allowing more scope for non-sociological explanations than Durkheim's earlier writings. It was important to see that individuals (conditioned, it was true, by society) had 'at every given point, a certain autonomy in relation to society'[86] – hence every new development in the forms and traditions of society, sacred as well as profane, and hence the rise of new ideas and customs. It was necessary to look at psychological processes in individuals, especially to explain the development of individual deviations and initiatives. Indeed, the role of the individual and the development of individual variations increased as religions advanced. In fact, Durkheim made use of psychological explanations (for example his account of 'contagiousness' in totemic cosmology). Finally, he disagreed with Durkheim's account of

81. Cited by Lalande, A., *Philosophical Review*, 13 (1913), p. 365.
82. ibid.
83. Goblet d'Alviella, 1913.
84. ibid., p. 210.
85. Höffding, 1914.
86. ibid., pp. 840–41.

the social origin of causation, stressing instead the role of the history of science in explaining this. Religious influences were here only of historical interest.

In the United States there were two critical reviews in the *American Journal of Sociology*. The first, by Webster,[87] argued that Durkheim exaggerated the importance of totemism as a social institution and also of the idea of *mana*, which was really a relatively advanced philosophical idea; in general, Durkheim's was an elaborate system that mistakenly attempted to explain 'the totality of primitive religion by reference to a single factor'.[88] In the second, Ulysses G. Weatherly[89] made four criticisms: first, that Durkheim tended to read back into the savage mind 'something of the abstruse mental processes of the critical scholar';[90] second, that he sought generalizations to cover 'the most heterogeneous and often contradictory facts'[91]; third, that he misapplied the sacred–profane distinction; and fourth, that his account of the origin of totemic groupings was unsatisfactory.

Elsewhere, Wallis[92] argued: (1) that primitive societies did not necessarily have primitive religions; (2) that 'native life' was not as uniform and undifferentiated as Durkheim supposed; (3) that Durkheim made use of an unacceptable 'principle of evolution'; (4) that his purportedly 'purely analytic and inductive method' amounted to beginning with a definition of religion and then collecting examples, so that one only got out of the analysis what had been put into it – and this led him to underestimate the differentiated character of totemism (revealed by Lang, van Gennep and Goldenweiser); (5) that his account of the origin of totemism was logically inadequate; and (6) that while he had shown the importance of the division between the sacred and the profane, the co-operation of individuals, the church, ritualistic phases and the plurality of the sacred, these were not *differentia* of religion.

87. Webster, 1913.
88. ibid., p. 846.
89. Weatherly, 1917.
90. ibid., p. 561.
91. ibid., p. 562.
92. Wallis, 1914.

Religion was not essentially social and the sociological point of view was only one among many. One needed to look at individual influences, especially to explain messianic religions. In general there was a need to 'explain what keeps [religion] going and to what element of our natures it appeals'[93]; and, *contra* Durkheim, it was necessary to introduce the concept of the supernatural or the supernormal into a definition of religion.

One of the most interesting and valuable discussions of Durkheim's sociology of religion took place at a meeting of the Union des Libres Penseurs et de Libres Croyants pour la Culture Morale, a group of undogmatic non-believers and believers, held early in 1914. This was devoted to a discussion of *The Elementary Forms*, before which Durkheim delivered an introductory (and impromptu) speech.[94] The report of this meeting is particularly valuable, partly because of the criticisms raised, but also because it clearly shows how Durkheim viewed the method appropriate to the sociology of religion, how he saw its implications for religion itself, and what his ideas were concerning the future of religion. For once, he allowed himself to indulge in prophetic speculation, at a time of renascent irrationalism and nationalism, about the nature and place of religion in the societies of the future.

In his speech, Durkheim specified how he wished his book to be studied and discussed. Addressing himself first to the non-believers in the audience, he argued that religion was not simply to be seen as a system of ideas, but as primarily a 'system of forces'.[95] The man who lived religiously was not just someone who saw the world in a certain way, knowing what others did not know: he was a man who felt within him an extraordinary power, a 'force which dominates him, but which, at the same time, sustains him and raises him above himself',[96] giving him greater strength to face life's difficulties and enabling him to bend nature to his will. Such a sentiment was too universal and too constant to be an illusion; an

93. ibid., p. 264.
94. 1919b. He had to leave early and did not stay for the discussion.
95. ibid., p. 98.
96. ibid., p. 99.

illusion could not last for centuries. Whence, then, came this force? It could not result from men's attempts to interpret natural phenomena, even the great cosmic powers; physical forces did not penetrate the inner life. It was moral forces that were in question; and for the non-believer, seeking to render religion rationally intelligible, the only possible source of such moral force was to be found in the coming together of people. His explanation of the collective origin of religion was, he observed, not just speculative; it arose out of facts and historical observation, it had inspired and given a useful guide to research, and it had served to interpret various phenomena in different religions. Thus it had stood the test of experience and thereby shown its vitality.

Finally, and most significantly, Durkheim urged the non-believer to 'confront religion in the state of mind of the believer'.[97] On this condition alone, he went on, could one hope to understand it:

> Let him experience it as the believer experiences it, for it only really exists in virtue of what it is for the latter. Thus whoever does not bring to the study of religion a sort of religious sentiment has no right to speak about it! He would be like a blind man talking about colours. Now, for the believer, the essence of religion is not a plausible or seductive hypothesis about man or his destiny. He sticks to his faith because it forms part of his being, because he cannot renounce it, so he thinks, without losing something of himself, without being cast down, without a diminution of his vitality, a lowering of his moral temperature.
>
> In a word, the characteristic of religion is the dynamogenic influence it exercises on men's minds. To explain religion is thus, above all, to explain this influence.[98]

Turning next to the believers present, Durkheim asked for their sympathy, and a certain freedom of thought and cartesian doubt. Let them at least forget provisionally the formulae in which they believed, if only to return to them later. The task was to uncover the reality which religious formulae expressed, all more or less inexactly. In this way they would not be

97. ibid., p. 101. This is the nearest Durkheim ever came to the principle of *Verstehen*.
98. ibid.

tempted to commit the unjust error of those believers who had characterized his manner of interpreting religion as thoroughly irreligious. Indeed, a rational interpretation of religion could not be thoroughly irreligious, since an irreligious interpretation of religion would be one which denied the very fact it sought to explain (this ingenious remark met with applause). Nothing was more contrary to the scientific method. His own account of the source of religious life should surely be acceptable to believers. They might certainly believe there to be another, higher religious life, with a quite different origin, but perhaps they could agree that there were religious forces within us and outside us that we could call into existence, indeed could not avoid arousing, by the very fact of thinking, feeling and acting in common.

Recently an orator had gestured prophetically at the heavens, saying that they were emptying and urging his hearers to turn their gaze towards the earth and look after their economic interests. This had been called impious, but for Durkheim it was simply false:

No, there is no reason to fear that the heavens will ever become quite empty; for it is we ourselves who fill them. And so long as there are human societies, they will provide from within themselves great ideals for men to serve.[99]

Durkheim then turned to the nature of religion in the future, once it had become more conscious of its social origins. Extreme caution was, of course, necessary in such conjecture, and one could not predict in what form such a religion would be expressed. But one could guess at the social forces that would engender it. The reason why contemporary religious life was at a low ebb, and why religious revivals were never more than superficial and temporary, was that 'our power of generating ideals has weakened'.[1] But this was because 'our societies' were undergoing a phase of profound disturbance, after an earlier period of equilibrium. The old ideals and the divinities which incarnated them were in the

99. ibid., p. 103.
 1. ibid., p. 104.

process of dying, because they no longer responded adequately to the new aspirations which were becoming evident; and the new ideals that would be necessary to guide men's lives were not yet born. 'We therefore find ourselves', Durkheim said, 'in an intermediary period, a period of moral indifference which explains the various manifestations that we see every day, in anxiety and sorrow.'[2]

Yet there was cause for reassurance, for, in the depths of society,

an intense life is growing and seeking outlets, which it will eventually find. We aspire to a justice higher than that expressed by any existing formulae. These obscure aspirations that now excite us will, however, some day come to be more clearly formulated, translated into clearcut formulae around which men will rally and which will form a focus of crystallization for new beliefs. As to the letter of those beliefs, there is no point in trying to discern this. Will they remain general and abstract, or will they be linked to certain persons who will incarnate them and represent them? That will depend on historical contingencies that one cannot foresee.

All that matters is that we should realize that, beneath the moral indifference that pervades the surface of our collective life, there are sources of commitment that our societies contain within themselves. One can even go further and say with some precision in which region of society these emerging forces are particularly in evidence: among the working class (*les classes populaires*).[3]

Durkheim concluded his speech by observing that it was inescapable that humanity must rely on its own resources; historically this idea had become ever more pervasive and it was unlikely to recede. It was troubling to a person used to relying on extra-human forces, but, once he realized that humanity could provide him with the support he needed, surely it was highly comforting, since the required resources were close to hand?

In the discussion, Gustave Belot repeated his criticisms mentioned above, observing that it was difficult for him to dispel the very intense conviction created in the audience by

2. ibid.
3. ibid.

the clarity and warmth of Durkheim's language. He emphasized the multiplicity of the forms, causes and functions of
religion, but his chief argument was against Durkheim's
claim that his sociology of religion did not destroy religion
itself, that his explanation of religion was compatible with
believing in it. Durkheim, Belot insisted, was (despite his
claim to the contrary) maintaining that all religions were
false, in so far as they did not accept his own theory. Who,
asked Belot, would continue to pray, if he knew he was
praying to no one, but merely addressing a collectivity that was
not listening? Where, he continued,

is the man who would continue to take part in communion if he
believed that it was no more than a mere symbol and that there was
nothing real underlying it?[4]

Religion, according to Durkheim, was the first form of the
conscience collective and as such a basis for social cohesion.
But today there were other institutions providing such a
basis, as Durkheim had himself shown in *The Division of
Labour*. Moreover, the *conscience collective* no longer required
religious symbols – and, in any case, religion divided societies
more than it unified them. Durkheim was thus destroying
religion by postulating as its essential function one that was
adequately fulfilled by other institutions and poorly by religion
itself. Finally, the notion of a science of the sacred was a self-
contradiction. It was, in short, impossible that the scientific
theory of religion could leave religion intact.

The next speaker was the Protestant pastor and professor
Marc Boegner, later to become head of the French Protestant
church and president of the World Council of Churches.
Boegner began by paying tribute to the way in which Durkheim had expressed the nature of the religious life; one seemed,
he remarked, 'to hear a believer testifying to what he believes
to be essential to his faith, to that which he holds most dear'.[5]
Boegner raised four questions in relation to Durkheim's
theory, which, together with Durkheim's written replies, are
worth reproducing in full.

4. ibid., p. 131.
5. ibid., pp. 134–5.

(1) BOEGNER: Is it legitimate to seek the essential elements of the religious life in its most rudimentary forms? In order to determine these elements, should one not take the greatest account of the most perfect and *realized* forms of that religious life?

DURKHEIM: I have explained in my *Formes élémentaires de la vie religieuse*, pages 3–12, the reasons why the study of a very simple religion seemed to me particularly instructive. It is because a science in its infancy must pose problems in their simplest form, and only later make them gradually more complicated. When we have understood very elementary religions, we will be able to move on to others. Moreover, the former have the advantage that, by reason of their simplicity, the essential elements are more apparent within them, and easier to discern.

On the other hand, it is very clear that the study of the most advanced forms of religious life also has very great advantages. I might even add that a certain knowledge of these more advanced forms is a help in understanding the simpler forms. But research must in the first instance concentrate on the latter.

(2) BOEGNER: Can the primitives of present-day Australia be regarded as genuine primitives? Surely primitive forms of religious life, when this has emerged, must have a certain spontaneity, and, in virtue of this, certain essential characteristics that are no longer to be found in the religious life of contemporary Australians, which has necessarily become ossified, at least to a certain extent, by remaining unchanged during many centuries?

DURKHEIM: There are no longer any 'genuine primitives': I said this on the first page of my book. There is no doubt that the Australians have a long history behind them, as have all known peoples. I chose them simply because I found among them a religion that surpassed in simplicity all others of which I knew and which it seemed to me could be explained without it being necessary to refer to an antecedent religion. If another religion is found that is still more simple, then let us study it, but for the time being it is useless to speak about this.

In the same way, it seems to me pointless to talk about changes that may have occurred within Australian religions in the course of history, given that we are ignorant of these. There are, however, some that we know about and others that we can reasonably guess at. The cults of the great gods seem to me to be relatively late, the phratry cults to have lost ground, etc.

(3) BOEGNER: Is it possible to recognize in the *conscience collective* of a given time all the elements which go to make up the religious

conscience of the great innovators of that time, of a Jeremiah or a Jesus, for example, who went against the tendencies of the collective religious *conscience* of their epoch?

DURKHEIM: The problem of great religious personalities and their role is certainly important. The study that I undertook did not consider it. I do not have to advance an hypothesis concerning such a complex problem, which has never been studied methodically.

(4) BOEGNER: Would the sociologist not find it interesting to study the social phenomena which determine the influence of a religion regarded as superior, such as Christianity, on the *conscience collective* of a tribe of pagan people (whether they believe in fetishism or animism), such influence operating through the individual minds that it penetrates? Examples might be Basutoland and Uganda.

DURKHEIM: The study here referred to would be among the most interesting. There is here a whole field of human experience, the importance of which is indisputable.[6]

ANTHROPOLOGICAL CRITICS

Among social anthropologists, there were noteworthy reviews of *The Elementary Forms* by Sidney Hartland,[7] Alexander Goldenweiser,[8] Bronislaw Malinowski[9] and Arnold van Gennep.[10] Hartland thought it a 'brilliant volume' which 'opens up a new chapter in the discussion of the origin of religion'[11] but thought Durkheim's case against animism and his view that primitive religions were not anthropomorphic to be unsustained. He also argued against Durkheim's view that if primitive religions were essentially illusory they could not be amenable to scientific study; indeed he argued that Durkheim's own theory entailed that the soul and spiritual existence were unreal. And, like many other critics, he held that Durkheim and his school 'attach too little weight to [the

6. ibid., pp. 142–3. I have rearranged these questions and answers which appear in the text in two separate lists.

7. Hartland, 1913.

8. Goldenweiser, 1915 (cf. 1913a (ii) (13)).

9. Malinowski, 1913.

10. Van Gennep, 1913.

11. Hartland, 1913, p. 92.

influence of external nature and the experiences of the indi-
vidual] upon what is assumed, rightly or wrongly, to be the
constitution of the human mind.'[12]

Goldenweiser's critique was comprehensive and largely
unfavourable. Durkheim's view that primitive man did not
distinguish between the natural and the supernatural showed
that 'he fundamentally misunderstands savage mentality'[13] and
his search for a reality underlying religion was misconceived.
Moreover, his definition of religion was a conceptual hybrid,
assimilating ritual with belief, and a body of believers with
a moral community. He questioned Durkheim's assumption
that a clan organization was *ipso facto* primitive and argued that,
in any case, primitiveness of clan organization was not necessarily correlated with primitiveness of religion. Moreover the
choice of Australia was unfortunate since the data were
notoriously unsoundly based. He also had a number of concrete points against Durkheim's theory of totemism: (1) a clan
name did not necessarily betoken solidarity and solidarity did
not necessarily lead to a name; (2) Australian art was of extra-
totemic origin; (3) cosmogony and totemism were only
indirectly related; (4) totemic complexes were really 'aggregates of various cultural features of heterogeneous psychological and historical derivation'[14]; and (5) the argument for
the historical priority of clan totemism was unconvincing – in
particular, what Durkheim called 'individual totemism' was
not a development out of clan totemism, and there were forms
of religion earlier and more universal than clan totemism.

Turning then to what he called Durkheim's theory of social
control, he objected to Durkheim's account of *mana*, *wakan*
and *orenda* and their positions in conceptual evolution, and also
to the derivation of the sacred from an inner sense of social
pressure – there must be pre-existing religious conceptions.
But Durkheim's main error in this connection was his 'mis-
conception of the relation of the individual to the social'.[15]

12. ibid., p. 96. Cf. Hartland, E. S., *Ritual and Belief* (London, 1914).
13. Goldenweiser, 1915, p. 720. Goldenweiser found Durkheim's book
'brilliant but unconvincing' (cited in Van Gennep, 1920, p. 10).
14. ibid., p. 724.
15. ibid., p. 727.

His conception of the social was at once too wide and too narrow. It was too wide in that it allowed individual factors to become altogether obscured ('The lives of the saints are one great argument against Durkheim's theory'[16]) and left isolated religious experience quite out of account. It was too narrow in so far as 'the only aspect of the relation of the individual to the social drawn upon in Durkheim's theory is the crowd-psychological situation'.[17] For Durkheim, society was a sublimated crowd. There was no consideration of the 'cultural type of the group, of the tribal or national or class patterns developed by history or fixed by tradition'.[18] Goldenweiser next turned to Durkheim's theory of ritual. This was the most satisfying part of his analysis but still open to two objections: first, that the intensity of religious belief was not correlated with complex ceremonialism ('The gods live not by ritual alone'[19]); and second, that Durkheim was guilty of behaviourism in attempting to account for the survival of the soul by means of ritualistic mentality.

Finally, with respect to the 'theory of thought', Goldenweiser described it as 'obviously artificial and one-sided'.[20] In the first place, the categories existed where a 'complex and definite social system' did not; there were other sources for them in experience and in the psychological constitution of man (even grammar could be seen as a conceptual shorthand for experience). In the second place, Durkheim's exclusive emphasis on the religious and ultimately on the social was 'unjustified in virtue of the rich variety of profane experience which is amenable to like conceptualization'.[21] Goldenweiser concluded that the central thesis of the book that the fundamental reality underlying religion is social 'must be regarded as unproved'.[22]

Malinowski made a number of the same points, though he

16. ibid., p. 728.
17. ibid.
18. ibid.
19. ibid., p. 731.
20. ibid., p. 733.
21. ibid.
22. ibid., p. 735.

regarded Durkheim's book as 'a contribution to science of the greatest importance' by 'one of the acutest and most brilliant living sociologists'.[23] While objecting to Durkheim's attempt to base a theory 'concerning one of the most fundamental aspects of religion' on the 'analysis of a single tribe, as described in practically a single ethnographical work',[24] declaring himself unconvinced that the distinction between the sacred and the profane was universal, and while registering his uneasiness about the assumption of totemism being the elementary form of religion, Malinowski found 'very interesting' Durkheim's conception of religion, which stressed 'the social nature of the religious' and was based on his theory of totemism, in which the 'god of the clan ... can be no other than the clan itself, but hypostasized and represented to men's imaginations under the perceptible form of vegetable and animal species which serve as totems'.[25]

But then Malinowski turned to the question of Durkheim's 'objective' method of 'treating social facts as things and avoiding individual psychological interpretations'.[26] Durkheim wrote of society as 'an active being endowed with will, aims and desires'.[27] This was either to be interpreted as 'an entirely metaphysical conception', conveying 'no scientific meaning', or else it referred to individual experience of a certain sort, in which case it would be 'perfectly empirical'.[28] But the latter interpretation did not yield an 'objective', non-psychological set of explanations. In his actual theory Durkheim 'uses throughout individual psychological explanations'.[29] Thus the source of religious ideas was to be found in 'big social gatherings' and their effects on individual minds. The sacred and divine were in fact 'psychological categories governing ideas originated in religiously inspired crowds'.[30]

23. Malinowski, 1913, p. 531.
24. ibid.
25. ibid., p. 527 (tr. S.L. from Durkheim, 1912a, p. 295).
26. ibid., p. 530.
27. ibid., p. 528.
28. ibid.
29. ibid., p. 530.
30. ibid.

Durkheim's views thus presented 'fundamental inconsistencies'. Society was 'the source of religion, the origin of the divine' – but in what sense? As a collective subject which 'thinks and creates the religious ideas'?[31] But that was metaphysical. In the sense that society was itself the 'god', as the totemic principle was the clan conceived under the aspect of a totem? But that reminded one of 'Hegel's Absolute, "thinking itself" under one aspect or another'. Or else as merely 'the atmosphere in which *individuals* create religious ideas'.[32] This last was the only scientifically admissible interpretation. Religious ideas were then only collective in the sense of being general, that is common to all members of the crowd. Their nature was to be understood, Malinowski insisted, 'by individual analysis, by psychological introspection, and not by treating those phenomena as "things"'.[33] Finally, he observed that tracing back the origins of all religious phenomena to crowd manifestations seemed 'to narrow down extremely both the forms of social influence upon religion, and the sources from which man can draw his religious inspiration'. 'Mental effervescence' in large gatherings could 'hardly be accepted as the only source of religion'.[34]

The most devastating of Durkheim's anthropological critics was the great ethnographer and folklorist Arnold van Gennep, who criticized *The Elementary Forms* on both empirical and theoretical grounds.[35] His empirical critique was both authoritative and severe (though some distinguished Australian specialists have, as we have seen, taken a more favourable view[36]). He wrote:

Since I have gone through the same documents as M. Durkheim in the course of the years, I believe I can assert that their theoretical value is less than the author thinks; he treats them as commentators

31. ibid., p. 529.
32. ibid.
33. ibid., p. 530.
34. ibid., pp. 530–31.

35. See also van Gennep, 1920. It is striking than van Gennep was ignored and excluded by Durkheim and his colleagues. M. Davy has confirmed that they did not take him seriously (personal communication).
36. For example Elkin and Stanner; see above, p. 479.

treat sacred texts, elucidating them with the aid of great erudition, but without asking whether three-quarters of the raw data are even worthy of confidence . . . this is bookish ethnography, carried out, following the method wrongly called German, in the way in which Greek and Latin texts are treated. This abundance of references to documents provided by sundry informants, police agents, unspecified colonists, obtuse missionaries, etc., is not worth much, for there are pages of M. Durkheim's book in which the impartial ethnographer is bound to put question marks beside each line: 'Is this certain? What is the value of the informant? What is the value of the document, or what exactly does it say?' Andrew Lang and Father Schmidt had already been led astray in the Australian hornet's nest; M. Durkheim has rushed into it in turn. Within ten years his whole Australian systematization will be completely rejected, and along with it the generalizations he has constructed on the most fragile set of ethnographic data of which I know. The idea he has derived from them of a primitive man (relatively; cf. his note on page 11) and of 'simple' societies is entirely erroneous. The more one knows of the Australians and the less one identifies the stage of their material civilization with that of their social organization, one discovers that the Australian societies are very complex, very far from the simple and the primitive, but very far advanced along their own paths of development.[37]

Anyone could see, van Gennep wrote, 'how M. Durkheim makes up for the lacunae in the evidence by innumerable hypotheses, always ingenious, and presented with a disconcerting sincerity'. However, once 'one refuses to accept one or another of these hypotheses, the rest crumbles'. Each of these interconnected hypotheses would virtually require 'a special book in order to show its factual emptiness and logical inadequacy'.

Leaving 'these unhappy Australians who have already played tricks on several theorists', van Gennep turned to his theoretical critique of Durkheim's work, the theoretical part of which he held to be 'full of solid truths'. Considering first the general theory of totemism, he endorsed Durkheim's critique of other theories as 'simple, rapid, exact', but accused his own of confusing totemism and fetishism in characterizing the former as the religion of an anonymous and impersonal force

37. Van Gennep, 1913, p. 389.

incarnated in, but not confounded with, particular animals or men or images. This definition only applied to totemism's basis; it suppressed all the difficulties of interpretation of details and precluded asking the questions: 'Why so many forms of totemism? What is true totemism?, etc.' In short it served

to open the door to all sorts of new discussions, but not to provide a definition that immediately illuminates all the obscurities which perplex us. A totem is already an individualized power: we are far from the 'fetishist' or 'impersonalist' stage.

On the other hand, what Durkheim said about this impersonal force and about 'dynamist primitive conceptions', van Gennep found . 'entirely right'. Primitive conceptions were 'clearly characterized by energy. Indeed, all religions are: what differs is the name we give to the sources and forms of energy, and the form in which it is represented.'[38]

Turning finally . to Durkheim's general theory of religion and its constituent elements, van Gennep observed that it depended directly on the results derived from the study of the Australians, thereby rendering 'his entire construction so fragile, since its bases are shaky'. But apart from this, Durkheim's well-known tendency to 'perceive the collective (social) element before all else and to give it first place' led him to neglect 'the influence, formative of institutions and beliefs, of various individuals'.[39] He had carefully shown the preponderant importance of society in the various religious phenomena he considered, but he went too far in calling society 'a being (*un être*)'. Though in the most primitive societies, 'social influence is more compelling than individual influence', the latter 'can always take its revenge'. Durkheim's illusion, van Gennep argued, was 'to see in society a natural reality ... subject to laws as necessary as physico-chemical laws; he even professed to see Australian societies as monocellular organisms:

I fear that M. Durkheim, despite his apparent care with ethnographic data, possesses only the metaphysical and still more the

38. ibid., p. 390.
39. A subject that had been investigated by van Gennep himself in his *Mythes et Légendes d'Australie* (1896), a work which Durkheim ignored.

scholastic sense; he accords true reality to concepts and words. Lacking the sense of life, that is, the biological and ethnographic sense, he turns living beings into scientifically dessicated plants, as in a herbarium.

From this position it was a short step to the denial of the individual's reality and of his dynamic contribution to the evolution of civilizations – a step, van Gennep claimed, which Durkheim happily took. Certainly, in semi-civilized societies, religion was the most 'social' phenomenon, since at this stage it encompassed everything – such as law, science, etc.; but

for that reason, and because the individual gradually becomes conscious of himself and becomes individualized, . . . the progress of humanity has consisted in the gradual secularization of all mental and practical activities, as they become separated and accordingly eliminate religion. As for the replacement of religion by another sociological imperative, I do not see its utility, or even its possibility.[40]

Last among the anthropologists, we may mention Radcliffe-Brown's criticisms of Durkheim. In August 1912 Radcliffe-Brown wrote a letter to Mauss,[41] in the course of which he said that he was 'somewhat disappointed by Professor Durkheim's latest work'. His chief criticisms of Durkheim were

that he has misunderstood the real nature of the Australian social organization, particularly the classificatory system (of which the phratries and classes are simply a part), and the clans (which are also, as I see it, a part of the classificatory system). He has also exaggerated the importance of the clan-emblem. The *waninga* and carved bull-roarer exist in many parts of Australia and are sacred, without being in any way associated with the totems. Such association seems to be confined to the tribes of the centre. I have collected a good deal of material for a study of symbolism in Australian tribes and I think it can be shown that in most cases this symbolism (*waninga*, ornamentation, etc.) is independent of totemism.

But he then went on:

I may say that I am in complete agreement with the view of sociology put forward in the *Année sociologique*, and I was the first person to

40. Van Gennep, 1913, p. 391.
41. Letter dated 6 August 1912. This letter was kindly made available to me by Professor Raymond Aron.

expound those views in England . . . In England Durkheim's views are either ignored or misunderstood. It is to be hoped that the new book will do something to alter this, but I am sorry, for that very reason, that it should contain much that I cannot help but regard as misinterpretation of the real facts.

Radcliffe-Brown was also in correspondence with Durkheim. A letter survives in which Durkheim replied to him,[42] thanking him for sending a letter together with a reprint of Radcliffe-Brown's article 'Three Tribes of Western Australia'[43] in which his criticisms of Durkheim's view of Australian social organization were elaborated with reference to Durkheim's 'Sur l'organisation matrimoniale des sociétés australiennes'.[44] Durkheim, in his reply, wrote that he was 'extremely glad to learn from you that we are in agreement concerning the general principles of the science. Nothing could have given me greater confidence in the method that I am trying to apply.'[45] Concerning Radcliffe-Brown's article, Durkheim wrote:

Without mentioning numerous points of detail which I have noted, what you say about matrimonial rules in Australia is certainly such as to make me reflect and hesitate. In order to know whether I should completely abandon the explanation which I have previously put forward concerning the organization in eight classes, it would be necessary for me to carry out a new study of the facts, which I cannot contemplate doing at the moment; for all my time is taken by my teaching which has just started again. But I recognize very clearly that the objection is a very strong one and I am very grateful to you for having pointed it out to me. The subject has to be investigated anew.[46]

42. Reprinted in Wolff, 1960, pp. 317–18: dated 9 November 1913.
43. *Journal of the Royal Anthropological Institute*, XLIII (1913), pp. 143–94.
44. 1905a (i).
45. 1960c, p. 318. There is another letter from Durkheim to Radcliffe-Brown, dated 12 January 1914, which gives similar expression to a sense of intellectual alliance. Durkheim wrote: 'I have read your lecture programme at Birmingham with much interest. It constitutes one more proof of the understanding (*entente*) which exists between us about the general conception of our science' (the letter, together with the lecture-programme, is among Radcliffe-Brown's papers at the Oxford University Institute of Social Anthropology).
46. 1960c, p. 318. For a discussion of Radcliffe-Brown's criticisms, see Peristiany, 1960.

It never was. Within two years France was at war and Durkheim's intellectual life effectively at an end. As we have seen, his methodological ideas and his work in the sociology of morality, knowledge and religion had undergone considerable development – partly under the stimulus of the wide-ranging criticisms we have considered above. In all these spheres, his thought was arrested and his achievement incomplete.

Chapter 26

Practical Concerns

Up to the outbreak of war, Durkheim continued to keep himself apart from direct political involvements, though not from active, occasionally vehement, controversy over current social and political issues. Always he took a clear and ruthlessly reasoned position that followed, more or less directly, from what he took to be sociologically established premises. For Durkheim a sociological perspective always had distinctive practical, social and political implications.

MARRIAGE AND SEX

For example, he brought to his discussion of the much-debated question of divorce law reform arguments based on the evolution of marriage and the family, and on their present nature and functions, as well as on the evidence of comparative statistics of suicide.[1] His general position was that, while fully accepting the principle of divorce under certain closely defined conditions, he was opposed to divorce by mutual consent, on the grounds that it would probably have 'a very dangerous influence on marriage and its normal functioning'.[2] He claimed to have shown in *Suicide* that quite generally the number of suicides varied with the number of divorces, and further that where the divorce rate was high, the bulk of the extra suicides were committed by married persons. Durkheim advanced the hypothesis that 'the practice of divorce strongly affects the moral environment resulting from the state of

---

1. See 1906a (35), 1906d and 1909f. Cf. Chapters 8 and 9, above.
2. 1906d, p. 549. Divorce had been established in France by a law of 1884, which had been applied with increasing leniency. In the early 1900s various publicists and politicians started campaigning for divorce by mutual consent (see 1906a (35)).

marriage',[3] which directly affected spouses and whose influence survived among the widowed, and was directly related to a tendency to suicide. This, he held, applied especially to men; since in existing societies 'the marriage state only weakly affects the woman's moral constitution',[4] and since she gained little from marriage, she was less harmed by the prevalence of divorce.

Durkhem's case was, therefore, that marriage exercised above all, on men, 'a moral influence from which individuals themselves gain; it provides them with a stronger attachment to life', while 'they part with it the more easily when they find it easier to break conjugal bonds'.[5] What was the nature of this influence? Marriage

by the rule to which it submits the passions, provides man with a moral disposition which strengthens his power of resistance. By giving his desires an object that is certain, definite and, in principle, invariable, it prevents them from becoming aggravated in the pursuit of ends that are always new and always changing, that become boring once they are attained, leaving nothing behind but weariness and disenchantment. It prevents the search after pleasures that are unattainable or disappointing; and it makes it much easier to attain that peace of mind, that internal equilibrium, which are th : essential conditions of moral health and of happiness. But it only produces these effects because it involves a system of rules that are respected, by means of which men are firmly bound.[6]

Allowing these bonds to be broken at will would render them fragile and ineffective:

A system of rules from which one can flee as soon as one has a fancy to do so ceases to be such. A curb from which one can free oneself so easily is no longer a curb that might moderate desires, and, in moderating them, appease them.[7]

3. 1906d, p. 550.
4. ibid., p. 551.
5. ibid., p. 552.
6. ibid.
7. ibid.

The result would be that a measure designed to alleviate the sufferings of married persons would end by 'demoralizing them and diminishing their attachment to life'.[8]

Furthermore, Durkheim went on to argue, marriage did not merely have repercussions on the husband and the wife: there were 'higher and graver interests at stake',[9] above all where there were children, and it was 'not enough merely to consider the mutual feelings of the parents and their material and moral well-being'.[10] In any case, their own view of their relations was 'a very poor criterion for judging the true state of those relations'.[11] Except where they were literally impossible, it was better to preserve the family. How many families were there in which 'husband and wife do not have for one another all the sympathy that could be desired, but where both still have a sufficient sense of their obligations usefully to fulfil their roles, while this attachment to a common task, by bringing them together in a mutual state of tolerance, renders their lives more supportable and easier'?[12] But to preserve this attachment, it must be seen as a strict duty, sanctioned by the law, the interpreter of the public conscience. Where would they derive 'the moral force needed to support courageously an existence whose joys must needs be somewhat austere, if public authority solemnly proclaims that they have the right to become free of it whenever they please'?[13] Thus divorce by mutual consent could only 'sap the springs of domestic life, break up a large number of families, and all this still without a corresponding increase in happiness or diminution of suffering for most married persons'.[14]

The argument went even further. If marriage was at the basis of the family, the functions of the family went far beyond the rearing of children. In primitive societies family life had

8. ibid.

9. ibid., p. 553.

10. ibid.

11. 1906a (35), p. 442. They were not in a position to decide whether their marriage was 'no longer able to fulfil its function' (ibid.).

12. 1906d, p. 553.

13. ibid.

14. ibid.

encompassed almost all forms of social activity – economic, religious, even legal. Although these various functions had since become differentiated and organized outside the family, it 'has kept something of its primitive role':

If it is no longer directly in control of these various manifestations of collective life, there is still none with which it has no connection. It is affected by the economic, religious, political, legal life of its members. All that affects them affects it. It has the task of affording them help in the efforts they make in these various directions, of stimulating them and guiding them, of restraining them and comforting them. It has the task of exercising over the whole of our life a moral influence which is of the utmost importance. That is its true function.[15]

Given this, together with the fact that the contemporary family was based upon the married couple, it was very important that it 'should not depend solely on the will of particular persons, on the caprice of their wishes'. It was essential that 'there should be a rule which dominates people's desires'.[16]

The same alliance of sociological acumen with strict Victorian morality is to be seen in Durkheim's views on sex. At a discussion of sex education at the Société de Philosophie,[17] he claimed that his historical and ethnographic researches had revealed to him the 'obscure, mysterious, forbidding character of the sexual act',[18] as well as the extreme generality of this way of regarding it. It was necessary to look at the sentiments, ideas and institutions which 'gave sexual relations their specifically human form'[19]; and it was due to 'our moral and social ideas of today'[20] that the sexual act appeared to us as mysterious. By this he meant that it could not

be assimilated to the actions of ordinary life, that it is exceptional, that, in some of its aspects, it is troubling and disconcerting,

15. 1909f, pp. 280–81.
16. ibid., p. 281.
17. 1911a. The paper was given by Dr Doléris of the Académie de Médecine, who advocated a 'rational education' in sexual matters by means of science.
18. ibid., p. 38.
19. ibid.
20. ibid.

awakening in us contradictory sentiments. That is to say, it shocks us, offends us, repels us, while at the same time it attracts us.[21]

How, Durkheim asked, could this contradictory, mysterious and exceptional character of the sexual act be preserved if it were spoken of quite openly, without any sort of precaution? What moral results would ensue 'if one encouraged young people to see in sexual relations nothing but the expression of a biological function, comparable to digestion and circulation'?[22] As in so much else, the religions had offered a symbolic and rationally indefensible expression of an important truth: 'the confessional symbol may imperfectly express the moral reality to which it corresponds; but that is not to say that it is devoid of all reality'.[23]

CHURCH AND STATE

Durkheim also brought his sociological perspective to bear on the issue of the separation of Church and State,[24] a measure finally enacted by Briand in December 1905, whereby the State recognized absolute liberty of conscience and no longer recognized, or contributed to the funds of, any religion. Durkheim was a good anticlerical, but with a difference. At a meeting of Paul Desjardins' Union pour la Vérité he caused a stir by observing that the Church was 'from a sociological point of view, a monstrosity'.[25] (The report of the proceedings indicates that 'this condensed formula of M. Durkheim's had a striking effect on the persons present at the discussion'.)[26] Desjardins, concerned to reconcile Catholics and freethinkers, tried to soothe ruffled feelings by reformulating this as meaning that the Church had something of the miraculous about it. But to this Durkheim responded,

That's the same thing . . . It is abnormal that an association so vast, so far-reaching, that is itself a grouping of such complex moral

21. ibid., p. 34.
22. ibid., p. 35.
23. ibid., p. 34.
24. 1905e.
25. ibid., p. 369. On the Union, see below.
26. ibid.

groups – in which, as a result, so many causes of differentiation should operate – should be subject to such absolute intellectual and moral uniformity. The effect of the law [of Separation] will be to let loose within this organism the sources of differentiation that have been muzzled for centuries. It is possible, in fact, that local groups will be less impeded than they have been in the past from developing their natural diversity.[27]

There was, he went on, a contradiction between the Church viewed as eternally hierarchical, and indeed military and monarchical, in structure, on the one hand, and the Separation of Church and State, giving rise to internal dispersive and decentralizing tendencies, on the other. The reign of opinion, even if qualified, was the essence of any democratic constitution, and 'if Separation awakened the opinion of the faithful, then there would certainly be some changes in the Church'.[28] In fact, in the short term at least, it had precisely the opposite effect: the Church's embattled unity only increased during this period of politically authorized persecution.

Durkheim was a regular attender at the Union pour la Vérité, founded in the early 1900s as a successor to the old Union pour l'Action Morale.[29] It was an association of academics, liberal Churchmen and politicians that was forbidden by its constitution from adhering 'to any church, philosophical school or political party, and in short to any grouping organized around a fixed doctrine'.[30] Its self-proclaimed objects were '(a) to maintain among its members, by a discipline of judgement and manners, the perpetual liberty of thought which the investigation of truth and the struggle for the right demand; and (b) to uphold in public life, by its example and propaganda, the active love of truth and right, and to promote the adoption of critical methods in general practice'.[31] Its main activities were the Libres Entretiens, held

27. ibid., p. 370.
28. ibid., p. 497.
29. See Besse, 1913, ch. XII, and Lalande, 'Philosophy in France', *Philosophical Review*, 15 (1906), pp. 261 ff.
30. Lalande, art. cit., p. 261.
31. ibid. Among the members attending the Libres Entretiens were Andler, Belot, Bouglé, Brunschvicg, Buisson, Paul Bureau, Darlu,

regularly in Paris, internal correspondence and *ad hoc* public and private meetings.

It was at the Libres Entretiens that Durkheim gave the fullest expression we have of his views on the two very different contemporary movements of administrative and revolutionary syndicalism, and on the militantly antipatriotic ideas associated with the latter. In the course of doing so, he elaborated further his distinctive understanding of socialism and its practical implications for the future organization of industrial societies. Since he never systematically set out these ideas in published form, it is worth attempting to reconstruct them in some detail. As always, he argued *ex cathedra* as a sociologist.

ADMINISTRATIVE SYNDICALISM

Administrative syndicalism was historically quite distinct from revolutionary and working-class syndicalism. It had begun as 'a revolt of State employees against the favouritism that was rampant in all public administrative services',[32] in particular against violations of the regulations concerning appointments and promotions. After the Law of Congregations of 1901, which established freedom of association for all secular purposes, professional associations began to form, alongside the militant unions of the Confédération Générale du Travail. These were the middle-class Syndicats de Fonctionnaires, whose primary aim was initially the defence of legal status against political inroads – 'associations of legal defence against political chicanery'.[33] The ideas of administrative syndicalism developed in the direction of demanding the autonomy and

Desjardins, Durkheim, Fontaine, Lalande, Lévy-Bruhl, Pécaut, Rauh, Vidal de la Blache. Politicians such as Millerand, Steeg and Benoist attended, as did a number of *abbés*.

32. Jubineau, *L'Idée de fédéralisme économique dans le socialisme français*, cited in Soltau, op. cit., p. 466. I am indebted to Soltau's discussion of this movement (ibid., pp. 465–72). Cf. also Laski, H. J., *Authority in the Modern State* (London and New York, 1919), ch. v.

33. The phrase is Hauriou's: cited in Soltau, loc. cit.

decentralization of the whole Civil Service and a similar organization of the whole economy, with the gradual limitation of the role of the State to financial control and the securing of efficiency. The movement was a broad response to what was seen as the breakdown of political authority and the parliamentary system, and to the ever-present threat, so powerful in those years, of anti-republican authoritarianism. It propagated ideas of economic federalism and functional groups or '*syndicats*' based on free contracts between themselves and the State. It was basically advocating a sort of loosely organized capitalism: it declared itself opposed to 'monopoly or State Socialism'[34] and held that 'economic questions are now in the forefront and the task is how to organize a freedom duly subordinated to economic relations and economic conditions'.[35] Since the State could not do this, it was necessary that private interests should organize themselves.

Durkheim was against the general tenor of administrative syndicalism.[36] His view was that the unplanned growth of '*syndicats*' throughout the society would gravely disorganize its most essential functions. Society would come to consist of professional federations, each with its own life, and within which each professional group would be sovereign on internal matters. The State would become absorbed into the professional groups themselves.[37] But such a development was 'contrary to the general direction of our historical evolution'.[38] The idea, he argued, had arisen in the nineteenth century that there was no essential distinction between private and public jobs, that men were all *fonctionnaires* of society. The '*syndicats*' were seen by the administrative syndicalists as a means of introducing this idea, though only partially, into economic life, where there was little sense of the social character of economic functions. The chaotic nature of economic relations resulted from the free play of the antagonistic

34. M. Leroy, cited in ibid., p. 468.
35. J. Paul-Bancour, cited in ibid., p. 472.
36. 1908d.
37. M. Cuvillier's lecture-notes of 1908–9 lecture-course on 'La Morale', repr. in Lukes, 1968b.
38. 1908d, p. 253.

interests of individuals, and the *syndicats* seemed to offer a hope of order. The hope was that the social interests served by each occupation would increasingly predominate over particular interests. The trouble was that 'the *syndicat* is, in the end, only a poor and imperfect image of real administrative organization'.[39]

One looked forward, Durkheim said, to a time when

in industry strikes would be rare, or even would be compulsorily referred to arbitration tribunals, when wage-earners would have more stability and would be less dependent on bargaining, on arbitrary decisions and on circumstances.[40]

The remedy of *syndicats* was worse than the evil it sought to cure, since it only reinforced the system of bargaining and free enterprise. The true solution was to 'elevate those functions called private to the dignity of public functions'.[41] Contemporary professional associations or *syndicats* were 'private, particular groups; in a single occupation one could have an unlimited number', and this absence of organizational unity and of hierarchy rendered them unfit for the task that they should fulfil. Instead Durkheim envisaged 'vast administrative corporations, strongly organized and unified'.[42] In general, there was, he thought,

a whole aspect of administrative life which is essential, namely, authority and hierarchy. There must be centres of command. One must not imagine that the authority that has been indispensable to all known societies, can suddenly turn out to be useless.[43]

THE FUTURE ORGANIZATION OF SOCIETY

Durkheim never worked out a detailed blueprint for the future organization of large-scale industry; as he wrote, 'the

39. ibid., p. 254.

40. ibid.

41. ibid., p. 261. Cf. Léon Duguit's view that 'the *syndicats* ought to be integrated into the State' (quoted in Hayward, 1960, p. 194).

42. ibid.

43. ibid., p. 265. Durkheim added, with some truth, that his ideas were, in fact, consonant with those of Guesde (ibid., p. 280). They were also consonant with those of Engels.

sociologist's task is not that of the statesman'.[44] But his
guiding ideas on this subject can be reconstructed from his
contribution to the *Entretien*, together with his lectures on
Professional Ethics and his preface to the second edition of
The Division of Labour.[45]

He envisaged the various industries throughout the country
grouped into separate categories based on similarity of type
and natural affinity. Each group would be presided over by an
administrative council, a sort of miniature parliament, nomi-
nated by elections. This would have the power, the extent of
which would have to be determined, to regulate matters that
concerned the industry in question – labour relations, labour
conditions, wages and salaries, relations of competing organizations with one another, questions of appointment and promotion, and so on. They would consist (given 'the present
state of industry') of representatives of employers and workers
(as was currently the case with arbitration tribunals), 'in proportions corresponding to the respective importance attributed
by opinion to these two factors of production'.[46] Without
being certain, Durkheim wondered whether these representatives would not have to be elected by distinct electoral
bodies at the base of the corporative organization, at least in so
far as their respective interests were in conflict.[47] In addition to
this central administrative council, there would be a place for the
growth of subsidiary and regional bodies under its jurisdiction.
The

general rules to be laid down by it might be made specific and adapted
to apply to various parts of the area by industrial boards. These
would be more regional in character . . . In this way economic life

44. 1902b, p. xxvii: tr. 1933b, p. 23.
45. 1908d; 1950a, pp. 46–51: tr. 1957a, pp. 37–41; and 1902b, pp.
xxvii–xxxvi: tr. 1933b, pp. 23–31.
46. 1902b, pp. xxviii–xxix fn.: tr. 1933b, p. 25 fn.
47. See 1950a, pp. 49–50: tr. 1957a, p. 39. He became more certain
about this by 1902; see 1902b, p. xxix fn.: tr. 1933b, p. 25 fn.: '. . . if it is
necessary that both meet in the directing councils of the corporation, it is
no less important that at the base of the corporative organization they
form distinct and independent groups, for their interests are too often
rival and antagonistic.'

would be organized, regulated and defined, without losing any of its diversity.[48]

The point was to develop

a structure that was comprehensive and national, uniform and at the same time complex, in which the local groupings of the past would still survive, but simply as agencies to ensure communication and diversity.[49]

The corporations would be statutory bodies and individual membership would be obligatory. They would be attached to, but distinct from, the State.

What would their functions be? First, they would enact industrial legislation, as a specific application of the law in general enacted by the State; thus they would deal with such matters as 'the general principles of the labour contract, of salary and wage remuneration, of industrial health, of all that concerns the labour of women and children, etc.'.[50] Second, they would be a suitable source for 'the provision of super-annuation and provident funds'[51] – more suitable than the State ('over-burdened as it is with various services, as well as being too far removed from the individual'[52]). Third, they would regulate labour disputes, a function requiring specialized and variable procedures. Lastly, they would have a more general function: that of acting as 'a source of life *sui generis*'.[53] They would encourage that solidarity and 'intellectual and moral homogeneity'[54] which comes from the practice of the same occupation. This would be evident in the provision of social security, and of technical and adult education, as well as in sport and recreation. These were the more obvious functions, but, Durkheim added, once they were formed, others would develop of their own accord and 'no one can forsee at what point this evolution would stop'.[55] There might, for

48. 1950a, p. 47: tr. 1957a, p. 37.
49. ibid., p. 47: tr. p. 38.
50. ibid., p. 50: tr. p. 40.
51. ibid.
52. ibid.
53. 1902b, p. xxx: tr. 1933b, p. 26.
54. ibid.
55. 1950a, p. 51: tr. 1957a, p. 40.

example, be a recasting of the laws of property, with a trans-ference of property rights from the family to the occupational group (for they would be both institutionally stable and closer to economic life). It was unlikely that the day would ever come when the means of production would be wholly divorced from the means of consumption, when all property rights and rights of inheritance would be abolished, and when the position of the employer would no longer exist – and it was impossible to predict what parts these would play in any future social structure.

Durkheim widened his speculations about the corporations to the point of envisaging a transformation of the political system based on functional representation; and in this he joins a whole tradition of French political thought that stretches from Saint-Simon through Proudhon and Louis Blanc to various present-day theorists of *planification* and others, on both right and left.[56] The corporation, he believed, was destined to become 'the basis or one of the essential bases of our political organization', and would be 'the elementary division of the State, the fundamental political unit'.[57] With the development of industrial society, there was a progressive weakening of the old social structure: territorial divisions, though they would not disappear entirely, were diminishing in importance, and the bonds attaching us to them were 'becoming daily more fragile and more slack'.[58] Increasingly they affected men only in so far as they affected their occupational interests. Political representation should ultimately be reorganized along func-tional lines and society, 'instead of remaining what it is today, an aggregate of juxtaposed territorial districts, would become a vast system of national corporations'.[59]

56. Cf. Hayward, 1960 and *Private Interests and Public Policy* (London, 1966), ch. 11 (q.v. for further references). A recent example is Pierre Mendès-France: see *La République moderne* (Paris, 1962), ch. 5. It is worth adding that Durkheim strongly influenced Joseph Paul-Bancour, author of *Le Fédéralisme économique* (Paris, 1900) and Prime Minister, briefly, in 1933, who adhered to a similar form of pluralist and syndicalist democracy.

57. 1902b, p. xxxi: tr. 1933b, p. 27 (S.L.).

58. ibid., p. xxxii: tr. p. 27.

59. ibid., p. xxxi: tr. p. 27. It should be evident that Durkheim's corporatism was very different from that of Maurras and the Action Française, which eventually issued in the Vichy Charte du Travail.

REVOLUTIONARY SYNDICALISM

Needless to say, Durkheim was much further removed from revolutionary than he was from administrative syndicalism. Nothing could have been less congenial to him than the anti-reformist, anti-intellectual and anti-bourgeois standpoint of the former, or the heroic myth-making of its theoreticians, though he mildly echoed its hostility to parliamentarism and party politics.

The theorists of revolutionary syndicalism, and in particular Georges Sorel, Édouard Berth and Hubert Lagardelle, had come to embrace and idealize the thinking and practice of the militant union activists within the C.G.T. Sorel and Berth, who had little influence among the unionists, were moving in an irrationalist and pro-royalist and nationalist direction, but Lagardelle remained at this time closer to the union movement and the Socialist party, editing the *Mouvement socialiste* from 1899 to 1914, which was an important international forum for the discussion of syndicalist ideas.[60] These were much influenced by the uncompromising anti-nationalist Gustave Hervé. Syndicalists in general agreed with Hervé (at least, until 1914) when he said that 'for the poor, nations are not loving mothers; they are harsh stepmothers . . . Our nation can only be our class'.[61] Socialists should, they believed, oppose all wars, whether offensive or defensive, by means of a revolutionary strike against the whole capitalist system.

Durkheim confronted these ideas at a Libre Entretien in 1905,[62] which was devoted to the question of whether there was an incompatibility between working-class consciousness and patriotism. Was anti-patriotism necessary to the class struggle? Lagardelle argued that it was, and, in reply, Durkheim observed that this position was derived from a more general set of assumptions: that a reconstruction of society was only possible by means of the destruction of existing nations, that present society consisted of two *blocs* and that one had to

60. Lagardelle was subsequently to become Minister of Labour in the Vichy government.
61. Quoted in Goldberg, *The Life of Jean Jaurès* (Madison, 1962), p. 378.
62. 1905e.

destroy the other. Thus it was necessary to examine the question of whether socialism and destructive revolution entailed one another.

Durkheim advanced three principal arguments against Lagardelle. In the first place, Lagardelle had argued that the necessary destruction of existing societies was a consequence of the growth of large-scale industry. But why should one assume that this growth was not part of the normal development of modern societies? Why should our societies necessarily be unable to achieve a relative harmony with the economic system? Why 'should it be impossible that legal and moral institutions should progress, parallel to this economic progress, in such a way as to achieve this harmony?'[63] In the second place, the whole theory of revolutionary syndicalism was based on the idea that the worker was exclusively a producer. This was to reduce him to an abstraction, altogether analogous to the old *homo oeconomicus* of the classical econommists; in fact, the worker participated in a whole 'intellectual and moral life' that was as necessary to him as the air he breathed.

In the third place, how could it be possible that tomorrow man should wish the destruction of society and the advent of barbarism? Man was man because he had a social life; how could he want to destroy society? It had been said, Durkheim continued

that if war broke out today between France and Germany, that would be the end of everything. The destructive revolution that is advocated would be a destructive movement worse than that.[64]

To destroy society was to destroy a civilization. Doubtless such catastrophes had often occurred in the past, but

man's intelligence should precisely have as its overriding aim the taming and muzzling of these blind forces, instead of letting them wreak destruction. I am quite aware then when people speak of destroying existing societies, they intend to reconstruct them. But these are the fantasies of children. One cannot in this way rebuild collective life; once our social organization is destroyed, centuries

63. ibid., p. 422.
64. ibid.

of history will be required to rebuild another. In the intervening period, there will be a new Middle Ages, a transitional period in which the old departed civilization will not be replaced by any other, or at least will only be replaced by a civilization that is incipient, uncertain and seeking to find itself. It will not be the sun of a new society that will rise, all resplendent with light over the ruins of the old; instead, men will enter a new period of darkness. Instead of hastening the advent of that period, it is necessary to employ all our intelligence so as to forestall it, or, if that is impossible, to shorten it and render it less sombre. And to do that we must avoid acts of destruction that suspend the course of social life and civilization.[65]

Certainly, Durkheim went on, he did not deny the individual's right to wish to live in a better society, but the anti-patriots were making war on *all* societies, since these were all capitalist. They thus accepted joyfully the prospect of the transitional epoch of which he had spoken – and that was a true enormity.

Lagardelle replied that intellectuals were irrelevant; the workers did not have to justify themselves before an intellectual like M. Durkheim. An intellectual could not understand their reasons. It was, he said,

up to M. Durkheim, who is a sociologist, to understand [workers' socialism], not to oppose it . . . The workers feel themselves to be outside the *patrie*. That conviction may scandalize us, but it is a fact . . .[66]

All maladies, observed Durkheim, were facts (at this there was laughter), but M. Lagardelle had not justified the anti-patriotic sentiment. Lagardelle answered that he could only describe it. Durkheim then observed that one must not lose one's reason and approve of a violent movement simply because it was violent. One had to reflect, and not abandon oneself blindly to one's emotions. Lagardelle replied that these ideas were the products of a spontaneous movement of the masses. Durkheim in turn replied – so what? Lagardelle then spoke of the capitalist régime as at a certain point engendering within

65. ibid., p. 423.
66. ibid., p. 424.

itself forces that were incompatible with capitalism itself and would lead to revolution. Durkheim replied that

> It would be necessary to show how the development of capitalism has suddenly produced this antagonism, that would necessarily bring with it the destruction of existing society.[67]

Slightly later in the discussion, Durkheim once more asked Lagardelle why moral, legal and political institutions could not evolve alongside economic life, so as to adapt to it and regulate it. Lagardelle replied that we were confronted by two régimes that were economically distinct: capitalist production contained forces that tended to destroy the capitalist régime and transform society. To this Durkheim responded by remarking that there had certainly been a greater relative change between the crafts of the Middle Ages and the manufacturing industry of the eighteenth century than between the eighteenth century and the large-scale industry of the present time. In any case, what Lagardelle forgot was the factor of consciousness: it was under the influence of the French Revolution that the new aspirations had been formed. The beginning of socialism was in the French Revolution. Lagardelle was the prisoner of the formulae of Marxist materialism. Lagardelle replied that the progressive evolution of capitalism was towards revolution. The worker was confined to the sphere of production, without property and subject to the arbitrary exploitation of capitalists. Everything depended on the worker's role as producer.

This discussion was leading nowhere, and Durkheim reverted to the question of the worker's supposed anti-patriotism by observing that there was more in common between the worker and the bourgeois than Lagardelle thought; they lived in the same social environment, they

> inhale the same moral atmosphere, they are, though they deny it, members of a single society, and, as a result, cannot but be impregnated with the same ideas.[68]

67. ibid., p. 427.
68. ibid., p. 433.

In the light of this, the notion of imminent and indispensable destruction was unintelligible. As for socialism, he concluded:

It is a question, in the end, of knowing whether socialism is miraculous, as it imagines, whether it is contrary to the nature of our societies, or whether it accords with their natural evolution, so that it does not have to destroy them in order to establish itself. It is to this latter view that history seems to me to point.[69]

These, then, were Durkheim's views about the issues of his time. He was in many ways both a moralistic conservative and a radical social reformer, who would qualify, on most definitions, as a socialist of sorts. His conservatism was sociologically based but rested ultimately on a view of human nature as being in need of limits and moral discipline. His socialism likewise rested on a fear of anarchy both within society and within the life of the individual. Social order and the mental equilibrium of the individual, based on maximum freedom of thought and distributive justice in social relations – these were his ultimate guiding preoccupations.

He was also, like so many of his generation prior to 1914, an optimist. His high-minded rationalism led him to believe, like Jaurès, in an internationalist future, though from the mid-1900s (say, from the fall of Delcassé in 1905) this looked increasingly unlikely. He believed, as Jaurès did, that, 'while awaiting the realization of international peace by socialist unity, socialists of all countries must each protect their own against possible acts of aggression'.[70] He also believed that they would do so, and eventually he was proved right. Yet he was never a nationalist though he was a patriot: as he said, in 1907, it was

to speak in nationalist terms to place French culture above all others, even though it be revolutionary . . . It would be a cause for despair if one were condemned to think of patriotism only in terms of putting France above all.[71]

As we have seen, he came to fear the outbreak of war with Germany as being 'the end of everything'. But when it came, he gave himself wholly to the national war effort.

69. ibid., p. 436.
70. (1898), quoted in Soltau, op. cit., p. 440.
71. 1908a (1), pp. 6–7. Contrast this with the misleading statements concerning Durkheim's 'nationalism' in Mitchell, 1931, and Peterson, 1963.

Chapter 27

The War

'ON the day when the flood of arms inundated us', recalled André Lalande, 'we felt for the most part as if a gigantic sea-wave had crossed the valley of the Seine and was about to dash upon the suburbs of Paris.'[1] German forces under Von Kluck swept through Belgium into northern France, but the French counter-attacked in early September, the Germans were contained and Paris was saved by the battle of the Marne. Durkheim wrote to Léon:

I don't have to tell you what satisfaction these latest events have caused me. But we are not at the end of our difficulties and our sacrifices; yet for the first time one has the sense that the *monstre de feu* has been hit . . .[2]

It seemed impossible he wrote

that Germany, even helped by Austria, should prevail over the entire world and the nature of things.[3]

The time was perhaps near when French territory would be freed; above all it was necessary to 'undermine their morbid arrogance – and their arrogance is their strength'.[4] The recent events he felt.

should revive your idealistic faith, which the brutality of the German attack may have disturbed. Never has the ideal to which we are all attached shown its strength more clearly. Therein has resided the value to us of our most effective allies, the English and Belgians; and it is because Germany, or rather Prussia, has combated this ideal with a brutality leaving no room for any doubt, that the

1. 'Philosophy in France', *Philosophical Review*, 25 (1916), p. 525.
2. Letter dated 15 September 1914.
3. ibid.
4. ibid.

Prussian regime is tottering. The regimes of Prussia and Austria are unnatural aggregates, established and maintained by force, and they have not been able gradually to replace force and compulsory subjection by voluntary support. An empire so constructed cannot last. The geography of Europe will be remade on a rational and moral basis. Russia herself is caught up in the movement – she is liberating Poland![5]

This optimism and idealism sustained him for the next two years.[6] Although his health was already seriously impaired by overwork,[7] he threw himself into the task of national defence, alongside his teaching which continued until 1916. As for the teaching, he had little enthusiasm for it. Most of the students were called up; indeed, of the 342 students at the École Normale Supérieure, 293 were eventually sent to the firing line and 104 were killed outright.[8] Of those that remained, Durkheim wrote that neither teachers nor students could show much interest in university life.[9] With national survival in jeopardy, with national morale to sustain and foreign support to win, especially in the neutral countries, and with his own son and son-in-law and five nephews in the army, Durkheim's attention lay elsewhere. Yet he still managed to write an article on sociology for the International Exhibition at San Francisco[10] and to edit and write part of a book explaining French universities to Americans.[11]

5. ibid.

6. A year later he was, for example, to write: 'If, then, at certain times of weariness, it should happen that we allow ourselves to sink into doubt and discouragement, let us think of the Serbs and the Belgians! These small states, devastated and ruined, remain a force to be reckoned with. They symbolize a whole aspect of the ideal for which we are fighting' (1916a, p. 120).

7. Davy, 1960b, p. 11. He was twice forced to take a holiday (ibid.).

8. Lalande, art. cit., p. 525. Many of the most promising Durkheimians died during the war: see the obituaries in the *Année*: *AS*, n.s. 1 and 2 (1925 and 1927).

9. Letter to Léon dated 30 October 1914.

10. 1915a.

11. 1918a. He took this work very seriously, as is shown by two long letters to Louis Havet in which Durkheim, as editor, sought to correct what he saw as misleading statements in Havet's account of the École des Hautes Études.

Durkheim's chief activities were writing and organizing. He organized a committee for the publication of studies and documents on the war,[12] which were, as he told Léon, to be sent 'to neutral countries and would neutralize, as far as possible, Germany's bold and lying propaganda'.[13] The Committee published two pamphlets by Durkheim himself: *Qui a voulu la guerre?*[14] and *L'Allemagne au-dessus de tout*.[15] The first, written with a noted *germaniste*, Ernest Denis, is a brief and incisive study of the events leading up to the war based on the available diplomatic documents. It is a careful and cool document, evaluating the respective responsibilities of France, England, Russia, Austria and Germany for the outbreak of war. In introducing it, the authors wrote that

In approaching the subject of this study, we must not forget that we are ourselves judge and a party in the debate, since our own country is concerned. We must therefore forewarn ourselves and above all our readers against a possible national *parti-pris*, however respectable that may be. For this reason, we shall confine ourselves to providing in the first place an objective and complete account of the events, without any mixture of evaluation. Only subsequently will we allow ourselves to draw any conclusions; but, at that stage, it will be easy for the reader to test, by the account which precedes them, the results that we will arrive at.[16]

The conclusions were that Austria provoked the war by issuing an unacceptable ultimatum to Serbia but drew back as a wider war became more and more menacing; and that it

12. The committee consisted of E. Lavisse (President), Durkheim (Secretary), C. Andler, J. Bédier, H. Bergson, É. Boutroux, E. Denis, J. Hadamard, G. Lanson, C. Seignobos and A. Weiss. It was formed by agreement with Raymond Poincaré and Marcel Sembat. For a discussion of the role of French academics in this propaganda work, see Mitchell, A, 'German History in France after 1870', *Journal of Contemporary History*, 2, 3 (1967), pp. 95–9.

13. Letter dated 30 October 1914.

14. 1915b: tr. 1915e. He appealed to the schoolteachers to help secure its widest possible circulation (Davy, 1960a, p. 19).

15. 1915c: tr. 1915f.

16. 1915a, p. 5. Some of his evidence was obtained directly from those who had taken part in these events (letter to Léon dated 12 February 1915).

was Germany who had initially encouraged Austria and sub-sequently pressed her to persevere. It was Germany who systematically directed the crisis towards war, refusing efforts to delay and offers of mediation, and ultimately declaring war on Russia and France. Germany was '*la grande coupable*'.[17] Allowing for its conditions of publication as a French war pamphlet, and given the restricted availability of diplomatic evidence, this pamphlet stands up remarkably well to the historical record. Indeed, some present-day historians are increasingly arguing precisely this case[18]: that in 1914 the German government was prepared to risk war in pursuit of the general aim of establishing Germany as a Great Power, and that it systematically encouraged Austria to provoke war with Serbia even when it saw that it could not be localized.

Durkheim's second pamphlet, *L'Allemagne au-dessus de tout*, was written as a study of 'German mentality', centring on the pan-germanist ideas associated with Heinrich von Treitschke. This was altogether less coolly written. He began by drawing a contrast between Treitschke's ideas (in which there was 'not one word of humanity'[19]) and humanitarian morality:

> For morality to us, that is to say, to all civilized nations, to all those who have been formed in the school of Christianity, has for its primary object the realization of humanity, its liberation from the servitudes that belittle it, its growth in loving-kindness and fraternity.[20]

In a democratic society, he wrote, 'the people and the State are simply two aspects of a single reality. The State is a people awakened to a consciousness of itself, of its needs and aspira-tions – a more complete and definite consciousness.'[21] In Germany there was 'between these two essential elements of

17. ibid., p. 61.
18. See especially Fischer, F., *Griff nach der Weltmacht* (Düsseldorf, 1961; 3rd edn 1964): tr. as *Germany's Aims in the First World War* (London, 1967); and the illuminating discussion by Joll, J., 'The 1914 Debate Continues', *Past and Present*, 34 (July 1966), pp. 100–13.
19. 1915c, p. 23.
20. ibid.
21. ibid., p. 27.

all national life a radical distinction and even a sort of contradiction'.[22] Treitschke assumed there to be a contradiction between the State and the individual, but in reality there was no such necessary antinomy. Individuals did not just care for their private interests; the State presupposed society, expressing, defining and regulating men's 'social sentiments'. The State depended on moral forces which themselves depended on treaties it had signed, as well as on the goodwill of its subjects and of foreign nationalities. Morality, seen not merely as a set of ideas but as forces which move and dominate men, was superior to the State, limiting its authority and its sovereignty. With these principles Durkheim contrasted the German 'public mentality', arguing that 'the war has been caused by the German staff with a barbarity unparalleled in history'.[23]

Turning to the analysis of this mentality, Durkheim wrote that there was evidently.

an intelligently organized system of ideas in the German mind which accounts for the actions of which one would like to believe Germany incapable. We are ... able to see where and how [these practical consequences] coincide with a certain form of German mentality.[24]

This was a 'system of ideas ... made for war'[25]: its basis was Germany's 'will to power'. Treitschke's doctrine, embodying a 'concrete and living sentiment',[26] was based on an idea of the State that rested on a certain disposition of the will. What were the sources of this myth of Germany as 'the highest terrestrial incarnation of divine power'? Durkheim found them to lie in a spiritual state, a 'morbid hypertrophy of the will, a kind of will-mania'.[27] The 'normal, healthy will, however vigorous, accepts the necessary relations of dependence inherent in the nature of things',[28] but the German will to power and world-domination was unbounded. But Durkheim,

22. ibid.
23. ibid., p. 38.
24. ibid., p. 41.
25. ibid., p. 42.
26. ibid., p. 44.
27. ibid.
28. ibid.

characteristically, saw this as transitory because unnatural:

> There is no state so great that it can govern eternally against the wishes of its subjects and force them by purely external coercion, to submit to its will. There is no state so great that it is not merged within the vaster system of other states, that does not, in other words, form part of the great human community, and that owes nothing to this. There is a universal conscience and a universal opinion, and it is no more possible to escape the empire of these than to escape that of physical laws, for they are forces which, when they are violated, react against those who offend them. A state cannot survive that has humanity arrayed against it.[29]

These were observations forged in the heat of war; but Durkheim was not, for the most part, affected by war hysteria nor, at all, by the aggressive integral nationalism evident in the Catholic and conservative sectors of French opinion. Although in September 1914 he was writing that 'in order to destroy Prussian militarism . . . it will be necessary seriously to invade Germany',[30] he was soon worrying about the dangers of a German military defeat:

> I do not think one has the right to [seek to prevent Germany from existing as a people], and I wonder if it is possible. It is contrary to the principle which we intend to apply. If the Poles must belong to Poland, the Alsatians to themselves or to France, the Germans must belong to Germany. All that matters is that Germany must be prevented from being Prussian, from being an essentially military empire. Unfortunately, I fear that we are not tending in this direction.[31]

In France, he wrote, the clerical party was seeking to turn the circumstances of the war to its own advantage:

> By an abominable paradox, it is said that this war spells the death of the pacific ideal, whereas it constitutes its triumph, above all if we win.[32]

29. ibid.
30. Letter to Léon dated 23 September 1914.
31. ibid., dated 2 October 1914.
32. ibid.

He was greatly concerned to contribute to what he called the 'moral sustenance of the country',[33] which, as the war dragged on, became increasingly important. As he wrote to Davy in late 1915, it was vital to 'remain calm, to rejoice in success, when it comes, but without abandoning oneself to such emotions, because of the extended efforts still needed, nor to the contrary emotions in case of difficulties'.[34] These sentiments colour the patriotic pamphlets entitled *Lettres à tous les Français*,[35] which he organized, writing a number of them himself. In the first he developed the theme to be found in them all: the need for 'patience, effort, confidence'.[36] It was, he wrote, only their inflexible will that would give Frenchmen victory in a struggle that could not quickly be brought to an end. In war the people's 'moral state' played 'a role of the utmost importance'.[37] In order that the nation should remain patient, calm and unshakeable in its decision, it was necessary

that we all sustain ourselves, that we all involve one another mutually, that we strengthen each other ceaselessly by speech and example in this patience and this firmness ... We must struggle against ourselves, against our nerves, against causes of all sorts that threaten our internal equilibrium and that of the country; and we must struggle too against similar weaknesses in others ... We do not belong to one another as in times of peace. We are accountable for the feelings we experience and, more still, for the language that we use. For if, in the flow of conversation, we let slip one word of discouragement, we diminish the courage of those around us ...[38]

He wrote to Léon in early 1915 that

events have shown that there is still a rich vitality in the country; this is worth infinitely more than those who represent and lead it. When a strong sentiment unites it, it shows itself capable of energy. What we must make sure of is that, when peace is re-established, this moral enthusiasm must be preserved. That will not be easy ...[39]

33. Davy, 1960b, p. 11.
34. Davy, 1960a, p. 19.
35. 1916a.
36. See Davy, 1919, p. 192.
37. 1916a, p. 12.
38. ibid., pp. 12–13.
39. Letter dated 30 March 1915.

And, in response to an 'Enquête sur la Politique de Demain' in the newspaper *La Dépêche de Toulouse*, he wrote:

> One of the results of this war, without parallel in history, will be to revive the sense of community (*aviver le sens social*), to render it more active and make the citizens more accustomed to combine their efforts and subordinate their interests to those of society – and all this in the economic sphere as much as in the other forms of human activity.[40]

Durkheim's own energy and enthusiasm were prodigious. He was an assiduous member of the following committees (among others): the Conseil de l'Université, the Comité des Travaux Historiques et Scientifiques, the Comité Consultatif de l'Enseignement Supérieure, the Comité aux Étrangers au Ministère de l'Intérieur, the Comité Français d'Information et d'Action auprès des Juifs des Pays Neutres, the Fraternité Franco-Américaine, the Pupiles de l'École Publique, the Comité des Publication des Études et Documents sur la Guerre, the Comité de Publication des Lettres à tous les Français, the Ligue Républicaine d'Alsace-Lorraine, the Société des Amis de Jaurès, and Pour la Rapprochement Universitaire.[41] In November 1914 he wrote to Léon that he did not have a moment to himself – 'I am working like a young man'[42]; in February 1915 he wrote that he had been leading a life that was 'more than active', adding that 'I can do no more than I am doing at present. I have twice had to stop in these last weeks.'[43] In March he wrote that the translation into seven languages of the war pamphlets, posing endless problems for him to solve, was filling his whole life: 'I do not think', he wrote, 'that I have worked so hard for twenty years.'[44]

Amidst all this activity, he was to receive a blow from which he would never recover. His son André, to whom he was greatly devoted, had just gained his *agrégation* when war

40. Quoted in Narquet, L., 'La Transformation de la Mentalité Française', *MF*, CXVII, 16 June 1918, p. 623. I have been unable to trace the original source of this quotation.

41. Davy, 1919, p. 193.

42. Letter dated 24 November 1914.

43. Letter to Léon dated 12 February 1915.

44. Letter to Léon dated 10 March 1915.

broke out and had been training to be a linguist under Antoine Meillet. He was one of the most brilliant of the youngest members of the *Année* group. Durkheim's letters are full of constant and anxious concern for him. Late in 1915 he was sent to the Bulgarian front and suddenly the family lost communication with him. On 10 January 1916 Durkheim wrote to Davy, telling him that he had just learnt that André had been declared missing in the retreat from Serbia. He continued:

I do not have to tell you of the anguish in which I am living. It is an obsession that fills every moment and is even worse than I supposed. Still, I have been preparing for this blow for a long time. My wife and I realized it above all when he left for Salonica.[45]

On the 14th, he wrote: 'Now I can see the expected moment approaching, I am afraid'[46]; and the next day, to Léon, referring to his continual scrutiny of the Bulgarian despatches: 'I am beginning to discern the insignificant signs over which I stop for a moment only to struggle against the opposite sensations that dominate me'.[47] Then, a month later, to Davy, still with no definite news, he wrote that he was haunted by 'the image of this exhausted child, alone at the side of a road in the midst of night and fog . . . that seizes me by the throat'.[48] Ten days later, he wrote to Léon, asking him to come and visit:

We will converse as before. But what I wish to avoid is conversations that may lead me back to that on which my thoughts find it all too easy to concentrate. The best rule, in such a case, is to set about one's task again as quickly as possible. It is the only way to prevent obsessions . . .

but then he added:

Nothing is so bad as endlessly analysing one's grief. I have allowed myself to do this too much . . . And that is why I ask my friends not to come and see me at this time, because of the circumstances in which I find myself. I am sure that on reflection you will agree with me.[49]

45. Cited in Davy, 1960a, p. 19. Cf. Davy, 1960b, p. 12.
46. ibid.
47. Letter dated 15 January 1916.
48. Cited in Davy, 1960a, p. 19.
49. Letter dated 28 February 1916.

Finally, in April, there was no longer any doubt; André's death and its circumstances were confirmed.[50] Durkheim wrote to Davy: 'It is at least a satisfaction to me to have discovered that I found comfort in the ideas that I teach', and added: 'Do not worry about us. We will recover, at least in so far as it is possible to recover, at any rate I hope so.'[51]

He went to Biarritz to recuperate, writing to Léon:

[The seaside] is of no interest to us. Personally, what I need is silence and meditation. I have profited from the over-active life I led in Paris. It proved to me that I was still able to interest myself in things although I no longer had a personal interest in them. Above all, it prevented the suffering from overwhelming me completely, driving it back and localizing it. From there it cannot be driven out. But it is perhaps possible to render it less acute. To this task I am applying myself. To achieve this, it is important that I should be left to myself for a while. I feel a great need for that.

It is truly incredible that the therapeutic of moral grief should still be as Epicurus described it. I am not aware that anything new has since been said on this subject. It is inconceivable that this should be the great human malady and that almost nothing should have been done to treat it. Of course I know that the religions are there, and that their practices are rich in experience that is unconscious and full of accumulated wisdom. But their wisdom is crude and empirical; nothing resembling ritual practices has been of use to me or seems effective to me. Everything remains to be done and yet although for several months I did not know . . . .[52] to what happens to me, one does not find the remedy for such ills in so short a time. I am none the less trying as methodically as I can. We will see what the results will be.

Apart from this, my recuperation is not pure contemplation. I have work to do. We are going to publish the *Lettres* in three volumes. There were two that were so bad that I had to rewrite

50. In his son's obituary, Durkheim was to write: 'André Durkheim was not only united to me by blood-ties. For a long time I was his sole teacher and I always remained closely associated with his studies. Very early he showed a marked interest in the researches to which I have devoted myself and the moment was near when he was about to become a companion in my work. The intellectual intimacy between us was thus as complete as possible' (1917a, p. 201).

51. Cited in Davy, 1960a, p. 19.

52. The writing here becomes indecipherable.

them. This is how I am occupied at the moment. It is almost finished. I am also concerned about the Jewish question in Russia, which I am studying for the first time. Add to that a correspondence that is several months behind. That is enough to fill my days and even my evenings. Ten o'clock has struck and my wife is calling me to order. I obey.[53]

Meanwhile, the uglier passions of war mounted within the country; and as a native of Alsace-Lorraine, and a Jew with a German name, Durkheim was the victim of at least two scurrilous attacks. The first was an item in the *Libre Parole* of 19 January 1916, referring to Durkheim as 'a *Boche* with a false nose, representing the *Kriegsministerium* whose agents are swarming throughout France'.[54] The second attack came in March from a senator, M. Gaudin de Vilaine, speaking at the *tribune* of the Senate, who demanded that the Commission charged with reviewing residence permits issued to foreigners should examine the situation of 'Frenchmen of foreign descent, such as M. Durkheim, a Professor at our Sorbonne, and without doubt representing, or so it has been claimed, the German *Kriegsministerium*'.[55] However, at a subsequent meeting Paul Painlevé, then at the Ministry of Public Instruction, protested indignantly at this accusation, in the following words:

M. Durkheim, Head of the School of French Sociology, has published a pamphlet about responsibilities for the war which has made the greatest impression in the neutral countries (*Très bien!* and applause). His son was killed gloriously on the field of honour at Salonica (loud applause). This is the man that it is sought to dishonour at the *tribune*. I shall say no more. I regret that to the wound caused by a German hand to M. Durkheim's heart there has today been added an even graver injury coming from a French hand (*Très bien!* and loud and unanimous applause).[56]

53. Letter dated 20 April 1916.
54. Cited in letter to Léon dated 26 January 1916.
55. Cited in Sarrailh, 1960, p. 9, and in Durkheim's dossier, Archives Nationales.
56. From Durkheim's dossier, Bordeaux. In the meantime Liard had written Painlevé a letter urging him to refute this 'odious accusation' and to accord Durkheim 'the public testimony of esteem and sympathy that he deserves' (dated 27 March 1916, in Durkheim's dossier, Archives Nationales).

The senator was then forced to withdraw his accusation by the unanimous disapproval of the Senate.

Despite his imperfect health, Durkheim continued his manifold activities during 1916. Davy recalls that he had withdrawn into 'an almost ferocious silence',[57] forbidding his friends to mention the source of his grief: 'do not', he said to Davy 'speak to me again about my son until I tell you that it has become possible'.[58] Léon recalled that he imposed on others a 'frightening silence, as glacial as death itself'.[59] He gave himself all the more unstintingly to all the various committees and organizations concerned with the war.[60] 'What we lack', he wrote to Davy, 'is a strong hand, an energetic will, that will stir up and gather together the forces [in the country] and direct them untiringly towards a fixed objective'.[61]

He had become thin and feverish, his eyes were hollow and his walk less assured.[62] He was trying to take up his lectures on *La Morale* again, but could not work continuously. He confided to Davy that he feared that he would never be able to complete his book on this subject.[63] On 7 October 1916 he wrote to Bouglé that he was just beginning 'my thirtieth year of lecturing and teaching and my thirty-fifth year of service since leaving the École', and there were still 'a certain number of things I would like to do'. As he was leaving one of his

57. Davy, 1960b, p. 12.
58. Davy, 1960a, p. 19.
59. Léon, 1917, p. 750.
60. For instance, according to Leon Trotsky, Durkheim was President of the Commission for Russian refugees, appointed by the Government. In this capacity, he conveyed a warning that the Government was preparing to expel Trotsky and his co-workers from France: Trotsky writes that Durkheim 'informed a representative of the refugees of the impending suppression of *Nashe Slovo* and the expulsion of the editors' (Trotsky, L., *Against Social Patriotism: An Open Letter to Jules Guesde*, dated October 1916, Paris, reprinted Colombo, Ceylon, 1952, p. 2). There seems every reason to believe that Durkheim was genuinely sympathetic to the Russians, and that Trotsky recognized this. (I am grateful to Professor Lewis S. Feuer for bringing this to my notice and for the reference.)
61. Davy, 1960a, p. 20.
62. Davy, 1919, p. 181.
63. Davy, 1960b, p. 12.

innumerable committee meetings late in 1916, after making a passionate speech, he had a stroke.[64] He was obliged to rest for several months and seemed to recover some of his former strength. America's entry into the war was a great relief to him: he wrote to Davy that 'more than ever it seems that things are going well for us'.[65] He took up some work again, though he could not contemplate the prospect of an hour's lecturing.[66]

In the early summer he spent some weeks at Fontainebleau in the peace and fresh air. While there, he said, in the course of a conversation, to Davy: 'I have the sensation of speaking to you about men and things with the detachment of someone who has already left the world.'[67] He died on the 15 November of that year at the age of fifty-nine, his work unfinished, having lost, in the course of the war, many of his closest collaborators and finest students.

64. Léon, 1917, p. 750.
65. Davy, 1960a, p. 20.
66. See ibid.
67. ibid.

Bibliography of Durkheim's Publications*

1885a   'Schaeffle, A., *Bau und Leben des sozialen Körpers: Erster Band*', *RP*, XIX, pp. 84–101 (review).

1885b   'Fouillée, A., *La Propriété sociale et la démocratie*', *RP*, XIX, pp. 446–53 (review).

1885c   'Gumplowicz, Ludwig, *Grundriss der Soziologie*', *RP*, XX, pp. 627–34 (review).

1886a   'Les Études de science sociale', *RP*, XXII, pp. 61–80 (review of H. Spencer, *Ecclesiastical Institutions*: part 6 of *Principles of Sociology*; A. Regnard, *L'État, ses origines, sa nature et son but*; A. Coste, Aug. Burdeau et L. Arréat, *Les Questions sociales contemporaines*; A. Schaeffle, *Die Quintessenz des Sozialismus*).

1886b   'DeGreef, Guillaume, *Introduction à la sociologie*', *RP*, XXII, pp. 658–63 (review).

1887a   'La Philosophie dans les universités allemandes', *RIE*, XIII, pp. 313–38, 423–40.

1887b   'Guyau, M., *L'Irréligion de l'avenir*', *RP*, XXIII, pp. 299–311 (review).

1887c   'La Science positive de la morale en Allemagne', *RP*, XXIV, pp. 33–58, 113–42, 275–84 (study of Wagner, Schmoller, Schaeffle, Ihering, Wundt, Post).

1887d   'Nécrologie d'Hommay', *L'Annuaire de l'Association des anciens élèves de l'École Normale Supérieure*, 9 January, pp. 51–5.

1888a   'Cours de science sociale: leçon d'ouverture', *RIE*, XV, pp. 23–48 (opening lecture of Durkheim's first course at Bordeaux entitled 'La Solidarité sociale' given during 1887–8). Also reprinted separately (Paris: Colin).

* This bibliography is, it is hoped, complete. In compiling it I have made use of those of Alpert, 1939a, and Cuvillier, 1959a. It includes a great many additional items and, in particular, all reviews (other than those of less than six lines). Where the authorship is in doubt, this is indicated. English translations are listed separately at the end (with the exception of 1905c and 1905d).

1888b 'Le Programme économique de M. Schaeffle', *REP*, II, pp. 3–7.

1888c 'Introduction à la sociologie de la famille', *AFLB*, pp. 257–81 (opening lecture of the 1888–9 course entitled 'La Famille: origines, types principaux').

1888d 'Suicide et natalité: étude de statistique morale', *RP*, XXVI, pp. 446–63.

1889a 'Lutoslawski, W., *Erhaltung und Untergang der Staatsverfassungen nach Plato, Aristoteles, und Machiavelli*', *RP*, XXVII, pp. 317–19 (review).

1889b 'Tönnies, F., *Gemeinschaft und Gesellschaft*', *RP*, XXVII, pp. 416–22 (review).

1890a 'Les Principes de 1789 et la sociologie', *RIE*, XIX, pp. 450–56 (review of Ferneuil, T., *Les Principes de 1789 et la science sociale*).

1892a *Quid Secundatus Politicae Scientiae Instituendae Contulerit* (Bordeaux: Gounouilhou) (tr. into French: 1937b and 1953a; tr. into English 1960b).

1893a 'Richard, G., *Essai sur l'origine de l'idée de droit*', *RP*, XXXV, pp. 290–96 (review).

1893b *De la division du travail social: étude sur l'organisation des sociétés supérieures* (Paris: Alcan) (tr. 1933b).

1893c 'Note sur la définition du socialisme', *RP*, XXXVI, pp. 506–12.

1894a 'Les Règles de la méthode sociologique', *RP*, XXXVII, pp. 465–98, 577–607; XXXVIII, pp. 14–39, 168–82.

1895a *Les Règles de la méthode sociologique* (Paris: Alcan) (the above articles, with slight modifications, and a preface) (tr. 1938b).

1895b 'L'Enseignement philosophique et l'agrégation de philosophie', *RP*, XXXIX, pp. 121–47.

1895c 'Crime et santé sociale', *RP*, XXXIX, pp. 518–23.

1895d 'L'Origine du mariage dans l'espèce humaine d'après Westermarck', *RP*, XL, pp. 606–23 (review of Westermarck's *History of Human Marriage*).

1895e 'Lo stato attuale degli studi sociologici in Francia', *RS*, III, pp. 607–22, 691–707.

1896a 'Letter to the editor of the *Revue de métaphysique et de morale*', *RMM*, IV, Supplément of 4 July, p. 20.

1897a *Le Suicide: étude de sociologie* (Paris: Alcan) (tr. 1951a).

1897b 'Il suicidio dal punto di vista sociologico', *Ri It S*, I, pp. 17–27 (a translation, with very slight modifications, of *Le Suicide*; pp. 1–15).

1897c 'Il suicidio e l'instabilità economica', *RS*, VII, pp. 529–47 (a translation of *Le Suicide;* pp. 264–88).

1897d 'Richard, G., *Le Socialisme et la science sociale*', *RP*, XLIV, pp. 200–205 (review).

1897e 'Labriola, Antonio, *Essais sur la conception matérialiste de l'histoire*', *RP*, XLIV, pp. 645–51 (review).

1897f Contribution to 'Enquête sur l'œuvre de H. Taine', *Revue blanche*, 13, pp. 287–91.

1898a *L'Année sociologique*, vol. I (i) Préface, pp. i–vii (tr. 1960c). (ii) Article: 'La Prohibition de l'inceste et ses origines', pp. 1–70 (tr. 1963a). (iii) Note: L'Anthroposociologie', p. 519. (iv) Reviews: (1) 'Kohler, Professor J., *Zur Urgeschichte der Ehe. Totemismus, Gruppenehe, Mutterrecht*', pp. 306–19. (2) 'Grosse, Ernest, *Die Formen der Familie und die Formen der Wirtschaft*', pp. 319–32. (3) 'Leist, *Alt-Arisches Jus civile, 2. Abteilung*', pp. 333–8. (4) 'Moret, A., *La Condition des Féaux en Égypte, dans la famille, dans la société etc.*', p. 338. (5) 'Acimovic, von Iovan, *Übersicht des serbischen Erbrechts*', p. 339. (6) 'Miler, Ernest, *Die Hauskommunion der Südslaven*', pp. 339–40. (7) 'Meynial, Éd., *Le Mariage après les invasions*', pp. 340–43. (8) 'Friederichs, Karl, *Familienstufen und Eheformen*', pp. 343–4. (9) 'Garufi, C. A., *Ricerche sugli usi nuziali nel medio evo in Sicilia*', p. 345. (10) 'Schulenburg, Emil, *Die Spuren des Brautraubes, etc.*', pp. 346–7. (11) 'Gunther, L., *Die Idee der Wiedervergeltung in der Geschichte, etc.*', pp. 347–51. (12) 'Kohler, J., *Studien aus dem Strafrecht, etc.*' pp. 351–3. (13) 'Mauss, Marcel, *La Religion et les origines du droit pénal*', pp. 353–8. (14) 'Baden-Powell, B. H., *The Indian Village Community*', pp. 359–63. (15) 'Jobbé-Duval, *La Commune annamite*', pp. 363–6. (16) 'Kovalewsky, Maxime, *Le Système du clan dans le pays de Galles*', p. 366. (17) 'Kohler, J., *Die Rechte der Urvölker Nordamerikas*', p. 389. (18) 'Tamassia, V., *Il " Dharna" in Germania ed in Grecia?*', pp. 389–90. (19) 'Gusakov, *Délits et contrats, étude d'histoire juridique*', p. 390. (20) 'Ratzel, Friedrich, *Der Staat und sein Boden geographisch beobachtet*', pp. 533–9.

1898b 'Représentations individuelles et représentations collectives', *RMM*, VI, pp. 273–302 (reproduced in 1924a).

1898c 'L'Individualisme et les intellectuels', *RB*, 4e série, X, pp. 7–13 (tr. 1969d).

1898d   'Letter to the Editor of the *American Journal of Sociology*',
        AJS, III, pp. 848–9.

1899a   *L'Année sociologique*, vol. II (i) Préface, pp. i–vi (tr. 1960c).
        (ii) Article: 'De la définition des phénomènes religieux',
        pp. 1–28. (iii) Note: 'Morphologie sociale', pp. 520–21.
        (iv) Reviews: (1) 'Smirnov, Jean, et Boyer, Paul, *Les
        Populations finnoises des bassins de la Volga et de la Kama*',
        pp. 226–9. (2) 'Meyer, Elard Hugo, *Deutsche Volkskunde*',
        pp. 302–6. (3) 'Hagelstange, Abel, *Süddeutsches Bauernleben
        im Mittelalter*', pp. 306–9. (4) 'Pandian, J. B., *Indian Village
        Folk, Their Works and Ways*', pp. 309–10. (5) 'Becke, Louis,
        Wild Life in Southern Seas', p. 310. (6) 'Rudeck, Wilhelm,
        Geschichte der öffentlichen Sittlichkeit in Deutschland', pp.
        310–13. (7) 'Schaible, K. Heinrich, *Die Frau im Altertum*',
        pp. 313–14. (8) 'Reibmayr, Albert, *Inzucht und Vermischung
        beim Menschen*', p. 314. (9) 'Ploss, H., *Das Weib in der Natur
        und Völkerkunde*', pp. 314–15. (10) 'Cunow, Heinrich, *Die
        ökonomischen Grundlagen der Mutterherrschaft*', pp. 316–18.
        (11) 'Kovalevski, M., *L'organizzazione del clan nel Daghestan*',
        pp. 318–20. (12) 'Smirnov et Boyer, *Les Populations
        finnoises des bassins de la Volga et de la Kama*', pp. 320–21.
        (13) 'Ciszewski, Stanilas, *Künstliche Verwandtschaft bei den
        Südslaven*', pp. 321–3. (14) 'Marçais, W., *Des Parents et des
        alliés successibles en droit musulman*', pp. 324–5. (15) 'Lefas,
        A., *L'Adoption testamentaire à Rome*', pp. 325–7. (16) 'Cornil,
        George, *Contribution à l'étude de la "Patria Potestas"*', pp.
        327–8. (17) 'Thomas, William I., *The Relation of Sex to
        Primitive Social Control*', pp. 328–9. (18) 'Flechter, A. C.,
        Häusliches Leben bei den Indianern', pp. 329–30. (19) 'Hut-
        chinson, Rev. H. N., *Marriage Customs in Many Lands*',
        pp. 331–4. (20) 'Loebel, D. Théophil, *Hochzeitsbräuche in
        der Türkei*', pp. 334–6. (21) 'Amram, David Werner, *The
        Jewish Law of Divorce according to Bible and Talmud*', pp.
        336–8. (22) 'Schnitzer, Jos., *Katholisches Eherecht*', pp. 339–
        41. (23) 'Meynial, Éd., *Le Mariage après les invasions*', pp.
        341–2. (24) 'Zocco-Rosa, A., *Sulle cerimonie nuziali dei
        Lusitani*', p. 343. (25) 'Bulow, v. W., *Die Ehegesetze der
        Samoaner*', p. 343. (26) 'McNair, Major, et Barlow, T. L.,
        *Customs and Ceremonies Observed at Betrothal and Wedding in
        the Pundjab*', p. 343. (27) 'Simcox, E. J., *Primitive Civiliza-
        tions or Outlines of the History of Ownership in Archaic
        Communities*', pp. 348–9. (28) 'Stefano, Gesmaro de, *II*

diritto penale nell'Hamasen (Eritrea) ed il Fethà Neghest', pp. 349–52. (29) 'Kohler, J., *Studien aus dem Strafrecht*', pp. 365–6. (30) 'Gatschet, Albert, *Die Osage Indianer*', p. 393. (31) 'Melching, Karl, *Die Staatenbildung in Melanesien*', p. 393. (32) 'Steinmetz, S. R., *Gli antichi scongiuri giuridici contro i debitori*', pp. 399–400. (33) 'Ratzel, Friedrich, *Politische Geographie*', pp. 522–32. (34) 'Vidal de la Blache, P., *La Géographie politique*', p. 532. (35) 'Von Mayr, G., *Statistik und Gesellschaftslehre. – II. Bevölkerungs-statistik*', pp. 533–6. (36) 'Rietschel, Siegfried, *Markt und Stadt in ihrem rechtlichen Verhältnis*', pp. 537–40. (37) 'Hegel, Karl, *Die Entstehung des deutschen Städtewesens*', pp. 540–42. (38) 'Meuriot, Paul, *Des Agglomérations urbaines dans l'Europe contemporaine*', pp. 542–6. (39) 'Kuczynski, R., *Der Zug nach der Stadt. Statistische Studien über Vorgänge der Bevölkerungsbewegung im deutschen Reiche*', pp. 546–9. (40) 'Barberis, L., *Lo sviluppo della rete ferroviaria degli Stati Uniti*', p. 550. (41) 'Ratzel, Friedrich, *Der Ursprung und das Wander der Völker, geographisch beobachtet*', p. 551. (42) 'Lapie, Paul, *Les Civilisations tunisiennes*', pp. 557–9. (43) 'Bortkewitsch, L. von, *Das Gesetz der kleinen Zahlen*', pp. 563–4. (44) 'Bennini, R., *Le Combinazioni simpatiche in demografia*', pp. 564–5.

1899b   Contribution to 'Enquête sur la guerre et le militarisme', *L'Humanité nouvelle*, May 1899, pp. 50–52.

1899c   Contribution to 'Enquête sur l'introduction de la sociologie dans l'enseignement secondaire', *RIS*, VII, p. 679.

1899d   Contribution to H. Dagan, *Enquête sur l'antisémitisme* (Paris: P. V. Stock), pp. 59–63.

1899e   'Merlino (Saverio), *Formes et essence du socialisme*, avec une préface de G. Sorel', *RP*, XLVIII, pp. 433–9 (review).

1899f   'Remarque sur la nature de la religiosité.' Fragment of a letter addressed on 11 May 1899 to Gaston Richard, cited in G. Richard, 'L'Enseignement de la sociologie à l'école normale primaire', *L'Éducateur protestant*, 1928, pp. 31–2.

1900a   *L'Année sociologique*, vol. III. Reviews: (1) 'Lindsay, S. M., *The Unit of Investigation in Sociology*', p. 160. (2) 'Villa, G., *La psicologia e le scienze morali*', p. 161. (3) 'Pareto, *I problemi della sociologia*', p. 163. (4) 'Giner, F., *Estudios y fragmentos sobre la teoria de la persona social*', pp. 182–3. (5) 'Ellwood, A., *Prolegomena to Social Psychology*', pp. 183–4. (6) 'Neukamp, Ernst, *Das Zwangsmoment im Recht in entwicklungsgeschichtlicher Bedeutung*', pp. 324–5. (7) 'Asturaro, A., *La scienza morale e la sociologia generale*', p. 330. (8) 'Spencer, Baldwin, et Gillen, F. J., *The Native Tribes of Central Australia*', pp. 330–36. (9) 'Boas, Franz, *The Social Organization and the Secret Societies of the Kwakiutl Indians*', pp. 336–40. (10) 'Parkinson, R., *Zur Ethnographie der nordwestlichen Salomo Inseln*', pp. 340-41. (11) 'Picard, E., *Les Pygmées*', pp. 341–3. (12) 'Schmidt, Max, *Über das Recht der tropischen Naturvölker Südamerikas*', pp. 344–6. (13) 'Buhl, D. Frants, *Die sozialen Verhältnisse der Israeliten*', pp. 346–8. (14) 'Conrady, Alexander, *Geschichte der Clanverfassung in den schottischen Hochlanden*', pp. 350–52. (15) 'Wilbrandt, M., *Die politische und soziale Bedeutung der attischen Geschlechter vor Solon*', pp. 352–4. (16) 'Courant, Maurice, *Les Associations en Chine*', pp. 354–6. (17) 'Starcke, C.-V., *La Famille dans les différentes sociétés*', pp. 365–70. (18) 'Junod, Henri A., *Les Ba-Ronga. Étude ethnographique sur les indigènes de la baie de Delagoa*', pp. 370–72. (19) 'Grenard, F., *Le Turkestan et le Tibet*', pp. 373–8. (20) 'Ritou, Étienne, *De la condition des personnes chez les Basques français jusqu'en 1789*', pp. 378–9. (21) 'Courant, Maurice, *Les Associations en Chine*', pp. 380–81. (22) 'Schmoller, G., *Die Urgeschichte der Familie: Mutterrecht und Gentilverfassung*', pp. 381–2. (23) 'Tamassia, N., *L'allevamento dei figli nell'antico diritto irlandese*', p. 382. (24) 'Mazzarella, Giuseppe, *La condizione giuridica del marito nella familia matriarcale*', pp. 383–5. (25) 'Holt, R. B., *Marriage Laws and Customs of the Cymri*', pp. 385–6. (26) 'Gürgens, Heinrich, *Die Lehre von der ehelichen Gütergemeinschaft nach livländischem Stadtrecht*', pp. 386–8. (27) 'Klugmann, N., *Vergleichende Studien zur Stellung der Frau im Altertum. I. Die Frau im Talmud*', pp. 388–9. (28) 'Marx, Victor, *Die Stellung der Frauen im Babylonien*', pp. 389–90. (29) 'Friederici, *Die Behandlung weiblicher Gefangener durch die Indianer von Nordamerika*', p. 390. (30) 'Lampérière, Anna, *Le Rôle social de la femme*', pp. 390–91. (31) 'Posado, A., *Feminismo*', p. 391. (32) 'Marro, *Le Rôle de la puberté*', p. 392. (33) 'Des Marez, Guillaume, *Étude sur la propriété foncière dans les villes du moyen âge*', pp. 393–5. (34) 'Cohn, Georg, *Gemeinderschaft und Hausgenossenschaft*', pp. 396–8. (35) 'Brentano, Lujo, *Die Entwicklung des englischen Erbrechts in das Grundeigenthum*', p. 398. (36) 'Veblen, Thorstein, *The Beginnings of Ownership*', p. 398. (37) 'Sée, H.,

Le Droit d'usage et les biens communaux en France au moyen âge', p. 399. (38) 'Hutter, *Der Abschluss von Blutsfreundschaft und Verträgen bei den Negern des Graslandes in Nordkamerun*', pp. 402–3. (39) 'Klemm, Kurt, *Ordal und Eid in Hinterindien*', p. 403. (40) 'Castelli, D., *Creditori e debitori nell'antica società ebraica*', pp. 403–4. (41) 'Steinmetz, *Das Verhältnis zwischen Eltern und Kindern bei den Naturvölkern*', pp. 445–7. (42) 'Wolf, Julius, *Das Verhältnis von Eltern und Kindern bei dem Landvolk in Deutschland*', pp. 447–8. (43) 'De Marchi, Attilio, *La beneficenza in Roma antica*', pp. 448–9. (44) 'Puini, C., *Del concetto d'uguaglianza nelle dottrine politiche del confucianesimo*', p. 449. (45) 'Lasch, Richard, *Religiöser Selbstmord und seine Beziehung zum Menschenopfer*', pp. 480–81. (46) 'Lasch, Richard, *Rache als Selbstmordmotiv*', p. 481. (47) 'Ratzel, Friedrich, *Anthropogeographie, Erster Teil: Grundzüge der Anwendung der Erdkunde auf die Geschichte*', pp. 550–58. (48) 'Dumont, Arsène, *Natalité et démocratie*', pp. 558–61. (49) 'Goldstein, J., *Die vermeintlichen und die wirklichen Ursachen des Bevölkerungsstillstandes in Frankreich*', pp. 561–3. (50) 'Prinzing, *Die Sterblichkeit der Ledigen und der Verheirateten*', p. 563. (51) 'Wolf, Julien, *Die Fruchtbarkeit der Ehe auf dem Lande im deutschen Reich*', pp. 563–4. (52) 'Brandt, Alexandre von, *L'Origine des villages à banlieue morcelée et des domaines agglomérés*', pp. 564–6. (53) 'Below, G. von, *Das ältere deutsche Städtewesen und Bürgertum*', pp. 566–70. (54) 'James, Edmond J., *The Growth of Great Cities in Area and Population*', p. 570. (55) 'Schoenherr, A., *Der Einfluss der Eisenbahnen auf die Bevölkerungszunahme im Königreiche Sachsen*', pp. 570–71. (56) 'Salvioni, G. B., *Zur Statistik der Haushaltungen*', pp. 571–3. (57) 'Conrau, *Der Hüttenbau der Völker im nordlichen Kamerungebiet*', pp. 573–4.

1900b   'La Sociologie en France au XIXe siècle', *RB*, 4e série, XII, pp. 609–13 (1ère période: Saint-Simon et Auguste Comte) and 647–52 (2ème période: de 1870 à 1900).

1900c   'La sociologia ed il suo dominio scientifico', *Ri It S*, anno IV, pp. 127–48 (tr. 1960c).

1901a   *L'Année sociologique*, vol. IV. (i) Article: 'Deux Lois de l'évolution pénale', pp. 65–95. (ii) Note: (1) 'Sociologie criminelle et statistique morale', pp. 433–6. (2) 'Technologie', pp. 593–4. (iii) Reviews: (1) 'Vierkandt, Alfred, *Das Kulturproblem*', pp. 128–9. (2) 'Tarde, G., *L'Esprit de groupe*', p. 136. (3) 'Palante, G., *L'Esprit de corps*', p. 137.

(4) 'Schultze, Fritz, *Psychologie der Naturvölker*', pp. 137–8. (5) 'Flachs, Adolf, *Rumänische Hochzeits- und Totengebräuche*', p. 178. (6) 'Ross, Edward Alsworth, *The Genesis of Ethical Elements*', pp. 308–9. (7) 'Gorst, Harold E., *China*', pp. 323–5. (8) 'Singer, H., *Die Karolinen*', pp. 327–8. (9) 'Reinecke, *Zur Kennzeichnung der Verhältnisse auf den Samoa-Inseln*', p. 328. (10) 'Henning, C. L., *Die Onondaga Indianer des Staates New-York*', p. 329. (11) 'Hutter, *Politische und Soziale Verhältnisse bei den Graslandstämmen Nordkameruns*', pp. 329–30. (12) 'Rocca, Félix de, *Les Zemskié Sobors*', pp. 330–32. (13) 'Commons, John R., *A Sociological View of Sovereignty*', p. 333. (14) 'Liebenam, W., *Städteverwaltung im Römischen Kaiserreiche*', pp. 337–8. (15) 'Stouff, Louis, *Les Comtes de Bourgogne et leurs villes domaniales*', pp. 338–9. *(16) 'Bellangé, Charles, *Le Gouvernement local en France et l'organisation du canton*', pp. 339–40. (17) 'Steinmetz, S. R., *Die neueren Forschungen zur Geschichte der menschlichen Familie*', pp. 340–42. (18) 'Cahuzac, Albert, *Essai sur les institutions et le droit malgaches*', pp. 342–5. (19) 'Escher, Arnold, *Der Einfluss des Geschlechtsunterschiedes der Descendenten im schweizerischen Erbrecht*', pp. 345–7. (20) 'Auffroy, Henri, *Évolution du testament en France*', pp. 348–52. (21) 'Hough, Walter, *Korean Clan Organization*', p. 352. (22) 'Flach, Jacques, *Les Institutions primitives. Les origines de la famille: Le Lévirat*', pp. 353–5. (23) 'Puini, C., *Il matrimonio nel Tibet*', pp. 355–6. (24) 'Roeder, Fritz, *Die Familie bei den Angelsachsen*', pp. 357–8. (25) 'Lefebvre, Charles, *Leçons d'introduction générale à l'histoire du droit matrimonial français*', pp. 358–62. (26) 'Winter, A. C., *Eine Bauernhochzeit in Russisch-Karelien*', pp. 362–3. (27) 'Esmein, A., *Trois Documents sur le mariage par vente*', p. 363. (28) 'Lourbet, Jacques, *Le Problème des sexes*', p. 364. (29) 'Fraser, J. G., *Suggestions as to the Origin of Gender in Language*', pp. 364–5. (30) 'Fuld, Ludwig, *Die Frauen und das Bürgerliche Gesetzbuch*', p. 365. (31) 'Schurtz, Heinrich, *Die Anfänge des Landbesitzes*', pp. 366–7. (32) 'Dultzig, Eugen v., *Das deutsche Grunderbrecht in Vergangenheit, Gegenwart und Zukunft*', pp. 367–9. (33) 'Boas, Franz, *Property Marks of Alaskan Eskimo*', p. 373. (34) 'Rakowski, Kasimir v., *Entstehung des Grossgrundbesitzes im XV. und XVI. Jahrhundert in Polen*',

* Unsigned – possibly by Durkheim.

pp. 373–4. (35) 'Glasson, *Communautés taisibles et communautés coutumières depuis la rédaction des coutumes*', p. 374. *(36) 'Grasshoff, Richard, *Das Wechselrecht der Araber. Eine rechtsvergleichende Studie über die Herkunft des Wechsels*', pp. 375–6. †(37) 'Chausse, A., *Les Singularités de la vente romaine*', pp. 376–7. (38) 'Lattes, Alessandro, *Il diritto consuetudinario nelle città lombarde*', pp. 418–19. (39) 'Vierkandt, A., *Die primitive Sittlichkeit der Naturvölker*', p. 422. (40) 'Bard, É., *Les Chinois chez eux*', pp. 422–3. (41) 'Kollmann, Paul, *Die soziale Zusammensetzung der Bevölkerung im deutschen Reiche*', pp. 436–8. (42) 'Prinzing, *Die soziale Lage der Witwe in Deutschland;* and *Grundzüge und Kosten eines Gesetzes über die Fürsorge für die Witwen und Waisen der Arbeiter*', pp. 438–40. (43) 'Fahlbeck, E., *Contributo allo studio demografico delle famiglie e delle generazioni umane*', p. 440. (44) 'Lindner, Friedrich, *Die unehelichen Geburten als Sozialphänomen*', pp. 441–3. (45) 'Fouillée, Alfred, *La France au point de vue moral*', pp. 443–5. (46) 'Rein, W., *Jugendliches Verbrechertum und seine Bekämpfung*', pp. 451–2. (47) 'Kellor, Frances A., *Psychological and Environmental Study of Women Criminals*', p. 452. (48) 'Marro, Antonio, *Influence of the Pubertal Development upon the Moral Character*', p. 452. (49) 'Tarnowski, E., *La mendicità in Russia*', pp. 460–61. (50) 'Lasch, Richard, *Die Behandlung der Leiche des Selbstmörders. Die Verbleibsorte der Abgeschiedenen Seelen der Selbstmörder*', pp. 462–3. (51) 'Lasch, Richard, *Der Selbstmord aus erotischen Motiven bei den primitiven Völkern*', p. 463. (52) 'Duprat, G.-L., *Les Causes sociales de la folie*', pp. 475–6. (53) 'Ratzel, Friedrich, *Das Meer als Quelle der Völkergrösse*', pp. 565–7. (54) 'Ratzel, F., *Der Ursprung und die Wanderungen der Völker geographisch betrachtet*', pp. 567–8. (55) 'Cauderlier, G., *Les Lois de la population et leur application à la Belgique*', pp. 569–74. (56) 'Beloch, Julius, *Die Bevölkerung im Altertum*', p. 574. (57) 'Beloch, Julius, *Die Bevölkerung Europas im Mittelalter*', p. 575. (58) 'Mariotti, A., *L'emigrazione italiana*', p. 575. (59) 'Kornemann, Ernst, *Zur Stadtentstehung in den ehemals keltischen und germanischen Gebieten des Römerreichs*', pp. 576–7. (60) 'Weber, Adna Ferrin, *The Growth of Cities in the Nineteenth Century*', pp. 577–82.

* Unsigned – by Durkheim and/or É. Lévy.
† Unsigned – by Durkheim and/or É. Lévy.

1901b   'De la méthode objective en sociologie', *RSH*, 11, pp. 3–17.
(The Preface to the 2nd edn. of *Les Règles*) (tr. 1938b).

1901c   *Les Règles de la méthode sociologique, revue et augmentée d'une
préface nouvelle* (2nd edn; Paris: Alcan) (tr. 1938b).

1901d   'Lettre au Directeur de la *Revue philosophique*', *RP*, LII,
p. 704.

1901e   'Simmel, G., *Philosophie des Geldes*', *NC*, 2e année, para. 406,
pp. 65–9 (review).

1901f   'Demolins, É., *Les Grandes Routes des peuples: essai de
géographie sociale. Comment la route crée le type social*', *NC*,
2e année, para. 1009, pp. 152–3 (review).

1901g   'Lambert, E., *La Tradition romaine sur la succession*', *NC*,
2e année, para. 1631, pp. 269–70 (review).

[1901h   Compte-rendu d'une conférence sur 'Religion et libre
pensée', devant les membres de la Fédération de Jeunesse
Laïque (donnée le 22 mai 1901), *La Petite Gironde*, 24 May
1901.]

1902a   *L'Année sociologique*, vol. v. (i) Article: 'Sur le totémisme',
pp. 82–121. (ii) Note: 'Civilisation en général et types de
civilisation', pp. 167–8. (iii) Reviews: (1) 'Seignobos, C.,
La Méthode historique appliquée aux sciences sociales', pp. 123–7.
(2) 'Novicow, *Les Castes et la sociologie biologique*', pp. 127–9.
(3) 'Espinas, A., *Être ou ne pas être ou du postulat de la
sociologie*', pp. 127–9 (items (2) and (3) reviewed together).
(4) 'Small, Albion W., *The Scope of Sociology*', pp. 133–4.
(5) 'Ward, Lester F., *La Mécanique sociale*', p. 137. (6)
'Simmel, Georg, *Philosophie des Geldes*', pp. 140–45. (7)
'Gumplowicz, *Aperçus sociologiques*', pp. 154–5. (8) '*Studii
sociologici*, publiées par le Dr Cosentini', p. 155. (9) 'Ellwood, Charles A., *The Theory of Imitation in Social Psychology*', pp. 155–6. (10) 'Ammon, Otto, *Der Ursprung der
sozialen Triebe*', p. 156. (11) 'Palante, *Le Mensonge de
groupe: étude sociologique*', p. 167. (12) 'Chailley-Bert, J.,
Java et ses habitants', pp. 184–5. (13) 'Dumont, Arsène,
La Morale basée sur la démographie', pp. 320–42. (14) 'Westermarck, E., *L'elemento morale nelle consuetudini e nelle leggi*',
pp. 326–7. (15) 'Kohler, J., *Rechte der deutschen Schutzgebiete. I. Das Recht der Herrero*', pp. 330–32. (16) 'Kohler,
J., *Rechte der deutschen Schutzgebiete. II. Das Recht der Papuas*',
pp. 332–3. (17) 'Kohler, J., *Rechte der deutschen Schutzgebiete. IV. Das Banturecht in Ostafrika*', pp. 333–4. (18)
'Rhys, J., et Brynmor-Jones, D., *The Welsh People*', pp. 334–5.

(19) 'Doniol, Henri, *Serfs et vilains au moyen âge*', pp. 336–9. (20) 'Sée, Henri, *Les Classes rurales et le régime domanial en France au moyen age*', pp. 339–42. (21) 'Fukuda, Tokuzo, *Die gesellschaftliche und wirtschaftliche Entwicklung in Japan*', pp. 342–7. (22) 'Milioukov, P., *Essais sur l'histoire de la civilisation russe*', pp. 358–9. (23) 'Abou'l-Hassan El-Maverdi, *Traité de droit public musulman*', pp. 362–3. (24) 'Sumner, W. G., *The Yakuts*', pp. 364–6. (25) 'Kohler, J., *Rechte der deutschen Schutzgebiete. II. Das Recht der Papuas*', pp. 366–8. (26) 'Kohler, J., *Rechte der deutschen Schutzgebiete. III. Das Recht der Marschallinsulaner*', pp. 368–71. (27) 'Darinsky, A., *Die Familie bei den kaukasischen Völkern*', pp. 371–3. (28) 'Lambert, Édouard, *La Tradition romaine sur la succession des formes du testament devant l'histoire comparative*', pp. 373–6. (29) 'Grenédan, J. Du Plessis de, *Histoire de l'autorité paternelle et de la société familiale en France avant 1789*', pp. 376–9. (30) 'Dupré la Tour, Félix, *De la recherche de la paternité en droit comparé et principalement en Suisse, en Angleterre et en Allemagne*', pp. 379–81. (31) 'Grasserie, Raoul de la, *La Famille artificielle*', p. 381. (32) 'Kovalewsky, Maxime, *La Gens et le clan*', pp. 381–2. (33) 'Rivers, W. H. R., *A Genealogical Method of Collecting Social and Vital Statistics*', p. 382. (34) 'Kohler, J., *Das Recht der Ba-Ronga*', pp. 382–3. (35) 'Binet, *Observations sur les Dahoméens*', p. 383. (36) 'Kaindl, R. F., *Bericht über neue anthropologische und volkskundliche Arbeiten in Galizien*', p. 383. (37) 'Muller, Otto, *Untersuchungen zur Geschichte des attischen Bürger- und Eherechts*', p. 383–7. (38) 'Marcou, Édmond, *De l' Autorisation maritale au XIIIe siècle comparée à celle du code civil*', pp. 387–9. (39) 'Kaindl, R. F., *Ruthenische Hochzeitsgebräuche in der Bukowina*', pp. 389–90. (40) 'Lolek, Emilian, *Vermahlungsbräuche in Bosnien und der Herzegovina*', p. 390. (41) 'Mazzarella, G., *Nuove ricerche sulla condizione del marito nella famiglia primitiva*', pp. 390–91. (42)'Mazzar ella, G., *L'esogamia presso i popoli semitici*', p. 391. (43) 'Muller, Joseph, *Das Sexuelle Leben der Naturvölker*', p. 392. (44) 'Ellis, Havelock, *Studies in the Psychology of Sex*', p. 392. (45) 'Beyerle, Konrad, *Grundeigentumsverhältnisse und Bürgerrecht im mittelalterlichen Konstanz*', pp. 393–4. (46) 'Van den Berg, L. W. C., *Het Inlandsche Gemeentewezen of Java en Madoera*', pp. 394–5. (47) 'Beauchet, L., *De la propriété familiale dans l'ancien droit suédois*', p. 395. (48) 'Friesen,

Heinrich Freiherr V., *Die Familienanwartschaften*', p. 396. (49) 'Seidel, H., *Pfandwesen und Schuldhaft in Togo*', pp. 396–7. (50) 'Marez, G. des, *La Lettre de foire à Ypres au XIIe siècle*', pp. 397–9. (51) 'Hopkins, Washburn, *On the Hindu Custom of Dying to Redress a Grievance*', pp. 399–400. (52) 'Bertillon, J., *Nombre d'enfants par famille*', pp. 435–6. (53) 'Prinzing, Friedrich, *Die eheliche Fruchtbarkeit in Deutschland*', pp. 436–7. (54) 'Dumont, Arsène, *De l'infécondité chez certaines populations industrielles*', p. 438. (55) 'Work, Monroe N., *Crime among the Negroes of Chicago*', pp. 449–50. (56) 'Lasch, Richard, *Die Anfänge des Gewerbestandes*', p. 514. (57) 'Demolins, Édmond, *Les Grandes Routes des peuples*', pp. 560–62. (58) 'Martonne, É. de, *Sur la toponymie naturelle des régions de haute montagne, en particulier dans les Karpates méridionales*', p. 562. (59) 'Goldstein, J., *Bevölkerungsprobleme und Berufsgliederung in Frankreich*', pp. 562–5. (60) 'Bertillon, Jacques, *Statistique internationale résultant des recensements de la population*', p. 565. (61) 'Cilleuls A. des, *La Population française en 1800 et en 1900*', pp. 565–6. (62) 'Sitta, P., *La popolazione della repubblica argentina*', p. 566. (63) 'Piolet, J. B., *La France hors de France*', pp. 566–7. (64) 'Pirenne, H., *Histoire de la Belgique*', pp. 567–71. (65) 'Buomberger, Ferdinand, *Bevölkerungs- und Vermögensstatistik in der Stadt und Landschaft Freiburg*', pp. 571–4. (66) 'Jullian, C., *À propos des "Pagi" gaulois avant la conquête romaine*', pp. 574–5. (67) 'Prinzing, Fr., *Die Kindersterblichkeit in Stadt und Land*', p. 576. (68) 'Mazzola, Ugo, *Il momento economico nell'arte*', p. 592. (69) 'Sorel, G., *La valeur sociale de l'art*', p. 592.

1902b   *De la division du travail social*, avec une nouvelle préface intitulée 'Quelques Remarques sur les groupements professionels' (2nd ed; Paris: Alcan) (tr. 1933b).

1902c   'Palante, G., *Précis de sociologie*', *RSH*, IV, pp. 114–15 (review).

1902d   Contribution to 'Enquête sur l'influence allemande: II – Sociologie et économie politique', *MF*, no. 156, t. XLIV, pp. 647–8 (December 1902).

1902e   'Demuth, E., *Die wechselseitigen Verfügungen von Todeswegen nach alamannisch-zürcherischem Recht*', *NC*, 3e année, para. 444, pp. 77–8 (review).

1902f   'Bauer, A., *Les Classes sociales*', *NC*, 3e année, para. 1453, pp. 257–8 (review).

1903a *L'Année sociologique*, vol. VI. (i) Article: 'De quelques formes primitives de classification: contribution à l'étude des représentations collectives', pp. 1–72 (with M. Mauss) (tr. 1963b). (ii) Notes: (1) 'Systèmes juridiques', p. 305 (with P. Fauconnet). (2) 'Organisation sociale', p. 316. (iii) Reviews: (1) 'Salvemini, G., *La storia considerata come scienza*', pp. 123–5. (2) 'Croce, B., *La storia considerata come scienza*', pp. 123–5. (3) 'Sorel, G., *Storia e scienze sociali*', pp. 123–5 (items (1), (2) and (3) reviewed together). (4) 'Vierkandt, A., *Natur und Kultur in sozialem Individuum*', pp. 145–6. (5) 'Steinmetz, S. R., *Der erbliche Rassen- und Volkscharakter*', pp. 146–7. (6) 'Wallis, Louis, *The Capitalization of Social Development*', p. 147. (7) 'Gumplowicz, L., *Una legge sociologica della storia*', p. 147. (8) 'Sergi, G., *L'evoluzione in biologia e nell'uomo*', pp. 147–8. (9) 'Robertis, R. Resta de, *La psicologia collettiva della scuola*', pp. 151–2. (10) 'Romano, P., *La pedagogia nelle sue relazioni con la sociologia*', pp. 151–2 (items (9) and (10) reviewed together). (11) 'Savigny, L. von, *Das Naturrechtsproblem und die Methode seiner Lösung . . .*, Saleilles, R., *École historique et droit naturel*', pp. 302–3. (12) 'Bonfante, P., *La progressiva diversificazione del diritto publico e privato*', pp. 304–5. (13) 'Kohler, J., *Rechte der deutschen Schutzgebiete*', pp. 306–8. (14) 'Conradt, L., *Die Ngumba in Südkamerun*', p. 308. (15) 'Koch, T., *Die Guaikurustämme*', p. 309. (16) 'Mazzarella, *Le istituzioni giuridiche di una tribu dell'America settentrionale*', p. 309. (17) 'Bogoras, W., *The Chukchi of Northern Asia*', p. 309. (18) 'Gautier, Victor, *La Langue, les noms et le droit des anciens Germains*', pp. 309–10. (19) 'Schurtz, Heinrich, *Altersklassen und Männerbünde*', pp. 317–23. (20) 'McGee, W. J., *The Seri Indians*', pp. 323–4. (21) 'Szanto, Emil, *Die Griechischen Phylen*', pp. 324–7. (22) 'Holzapfel, L., *Die drei ältesten römischen Tribus*', pp. 324–7 (items (21) and (22) reviewed together). (23) 'Wittich, Werner, *Die Frage der Freibauern*', pp. 331–3. (24) 'Guilhiermoz, P., *Essai sur l'origine de la noblesse en France*', pp. 333–7. (25) 'Viollet, Paul, *Les Communes françaises au moyen âge*', pp. 337–41. (26) 'Loncao, E., *La genesi sociale dei communi italiani*', pp. 341–2. (27) 'Lavallée, A., *Notes ethnographiques sur divers tribus du sud-est de l'Indo-Chine*', pp. 342–3. (28) 'Nicholas, F. C., *The Aborigines of the Province of Santa Maria*', p. 343. (29) 'Rundstein, S., *Die vergleichende Methode in ihrer An-*

wendung auf die slawische Rechtsgeschichte', pp. 343–5. (30) 'Marchand, Lucien, *Les Gard'orphènes à Lille*', p. 345. (31) 'Caillemer, R., *Origines et développement de l'exécution testamentaire*', pp. 345–50. (32) 'Crawley, Ernest, *The Mystic Rose. A Study of Primitive Marriage*', pp. 352–8. (33) 'Thomas, Wilson, *Der Ursprung der Exogamie*,' pp. 358–9. (34) 'Esmein, A., *Les Coutumes primitives dans les écrits des mythologues grecs et romains*', pp. 359–61. (35) 'Révész, Géza, *Das Trauerjahr der Witwe*', pp. 361–5. (36) 'Weitzecker, G., *La donna fra i Basuto*', p. 365. (37) 'Lefebvre, C., *Le Mariage civil n'est-il qu'un contrat?*' pp. 365–6. (38) 'Rullkoeter, William, *The Legal Protection of Woman among the Ancient Germans*', pp. 366–7. (39) 'Courant, Maurice, *En Chine*', pp. 367–9. (40) 'Vierkandt, Alfred, *Die politischen Verhältnisse der Naturvölker*', pp. 372–3. (41) 'Francotte, Henri, *Formation des villes, des états, des confédérations et des ligues dans la Grèce ancienne*', pp. 373–6. (42) 'Iovanovic, Milan Paul, *Die agrarischen Rechtsverhältnisse im türkischen Reiche*', pp. 383–5. (43) 'Huvelin, P., *Les Tablettes magiques et le droit romain*', pp. 388–90. (44) 'Loncao, Enrico, *L'inviolabilità del domicilio nell'antico diritto germanico*', pp. 413–14. (45) 'Vecchio, G. del, *L'evoluzione dell'ospitalità*', p. 414. (46) 'Pouzol, Abel, *La Recherche de la paternité*', pp. 415–18. (47) 'Dépinay, J., *Le Régime dotal*', pp. 418–20. (48) 'Griveau, Paul, *Le Régime dotal en France*', pp. 418–20 (items (47) and (48) reviewed together). (49) 'Buomberger, F., *Die schweizerische Ehegesetzgebung im Lichte der Statistik*', pp. 420–22. (50) 'Prinzing, Friedrich, *Die Ehescheidungen in Berlin und anderwärts*', pp. 422–3. (51) 'Prinzing, Friedrich, *Die uneheliche Fruchtbarkeit in Deutschland*', p. 423. (52) 'Schrader, Franz, *Le Facteur planétaire de l'évolution humaine. Lois terrestres et coutumes humaines*', pp. 539–40. (53) 'Coste, *Le Facteur population dans l'évolution sociale*', pp. 540–41. (54) 'Verrijn Stuart, C. A., *Untersuchungen über die Beziehung zwischen Wohlstand, Natalität und Kindersterblichkeit in den Niederlanden*', pp. 546–7. (55) 'Ottolenghi, C., *La popolazione del Piemonte nel secolo XVI*', p. 549. (56) '*Xe Congrès international d'hygiène et de démographie: Paris 1900*', pp. 549–50. (57) 'Fournier de Flaix, E., *Statistique et consistance des religions à la fin du XIXe siècle*', pp. 550–51. (58) 'Jullian, Camille, *Notes gallo-romaines*', p. 552. (59) 'Allendorf, Hans, *Der Zuzug in die Städte*', pp. 552–6.

(60) 'Meuriot, P., *La Population de Berlin et de Vienne d'après les dénombrements récents*', pp. 556–7. (61) 'Coste, A., *De l'influence des agglomérations urbaines sur l'état matériel et moral d'un pays*', p. 557.

1903b   'Pédagogie et sociologie', *RMM*, XI, pp. 37–54 (reproduced in 1922a) (opening lecture of 1902–3 course on 'L'Éducation Morale').

1903c   'Sociologie et sciences sociales', *RP*, LV, pp. 465–97 (with P. Fauconnet) (abridged tr. 1905d).

1903d   'Lang, A., *Social Origins* and Atkinson, J. J., *Primal Law*', *Folklore*, XIV, pp. 421–5. (review).

1903e   'Letourneau, C., *La Condition de la femme dans les diverses races et civilisations*', *NC*, 4e année, para. 289, pp. 65–6 (review).

1903f   'Markovic, M., *Die serbische Hauskommunion (Zadruga) und ihre Bedeutung in der Vergangenheit und Gegenwart*', *NC*, 4e année, para. 837, pp. 199–200 (review).

1904a   *L'Année sociologique*, vol. VII. Reviews: (1) 'Ross, Edward Alsworth, *Moot Points in Sociology. I. The Scope and Task of Sociology*', pp. 158–9. (2) 'Steinmetz, S. R., *Die Bedeutung der Ethnologie für die Soziologie*', pp. 159–60. (3) 'Allin, Arthur, *The Basis of Sociality*', p. 185. (4) 'Lambert, Édouard, *La Fonction du droit civil comparé*', pp. 374–9. (5) 'Lévy-Bruhl, L., *La Morale et la science des mœurs*', pp. 380–84. (6) 'Steinmetz, S. R., *Rechtsverhältnisse von eingeborenen Völkern in Afrika und Oceanien*', pp. 389–94. (7) 'Merker, M., *Rechtsverhältnisse und Sitten der Wadschagga*', pp. 394–6. (8) 'Lang, Andrew, *Social Origins*', pp. 407–11. (9) 'Atkinson, J. J., *Primal Law*', pp. 407–11. (items (8) and (9) reviewed together). (10) 'Oberziner, Giovanni, *Origine della plebe romana*', pp. 412–13. (11) 'Amadori-Virgili, Giovanni, *L'istituto famigliare nelle società primordiali*', pp. 416–17. (12) 'Wilutzky, Paul, *Vorgeschichte des Rechts*', pp. 417–18. (13) 'Thal, Max, *Mutterrecht, Frauenfrage und Weltanschauung*', p. 418. (14) 'Niese, Richard, *Das Personen- und Familienrecht der Suaheli*', pp. 420–23. (15) 'Markovic, Milan, *Die serbische Hauskommunion (Zadruga) and ihre Bedeutung in der Vergangenheit und Gegenwart*', pp. 425–7. (16) 'Stockar, Hans, *Über den Entzug der väterlichen Gewalt im römischen Recht*', pp. 427–8. (17) 'Glasson, E., *Histoire du droit et des institutions de la France*', pp. 428–33. (18) 'Letourneau, C., *La Condition de la femme dans les diverses races et civilisations*', pp. 433–4. (19) 'Gaudefroy-Demombynes, *Les Cérémonies du mariage chez les indigènes de l'Algérie*', pp. 435–6. (20) 'Pidoux, Pierre-André, *Histoire du mariage et du droit des gens mariés en Franche-Comté*', pp. 436–8. (21) 'Bauer, Max, *Das Geschlechtsleben in der deutschen Vergangenheit*', pp. 438–40. (22) 'Khamm, Karl, *Der Verkehr der Geschlechter unter den Slaven in seinen gegensätzlichen Erscheinungen*', p. 440–41. (23) 'Budanov, V., *L'Autorité dans la Russie ancienne*', pp. 447–50. (24) 'Pirenne, H., *L'Histoire de la Belgique*', pp. 453–4. (25) 'Girault, Arthur, *Les Bambaras*', p. 464. (26) 'Duprat, G.-L., *Le Mensonge*', pp. 512–13. (27) 'Prinzing, Friedrich, *Die Wandlungen der Heiratshäufigkeit und des mittleren Heiratsalters*', pp. 520–21. (28) 'Loewenstimm, August, *Aberglaube und Verbrechen*', p. 523. (29) 'Simmel, Georg, *Über räumliche Projectionen sozialer Formen*', p. 646–7. (30) 'Simmel, Georg, *The Number of Members as Determining the Sociological Form of the Group*', pp. 647–9. (31) 'Cauderlier, G., *Les Lois de la population*', p. 651. (32) 'Lang, Hans, *Die Entwicklung der Bevölkerung in Württemberg*', pp. 651–4. (33) 'Turquan, Victor, *Contribution à l'étude de la population et de la dépopulation*', p. 655. (34) 'Maurel, É., *Causes de notre dépopulation*', p. 655. (35) 'Prinzing, F., *Die Kindersterblichkeit in Österreich*', pp. 655–6. (36) 'Reisner, Wilhelm, *Die Einwohnerzahl deutscher Städte in früheren Jahrhunderten*', pp. 655–7. (37) 'Vandervelde, É., *L'Exode rural et le retour aux champs*', pp. 658–62. (38) 'Meuriot, Paul, *Du Centre mathématique d'une population*', p. 662. (39) 'Schultz, Alwin, *Das Häusliche Leben der europäischen Kulturvölker*', pp. 664–5. (40) 'Durkheim, Émile, *Pédagogie et sociologie*', pp. 683–6. (41) 'Barth, Paul, *Die Geschichte der Erziehung in soziologischer Beleuchtung*', pp. 683–6 (items (40) and (41) reviewed together).

1904b   'La Sociologie et les sciences sociales', *RIS*, XII, pp. 83–4 (*résumé d'une conférence;* followed by discussion, pp. 86–7).

1904c   'Lambert, É., *La Fonction du droit civil comparé:* (1) *les conceptions étroites et unilatérales*', *NC*, 5e année, para. 43, pp. 10–12 (review).

1904d   'Réponse à M. Lang', letter in *Folklore*, XV, pp. 215–16.

1904e   Contribution to 'L'Élite intellectuelle et la démocratie', *RB*, 5e série, t. 1, no. 23, pp. 705–6 (4 June 1904).

1905a   *L'Année sociologique*, vol. VIII. (i) Article: 'Sur l'organisation matrimoniale des sociétés australiennes', pp. 118–47.

(ii) Reviews: (1) 'Thomas, William, *Der Mangel an Generali-sationsvermögen bei den Negern*', p. 198. (2) 'Pelisson, Maurice, *La Sécularisation de la morale au XVIII siècle*', pp. 381–2. (3) '*Reports of the Cambridge Anthropological Expedition to Torres Straits*', pp. 382–91. (4) 'Koehler, Arthur, *Verfassung, soziale Gliederung, Recht und Wirtschaft der Tuareg*', pp. 392–3. *(5) 'Cook, S. A., *The Laws of Moses and the Code of Hammurabi*', pp. 393–5. *(6) 'Daiches, S., *Altbabylonische Rechtsurkunden aus der Zeit der Hammurabi-Dynastie*', pp. 393–5. (7) 'Lot, Ferdinand, *Fidèles ou vassaux?*', pp. 403–4. (8) 'Kruyt, Alb. C., *Beobachtungen an Leben und Tod, Ehe und Familie in Zentralcelebes*', pp. 408–9. (9) 'Tsugaru, Fusamaro, *Die Lehre von der japanischen Adoption*', pp. 409–13. (10) 'Engelmann, Jean, *Les Testaments coutumiers au XVe siècle*', pp. 413–14. (11) 'Penot, Joseph, *Évolution du mariage et consanguinité*', p. 415. (12) 'Nietzold, Johannes, *Die Ehe in Ägypten zur ptolemäisch-römischen Zeit*', pp. 415–18. (13) 'Ruggiero, Roberto de, *Studi papirologici sul matrimonio et sul divorzio nell'Egitto greco-romano*', pp. 418–19. (14) 'Mielziner, M., *The Jewish Law of Marriage and Divorce*', pp. 419–21. (15) 'Twasaky, Kojiro, *Das japanische Eherecht*', pp. 421–5. (16) 'Sakamoto, Saburo, *Das Ehescheidungsrecht Japans*', pp. 421–5 (items (15) and (16) reviewed together). (17) 'Bartsch, Robert, *Die Rechtsstellung der Frau als Gattin und Mutter*', pp. 425–7. (18) 'Typaldo-Bassia, A., *La Communauté de biens con-jugale dans l'ancien droit français*', pp. 427–9. (19) 'Saguez, Eugène, *Étude sur le droit des gens mariés dans les coutumes d'Amiens*', pp. 429–31. (20) 'Kulischer, E., *Untersuchungen über das primitive Strafrecht*', pp. 460–63. (21) 'Usteri, P., *Achtung und Verbannung im griechischen Recht*', p. 464. (22) 'Glotz, Gustave, *La Solidarité de la famille dans le droit criminel en Grèce*', pp. 465–72. (23) 'Huvelin, P., *La Notion de l'* "*Injuria*" *dans le très ancien droit romain*', pp. 472–4. (24) 'Leonhard, R., *Der Schutz der Ehre im alten Rom*', pp. 472–4. (items (23) and (24) reviewed together). (25) 'Dareste, R., *Les Anciennes Coutumes Albanaises*', pp. 474–5. †(26) 'Kwiatkowski, E. von, *Die Constitutio Criminalis Theresiana*', pp. 475–6. †(27) 'Labriola, Teresa, *Ragione e sviluppo della*

---

* Items (5) and (6) reviewed together, but unsigned – probably by Durkheim or P. Fauconnet.

† Unsigned – by Durkheim or P. Fauconnet.

giustizia punitiva', pp. 476–7. *(28) 'Loening, R., *Geschichte der strafrechtlichen Zurechnungslehre'*, pp. 477–9. *(29) 'Kurella, H., *Die Grenzen der Zurechnungsfähigkeit und die Kriminal-Anthropologie'*, p. 479. *(30) 'Glotz, G., *L'Ordalie dans la Grèce primitive'*, pp. 480–83. (31) 'Grierson, Hamilton P. J., *The Silent Trade'*, pp. 483–6. (32) 'Prinzing, Friedrich, *Heiratshäufligkeit und Heiratsalter nach Stand und Beruf'*, pp. 487–8. (33) 'Stchoukine, Ivan, *Le Suicide collectif dans le Raskol russe,'* pp. 499–500. (34) 'Rost, Hans, *Der Selbstmord in den Städten'*, p. 502. (35) 'Juglar, Clément, *Tableau des naissances'*, pp. 616–17. (36) 'Kiaer, A. N., *Statistische Beiträge zur Beleuchtung der ehelichen Fruchtbarkeit'*, pp. 618–19. (37) 'Casagrandi, O., *La popolazione, le nascite, le morti a Roma negli ultimi due secoli'*, pp. 619–20. (38) 'Klatt, Max, *Die Alters- und Sterblichkeitsverhältnisse der preussischen Richter und Staatsanwälte'*, p. 620. (39) 'Wagner, Eduard, *Die Bevölkerungsdichte in Südhannover und deren Ursachen'*, p. 625. (40) 'Dade, Heinrich, *Die landwirtschaftliche Bevölkerung des deutschen Reichs um die Wende des 19. Jahrhunderts'*, pp. 625–6.

1905b   Contribution to 'La Morale sans Dieu: essai de solution collective', *La Revue*, LIX, pp. 306–8.

1905c   'On the Relation of Sociology to the Social Sciences and to Philosophy', *SP*, 1, Macmillan, London (abstract of a paper laid before the Sociological Society at the School of Economics and Political Science, University of London, 20 June 1904, pp. 197–200, and reply to criticisms,† p. 257).

1905d   'Sociology and the Social Sciences', *SP*, 1, London, pp. 258–80 (with P. Fauconnet) (abridged translation of 1903c, omitting pp. 473–84).

1905e   Contribution to discussion: 'Sur la séparation des églises et de l'état', in *Libres entretiens*, 1ère série, pp. 369–71, 496–

---

* Unsigned – by Durkheim or P. Fauconnet.

† By B. Bosanquet, J. H. Bridges, E. Reich, Shadworth Hodgson, J. A. Hobson, J. M. Robertson, L. T. Hobhouse, P. Barth, M. Bernès, L. Lévy-Bruhl, J. Bryce, J. Bury, S. J. Chapman, Combe de Lestrade, Prof. Cosentini, C. Gide, B. Crozier, R. Dareste, A. Fouillée, C. J. de J. Stuart-Glennie, J. H. Harley, Profs. Ingram, Kovalevsky, Latta, A. Loria, J. H. Muirhead, H. Osman Newland, J. S. Nicholson, A. S. Pringle-Pattison, B. Russell, W. R. Sorley, L. Stein, S. R. Steinmetz, J. L. Tayler, F. Tönnies, L. Winiarski and R. Worms.

500, and to discussion 'Sur l'Internationalisme: définition des termes: Internationalisme économique; patriotisme national et lutte des classes', in *Libres entretiens*, 2e série, pp. 17, 27, 30–33, 35, 39–42, 45, 56–7, 147–8, 150, 153, 412, 425–34, 436, 480–84.

1906a *L'Année sociologique*, vol. IX. Reviews: (1) 'Tarde, G., *L'Interpsychologie*', pp. 133–5. (2) 'Xenopol, A. D., *Sociologia e storia*', pp. 139–40. (3) 'Andreotti, A., *L'induzione sociologica nello studio del diritto penale*', pp. 141–2. (4) 'Matteucci, U., *Intorno al riconoscimento della sociologia come scienza autonoma*', pp. 141–2 (5) 'Matteucci, U., *L'insegnamento della sociologia*', pp. 141–2. (items (3), (4) and (5) reviewed together). (6) 'Toniolo Giuseppe, *L'odierno problema sociologico*', pp. 142–3. (7) 'Carini, P., *Saggio di una classificazione delle società*', pp. 143–4. (8) 'Ribot, T., *La Logique des sentiments*', pp. 156–8. (9) 'De Robertis, R. Resta, *L'anima delle folle*', pp. 159–60. (10) 'Hoeffding, Harald, *On the Relation between Sociology and Ethics*', pp. 323–4. (11) 'Bayet, Albert, *La Morale scientifique*', pp. 324–6. (12) 'Kohler, Josef, *Zum Rechte der Tshinuk*', pp. 330–31. (13) 'Merker, M., *Die Masai. Ethnographische Monographie eines ostafrikanischen Semitenvolkes*', pp. 331–7. (14) 'Farjenel, Fernand, *Le Peuple chinois. Ses mœurs et ses institutions*', pp. 338–9. (15) 'Grenard, F., *Le Tibet, le pays et les habitants*', pp. 339–40. (16) 'Dareste, R., *La Loi des Homérites*', pp. 340–42. (17) 'Chadwick, H. Munro, *Studies on Anglo-Saxon Institutions*', pp. 345–6. (18) 'Hitier, Joseph, *La Doctrine de l'absolutisme*', pp. 353–5. (19) 'Howitt, A. W., *The Native Tribes of South-East Australia*', pp. 355–68. (20) 'Kohler, Josef, *Aus dem malayischen Recht*', pp. 368–9. (21) 'Kovalewsky, Maxime, *Le Clan chez les tribus indigènes de la Russie*', p. 369. (22) 'Doutté, Édmond, *L'Organisation domestique et sociale chez les H'âh'a*', pp. 369–72. (23) 'Lévy, Louis-Germain, *La Famille dans l'antiquité israélite*', pp. 372–3. (24) 'Duarte, José Castillejo y, et Ruben, Ernst, *Die Hausgemeinschaft im heutigen spanischen Gewohnheitsrechte*', pp. 375–7. (25) 'Platon, G., *Du droit de la famille dans ses rapports avec le régime des biens en droit andorran*', pp. 375–7. (items (24) and (25) reviewed together). (26) 'Kohler, Josef, *Zur Urgeschichte der Ehe*', pp. 378–80. (27) 'Westermarck, Edward, *The Position of Women in Early Civilization*', p. 380. (28) 'Hermann, E., *Zur Geschichte des Braut-*

kaufs bei den indogermanischen Völkern', pp. 381–3. (29)
'Behre, Ernst, *Die Eigentumsverhältnisse im ehelichen Güter-recht des Sachsenspiegels und magdeburger Rechts'*, pp. 383–4.
(30) 'Howard, George Elliott, *A History of Matrimonial Institutions'*, pp. 384–92. (31) 'Kelles-Krauz, Casimir de, *L'Origine des interdictions sexuelles'*, pp. 393–4. (32) 'Guiraud, P., *La Propriété primitive à Rome'*, pp. 398–400. (33) 'Dereux, George, *De l'interprétation des actes juridiques privés'*, pp. 418–20. (34) 'Spann, Othmar, *Die Stiefvaterfamilie unehe-lichen Ursprungs. Zugleich eine Studie zur Methodologie der Unehelichkeits-Statistik'*, pp. 435–8. (35) 'Valensi, Alfred, *L'Application de la loi du divorce en France'*, pp. 438–43.
(36) 'Frauenstaedt, Paul, *Zwanzig Jahre Kriminalstatistik'*, pp. 448–9.

1906b   'La Détermination du fait moral', *BSFP*, VI, Séances du 11 février et du 22 mars 1906, pp. 169–212 (reproduced, with excerpts from the discussion, in 1924a).

1906c   'L'Évolution et le rôle de l'enseignement secondaire en France', *RB*, 5e série, V, pp. 70–77 (reproduced in 1922a) (opening lecture of 1905–6 course on 'Formation et développement de l'enseignement secondaire en France'.

1906d   'Le Divorce par consentement mutuel', *RB*, 5e série, V, pp. 549–54.

[1906e   Summary by A. Lalande of a lecture by Durkheim on religion and morality, delivered at the École des Hautes Études in the winter of 1905–6, *Philosophical Review* (New York), XV, pp. 255–7.]

1907a   *L'Année sociologique*, vol. X. Reviews: (1) 'Jankelevitch, Dr S., *Nature et société'*, pp. 171–4. (2) 'Naville, Adrien, *La Sociologie abstraite et ses divisions'*, p. 176. (3) 'Fouillée, Alfred, *Les Éléments sociologiques de la morale'*, pp. 352–69.
(4) 'Belot, Gustave, *En quête d'une morale positive'*, pp. 352–69. (5) 'Landry, Adolphe, *Principes de morale rationnelle'*, pp. 352–69 (items (3), (4) and (5) reviewed together). (6) 'Miceli, V., *Il diritto quale fenomeno di credenza collettiva'*, p. 381. (7) 'Colozza, M., *Le fonti del diritto e la credenza'*, p. 381. (8) 'Brugi, R., *Il diritto greco classico et la sociologia'*, pp. 381–2. (9) 'Richard, G., *Les Lois de la solidarité morale'*, pp. 382–3. (10) 'Westermarck, Edward, *The Origin and Development of the Moral Ideas'*, pp. 383–95. (11) 'Meyer, Félix, *Wirtschaft und Recht der Herero'*, pp. 395–8. (12) 'Irle, J., *Die Herero'*, pp. 395–8 (items (11) and (12) reviewed

together). (13) 'Kohler, Josef, *Über das Recht der Herero*', p. 398. (14) 'Kohler, Josef, *Zum Rechte der Papuas*', pp. 398–9. (15) 'Farjenel, F., *La Morale chinoise. Fondement des sociétés d'Extrême-Orient*', p. 399. (16) 'Lang, Andrew, *The Secret of the Totem*', pp. 400–409. (17) 'Frazer, J. G., *Lectures on the Early History of the Kingship*', pp. 411–15. (18) 'Moore, Levis, *Malabar Law and Custom*', pp. 420–44. (19) 'D'Arbois de Jubainville, H., *La Famille celtique*', pp. 424–7. (20) 'Engert, Thad., *Ehe- und Familienrecht der Hebräer*', pp. 427–9. (21) 'Lefebvre, Charles, *Cours de doctorat sur l'histoire matrimoniale française*', pp. 429–33. (22) 'Dainville, Albert de, *Des Pactes successoraux dans l'ancien droit français*', pp. 433–4. (23) 'Guigon, Henri, *La Succession des bâtards dans l'ancienne Bourgogne*', pp. 435–6. (24) 'Bryce, James, *Marriage and Divorce*', pp. 436–7. (25) 'Rol, Auguste, *L'Évolution du divorce*', pp. 437–8. (26) 'Mallard, Henri, *Étude sur le droit des gens mariés*', pp. 438–9. (27) 'Blau, Bruno, *Die Kriminalität der deutschen Juden*', pp. 494–5. (28) 'Krose, H. A., *Der Selbstmord im 19. Jahrhundert nach seiner Verteilung auf Staaten und Verwaltungsbezirke*', pp. 499–500.

1907b 'Lettres au Directeur de la *Revue néo-scolastique*', RNS, XIV, pp. 606–7, 612–14.

1907c Contribution to *La Question religieuse: enquête internationale*, MF, LXVII, p. 51 (reprinted in volume of same title edited by Fr. Charpin, 1908, pp. 95–7).

1907d Contributions to discussion: 'Sur la réforme des institutions judiciaires: l'enseignement du droit', in *Libres entretiens*, 3e série, pp. 361, 366, 371–3, 388–91, 394, 397–9, 414–17, 419–21.

1907e Article on O. Hamelin in *Le Temps*, 18 September 1907.

[1907f 'Cours d'Émile Durkheim à la Sorbonne', *Revue de philosophie* VII: no. 5, pp. 528–39; no. 7, pp. 92–114; and no. 12, pp. 620–38. Summary by P. Fontana of 1906–7 lecture course: 'La Religion: Origines'.]

1907g Contribution to 'Débat sur les rapports de l'ethnologie et la sociologie', *Bulletin du Comité des Travaux historiques et scientifiques. Section des sciences économiques et sociales*, 1907, pp. 199–200.

1908a Contribution to discussions of: (1) 'Pacifisme et patriotisme', séance du 30 décembre 1907, pp. 44–9, 51–2, 66–7, 69. (2) 'La Morale positive: examen de quelques difficultés', séance du 26 mars 1908, pp. 189–200. (3)

'L'Inconnu et l'inconscient en histoire', séance du 28 mai 1908, pp. 229–45, in *BSFP*, VIII.

1908b   'Aux lecteurs de *l'Année sociologique*', in Bouglé, C., *Essais sur le régime des castes* (Paris: Alcan), pp. v–viii.

1908c   Contribution to discussions of: (1) 'De la position de l'économie politique dans l'ensemble des sciences sociales' in *Bulletin de la Société d'économie politique*, séance du 4 avril 1908, pp. 61–73. (2) *Ditto* in *Journal des économistes*, XVIII, avril 1908, pp. 113–15, 117–20.

1908d   Contributions to discussion: 'Sur l'état, les fonctionnaires et le public: le fonctionnaire citoyen; syndicats de fonctionnaires', in *Libres entretiens*, 4e série, pp. 137–8, 140, 142–5, 148, 150–52, 161–3, 169–70, 176, 190, 194–7, 243, 245, 252–6, 257–9, 261–6, 272, 275, 279–81, 283, 292–5.

1908e   Contribution to 'Enquête sur l'impuissance parlementaire', *La Revue*, LXIII, pp. 396–7.

1908f   Contribution to 'Enquête sur la sociologie', *Les Documents du progrès*, 2e. année, février, pp. 131–3.

1909a   Contribution to discussions of: (1) 'Science et religion', séance du 19 novembre 1908, pp. 56–60. (2) 'L'Efficacité des doctrines morales', séance du 20 mai 1909, in *BSFP*, IX, pp. 56–60.

1909b   'Note sur la spécialisation des facultés des lettres et l'agrégation de philosophie', *RIE*, LVII, pp. 159–61.

1909c   'Examen critique des systèmes classiques sur les origines de la pensée religieuse', *RP*, LXVII, pp. 1–28, 142–62 (corresponding to chs. II and III of 1912a).

1909d   'Sociologie religieuse et théorie de la connaissance', *RMM*, XVII, pp. 733–58 (Introduction to 1912a. As incorporated in the volume, section III of this article – pp. 754–8 – is omitted).

1909e   'Sociologie et sciences sociales', in *De la méthode dans les sciences* (1ère série; Paris: Alcan), pp. 259–85.

1909f   Contributions to discussion: 'Mariage et divorce', in *Libres entretiens*, 5e série, pp. 258–9, 261–2, 266–7, 270, 273, 277–9, 279–83, 293.

1910a   *L'Année sociologique*, vol. XI. (i) Préface, pp. i–iii. (ii) Notes: (1) 'Les Conditions sociologiques de la connaissance', pp. 41–2 (with C. Bouglé). (2) 'Systèmes religieux des sociétés inférieures', pp. 75–6 (with M. Mauss). *(3) 'Sys-

* Unsigned – probably by Durkheim.

tèmes juridiques et moraux', pp. 286–8. (iii) Reviews: (1)
'Meyer, Eduard, *Geschichte des Altertums*', pp. 5–13. (2)
'Jérusalem, Wilhelm, *Soziologie des Erkennens*', pp. 42–5.
*(3) 'Strehlow, C., *Die Aranda und Loritja-Stämme in
Zentral-Australien*', pp. 76–81. (4) 'Marzan (de), *Le Totémisme
aux îles Fiji*', pp. 105–6. (5) 'Rivers, W. H. R., *Totemism in
Fiji*', pp. 105–6 (6) 'Seligmann, *Note on the Totemism in
New Guinea*', p. 105–6 (items (4), (5) and (6) reviewed
together). (7) 'Wundt, W., *Die Anfänge der Gesellschaft*',
pp. 291–3. (8) '*Reports of the Cambridge Anthropological
Expedition to Torres Straits. VI*', pp. 297–304. (9) 'Thomas,
Northcote, W., *Kinship Organization and Group Marriage in
Australia*', pp. 335–43. (10) 'Stanischitsch, Alexa, *Über
den Ursprung der Zadruga*', pp. 343–7. (11) 'Launspach,
C. W. L., *State and Family in Early Rome*', pp. 347–8. (12)
'Obrist, Alfred, *Essai sur les origines du testament romain*',
pp. 352–5. (13) 'Roberts, Rob., *Das Familien-Sklaven und
Erbrecht im Qorân*', pp. 355–7. (14) 'Kohler, Joseph,
Über Totemismus und Urehe', pp. 359–61. (15) 'Kohler,
Joseph, *Eskimo und Gruppenehe*', pp. 359–61. (16) 'Kohler,
Joseph, *Nochmals über Gruppenehe und Totemismus*', pp.
359–61 (items (14), (15) and (16) reviewed together). (17)
'Crawley, A. E., *Exogamy and the Mating of Cousins*', pp.
361–2. (18) 'Lang, A., *Australian Problems*', pp. 361–2
(items (17) and (18) reviewed together). (19) 'Weber,
Marianne, *Ehefrau und Mutter in der Rechtsentwicklung*',
pp. 363–9. (20) 'Richard, Gaston, *La Femme dans l'histoire*',
pp. 369–71. (21) 'Stoll, Otto, *Das Geschlechtsleben in der
Völkerpsychologie*', pp. 375–83. (22) 'Bouglé, C., *Essais sur
le régime des castes*', pp. 384–7. (23) 'Cramer, Julius, *Die
Verfassungsgeschichte der Germanen und Kelten*', pp. 387–95.
(24) 'Schwerin, Claudius von, *Die Altgermanische Hundert-
schaft*', pp. 387–95 (items (23) and (24) reviewed together).
(25) 'Preuss, H., *Die Entwicklung des deutschen Städtewesens*',
pp. 396–401. (26) 'Lasch, Richard, *Der Eid. Seine Entstehung und Beziehung zu Glaube und Brauch der Naturvölker*',
pp. 460–65. (27) 'Friederici, Georg, *Der Tränengruss der
Indianer*', pp. 469–70. (28) 'Buschan, Georg, *Geschlecht und
Verbrechen*', pp. 492–4. (29) 'Krose, H. A., *Die Ursachen der
Selbstmordhäufigkeit*', pp. 511–15.

* With M. Mauss.

584   *Bibliography of Durkheim's Publications*

1910b   Contribution to discussion of: 'La Notion d'égalité sociale', séance du 30 décembre 1909, in *BSFP*, x, pp. 59–63, 65–7, 69–70.

1911a   Contribution to discussion of: 'L'Éducation sexuelle', séance du 28 février 1911, in *BSFP*, xi, pp. 33–8, 44–7.

1911b   'Jugements de valeur et jugements de réalité', in *Atti del IV Congresso Internazionale di Filosofia* (Bologna: 1911), vol. I, pp. 99–114 (published also in *RMM*, xix, pp. 437–53; reproduced in 1924a).

1911c   Articles: (1) 'Éducation', pp. 529–36, (2) 'Enfance', pp. 552–3 (with F. Buisson), (3) 'Pédagogie', pp. 1538–43, in *Nouveau Dictionnaire de pédagogie et d'instruction primaire publié sous la direction de F. Buisson* (Paris: Hachette) (1 and 3 reproduced in 1922a).

1911d   'Préface', in Hamelin, O., *Le Système de Descartes, publié par L. Robin* (Paris: Alcan), pp. v–xi.

1912a   *Les Formes élémentaires de la vie religieuse: le système totémique en Australie* (Paris: Alcan) (tr. 1915d).

1912b   Contributions to discussion of: 'Sur la culture générale et la réforme de l'enseignement', in *Libres entretiens*, 8e série, pp. 319–70, 322, 332.

1913a   *L'Année sociologique*, vol. xii. (i) Notes: (1) 'Sur la notion de civilisation', pp. 46–50 (with M. Mauss). (tr. 1971a). (2) 'Sur les systèmes religieux des sociétés inférieures', pp. 90–91. (3) 'Sur les systèmes juridiques', pp. 365–6. (4) 'Sur les systèmes juridiques tribaux', pp. 379–80. (ii) Reviews: (1) 'Richard, Gaston, *La Sociologie générale et les lois sociologiques*', pp. 1–3. (2) 'Belliot, R. P. A., *Manuel de sociologie catholique*', p. 14. (3) '*Le premier congrès allemand de sociologie*', pp. 23–6. (4) 'Berr, Henri, *La Synthèse en histoire*', pp. 26–7. (5) 'Boas, Franz, *The Mind of the Primitive Man*', pp. 31–3. (6) 'Lévy-Bruhl, *Les Fonctions mentales dans les sociétés inférieures*', pp. 33–7. (7) 'Durkheim, Émile, *Les Formes élémentaires de la vie religieuse*', pp. 33–7 (items (6) and (7) reviewed together). (8) 'Wundt, Wilhelm, *Elemente der Völkerpsychologie*', pp. 50–61. (9) 'Patten, *The Social Basis of Religion*', pp. 79–80. (10) 'Visscher, H., *Religion und soziales Leben bei den Naturvölkern*', pp. 83–8. *(11) 'Frazer, *Totemism and Exogamy*', pp. 91–8. *(12) 'Durkheim, *Les Formes élémentaires de la vie religieuse*', pp. 91–8 (items (11) and (12)

* With M. Mauss.

reviewed together). (13) 'Goldenweiser, A. A., *Totemism, an Analytical Study*', pp. 100–101. (14) 'Claus, Heinrich, *Die Wagogo*', pp. 134–5. (15) 'Deploige, Simon, *Le Conflit de la morale et de la sociologie*', pp. 326–8. (16) 'Fletcher, Alice C., et La Flesche, Francis, *The Omaha Tribe*', pp. 366–71. *(17) 'Endle, Sidney, *The Kacharis*', pp. 375–8. (18) 'Hutereau, A., *Notes sur la vie familiale et juridique de quelques populations du Congo belge*', pp. 380–84. (19) 'Calonne-Beaufaict, A. de, *Les Ababua*', pp. 380–84 (items (18) and (19) reviewed together). †(20) 'Torday et Joyce, *Notes ethnographiques sur les peuples communément appelés Bakuba, ainsi que sur les peuplades apparentées, les Bushongo*', pp. 384–90. †(21) 'Hilton-Simpson, *Land and Peoples of the Kasai*', pp. 384–90 (items (20) and (21) reviewed together). (22) 'Roscoe, John, *The Baganda, Their Customs and Beliefs*', pp. 390–94. (23) 'Guttmann, Bruno, *Dichten und Denken der Dschagga-Neger*', pp. 394–7. (24) 'Hollis, *The Nandi*', pp. 395–7. (25) 'Hobley, C. W., *Ethnology of Akamba and other East African Tribes*', pp. 395–7 (items (23), (24) and (25) reviewed together). (26) 'Seligmann, C. G., and Brenda, Z., *The Veddas*', pp. 400–402. (27) 'Bogoras, W., *The Chukchee. III. Social Organization*', pp. 402–5. (28) 'Hartland, E. Sidney, *Primitive Paternity*', pp. 410–14. (29) 'Gebhard, Richard, *Russisches Familien- und Erbrecht*', pp. 424–6. (30) 'Avebury, Lord, *Marriage, Totemism and Exogamy*', p. 429. (31) 'Frazer, *Totemism and Exogamy*', pp. 429–32. (32) 'Opet, Otto, *Brauttradition und Consensgespräch in mittelalterischen Trauungsritualen*', p. 433. (33) 'Neubecker, F. K., *Die Mitgift in rechtsvergleichender Darstellung*', p. 434. (34) 'Aubéry, Gaëtan, *La Communauté de biens conjugale*', pp. 434–7. (35) 'Laborde, Laurent, *La Dot dans les fors et coutumes du Béarn*', pp. 437–8. (36) 'Bloch, G., *La Plèbe romaine*', pp. 441–3. (37) 'Brunhes, Jean, *La Géographie humaine*', pp. 818–21.

1913b   Contribution to discussion of: 'Le Problème religieux et la dualité de la nature humaine', séance du 4 février 1913, in *BSFP*, XIII, pp. 63–75, 80–87, 90–100, 108–11 (discussion of 1912a).

1914a   'Le Dualisme de la nature humaine et ses conditions sociales', *Scientia*, XV, pp. 206–21 (tr. 1960c).

* With M. Mauss.
† With M. Bianconi.

1914b Contributions to discussion of: 'Une nouvelle position du problème moral', séance du 2 janvier 1914, *BSFP*, xiv, pp. 26–9, 34–6.

1915a 'La Sociologie', in *La Science française* (Paris: Ministère de l'Instruction Publique et des Beaux-Arts), vol. I, pp. 39–49 (reprinted separately in *La Science française*, vol. 1, Paris: Larousse) (tr. 1960c). Written for the 'Exposition universelle et internationale de San Francisco'.

1915b *Qui a voulu la guerre?: Les origines de la guerre d'après les documents diplomatiques* (Paris: Colin) (with E. Denis) (tr. 1915e).

1915c *L'Allemagne au-dessus de tout: la mentalité allemande et la guerre* (Paris: Colin) (tr. 1915f).

1916a *Lettres à tous les Français* (Paris: Comité de publication). 1st letter: 'Patience, effort, confiance'; 5th letter: 'Les alliés de l'Allemagne en Orient: Turquie, Bulgarie'; 10th letter: 'Les Forces italiennes – la Belgique, la Serbie, le Monténégro' (the last section by Durkheim); 11th letter: 'Les Forces françaises'.

1916b 'Notice sur Robert Hertz', *L'Annuaire de l'Association des anciens élèves de l'École Normale Supérieure*, pp. 116–20.

1917a 'Notice sur André-Armand Durkheim', *L'Annuaire de l'Association des anciens élèves de l'École Normale Supérieure*, pp. 201–5.

PUBLISHED POSTHUMOUSLY

1917b Contributions to discussion of: 'Vocabulaire technique et critique de la philosophie', *BSFP*, xv, pp. 1–2 ('Sacre'), p. 57 ('Société').

1918a *La Vie universitaire à Paris* (Paris: Colin) (with others) (Préface; Première partie, chs. I et II; Deuxième partie, introduction signed by Durkheim).

1918b 'Le "Contrat Social" de Rousseau', *RMM*, xxv, pp. 1–23, 129–61 (reproduced in 1953a; tr. 1960b).

1919a 'La Pédagogie de Rousseau', *RMM*, xxvi, pp. 153–80.

1919b Contribution to Abauzit, F., et al. *Le Sentiment religieux à l'heure actuelle* (Paris: Vrin). Meetings and discussions of the Union de Libres Penseurs et de Libres Croyants pour la Culture Morale during Winter of 1913–14. Durkheim's contribution is to meeting of 18 January 1914 on 'La Con-

ception sociale de la religion', pp. 97–105 and 142–3.*
(Reproduced in *Archives de sociologie des religions*, 27 (1969),
pp. 73–7, and 30 (1971), pp. 89–90.)

1920a 'Introduction à la morale', *RP*, LXXXIX, pp. 79–97, with
note by M. Mauss (intended as part of projected work on
La Morale).

1921a 'La Famille conjugale: conclusion du cours sur la famille',
RP, XC, pp. 1–14 (last lecture in the 1891–2 course at
Bordeaux entitled 'La Famille (à partir de la famille
patriarcale)'). Edited with note by M. Mauss (tr. 1965a).

1921b 'Définition du socialisme', *RMM*, XXVIII, pp. 479–95,
591–614 (reproduced in 1928a).

1922a *Éducation et sociologie*, Introduction by P. Fauconnet (Paris:
Alcan) (reproduces 1911C1, 1911C3, 1903b, 1906c) (tr. 1956a).

1923a 'Histoire du socialisme: le socialisme au XVIIIe siècle',
RMM, XXX, pp. 389–413 (reproduced in 1928a).

1924a *Sociologie et philosophie*, Preface by C. Bouglé (Paris: Alcan)
(reproduces 1898b, 1906b, 1911b) (tr. 1953b). (References
in text are to new edition, Paris, 1951.)

1925a *L'Éducation morale*, Foreword by P. Fauconnet (Paris:
Alcan) (tr. 1961a).

1925b 'Saint-Simon, fondateur du positivisme et de la sociologie',
RP, XCIX, pp. 321–41 (reproduced in 1928a).

1926a 'Critiques de Saint-Simon et du Saint-Simonisme', *RMM*,
XXXIII, pp. 433–54 (reproduced in 1928a).

1928a *Le Socialisme*, edited with Introduction by M. Mauss (Paris:
Alcan) (includes 1921b, 1923a, 1925b and 1926a; tr. 1958b).
Reprinted in 2nd edn with Preface by Birnbaum, P. (Paris:
Presses Universitaires de France, 1971).

1933a 'La Sociologie', in *La Science française* (Nouvelle edition
entièrement refondue; Paris: Larousse), vol. I, pp. 27–35
(reprint of 1915a, followed by a note on 'La Sociologie en
France depuis 1914', by M. Mauss, pp. 36–47).

1937a 'Morale professionnelle', *RMM*, XLIV, pp. 527–44, 711–
38, with note by M. Mauss (included in 1950a; tr. 1957a).

1937b 'Montesquieu: sa part dans la fondation des sciences
politiques et de la science des sociétés', translated from the
Latin by F. Alengry, *Revue d'histoire politique et constitu-
tionnelle*, I, pp. 405–63 (translation of 1892a).

* The other contributions included are from Gustave Belot and Marc
Boegner.

1938a   *L'Évolution pédagogique en France*, Introduction by M. Halbwachs (Paris: Alcan). Volume I: *Des origines à la renaissance*; Volume II: *De la renaissance à nos jours*.

1950a   *Leçons de sociologie: physique des mœurs et du droit*, Foreword by H. N. Kubali; Introduction by G. Davy (Istanbul: L'Université d'Istanbul, 'Publications de l'Université, Faculté de Droit', no. 111; and Paris: Presses Universitaires de France) (tr. 1957a).

1953a   *Montesquieu et Rousseau, précurseurs de la sociologie*, Foreword by A. Cuvillier; Introductory note by G. Davy (Paris: Marcel Rivière, 'Petite Bibliothèque Sociologique Internationale') (new translation by A. Cuvillier of 1892a, replacing 1937b together with reprint of 1918b) (tr. 1960b).

1955a   *Pragmatisme et sociologie*. Cours inédit prononcé à la Sorbonne en 1913–14 et restitué d'après des notes d'étudiants et avec Préface par A. Cuvillier (Paris: Vrin) (tr. 1960c – in part).

1958a   'L'Etat', *RP*, CXLVIII, pp. 433–7 (presented by Raymond Lenoir).

1959a   'La Démocratie' (in Spanish translation), *Revista mexicana de sociologia*, 21, pp. 819–30 (presented by Raymond Lenoir).

1960a   'Les Raisons d'être, morale de la société en général', *Annales de l'Université de Paris*, no. 1, pp. 54–6 (presented by Raymond Lenoir).

1962a   'La Société politique' (in Spanish translation), *Revista mexicana de sociologia*, 24, pp. 9–13 (presented by Raymond Lenoir).

1967a   'Discours aux lycéens de Sens'. Discours prononcé à la distribution des prix du Lycée de Sens, le 6 août 1883. Preceded by introduction by Tiryakian, E.A., *CIS*, XLIII, pp. 25–32 (found in the Archives d'Épinal).

1969a   Reproduction of 1919b in *Archives de sociologie des religions*, 27, pp. 73–7, and 30, pp. 89–90.

1969b   'Une Lettre inédite d'Émile Durkheim', *AS*, 3ᵉ série (1967), p. 14. Also reprinted in *RP*, XCIV, p. 381. (Letter to Lévy-Bruhl, presented by Georges Davy.)

1969c   *Journal sociologique*, with Introduction and Notes by J. Duvignaud (Paris: Presses Universitaires de France). Selection of Durkheim's articles, notes and principal reviews in the *Année sociologique*.

1970a   *La Science sociale et l'action*, Introduction and presentation by J.-C. Filloux (Paris: Presses Universitaires de France). Collection of articles by Durkheim (1888a, 1900b, 1909e,

1885b, 1886a, 1890a, 1893c, 1897d, 1897e, 1898c, 1904e, 1905e, 1908a(1), 1919b, 1914a).

1970b   'Lettre inédite d'Émile Durkheim à Lucien Lévy-Bruhl', *RP*, xcv, pp. 163–4.

1973a   'Lettres d'Émile Durkheim à Georges Davy' and 'Lettres d'Émile Durkheim à Lucien Lévy-Bruhl', in Davy, 1973.

ENGLISH TRANSLATIONS*

1915d   *The Elementary Forms of the Religious Life: A Study in Religious Sociology.* Translation of 1912a by J. W. Swain (London: Allen and Unwin; New York: Macmillan).

1915e   *Who Wanted War? The Origin of the War according to Diplomatic Documents.* Translation of 1915b (Paris:Colin).

1915f   *'Germany Above All': German Mentality and the War.* Translation of 1915c (Paris: Colin).

1933b   *The Division of Labor in Society.* Translation of 1893b (1902b) by G. Simpson (New York: Macmillan). (Translation seriously defective.)

1938b   *The Rules of Sociological Method.* Translation of 1895a (1901c) by S. A. Solovay and J. H. Mueller and edited with Introduction by G. E. G. Catlin (Chicago: University of Chicago Press, republished 1950 by Glencoe, Ill.: Free Press of Glencoe). (Translation defective – note omission of paragraph crucial to the argument at foot of page 10.)

1951a   *Suicide: A Study in Sociology.* Translation of 1897a by J. A. Spaulding and G. Simpson and edited with Introduction by G. Simpson (Glencoe, Ill.: Free Press of Glencoe; and (1952) London: Routledge and Kegan Paul).

1953b   *Sociology and Philosophy.* Translation of 1924a by D. F. Pocock with Introduction by J. G. Peristiany (London: Cohen and West; and Glencoe, Ill.: Free Press of Glencoe).

1956a   *Education and Sociology.* Translation of 1922a by S. D. Fox with Introduction by translator and Foreword by T. Parsons (Glencoe, Ill.: Free Press of Glencoe).

1957a   *Professional Ethics and Civic Morals.* Translation of 1950a by C. Brookfield (London: Routledge and Kegan Paul).

* The quality of these varies from the very poor indeed to the excellent. Particular caution is recommended in the cases of 1933b and 1938b. We urgently need a standard English edition of Durkheim's works.

1958b   *Socialism and Saint-Simon.* Translation of 1928a by C. Sattler and edited with Introduction by A. W. Gouldner (Yellow Springs, Ohio: Antioch Press; and (1959) London: Routledge and Kegan Paul).

1960b   *Montesquieu and Rousseau: Forerunners of Sociology.* Translation of 1953a by R. Manheim with Foreword by H. Peyre (Ann Arbor, Mich.: University of Michigan Press).

1960c   Translations in *Émile Durkheim, 1858–1917: A Collection of Essays, with Translations and a Bibliography,* edited by Kurt H. Wolff. Translations of hitherto unpublished letter from Durkheim to Radcliffe-Brown by J. G. Peristiany; of 1914a by Charles Blend; of 1898a (i) and 1899a (i) and of 1900c by Kurt H. Wolff; of 1915a by Jerome D. Folkman; and of lectures 1, 2, 3, 4, 5, 13 and 14 in 1955a by Charles Blend (Columbus, Ohio: Ohio State University Press). (See Wolff, 1960.)

1961a   *Moral Education: A Study in the Theory and Application of the Sociology of Education.* Translation of 1925a by Everett K. Wilson and Herman Schnurer and edited with Introduction by Everett K. Wilson (New York: Free Press of Glencoe).

1963a   *Incest: The Nature and Origin of the Taboo* (together with A. Ellis, *The Origins and Development of the Incest Taboo*). Translation of 1898a(ii) with Introduction by Edward Sagarin (New York: Lyle Stuart).

1963b   *Primitive Classification.* Translation of 1903a and edited with Introduction by Rodney Needham (London: Cohen and West; and Chicago: University of Chicago Press).

1965a   'A Durkheim Fragment: the Conjugal Family'. Translation of 1921a by G. Simpson, with note, in *AJS*, LXX, 5, pp. 527–36.

1969d   'Individualism and the Intellectuals'. Translation of 1898c by S. and J. Lukes, with note, in *Political Studies*, XVII, pp. 14–30.

1971a   'Note on the Notion of Civilization'. Translation of 1913a (i) (1) by Benjamin Nelson with introduction, in *SR^{ch}*, 38, pp. 808–13.

Comprehensive Bibliography of Writings on or Directly Relevant to Durkheim

Adams, G. P., 1916, 'The Interpretation of Religion in Royce and Durkheim', *Philosophical Review*, 25, pp. 297–304.

Adorno, T. W., 1967, Introduction to Durkheim, *Soziologie und Philosophie* (Frankfurt). (German tr. of Durkheim, 1924a.)

Aimard, G., 1962, *Durkheim et la science économique* (Paris).

Alberoni, F., 1964, 'Riflessioni su Durkheim: individuo e società', *Studi di sociologia*, 2, pp. 125–46.

Allardt, E., 1968, 'Émile Durkheim: sein Beitrag zur politischen Soziologie', *KZS*, 20, pp. 1–16.

Allport, F. H., 1924, 'The Group Mind Fallacy in Relation to Social Science', *Journal of Abnormal and Social Psychology*, 19, pp. 60–73.

Alpert, H., 1937, 'France's First University Course in Sociology', *ASR*, 2, pp. 311–17.

——, 1938, 'Durkheim's Functional Theory of Ritual', *Sociology and Social Research*, 23, pp. 103–8 (reprinted in Nisbet, 1965).

——, 1939a, *Émile Durkheim and His Sociology* (New York; republished 1961).

——, 1939b, 'Émile Durkheim and Sociologismic Psychology', *AJS*, 45, pp. 64–70.

——, 1939c, 'Explaining the Social Socially', *Social Forces*, 17, pp. 361–5.

——, 1941, 'Émile Durkheim and the Theory of Social Integration', *Journal of Social Philosophy*, 6, pp. 172–84.

——, 1958, 'Émile Durkheim, Enemy of Fixed Psychological Elements', *AJS*, 63, pp. 662–4 (Durkheim-Simmel commemorative issue).

——, 1959, 'Émile Durkheim, A Perspective and Appreciation', *ASR*, 24, pp. 462–5.

——, 1960, See under Tiryakian et al.

Andler, C., 1896a, 'Sociologie et démocratie', *RMM*, 4, pp. 243–56. Critique of Bouglé, 1896b.

——, 1896b, 'Réponse aux objections', *RMM*, 4, pp. 371–3.

Apchié, M., 1936, 'Quelques Remarques critiques sur la sociologie d'Émile Durkheim', *APDSJ*, 6, pp. 182–95.

Aron, R., 1960, see under Divers.

——, 1967, *Les Étapes de la pensée sociologique* (Paris), tr. as *Main Currents in Sociological Thought*, London, 1965 and 1968.

——, 1971, *De la condition historique du sociologue*. Leçon inaugurale au Collège de France (Paris).

Aron, R., Demangeon, A., Meuvret, J., et al., 1937, *Les Sciences sociales en France: enseignement et recherche* (Paris).

Azevedo, T. de, 1959, see under De Azevedo.

Baracani, N., 1970, 'Bibliographie durkheimienne', *Communautés, Archives internationales de sociologie de la coopération et du développement*, 28, pp. 161–223.

Barnes, H. E., 1920, 'Durkheim's Contribution to the Reconstruction of Political Theory', *PSQ*, 35, pp. 236–54.

Barnes, H. E., and Becker, H., 1938, *Social Thought from Lore to Science* (New York), republished as Becker, H., and Barnes, H. E. (with assistance of Benoît-Smullyan, É., and others), *Social Thought from Lore to Science* (3rd edn 3 vols., Dover Publications, New York: 1961); see especially vol. 3, ch. 22 (contributed by É. Benoît-Smullyan) on 'Sociology in the French Language' (page references to this edition).

Barnes, J. A., 1966, 'Durkheim's Division of Labour in Society', *Man*, 1, 2, pp. 158–75.

Barth, P., 1897, *Die Philosophie der Geschichte als Soziologie* (Leipzig, 4th edn, 1922), vol. 1, pp. 628–42.

Bayet, A., 1903, 'La Philosophie de Durkheim', *RB*, 19, pp. 693ff.

——, 1907, 'Sur la distinction du normal et du pathologique', *RP*, 63, pp. 67–80.

——, 1923, *Le Suicide et la morale* (Paris).

——, 1925, *La Science des faits moraux* (Paris).

——, 1926, 'Émile Durkheim: *L'Éducation morale*', *RP*, 102, pp. 304–9.

Bellah, R. N., 1959, 'Durkheim and History', *ASR*, 24, pp. 447–61 (reprinted in Nisbet, 1965).

——, 1960, see under Tiryakian et al.

——, 1973, *Émile Durkheim on Morality and Society*. Selected Writings, edited and with an Introduction by Robert N. Bellah (Chicago and London).

Belot, G., 1894, 'L'Utilitarisme et ses nouveaux critiques', *RMM*, 2, pp. 404–64.

——, 1898, 'Émile Durkheim: *L'Année sociologique*', *RP*, 45, pp. 649–57.

——, 1900, 'La Religion comme principe sociologique', *RP*, 49, pp. 288–99.

——, 1903, 'Émile Durkheim: *L'Année sociologique*', *RP*, 55, pp. 96–103.

——, 1905–6, 'En quête d'une morale positive', *RMM*, 13, pp. 39–74, 561–88, 727–63; and 14, pp. 163–95 (cf. Durkheim, 1907a (4)).

——, 1907, *Études de morale positive* (Paris), t. 2, section 4, pp. 116–33.

——, 1913, 'Une Théorie nouvelle de la religion', *RP*, 75, pp. 329–79.

Bendix, R., 1971, 'Two Sociological Traditions', in Bendix, R., and Roth, G., *Scholarship and Partisanship* (Berkeley, Los Angeles and London). A comparison of Durkheim and Weber.

Benoît-Smullyan, É., 1937, *The Development of French Sociologism and Its Critics in France* (unpublished doctoral dissertation: Widener Library, Harvard University and Library of University of Wisconsin).

——, 1938, see under Barnes and Becker.

——, 1948, 'The Sociologism of Émile Durkheim and his School', in H. E. Barnes (ed.), *An Introduction to the History of Sociology* (Chicago) (abridged paperback edition: Phoenix Books, Chicago and London, 1966).

Benrubi, J., 1933, *Les Sources et les courants de la philosophie contemporaine en France* (Paris), pp. 153–76.

Bentley, A. F., 1926, 'Simmel, Durkheim and Ratzenhofer', *AJS*, 32, pp. 250–56.

Bernès, M., 1895, 'Sur la méthode en sociologie', *RP*, 39, pp. 238–57.

Besse, Dom, 1913, *Les Religions laïques* (Paris), chapter on 'M. Durkheim en Sorbonne'.

Bierstedt, R., 1966, *Émile Durkheim* (New York and London). Short biography, selective bibliography, selections with commentary.

Birnbaum, P., 1969, 'Cadres sociaux et représentations collectives dans l'œuvre de Durkheim: l'exemple du socialisme', *RFS*, 10, pp. 3–11.

——, 1971, Preface to 2nd edn of Durkheim, 1928a.

Birou, A., 1959, 'Religion and Ideal in the Thought of Durkheim'. See under Divers.

Blondel, C., 1913, *La Conscience morbide: essai de psychopathologie générale* (Paris). Synthesis of thought of Durkheim and Bergson.

——, 1927, 'La Psychologie selon Comte, Durkheim et Tarde', *Journal de psychologie normale et pathologique*, 24, pp. 381–3, 387–99 and 493–520.

——, 1928, *Introduction à la psychologie collective* (Paris).

——, 1933, *Le Suicide* (Strasbourg).

Bohannan, P., 1960, 'Conscience Collective and Culture', in Wolff, 1960.

Bouglé, C., 1896a, *Les Sciences sociales en Allemagne: le conflit des méthodes* (Paris; 3rd edn, 1912).

——, 1896b, 'Sociologie et démocratie', *RMM*, 4, pp. 118–28.

——, 1896c, 'Sociologie, psychologie et histoire', *RMM*, 4, pp. 362–70. Reply to Andler, 1896a.

——, 1897, Review of Durkheim, 1898b, *AS*, 2, pp. 152–5.

——, 1899, *Les Idées égalitaires. Étude sociologique* (Paris).

——, 1901, 'Remarques sur l'origine des castes', *AS*, 4, pp. 1–64 (repr. in Bouglé, 1908).

——, 1903, 'Revue générale des théories récentes sur la division du travail', *AS*, 6, pp. 73–122 (reprinted in Bouglé, 1907).

——, 1904, *La Démocratie devant la science* (Paris).

——, 1905, 'Individualisme et sociologie', *RB*, 5ᵉ série, t. 4, no. 18, pp. 553–5, and no. 19, pp. 587–9.

——, 1907, *Qu'est-ce que la sociologie?* (Paris).

——, 1908, *Essais sur le régime des castes* (Paris).

——, 1922, *Leçons du sociologie sur l'évolution des valeurs* (Paris), translated as *The Evolution of Values* by H. S. Sellars (New York, 1926) (2nd edn, 1929).

——, 1924, 'Le Spiritualisme d'Émile Durkheim', *RB*, 62, pp. 550–53, reproduced as introduction to Durkheim, 1924a.

——, 1925, 'Die Philosophischen Tendenzen der Soziologie Durkheims', *Jahrbuch für Soziologie*, Bd 1.

——, 1930a, 'The Present Tendency of the Social Sciences in France', in L. D. White (ed.), *The New Social Sciences*.

——, 1930b, see under Divers.

——, 1930c, 'Émile Durkheim', *Encyclopedia of the Social Sciences*, 5, pp. 291–2.

——, 1935, *Bilan de la sociologie française contemporaine* (Paris).

——, 1936, 'La Méthodologie de F. Simiand et la sociologie', *AnS*, série A, fasc. 2, pp. 5–28.

——, 1937, see under Aron et al.

——, 1938, *Humanisme, sociologie, philosophie: remarques sur la conception française de la culture générale* (Paris), especially ch. 11.

Bouglé, C., and Déat, M., 1921, *Le Guide de l'étudiant en sociologie* (Paris).

Bourdieu, P., and Passeron, J. C., 1967, 'Sociology and Philosophy in France since 1945: Death and Resurrection of a Philosophy without Subject', *SRᶜʰ*, 34, 1, pp. 162–212.

Bourgin, H., 1938, *De Jaurès à Léon Blum. L'École Normale et la politique* (Paris), especially pp. 215–27.

——, 1942, *Le Socialisme universitaire* (Paris), pp. 72–9.

Branford, V., 1918, 'Durkheim, a Brief Memoir', *SR*, 10, pp. 77–82.

Bristol, L. M., 1915, *Social Adaptation* (Cambridge).

Brunschvicg, L., 1922, *L'Expérience humaine et la causalité physique* (Paris), chs. 9 and 10: critique of Durkheim's sociological theory of knowledge.

——, 1927, *Le Progrès de la conscience dans la philosophie occidentale* (Paris), bk 7: 'Les Synthèses sociologiques'.

Brunschvicg, L., and Halévy, É., 1894, 'L'Année philosophique, 1893', *RMM*, pp. 564–90.

Bureau, P., 1923, *La Science des mœurs: introduction à la méthode sociologique* (Paris). See especially preface for attack on Durkheim's 'apriorism'.

Cantécor, G., 1904, 'La Science positive de la morale', *RP*, 57, pp. 225–41 and 368–92.

Cantoni, R., 1963, 'La sociologia religiosa di Durkheim', *Quaderni sociologici*, 12, 3, pp. 239–71 (in Italian).

Case, C. M., 1924, 'Durkheim's Educational Sociology', *Journal of Applied Sociology*, 9, pp. 30–33.

Catlin, G. E. C., 1938, 'Introduction to the Translation', Durkheim, 1938b, pp. x–xl.

Cazeneuve, J., 1958, 'Les Zunis dans l'œuvre de Durkheim', *RP*, 83, pp. 452–61.

——, 1960a, 'Le Centenaire de Durkheim', *Table ronde*, no. 145, p. 137.

——, 1960b, see under Divers.

——, 1968, 'Lucien Lévy-Bruhl', *IESS*.

Chazel, F., 1967, 'Considérations sur la nature d'anomie', *RFS*, 8, pp. 151–68.

Chulliat, C., 1956, 'Le Play et Durkheim: essai de synthèse', in *Recueil d'études sociales à la mémoire de Frédéric Le Play* (Paris), pp. 15–22.

Clark, T. N., 1968a, 'Émile Durkheim and the Institutionalization of Sociology in the French University System', *EJS*, 9, pp. 37–71.

——, 1968b, 'The Structure and Functions of a Research Institute: the *Année sociologique*', *EJS*, 9, pp. 72–91.

——, 1973, *Prophets and Patrons: The French University and the Emergence of the Social Sciences* (Cambridge, Mass.).

Clifford-Vaughan, M., and Scotford-Morton, M., 1967, 'Legal Norms and Social Order: Petrazycki, Pareto, Durkheim', *BJS*, 18, pp. 269–77.

Conze, E., 1927, 'Zur Bibliographie der Durkheim-Schule', *Kölner Vierteljahrshefte für Soziologie*, 6, pp. 279–83.

Coser, L. A., 1960, 'Durkheim's Conservatism and Its Implications for his Sociological Theory', in Wolff, 1960.

——, 1971, *Masters of Sociological Thought* (New York), chapter on Durkheim.

Cunnison, I., 1948, 'Durkheim's Place in the Development of Social Anthropology' (paper read at seminar; typescript deposited in Library of Institute of Social Anthropology, Oxford).

Cuvillier, A., 1948, 'Durkheim et Marx', *CIS*, 4, pp. 75–97; reproduced in *Partis pris sur l'art, la philosophie, l'histoire* (Paris, 1956).

——, 1953, *Où va la sociologie française? Avec une étude d'Émile Durkheim sur la sociologie formaliste* (1900c) (Paris).

——, 1954, 'Les *Leçons de sociologie* d'É. Durkheim', *Les Études philosophiques*, 9, reproduced in *Partis pris sur l'art, la philosophie, l'histoire* (Paris, 1956).

——, 1955, Preface to Durkheim, 1955a.

——, 1958, 'É. Durkheim et le pragmatisme', in *Sociologie et Problèmes actuels* (Paris; 2nd edn, 1961).

——, 1959a, 'Bibliography of Works of Durkheim', see under Divers.

——, 1959b, 'É. Durkheim et le socialisme', *Revue socialiste*, 122, pp. 33–43.

——, 1959c, 'Émile Durkheim and His Conception of Sociology', see under Divers.

D'Araujo, Oscar, 1899, 'Durkheim and Comte', *Revue occidentale*, n.s., 20, pp. 305–10.

Davis, M., 1909, *Psychological Interpretations of Society* ('Studies in History, Economics and Public Law', vol. 33, no. 2, Columbia University, New York).

Davy, G., 1911a, *Durkheim, choix de textes avec étude du système sociologique* (Paris).

——, 1911b, 'La Sociologie de M. Durkheim', *RP*, 72, pp. 42–71 and 160–85.

——, 1919, 'Émile Durkheim: l'homme', *RMM*, 26, pp. 181–98.

——, 1920, 'Émile Durkheim: l'œuvre', *RMM*, 27, pp. 71–112.

——, 1922, *La Foi jurée. Étude sociologique du problème du contrat, la formation du lien contractuel* (Paris).

——, 1924a, 'La Sociologie', in Dumas, G., *Traité de psychologie* (Paris), t. 2.

——, 1924b, *Sociologie politique* (Paris).

——, 1925, 'Vues sociologiques sur la famille et la parenté d'après Émile Durkheim', *RP*, 100, pp. 79–117 (republished in Davy, 1931, q.v. for page references).

——, 1926, 'La Sociologie française de 1918 à 1925', *Monist*, reproduced as Introduction to Davy, 1931.

——, 1928, 'Sociology' in Scharb (ed.), *Philosophy Today* (Chicago).

——, 1930, see under Divers.

——, 1931, *Sociologues d'hier et d'aujourd'hui* (Paris, 2nd edn, 1950). Collection of previously published articles (with additional note on Lévy-Bruhl).

——, 1949, 'L'Explication sociologique et le recours à l'histoire d'après Comte, Mill et Durkheim', *RMM*, 54, pp. 330–62.

——, 1950, Introduction to Durkheim, 1950a.

——, 1952, 'Le Social et l'humain dans la sociologie durkheimienne', *RP*, 142, pp. 321–50.

——, 1957, 'In Memoriam: Émile Durkheim', *AS*, 3e série, pp. vii–x.

——, 1960a, see under Divers.

——, 1960b, 'É. Durkheim', *RFS*, 1, pp. 3–24.

——, 1967, 'Célestin Bouglé (1870–1940)', *RFS*, 7, pp. 3–13.

——, 1973, *L'Homme, le fait social et le fait politique* (Paris).

Davy, G., and Moret, A., 1923, *Des clans aux empires* (Paris).

De Azevedo, T., et al., 1959, *Atualidade de Durkheim* (Publicações da Universidade da Bahia, Brazil).

De Gaudemar, P., 1969, 'Les Ambiguités de la critique durkheimienne du pragmatisme', *La Pensée*, 145, pp. 81–8.

De Grazia, S., 1947, Introduction to 'On Suicide' (extract), in *University Observer*, 1, pp. 51–60.

De Gré, G. L., 1943, *Society and Ideology: An Inquiry into the Sociology of Knowledge* (New York), ch. iii, pp. 54–84.

Deledalle, G., 1959, 'Durkheim et Dewey: un double centenaire', *Les Études philosophiques*, n.s. 4, pp. 493–8.

Dennes, W. R., 1924, *The Method and Presuppositions of Group Psychology* (Berkeley: Los Angeles), ch. iii, 'Durkheim'.

Deploige, S., 1911, *Le conflit de la morale et de la sociologie* (Louvain; 3rd edn, 1923; tr. as *The Conflict between Ethics and Sociology*, St Louis and London, 1938) (cf. 1913a (ii) (15)).

De Roberty, E., 1914, 'Les nouveaux courants d'idées dans la sociologie contemporaine', *RP*, 77, pp. 1–31.

Desroche, H., 1969, 'Retour à Durkheim? D'un texte peu connu à quelques thèses méconnues', *Archives de sociologie des religions*, 27, pp. 79–88.

Divers, 1930, 'L'œuvre sociologique d'Émile Durkheim', *Europe*, 22, pp. 281–304. Contributions by Bouglé, Davy, Granet, Lenoir, Maublanc.

——, 1951, 'In Memoriam: Fauconnet, Bouglé, Granet', *AS*, 3, pp. xi ff.

——, 1959, Special Issue for Durkheim's Centenary, *Revista mexicana de sociologia*, 21, 3 (Mexico), p. 790–1149. Fourteen articles on Durkheim and Bibliography (listed separately; all in Spanish).

——, 1960, *Centenaire de la naissance de Durkheim:* Avant-propos par Cazeneuve, J., Allocutions par Sarrailh, J., Janne, H., Davy, G., Lalande, A., Lacroze, R., Aron, R., Gurvitch, G., Lévy-Bruhl, H., Le Bras, G., Lévi-Strauss, C., et note sur un texte inédit par Lenoir, R., et Durkheim 1960a, *Annales de l'Université de Paris*, 1, pp. 3–54.

——, 1970, 'Émile Durkheim relu et enrichi', *Le Monde*, 3 et 4 mai, 1970, supplément au numéro 7869, pp. iv–v. Articles by Baudelot, C., Establet, R., Chazel, F., Lecuyer, B., Snyders, G., and Ziegler, J.

Dohrenwend, B. P., 1959, 'Egoism, Altruism, Anomie: A Conceptual Analysis of Durkheim's Types', *ASR*, 24, pp. 466–72.

Douglas, J. D., 1966, 'The Sociological Analysis of Social Meanings of Suicide', *EJS*, 7, 2, pp. 249–75.

——, 1967, *The Social Meanings of Suicide* (Princeton).

Dubar, C., 1969, 'La Méthode de Marcel Mauss', *RFS*, 10, pp. 515–21.

Duguit, L., 1893, 'Un Séminaire de sociologie', *RIS*, 1, pp. 201–8.

Duncan, H. D., 1960, 'The Development of Durkheim's Concept of Ritual and the Problem of Social Disrelationships', in Wolff, 1960.

——, 1969, *Symbols and Social Theory* (New York), especially chs. 12 and 13.

Duprat, G. L., 1926, 'La Psycho-sociologie en France', *Archiv für Geschichte der Philosophie und Soziologie*, 37, pp. 133–60.

——, 1932, 'Auguste Comte et Émile Durkheim', *Sozialwissenschaftliche Bausteine*, Band 4, pp. 109–40 (Jena).

Duvignaud, J., 1965, *Durkheim: sa vie, son œuvre, avec un exposé de sa philosophie* (Paris). Selected texts with Introduction.

——, 1969, Introduction to Durkheim, 1969c.

Elliot, M., and Merill, F., 1934, *Social Disorganization* (New York). See Appendix on social disorganization in French sociology.

Ellwood, C. A., 1916, 'Objectivism in Sociology', *AJS*, 22, pp. 289–305.

Essertier, D., 1927a, *Les Formes inférieures de l'explication* (Paris).

——, 1927b, *Psychologie et sociologie* (Paris).

——, 1929, *La Psychologie* (Paris).

——, 1930, *La Sociologie* (Paris).

Essertier, D., and Bouglé, C., 1934, 'Sociologie et psychologie: remarques générales', *AnS*, Sér. A., fasc. 1, pp. 121–48.

Evans-Pritchard, E. E., 1960, Introduction to R. Hertz, *Death* and *The Right Hand* tr. R. and C. Needham (London).

——, 1965, *Theories of Primitive Religion* (Oxford), especially ch. 3: 'Sociological Theories'.

Faublée, J., 1964, 'Henri Berr et *l'Année sociologique*', *Revue de synthèse*, 3e série, 35, pp. 68–74.

Fauconnet, P., 1898, Review of Durkheim, 1897a, *RP*, 35, pp. 618–38.

——, 1920, *La Responsabilité* (Paris).

——, 1922, 'L'œuvre pédagogique d'Émile Durkheim', *RP*, 93, pp. 185–209, reprinted and tr. in *AJS*, 28, pp. 529–53 (1923), used as Introduction to Durkheim, 1922a, q.v. for page references.

——, 1927, 'The Durkheim School in France', *SR*, 19, pp. 15–20.

Fauconnet, P., and Mauss, M., 1901, 'Sociologie', in *La Grande Encyclopédie*, 30, pp. 165–76 (Paris).

Ferreira, L. P., 1959, 'Synthesis of the Contribution of Durkheim to Sociology', see under Divers.

Filloux, J. C., 1963, 'Durkheimism and Socialism', *The Review: A Quarterly Journal of Pluralist Socialism*, 5, 2, pp. 66–85.

——, 1965, 'Notes sur Durkheim et la Psychologie', *Bulletin de Psychologie* (Groupe d'Études de Psychologie de l'Université de Paris), 244, 19, 1, pp. 40–51.

——, 1970, Introduction and notes to Durkheim, 1970a.

——, 1971, 'Démocratie et société socialiste chez Durkheim', *Cahiers Vilfredo Pareto: Revue européenne de sciences sociales*, 25, pp. 29–48.

Fletcher, R., 1971, *The Making of Sociology* (London), vol. 2, pp. 245–380.

Floud, J., 1965, Review of Durkheim, 1938a, *JSSR*, 4, pp. 250–52.

Fohlen, C., 1968, 'François Simiand', in *IESS*.

Foskett, J. D., 1939, *Émile Durkheim and the Problem of Social Order* (Ph.D. dissertation, Department of Sociology and Social Institutions, University of California, Berkeley).

——, 1940, 'É. Durkheim's Contribution to the Problem of Social Order', *Research Studies of the State College of Washington*, vol. 8.

Fouillée, A., 1905, *Les Éléments sociologiques de la morale* (Paris). Critique of Durkheim: pp. viii ff., 159–75 and 238–86 (cf. Durkheim, 1907a (3)).

Fox, S. D., 1956, Introduction to Durkheim, 1956a.

Friedmann, G., 1955, 'La Thèse de Durkheim et les formes contemporaines de la division du travail', *CIS*, 19, pp. 45–58, reprinted in *Le Travail en miettes* (Paris), trans. *The Anatomy of Work* (London: 1961) as ch. 5, 'Durkheim's Theories: Contemporary Forms of the Division of Labour'.

——, 1968, 'Maurice Halbwachs', in *IESS*.

Gabel, J., 1963, 'An Inductive Vindication of Historical Materialism', Introduction to translated reprint of Jaszi, O., 1906.

Gaudemar, P. de, 1969, see under De Gaudemar.

Gehlke, C. E., 1915, *Émile Durkheim's Contributions to Sociological Theory* (New York).

Gennep, A. van, see van Gennep.

Giddens, A., 1965, 'The Suicide Problem in French Sociology', *BJS*, 16, 1, pp. 1–18.

——, 1966, 'A Typology of Suicide', *EJS*, 7, 2, pp. 276–95.

——, 1970, 'Durkheim as a Review Critic', *SR*, 18, pp. 171–96.

——, 1971a, 'The "Individual" in the Writings of Durkheim', *EJS*, 12, pp. 210–28.

——, 1971b, *Capitalism and Social Theory* (Cambridge). Chapters on Durkheim.

——, 1971c, 'Durkheim's Political Sociology', *SR*, n.s., 19, pp. 477–519.

——, 1972, *Émile Durkheim: Selected Writings* (Cambridge). Translated and with an introduction by the editor.

Gilbert, R., n. d., *Durkheim* (Collection 'Problèmes': Paris).

Ginsberg, M., 1936, Ch. 16: 'The Place of Sociology'.

——, 1951, Ch. 4: 'Durkheim's Ethical Theory' (reprinted in Nisbet, 1965).

——, 1953, Ch. 9: 'The Individual and Society'.

——, 1955, Ch. 14: 'Durkheim's Theory of Religion', in *On the Diversity of Morals* (London, 1956).

Gisbert, P., 1959, 'Social Facts and Durkheim's System', *Anthropos*, 54, pp. 353–69.

Goblet d'Alviella, Le Comte, 1913, 'La Sociologie de M. Durkheim et l'histoire des religions', *Revue de l'histoire des religions*, 67 pp. 192–221.

Gold, M., 1958, 'Suicide, Homicide and the Socialization of Aggression', *AJS*, 63, pp. 651–61.

Goldenweiser, A. A., 1915, Review of Durkheim, 1912a, *American Anthropologist*, 17, pp. 719–35.

——, 1917, 'Religion and Society: A Critique of Durkheim's Theory of the Origin and Nature of Religion', reprinted as pt 4, ch. 1, of *History, Psychology and Culture* (New York, 1933).

——, 1923, *Early Civilization: An Introduction to Anthropology* (New York), ch. 16: Critique of Durkheim.

Goody, J., 1961, 'Religion and Ritual: The Definitional Problem', *BJS*, 12, pp. 142–64. Critique of Durkheim's use of the distinction between the sacred and the profane.

Gouldner, A. W., 1958, Introduction to Durkheim, 1958a.

Granet, M., 1930, see under Divers.

Grazia, S. de, 1947, see under De Grazia.

Gré, G. L. de, 1943, see under De Gré.

Gugler, J., 1961, *Die Neuere Französische Soziologie* (Neuwied).

——, 1968, 'Georges Davy', in *IESS*.

Guitton, J., 1968, *Regards sur la pensée française: 1870–1940* (Paris).

Günzel, K., 1934, *Die Gesellschaftliche Wirklichkeit: Eine Studie der Émile Durkheims Soziologie* (Ohlau i Schl., Eschenhagen).

Gurvitch, G., 1937, 'La Science des faits moraux et la morale théorique chez É. Durkheim', *APDSJ*, 7, pp. 18–44. Repr. in Gurvitch, *Essais de sociologie* (1938) and *La Vocation actuelle de la sociologie* (1950).

——, 1938, *Essais de sociologie* (Paris), republished in a revised and augmented form as *La Vocation actuelle de la sociologie*, 1950; 2nd edn, 2 vols., 1957–62. In particular: 'Le Problème de la conscience collective dans la sociologie de Durkheim'; 'La Science des faits moraux et la morale théorique chez É. Durkheim'; 'Les Faux Problèmes de la sociologie au XIXe siècle'.

——, 1939, 'The Sociological Legacy of L. Lévy-Bruhl', *Journal of Social Philosophy*, 5, pp. 61–70. Discusses theoretical disagreements between Durkheim and Lévy-Bruhl.

——, 1959, 'Pour le centenaire de la naissance de Durkheim', *CIS*, 6, pp. 3–10.

——, 1960, see under Divers.

Halbwachs, M., 1913, *La Classe ouvrière et les niveaux de la vie* (Paris).

——, 1918, 'La Doctrine d'Émile Durkheim', *RP*, 85, pp. 353–411. A particularly clear and authoritative summary.

——, 1924, *Les Origines du sentiment religieux d'après Durkheim* (Paris), republished and translated as *Sources of Religious Sentiment* (tr. Spaulding, J. A., New York: 1962).

——, 1925, *Les Cadres sociaux de la mémoire* (Paris).

——, 1930, *Les Causes du suicide* (Paris).

——, 1933, *L'Évolution des besoins dans les classes ouvrières* (Paris).

——, 1938a, Introduction to Durkheim, 1938a.

——, 1938b, *Morphologie sociale* (Paris).

——, 1939, 'Individual Consciousness and the Collective Mind', *AJS*, 44, pp. 812–22.

——, 1950, *La Mémoire collective* (Paris, 2nd edn, 1968).

Harris, M., 1968, *The Rise of Anthropological Theory* (New York), ch. 18.

Hart, H. L. A., 1967, 'Social Solidarity and the Enforcement of Morals', *University of Chicago Law Review*, 55, pp. 1–13.

Hartland, E. S., 1913, Review of Durkheim, 1912a, *Man*, 13, 6, pp. 91–6.

Hayward, J. E. S., 1960, 'Solidarist Syndicalism: Durkheim and Duguit', *SR*, n.s. 8, pp. 17–36 and 185–202.

Hermansen, R., 1927, 'El sociologo Frances Emilio Durkheim', *Atenea*, año 4, pp. 205–14.

Herr, L., 1893, Review of Durkheim, 1893b, *Revue universitaire*, 2, 1, p. 581.

——, 1894, Review of Durkheim, 1895a, *Revue universitaire*, 3, 2, pp. 487–8.

Hertz, R., 1907, 'Contribution à une étude sur la représentation collective de la mort', *AS*, 10, pp. 48–137: repr. in Hertz, 1928; tr. Needham, R. and C., in *Death* and *The Right Hand* (London, 1960).

——, 1909, 'La Prééminence de la main droite', *RP*, 68, pp. 553–80: repr. in Hertz, 1928; tr. in *Death* and *The Right Hand*.

——, 1928, *Mélanges de sociologie religieuse et folklore* (Paris).

Hinkle, R. C. (Jr), 1960, 'Durkheim in American Sociology', in Wolff, 1960.

Höffding, H., 1914, Review of Durkheim, 1912a, *RMM*, 22, pp. 828–48.

Holland, R. F., 1970, 'Suicide as a Social Problem: Some Reflections on Durkheim', *Ratio*, 12, pp. 116–24.

Honigsheim, P., 1960a, 'The Influence of Durkheim and His School on the Study of Religion', in Wolff, 1960.

——, 1960b, 'Reminiscences of the Durkheim School', in Wolff, 1960.

Horton, J., 1964, 'The Dehumanization of Anomie and Alienation', *BJS*, 15, pp. 283–300.

Horton, R., 1973, 'Lévy-Bruhl, Durkheim and the Scientific Revolution', in Horton, R., and Finnegan, R. (eds.), *Modes of Thought* (London).

Hubert, H., 1905, 'Étude sommaire de la représentation du temps dans la religion et la magie' (*École pratique des hautes études, section des sciences religieuses*, pp. 1–39); repr. in Hubert and Mauss, 1909.

——, 1932, *Les Celtes et l'expansion celtique à l'époque de la Têne* (Paris).

Hubert, H., and Mauss, M., 1899, 'Essai sur la nature et la fonction du sacrifice', *AS*, 2, pp. 29–138; repr. in Hubert and Mauss, 1909, and Mauss, 1968–9; tr. Halls, W. D., as *Sacrifice: Its Nature and Function* (London, 1964) with Foreword by E. E. Evans-Pritchard.

——, 1904, 'Esquisse d'un théorie générale de la magie', *AS*, 7, pp. 1–146; repr. in Mauss, 1950.

——, 1909, *Mélanges d'histoire des religions* (Paris; 2nd edn., 1929), containing Préface; Hubert and Mauss, 1899; 'L'Origine des pouvoirs magiques dans les sociétés australiennes'; and Hubert, 1905.

Hubert, R., 1938, 'Essai sur l'histoire des origines et des progrès de la sociologie en France', *Revue de l'histoire de la philosophie et d'histoire générale de la civilisation*, n.s., 6, pp. 111–55 and 281–310.

Hueso, V., 1911, *La educación moral en la escuela primaria, segun Durkheim* (Paris), forming vol. 18 of Anales of 'Junta para Ampliación de Estudios é Investigaciones científicas' (Madrid, 1916).

Hughes, E. C., 1928, 'Personality Types and the Division of Labour', *AJS*, 33, pp. 754–68.

Hughes, H. S., 1958, *Consciousness and Society* (New York).

Humphreys, S. C., 1971, 'The Work of Louis Gernet', *History and Theory*, 10, pp. 172–96.

Huvelin, P., 1907 'Magie et droit individuel', *AS*, 10, pp. 1–47.

Indan, F., 1960, *Pozytywizm Etyczny Emila Durkheima* ('le Positivisme éthique d'Émile Durkheim') (*Towarzystwo Naukowe w Torunio Prace Wydzialu Filologiczno – Filozoficznego*, t 9, zeszyt 1, Torun, Poland), with résumé in French.

Jacovella, O., 1925, 'Sociologia e pedagogia in Emilio Durkheim', *Rivista pedagogica*, 18, pp. 280–309, 445–73, 536–86.

Jaszi, O., 1906, 'An Inductive Vindication of Historical Materialism,' first publ. in the review *Huszadik Szazad* (Budapest) and repr. (in English) with an introduction by J. Gabel in *The Review: A Quarterly of Pluralist Socialism* (Brussels), 5, 2, pp. 51–65. Discusses Mauss and Beuchat, 1906, in the light of the Marxist theory of historical materialism.

Johnson, B. D., 1964, *Émile Durkheim and the Theory of Social Integration* (unpublished M.A. thesis, University of California, Berkeley).

——, 1965, 'Durkheim's One Cause of Suicide', *ASR*, 30, 6, pp. 875–86.

Jyan, Choy, 1926, *Étude comparative sur les doctrines pédagogiques de Durkheim et de Dewey* (Lyon).

Kagan, G., 1938, 'Durkheim et Marx', *Revue de l'histoire économique et sociale*, 24, 3, pp. 233–45.

Karady, V., 1968, 'Présentation de l'édition', in Mauss, 1968–9.

Kardiner, A., and Preble, E., 1961, *They Studied Man* (London), chapter on Durkheim, pp. 108–33.

Kattsoff, L. O., 1954, 'Methodological Commentaries on Sociology', *Revista mexicana de sociologia*, 16, pp. 185–95 (in Spanish).

Kon, I. S., 1968, *Der Positivismus in der Soziologie* (E. Berlin), Ch. 4.

König, R., 1956, 'Drei Unbekannte Werke von É. Durkheim', *KZS*, 8, pp. 642–7.

——, 1958, 'É. Durkheim', *KZS*, 10, pp. 561–86.

——, 1961, Émile Durkheim, *Die Regeln der soziologischen Methode*, herausgegeben und eingeleitet von René König (Neuwied and Berlin). German translation of 1901c.

——, 1962, 'Die Religionssoziologie bei Émile Durkheim', *Probleme der Religionssoziologie*, ed. by D. Goldschmidt and J. Matthes, Sonderheft 6 der *KZS*, pp. 36–49 (Köln and Opladen).

Kroeber, A. L., 1935, 'History and Science in Anthropology', *American Anthropologist*, n.s., 37.

Kruijt, J. P., 1958, 'Het Sociologisme van É. Durkheim', *Mens en Maatschappij*, 33, pp. 3 ff. (Amsterdam) (in Dutch).

Kubali, H. N., 1950, Preface to Durkheim, 1950a.

Kurauchi, K., 1960, 'Durkheim's Influence on Japanese Sociology', in Wolff, 1960.

LaCapra, D., 1972, *Émile Durkheim: Sociologist and Philosopher* (Ithaca and London).

Lacombe, P., 1911, 'Études sur la génésique, le totémisme et l'exogamie d'après Émile Durkheim', *RSH*, 23, pp. 1–19 and 165–78.

Lacombe, R., 1925, 'L'Interprétation des faits matériels dans la méthode de Durkheim', *RP*, 99, pp. 369–88.

——, 1926a, *La Méthode sociologique de Durkheim* (Paris).

——, 1926b, 'La Thèse sociologique en psychologie', *RMM*, 33, pp. 351–77.

Lacroze, R., 1960a, 'Émile Durkheim à Bordeaux', *Actes de l'Académie Nationale des Sciences, Belles-Lettres et Arts de Bordeaux*, 4e série, 17, pp. 1–6.

——, 1906b, see under Divers.

Ladd, J., 1957, *The Structure of a Moral Code* (Cambridge, Mass.), especially pp. 4–9 ff.

La Fontaine, A. P., 1926, *La Philosophie d'É. Durkheim* (*Sociologie générale*) (Paris).

Lalande, A., 1960, see under Divers.

Landry, A., 1906, *Principes de morale rationelle* (Paris) (cf. Durkheim, 1907a (5)).

Lang, A., 1904, 'Dr Durkheim on "Social Origins"', *Folklore*, 15, pp. 100–102.

Lasserre, P., 1913, *La Doctrine officielle de l'université* (Paris), pp. 173–246.

Lear, E. N., 1961, 'Émile Durkheim as Educator', *Journal of Educational Sociology*, 34, pp. 193–204.

Le Bras, G., 1960, see under Divers.

——, 1966, 'Note sur la sociologie religieuse dans *l'Année sociologique*', *Archives de sociologie des religions*, 21, pp. 47–53.

Leguay, P., 1912, 'M. Émile Durkheim', *Universitaires d'aujourd'hui* (Paris).

Lenoir, R., 1918, 'Émile Durkheim et la conscience moderne', *MF*, 77, pp. 577–95.

——, 1930, see under Divers.

——, 1959, 'Émile Durkheim and the Social Environment of His Time', see under Divers.

——, 1960, see under Divers.

Leuba, J. H., 1913, 'Sociology and Psychology: The Conception of Religion and Magic and the Place of Psychology in Sociological Studies', *AJS*, 19, pp. 323–42. Discussion of views of Durkheim and of Hubert and Mauss.

Lévi-Strauss, C., 1945, 'French Sociology', in Gurvitch, G., and Moore, W. E., *Twentieth Century Sociology* (New York).

——, 1949, *Les Structures élémentaires de la parenté* (Paris; 2nd edn, 1967), tr. as *The Elementary Structures of Kinship* by Bell, J. H., Sturmer, J. R. von, and Needham, R. (London, 1969).

——, 1950, Introduction to Mauss, M., *Sociologie et anthropologie* (Paris).

——, 1960, 'Ce que l'ethnologie doit à Durkheim', see under Divers.

——, 1962a, *Le Totémisme aujourd'hui* (Paris), tr. as *Totemism* by R. Needham (London, 1964).

——, 1962b, *La Pensée sauvage* (Paris), tr. as *The Savage Mind* (London, 1966).

Lévy-Bruhl, H., 1937, 'Rapports du droit et de la sociologie', *APDSJ*, 7, pp. 21–5.

——, 1951, 'In Memoriam: Marcel Mauss', *AS*, 3e série, pp. 1–4.

Lévy-Bruhl, L., 1903, *La Morale et la science des mœurs* (Paris), translated as *Ethics and Moral Science* (London, 1905).

——, 1910, *Les Fonctions mentales dans les sociétés inférieures* (Paris).

——, 1922, *La Mentalité primitive* (Paris).

——, 1927, *L'Âme primitive* (Paris).

——, 1931, *Le Surnaturel et la nature dans la mentalité primitive* (Paris).

——, 1935, *La Mythologie primitive* (Paris).

——, 1938, *L'Expérience mystique et les symboles chez les primitifs* (Paris).

——, 1949, *Les Carnets de Lucien Lévy-Bruhl* (Préface de Maurice Leenhardt) (Paris).

Lourau, R., 1969, 'La Société institutrice (Durkheim et les origines de la science de l'éducation)', *Les Temps modernes*, 24, pp. 1648–64.

Lowie, R. H., 1924, *Primitive Religion* (New York).

——, 1937, *The History of Ethnological Theory* (New York), ch. xii, pp. 196–229.

Lukes, S. M., 1966, 'On the History of Sociological Theory', *BJS*, 17, pp. 198–203.

——, 1967a, 'Alienation and Anomie', in Laslett, P., and Runciman, W. G., *Philosophy, Politics and Society*, Series III (Oxford).

——, 1967b, 'Some Problems about Rationality', *EJS*, 7, pp. 247–64.

——, 1968a, 'Marcel Mauss', in *IESS*.

——, 1968b, *Émile Durkheim: An Intellectual Biography* (thesis presented for degree of Doctor of Philosophy, deposited at Bodleian Library, Oxford), 2 vols.

——, 1968c, 'Methodological Individualism Reconsidered', *BJS*, 19, pp. 119–29.

——, 1969, Introduction to Durkheim, 1969d.

——, 1971, 'Prolegomena to the Interpretation of Durkheim', *EJS*, pp. 183–209.

——, 1973, 'On the Social Determination of Truth', in Horton, R., and Finnegan, R. (eds.), *Modes of Thought* (London).

Lupu, I., 1931, *Die Grundlagen der Gesellschaft, das Recht und die Religion in der Durkheimschule: Ihr besonderer Widerhall in der Jenenser Jerusalemschen Soziologie* (Iasi: Viata Romacascâ).

Mac Kensie, J. S., 1925, 'L'Éducation morale d'Émile Durkheim', *Litteris*, pp. 185–96 (December).

Maclean, Y. Estenos, R., 1959, 'The Importance of Émile Durkheim in the History of Sociology', see under Divers.

Madge, J., 1962, *The Origins of Scientific Sociology* (London). Ch. 1: 'Suicide and Anomie'.

Malinowski, B., 1913, Review of Durkheim, 1912a, *Folklore*, 24, pp. 525–31.

——, 1925, 'Magic, Science and Religion', in Needham, J. (ed), *Science, Religion and Reality* (New York).

——, 1926, *Crime and Custom in Savage Society* (London and New York).

Mariça, G. E., 1932, *Émile Durkheim: Soziologie und Soziologismus: Sozialwissenschaftliche Bausteine, Band 6* (Jena).

Marjolin, R., 1937, 'French Sociology: Comte and Durkheim', *AJS*, 42, pp. 693–704, and corrections, pp. 901–2.

Maritain, J., 1930, *Religion et culture* (Paris).

Masson-Oursel, P., 1947, 'La Sociologie de Durkheim et la psychoanalyse', *Psyché: Revue internationale de psychoanalyse et des sciences de l'homme*, 2, pp. 1439–42.

Maublanc, R., 1930, see under Divers.

Mauchaussat, G., 1928, 'Sur les limites d'interprétation sociologique de la morale', *RMM*, 35, pp. 347–79.

Maunier, R., 1920, *Manuel bibliographique des sciences sociales et économiques* (Paris).

Maus, H., 1956, *A Short History of Sociology* (Stuttgart; first publ. in English, London, 1962). Ch. 11, 'Durkheim, His School and His Opponents'.

Mauss, M., 1909, *La Prière* (distributed privately); repr. in Mauss, 1968–9.

——, 1920, Introduction to Durkheim, 1920a.

——, 1924, 'Rapports réels et pratiques de la psychologie et de la sociologie', *Journal de psychologie*, 21, pp. 892–922; repr. in Mauss, 1950.

——, 1925a, 'In memoriam, l'œuvre inédite de Durkheim et de ses collaborateurs', *AS*, n.s., 1, pp. 7–29; repr. in Mauss, 1968–9.

——, 1925b, 'Essai sur le don', *AS*, n.s., 1, pp. 30–186; repr. in Mauss, 1950; tr. by Cunnison, I., as *The Gift* (London, 1954), with Introduction by E. E. Evans-Pritchard.

——, 1927a, 'Notices biographiques', *AS*, n.s., 2, pp. 3–9; repr. in Mauss, 1968–9.

——, 1927b, 'Division et proportions des divisions de la sociologie', *AS*, n.s., 2, pp. 95–176; repr. in Mauss, 1968–9.

——, 1928, Introduction to Durkheim, 1928a; repr. in Mauss, 1968–9.

——, 1932, 'La Cohésion sociale dans les sociétés polysegmentaires', *Bulletin de l'Institut français de sociologie*, 1, pp. 49–68; repr. in Mauss, 1968–9.

——, 1934, 'Fragment d'un plan de sociologie générale descriptive. Classification et méthode d'observation des phénomènes généraux de la vie sociale dans les sociétés de types archaïques (phénomènes spécifiques de la vie intérieure de la société)', *AnS*, sér. A, fasc. 1, pp. 1–56; repr. in Mauss, 1968–9.

——, 1937, Introduction to Durkheim, 1937a; repr. in Mauss, 1968–9.

——, 1947, *Manuel d'ethnographie*. Edited by Paulme, Dénise (Paris). An edited record, made from shorthand notes, of a course given at the Institut d'Ethnologie de l'Université de Paris (2nd edn, Paris, 1967).

——, 1950, *Sociologie et anthropologie* (Paris, 3rd edn, 1966). A collection of reprinted articles with Introduction by C. Lévi-Strauss.

——, 1968–9, *Œuvres*, présentation de V. Karady, 3 vols. (Paris).

Mauss, M., and Hubert, H., 1899, see Hubert and Mauss, 1899.

——, ——, 1904, see Hubert and Mauss, 1904.

——, ——, 1909, see Hubert and Mauss, 1909.

Mauss, M., and Fauconnet, P., 1901, 'Sociologie', *La Grande Encyclopédie*, 30, pp. 165–76.

Mauss, M., and Durkheim, É., 1903, see under Durkheim 1903a (i).

Mauss, M., and Beuchat, H., 1906, 'Essai sur les variations saisonnières des sociétés eskimos. Étude de morphologie sociale', *AS*, 9, pp. 39–132; repr. in Mauss, 1950, 3rd edn, 1966.

Mawson, A. R., 1970, 'Durkheim and Contemporary Pathology', *BJS*, 21, pp. 298–313.

Maybury-Lewis, D. H. P., 1965, 'Durkheim on Relationship Systems', *JSSR*, 4, pp. 253–60.

Mazel, H., 1899, 'Sociologues contemporains', *MF*, 29, pp. 662–91. On Durkheim, see pp. 675–91.

Meillet, A., 1906, 'Comment les mots changent de sens', *AS*, 9, pp. 1–38.

Mendieta y Nunez, L., 1959a, 'A Short Panegyric Essay in Honour of É. Durkheim', see under Divers.

——, 1959b, 'Émile Durkheim: the State and Democracy', see under Divers (reprinted in *JSSR*, 3, pp. 255–60).

Merton, R. K., 1934a, 'Durkheim's Division of Labour in Society', *AJS*, 40, pp. 319–28 (reprinted in Nisbet, 1965).

——, 1934b, 'Recent French Sociology', *Social Forces*, 12, pp. 537–45.

Mitchell, M. M., 1931, 'Émile Durkheim and the Philosophy of Nationalism', *PSQ*, 46, pp. 87–106.

Monnerot, J., 1946, *Les Faits sociaux ne sont pas des choses* (Paris).

Morrish, J., 1967, *Disciplines of Education* (London). Section on Durkheim.

Murroni, B., 1960, 'La nozione di conscienza collettiva nella sociologia di sturzo con riferimento alla sociologia di Durkheim', *Sociologia* (Milan), 5, pp. 384–410.

Naegele, K. S., 1958, 'Attachment and Alienation: Complementary Aspects of the Work of Durkheim and Simmel', *AJS*, 62, pp. 580–89.

Needham, R., 1963, Introduction to Durkheim, 1963b.

Nelson, B., 1971, Introduction to Durkheim, 1971a.

Neyer, J., 1960, 'Individualism and Socialism in Durkheim', in Wolff, 1960.

Nisbet, R. A., 1943, 'The French Revolution and the Rise of Sociology in France', *AJS*, 49, pp. 156–64.

——, 1952, 'Conservatism and Sociology', *AJS*, 58, pp. 167–75.

——, 1965, *Émile Durkheim* (Englewood Cliffs, N. J.), with Selected Essays by Merton, R. K. (repr. of Merton, 1934a), Selvin, H. C. (revised version of Selvin, 1958), Ginsberg, M. (repr. of Ginsberg, 1951), and Bellah, R. (repr. of Bellah, 1959).

——, 1966, *The Sociological Tradition* (New York).

——, 1974, *The Sociology of Émile Durkheim* (New York).

Norrish, P. J., 1957, 'Unanimist Elements in the Work of Durkheim and Verhaeren', *French Studies*, 11, pp. 38–49.

North, C. C., 1926, *Social Differentiation* (Chapel Hill), pt 4.

Nye, D. A., and Ashworth, C. E., 1971, 'Émile Durkheim: Was he a Nominalist or a Realist?' *BJS*, 22, pp. 133–48.

Olsen, M. D., 1965, 'Durkheim's Two Concepts of Anomie', *Sociological Quarterly*, 6, 1, pp. 37–44.

Ottaway, A. K. C., 1955, 'The Educational Sociology of Émile Durkheim', *BJS*, 6, pp. 213–27.

Ouy, A., 1926, 'L'Éducation morale', *RIS*, 34, pp. 199–206.

——, 1927, 'La Méthode sociologues de Durkheim', *RIS*, 35, pp. 371–83 (review of Lacombe, 1926a).

——, 1939, 'Les Sociologues et la sociologie: Deuxième partie, le sociologisme, Émile Durkheim', *RIS*, 47, pp. 245–75.

Parodi, D., 1909, *Traditionalisme et démocratie* (Paris). Discusses conservative implications of Durkheim's doctrines.

——, 1919, *La Philosophie contemporaine en France* (Paris, 2nd edn, 1926), ch. 5, 'Émile Durkheim et l'école sociologique', pp. 113–60.

Parsons, T., 1937, *The Structure of Social Action* (New York, 2nd edn, 1949), especially chs. 8–12.

——, 1960, 'Durkheim's Contribution to the Theory of Integration of Social Systems', in Wolff, 1960.

——, 1968, 'Émile Durkheim', in *IESS*.

Pécaut, F., 1918, 'Émile Durkheim', *Revue pédagogique*, n.s., 72, pp. 1–20.

——, 1920, 'Un Spiritualisme scientifique: la philosophie d'Émile Durkheim', *Revue de l'enseignement français hors de France*, 2.

——, 1921, 'Auguste Comte et Émile Durkheim', *RMM*, 28, pp. 639–55.

Péguy, C., 1897, Review of Durkheim, 1897a, *Revue socialiste*, 155, pp. 635–6 (November). Published under the pseudonym 'Pierre Deloire', which Péguy used for all his articles in the *Revue socialiste* except the first.

——, 1906, 'De la situation faite à l'histoire et à la sociologie dans les temps modernes', *Cahiers de la quinzaine*, 3e cahier de la 8e série. 'De la situation faite au parti intellectuel dans le monde moderne', ibid., 5e cahier de la 8e série (repr. in *Œuvres en prose*, Paris, 1959, pp. 991–1078; also in *Situations*, Paris, 1940).

Peristiany, J. G., 1953, Introduction to Durkheim, 1953b.

——, 1960, 'Durkheim's Letter to Radcliffe-Brown', in Wolff, 1960.

Perry, R. B., 1921, 'Des Formes de l'unité sociale', *Congrès des sociétés philosophiques américaines, anglaises, belges, italiennes et françaises. Communications et discussions* (Paris), pp. 445–70. Followed by discussion by Lenoir, Fauconnet, Pécaut and Perry, pp. 470–73.

——, 1926, *General Theory of Value* (New York). Especially chs. 14–17.

Petersen, C., 1944, *Émile Durkheim: En Historisk Kritisk Studie: Med Særligt Hensyn til hans Almindelige Sociologi eller Samfunds Filosofi* ('Émile Durkheim: A Historical Critical Study with Special Regard to his General Sociology or Social Philosophy') (Copenhagen).

Peterson, R. A., 1963, Comment on Steeman, 1963, *JSSR*, 3, pp. 108–10.

Peyre, H., 1960a, 'Durkheim: The Man, His Time and His Intellectual Background', in Wolff, 1960.

——, 1960b, Foreword to Durkheim, 1960b.

Piaget, J., 1928, 'Logique génétique et sociologie', *RP*, 105, pp. 167–205.

——, 1932, *Le Jugement moral chez l'enfant* (Paris), tr. as *The Moral Judgment of the Child* (London), especially ch. 4.

Pierce, A., 1960, 'Durkheim and Functionalism', in Wolff, 1960.

Pizzorno, A., 1962, Introduction to Italian translation of Durkheim, 1902b (Milan).

——, 1963, 'Lecture actuelle de Durkheim', *EJS*, 4, 1, pp. 1–36, repr. and tr. from *Quaderni sociologici*, 12, 3, pp. 272–309.

Poggi, G., 1971, 'The Place of Religion in Durkheim's Theory of Institutions', *EJS*, 12, pp. 229–60.

——, 1972, *Images of Society: Essays on the Sociological Theories of Tocqueville, Marx and Durkheim* (Stanford).

Porras, D., 1962, 'Durkheim and Sociology', *Revista mexicana de sociologia*, 24, 1, pp. 225–34.

Radcliffe-Brown, A. R., 1952, *Structure and Function in Primitive Society* (London). Ch. vi, 'The Sociological Theory of Totemism'; ch. viii, 'Religion and Society'; ch. ix, 'On the Concept of Function in Social Science'.

Ransøy, O., 1957, *Durkheim og andre on selvmord og sosial struktur* ('Durkheim and Others on Suicide and Social Structure') (Oslo, University of Oslo, Inst. of Sociology).

Ranulf, S., 1939, 'Scholarly Forerunners of Fascism', *Ethics*, 50, pp. 16–34. Includes an important letter from Mauss.*

——, 1955, 'Methods of Sociology: with an Essay: Remarks on the Epistemology of Sociology', *Acta Jutlandica, Amskrift for Aarhus Universitet*, 27.

Rauh, F., 1904, 'Science et conscience', *RP*, 57, pp. 359–67.

Recaséns Siches, L., 1959, 'Estimate of Durkheim', see under Divers.

Richard, G., 1912, *La Sociologie générale* (Paris).

——, 1923, *L'Athéisme dogmatique en sociologie religieuse* (7e cahier de la *Revue d'histoire et de philosophies religieuses*) (Strasbourg).

——, 1928, 'Nouvelles Tendances sociologiques en France', *RIS*, 36, pp. 648 ff.

——, 1930, 'La Pathologie sociale d'É. Durkheim', *RIS*, 38, pp. 113–26.

——, 1932, 'Auguste Comte et Émile Durkheim', *RIS*, 40, pp. 603–12.

——, 1935, 'Avant-propos inédit, écrit spécialement par M. Gaston Richard à l'occasion de ce numéro exceptionnel', *RIS*, Supp. 43, pp. 9–33. Account of Richard's career.

Richter, M., 1960, 'Durkheim's Politics and Political Theory', in Wolff, 1960.

Roberty, E. de, 1914, see under De Roberty.

Rossi, P. H., 1958, 'Émile Durkheim and George Simmel', *AJS*, 62, p. 579.

Rumney, J., 1934, *Herbert Spencer's Sociology: A Study in The History of Social Theory* (London). See especially pp. 81–91 on Spencer and Durkheim.

Runciman, W. G., 1969, 'The Sociological Explanation of "Religious" Beliefs', *EJS*, 10, pp. 149–91.

Salomon, A., 1960, 'Some Aspects of the Legacy of Durkheim', in Wolff, 1960.

Sarrailh, J., 1960, see under Divers.

* See p. 338 n. 71 of the present work.

Schaub, E., 1920, 'A Sociological Theory of Knowledge', *Philosophical Review*, 29, pp. 319–39.

Schatz, A., 1907, *L'Individualisme économique et sociale* (Paris), ch. viii, 'L'Individualisme sociologique'.

Schnore, L. F., 1958, 'Social Morphology and Human Ecology', *AJS*, 63, pp. 620–34.

Scrivoletto, A., 1970, *Il Metodo sociologico di Emile Durkheim* (Milan).

Seger, Imogen, 1957, *Durkheim and His Critics on the Sociology of Religion* (Monograph Series, Bureau of Applied Social Research, Columbia University, New York). A particularly useful survey.

Selvin, H. C., 1958, 'Durkheim's *Suicide* and Problems of Empirical Research', *AJS*, 63, pp. 607–19 (revised version in Nisbet, 1965).

Sholtz, J., 1935, 'Durkheim's Theory of Culture', *Reflex*.

Sicard, E., 1960, 'Essays on the Social Setting of Émile Durkheim's Works', *Revista mexicana de sociologia*, 21, pp. 893–956, and 23, pp. 465–90 (1961) (in Spanish).

Siches, L. R., 1959, 'Balance sobre Durkheim', see under Divers.

Simiand, F., 1895, 'L'Année sociologique 1897', *RMM*, 6, pp. 608–53; see pp. 644–9 on Durkheim, 1895a, and pp. 651–3 on *AS*, Première Année.

——, 1903, 'Méthode historique et science sociale', *RSH*, 6, pp. 1–22, 129–57.

——, 1912, *La Méthode positive en science économique* (Paris).

——, 1922, *Statistique et expérience* (Paris).

——, 1932a, *Le Salaire, l'évolution sociale et la monnaie* (Paris). 3 vols.

——, 1932b, *Les Fluctuations économiques à longue période et la crise mondiale* (Paris).

——, 1934, 'La Monnaie, realité sociale', *AnS*, Sér. A., Fasc. D., pp. 1–58; discussion, pp. 59–86.

Simon, W. M., 1963, *European Positivism in the Nineteenth Century* (Ithaca, New York).

Simpson, G., 1933a, 'An Estimate of Durkheim's Work', *The Division of Labor in Society* (New York) (omitted in subsequent editions).

——, 1933b, 'Émile Durkheim's Social Realism', *Sociology and Social Research*, 28, pp. 2–11.

——, 1933c, Introduction to Durkheim, 1933b.

——, 1950, 'Methodological Problems in Determining the Aetiology of Suicide', *ASR*, 16, pp. 658–63.

——, 1963, *Émile Durkheim* (selections from his work, with an introduction and commentaries).

Small, A. W., 1898, Comments on Durkheim, 1898a, *AJS*, 3, p. 700.

——, 1899, Comments on Durkheim, 1899a, *AJS*, 5, p. 124.

——, 1900, Comments on Durkheim, 1900a, *AJS*, 6, pp. 276–7.

——, 1902a, Review of Durkheim, 1902b, *AJS*, 7, pp. 566–8.

——, 1902b, Comments on Durkheim, 1902a, *AJS*, 8, pp. 277–8.

——, 1905, Comments on Durkheim, 1905a, *AJS*, 11, pp. 122–33.

——, 1924, Review of Durkheim, 1922a, *AJS*, 29, pp. 608–9.

Sorel, G., 1895, 'Les Théories de M. Durkheim', *Le Devenir social*, 1, pp. 1–26 and 148–80.

Sorokin, P., 1928, *Contemporary Sociological Theories* (New York and London), ch. viii, section 4, pp. 463–80.

Spencer, R. F., 1958, 'Culture Process and Intellectual Current: Durkheim and Ataturk', *American Anthropologist*, 60, pp. 640–57.

Stanner, W. E. H., 1967, 'Reflections on Durkheim and Aboriginal Religion', in Freedman, M. (ed.), *Social Organization: Essays Presented to Raymond Firth* (London).

Starcke, C. N., 1932, *Laws of Social Evolution and Social Ideals* (Copenhagen), especially pp. 294–315.

Steeman, T. M., 1963, 'Durkheim's Professional Ethics', *JSSR*, 2, pp. 163–81.

Stoetzel, J., 1957, 'Sociology in France: An Empiricist View', H. Becker and A. Boskoff, *Modern Sociological Theory in Continuity and Change* (New York).

Stone, G. P. and Faberman, H. A., 1967, 'On the Edge of Rapprochement: Was Durkheim Moving toward the Perspective of Social Interaction?', *Sociological Quarterly*, 8, pp. 149–64.

Sumpf, J., 1965, 'Durkheim et le problème de l'étude sociologique de la religion', *Archives de sociologie des religions*, 20, pp. 63–73.

Tarde, G., 1893, 'Questions sociales', *RP*, 35, pp. 618–38.

——, 1894, 'Les Deux Éléments de la sociologie', Lecture faite au 1er Congrès International de Sociologie 1894, *Annales de l'Institut international de sociologie*, t. 1., p. 895ff., repr. in Tarde, 1898a, pp. 63–94.

——, 1895a, *La Logique sociale* (Paris).

——, 1895b, 'Criminalité et santé sociale', *RP*, 39, pp. 148–62, repr. in Tarde, 1898a, pp. 136–58.

——, 1895c, 'La Sociologie élémentaire', *Annales de l'Institut international de sociologie*, t. 2.

——, 1895d, *Essais et mélanges sociologiques* (Paris).

——, 1898a, *Études de psychologie sociale* (Paris).

——, 1898b, *Les Lois sociales*, (Paris).

——, 1901, 'La Réalité sociale', *RP*, 52, pp. 457–79.

Taylor, S., 1963, 'Some Implications of the Contribution of É. Durkheim to Réligious Thought', *Philosophical and Phenomenological Research*, 24, 1, pp. 125–34.

Telezhnikov, F., 1928, 'É. Durkheim o predmete i Metode Sociologii', *Vestnick Kommunisticheskoi Akademii*, 30, pp. 159–88 (in Russian).

Timashieff, N., 1955, *Sociological Theory: Its Nature and Growth* (Garden City, New York).

Tiryakian, E. A., 1962, *Sociologism and Existentialism: Two Perspectives on the Individual and Society* (Englewood Cliffs, N. J.).

——, 1964a, 'Introduction to a Biographical Focus on Émile Durkheim', *JSSR*, 3, 2, pp. 247–54.

——, 1964b, 'Durkheim's Two Laws of Penal Evolution', *JSSR*, 3, 2, pp. 261–6.

——, 1965, 'A Problem for the Sociology of Knowledge: The Mutual Unawareness of Émile Durkheim and Max Weber' (paper presented at the annual meeting of the American Sociological Association), *EJS*, 7, 2, pp. 330–36.

——, 1967, Introduction to Durkheim, 1967a.

Tiryakian, E. A., Bellah, R. N., and Alpert, H., 1960, 'On Durkheim: An Exchange', *ASR*, 25, pp. 406–8.

Tönnies, F., 1898, Review of Durkheim, 1895a, *Archiv für Systematische Philosophie*, Band IV, pp. 495–9 (repr. in Tönnies, 1929, pp. 274–6).

——, 1929, *Soziologische Studien und Kritiken* (Jena), vol. 3, pp. 215–17; 274–6; 305–6.

Tosti, G., 1898a, 'The Delusions of Durkheim's Sociological Objectivism', *AJS*, 4, pp. 171–7.

——, 1898b, 'Suicide in the Light of Recent Studies', *AJS*, 3, pp. 464–78.

Tufts, J. H., 1896, 'Recent Sociological Tendencies in France', *AJS*, 1, pp. 446–56.

Van Gennep, A., 1913, Review of Durkheim, 1912a, *MF*, 101, pp. 389–91.

——, 1920, *L'État actuel du problème totémique* (Paris).

Vialatoux, J., 1939, *De Durkheim à Bergson* (Paris).

Viano, C. A., 1963, 'La dimensione normativa nella sociologia di Durkheim', *Quaderni sociologici*, 12, 3, pp. 310–53.

Villegas, O. U., 1959, 'Durkheim's Sociological Method in its Application to the Study of Suicide', see under Divers.

Wallis, W. D., 1914, 'Durkheim's View of Religion', *Journal of Religious Psychology*, 7, pp. 252–67.

Wallwork, E., 1972, *Durkheim, Morality and Milieu* (Cambridge, Mass.).

Weatherly, U. G., 1917, Review of Durkheim, 1912a, *AJS*, 18, pp. 843–6.

Webb, C. C. J., 1916, *Group Theories of Religion and the Individual* (London).

Webster, H., 1913, Review of Durkheim, 1912a, *AJS*, 18, pp. 843–6.

Weiss, H. P., 1964, 'Durkheim, Denmark and Suicide', *Acta Sociologica*, 7, pp. 264–78.

Wilson, E. M., 1934, 'Émile Durkheim's Sociological Method', *Sociology and Social Research*, 18, pp. 511–58.

Wilson, E. K., 1961, Introduction to Durkheim, 1961a.

——, 1963, 'L'Influence de Durkheim aux États-Unis: recherches empiriques sur le suicide', *RFS*, 4, 1, pp. 3–11.

Wirth, L., 1938, 'Social Interaction: The Problems of the Individual and the Group', *AJS*, 44, pp. 965–79.

Wolff, K. H., 1958, 'The Challenge of Durkheim and Simmel', *AJS*, 62, pp. 590–96.

——, 1960, *Émile Durkheim* (1858–1917) (Ohio). A collection of essays by Peyre, H., Neyer, J., Bohannan, P., Duncan, H. D., Parsons, T., Pierce, A., Richter, M., Coser, L. A., Honigsheim, P., Salomon, A., Hinkle, R. C., Kurauchi, R., and Peristiany, J. G., with translations of writings by Durkheim and a Bibliography. Republ. as *Essays on Sociology and Philosophy* (New York and London, 1964).

Wolin, S. S., 1960, *Politics and Vision: Continuity and Innovation in Western Political Thought* (Boston, 1960; London, 1961), Chapter 10.

Worms, R., 1893, Review of Durkheim, 1893b, *RIS*, 1, pp. 359–60.

——, 1907, *Philosophie des sciences sociales* (Paris), 3 vols.

——, 1917, 'Émile Durkheim', *RIS*, 25, pp. 561–8.

——, 1921, *La Sociologie, sa nature, son contenu, ses attaches* (Paris).

Worsley, P. M., 1956, 'É. Durkheim's Theory of Knowledge', *SR*, n.s., 4, pp. 47–62.

Appendix A
Courses of Lectures given by Durkheim at Bordeaux and Paris*

1887–8 Cours public de science sociale: La Solidarité sociale.
Conférence de pédagogie.

1888–9 Cours public de sociologie: (1) La Famille, origines, types principaux; (2) Morale et philosophie du droit chez Kant.
Conférence de pédagogie: Explication des auteurs.
Éducation de l'intelligence.

1889–90 Cours public de sociologie: Le suicide.
Conférence de pédagogie: Histoire de la pédagogie.
Éducation morale.

1890–91 Cours public de sociologie: Physiologie du droit et des mœurs [La Famille].
Conférence de pédagogie: Pédagogie française au XVIIIᵉ et XIXᵉ siècle.
Éducation intellectuelle.

1891–2 Cours public de sociologie: La Famille (à partir de la Famille patriarcale).
Conférence de pédagogie: L'Éducation et la pédagogie dans l'antiquité.
Pédagogie pratique.

1892–3 Cours de sociologie: La Sociologie criminelle.
Conférence de pédagogie: La Pédagogie au XIXᵉ siècle.
Cours de psychologie appliquée à l'éducation.

---

* This list, which is as complete as possible on available evidence, supersedes the selective list given in Alpert, 1939a, pp. 64–6. In compiling it, I have made use of the *Annuaire des Facultés de l'Université de Bordeaux*, the *Revue universitaire*, the *Revue de philosophie*, the *Revue internationale de sociologie*, the supplements of the *RMM*, the various introductions and prefaces to Durkheim's works, and Mauss, 1925a. Where these indications differ, I have stated Mauss's information in square brackets: he cannot necessarily be relied upon for strict accuracy in information of this kind. On the other hand, the printed announcements may be misleading.

1893-4 Cours de sociologie: La Sociologie criminelle (suite): La Peine; La Responsabilité; La Procédure.
Cours de psychologie appliquée à l'éducation.
Exercices pratiques pour les candidats de l'agrégation de philosophie.

1894-5 Cours de sociologie: La Religion.
Conférence de psychologie.
Exercices pratiques pour les candidats de l'agrégation de philosophie.

1895-6 Cours de sociologie: l'Histoire du socialisme [La Famille].
Conférence de psychologie: Les Émotions; L'Activité.
Exercises pratiques pour les candidats de l'agrégation de philosophie.

1896-7 Cours de sociologie: Physique générale des mœurs et du droit.
Conférence de psychologie.
Exercices pratiques pour les candidats de l'agrégation de philosophie.

1897-8 Cours de sociologie: Physique générale des mœurs et du droit.
Conférence de psychologie.
Exercices pratiques pour les candidats de l'agrégation de philosophie.

1898-9 Cours de sociologie: Physique générale des mœurs et du droit. [Théorie de l'obligation, de la sanction et de la moralité.]
Cours de pédagogie: L'Éducation morale.
Exercices pratiques pour les candidats de l'agrégation de philosophie.

1899-1900 Cours de sociologie: Physique générale des mœurs et du droit (fin) (La Peine; La Responsabilité).
[Morale civique et professionelle; Organisation domestique et la morale domestique.]
Cours de pédagogie: L'Éducational morale.
Exercices pratiques pour les candidats de l'agrégation de philosophie.

1900-1901 Cours de sociologie: Les Formes élémentaires de la religion.
Cours de pédagogie: L'Éducation intellectuelle.
Exercices pratiques pour les candidats de l'agrégation de philosophie.

1901-2 Cours de sociologie: Histoire des doctrines sociologiques.
Cours de pédagogie: Psychologie appliquée à l'éducation.
Exercices pratiques pour les candidats de l'agrégation de philosophie.

PARIS

1902-3 [Physiologie du droit et des mœurs. Pt I: Morale de la société.]
[L'Organisation domestique.]
L'Éducation morale.
Conférences sur la pédagogie de la renaissance.
Exercices pratiques pour les candidats à l'agrégation de philosophie.

1903-4 [Physiologie du droit et des mœurs. Pt II: Morale des groupes spéciaux de la société: Famille, groupes professionels, etc.]
La Pédagogie au commencement du XIXe siècle (Pestalozzi et Herbart).
De l'enseignement de la morale à l'école primaire.
Exercices pratiques pour les candidats à l'agrégation de philosophie.

1904-5 La Morale (incl. Morale civique et professionelle).
L'Histoire de l'enseignement secondaire en France.*

1905-6 [La Famille.]
Formation et développement de l'enseignement secondaire en France.*
L'Éducation intellectuelle à l'école primaire.
Exercices pour la préparation au diplôme d'études et à l'agrégation.

1906-7 La Religion: Origines (Cours public).
Formation et développement de l'enseignement secondaire en France.*
L'Éducation morale à l'école.

1907-8 L'Évolution du mariage et de la famille.
Formation et développement de l'enseignement secondaire en France.*
L'Enseignement de la morale à l'école.

⋅

* Delivered at the École Normale Supérieure (see 1938a).

1908–9 La Morale.
[Physiologie du droit et des mœurs, Pt I: Morale de la société.]
[L'Organisation domestique.]
Formation et développement de l'enseignement secondaire en France.*
Histoire des doctrines pédagogiques.

1909–10 La Morale (suite).
[Physiologie du droit et des mœurs, Pt II: Morale des groupes spéciaux de la société: Famille, groupes professionels, etc.]
[La Famille.]
Formation et développement de l'enseignement secondaire en France.*
Histoire des doctrines pédagogiques.

1910–11 La Morale (suite) – Droit de propriété – Morale contractuelle – Morale individuelle.
L'Enseignement secondaire en France.*
L'Éducation intellectuelle.

1911–12 Théorie des transactions dans la responsabilité. L'Éducation morale à l'école.
Formation et développement de l'enseignement secondaire en France.*
Exercices pour les étudiants à la licence.

1912–13 Formation et développement de l'enseignement secondaire en France.*

1913–14 Pragmatisme et sociologie.
L'Enseignement de la morale à l'école.
Exercices pratiques pour les candidats à la licence.

1914–15 La Morale (incl. Morale civique et professionelle) (?)
[La Morale théorique.]

1915–16 La Philosophie sociale d'Auguste Comte.
[La Morale civique et professionelle.]
Les Grands Doctrines pédagogiques du XVIIIe et du XIXe siècle.
Exercices pratiques pour les candidats de la licence.

* Delivered at the École Normale Supérieure (see 1938a).

Appendix B
Durkheim as Examiner

CONTENTS

During his career at Paris, Durkheim regularly sat on juries to examine doctoral theses. Reports of the oral examinations appear in the supplements to the *Revue de métaphysique et de morale* and in the *Revue de philosophie* (henceforth *RMM* and *R de P*). There follows a translation of all Durkheim's contributions on these occasions, introduced by a summary account of the context of the discussion, where necessary. These contributions are set out chronologically under journal, volume, month and year, together with the author and title of the thesis being examined. Where reports appear in both journals, the longer report is selected. (All candidates received their doctorates.)

S.L.

1. *RMM, Volume XI, July 1903*
M. Ribéry. *Essay on Characters**

The thesis deals with the classification of characters, seeking for a natural hierarchy of the elements of character. It attempts to provide a classification of temperaments, which are held to be dependent upon the laws of life, a classification which reproduces the order of nature. M. Ribéry claims to have improved upon Ribot's work on this subject.

DURKHEIM: I will ask you first why you have employed the deductive method. I am aware that, in a chapter in your book, you cover yourself by invoking the authority of J. S. Mill, who in effect recommends this method. But your argument does not seem to me to be sufficient. It seems to me, on the contrary, that in a science such as that of ethology, that is, in what one might call the science of individuals, the method needed is that which begins from observation.

Ribéry replies at length, saying that, according to Mill, the science of ethology begins from general laws, discovered by observation. He himself holds that it is necessary to begin with *a priori* ideas: particular observations may be biased and misleading. The time for observation is when a set of classifications has been established.

DURKHEIM: You say that emotion is altruistic. I shall ask you now, therefore, how you manage to deduce altruism from emotion.

RIBÉRY: I do not deduce altruism from emotion, but I assert simply that emotion is altruistic.

DURKHEIM: Could you give an example?

RIBÉRY: I might give as an example woman who is more altruistic than man.

DURKHEIM: Why do you say that the affective type, which corresponds to the sanguine temperament, is altruistic since emotion, according to you, is not present in the affective type?

RIBÉRY: I did say that the sanguine temperament is altruistic. Its altruism is very modified. The sanguine type is a sensitive type, and what is predominant in his case is sensation. But sensation

*That is, character-dispositions, the subject of ethology.

is no less the point of departure for emotion. It is not surprising therefore that there is in his case as it were the appearance of altruism.

DURKHEIM: The examples which you take, whether from literature or from history, do not appear to me to be very conclusive. So far as historical persons are concerned, we in general do not know them except as transformed by legend. And as to persons taken from literature, in any case imaginary beings, they can prove nothing at all.

RIBÉRY: The choice of examples is in fact very difficult and has given me much trouble. Historical persons have this advantage for a general study such as I have undertaken, that they are known by all. Moreover, modern historical criticism permits us to know about them today or at least a certain number of them with sufficient precision. As to persons taken from literature, they have not existed, it is true; but the writers and the poets who have created them have observed, and their observations, although they do not have a properly scientific end, none the less have a very great value.

DURKHEIM: I will now ask you why you did not think of making habit one of the principal elements in your classification.

RIBÉRY: Habit certainly plays a very great role in the life of man. But this power of inhibition is not primitive in man. The power of inhibition only establishes itself in us little by little by successive conquests. It is therefore through the power of inhibition that I might have been led to make of habit one of the fundamental elements of my classification, but if I have not spoken at the beginning of the power of inhibition, it is precisely for the very reason that this power does not appear until fairly late.

DURKHEIM: Finally, in your scheme, you say that the educator must define the distinct character of the child and that he must constantly have before his eyes this distinct or ideal character. Do you not think that the end which the educator should pursue lies outside the child?

RIBÉRY: It is certainly true, on the one hand, that the child must be prepared for life. But it is no less true that the educator has the duty to respect the individual nature of each person. The problem will therefore be the following: given a particular determinate individual and determinate environment, how to adapt in the best possible manner that individual to that environment.

DURKHEIM: But you have not observed yourself that the rules which you derived from your classification seemed to have the effect of developing characters?

RIBÉRY: I said that the rules which one may draw from the classification can only produce undesirable effects if one misapplies them.

2. *RMM, Volume XII, May 1904*

M. Albert Lévy. *Stirner and Nietzsche*

Lévy criticizes the view that Stirner and Nietzsche were exponents of a similar 'individualism', on the grounds that Stirner was a Left-Hegelian and Nietzsche a disciple of Schopenhauer. Nietzsche did not know Schopenhauer's work. Besides their doctrines differ profoundly.

Durkheim praises Lévy's thesis, 'his method, his *conscience*', and asks, 'Do you not think all the same that there is between Schopenhauer's and Nietzsche's thought a development, an advance, and that at bottom it is really the same thought in different forms; they are two mythologies of the individual, two variations on the same theme?'

3. *R de P, Volume IV (2), October 1904*

M. Glotz. *Solidarity of the Family in the Criminal Law of Ancient Greece**

M. Glotz argues that Greek law evolved very rapidly and his thesis is a study of this evolution with particular reference to the criminal law. He distinguishes three periods: (1) the *legendary period*, in which the family *acts* (active solidarity) or is responsible (passive solidarity) for acts committed by any of its members or by its animals; (2) a second period in which passive solidarity declines, with the family rejecting the guilty from its bosom. In this period individual responsibility begins to appear; (3) a third period in which the principle of individual responsibility is formulated, while at the same time the rights of the family are limited; crime is conceived as a social offence, and public action against it replaces private action.

* Cf. 1905a (ii) (22).

This general evolution is linked to general features of Greek life. The possibility is suggested that it was because the Greek people were never enclosed in a too powerful religious formalism that social forces were able to act unhindered and spontaneously transform the criminal law. In the rapidity and precision of the evolution, one must see, once more, the Greek miracle.

M. Durkheim is pleased to observe that historians are taking more and more account of the truth that between history and sociology there is no watertight division.

DURKHEIM: The value of your work derives less from its general theme, which is a little thin in relation to the breadth of the rest, than from the great mass of very intesting questions which it raises. I have been pleased to find in your thesis a mistrust of easy, so-called rational solutions in the explanation of social facts. You are aware that ancient institutions rested upon ideas that were not clear and simple, but on the contrary very confused, so that we have great difficulty in rendering them intelligible, although it is at the very least indispensable to try. In order to understand ancient institutions it is necessary, however difficult it may be for us, to attempt to reproduce the ancient way of thinking. Comparative studies can help us here; they are thus the best propaedeutics for the examination of particular problems. I therefore have only praise for your method on this point.

Nevertheless, I have one reservation to make. Your liking for new solutions is not always accompanied by a sufficiently critical attitude; the proofs which you invoke are not always very substantial; and the use you make of certain texts is astonishing; finally (and the reproach I am now making is one I have myself sometimes deserved) you are not always sufficiently prudent in the comparisons that you make.

According to you, it is the γένος which was, originally, the organ of collective prosecution of crime and which remained its principal agent; but you have made the mistake of confusing under the same name very different familial organizations. In effect, γένος sometimes designates a *monarchical* organization (omnipotence of the father), sometimes a group organized *democratically* where the father has more limited rights and is subject to a rigorous control. As a result of this ambiguity, there are a good number of regrettable confusions in your thesis.

Your chapter on the αἰδώς is very interesting; but you have not brought out the religious character of the αἰδώς.

You say that the theory of pollution was a late development; but this is not correct; there is, as you know, no religion without the idea of pollution, but according to you it was originally only a matter of physical pollution. That is a heresy. Originally, material and religious purity were not distinct.

In the explanation of the evolution of responsibility, you have neglected a very important factor. If certain crimes became public crimes, they became, at the same time, less important; crimes against the individual were originally considered as sacrilegious, which was why the whole family of the criminal was responsible for them. It is an important fact which one must not neglect. For crimes considered to be sacrilegious, this collective responsibility has always existed. Thus one can say collective responsibility has disappeared only because certain crimes have lost their importance, and in relation to these crimes only. There is here an important element which must be taken account of in the study of the evolution of collective responsibility.

4. *R de P, Volume V (1) April 1905*

M. L-Germain Lévy.   *The Family in Ancient Israel**

This thesis is a study of the Israelite (not Jewish) family – that is, what one finds when one goes back as far as possible to the origins of Judaism. A number of different questions are studied: (1) *The relations between the family and religion*. Religion pervades all institutions. Lévy rejects the hypothesis of totemism and of the cult of the dead. He adheres to the idea of power, life and fecundity as incarnated in Jehovah. The family in general consists of three groups: the family *stricto sensu*, the clan and the tribe. The clan is the oldest, comprising several families *stricto sensu*. The clan is founded on community of blood. Slaves are admitted into the family. Lévy also studies *clients*. (2) *Solidarity*. The clan forms a closed group all of whose members are solidary. There are three forms of solidarity: juridicial solidarity (vendetta), historical solidarity (genealogy, the importance of names), and territorial solidarity (collective property). (3) *Marriage*. Lévy rejects the hypothesis of the matriarchate. The father is always the chief of the family; the woman has no rights, not even a personality. Various questions are studied concerning marriage: the different types of marriage, laws and rights in relation to marriage, the relations between parents and children, and succession.

* Cf. 1906a (23).

Lévy seeks to show how the Israelite family has evolved under the influence of the idea of *God*, etc.

DURKHEIM: M. Lévy has included in his thesis important texts relating to the question he has studied. He has also made an attempt to interpret these texts as impartially as possible. Doubtless it is impossible ever to arrive at complete impartiality, and M. Lévy sometimes allows himself to believe that the Jewish people was a people apart; nevertheless, in a general way, the thesis is satisfactory in this respect.

But M. Durkheim finds that the actual execution of the thesis is not altogether happy: its design is defective; the texts are grouped in a somewhat artificial fashion.

DURKHEIM: For example, under the title 'Familial solidarity' one finds that vendetta, genealogy and property are all studied. Now, it is certainly the case that these are very different phenomena. For example, the solidarity which is expressed in the practice of vendetta is a solidarity between persons, while that relating to property is a solidarity between things and persons. Again, one finds a chapter on the family *in general*; and it is in a different chapter that the mutual relations between kinsmen are studied. One finds the same uncertainty in the arrangement of details; one sees the same questions reappearing in different parts of the thesis; the *levirate*, for example. And there is another fault of the same kind: the question of the vendetta and the penal law are studied and confused in the same chapter, although they are essentially distinct.

LÉVY: In both cases punishment is inflicted by the collectivity.

DURKHEIM: Yes, but by essentially different collectivities. The quotations are generally exact, but the interpretations provided are often arbitrary. For example, you say that if, in certain cases, the mother seems to play a more important role than the father, this is because the latter, having several wives, is suspected of partiality *vis à vis* one or other of his children. But the text which you cite does not say any such thing. Your explanation is an arbitrary supposition. Likewise, with respect to the marriage of *sadiqa* (p. 151), you rely, in order to assert its existence, on three texts which are in no way conclusive. In the first, for example, it is not a question of a legitimate wife, but rather of a concubine.

M. Durkheim next examines the very basis of the thesis. The first part is devoted to the relations between religion and the family. Without in the least denying the existence of such relations, M. Durkheim finds that the manner in which this development is presented in the thesis gives it the appearance of a digression. One does not see, in effect, in what way M. Lévy's conclusions on this question affect the rest of the thesis. For example, M. Lévy rejects totemism. In what way would the conclusions of the thesis have been changed if M. Lévy had accepted it?

M. Lévy replies that the Jewish family had not evolved in the same ways as the families of peoples in which totemism is to be found. He adds that, furthermore, since he was studying the Israelite family, it was necessary that he should examine this question of totemism, which had been posed before him by those who had previously studied the Israelite family.

DURKHEIM: This question still remains external to the thesis. Besides, totemism, which was found in Hebraic societies, goes back to a period well before that which you have studied. Thus, it was not part of your subject.

And in any case, on this very question it seems to me that you make a mistake. One can no longer, as you seem to think, maintain today, as was once maintained, that all species of religion have passed through the totemic phase. For no one today maintains any longer that every new society which forms begins its evolution anew by starting with totemism; it is only a question of knowing if the society that one is considering began early enough in the scale of evolution such that one may find in it beliefs that are genuinely inferior.

Besides, the arguments with which you reject totemism in connection with Hebraic society are not convincing. The attitude which one should have in this matter is the following: totemism is a form so constant among primitive religions that, when one finds traces such as those you indicate yourself, there is a strong presumption in favour of a totemic origin. One example will suffice to show the inadequacy of your arguments. There are, you say, names of animals given to individuals which are not *taboo*. That proves nothing. The animal designated might have been *taboo* at an earlier period. And I can adduce as a virtually decisive argument in favour of the totemichypo thesis: that in Hebraic society we find many clans designated by the names of animals.

With respect to the primitive religious ideas of the Hebrews, I agree with you that certain instruments of the cult seem to make allusion to a phallic cult but I believe that you are looking for your demonstration a little too far afield, and that it should not give you so much trouble; for all religions have begun with the cult of life. They have all always had the aim of sustaining the life of men and gods.

You deny any trace in Hebraic society of the *uterine* family where filiation is through the woman. I wonder whether the text, 'You will leave your father and your mother so as to follow your wife' does not relate to this form of family. Other factors also seem to me to be explained by the same hypothesis: in the first place, the fact that he was permitted to marry his paternal sister; and again the fact of the independence he experienced from his wife. For I have noticed that, in general, this independence is linked to the existence of the uterine family.

You assert the existence of marriage by *capture* in the society you have studied. But the text which you cite speaks nowhere of marriage but only of the abduction of women. For the latter to become regular spouses, it would be necessary for them to undergo certain rites. Thus *capture* does not itself bring about marriage.

You do not distinguish, as you should have done, the *levirate* and the *goël*. There are great differences between these two. The *levirate* was obligatory: furthermore, it was imposed on brothers who lived together. The duty of the *goël* was not subject to this condition.

5. *R de P*, Volume *V* (*1*), May *1905*

M. Gockler.   *The Pedagogy of Herbart*

M. Gockler first justifies his choice of subject. It is practically important, has been much misunderstood and thus demands to be expounded as a whole. The principal parts of the thesis are as follows: (1) Life and origins of ideas, influences, etc.; (2) Exposition of ideas. Herbart's doctrine is based on psychology (means) and ethics (end). Regarding ethics, the basis of all morality is aesthetic judgement applied to the relations between human wills (which are of five different types); the object of all education is to form a powerful moral character. The educator acts on the will, directly by means of discipline, and indirectly by means of ideas. Herbart's theory of interest asserts that the educator must elaborate a multiple and well-balanced interest. Above all, education takes place in the family. The school is seen as an important auxiliary.

The third part of Gockler's thesis is (3) a discussion of Herbart's views. Gockler is in favour of these. They lead to a consideration of what is durable and can excite interest, as opposed to knowledge pure and simple. These ideas are conducive to mental stability; they imply an education which seeks to establish a unity and harmony of the mental life of young people by means of methodical concentration. The only way of resolving questions relative to teaching and education is by demanding that all those who devote themselves to teaching the young should become as familiar as possible with pedagogy.

DURKHEIM: The study which M. Gockler has just presented fills a real gap in the literature, not only in France but also in Germany. The few truly objective works that have been written so far on Herbart have most often been too condensed and dry; they slur over the difficulties of the doctrine which they expound, and rarely confront them. M. Gockler, on the contrary, has not tried to conceal any of them. He has constantly confined himself to following his author with a great concern to be impartial and impersonal; he has achieved a work that is very precise and very honest. On the other hand, he has assimilated so well Herbart's thought, which is admittedly sometimes so difficult to grasp, that he moves within it with ease. But perhaps, for that very reason, he does not sufficiently foresee the difficulties which a French reader may find with it.

M. Durkheim also praises M. Gockler for having criticized Herbart with impartiality, and for judging him not as a docile disciple, but in a spirit which enables him entirely to keep his independence in face of a doctrine which he has deepened and whose value he fully appreciates. M. Durkheim adds also that M. Gockler has been able to collect, at the end of his thesis, information that is both useful and interesting; and that the style is not only correct but often even elegant.

In sum M. Gockler's thesis displays very fine qualities, and the general impression it creates is excellent.

M. Durkheim next indicates what criticisms he thinks this thesis merits.

In order to expound Herbart's pedagogy, he says, you have followed the following plan: (1) moral and psychological bases of Herbart's pedagogy; (2) you have sought to show how from the theories posed initially your author's pedagogy is derived. This method seems, at first sight, perfectly legitimate. But let us look at it more closely. This way of proceeding leads one to believe that the pedagogy is *deduced* from moral principles and psychological knowledge. Now, it is quite certain that it is not by a *deduction* of this type that pedagogy is established, and this is as true of Herbart as of other educational theorists. For neither psychology nor ethics offers a certainty and a scientific exactitude that are sufficient to serve as a basis and a point of departure for such a deduction. Further, in fact, pedagogues have not begun from psychological and ethical theories; educational theorists have begun from practice; it is here that they have acquired a more or less clear apprehension of what education ought to be. Psychology only intervenes subsequently, to provide a framework of argument, and to shore up practices that had been suggested in other ways. I hasten to say that it is very lucky that things have happened thus, for psychology has only tended in a scientific direction since very recently, and as for what there is of the science of morality, this is only just being born. What I have just suggested is true in a general way for all educators, and in particular for Herbart, who began, not from psychology and ethics, but indeed from *pedagogy*. Your exposition thus gives a picture of the doctrine which it presents to us that does not correspond to its historical formation. If it were to have been fully accurate, it would have been preferable if you had, in your exposition, reproduced the genesis of the doctrine. That is to say that, starting from the pedagogical ideas of Herbart, you should have introduced psychology and ethics only at the point at which your author appealed to them in order to support his educational doctrines.

GOCKLER: I have followed the plan adopted by Herbart himself in his work; moreover, one cannot understand his pedagogical ideas unless one knows his theories about morality and psychology.

DURKHEIM: That's true, but the question is to what extent such knowledge is indispensable. Now, it is true to say that the plan which you have followed could not, in this respect, give you any indication, nor provide any limits for you. For if you begin, for example, by expounding psychology, what reason would you have for restricting yourself to the examination of such and such particular questions? The result is that your exposition sins at the same time through excess and through default. For example, you tell us about the notion of the soul according to Herbart.

Now, I am convinced that this notion remains wholly external to his pedagogy and that, in order to expound this latter, it is at no point necessary to appeal to the idea of the soul. You would have seen this immediately, if you had begun from the pedagogy. You would not then, I think, have encountered this idea at any point. For, since, according to Herbart, the soul does nothing, the notion remains for him practically useless. You will see by this that the method of exposition which you have followed puts a great distance between you and pedagogy. On the other hand, this same method has led you to make no reference to the theory of the *faculties*. Herbart's attitude in relation to this question is, however, most important; it admits that mental life reduces itself entirely to *représentations*; and consequently, if one concedes the existence of faculties, that is to say something other than *représentations*, his whole theory collapses ... and this question which you have left on one side in your exposition of the doctrine is so important that, in your critical section, you have indeed been compelled to introduce it.

Another criticism: in order to carry out your exposition, you have collated texts, in such a way that your personality does not intervene. I recognize that this method would be the ideal method; but it meets with practical difficulties that are insurmountable, especially in the case of an author as difficult as Herbart. For the texts, if one does not think them through anew on one's own account and if one does not rearrange them somewhat, are very difficult to harmonize with one another. This is even more evident when they come from different works.

Moreover, it happens that the texts which you cite include terms whose sense you have not yet given.

Thus, on p. 161, you assign as an end for education 'multiple and well-equilibrated interest', without seeing that you are presupposing as given something which has not yet been treated.

Likewise, on p. 182, when you speak of 'the aesthetic representation of the world'.

M. Gockler replies that in that also he has followed the order of exposition adopted by Herbart.

DURKHEIM: It was not indispensable to the end which you set yourself to reproduce this order, it if was of such a nature as to create obscurities.

You have devoted to the question of *multiple interest*, of the *encyclopaedic character of culture*, an entire chapter (second part, chapter VI). Now, it is only at the end of this chapter that one finds presented, and very sketchily, the reasons invoked in favour of this culture. It was nevertheless very important to know what these reasons are; and I wonder whether the criticisms which you direct against this conception do not really derive from the rapidity with which you have passed over these reasons.

You have not made a special study of the notion of *aesthetic representation of the world*, to which Herbart, in fact, attributed much importance, and of which he speaks in very strong terms.

GOCKLER: The reason is that Herbart himself seems to have renounced this theory; at least he did not keep this designation: 'aesthetic representation of the world'.

DURKHEIM: I wonder whether it is not just this designation that disappeared. I think that the theory itself was retained. In any case the question deserves to have been examined: did Herbart abandon this theory, or did he not? If he did, for what reason, and what elements of it did he retain?

I have already shown that your method, which consists in bringing the texts together without interpreting them, often leaves the reader in a state of great perplexity. It often happens that you confront him with difficulties, which you do not try to resolve. For example, on p. 224, you give us the definition of *analytic* and *synthetic* teaching. These definitions are obscure, and you make no attempt to clarify them. Herbart says that analysis begins from given phenomena, and by its own means leads us to isolated characteristics, to forms, that is to say, to the *abstract*. But one does not at all see how he could believe that analysis, reduced to its own powers, has the capacity to enable us to attain the abstract, having started from the concrete.

GOCKLER: Analytic teaching consists in decomposing matter furnished by experience, in order to arrive thereby at determining its specific and abstract features.

DURKHEIM: But in order to arrive at the abstract notion, one must, after having used an analysis which decomposed given concrete matter into concrete elements, turn to synthesis which, by the bringing together and combination of elements obtained in the course of different analyses, thereby produces abstract notions. One does not therefore pass, by means of analysis alone, from the concrete to the abstract; one must also appeal to synthesis.

GOCKLER: It is true that, according to Herbart, as I have said in the passage of my thesis concerning this matter, analytic teaching does not abstain from a recourse to synthesis as well. But the opposition between these two modes of teaching is not thereby abolished, for this consists above all in the fact that, according to him, synthetic teaching proceeds primarily by deduction: it begins from principles which it develops.

DURKHEIM: I do not believe that one can express Herbart's thought in this way. For synthetic teaching enriches the knowledge of the pupil, and that is sufficient to ensure that it does not consist merely of deduction pure and simple. The true idea which I believe to be at the root of Herbart's theory on this question is that in analytic teaching it is above all the student who works; in synthetic teaching it is the master who acts in a positive manner on the pupil, yet without this influence going so far as to form in the mind of the pupil the whole logical organization of knowledge; that remains the work of the pupil.

Another difficulty: what relation is there between the two forms of teaching and the four *formal degrees* of which Herbart speaks elsewhere? Are these four forms to be found in each of the two modes of teaching?

M. Gockler thinks that they are.

M. Durkheim then passes to the examination of the critical part of M. Gockler's thesis. He wonders whether Herbart deserves the reproach, advanced by M. Gockler, of having assigned contrary ends to education, maintaining that it should seek to realize at the same time *multiple culture* and *morality*. M. Durkheim does not see these two ends as contrary; for in order that man be moral, he needs to know how to come to terms with his place in the world, and this knowledge requires an encylopaedic culture.

M. Gockler replies that he does not consider these two ends as contrary, but merely as heterogeneous.

DURKHEIM: In the chapter on psychology, you said that the psychologists have all attacked Herbart. That is not correct. Ribot wrote a fine eulogy of him (see *La Psychologie allemande contemporaine*). He saw that, in effect, Herbart substituted the notion of *représentation* for that of *faculty* and thus opened the way to the scientific study of psychological phenomena. The psychology of Herbart was, taken as a whole and in its spirit, more scientific than that of the English associationist school.

I was surprised to find expressed in your thesis the idea that, in so far as one accepts determinism, morality is impossible. Without entering in this connection into a discussion which has often been pursued, I will merely remind you that it is more and more generally accepted that it is not necessary to make morality depend on a thesis that is so insecurely founded as that of liberty (freewill – S. L.).

Finally, M. Durkheim wonders how it is to be explained that, despite its very great obscurity, Herbart's theory has had considerable influence in practice.

M. Gockler explains this by saying that the disciples of Herbart have applied themselves to disengaging the essential principles of his doctrines, and to making clear their practical value.

M. Durkheim believes that to this explanation one must add the following one: it is probable that at a certain moment in time an intense need was felt in Germany for a rational system of education. And it was this need which found satisfaction in the theories of Herbart.

6. *RMM Volume XIII, July 1905*

M. Hubert Bourgin. *Fourier: A Contribution to the Study of French Socialism*

The thesis is about the historical role of Fourier and his influence on French socialism. It is a simultaneous investigation of the work of Fourier, the work of the Fourierists, socialist doctrines of the nineteenth century and nineteenth-century economic history. Bourgin avoids a 'personal and subjective critique'. In his view Fourier's doctrine was a critique of contemporary society and an anticipation of future society, and thus the sole method of admissible criticism would be an essay of verification and explanation by the study of contemporary and future evidence. But this evidence is not today sufficiently known except in a very incomplete and inadequate manner. To avoid error, it is best to wait till social science has developed; therefore M. Bourgin abstains from this task and confines himself to the details of experience which explain the details of Fourier's doctrine. But he also considers the doctrine's influence, particularly in the form of the Fourierist school. His conclusion is that it had a much greater influence on socialism than on social development.

Durkheim praises the sureness, the impartiality and the honesty of M. Bourgin's work; he congratulates him on refusing to expound the uncertain results of the critique which he had begun. The importance accorded to the study of influence is explained by the fact that the doctrine of Fourier is a practical doctrine, made for action. What is lacking, in the study of the doctrine, is a positive basis in the facts. Doubtless there were great difficulties of method here, but perhaps one might have been able to triumph over them. Thus, M. Bourgin might have been able to study and describe the chief currents of contemporary ideas to which Fourier's thought belonged.

Bourgin replies that he does not think that these currents of ideas could have been scientifically accounted for. The study of great doctrines has only begun: but the whole study of their propagation, their dispersion, their diffusion within society is still to be undertaken. This question has not even been explored.

Durkheim says he does not wish to be misunderstood. It is not a question of sources but only of intellectual currents: this study does not demand the historical exactness that the study of sources demands.

Bourgin is also of the opinion that the question of sources is not what is at issue here: but he maintains that currents of ideas, as Durkheim defines and understands them, cannot be at present known in a scientific manner.

By way of examples Durkheim mentions the socialist messianism which one finds in Saint-Simon as well as Fourier, and the petit-bourgeois sentiments which are evident in both. On the other hand, the proletarian sentiment is manifest in Fourier but not in Saint-Simon.

Bourgin explains this difference by the different conditions they experienced: Fourier saw at close hand the poverty of the Lyonnais proletariat from 1790 to 1793 and from 1832 to 1834.

Finally M. Durkheim thinks that one point deserves to be clarified in the relation between Fourierism and Saint-Simonism. The doctrine of Fourier contributed to the sensual doctrine of Enfantinism; yet the doctrine of the rehabilitation of the flesh was already present in the thought of Bazard.

Bourgin agrees. He only wished to show the way in which Fourierism contributed to the corruption of Saint-Simonism.

7. *RMM Volume XIV, July 1906*
M. Aslan.   *The Ethics of Guyau*

Aslan discusses Guyau's attempt to arrive at a science of morality. He criticizes Guyau from a point of view very sympathetic to

Durkheim, that is of being unscientific. Guyau's method is one of 'poetic intuition' confirmed by conveniently chosen examples, rather than an induction based on long and methodical investigation. He is inconsistent and vague. He reduces obligation and sanction to material forces and he slides over difficulties. He wants to derive the social from the individual, but he only succeeds in suppressing what is specific in the social. All that remains of value in Guyau is his rejection of all metaphysical systems of ethics.

The philosopher, Séailles (one of Durkheim's fellow examiners), defends Guyau's metaphysical conception of 'the principle of life', his *a priori* moral ideal, and the priority he accords the individual. (Séailles is in effect attacking Durkheim.) Aslan replies by quoting one of Guyau's formulae: 'The social sentiment is born from the nature of our brain which is fashioned by our acts'. Yet where, he asks, do these acts come from? – From society.

Séailles says that, of course, in order to have a social individual, you need society, and society needs individuals; but society gives increasing emphasis to the individual. Individuality has become more and more pronounced: where the *conscience collective* is strong, moral ideas are average ideas, but the *conscience collective* has fragmented into many individual *consciences*, which can only communicate by reason. In developed and civilized societies, morality does not consist in conforming to society, but in being ahead of its time. To be moral is to anticipate one's epoch. It is in the moral order that one kills inventors.

DURKHEIM: Or one hands them over to the correctional police.

SÉAILLES: Humanity is characterized by the substitution of personal development for the *conscience collective*. The great moral *consciences* are those which resist social pressure. Your theory – that of the sociologists – has been very useful, in this sense, that it has advanced a certain number of ideas that were at one time not discussible, but it must not be exclusive.

ASLAN: You admit that social explanation is valid for primitive societies. Why not for contemporary societies?

SÉAILLES: Why? I assert an evolution, in the course of history, from collective imagination to the progressive individualization of *consciences*. In our modern societies, which are so complex and diverse in their elements, there are many points of view about life: often facts do not support us, and we are reduced to having to decide by the old appeal to conscience.

DURKHEIM: I will not argue with your thesis: I believe we are in agreement on its principal ideas. I have been astonished that it has not been understood that such a thesis in no way implies the negation of individuality. It is impossible to explain the whole of the individual by the social, but nor can one succeed in explaining the social by the individual. The social as such must be explained by the social. The sociological point of view thus implies that the two terms 'individual' and 'society' are postulated from the beginning as inseparable.

8. *RMM, Volume XVI, March 1908*
M. d'Allonnes. *The Psychology of a Religion*

This thesis is a study in the psychology of fanaticism, and in particular of Pastor Guillaume Monod and his followers. It is presented as an investigation into 'morbid religious contagion'.

DURKHEIM: You have chosen a subject that is attractive, but dangerous. After having read you, I see only imperfectly what conclusions your work leads to. The six propositions which are the conclusions of your thesis only contain one which is of interest to psychology. The gap between the title and the content of the book is so great that I was not able to find your thesis in your summary. I wonder if this confusion does not arise out of the variations which your thought has undergone. I therefore ask you: what important psychological propositions have you established?

D'ALLONNES: As a matter of general method, I have avoided including chapters consisting of general ideas based on my data. What I want to achieve is that the psychology of inspiration develops little by little from facts that are studied. I have not written a dogmatic book, but a work of observation. I observe the founder of a religion in the first part; in the second part I study the formation of a synthesis of cults and beliefs which is such that one can call it a religion.

DURKHEIM: You attribute unusual importance to the group of the Monodists. You speak of the doctrine of the author in terms that are scarcely proportionate to the value of that doctrine. You are really engaged in Monodist apologetics. You discuss the doctrine of Monod, without citing any text to support your assertions. This man believes himself to be a God and he borrowed from

Australia a doctrine of the reincarnation of souls! Monod's own ideas appear to me to be very meagre. Monod created a religion in order to prove that he was God. The only idea having any interest is the idea of salvation. What was it that persuaded Monodists and brought about their conversion?

D'ALLONES: There were several Monodists persuaded by the doctrine of Monod.

DURKHEIM: What is it that justifies the epithets of 'beauty' and 'novelty' which you apply to this doctrine?

D'ALLONNES: It is beautiful, it has a certain elegant aspect, it is part of the radiance of Monod, who was personally beautiful, beautiful in his energy.

DURKHEIM: I am asking you in what respect this doctrine, in itself, is beautiful and new.

D'ALLONNES: It can appear beautiful to religious spirits.

DURKHEIM: From the general point of view of believers?

D'ALLONNES: One finds in Monodism the doctrine of redemption, the great Christian ideas, the idea of a personal Messiah.

DURKHEIM: But then, it had only to remain in the temple! I would love to have known how many Monodist churches there have been, and what was their geographical distribution. This would have shed light on the whole study. Were the two hundred persons collected together? Or separated?

D'ALLONNES: These were above all phenomena of individual contagion.

DURKHEIM: One can therefore scarcely speak of religion.

D'ALLONNES: Protestantism is an individualist religion.

DURKHEIM: Let us not confuse the content of a belief from the collective character of that belief. These are distinct. Your theological argument consists in saying that Monod reasoned like a good theologian, in order to prove that he was Christ. His exegesis is correct. That is the question which preoccupies you constantly, and you are always returning to it and it wearies you. It takes up almost a third of your book. Suppose that all the arguments *are* sound – what then follows for religious psychology?

D'ALLONNES: The problem is to know if I am dealing with the normal or the pathological: is this a normal case, in so far as a Messiah is normal?

DURKHEIM: I do not see why this theological study is necessary for you. The biblical prophets do not provide any exegesis. The mental mechanism of Monod is distinct from all this theological argument. The question is to know if one prophet resembles another prophet.

D'ALLONNES: There are two groups of prophets, artificial prophets and natural prophets. Monod is not a great inspired prophet. He is an artificial prophet.

DURKHEIM: I come to the large question. It might either be a case of prophetic genius or prophetic madness. You distinguish these in accordance with the effects of the preaching. You have replied to M. Dumas: 'We are not on the same ground when we judge the normal and the abnormal.' But it is necessary to be in turn on each of these grounds and not to confuse them. You assert that there are madmen who have rendered social services but although they have rendered those social services, they are none the less mad. You come back in short to saying that among the abnormal, some are socially sterile and others socially useful and that there is therefore a need to distinguish the individually abnormal and socially abnormal, and the question that requires answering is whether the individually abnormal can be socially normal. To this you reply affirmatively.

D'ALLONNES: I believe I have provided a solution to the relations of the normal and the abnormal. So far as the distinction between normal and abnormal is concerned two ideas are present. The distinction in question can be of a medical order: the students of mental diseases proceed as clinicians by definitions that are too broad; the doctor always proceeds imprecisely. On the other hand the distinction can be of a psychological nature. The psychologist seeks to identify the directly abnormal phenomenon without including in it neighbouring phenomena which are distinct. On the contrary he equally seeks to track down the normal at the core of phenomena considered imprecisely by the medical profession. That is what I have done.

DURKHEIM: Unfortunately, if the socially normal is that which meets with social adhesion, your case is hardly normal: you have taken a prophet who did not succeed.

9. *RMM. Volume XVII, March 1909*

M. Mangé. *Systematization in the Sciences: Its Conditions and Its Principles*

M. Mangé argues for apriorism in science, for the use of preconceived ideas. Durkheim pays homage to the sincerity and to the philosophical passion of the author, who argues that the method which postulates an ideal science is mistaken. One needs to know what *in fact* science is, that is what the sciences are. 'If there is any discordance between science constructed abstractly and the sciences as they really are, which concerns you? Sciences as they are, the method which science ought to employ, or the philosophical systematization of the sciences?'

MANGÉ: It is a question of philosophical science, or of scientific philosophy; of the conditions that must be fulfilled if science wishes to become systematized. There is science which collects evidence and that which co-ordinates it, that is, *systematic science*. What I provide is a *method of discovery*, not of facts, not even of laws, but of *principles*.

DURKHEIM: Science systematizes spontaneously.

10. *RMM, Volume XVII, May 1909*

M. Cramaussel. *The First Intellectual Awakening of the Child*

This thesis argues that the intellectual life of the child begins with sensation and continues with intuition, the concept, judgement and finally reasoning. Sensation is pure and precise; from the intuition stage onwards, thought progressively adapts to the world. He derives the pedagogical conclusion that the educator should not impose concepts and artificial judgements on the child. Durkheim praises the sincerity of the observations, the subtlety of the analysis, indeed the very subject which the author has been concerned with both as a man and as a philosopher. He summarizes M. Cramaussel's idea that there really is a first phase of intellectual life, a period characterized by the intellectuality of infantile thinking. He asks for several clarifications relating to the method followed. How have the observations been made? Are the data transcribed immediately or on the basis of more or less distorting memories? The author has observed only four children, so that, sometimes, a generalization rests on one sole fact. He should have brought his observations into line with those of his predecessors. Finally he has not treated the interesting question of both the child's hatred and his love of novelty.

CRAMAUSSEL: The observations were noted down as soon as they were made. When facts have been indicated to me by others, I have myself observed them experimentally. I have compared others' observations with my own but without confusing theirs with mine. If the data are few, they are typical, selected from a mass of others. If the child is antagonistic to novelty, it is because he likes organization, solidarity. If he loves novelty it is because he has the world to discover.

DURKHEIM: You have taken the framework for your observations from adult psychology, and without it you would perhaps have found something else, some other reality. You speak of pure sensation unmixed with association: but there is no such thing to be observed. What do you mean by intuition? How is your intuition different from perception? It is an objectification, a spontaneous projection which confronts the child with a new reality. Your intuition is clearly distinct from the concept but much less from perception.

CRAMAUSSEL: There is nothing more in attention, memory, association, intuition itself, the act of synthesis, than sensations grouped together rather than being isolated.

There is nothing new from the moment that one separates out the identical elements (partial identity). Adult perception implies association and an operation of the mind; a child's intuition occurs spontaneously, incidentally, without any mental labour.

DURKHEIM: For you, the child begins with clear, distinct states, which become confused later. Yet the whole of intellectual progress is towards clearness and distinctness; the child is flooded, lost in the unknown and the uncomprehended, as though in a strange country: and it is that which you see as joy and facility. Your whole theory is based on an impressionistic interpretation of the child's smile.

CRAMAUSSEL: This interpretation has objective physiological grounds. The same muscular state does not accompany both the animal's smile of digestion and the intellectual smile of childish intuition. The child, when he wants to, is capable of distinguishing even very closely related species, such as the goat and the chamois.

He perceives identities and differences when these are *useful* to him and he can always come back to these distinctions.

DURKHEIM: That is hardly likely, as long as he does not possess language, that instrument of discrimination. Your work explains survival by primitive adaptation and postulates reason as the starting-point; it is dominated by a metaphysical idea, the teleological idea of an organizing Nature.

11. *RMM, Volume XVIII, January 1910*
M. Pradines. *The Principles of Every Philosophy of Action*

The candidate begins by saying that he has lived his work as much as thought it. This thesis asks how is action possible and intelligible. It advances a sort of rational pragmatism in which reason derives from action and expresses it. It includes a theory of liberty and of the good.

DURKHEIM: You have a remarkable facility in handling concepts, and your book bears witness to an undeniable power of meditation. All the same I am surprised that you have really 'lived' it. Certainly, you are the only judge of that, but I have the impression that, rather than living your thought, you have considered it as if it were an image that is foreign to your personality. By this exclusively intellectual consideration, I refer to those ideas considered in the aggregate, which Rauh indicated,* and also those 'brilliant phrases'. I would like to forget your talent and judge your work, as one should judge every philosophical work, objectively. I will not weigh up the value of different methods, for your thought avoids all method. The aim of every method is to enable one to think straight; but I do not see that you have submitted your reason to any control whatever. What about the control of the facts? I have looked in vain throughout the whole of your book for a single instance taken either from common experience or personal experience. But let us leave this point: you are not a scientist, but a dialectician. I do not scorn dialectics, but I want people to understand themselves, and also that they should make themselves understood. What is one to think of a dialectician who does not define the notion he plays with, who speaks of Nature and of Reason without remembering that

---

* The reference is to an earlier observation by Durkheim's fellow-examiner, Félix Rauh.

distinguished thinkers have seen reason as part of nature, and who forgets to define the meaning of the terms 'law', 'good', 'obligation'? The same vagueness is to be found in your allusions to moral doctrines. Thus you appear not to have considered but merely to have dreamt your thought. Also you summarized it in formulae that are decisive but vague, and hardly convincing, bearing out what Fustel de Coulanges once said to me 'to philosophize is to think what one wants'.

PRADINES: You will find in the first part of my work the definition of certain words which I use without commentary in the second. Besides I believe that there are ideas which one can only define by means of examples and antitheses: their meaning, being too rich, overflows logical categories: such are the antithetical terms of reason and nature ...

DURKHEIM: Do you mean that one does not have to define them?

PRADINES: Yes.

DURKHEIM: How then will we be able to understand ourselves? Will you be able to understand yourself? What, at least, do you mean by 'nature'? Does social nature form part of it? ... The whole question resides here: if social phenomena are in nature, then moral phenomena, of which social phenomena are at least an expression, are also in nature, and are thus [not] free and undetermined.*

PRADINES: I understand by nature observable nature.

DURKHEIM: Where do you put social phenomena?

PRADINES: I think that to a certain extent society can impose laws on observable nature.

DURKHEIM: It is then a form of nature, social nature, and not beyond nature and reason. What becomes of your antithesis? You assert that there is an interpenetration of the two concepts which you have artificially separated. What is one to say of your idea of 'law'? I think that you mean by this a general law. Now law and generality may be distinct: Hamelin has shown this. Do you not think that there can be a law of the particular?

* The transcript does not include 'not', but this seems to be required by the sense (S.L.).

PRADINES: Certainly.

DURKHEIM: I was expecting this *volte-face*. Sometimes you oppose laws, seen as general, to the particular; sometimes you believe that there is only a law of the particular.

PRADINES: Every law is general: but its object is the particular . . .

DURKHEIM: The question is: is the particular as such intelligible? Or does there exist in it some irreducible element which escapes laws? The term 'law', so ill-defined, serves as a basic for your dialectic. This is in fact the essence of your thesis: law expresses what is; action is what does not yet exist: therefore law annihilates action. I do not understand this logic according to which law would exclude action; you only reach this result by a sophism. There are two sorts of laws. If a physical law expresses what is, one must say of the moral law that it expresses what does not yet exist. It is the illegitimate extension of what concerns law to what concerns the moral rule that constitutes the sophism at the root of your system; and it is explained by an equivocation over a word which you, in your capacity as a dialectician, have neglected to define.

PRADINES: My aim was precisely to denounce the equivocation involved in this misleading distinction between law and rule. I have shown that all systems accept it, but they all end, in effect, by confusing law and rule: they are indiscernible concepts, the rule – or ideal – applying to the pure abstraction of ourselves.

DURKHEIM: Does the rule exist, yes or no?

PRADINES: No, in the meaning of systems.

DURKHEIM: What moralist has confused rules with the laws?

PRADINES: Plato, in the *Phaedo*.

DURKHEIM: The errors, whether conscious or involuntary, of our predecessors matter little. I say that the moralists have distinguished the generalization of what is from what ought to be, laws from the ideals. You would not have the right to identify moral law and physical law unless all moralists admitted that the rule was realized in fact: the moral law and the physical law will not be a conventional summary of what is unless all moralists and yourself admit that all men practise the rules of morality. You say to the empiricist: your rule expresses individual nature; to the sociologist: yours expresses social nature. A rule does not exist any the less merely because of men's actions: and the criminal who disobeys it shows that it is an ideal. In brief, there is a sense in which 'we' are subject to physical laws, and another in which 'we' perform the moral law: we are double.

PRADINES: I wanted to put an end to this dualism.

DURKHEIM: You have not succeeded. Reason, you say, unifies the tendencies in the moral law just as in the physical law it unifies natural phenomena, but do you not see that this antagonism is in us, in ourselves? What difficulty is there here? How can one imagine that a dialectical trick will unify this dualism, which all thinkers before you have expressed, each in his own language, some tracing the social to the perceptible, others opposing the rational to the individual, but all seeing one characteristic, the most profound of all moral characteristics. You who claim to have so keen an apprehension of complexity, how is it that you have not felt that there is always in us something which is elevating while another part of us draws us in an opposite direction?

PRADINES: It has seemed to me that classical rationalism was wrong not to put an end to this undeniable dualism.

DURKHEIM: Such a solution is impossible. You have found in all systems an internal opposition. You have denounced this as a contradiction; you should have seen that this contradiction is in life itself.

12. *RMM, Volume XVIII, March 1910*
M. Mendousse. *From Animal Training to Education*

This thesis is a study in the psychology of adolescence. The author attempts to put in relation with one another ideas on education and on animal training; contending that the first is concerned with the progressive submission to internal discipline, the second with the submission to external discipline.

DURKHEIM: The merit of your thesis is that it is dominated by an idea. I might add that it is full of wisdom and thoughtfulness. One cannot read it without feeling attracted to the author. The documentation of the first part is very rich, and the form is acceptable and sound; on the other hand there are numerous printing errors.

However, your subject is very general; you are obliged to provide a sort of philosophy of education. In one single work, it is difficult to tackle so many questions directly; perhaps you might have been able to find an angle from which to approach them. You expose yourself to remaining within generalizations and it is this which provides the contrast between the first and the second part of your thesis: the second is a somewhat lengthy dissertation, the academic analysis of an idea.

MENDOUSSE: One can define accurately the concept of training. I have raised the question of finding an angle. As to the difference between different ages, this is based on evidence.

DURKHEIM: Yes, you have considered the matter, but you were not able to provide sufficient proof. One of these ages would have sufficed.

MENDOUSSE: I have studied in my large thesis what was specifically appropriate to each age.

DURKHEIM: Apart from this question of the difference between ages, there remains the question of education, which is immense as you pose it. Indeed, you have a positive conception of education, but you have gone beyond the subject thus understood.

There is a chapter in your work (the first of the second part) which should summarize the whole history of pedagogy. And there are some very disputable points there. The history of pedagogy has certainly not come to an end; these studies do not go far enough for one to be able to come to such summary conclusions. Look at page 92. Port-Royal, which was pessimistic, provided the most liberal type of education; and indeed it has always been so. Your judgement of these Jesuits is altogether unjust. Do you think that from the end of the sixteenth century all the great Frenchmen have been brought up like parrots?

MENDOUSSE: Let us take Descartes and Voltaire. There is no relation between the education they have received and their own theories.

DURKHEIM: As for Descartes, I would attribute to the Jesuits a very great role. There was a wisdom latent in the Jesuit education.

The Jesuits only retained from Greek and Latin culture what was humane in it in order to prevent pagan culture from producing its pagan results. This is self-evident. It is true that historical ignorance also contributed to this.

You say further: the child is good from the start for Pestalozzi; but this formula has to be interpreted. And, for example, Rousseau never said that the child was naturally good, but he maintained that he was neither good nor bad. You will no doubt cite me a text, but that text must be placed within the context of the whole doctrine. According to Pestalozzi there is a natural progression from the plant to man.

Finally, you make of training the essential part of education. I fear this is an error. What you call liberty almost entirely escapes education. Here is the great difference between training and education: you have shown that training can only develop instinct, and that the aim of education is to repress instinct. There is therefore between training and education a constant antagonism. This is the significance of social life: for the creature of instinct it is necessary to substitute a being who does violence to these instincts.

MENDUOSSE: I think that the difference which you postulate between instinct and reason . . .

DURKHEIM: I have not spoken of reason.

MENDUOSSE: Whence then comes the power to resist instinct? I think that man yielding to the natural bent of his instincts is a general phenomenon.

DURKHEIM: Explain to us how the child, being egoistic, can come to sacrifice himself.

MENDOUSSE: I believe that the individual can come to do this by a development of instinct. Environment is insufficient: without the educator, it would only produce commonplace minds.

DURKHEIM: The educator forms part of the environment. There are 36 educators.

MENDOUSSE: I believe that every individual by his own powers . . .

DURKHEIM: . . . would create language?

MENDOUSSE: No, but the acquisition of language is a form of training.

DURKHEIM: Are these things comparable?

MENDOUSSE: I think so.

DURKHEIM: You think that, as soon as there is pressure, there is training. But there are different sorts of training. Training inculcates habits, education inculcates rules. Rules are not habits. We can practise rules which are not habitual to us. Do you know of rules followed by animals?

MENDOUSSE: Which proves that the rule is not exclusively social. It is the individual who needs a rule.

DURKHEIM: Is it not children who ask for the breast every two hours?

MENDOUSSE: They do not know how to ask for it.

DURKHEIM: It is the specific nature of man to follow rules. One knows how difficult it is to inculcate in the child the feeling for a rule. There is no education without moral authority, which distinguishes training from education.

13. *RMM, Volume XIX, January 1911*

M. Segond. *Prayer: A Study in Religious Psychology**

The thesis begins from a distinction between religion and magic, and it argues that prayer is at the centre of religious life. It employs a method of empathy with those who know prayer by experience, especially mystics. Prayer, it is argued, is an individual phenomenon, a sentiment of indefinable universalizable presence. It must be studied from the inside. In prayer inspiration is essential; it engages the whole personality and reveals man to himself by a process of self-examination. This self-examination is advocated by philosophers but it is only fully practised by mystics. Their silence is the awareness, not of emptiness, but of the self, together with the feeling of self-transcendence and communication with a Beyond.

Durkheim asks for a preliminary explanation of the meaning of the distinction which Segond makes between religious phenomena and magical phenomena. Segond explains that in magical phenomena, according to the believer, God's favours are mechanically induced, while in the religious act the subject's own activity intervenes.

DURKHEIM: The traditional definition lays down that there is a religion when there is a spiritual intermediary, a *conscience*, and that there is magic when a practice is held to act automatically, but this definition is very disputable.

* Cf. Review by Mauss: *Année sociologique*, XII, pp. 238–40.

SEGOND: The two points of view are reconcilable within the same activity. Take the prayer of incantation: when the name of God is held to act by itself there is magic.

DURKHEIM: No: even according to the traditional definition, since a spiritual being intervenes, albeit in a constrained manner, it is held to be a religious phenomenon. But we cannot discuss this distinction; it would take us too far afield.

You have written a sincere work, in which you have described and classified observations of the prayers of specified subjects, with a detachment that is more real in your book than in your thoughts. I will reproach you for having reproduced in your descriptions the terminology of the mystic without taking sufficient care to explain it. This procedure is troubling for one who has studied religious thought in another manner. Your conclusion is more personal: it might have entered into your book more as a result of those feelings which serve as its basis. Let us define your aim and your method: it is a question of studying prayer as an internal experience (page 32) as it appeared not to any particular mind but to the mind of the worshipper considered *in abstracto*. Therefore you have taken rather scattered examples and in this sense you have cut yourself off from a sociological point of view, which studies determinate *consciences* in groups. You, on the contrary, study prayer in the human *conscience* in general: that does not seem easy, but *a priori* I do not want to say it is impossible. Meanwhile, what is the nature of your procedure? All *consciences* do not have the same experiences and I do not find in your descriptions any states which I have not been able personally to experience. In order to define a human state, it is necessary to classify types or to take a rudimentary form on which the complex throws light. Now you have taken Christian, mystical contexts, but is this something other than a *particular* mental state? Your historical exposition is inadequate to prove the contrary; you there discover forms that by definition you have postulated as fundamental. It is not sufficient to point to forms that are analogous to those which you have studied, in a rapid and hurried review.

SEGOND: I know that a collective mental state is nothing but the echo in diverse individual *consciences* of social influences that are identical for this diverse *conscience*. But I was able to put myself in the place of the psychologist and take an internal point of view.

DURKHEIM: Let us not engage in this discussion of points of view. Let us study your manner of procedure. Why did you choose mystics?

SEGOND: The method which I have followed is a method of investigation. I have studied mystic thought, and left aside the rudimentary forms of religion because in their case it is difficult to grasp the nature of prayer: among the Australian tribes, for example, its very existence is in dispute.

DURKHEIM: Practical difficulties do not constitute excuses. In studying a restricted milieu how do you study a human state? You recognize that experiences are different.

SEGOND: Without doubt, but there is a mystic tradition in which there are discernible experiences that are relatively more homologous. How is one to proceed otherwise if one wants to study a religious sentiment?

DURKHEIM: I shall carry out this study as I am able to, but we are discussing your procedure. In brief, the chief characteristic of prayer for you is silence. Nevertheless, in general it is expressed – without, I agree, its necessarily being a request. The existence of a ritual form of words is a phenomenon that is relatively common: by means of it man is strengthened; by words his mental situation is stabilized. You neglect the role of words.

SEGOND: I have not left this out, as you assert, for I cite formalized prayers. But while one may begin with the form of words, one must above all seek its meaning and see whether there is not something else which is more important. Silence is an element of this kind: silence in the mystical sense of the casting-off by the soul of all that is external to it.

DURKHEIM: You have not treated the special problem of the ritual form in prayer.

SEGOND: I have had some difficulty in dealing with it but I discuss it in the historical part of my work.

DURKHEIM: You speak of the mental state as the worshipper thinks he apprehends it within himself: this is legitimate. But this state is superficial, since you allow for the existence of the unconscious. Therefore, if you do not *interpret* these superficial data, you will not gain an understanding of reality.

SEGOND: One cannot speak of such a division between super-ficial psychological facts and others which are more real. Psychology can only be developed by this method of asking questions of the mind.

DURKHEIM: That is the point of my objection: mystics do not understand the essence of prayer. You have to look for it.

SEGOND: Who knows this essence?

DURKHEIM: We do, when we study phenomena.

SEGOND: Phenomena are not minds.

DURKHEIM: Let us leave that aside. Psychology exists; and our memory and our sensations, which appear to us to be simple, are complex phenomena for the psychologist who analyses them. And you are engaged on a similar study when on page 201 you say that the subjective element is the essential one.

SEGOND: There is no general psychology able to impose its cate-gories upon the various special psychologies. I only wanted to undertake religious psychology.

DURKHEIM: But you maintain that the subjective element is the most profound: 'we consider the psychological aspects to be the most profound . . . I take the point of view of mysticism'. You claim to have arrived at an objective conception. One can do this (only) by showing that psychological facts are other than they appear to the subject.

SEGOND: I adhere to the immediate psychological method. I wanted only to describe, to say what mystics experience, and for this reason I have appealed to mystics, to their testimony, to that of Bossuet, for example, or of Ignatius de Loyola.

DURKHEIM: You in fact go beyond this subjective point of view. How do you know, if not by interpretation, what took place in the minds of the Jews, as they sang the psalms? Finally I will raise the question of the views that you attribute to me on the issue of subjective religion being only an 'epiphenomenon': I have written an article to prove that this word does not have any sense.* You attribute to me also the view that prayer is not essential to the cult.

* Durkheim is referring to 1898b.

SEGOND: I do not wish to attribute these (exact) statements to you but merely to summarize your thought. I am referring to page 10 of the 'Definition of Religious Phenomena' in the second volume of the *Année sociologique*.*

DURKHEIM: I do not have prayer in mind in that text.

SEGOND: You spoke of religious forms in which the idea of a superior being does not figure, and you define prayer as a practice, related to a dogma and consequently subordinate to it.

DURKHEIM: I have never thought that: beginning with Christianity, prayer is indeed the rite *par excellence*. It is precisely this point that constitutes my principal objection to your thesis: its very choice of subject-matter.

14. *RMM, Volume XX, July 1912*

M. Terraillon. *Honour: Sentiment and Moral Principle*

This thesis is a study of the idea of honour as found in the work of philosophers, novelists, publicists and playwrights. It argues that honour is half-way between egoism and altruism, in the region of the 'moi sociale'. Its essence is summed up in the phrase 'Act in a way worthy of your role'. The thesis contains studies of different sorts of honour.

DURKHEIM: The subject is a fine one and one cannot congratulate M. Terraillon too much for having chosen it. But by reason of the very difficulty of the problem, it would have been best to have given at the outset a definition of honour. In the absence of this, honour is often confused with the causes on which it may depend. As the expression 'lose one's honour' and 'have the honour to' show, it is a certain state of the subject, and it is just this mental state that should have been analysed. As to the supposed conflicts between honour and duty, all the examples cited can be advanced in support of the contrary thesis, since they only appear to indicate conflicts between duties.

Can one, on the other hand, maintain that honour only exists in particular groups? Hasn't the honest man as such the right to honour? There is a close link between this idea and day-to-day honesty. Thus the problem should be posed differently, in terms

* 1899 (ii).

of everyone's honour, as distinct from particular sorts of honour. As to this general honour, it transcends special or professional honour. It is common to all civilized groups and might be called human honour. M. Terraillon should have studied this.

Appendix C

Contributing Editors of
The *Année sociologique*, Vols. 1 – 12*

É. Durkheim (1, 2, 3, 4, 5, 6, 7, 8, 9, 10, 11, 12).
G. Simmel (1).
G. Richard (1, 2, 3, 4, 5, 6, 7, 8, 9, 10).
É. Lévy (1, 2, 3, 4, 5, 6, 7, 8, 9, 10, 11, 12).
C. Bouglé (1, 2, 3, 4, 5, 6, 7, 8, 9, 10, 11, 12).
P. Fauconnet (1, 2, 3, 4, 5, 6, 7, 8, 9, 10, 11, 12).
H. Hubert (1, 2, 3, 4, 5, 6, 7, 8, 9, 10, 11, 12).
P. Lapie (1, 2, 3, 4, 5, 6, 7, 8, 9, 10, 11).
M. Mauss (1, 2, 3, 4, 5, 6, 7, 8, 9, 10, 11, 12).
A. Milhaud (1).
H. Muffang (1, 2, 3).
D. Parodi (1, 2, 3, 4, 5, 6, 7, 8, 9, 10, 11, 12).
F. Simiand (1, 2, 3, 4, 5, 6, 7, 8, 9, 10, 11, 12).
M. Foucault (2, 7).
F. Ratzel (3).
(?) Sigel (3).
S. R. Steinmetz (3).
J. Charmont (4).
A. Aubin (4, 5, 6, 7, 8, 9, 10, 11, 12).
H. Bourgin (4, 5, 6, 7, 8, 9, 10, 11, 12).
A. Meillet (5, 6, 7, 8, 9, 10, 11, 12).
R. Hourticq (5, 6, 7, 8, 9, 10, 11, 12).
E.-Cl. Maître (5).
P. Huvelin (6, 7, 8, 9, 10, 11, 12).
C. Lalo (7).
M. Halbwachs (8, 9, 10, 11, 12).
R. Hertz (8, 9, 10, 11, 12).
A. Vacher (8, 9).
G. Bourgin (8, 9, 10, 11, 12).
A. Bianconi (10, 11, 12).
M. David (11, 12).

* The numbers in brackets give the volumes to which each person
listed contributed. (This is not always accurately indicated by the names
listed on the title-page of each volume.)

G. Davy (11, 12).
L. Gernet (11, 12).
J. Ray (11, 12).
J. Reynier (11, 12).
Ph. De Félice (11, 12).
J.-P. Lafitte (11).
A. Demangeon (12).
Ed. Doutté (12).
G. Gelly (12)
H. Jeanmaire (12).
E. Laskine (12).
P. Roussel (12).
J. Marx (12).
H. Beuchat (12).

Name Index

Abelard, 382
'Agathon' (H. Massis and A. de Tarde), 363, 372, 501 n. 25
Alcuin, 380 n. 4
Andler, Charles, 76, 314, 328 n. 34, 497, 535 n. 31, 549 n. 12
Aristotle, 104, 106, 264, 436
Aron, R., 339 n. 71
Aslan, 636-7
Aubin, A., 655

Bachofen, J. J., 180
Baldwin, J. M., 303 n. 20
Barrès, Maurice, 71, 334-5, 375
Barth, Paul, 397
Bauer, A., 21 n. 83
Bayet, A., 224
Bazard, Saint-Armand, 636
Bédier, J., 549 n. 12
Belot, Gustave, 45, 317, 395, 405 n. 79, 497, 535 n. 31; on Durkheim's view of morality, 501, 502-3, 504, 511, 517-18
Benoist, C., 536 n. 31
Bentham, Jeremy, 112, 146
Bergson, Henri, 44, 75, 358, 495, 505, 549; on Durkheim, 52, 501 n. 25; rivalry with Durkheim of, 363, 370, 371 n. 30; and James, 486, 487, 489
Bernard, Claude, 73 and n. 41
Bernès, Marcel, 314, 497
Bernstein, E., 323 n. 11
Berr, Henri, 376, 394
Bersot, Ernest, 53
Berth, Édouard, 542
Bertillon, Jacques, 395
Besse, Dom, 363, 373, 374
Beuchat, Henri, 402, 656
Bianconi, A., 655
Blanc, Louis, 541
Blanqui, Auguste, 198
Bloch, Marc, 232 n. 27, 403
Blondel, Charles, 403

Blondel, Maurice, 45
Blum, Léon, 327 n. 31, 328 and n. 34
Boas, Franz, 303 n. 20, 452
Boegner, Marc, 518-20
Boissier, Gaston, 53
Borel, Émil, 376
Bouglé, Célestin, 314, 357, 364, 353 n. 31; on Durkheim, 72, 300; Durkheim's letters to, 80, 139, 193 n. 13, 234 n. 25, 290, 292, 294, 316, 348, 368 n. 21, 404 n. 72, 405 n. 79, 558; and Année sociologique, 291, 327, 655; work of, 401
Bourgeois, Léon, 350, 352-3, 354 n. 37
Bourget, P. C. J., 75
Bourgin, Georges, 328 n. 34, 403, 655
Bourgin, Hubert, 292 n. 16, 320-21 and n. 4, 322, 655; and Dreyfus Affair, 328; and socialism, 328 n. 34, 329, 330; on Durkheim, 367, 369 and n. 25, 376-7; doctoral examination of, 635-6
Boutroux, Émile, 53, 358, 366, 406, 549 n. 12; influence on Durkheim of, 57-8, 73, 233, 206; examines Durkheim, 296, 297, 298
Briand, Aristide, 534
Brochard, Victor, 298, 366
Brunetière, Ferdinand, 75, 197, 335-8, 344
Brunot, Ferdinand, 45
Brunschvicg, Léon, 339 n. 71, 358 n. 47, 504, 535 n. 31
Buisson, Ferdinand, 350, 354, 360, 365, 366, 535 n. 31
Bureau, Paul, 535 n. 31
Burke, Edmund, 77-8 and n. 59

Cabet, Étienne, 198
Campanella, T., 250
Cantécor, G., 501
Charcot, J. M., 54
Charmont, J., 655

Subject Index

abnormal forms, see normality

L'Allemagne au-dessus de tout, see Germany Above All

Alliance pour l'Accroissement de la Population Française, 194–5

Alsace-Lorraine, 39, 99

altruism, 23, 185 n. 28, 622; and suicide 206, 207, 209–10, 213, 214, 218, 222, 225; and morality, 417

ambiguities in Durkheim's thought, in *représentation*, 7, 465; in 'social realism', 11; in definition of social facts, 12–13, 15; in psychology, 16–19; in social-individual distinction, 20–21; in discussion of morality, 416–18, 430, 431; in discussion of knowledge, 440; in 'primitivity' of religion, 455; on decline of religion, 474–7; in discussion of truth, 495–6

America, American thought, 171 n. 65, 303, 441; ethnography, 180, 237–8, 450–52; influence on Durkheim of, 237–8; and individualism, 351; sociology in, 392, 397; response to Durkheim's work, 513–14; and the war, 559

American Indians, 441, 453, 478, 480

American Journal of Sociology, 397, 513

analogy, 314 n. 77; of mental states, 7; of 'creative synthesis', 19–20; of medicine, 30, 430 n. 11; organic, 35, 82–3, 94, 148, 177, 178 n. 98, 233 n. 31, 269–85, 457; of electricity, 35, 215–16; mechanical, 148; of tree, 149 n. 49; experimental, 457; between moral and sacred, 413, 419, 503

anarchism, 224, 245, 324, 325

anarchy, 336–7, 343, 546

ancestor-worship, 62

Ancient City, The (Fustel de Coulanges), 59, 60–63, 238

Anglican church, 208

Année sociologique, 99 n. 4, 100, 179, 243, 248, 257, 289–95, 312, 501, 527, 655–6; foundation of, 289; aims of, 290–91; development of, 291–2; group associated with, 294, 300, 365; policy of, 294–5; criticisms of, 317

anomie, 18, 23, 164; industrial, 172–4, 211, 326; and cultural tradition, 198; and suicide, 207, 210–12, 213, 214, 218, 222–3, 225; suggested solution to, 265–6

anti-clericalism, 48, 320, 333, 334, 347, 349, 374, 534

anti-semitism, 41 and n. 14, 321 n. 4, 336, 557–8; Durkheim on, 345–7

'Après le procès' (Brunetière), 335

Arabia (ancient), 239

Archiv für Sozialwissenschaft und Sozialpolitik, 397

arguments characteristic of Durkheim's thought, 30–33; *petitio principii*, 31, 136, 201, 454, 480, 481; argument by elimination, 31–3, 168, 203, 416, 480; treatment of evidence, 33–4, 446

army, the, and suicide, 210; and Dreyfus Affair, 336, 337; *and see* militarism

art, 469–70

Arunta, 33, 190, 473

Aurore, L', 335, 347

Austria, 547, 549–50

Australian aboriginal societies, 33, 240, 244, 477–8, 519, 526–7, 528; section systems, 186, 189–90; and sociology of knowledge, 439, 441; and sociology of religion, 452–3, 455, 464, 473, 477–8, 479

authoritarianism, 259, 498, 537

authority, 538; and constraint, 12, 13; of moral rules, 114–15, 504; .in education, 116, 135–6; in Rousseau, 286; of collective *représentations*, 338